P9-ASB-447

ANNALS OF COMMUNISM

Each volume in the series Annals of Communism will publish selected and previously inaccessible documents from former Soviet state and party archives in a narrative that develops a particular topic in the history of Soviet and international communism. Separate English and Russian editions will be prepared. Russian and American scholars work together to prepare the documents for each volume. Documents are chosen not for their support of any single interpretation but for their particular historical importance or their general value in deepening understanding and facilitating discussion. The volumes are designed to be useful to students, scholars, and interested general readers.

The Road to Terror

*Stalin and the Self-Destruction
of the Bolsheviks, 1932–1939*

J. Arch Getty
and
Oleg V. Naumov

Translations by Benjamin Sher

Yale University Press

New Haven and London

Documents that are held by the Russian Center for the Preservation and Study of Documents of Recent History (RTsKhIDNI), the Central Repository of Recent Documentation (TsKhSD), and the State Archive of the Russian Federation (GARF) are used with the permission of these archives.

Published with assistance from the Louis Stern Memorial Fund.

Designed by James J. Johnson and set in Sabon and Melior Roman types by
The Composing Room of Michigan, Inc., Grand Rapids, Michigan
Printed in the United States of America by Vail-Ballou Press, Binghamton, New York.

Library of Congress Cataloging-in-Publication Data

Getty, J. Arch (John Arch), 1950–
    The road to terror : Stalin and the self-destruction of the
Bolsheviks, 1932–1939 / J. Arch Getty and Oleg V. Naumov ;
translations by Benjamin Sher.
        p.   cm. — (Annals of communism)
    Includes bibliographical references and index.
    ISBN 0-300-07772-6 (cloth : alk. paper)

    1. Political purges—Soviet Union—History—Sources. 2. Soviet
Union—Politics and government—1917–1936—Sources. 3. Soviet
Union—Politics and government—1936–1953—Sources.
4. Kommunisticheskaia partiia Sovetskogo soiuza—Purges—Sources.
5. Terrorism—Soviet Union—Sources. 6. Stalin, Joseph, 1879–1953—
Sources. I. Naumov, Oleg V. II. Title. III. Series.
DK267.G45   1999
947.084′2—dc21   99-17696

A catalogue record for this book is available from the British Library.

10 9 8 7 6 5 4 3 2 1

Yale University Press gratefully acknowledges the financial support given for this publication by the National Endowment for the Humanities and Open Society Fund (New York).

This volume has been prepared with the cooperation of the Russian Center for the Preservation and Study of Documents of Recent History (RTsKhIDNI) of the State Archival Service of Russia in the framework of an agreement concluded between RTsKhIDNI and Yale University Press.

For Nancy

Contents

Preface

Writing a history of the Soviet terror of the 1930s closely based on archival documents is no easy undertaking. The directors of the terror machine were unashamed and unafraid of a negative historical verdict. They recorded and documented almost everything they did. This helps the historian, but the official language of these texts can never capture the cruelty, suffering, and pathos inflicted and endured. We always run the risk of presenting a terrible human drama in humdrum bureaucratic language.

Another difficulty in writing such a book is perhaps less obvious. What used to be a paucity of sources has become an embarrassment of riches. This forces us to be selective and to discuss only documents that are somehow important in their own right or representative of various genres in what is now a huge documentary source base. Previously, scholars included absolutely every document in their analysis; we must now pick and choose and, inevitably, leave something out.

More and more archival documents have come to light in the ongoing process of documentary declassification in the former Soviet Union. Since 1991 new groups of important sources were sometimes opening to researchers as often as every few months. Although we welcomed these new insights, we found ourselves hard-pressed to decide when to finish the writing and send the work to press. What if some vitally important document that supported or contradicted one of our findings suddenly appeared after the book was finished? This happened more than once, and the present book has thus been nearly five years in the making.

It has been nearly fifteen years since I wrote *Origins of the Great Purges,* at a time when no Moscow archives were available and when our field's interpretive horizons were narrower than they are today. Scholars have since produced a large number of exciting and brilliant studies, and what seemed strident revisionism in the early 1980s is now old hat.

No one is surprised anymore to read that the Soviet state was not an efficient, monolithic, omnipotent machine. Nobody bats an eye at discussions of the leadership's poor (or nonexistent) planning or at the unintended consequences of their policies. Chaos and inefficiency in the Stalinist hierarchy are now included in the conventional wisdom. Although there is still disagreement aplenty, no one thinks it irrelevant to write about women, peasants, or local party organizations. Few today are outraged to read about them and other social groups trying to articulate their interests to a state that had to take them into account. Nobody believes any longer that the history of the Stalin period is synonymous with Stalin's personality or purported desires. A recent influential book described Stalinism as a complex, interactive "civilization" without provoking violent academic attack. Totalitarianism has become more a subject for historiographical and sociological analysis than an obligatory creed or framework for analysis.

The sudden availability of new archival sources has obliged me to rethink a number of the points about the terror that I had suggested before. The distinction I drew between the party membership purges of the early 1930s and the terror later in the decade was too flat and lacking in nuance. I had written that these purges *(chistki)* of 1933–36 were simple party membership screenings aimed at members who were apolitical hangers-on, petty criminals, or crooked bureaucrats. Fifteen years ago, it did not seem that these party screenings involved any significant participation by the secret police (NKVD).

The real situation was much more complex. The fact that the largest category of people expelled in these operations ("passive" party members) did not even figure in Moscow's original target list should signal a complicated situation. I still believe that the screenings and the terror were quite different; they mainly affected different groups, and if the former were purges, the latter often brought a purging of the purgers. But the differences are best understood not so much in terms of central intent or incidence (both of which are hard to define) but rather in terms of conflict and contested language. Working without Moscow archives, I was not able to apprehend or historicize the complicated and politicized uses of language inside the system.

Labels—really tropes—like *Trotskyist* were filled and refilled with content by different people at different times and used to ascribe meanings to various operations and events. Thus when some Moscow leaders demanded a purge of "Trotskyists," they had very different understandings of those targets in 1933, 1935, 1936, and 1937. Others in Moscow, and those receiving the orders in the provinces, were able to contest the meanings of such epithets, thereby shaping the Politburo's shifting intentions to their own benefit. One person's "Trotskyist" or "wrecker" was another person's arbitrary bureaucrat or disobedient worker, and there were ongoing struggles to define the "enemy."

It is now clear from the new documents that the secret police were involved, lurking in the shadows of these "party housekeeping" efforts. But just as the prescribed targets of the screenings were disputed, so were the roles of party and police. Some local party leaders tried to exclude local secret police from the party purges; others sought to unload the entire operation onto the police. The new documents show that local party and police agencies and their Moscow godfathers struggled with one another in turf battles over which of the two was the proper "political" agency. In these contests, political actors again advanced different ideas about who was the "enemy."

In spite of some misreadings and misunderstandings of earlier work, Stalin's guilt for the terror was never in question. We can now see his fingerprints all over the archives. Although he approved suggestions and draft documents from others as often as he launched his own initiatives, he played the leading role in the terror. But even with the new documents, that role remains problematic and hard to specify.

Until 1937 he seems to have been neither the bureaucratic moderator that I suggested nor the careful planner that others claimed. The sources show neither a master plan to carry out the terror nor a "liberal opposition" that tried to stop it. These themes are developed at length in the book, but suffice it to say here that the various initiatives that collectively preceded the terror were often ad hoc, reactive, and mutually contradictory. As such, they can no longer be seen as parts of a single plan. Stalin worked assiduously toward the goal of enhancing his power and centralizing authority in Moscow. Even when he was not the author of events, he was a master of turning them to his own personal and political advantage. But even in Stalin's office, there were too many twists and turns, too many false starts and subsequent embarrassing backtrackings to support the idea that the terror was the culmination of a well-prepared and long-standing master design. Stalin was not sure exactly what kind of repression he wanted or how to get it until rather late in the story. He seems not to have decided on a wholesale massacre until early in 1937. But when he did, his uncertainty was replaced by a fierce determination to root out all sources of real or imagined disloyalty.

With the new documents, Stalin's serpentine and convoluted road to terror can no longer be explained by organized resistance to him. The notion that we have clung to for so long—that there must have been "liberal" or "decent" Bolsheviks who tried unsuccessfully to stop Stalin's plan for terror—is no longer tenable. Instead, the real picture is even more depressing than a heroic but futile resistance to evil. At every step of the way, there were constituencies both within and outside the elite that supported repression of various groups, sometimes with greater vehemence than Stalin did. The terror was a series of group efforts (though the groups changed frequently) rather than a matter of one man intimidating everyone else. This finding by no means takes Stalin off the hook or lessens his guilt. But it does mean that the picture is more complex. Repression was as much a matter of consensus as of one man's dementia, and this is somehow even more troubling.

The new documentation has confirmed other aspects of the terror that I have suspected for some time. For one thing, the archival evidence from the secret police rejects the astronomically high estimates often given for the number of terror victims. Certainly, the numbers are still terribly large, and even the more modest figures from the archives do not make the terror any more palatable or easy to understand. We should not need to artificially run up the score to tens of millions of victims to realize the horror of Stalinism.

Some documents in currently open archives remain secret, and today a disturbing trend toward reclassification runs in contradiction to the "desecretization" process, as it is called in Russia. Important archival collections, including those of the secret police and the president of the Russian Federation, are still closed at this writing. As always in history, every point of interpretation is subject to confirmation or refutation by new sources that have yet to appear. A few years ago, we thought that the opening of the Soviet archives would suddenly explain everything. Now we know that archival secrets reveal themselves to us like layers of an onion. As each group of new sources appears, another layer comes off. Although we have not yet reached a center where we would have final answers, the documents presented here bring us closer than ever before.

J. Arch Getty

Acknowledgments

Research for this book was supported in part by a grant from the International Research and Exchanges Board, with funds provided by the U.S. Department of State (Title VIII program) and the National Endowment for the Humanities. I received additional support from the National Endowment for the Humanities and from the University of California at Riverside's Academic Senate.

People who have influenced this work in various ways, either personally or through their scholarship, are too numerous to mention; still, I cannot fail to recognize the influence of Ken Bailes, Robert McNeal, Jeff Burds, Bill Chase, Sheila Fitzpatrick, James Harris, Hiroaki Kuromiya, Roberta Manning, Alec Nove, Lewis Siegelbaum, Peter Solomon Jr., Ronald Suny, and Lynn Viola. I only wish that Ken and Bob were still among us. They helped me tremendously in the early stages of my work, and I would have liked to show them this book.

I have benefited greatly from conversations with Viktor Bortnevski, F. I. Firsov, O. V. Khlevniuk, V. A. Kozlov, O. V. Naumov, V. P. Naumov, A. P. Nenarokov, A. A. Ovsiannikov, A. K. Sokolov (and the *rebyata* in his laboratory), B. A. Starkov, and V. N. Zemskov. I received indescribable additional help from T. V. Goriacheva, N. V. Muraveva, L. V. Poliakov, Irina Renfro, and N. P. Yakovlev. Alice, Earl, and Floyd know what they did.

I owe a unique debt to my friend and colleague Gábor T. Rittersporn, who aided me in all the above categories. I will always feel fortunate at being able to tap the deep knowledge of the 1930s and of Soviet culture of all kinds which he so generously shares.

Benjamin Sher has my heartfelt thanks for his careful and sensitive translations, which capture sense and mood as well as language. Against all odds, he managed to maintain good cheer through a maze of texts that, schooled in the Russian literary language as he is, he found ghastly and depressing. He is especially to be commended for his renderings of the prose of N. I. Yezhov, whose texts, aside from their odious content, were crude and ungrammatical.

None of the organizations or people mentioned above are responsible for the views expressed in this book. They deserve due credit for anything good in what follows; I alone am to blame for any errors.

Finally, I could not have completed this work without the warm and tolerant support of my family. Nancy, Amanda, Jessica, and John tolerated Moscow, my absences when I was there without them, and my occasional mental absences when I was at home with them.

J. Arch Getty

Translator's Acknowledgments

I would like to express my very special debt of gratitude to my wife, Anna Sher, who, as a native of Moscow, served as my Russian consultant and English proofreader on this project. Without her conscientious, meticulous, and insightful scrutiny of the entire text in both languages, these translations would have been far less successful in accurately rendering what is often maddeningly obscure, inconsistent, or just muddled up.

My deep thanks to Alexander Wentzell and Alexandra Raskina, originally of Moscow, for their kind and unselfish help in deciphering some of the especially arcane linguistic and historical puzzles in the text. My thanks to Sam Ramer of Tulane University for his illuminating comments on certain aspects of Russian history. My thanks to Jeanette Hornot, who served as my secretary on part of the project, for her professional skills, industriousness, and inexhaustible patience.

My thanks to J. Arch Getty of the University of California, Riverside, and to Jonathan Brent, editorial director at Yale University Press, for giving me the rare privilege of serving as a translator on this unprecedented archival journey into the "whirlwind" of the 1930s. Their support and encouragement have been a blessing throughout.

Finally, my thanks as always to my mother, Helen Sher, for her devotion and support over the years.

Benjamin Sher

Notes on Transliteration and Terminology

In transliterating from Russian to English we have used a modified version of the standard Library of Congress system in the text and documents. Soft and hard signs have been omitted, and the following changes have been imposed.

In final position:
    ii in the LOC system becomes y (Trotsky, not Trotskii)
    iia = ia (Izvestia, not Izvestiia)
    nyi = ny (Nagorny, not Nagornyi)
In initial position:
    E = Ye (Yezhov, not Ezhov)
    Ia = Ya (Yaroslavsky, not Iaroslavsky)
    Iu = Yu (Yudin, not Iudin)

In citations and translator's notes, we have followed the Library of Congress system.

In the 1930s the Communist Party was known as the All-Union Communist Party (Bolshevik) [*Vsesoiuznaia Kommunisticheskaia Partiia (bol'shevikov)*], or VKP(b) in its Russian acronym. In practice, its highest policy-making body was the *Politburo,* which in the 1930s consisted of roughly ten full (voting) members and five candidate (nonvoting) members. In the beginning of the period covered by this study, it met about once a week; by the end of the period it was meeting about once a month. Each meeting technically had dozens or even hundreds of items on the agenda, but increasingly these were decided without formal meetings, by polling the members. Politburo meetings produced *protocols,* which are outlines of the questions discussed, often with an indication of the decision reached and sometimes with attachments or appendixes. It is not known whether minutes were taken in the Politburo; at this writing no such documents have been located in Soviet archives. Other top party committees included the *Secretariat* and *Orgburo,* both of which were largely concerned with personnel assignments.

The *Central Committee* of the VKP(b) (of which the Politburo, Orgburo, and Secretariat were formally subcommittees) consisted of about seventy full voting members and about seventy candidate members in the 1930s. A meeting of the Central Committee (hereafter CC) took place from two to four times a year and was known as a *plenum.* Minutes *(stenograms)* were taken at CC plena, and many of them are available in Russian archives.

Below the level of the CC, the party was divided into a hierarchy of regional party committees based on regions, territories, districts, and places of work. These bodies also conducted plena, but the real work was usually done in an inner executive committee known as a *buro.*

Parallel with this hierarchy, and subordinate to the CC, was another structure of party committees known as the *Party Control Commission* (KPK). The KPK was charged with various kinds of inspection and discipline in the party apparatus. Its mission was to investigate and punish cases of ideological deviance, corruption, and violation of party rules.

A parallel state apparatus was formally separate from the party but in reality subordinate to it. The state structure, ostensibly the government of the USSR, was in fact closely controlled by the party and was used to implement and execute party decisions. At the top of the hierarchy was a *Congress of Soviets,* with hundreds of delegates, and the formal legislative power resided in a *Central Executive Committee* (TsIK) of Soviets, consisting of several dozen members. Day-to-day administration and confirmation of legislation at this level was conducted by the *Presidium of the Central Executive Committee,* whose chairman served as nominal president of the USSR. Below the Central Executive Committee and formally subordinated to it was the government cabinet, known in this period as the *Council of People's Commissars (Sovnarkom),* which consisted of ministers ("commissars") representing various branches of the economy and state administration. Finally, below this central state structure was a hierarchy of elected regional, city, and district *soviets,* which might be thought of as organs of local administration.

The territorial structures and designations of the USSR can be confusing. The USSR was a union of republics, with each republic being the political organization of a nationality. The Russian Republic (RSFSR) and the Ukrainian Republic (USFSR) were the largest of a series of "states" that included Belorussia, Georgia, Armenia, Uzbekistan, and the other constituent republics of the USSR. The RSFSR was clearly the most powerful, and its administration overlapped in general with that of the USSR.

Each republic was divided into regional units, each of which was known as an *oblast'* (region) or a *krai* (territory). Thus at various times in the 1930s the RSFSR consisted of between seventy-five and ninety regions and territories. Although technically all republics were on an equal footing, in practice the status attached to a major region or territory of the RSFSR was equal to that of a non-Russian republic. The next subdivision (into which regions and territories were divided) was known as a *raion* (district). Districts could be rural or urban, perhaps roughly equivalent to counties or boroughs. Cities had separate administrations that fell between district and regional or territorial level.

Republics, regions, territories, cities, and districts each had party committees, party control commissions, and state bodies. Their titles, acronyms, and the translations used in this book are summarized below:

Russian territory	English usage	Political organization	Acronym
oblast'	region	regional (party) committee	*obkom*
		regional (party) control commission	*oblkk*
		regional (state) executive committee	*oblispolkom*
krai	territory	territorial (party) committee	*kraikom*
		territorial (party) control commission	*kraikk* or *kkk*
		territorial (state) executive committee	*kraiispolkom*
raion	district	district (party) committee	*raikom*
		district (party) control commission	*raikk* or *rkk*
		district (state) executive committee	*raiispolkom*
gorod	city	city (party) committee	*gorkom*
		city (party) control commission	*gorkk*
		city (state) executive committee	*gorispolkom*

A Note on the Documents

The vast majority of documents used or cited here are from the Russian Center for the Preservation and Study of Documents of Recent History (*Rossiiskii Tsentr Khraneniia i Izucheniia Dokumentov Noveishei Istorii,* hereafter RTsKhIDNI), the former Central Party Archive of the Institute of Marxism-Leninism of the Central Committee of the Communist Party (TsPA IML pri TsK KPSS).[1] Some documents are from the Central Repository of Recent Documentation (*Tsentr khraneniia sovremennoi dokumentatsii,* hereafter TsKhSD), the former archive of the General Department of the Central Committee, and from the State Archive of the Russian Federation (*Gosudarstvennyi arkhiv Rossiiskoi Federatsii,* hereafter GARF), the main archive of central state institutions. Russian archival documents are cited and numbered by collection *(fond* or *f.),* inventory *(opis'* or *op.),* file *(delo* or *d.),* and page *(list* or *l.,* or in plural, *ll.):* thus, for example, RTsKhIDNI, f. 17, op. 165, d. 47, l. 3.

Many of these documents were too long to be reproduced in full in this volume. Our editorial excisions are given by standard ellipses: . . .

Sometimes, ellipses appeared in the original documents; these are given by ellipses in parentheses: (. . .)

---

1. For an outline of the history and holdings of the archive, see J. Arch Getty, "Researcher's Introduction to RTsKhIDNI," in J. Arch Getty and V. P. Kozlov, eds., *Rossiiskii Tsentr Khraneniia i Izucheniia Dokumentov Noveishei Istorii: Kratkii Putevoditel',* Moscow, 1993, v–xix.

Breaks in speech, when a speaker trailed off or was interrupted, are given by a standard dash:—

Within the documents, all text in brackets [ ] is from the translator or authors.

Unless otherwise noted, all documents cited here exist in the archives as typescripts, formally certified by party clerical officials as originals, as exact copies of original documents, or as typed versions of drafts or dictation. Sometimes variant texts of a document (or rough drafts and a final version) exist. When differences among versions are significant, we have noted them in the text and have presented two versions of the document.

Archival texts recording the meetings of the party's Central Committee were deliberately prepared in several versions. The "uncorrected stenogram" was the raw minute of the meeting. Speakers then had the right to revise and extend their remarks and correct mistakes in the original transcription; this produced the "corrected stenogram." Finally, the Central Committee Secretariat edited the corrected minutes and prepared a printed "stenographic report" for distribution to ranking party officials. Digests and edited versions of these transcripts were circulated to lower party bodies for explanation to the party membership. In the process of producing these texts for distribution, the party leadership sometimes took considerable liberties with the corrected stenogram. These editorial changes are noted in the text. Unless otherwise noted, we have used the corrected stenogram of Central Committee plena as the best reflection of the speakers' intentions.

Soviet Organizational Acronyms and Abbreviations

AKhU — Administrative-Economic Directorate

Bund — General Jewish Workers' Union for Lithuania, Poland, and Russia

CC — Central Committee. *See* TsK

CCC — Central Control Commission. *See* TsKK

ChK (Cheka) — Extraordinary Commission for Combating Counter-revolution and Sabotage (1918–22): political police, predecessor of GPU, OGPU, NKVD, MGB, KGB

Comintern — Communist International (1919–43): an international, revolutionary, proletarian organization to which the Communist parties of various countries belonged

ECCI — Executive Committee of the Communist International

Glavdortrans — Main Administration for Highways, Unpaved Roads, and Motor Transport in the RSFSR

Glavpolitizdat — Main Publishing House for Political Literature

Glavpolitprosvet — Main Committee for Politics and Education

Glavtransmash — Main Administration for Machinery Construction in Transport

Glavtsesskom — Main Concessionary Committee

gorkom — City Committee of the VKP(b)

Gosbank — State Bank

Gosplan — State Planning Commission

GPU	State Political Directorate attached to the Council of People's Commissars (SNK) of the USSR: successor to Cheka and predecessor of OGPU and NKVD
GUGB	Main Administration for State Security of the NKVD of the USSR
GUPVO	Chief Directorate of the Political-Military Section
IKP	Institute of Red Professors
INO	Department for Foreign Affairs of the NKVD of the USSR
IPO	Ivanovo Industrial Province
Knigotsentr	Central organization responsible for the publication and dissemination of books
kolkhoz	Collective farm
Komakademia	Communist Academy
Komsomol	All-Union Leninist Youth League (VLKSM): a party organization for young people in the USSR
Komzag	Committee for (State) Procurement
KPK	Commission of Party Control attached to the Central Committee of the VKP(b)
kraikom	Territorial Committee of the VKP(b)
MCC	Moscow Control Commission
MGK	Moscow City Committee of the VKP(b)
MGU	Moscow State University
MK	Moscow Regional Committee of the VKP(b)
Mossovet	Moscow Council of Workers' Deputies
NKID	People's Commissariat for Foreign Affairs
NKLP	People's Commissariat for Light Industry
NKO	People's Commissariat for Defense
NKPS	People's Commissariat for Transport and Communications
NKS	People's Commissariat for Communications
NKTP	People's Commissariat for Heavy Industry
NKVD	People's Commissariat for Internal Affairs
NKVod	People's Commissariat for Water Transport
NKYu	People's Commissariat for Justice
NKZ	People's Commissariat for Health
Narodny Komissar	head of a People's Commissariat; equivalent to minister
NTU VSNKh	Scientific-Technical Board of the Supreme Council for the National Economy

obkom	Regional Committee of the VKP(b)
oblispolkom	Regional Executive Committee
oblplan	Regional Planning Commission
OGIZ	Association of State Publishing Houses for Books and Periodicals
OGPU	Unified State Political Directorate attached to the Council of People's Commissars (SNK) of the USSR: successor to Cheka and GPU and predecessor of NKVD
ONO	Department of Education (i.e., of local authority)
Orgburo TsK VKP(b)	Organizational Bureau of the CC of the VKP(b)
ORPO	Department of Leading Party Organs of the CC of the Russian Communist Party (Bolshevik)
Politburo TsK VKP(b)	Political Bureau of the CC of the VKP(b)
politotdel	Political Department
PP OGPU	Plenipotentiary Bureau of the OGPU
Prezidium TsKK (or KPK)	Supreme Governing Organ of the Central (after 1934, Party) Control Commission of the VKP(b)
Profintern	Red International of Trade Unions
RaiZO	District Department of Agriculture
Revvoensovet (RVS)	Revolutionary Military Council
RIK	District Executive Committee
RKKA	Workers' and Peasants' Red Army
Selmash	Factory for the Manufacture of Agricultural Machinery
Selsovet	Village Council
SKK	North Caucasus Territory
SNK	Council of People's Commissars
Tsentrarkhiv	Central Board for Archives
Tsentrsoyuz	Central Union of Consumer Associations
TsIK	Central Executive Committee of the USSR
TsK	Central Committee of the Communist Party
TsK ISKUSSTV	Central Committee of the Trade Union of Artists
TsKK	Central Control Commission of the VKP(b)
TsK MOPR	Central Committee of the International Organization for Assistance to Revolutionary Fighters
TsUSTRAKh	Central Board for Insurance

UNKVD	Regional Directorate of the NKVD
UPK	Criminal Law Procedure Code
VChK	All-Russian Extraordinary Commission for Combating Counterrevolution and Sabotage (1918–22)
VKP(b)	All-Union Communist Party (Bolshevik)
VSNKh	Supreme Council for the National Economy of the USSR
VTsSPS	All-Union Central Council of Trade Unions

The Road to Terror

Party Documents and Bolshevik Mentality

ALEXANDER YULEVICH TIVEL, enemy of the people, was executed by a firing squad of the Soviet secret police on a day in early March 1937, a day that did not shake the world.

A journalist and editor, Tivel was a midlevel bureaucrat, a minor figure whose records in no way stand out in the archives of his era. We shall not meet him in the corridors of Stalinist power. But precisely on that account his story is worth telling: he is a kind of Soviet Everyman. For some reason—or for no reason—Tivel became one of three-quarters of a million citizens executed during 1937 and 1938, many without trial or other legal proceedings, all in the name of cleansing the Communist Party and the Soviet Union of various vaguely "counterrevolutionary" elements. His biography is the story of Stalinist terror writ small.

Tivel was born just before the turn of the century in Baku, not far from where a young Stalin was pursuing his career as an underground revolutionary. His parents were white-collar employees of a joint-stock company, but Alexander's life possibilities had seemed limited by his birth into a Jewish family in the provinces. He was a clever boy, though, and at an early age had somehow managed to learn a passable amount of English, German, and French.

He was also political. At age sixteen he had joined a Zionist student organization in Baku. With two strikes against him—the Imperial system had little use for politically active Jews from non-Russian regions of the empire—he finished high school at age eighteen and wondered what he would do with his life. As it turned out, the determining factor was his graduation year of 1917, the year of the Russian Revolution.

We do not know what role he played in the dramatic events of that year, but in 1918 he was working first in the military office of the Piatigorsk Soviet, then in Moscow in the propaganda department of the new Bolshevik government. By the end of the year he had joined the editorial staff of the Soviet government's press agency, ROSTA. During the Russian Civil War (1918–21), he served as a correspondent for ROSTA and for several Soviet newspapers in Moscow, the Volga region, and Tashkent. His editing and language skills made him valuable to a new regime desperate for such talents.

After the civil war, Alexander Tivel worked as an editor and writer in Moscow for the Communist International (Comintern), where he met and married Eva Lipman. In 1925 he moved to Leningrad to work in the foreign news department of *Leningradskaia pravda,* but in 1926 it was back to Moscow for editorial work in the Secretariat of the Central Committee of the Communist Party and in the CC's Department of Culture and Propaganda. Although he had previously worked for the Communist press, he had never joined the party. But his new job in the apparatus of the Central Committee required him to be a member. His editorial experience and knowledge of languages made him a valued worker, and by special order of the CC Secretariat he was admitted directly to the party in December 1926, without the required period of candidate membership. During the next ten years, Tivel continued to work in Moscow party headquarters, eventually rising to the position of assistant chief of the International Information Bureau of the CC.

On the surface, his record seemed exemplary. True, between 1930 and 1936 Tivel had received three party reprimands for minor infractions like misplacing telegrams or losing his party card, but it was not unusual for party members to have several such small blots on their records. Behind the scenes, however, top party leaders, ever more apprehensive, were scrutinizing the records of lower-ranking bureaucrats. Normal work relationships with political dissidents or with losers in political intrigues were increasingly examined and given sinister interpretations. Tivel had two such suspicious associations in his past. During his year in Leningrad back in 1925, he had worked with followers of the leftist oppositionist Grigory Zinoviev. Tivel had been in the wrong place at the wrong time: because Zinoviev was party boss of Leningrad at the time, his supporters had naturally controlled the newspaper where Tivel worked. And by 1936 Tivel's immediate supervisor in the information bureau was the ex-Trotskyist Karl Radek, a well-known and bitingly sarcastic critic of Stalin in the 1920s.

Suspicions reached new heights in the aftermath of the August 1936 show trial of Zinoviev and other former leftists. The dissidents had been sentenced to death, and in the wake of the trial those like Radek who had sided with the leftists came under intense scrutiny. At the end of August, Radek was arrested. Tivel was taken by the secret police (NKVD) at the same time. His wife and young son never saw him again.

Tivel spent the next six months in prison under interrogation. We do not know whether he was physically tortured by his interrogators, but there is ample evidence that countless others were. Even high-ranking officials under arrest were beaten or, as Molotov would put it, "worked over."[1] Ten years later, a high-ranking police official described interrogation procedures in a letter to Stalin. First, prisoners were offered better conditions—better food, mail, and so on—in return for a confession. If that failed, appeals to the prisoner's conscience and concern for his family followed. The next step was a solitary-confinement cell without exercise, a bed, tobacco, or sleep for up to twenty days. Food was limited to three hundred grams of bread per day, with one hot meal every third day. Finally, the use of "physical pressure" was authorized in accordance with a Central Committee decree of 10 January 1939.[2] These procedures refer to a later, less terrible period; the routine would hardly have been lighter in the 1930s, when Tivel was in custody.

1. Feliks Chuev, *Sto sorok besed s Molotovym,* Moscow, 1991, 410–12.

2. Memo from V. Abakumov to Stalin, 17 July 1947. *Tsentral'naia khraneniia sovremennoi dokumentatsii* (hereafter TsKhSD), *fond* 89, *opis'* 18, *delo* 12. A copy of the 1939 CC circular authorizing "physical pressure" has not yet been located.

In 1936 the Stalinist leadership's paranoia reached new heights. A wave of arrests engulfed former party dissidents of both the left and the right. Many prominent Bolsheviks with oppositional pasts, including the diplomat Grigory Sokolnikov and Deputy Commissar of Heavy Industry Georgy Piatakov, found themselves in prison. All were accused of the most fantastic crimes: sabotage, espionage, and a variety of other treasonable actions. The Bolshevik elite was consuming itself.

Even within the precincts of the Central Committee where Tivel had worked, the wave of suspicion reached ludicrous proportions. In one of the paranoid waves, someone remembered that two party workers in the central apparatus, young women named Toropova and Lukinskaya, had been seen with Tivel at a social event. M. F. Shkiryatov, the high-ranking chairman of the Party Control Commission, dashed off a memo to the NKVD requesting that Tivel be asked about the women and expressing frustration that "we cannot verify everybody with whom Tivel danced."

On 7 March 1937 the NKVD replied that Alexander Tivel had reported nothing incriminating about the women. But the Military Collegium of the Supreme Court convicted Tivel not only of knowing about terrorists' intentions to assassinate Bolshevik leaders but of directly "preparing to commit a terrorist act against [NKVD chief N. I.] Yezhov." Tivel was probably executed on the same day. Unlike many others who were badgered and tortured by the NKVD, he had not confessed.

But the Tivel story does not end here. The terror that swallowed individuals also destroyed their families. Immediately after Tivel's arrest, his wife had been fired from her job "for political motives," and she now found it impossible to find any work with this notation on her record. Shortly thereafter she was evicted from her Moscow apartment, and, facing destitution "on the streets," she and her sickly young son moved into her mother's crowded flat. But in May 1937 Eva Tivel and her son were banished from Moscow altogether and exiled to the far-off Omsk region of Siberia. Her mother lost her apartment and was exiled along with her daughter and grandson, apparently for sheltering them.

In October 1937 Eva Tivel was herself arrested in Omsk. After eight months in the Tobolsk jail, she was sentenced by the NKVD's

Special Board (which had the power to pass sentences even on people who had committed no crime) to eight years in a labor camp for being a "member of the family of a traitor to the Motherland." The savage human destruction of the terror did not stop even there. Shortly after Eva's arrest, the NKVD arrived at her mother's apartment and took the Tivels' nine-year-old son to an orphanage. He did not see his mother again until he was in his mid-twenties.

After completing her eight-year sentence in the camps, Eva, like so many others, received an additional term: eight more years in Siberian exile. She was freed only in 1953, the year of Stalin's death, and returned to Moscow.

She soon began a campaign to have her husband's name cleared. Like millions of others who continued for decades to suffer from the terror of the 1930s, their twenty-five-year-old son was still officially labeled a "child of an enemy of the people." From the beginning of 1955, Eva began to write letters to various authorities seeking posthumous rehabilitation of Alexander Tivel "in order to remove this false conviction from the father of my son." The process moved slowly, and Eva joined the legion of widows, relatives, and former convicts who trudged from office to office in search of justice. Finally, on 23 May 1957, twenty years after Tivel's execution and after Eva's many letters and appeals, Tivel's sentence and party expulsion were overturned. In the laconic language that always hid so much, the USSR Supreme Court held only that his 1937 conviction "had been based on contradictory and dubious materials."[3]

Questions and Culprits

The fate of the obscure Alexander Tivel illustrates many of the elements of the terror process: innocent personal and work connections became crimes that spurred insane and paranoid investigations. The suffering of the Alexander Tivels and their families have been well documented in a huge corpus of powerful memoir literature—Evgenia Ginzburg's *Into the Whirlwind,* Anna Larina's *This I Cannot Forget,* and Alexander Solzhenitsyn's *Gulag Archipelago,*

3. Tivel's story is contained in his party file in RTsKhIDNI, f. 589, op. 3, d. 1466.

to name a few. Honest, loyal people had their lives destroyed. Relatives were persecuted, and descendants lived with stigma and tragedy for decades.

The Great Terror of the 1930s in the Soviet Union was one of the most horrible cases of political violence in modern history. Millions of people were detained, arrested, or sent to prison or camps. Countless lives, careers, and families were permanently shattered. Beyond this, the experience left a national trauma, a legacy of fear that lingered for generations. Although we have good documentation and powerful portrayals of the process from its victims, until the recent opening of some of the political archives of the former Soviet Union we were forced to guess about the process at the other end. We have not been able to write the history of the origins of the terror among those who administered it. The laconic official documents at our disposal until recently have been tips of the icebergs of Soviet political history. Our memoir literature has been able to make us feel the pain of those victimized, but the victims of the terror have for the most part been unable to tell us much about the policies and people who carried it out. Few who survived the terror were highly placed at its inception, and until recently, those who were had not spoken up.

What led the Soviet Communist Party elite to destroy its own? Why were useful, politically harmless people like Alexander and Eva Tivel destroyed in what might otherwise have been a historically common internecine fight? Why did it take so long, even after Stalin's death, to begin to reverse the miscarriages of justice? What was the mind-set of the Stalinist and post-Stalinist party elite?

The figure of Iosif Vissarionovich Stalin hovers like a specter over these events. As the most powerful political leader of the state and the center of a growing quasi-religious cult, he was personally responsible for much of the bloodshed. His motives and plans and the exact sequence of his actions are still not completely clear, but evidence of his enormous guilt is ample. Although we do not have a diary or journal, a clear list of his orders and commands, or many documents with his signature, we have enough to posit for him a vicious and cold participation in the killing.

Stalin's power grew dramatically throughout the 1930s; by the end of the decade he was a virtual autocrat. Russia had always been a country ruled by men rather than laws, but more and more people came to depend on Stalin or other leaders to guide their behavior and solve their problems. This process, though, was uneven and characterized by zigs and zags. Sometimes Stalin was a referee or makeweight, balancing various interests and groups against each other. He made and changed alliances with different groups at different times, either by explicit pronouncements or by implicitly allowing them to use his name and authority. At other times, he directly asserted his personal authority. Although by the end of the decade he was unquestionably the supreme leader, he was never omnipotent, and he always functioned within a matrix of other groups and interests.

Stalin was the central person in the politics and political violence of the 1930s. But his was not the only or even perhaps the most interesting role in the tragedy. In the witch-hunts of the seventeenth century, to which the Stalinist terror bears many similarities, a small number of authoritative persons identified the victims and organized their execution. Behind and around them, though, were other groups and constituencies—among them, members of religious and political hierarchies, policemen of various kinds, and ordinary citizen-members of "the crowd"—who abetted the proceedings, acquiesced in the process, or simply looked on, conceding that such ruthlessness was necessary, reasonable, or at least acceptable.

"No ruler has ever carried out a policy of wholesale expulsion or destruction without the cooperation of society," wrote H. R. Trevor-Roper about the witch-hunts. "Great massacres may be commanded by tyrants, but they are imposed by peoples. . . . Afterwards, when the mood has changed, or when the social pressure, thanks to the blood-letting, no longer exists, the anonymous people slinks away, leaving public responsibility to the preachers, the theorists, and the rulers who demanded, justified, and ordered the act."[4]

Our curiosity and attention must be drawn to those who helped, approved, or simply accepted the necessity of fatal purges of perceived enemies. Both colonial America and Stalinist Russia had

4. H. R. Trevor-Roper, *The European Witch-Craze of the Sixteenth and Seventeenth Centuries and Other Essays*, New York, 1968, 114–15.

bureaucratic constituencies and popular masses who went along with the bloodletting and who thought it right and even proper.

When we reflect on the terror of the 1930s and ask, "What made it possible?" we must look beyond Stalin's personality for answers. It is possible, after all, to analyze and even on some level to understand a homicidal maniac or serial murderer. Accounts of the deeds of such sociopaths are depressingly common in today's newspapers, and the tools of modern psychoanalysis give us quite a few clues to the motivations of these criminals. In the case of Stalin, a good bit has been written on his presumed personality.[5] Yet to understand how a generalized terror erupted in the USSR in the 1930s we must look farther afield. Why were his orders carried out? Why was there fertile soil for terror to grow? Even if we decide that Stalin was always the main actor, unless we study society and the political system, the scale and spread of the terror must remain incomprehensible.

The party was the state. It had the power, within broad parameters, to change the entire direction of economic and social policy. It had a monopoly on political organization, control of the press, courts, army, and police. The party established and defended the only permissible ideology; it suppressed and controlled traditional religion and promulgated its own system of beliefs in the communist millennium, complete with saints and demons. Yet the party, which could have stopped the terror, actively cooperated in its own destruction. It embarked on a series of policies that disorganized the regime, fractured society, and destroyed the party itself. This bears explaining.

The Bolshevik Party was a product of idealistic, egalitarian, and socially progressive strands in the Russian intelligentsia and working class. By the 1930s much of the original idealism had been lost or transformed, as Bolshevik revolutionaries became state officials. But even the remaining idealists—and there were many—supported and followed policies that facilitated terror, not only against traditional "enemies" but against themselves. This, too, requires an explanation.

5. The best work on this subject is Robert C. Tucker, *Stalin as Revolutionary, 1879-1929: A Study in History and Personality,* New York, 1973.

The terror of the 1930s had many components and aspects—
social and class conflicts, perceived foreign threats, economic dis-
location, popular moods and beliefs, Stalin's personality, and
others. We focus here on the political leadership not in order to
exclude other factors but rather to shed some light on them. At
various times, the party was the administrative tool for Stalin's
policies, the forum for conflicting and feuding bureaucracies, and
the only politically articulate stratum of a politically fractured society. It was the priesthood, the military commander, the chief of
police, and the sole landowner. In various ways its composition
was representative of society, including as it did workers, peasants,
foremen, collective farm chairmen, local political bosses, economic
administrators, and others in a wide array of social and political
roles. Through a study of the party it will be possible to make some
broader statements about the relationship between terror and society at large.

Why did the state acquiesce and participate in its own destruction? Why did the elite of the regime approve policies that ultimately weakened its hold on power? Why did large segments of
society—including not only rank-and-file communists but also the
general public—accept the propositions that the country was infiltrated with spies and saboteurs and that Lenin's Old Bolshevik
comrades-in-arms were traitors? Why did so many people believe
that a national witch-hunt was necessary? Why did large numbers
of regime supporters continue to believe in Stalin, the Bolshevik
Party, and the necessity for repression even after they themselves
had spent years in labor camps as victims of that very system?

Historians have often posed another question: How did one man
manage to inflict such wholesale terror on an experienced political
elite? The literature treats of Stalin's careful plans, his cunning,
deception, threats, and blackmail.[6] In some views, Stalin simply
decided to kill a lot of people and then tricked or intimidated large
numbers of otherwise intelligent people into helping him do it.
Society plays no role in these explanations, and there is no real
politics at work here. The only factors worth mentioning are the
plans of the ruler; everyone else was a passive recipient. Many basic

6. See, for example, Robert C. Tucker, *Stalin in Power: The Revolution from
Above, 1928–1941*, New York, 1990, ch. 17.

accounts of the terror operate at this interpretive level: once one decides who is guilty, there are no more questions to ask, and research becomes the further enumeration of foul deeds by the evil prince.[7]

Historians are supposed to study events not simply to record them and to pronounce this or that person good or evil. In the broadest sense, they study phenomena in order to understand human behavior. They try to place persons and events in their contexts and study their actions. To do this it is necessary to discern how historical participants interpreted and interacted with their environments. We must try to understand the social, political, and economic system in which people of the Soviet Union lived and worked in the 1930s, as well as the backgrounds, experiences, preconceptions, and beliefs that those people brought to politics. Finally, and most difficult, we must study the actions of persons, especially political actors, as they interacted with their environments. By presenting these documents in light of such questions, we hope to give some insight into the most difficult question of the terror: How was it all possible?

Important elements of politics in the 1930s include the steady accumulation of power in the hands of the central Moscow party leadership, the role of the party elite as a distinctive stratum, the increasing level of fear and apprehension among that elite about their position in society, and the growing momentum of repression. That momentum was propelled by certain groups that wanted to increase or decrease repression, by traditional Bolshevik Party unity that mutated into a fanatical party discipline, by customary practices of scapegoating, and by the transformation of political sins into judicial crimes.

One key to these processes is the position and corporate self-interest of the party elite. Since the early 1920s, full-time professional party leaders had become the administrators of the country. They became accustomed to giving commands, enjoying privileges, and living well. The process of the formation of an official social

7. For examples see Robert Conquest, *The Great Terror: A Reassessment,* Oxford, 1990; Oleg V. Khlevniuk, *1937: Stalin, NKVD i sovetskoe obshchestvo,* Moscow, 1992; and Oleg V. Khlevniuk, *Politbiuro: Mekhanizmy politicheskoi vlasti v 1930-e gody,* Moscow, 1996.

stratum had begun. This had been the gist of Leon Trotsky's critique of the Stalin regime and one of the reasons the ruling elite had been so fierce in its destruction of Trotsky's group. This ruling segment of the party, its elite, became more and more conscious of itself as a group separate from the party rank and file and from the population in general. Self-selected and replenished by a system of hierarchical personnel appointments, or *nomenklatura,* the party elite enjoyed increasing power, prestige, and privilege as time went on.

Technically, the word *nomenklatura* refers to the list of positions, appointment to which requires confirmation by a superior party body. Thus, the nomenklatura of the Central Committee was the list of high positions reserved for CC confirmation. With time, however, the word became a collective noun referring to the ruling stratum of the party itself.

This nomenklatura in turn comprised several strata with different interests. It included members and staffs of the Politburo and Central Committee, first secretaries of regional party committees, and full-time paid officials and organizers at many levels down to urban and rural districts. These various subgroups had differing parochial interests that sometimes conflicted with those of other nomenklatura groups, but they shared a group identity as insiders. They were the ones with power, great or small, whose membership in the ruling caste distinguished them from the multitudinous outsiders.

The nomenklatura's motives were varied. On one level, they jealously protected their position as the elite. If the regime fell, their various privileges and immunities would disappear. The more exclusive and authoritative they could be, the more secure were their personal fortunes. On another level, though, there is no reason to believe that they were not also true believers in communism. In fact, there was little contradiction between the two. In the worldview they had constructed, the future of humanity depended on socialism. Socialism in turn depended on the survival of the Soviet revolutionary experiment, which depended on keeping the Bolshevik regime united, tightly disciplined, and in control of a society that frequently exhibited hostility to that regime. The long-standing Bolshevik self-image as "midwives of the revolution" was alive and well throughout the 1930s. Even without crass self-interest as a conscious motive, this tradition made it easy to equate nomenklatura power with the good of the country.

Stalin was simultaneously creator, product, and symbol of the nomenklatura. As chief of Central Committee personnel, he controlled the most important appointments. But he was also a product and representative of the new official stratum; its members supported him as much as he supported them. As several scholars have noted, Stalin had "won over a majority cohort of high and middle-ranking party leaders" rather than creating that cohort.[8] Trotsky agreed, and always maintained that Stalin was simply the representative of the new official stratum.

His growing personality cult was more than ego gratification. It was the symbol of the unity, common purpose, and unerring political guidance that the nomenklatura wished to project to the public. Stalin's cult helped to cloak their privileges, conflicts, and mistakes behind a banner of wise leadership and teaching. Our documents will allow us to study the roles and interests of both Stalin and the nomenklatura, not only when they coincided but also when they came into conflict.

Schisms in the party, which were neither necessarily about ideology nor limited to the articulate political strata, are an important key to this story. Fault lines ran not so much between "right" and "left," as they had in the 1920s, but horizontally between strata. The party was by no means a united organization, and there are several ways to break it down into its component groups.

One crack ran between party and society. Bolsheviks, more or less united around a conception of socialism and more or less bound by party discipline, followed the Leninist tradition of presenting a single party face to the outside. That outside included not only foreigners but also the nonparty Russian public. Party unity was always seen as the key to Bolshevik survival, and when the chips were down party members of all ranks were enjoined to close ranks against the "class enemy."

Another crack ran inside the party between the regional and local party leaderships and the rank-and-file members. Territorial "fam-

---

8. James Hughes, "Patrimonialism and the Stalinist System: The Case of S. I. Syrtsov," *Europe-Asia Studies*, 48(4), 1996, 551–68. See also Tucker, *Stalin as Revolutionary*, 303–4.

ily circles," maintained by patronage and mutual protection, used the rank-and-file membership as their foot soldiers. Party secretaries, as members of the nomenklatura, insisted on iron discipline and obedience from their party troops, dismissing all criticism and attempts by underlings to play a role in local or regional politics. In turn, the rank and file who were not members of the local family circle resented their chiefs; when given the chance by (and protection of) Moscow officials, they often unleashed a torrent of criticism of their chiefs. This tactic of inciting criticism from below was risky for the party in general and, as we shall see, was used only as a last resort.

Although the regional "great lords" of the party were themselves part of the nomenklatura, they often found themselves in conflict with other elements of that elite. In particular, attempts by the Moscow elite and Stalin to centralize all elements of political and social life put Moscow leaders in conflict with their fellow bosses out in the provinces, who were anxious to protect their local patronage and power networks. Nevertheless, through most of the 1930s, this crack had to be kept hidden from the party rank and file and especially from the general population. Just as the party determined to present a united face to the country, the feuding groups within the elite usually felt a strong need to present a united front to the "party masses."

Stalin and his Politburo made up another collective player in the matrix, with their own interests. They sided with the centralization-minded elements of the elite nomenklatura when their interests coincided, but at other times they united with the regional chiefs. Again, as with the central and regional elites, Stalin and the Politburo were part of the broader governing stratum; more often than not they closed ranks with that stratum rather than with the party rank and file. Although these component groups of the elite feuded with one another and combined and recombined in various coalitions, their fears of splitting the party or revealing internal divisions to the outside world provided a strong incentive to keep their squabbles hidden.

Usually the party was able to present a united face to the outside world. But given the fractures and conflicting interests among segments of the party, several alliances and oppositions were possible.

Thus in 1933 and 1935 Stalin and the Politburo united with all levels of the nomenklatura elite to screen, or purge, a helpless rank and file. The regional leaders then used those purges to consolidate their machines and expel "inconvenient" people. This, in turn, brought about another alignment in 1936, in which Stalin and the Moscow nomenklatura sided with the rank and file, who complained of repression by the regional elites. In 1937 Stalin openly mobilized the "party masses" against the nomenklatura as a whole; this provided an important strand in the Great Terror's destruction of the elite. But in 1938 the Politburo changed alignments and reinforced the authority of the regional nomenklatura as part of an attempt to restore order in the party during the terror.

If the matter were not so serious and the human toll not so great, we might feel comfortable seeing this as a form of gamesmanship, in which the various players jockeyed with one another in a system bound by rules they did not always control. Even Stalin's room for maneuver was limited. At various times, for example, he wanted to reduce the authority of certain elite groups. Yet the regime needed these elites to maintain power and run the country. His dilemma, therefore, was to find ways to rein in other players' powers without advertising elite discord to the spectators outside the arena of politics. Sometimes the play became very risky. At one point, Stalin would attempt to co-opt antibureaucratic sentiments of the party rank and file and the public as weapons against parts of the elite. This not only threatened to open elite politics to public scrutiny but also risked discrediting the entire Bolshevik regime, of which Stalin himself was a part. Fine lines had to be walked, and Stalin and others adjusted their initiatives and statements in various ways to cope with these constraints. Finally, in 1937, Stalin broke all the rules of the game—indeed, destroyed the game completely—and unleashed a terror of all against all.

The actors in this tragedy, therefore, include not only Stalin but a variety of subleaders and interest groups both within and without the elite. At least as important as the actors is the setting and environment in which the actions take place, a setting that included Bolshevik traditions of intolerance, fanatical unity against opponents, and easy recourse to violence.

But as we suggest in Chapter 1, something new had been added at the beginning of the 1930s. This "new situation," as the Stalinists called it, was the disastrous position in which the Stalinist leadership found itself after the 1929–32 period of famine, repression, and social upheaval that its collectivization and industrialization policies had caused. Although they publicly celebrated the victory of their new policies, in their inner councils the Stalinist leaders felt more anxiety than confidence, and they perceived that their position was more fragile than secure. This heightened level of insecurity, in light of Bolshevik traditions and Stalin's personality, is important in trying to understand the terror.

Stalinist Mentalities, Language, and the Question of Belief

In the 1930s the Stalinists never felt that they really controlled the country. Transportation and communication were poor, and the regime's representatives were few in number, especially outside the cities. There was not even a telephone line to the Soviet Far East until the 1930s. In the relatively developed European part of Russia, most communications with party committees were by telegraph or letters delivered by couriers on motorcycles. Weather, mud, and snow isolated numerous villages from any contact with the regime for months out of the year. Local party officials frequently interpreted and misinterpreted Moscow's directives in ways that suited their local purposes. The Central Committee complained constantly throughout the decade about the lack of "fulfillment of decisions" and spent a great deal of time creating mechanisms to check up on miscreant and disobedient local leaders.[9]

Established regimes that rest on a base of general popular acceptance and consensual order do not need to resort to terror; they can rely on consensus to ensure stability and compliance. As Pierre Bourdieu has noted, "Once a system of mechanisms has been constituted capable of objectively ensuring the reproduction of the existing order by its own motion, the dominant class have only to *let the system they dominate take its own course* in order to exercise their domination; but until such a system exists, they have to work

9. For a discussion of breakdowns in the party chain of command, see J. Arch Getty, *Origins of the Great Purges: The Soviet Communist Party Reconsidered, 1933–1938*, New York, 1991.

directly, daily, personally, to produce and reproduce conditions of domination which are even then never entirely trustworthy."[10] The Bolsheviks, even into the 1930s, never enjoyed this level of acceptance and constantly feared for the safety of their regime.

The regime's monopoly on force, the sheer scale of the terror, and the grim, mechanical efficiency attributed to the secret police have produced a literature dominated by images of a monstrous, omnipotent "terror machine." Indeed, from the vantage point of the victim, or that of observers who associate themselves with the victim, the objective reality seems clear. To civilians killed by an artillery barrage, the force seems huge and powerful. Yet to those firing the shots, the nature of the persons targeted might seem quite different; they are perceived as inhuman, evil, threatening. The weapons of the state might seem dubious or even weak. Ultimately, of course, there is no difference: people are killed by a terrible mechanical process. But for an understanding of the event as phenomenon, the subjective perceptions of those administering terror are important. Studies of the terror that have dealt at all with the motives of those carrying it out have simply portrayed evil men who killed a lot of people. Without necessarily discarding such characterizations, we shall suggest that those men were also, collectively, frightened of their surroundings. And most of them were as afraid of political and social groups below them as of authorities on high.

This was a political system in which even Politburo members carried revolvers. Recalling in the 1930s their formative experiences in the civil war, the Stalinists always believed themselves figuratively surrounded, constantly at war with powerful and conniving opponents. Twenty years after the event, they reflexively fell back on civil war metaphors and branded all categories of enemies as "White Guards."

On the surface it should not be surprising that those who launched a terror should see the operation as a defensive one. Hitler, in his public statements about Jews, always cast them in the role of the aggressor, the conspirator, the danger. At this level, Stalin's and Hitler's anxious public discourses about "the other"

10. Pierre Bourdieu, *Outline of a Theory of Practice*, Cambridge, 1977, 190.

were similar. But the Soviet documents examined here were never meant for public consumption. They represent the private discussions and deliberations of the nomenklatura, the members of the ruling insiders' club, and therefore reflect the private attitudes and worldviews of that group.

Of course, even if regime anxiety partly inspired the Bolshevik recourse to terror, the awful results of that terror remain unchanged. There is no defense or excuse for the Stalinists; given the scale of the suffering they caused, there can be none. But if we are interested in the "why" surrounding the terror (or that part of it sponsored from above), we must inquire into the leadership's construction of reality and their place in it.

Clifford Geertz has written that "a religion is: (1) a system of symbols which acts to (2) establish powerful, pervasive, and long-lasting moods and motivations in men by (3) formulating conceptions of a general order of existence and (4) clothing these conceptions with such an aura of factuality that (5) the moods and motivations seem uniquely realistic." Although Geertz believed that religion differs from ideology insofar as it appeals to transcendent or cosmic authority, one could argue that the Stalinists' adherence to a form of Marxism-Leninism and their belief that they were agents of historical forces come very close to fulfilling such a definition of religion. Like religion, ideologies are "systems of interacting symbols, as patterns of interworking meanings." Ideology is, therefore, a kind of template or a "perspective" or "orientational necessity" for organizing and shaping a complicated reality. And because ideologies are inherently advocative, they "transform sentiment into significance and so make it socially available." Significantly for our purposes in the Soviet 1930s, Geertz also notes that ideologies become important in times of crisis.[11]

Much of our story in this book involves Stalinist attempts to create an interpretive template, a collective representation of reality that made sense of a society in crisis, as well as a corresponding rationale for a dominant hegemony to control that society. As many social theorists have shown, elites attempt to control societies by creating and promulgating an ideology—a "master discourse"

11. Clifford Geertz, *The Interpretation of Cultures*, New York, 1973, 90–91, 202–6, 219–20.

or "master narrative" for society to follow. Whether we call it a ruling myth, transcript, or hegemonic ideology, elites everywhere support basic systems of beliefs and assumptions.[12] Whether they are about democracy, socialism, fascism, patriarchy, or religion, these systems provide an organizing thought pattern and validation of the existing order (even if that order be revolutionary). They seek to legitimize the existing class and status order: "This is the way things are and this is the way things should be." They also provide a "self-portrait of dominant elites as they would have themselves seen."[13] The belief systems facilitate a unified elite self-representation, cohesion, and integration, and they offer a means of social control by insisting that citizens adhere to them; they thereby provide a definition of heresy in the form of nonadherence.

The documents that we have assembled provide not just a chronicle of orders and decrees. Taken together, they form a kind of discourse, a conversation of the elite and an implicit negotiation among its various levels and constituencies. Some of these documents were meant for public promulgation and in that sense make up a strand that highlights the relationship between leaders and the led. Other documents are more complex creations that were edited and altered in particular ways for particular audiences in attempts to produce specified political lines for particular groups. Studying this body of texts, we believe, can reveal a great deal about the Stalinist system and the groups that interacted within it.

Before proceeding further, we should note that we use *discourse* in its established meaning as an orderly expression of thought, rather than in the sense developed by some recent social theorists. We also use the word to describe spoken or written exposition of one's stance on a topic, often presented for persuasive purpose. Postmodernist "discourse" in the historical sense, among other things, refers to the construction of the past by a historian's use of language and indeed to the exclusive power of language to create what we apprehend as historical reality. In our writing of history, though, we make no assumptions that knowledge of the past exists only through language about it, that "reality" is merely a discursive

12. For a discussion of "transcripts" see James C. Scott, *Domination and the Arts of Resistance*, New Haven, 1990.
13. Scott, *Domination*, 18.

strategy, or that science and reality depend entirely on cultural context. At the same time, though, we shall see that as a dominant, hegemonic, and obligatory political discourse, Stalinist ideology was a powerful force in helping to shape the social world with which it interacted.

A good deal has been written on the function of discourse in the construction of social identities, which, many believe, are inseparable from the language that shapes them.[14] For Michel Foucault and others, discourse consists of patterns, conversations, and ideas functioning at all levels of society to create meaning. Our story here is confined to the elite and its creation of dominant ideologies or master narratives. Construction of such narratives is not usually the product of some intentional conspiracy to control society. Most often it is unconscious; elites promulgate them, and very often believe them. The fact that these symbolic systems also play a functional role of social control may be apparent to some, but to most they are simply self-apparent a priori religious or political "universal truths."

The texts presented here differ from many analogous elite ideologies or religions. Like religious belief systems, Bolshevik discourse was all-encompassing, with explicit heuristic, moral, and normative aspects. But unlike some other historical examples, the Bolshevik master worldview was deliberately created and maintained.

The documents of the Bolshevik elite thus provide a unique case study in the deliberate and intentional production and refinement of a prescribed belief system. Ideological definition was an important part of Bolshevik tradition and Stalinist rule. Lenin spent much of his life producing and debating political programs. For the Bolsheviks before the revolution (and especially for the intellectual leaders in emigration), hairsplitting over precise points of revolutionary ideology was much of their political life. To a significant extent, Bolshevik politics had always been inextricably bound with creating and sharpening texts.

---

14. See Lewis H. Siegelbaum and Ronald Grigor Suny, "Class Backwards? In Search of the Soviet Working Class," in Lewis H. Siegelbaum and Ronald Grigor Suny, eds., *Making Workers Soviet: Power, Class, and Identity*, Ithaca N.Y., 1994, 1–26; Gareth Stedman Jones, *Languages of Class: Studies in English Working Class History, 1832–1982*, Cambridge, 1983.

Statements emanating from the top Stalinist leadership were produced and written with great care and were intended to provide rules and parameters for political and social behavior according to the needs of those creating them. Phrasing was exact, reflecting prescribed linguistic formulations and agreed-upon slogans and phrases. Thus the Central Committee announced the official slogans of the season, which were then republished for study across the country.[15] Typically, *Pravda* issued a list of numbered official slogans on New Year's Day. Individuals, even high officials, were taken to task for using incorrect or unapproved formulations. As we shall see, variant texts of the same document were produced for mandatory consumption by different audiences in an attempt precisely to shape the behavior of those audiences through multiple narratives. In turn, texts from on high were studied and combed by those below for explicit rules and implicit codes and clues to guide political life. The relations among written laws and regulations, transcripts of authoritative political meetings, and speeches often held the key to proper behavior, and the successful politician was the one who best understood the relative powers of various texts.

Stalinist construction of dominant (and eventually obligatory and monopoly) narrative was carried out quite deliberately as a means of social control and transformation. It even had a name: the General Line. It had agencies of propaganda and censorship and a professional network of ideological agitators. Indeed, the Stalinist equivalent of a ministry of education was called the Commissariat of Enlightenment. Stalinist rhetoric was hegemonic and claimed to be monopolistic. Official texts and transcripts tolerated no competing discourses, branding them "enemy propaganda" and equating their creation or distribution with treasonous acts. Competing ideologies and texts, whether oral or written, were considered to be not simply heretical or slanderous but rather equivalent to overt political rebellion. Hostile language and hostile actions were similarly interpreted. The regime had mechanisms to enforce adherence to the dominant line, including the party and the secret police. Deviation from the line was even a specific state crime: anti-Soviet agitation.

15. To take only one local example, see *Rabochii put'* (Smolensk), Oct. 30, 1936, p. 1.

Because Stalinist rhetoric was a purposeful and deliberate production, we are tempted to think that those producing it were completely cynical politicians who in no way believed what they were broadcasting to society. We are perhaps inclined to think that they could not possibly have credited such widespread conspiracies of traitors, spies, and saboteurs. These documents show that this question of belief is a complicated one, connected to collective representations common to both the elite and the general population.

One approach to the question of elite belief is through its use of symbols. Stalinist rhetoric was attributive rather than strictly definitional in its creation of categories, symbols, and images. The best illustrations can be seen in the definition of enemies. The loud and prolonged attacks on "kulaks" (well-to-do peasants) and "Trotskyists" (leftist political dissidents in the 1920s) make little sense in terms of definitional categories. The regime itself could never define precisely who was a kulak according to its own purported criteria about size of farm, number of animals, and so forth. Yet despite this apparent contradiction, the regime continued to attack and denounce kulaks and even to specify quotas for repression. Similarly, the vast majority of those accused and persecuted as Trotskyists had absolutely no allegiance to Trotsky or connection to any Trotskyist program. Even faced with what we can clearly see is a non sequitur, the regime continued to destroy "Trotskyists" who had no real-world connection to Trotskyism.

Given the self-understanding and political traditions of the Bolsheviks, such blanket labels were not really mendacious or contradictory. According to the well-known formula, anyone who opposed the Bolsheviks was objectively and by definition opposing the revolution, opposing socialism, and opposing human welfare, regardless of that person's subjective intent. All those who opposed collectivization, therefore, might as well be kulaks because their opposition had the same effect as actual kulak resistance. All those who opposed, or might oppose, the Stalin Revolution and general line in the 1930s might as well be Trotskyists because the objective effects of their stance were just as harmful as tangible resistance.

Labels (really symbolic codes) like *kulak* or *Trotskyist*, along with many others we shall meet, like the "politically careless" official, the "heartless bureaucrat," the "provocateur," and the "little person," represented not so much categories as tropes, or metaphors, meant to carry symbolic content that changed over time. Rebels are labeled bandits; reluctant peasants become kulaks; dissenters become Trotskyists. Any unauthorized political group becomes ipso facto a "counterrevolutionary organization." As Geertz observes, "The power of a metaphor derives precisely from the interplay between the discordant meanings it symbolically coerces into a unitary conceptual framework and from the degree to which that coercion is successful in overcoming the psychic resistance such semantic tension inevitably generates in anyone in a position to perceive it."[16] But neither the identification nor the analogy were necessarily false for the Stalinists. One of the big surprises in these documents is that the Stalinists said the same things to each other behind closed doors that they said to the public: in this regard their "hidden transcripts" differed little from their public ones.

The Stalinists were themselves prisoners of the symbolic construction—the ideology—that they created. They were ultimately no more capable of escaping it than is the priest of any religion. As Bourdieu puts it, "The 'great' are those who can least afford to take liberties with the official norms. . . . The price to be paid for their outstanding value is outstanding conformity to the values of the group, the source of all symbolic value."[17]

This observation suggests a second approach, beyond the symbolic, to the question of elite belief. The language used in official—and, it is revealing to note, unofficial—texts reflects a particular and ideologically charged view of the world. It uses a peculiar political vocabulary and class-laden prose unique to the Lenin-Stalin political culture. The language is one of symbol-laden political codes that readers with varying levels of sophistication understood in various ways. In addition, these texts reflect a view of the world through a Bolshevik prism that interpreted reality in a special way. In this view of things, for example, persons and events were seen as manifestations of class forces. The world was divided sharply and exclusively into friends and enemies, orthodox and

16. Geertz, *Interpretation of Cultures*, 211.
17. Bourdieu, *Outline of a Theory of Practice*, 193–94.

heretical. Small political initiatives or deviations were portrayed as major attacks by enemy forces.

As Stephen Kotkin has shown, use of such language—"speaking Bolshevik"—was an obligatory part of functioning in Stalinist society.[18] Using the official mode of speech was a way to survive and maneuver within the Stalinist system and was practiced by everyone from the poorest peasant to the most senior official. It was a way in which individuals reacted to and made their way within the prescribed parameters of the system. Without a doubt, whether they were producing official documents, writing letters, or speaking at party meetings, many members of the Stalinist elite consciously "spoke Stalinist" as a matter of group conformity and even individual survival. Even more pragmatically, it was important for the top leaders to use the official language because they were producing texts for use by others at lower positions in the party hierarchy and in society. If they expected everyone to use the *lingua stalina,* they had to use it themselves.

Beyond such considerations of self-interested, utilitarian deployment of language for political or individual purposes, it may be useful to think of another possible effect of language: its impact on the self-understanding and consciousness of those using it.[19] On a basic level, this has been understood for millennia. Educational systems stressing recitation, as well as religious practices of liturgical repetition, have long been based on the simple notion that if people repeat something often enough in a particular form, they will come to believe it. Employing language in this way, therefore, is more than using it as a personal tool. It involves complex processes of identity shaping and formation and the creation of personal subjective meaning through use of language. Belief, therefore, can be understood as a dynamic and evolving process as much as an a priori motivation.

In some of the scenes examined here, this phenomenon can be

18. Stephen Kotkin, *Magnetic Mountain: Stalinism as a Civilization,* Berkeley, 1995.

19. For such considerations see Veronique Garros, Natalia Korenevskaya, and Thomas Lahusen, *Intimacy and Terror,* New York, 1995; and Jochen Hellbeck, "Fashioning the Stalinist Soul: The Diary of Stepan Polubnyi (1831–1939)," *Jahrbücher für Geschichte Osteuropas,* 44, 1996, 344–73. See also Hellbeck's review of Kotkin's book, ibid., 456–63.

examined closely. For example, plena of the Central Committee were secret, closed-door ceremonies with formalized and repetitious speech at a special time and place, in a setting that any anthropologist would recognize as a ritual. Like participation in any ritual or performance, participation in these meetings allowed CC members to affirm the corporate nature and authority of the organization, to represent themselves as members of that body, to legitimize the regime, and ultimately to create a particular meaning for their roles and persons. As they used language instrumentally and obligatorily, they were also being shaped by that language. Their identities were a product of the texts they created just as much as that language was a tool for individual advancement.

Documents and Texts

We present documents of the Communist Party of the Soviet Union from the period 1932–39. The party ratified, validated, and to some extent administered the terror. And it was the party that, as a group or institution, suffered most from it. At every step of the way, the party's Politburo, Central Committee, and other leading bodies took the decisions, adopted the "theses," and made the policies that provided the political and ideological justification for a terror that decimated the party itself.

These fascinating texts chronicle the major political watersheds and many of the less obvious twists and turns of Stalinist politics in the period. But they do more than that. The relation between documents and politics is a two-way street. Not only do these documents reflect political events, they actually influenced those events in important ways. As elements of the ongoing creation of a Stalinist worldview, they helped to create the ideological environment and preconditions for the terror itself and may also help explain why the scars were so deep and the trauma so long-lasting.

Our documents are mostly the central records of the Bolshevik Party: high-level letters, directives and memoranda, minutes of closed party meetings, and correspondence between higher and lower party bodies. The vast majority of these texts are from the files of the party Central Committee and its Politburo and Secretariat; nearly all are recently declassified and previously unpublished. Many of our key documents are from previously secret transcripts of the plena of the Central Committee or other party bodies. These were the forums where party leaders spoke, discussed policy, and even debated with one another.

These files provide an unprecedented inside view of the working and thinking in the party during one of the most tumultuous and violent periods of its history. They allow us to peel back the layers of propaganda and obfuscation with which the party (and its enemies) have covered and distorted these events, and they give us the opportunity to peek inside the mind of Bolshevism to a greater degree than before.

These texts show the major landmarks of the terror. They describe the main turning points, reveal the statements of important actors, and give new information on the numbers and characteristics of the victims. Some of these papers are remarkable: in addition to numerous secret speeches of leaders, we find Stalin's signature on documents authorizing mass executions, his remark to N. I. Bukharin that a possible decision to shoot him was "nothing against you personally," and a variety of documents about Yezhov, who ran the secret police during the terror.

But the sensational nature of many of these documents is not necessarily the most important thing about them. Many of them are ambiguous and susceptible of differing and contradictory interpretations. Like all historical documents they can be read in various ways. Rarely do they provide glib or simple answers to key questions. They do not tell us who organized the murder of S. M. Kirov in 1934. They do not tell us exactly when Stalin became convinced that mass terror was necessary, nor do they fully illuminate his thoughts. They do not prove whether there was a plan to conduct terror or the extent to which conscious plans were made to facilitate it. Scholars and readers will still have to make their own judgments about such questions, but at least now they will have more to go on.

When we find dramatic and unambiguous "smoking guns" in historical documents, they sometimes allow us to answer specific questions or to attribute praise or blame. But fortunately or unfortunately, smoking guns are rare in historical research, and real historical study rarely proceeds on such a basis. We still need to interpret and explain what things mean and why things happened as they did. Even if we had documents conclusively documenting every step of Stalin's thinking and action, even if they proved or disproved a premeditated plan for terror, even if we had an imaginary secret Stalin diary, we would still have work to do in the areas of interpretation and understanding. We would be able to show conclusively who threw what switch when; we would know a lot of the details. That would be no small step, but it would not in itself answer deeper questions about the phenomenon of terror and the mentalities that inspired it.

The objective realities of the 1930s were perhaps not as important as the Bolsheviks' perceptions of them, not least because the Bolsheviks acted on their perceptions. Like all politicians, the Bolsheviks interpreted their world and created representations of it that were, for them, reality. Our documents, particularly the secret internal ones, give the impression that many believed much of what they said: their collective representation of the world was both a product of these texts and a guide to their words and deeds. This implies neither a crude subjectivism nor a moral relativism. That the Bolsheviks functioned within sets of beliefs and perceptions does not absolve them of moral responsibility for the repression and destruction of lives their policies caused. This is precisely why our documents are priceless treasures. They provide a look into the Bolshevik mind. We see here what Bolshevik leaders said to one another behind closed doors and outside the public arena. We may to some extent gauge what they thought, apart from what they wanted the public (or historians) to think.

Some certainly believed their own rhetoric, and some did not. But virtually the entire elite (and even its victims) shared ideas about what constituted treason and conspiracy that differed sharply from ours. It is possible that we and the Bolsheviks may well agree on the facts of a particular "case," but we still would have diametrically opposed notions of criminality attached to the matter. Their "truth" was different from ours, and it was perfectly possible for them sincerely to accept someone's guilt where we see no offense.

Even if we assumed, for the sake of argument, a complete cynicism on the part of the Bolsheviks and began with the assumption that they manufactured a convenient transcript about themselves or their enemies, we should still have important questions to answer. Why in this case would they feel the necessity to frame their policies in Manichaean terms of conspiracy? Why would they speak to one another in their private councils in a code language they all knew was false? What was it about them and their society that forced them to behave as they did?

In this sense, it is not vitally important to establish conclusively, on the basis of the documents, whether Bolsheviks regularly lied to themselves and to one another, or whether they believed anything of what they said. The very existence of these texts, along with an analysis of their contents, images, and language, already tells us a great deal about Stalinist thinking. Objections to using Stalinist texts because Stalinists were liars miss the point. It is not crucial, even if it were possible, to establish whether or how often the Stalinists believed what they said and wrote. Regardless of their relation to "truth" or "reality," the texts can tell us at a minimum what their authors wanted others to think. In heeding these accounts, we will move closer to answering a central question: How was all this possible?

More than a few caveats are in order. First, our study does not touch on all questions relating to the terror. Because our sources are predominantly internal political records of the upper Communist Party, we are unable to deal comprehensively with foreign policy, agricultural or industrial affairs, or cultural matters. We rather focus on party policy as it relates to internal repression of perceived and identified "enemies," and hope that this exercise may shed some light on other areas. Our concentration on high politics in this collection does not imply that other factors were unimportant or even less important. Local conflicts between leaders and led, social and status conflicts on the shop floor or the kolkhoz, populist resentment from below, even popular culture played active roles that have been documented in other studies. But because of the categories of documents we present, these important elements cannot receive a great deal of attention here except as the objects of central concerns and policies. This is a bias of the source base, not necessarily a reflection of historical reality.

Second, even within a subject focus, all scholars are necessarily selective in their use of sources. Because our subject is the Communist Party, nearly all our documents are from the former Central Party Archive of the Soviet Communist Party, which is technically responsible for party documents for the period to 1953. Accordingly, we have not made use of the collections in the various state, economic, and cultural archives.

Similarly, for a variety of reasons we have not used much of the large corpus of memoir literature. This reflects no claim that Stalinist archival documents are inherently trustworthy or that they are inherently superior to literary accounts in general. Because of the special relation of Stalinist discourse to the truth (or more accurately because the Stalinists were "creating truth" through their documents), archival documents must be handled with utmost critical care. With that in mind, it is important also to observe that they were produced by the people in power. On the other hand, the vast majority of existing memoir accounts were not written by persons in a position accurately to report the maneuvers of high politics that we are studying. Much of the information they provide is in the form of second- or thirdhand gossip and hearsay. Even available secret police memoirs were written by agents stationed outside the USSR during the 1930s and written decades later.[20] Not only are such memoirs suspect because of their distance from the events they discuss; they also contain major mistakes and errors of fact. For example, concerning only some key events of the terror discussed in this volume, the two most important police memoirs misdate (sometimes by years) the Riutin opposition, the purge of 1933, the implication of Marshal Tukhachevsky, the arrest of Piatakov, and the execution of the army generals in 1937.[21]

Memoirs of victims who were not part of the elite or who were far removed from the seat of power, although they contain poignant and revealing material, cannot be taken as sources for central decision making even when they provide tantalizing rumors re-

20. For an analysis of this literature and its limitations see Getty, *Origins*, 211–21.

21. See Walter G. Krivitsky, *In Stalin's Secret Service*, New York, 1939, 181, 183, 241, 242; and Alexander Orlov, *The Secret History of Stalin's Crimes*, New York, 1953, 178, 310.

peated in the labor camps. By contrast, Molotov's and Kagano-vich's memoirs, although they were written decades after the events they recount, are more important sources because of the key positions their authors held in the 1930s. Nevertheless, they deserve the most strict critical treatment because of their ideological and self-serving nature.

The massive and voluminous nature of the party archives forced a strict and sometimes painful selectivity on us. We have, for example, avoided reproducing documents that are well-known and already published in English; in such cases the reader is referred to easily available editions. This collection is *representative* of the currently available source base of documents of the party leadership in the 1930s; it can by no means be considered complete or comprehensive. Our working group of American and Russian scholars and archival specialists tried at every step to select documents that fairly represented trends or groups of documents, and, within long individual documents, tried to retain the most significant sections for publication here. We can only hope that these selections help to provide a fuller answer to the question, "How was this all possible?"

I
Closing Ranks

CHAPTER ONE

The New Situation, 1930–32

I believe that the implementation of a plan of such exceptional difficulty as that which confronts us in 1931 demands solid unity between the top echelons of the Soviet and party leadership. Not the slightest cleft should be permitted.—V. V. Kuibyshev, 1930

THESE WERE TERRIBLE YEARS in the Soviet Union. In 1932, the fifteenth year of the revolution, the country faced the paradox of rapid industrial expansion combined with the starvation of millions of people. How had things come to such a pass?

In 1917 the Bolsheviks had come to power in a relatively backward country suffering through a wartime crisis. As Marxists, they believed that socialism was the inevitable future for mankind but that it depended on the existence of an advanced economy. As Leninists, they were convinced that this future could be brought about through a highly disciplined party of professional revolutionaries acting as "midwives of history" to guide the masses toward their future. These beliefs associated with the Leninist version of Marxism were understood differently by various groups within the Bolshevik Party, but by and large they were fundamentals of Bolshevism and crucial factors in the futures of both the party and the country.

Almost immediately, the new regime was plunged into the three-year civil war that pitted the Reds (Bolsheviks and their allies) against the Whites (politically, almost everyone else). More than a dozen capitalist states backed the Whites against the Bolsheviks in a war characterized by almost unimaginable violence and cruelty on both sides. Torture and massacres of prisoners were common, epidemic and famine racked the country, and the economic base of the country was undermined.

The civil war was an important formative experience for the Bolsheviks. To stay in power—to save the Revolution—they had launched a Red Terror and organized a secret police (Cheka) with unlimited powers to arrest, try, and execute. The war had forced on the Bolsheviks a kind of military discipline that placed a premium on obedience, strict party unity, and a combative mentality. Words like *implacable* and *pitiless* entered the Bolshevik vocabulary as positive descriptives for party members. Moreover, the life-and-death struggle against domestic and foreign enemies of the Revolution had nurtured in their minds a kind of siege mentality that made them see enemies and conspiracies everywhere and allowed little in the way of compromise or toleration. Concerns for legality and civil rights were seen as "rotten liberalism," which was dangerous to the Revolution, and it was in this period that the Bolsheviks banned other parties and took monopolistic control of the press. The Reds won the civil war in 1921, but these wartime measures were continued indefinitely. The regime never felt confident about its hold on power; domestic and foreign enemies were still out there, and to weaken the state seemed an unnecessary risk. Intolerance, quick recourse to violence and terror, and generalized fear and insecurity were the main legacies of the civil war. The ends justified the means, and it was the civil war that turned revolutionaries into dictators.[1]

Indeed, so concerned were the Bolsheviks with maintaining iron discipline in their own ranks that at the very moment of victory they passed a resolution banning the formation of factions within their own party. Lenin's ideas of party organization, known as democratic centralism, held that party policies should be adopted democratically, but once a decision was taken it was the duty of all party

1. On the civil war see Diane P. Koenker, William G. Rosenberg, and Ronald G. Suny, eds., *Party, State, and Society in the Russian Civil War: Explorations in Social History,* Bloomington, Ind., 1989; Peter Kenez, *Civil War in South Russia, 1919–1920,* Berkeley, 1977. An unsurpassed early work is William Chamberlin, *The Russian Revolution* (vol. 2), London, 1935.

members publicly to defend and support those policies whether or not they personally agreed with them. Rather loosely observed in the party before and during 1917, these norms received strong reinforcement in the desperate emergency of the civil war, and party leaders of all kinds had little trouble institutionalizing them as a "ban on fractions" at the Tenth Party Congress in early 1921.

Economically, the Bolsheviks faced a bleak outlook at the end of the civil war. During that struggle, their policies had been a patch-work of nationalizations, labor mobilizations, food requisitions, and state-sponsored barter known as state capitalism or, later, War Communism. The Russian peasants, a large majority of the popula-tion, had in their own spontaneous revolution seized and redis-tributed the land during 1917. They tolerated Bolshevik forced grain requisitions during the war only because the alternative was a restoration of the Old Regime with its landlords. But with the passing of the wartime emergency the peasants were unwilling to sacrifice their harvests for the Bolshevik state, and a series of revolts convinced Lenin of the need to placate peasant farmers to save the regime.[2]

The result was the New Economic Policy (NEP), adopted in 1921. Free markets were allowed in agriculture and in small and medium industry (the Bolsheviks retained nationalized heavy in-dustry in their own hands). Lenin saw this concession to capitalism as a necessary measure to appease the peasants and to allow market forces to help rebuild the shattered economy. NEP always enjoyed mixed popularity among the Bolsheviks. It was variously charac-terized as a "retreat" or a "breathing spell" on the road to social-ism, and the emphasis given to one or the other characterization reflected a party member's political views.[3]

For some "moderate" or "rightist" Bolsheviks, NEP was a stra-tegic retreat that implied a fairly long road to the eventual socialist

2. See Orlando Figes, *Peasant Russia, Civil War: The Volga Countryside in Revolution, 1917–1921,* Oxford, 1989; Silvana Malle, *The Economic Organiza-tion of War Communism, 1918–1921,* New York, 1985.

3. Stephen F. Cohen, *Bukharin and the Bolshevik Revolution: A Political Biog-raphy, 1888–1938,* New York, 1975; Lewis H. Siegelbaum, *Soviet State and Society Between Revolutions, 1918–1929,* New York, 1992; Sheila Fitzpatrick, Alexander Rabinowitch, and Richard Stites, eds., *Russia in the Era of NEP: Explorations in Soviet Society and Culture,* Bloomington, Ind., 1991.

goal. Traversing that long evolutionary path would require patient socialist indoctrination of the population, education, and above all, cultivation of the goodwill of the peasant majority along the way as it "grew into" socialism. For more "leftist" Bolsheviks, NEP was a tactical breathing spell, a temporary rest period before restarting the socialist offensive. For these leftists, who believed that reaching socialism was a revolutionary process that would inevitably involve a "class struggle" with "capitalist elements" among the peasantry, NEP was always a dangerous concession to capitalism.

Regardless of their political disposition toward the mixed economy of NEP, virtually all Bolsheviks agreed that the basic problem was an economic one. If Russia was to reach socialism, the country would have to undergo a dramatic industrial expansion. Marx had taught that socialism followed developed capitalism and was based on a modern technological and industrial base. Nobody in the party believed that Russia was anywhere near that stage, so the question was how (and how fast) to industrialize.

Rightist Bolsheviks, who clustered around economic theoretician and *Pravda* editor Nikolai Bukharin (and eventually trade union leader Mikhail Tomsky and Premier Aleksei Rykov), saw NEP as a long-term strategy in which the party should maintain its alliance *(smychka)* with an increasingly prosperous peasantry. Funds for industrialization would be generated by rational taxation and the general growth of the economy. Leftist Bolsheviks, on the other hand, favored "squeezing" resources from the peasantry at a faster rate. Led by Communist International chief and Leningrad party boss Grigory Zinoviev, Moscow party chief Lev Kamenev, and the brilliant Leon Trotsky, the leftists were impatient with what they considered the coddling of the peasantry and pressed for a more militant and aggressive industrial policy. Rightists accused them of courting disaster by provoking the peasantry. Leftists retorted by arguing that the rightist version of NEP was a sellout to capitalist elements that were holding the Bolsheviks hostage and delaying industrialization.

Overlaying and sharpening these disagreements was a classic struggle for succession that followed Lenin's death in 1924. Based on personal loyalties, patron-client networks, and sometimes policy platforms, Bolshevik leaders began to gravitate to various high personalities of the party who contended for Lenin's mantle. Bukharin spoke for the pro-NEP rightist Bolsheviks. Zinoviev became the leading spokesman for the more aggressive economic leftists. Trotsky, always an iconoclast, took varying—although generally leftist—positions on economic questions but was best known as an advocate of antibureaucratism and increased party democracy.

Iosif Stalin, as general secretary of the party, had influence among the growing apparat, or full-time corps of professional party secretaries and administrators. The party had grown tremendously from a relatively small membership in early 1917. As it became larger and more complex and took on the tasks of government rather than those of insurrection, Lenin and other leaders saw the need to regularize the party's structure. Toward the end of the civil war the party's governing body, the Central Committee, formed three subcommittees to carry out the party's work between sittings of the full body. The Political Bureau (Politburo) was to decide the grand strategic questions of policy. An Organizational Bureau (Orgburo) was to organize implementation of these decisions by assigning cadres to the necessary tasks. Finally, a Secretariat was charged with the day-to-day mundane matters of handling correspondence and communication, moving paperwork through the party bureaucracy, and preparing agendas for the other bodies. Stalin, pushed forward by Lenin as a good organizer, sat on all three subcommittees.[4]

Most party leaders believed that the Politburo would be the locus of real political power, and to a great extent it was. But as the struggle for personal influence heated up in the 1920s, real power—as is always the case in a large organization—was as much a question of patronage as of theory, and from his vantage in the Orgburo and Secretariat, Stalin was able to influence personnel appointments throughout the party. While the other leaders stood on economic policy platforms and theoretical formulations, Stalin's power was that of the machine boss. Throughout the country, territorial-based party committees were led by a network of party secretaries who, in theory, carried out the Politburo's policy in the

4. Robert H. McNeal, *Stalin: Man and Ruler*, Oxford, 1988.

provinces. More and more in the 1920s, this full-time party secretarial apparatus looked to Stalin as its leader.[5]

And he was an attractive leader for many reasons. Unlike the
other top leaders, Stalin was not an intellectual or theoretician. He
spoke a simple and unpretentious language appealing to a party
increasingly made up of workers and peasants. His style contrasted
sharply with that of his Politburo comrades, whose complicated
theories and pompous demeanor won them few friends among the
plebeian rank and file. He also had an uncanny way of projecting
what appeared to be moderate solutions to complicated problems.
Unlike his colleagues, who seemed shrill in their warnings of fatal
crises, Stalin frequently put himself forward as the calm man of the
golden mean with moderate, compromise solutions.

The personal struggle for power among the Olympian Bolshevik
leaders was complicated but can be summarized quickly. Beginning
in 1923, Trotsky launched a trenchant criticism of Stalin's "regime
of professional secretaries," claiming that they had become ossified
bureaucrats cut off from their proletarian followers. Trotsky also
argued that the survival of the Bolshevik regime depended on receiving support from successful workers' revolutions in Europe,
and he accused Stalin and other leaders of losing interest in spreading the revolution. To the other Politburo leaders, Trotsky seemed
the most powerful and the most dangerous. By common recognition he was, after Lenin, the most brilliant theoretician in the party.
More important, he was the leader of the victorious Red Army and
regarded as personally ambitious and a potential Napoleon of the
Russian Revolution.

Bukharin, Zinoviev, Kamenev, and Stalin closed ranks to isolate
Trotsky, accusing him of trying to split the party because of his
personal ambition to lead it. They argued that Trotsky was only
using "party democracy" as a phony political issue: during the civil
war he had never been for anything less than iron discipline. Now,
they charged, his criticism weakened party unity. Stalin in particular played a nationalist card by noting that the world revolution
was not coming about as soon as they had thought, and in any case
"we" Bolsheviks and "we" Soviet people do not need the help of

5. See Graeme Gill, *The Origins of the Stalinist Political System*, Cambridge,
1990, for the development of party organization.

foreigners to build socialism. "Socialism in One Country" was a real possibility, he argued, and Trotsky's insistence on proletarian revolutions abroad betrayed a lack of faith in the party's and country's possibilities. Faced with the unity of the other Politburo members, the party's near-religious devotion to party unity and discipline, and Stalin's influence among the party apparatus, Trotsky could not win. He was stripped of his military post in 1924 and gradually marginalized in the top leadership.[6]

The following year Zinoviev and Kamenev split off from the "party majority" by launching a critique of NEP from the leftist point of view. They said that the NEP policy of conceding constantly increasing grain prices to the peasantry was depriving the state of capital for industrialization, bankrupting industry, confronting the proletariat with high bread prices, and indefinitely postponing the march to socialism. In 1926 Trotsky joined Zinoviev and Kamenev in the New or United Opposition. To the Leningrad and Moscow machine votes controlled by Zinoviev and Kamenev, Trotsky brought the remnants of his supporters.

Stalin and Bukharin denounced this United Opposition as another attempt to split the party by challenging the existing policy and violating the "centralism" part of democratic centralism. Moreover, they defended NEP as the only viable and safe policy. Their arguments seemed far less incendiary than those of the left. Bukharin's impressive pragmatic and theoretical defense of "Lenin's" NEP, combined with Stalin's low-key pragmatic approach, were a formidable combination. The votes from the party secretarial apparatus—loyal to Stalin and not eager to provoke a dangerous turn in party policy—won the day, and the United Opposition went down to defeat in 1927.[7]

In a final bid for power, followers of Trotsky organized a street demonstration on the anniversary of the October Revolution in 1927 to protest the Central Committee majority and defend the leftists. Stalin and Bukharin used the police to break up this demonstration, characterizing it as an illegal and disloyal blow against the

6. The classic work on Trotsky is still Isaac Deutscher, *The Prophet* (3 vols.), Oxford, 1959.

7. See Robert V. Daniels, *The Conscience of the Revolution: Communist Opposition in Soviet Russia*, New York, 1969.

party. It was one thing to disagree with the leadership by voting against it in conferences and congresses, but quite another to take to the streets. Such a move horrified the party majority because it threatened to take the inner-party struggle into the public eye, where real enemies, disgruntled workers, and discontented "elements" of all kinds could take advantage of the friction in the party to threaten the regime as a whole. Trotsky seemed to be putting his own interests above those of the Bolshevik government, thereby putting the entire Revolution in danger. As we shall see, any attempt to carry politics outside the confines of the party was, to the Bolsheviks, the one unpardonable sin. Zinoviev and Kamenev were stripped of their most powerful positions. Trotsky was expelled from the party and exiled to Central Asia. In 1929 he was deported from the country.

Bukharin and Stalin were in charge. Bukharin handled theoretical matters and the powerful party press. His associates Tomsky and Rykov ran the trade unions and the government ministries. Stalin, for his part, led the growing party apparatus aided by a corps of Old Bolshevik lieutenants that included Viacheslav Molotov, Lazar Kaganovich, Kliment Voroshilov, and Sergo Ordzhonikidze. By all accounts, Stalin and Bukharin became close friends in this period. They called each other by familiar nicknames neither of them had used for Trotsky, Zinoviev, or Kamenev, and their arduous but successful struggle against the left certainly was a source of personal bonding. Their families saw each other socially, and Bukharin was a frequent guest in Stalin's home, sometimes spending entire summer months at Stalin's country house.[8]

But the political victory did not mean that the economy of NEP was working satisfactorily. Paying high prices for the peasants' grain drained the treasury and was not increasing the market for industrial goods by raising peasant buying power. After repairing the industrial base and reaching the level of 1914, industrial growth was stagnating. Workers faced high food prices and intensification of labor discipline from various "labor rationalizations" designed to increase efficiency. By the late 1920s, unemployment had reared its head, threatening the Bolsheviks' social base of support within

8. See the memoirs of Stalin's daughter: "Nikolai Bukharin, whom everyone adored, often came for the summer." Svetlana Alliluyeva, *Twenty Letters to a Friend,* New York, 1967, 31.

the working class. The real and immediate threat, however, and the factor that would change everything, came from agriculture.

Despite what the Bolsheviks considered to be favorable prices, the Russian peasantry was not marketing an adequate quantity of grain to satisfy urban and military needs. The reasons for this were complicated, but they included poor agricultural technology, bad harvests, and peasants playing the market by holding back grain to force higher prices. To Stalin in particular, all this smelled of peasant sabotage, and he doubtless began to wonder (but never to admit) whether perhaps the leftists had not been correct about the impossibility of allying with the peasants forever.

Beginning in 1927 Stalin sponsored a countrywide series of forced grain requisitions. Squads of Bolshevik loyalists fanned out across the countryside, and local party officials were mobilized to force peasants to market their grain reserves at fixed prices. Bukharin was horrified. He was not a blind partisan of the market and had been in favor of a controlled squeezing of the well-to-do peasant *(kulak)*. But Stalin's "extraordinary measures" went too far, striking at the "middle peasant" as well; such radical and voluntarist campaigns threatened to alienate the peasantry as a whole and to destroy the market foundations of NEP. Bukharin, Rykov, and Tomsky protested in the Politburo.[9]

Tempers flared, positions hardened, and the gulf between Stalin and Bukharin widened quickly. Neither side would compromise, and a break became inevitable. The Stalin faction accused Bukharin and his comrades of forming a propeasant "right opposition" against the "majority policy" of the Central Committee. In a series of Politburo and CC meetings in 1928 and 1929, Stalin was able to mobilize enough votes to defeat the rightists by portraying the situation as a potentially fatal crisis for the regime. By 1930 Bukharin, Rykov, and Tomsky were stripped of their key positions. But unlike the leftists, the right opposition went quietly. They did not take the struggle outside the party corridors and never attempted to mobilize support "outside" in society. Rykov later said that the rightists had been afraid of provoking a civil war.[10] Ac-

9. See Cohen, *Bukharin;* and Michal Reiman, *The Birth of Stalinism: The USSR on the Eve of the Second Revolution,* trans. George Saunders, Bloomington, Ind., 1987.

10. Rykov told this to the American newspaper reporter William Reswick. W. Reswick, *I Dreamt Revolution,* Chicago, 1956, 254.

cordingly, their treatment in defeat was much milder. They recanted their "mistakes" in party forums and with good party discipline affirmed their support for Stalin's line. Although they were removed from the Politburo, they remained on the Central Committee and were not expelled from the party. Those of their followers who refused to recant were expelled, and a few of the most recalcitrant were arrested.

Their power now unchallenged, the Stalinists plunged ahead with a truly radical Second Revolution, sometimes called the Stalin Revolution. In agriculture, the "extraordinary measures" of 1927–28 became a violent campaign of "dekulakization," in which hundreds of thousands of peasant families were deprived of their farms and deported to distant regions. By 1930 dekulakization had become the "full collectivization" of agriculture. Private farming and private property were ended, and agricultural production was organized into state-controlled collective farms. The public goal was to end capitalism and bring about the long-awaited socialism. The private goal was to end the economic power of the peasantry and establish control over food production.[11]

At the same time, the Stalinists abolished capitalism in industry and trade. All production was nationalized, and growth was to be planned without market mechanisms according to Five Year Plans of the national economy. Based on the notions that socialism could be built immediately and that national defense required quick growth, industrialization was to be carried out at a breakneck pace. Production targets were set extremely high, and the country was mobilized for the campaign of development. A new "Soviet technical intelligentsia" was to be created to staff industry. Professional engineers trained under the old regime but still working in industry ("bourgeois specialists") were pushed aside, removed, and arrested in large numbers to make way for a new generation of rapidly trained and politically loyal Red Engineers. Factory workers were taken from production and sent to school in large numbers to staff

11. See Moshe Lewin, *Russian Peasants and Soviet Power: A Study of Collectivization*, London, 1968; R. W. Davies, *The Socialist Offensive: The Collectivization of Soviet Agriculture, 1929–1930*, Cambridge, Mass., 1980; Sheila Fitzpatrick, *Stalin's Peasants: Resistance and Survival in the Russian Village After Collectivization*, Oxford, 1994.

this new cadre in a kind of massive affirmative action program for the proletariat.[12]

The Stalin Revolution was an enthusiastic campaign, not a policy. Scientific industrial "norms" and rational calculations of agricultural potential were cast aside in favor of impassioned mobilization. "Bolsheviks can storm any fortresses" became a watchword of the new revolution; speed and quantity, rather than accuracy and quality, became the criteria for success. Cautious warnings were denounced as sabotage or "capitalist wrecking," and careful analysis was suspect. No one could stand aside in the great push for modernization and socialism. The period of the first Five Year Plan (1928–32) was one of exuberance and excitement. Millions of workers went to school and moved into management. Millions of young peasants escaped the villages and flocked to new lives in construction. Young people volunteered in large numbers to work for the common effort, to help with collectivization, and to improve their work qualifications. For the young Nikita Khrushchevs and Leonid Brezhnevs, this was the best of times. It was the period of optimism and dynamism and the time that launched their careers. The enthusiastic upward mobility for plebeians looked very much like the fruition of the revolution: the workers were taking power and building socialism!

The Bolsheviks believed that they were involved in a life-or-death "class war" against the remaining "capitalist elements" in society. They issued slogans about class warfare and constantly stressed the need to win a quick victory, not only for the sake of socialism but to prevent an expected foreign intervention by capitalist states eager to protect their kulak and capitalist class allies. Party discipline took on an even more military character than before; party "mobilizations" on this or that "front," to storm this or that fortress, were always in the air. Even the military tunic of civil war days came back into fashion for party leaders and militants.

The first Five Year Plan was a resounding success. Production indexes in mining, steel, and chemicals increased severalfold in four years. Factories and mines materialized everywhere, and the country was proud of the new giant dams, plants, and railroads whose

12. Sheila Fitzpatrick, *Education and Social Mobility in the Soviet Union, 1921–1934*, New York, 1979.

construction contrasted so sharply with the industrial doldrums of the Great Depression in the West. Unemployment disappeared, and although real wages actually fell (another casualty of capital accumulation), education, opportunity, and mobility were available to everyone willing to work. In the lives of the rapidly increasing urban masses, on the factory wall charts of production, and in the rapidly growing network of educational institutions, everything was onward and upward.

But judged according to its effect on the lives of the peasantry, the agricultural part of the Stalin Revolution was an unqualified disaster, provoking one of the greatest human tragedies of modern times. Wild radical collectivizers descended on the villages, closing churches and attacking priests and other traditional village leaders. Grain was seized without any regard for peasants' need for food and seed. Any resistance was attributed to "kulak sabotage" and was met by deportation to Siberia, arrest, or execution. Many peasants were unable to plant because the seed had been taken; others refused to plant in protest. Rather than give up their animals to the new collective farms, peasants slaughtered horses, cows, pigs, and sheep in huge numbers. When the meat was gone the peasants starved. Soviet meat production would not recover for decades. The loss of animal traction power, and the regime's inability to provide tractors in adequate numbers, paralyzed agriculture. The regime's inability or unwillingness to calculate rational targets for planting and harvesting, along with the chaos in the countryside that was partly effect and partly cause of the government's miscalculation, hamstrung agriculture across the land, and bad weather was the coup de grâce, producing mass starvation. Millions died from hunger, disease, or the terrible conditions of remote exile.

By and large, party militants had responded loyally to the Stalinist "socialist offensive" of 1929–34. Believing that they were fighting the final battle for the communist millennium, masses of party members responded enthusiastically to the leadership's calls for rapid collectivization and escalating industrial production targets. In some cases, local militants' zeal outstripped the plans of the center, and Moscow often had to rein in excessive dekulakizations, forcible collectivization, and ultraleftist zeal in persecuting religion. At other times, local party officials and activists balked at the grain requisitions and more extreme forms of dekulakization and collectivization. Most of the time, though, the hard-line activities of party collectivizers on the ground were a reflection of the extreme policies of the Stalin leadership. The result was a disastrous famine and social violence and persecution on an unimaginable scale.

As we have seen, the "right opposition" of N. I. Bukharin, M. P. Tomsky, and A. I. Rykov had opposed the leftist course of collectivization back in 1928. But it had been defeated by 1929, and its leaders had recanted their mistakes in order to remain in the party. These mandatory recantations were designed not only to show a united face to the world but also to "disarm" the lower-level followers of the leading oppositionists. Former dissident leaders were required to show their orthodoxy in order to demonstrate to their former adherents that resistance was wrong and to confirm the correctness of the Stalinist party line. One scholar has aptly described such public apologies as a ritual payment of "symbolic taxes" or "symbolic capital," through public display of acceptance of error in order to reaffirm the status quo.[13]

The former dissidents were further expected to work loyally and diligently to fulfill that line and to combat the party's enemies. This was the essence of party discipline, as the Bolsheviks understood it. The following document is one of N. I. Bukharin's recantations. In 1930, however, such rituals did not have the solemnity that they would take on later. Oppositionists could still recant in a virtual colloquy with the Stalinist audience; Bukharin's text contained puns, and his reference to executing dissidents drew laughter.

Document 1

N. I. Bukharin's speech to a joint plenum of the CC and CCC of the VKP(b), 19 December 1930[14]

Bukharin: . . . I shall endeavor to reveal, in the course of analyzing the economic processes currently in place and in analyzing the whole system of scheduled figures established for the year 1931, the fundamental mistakes

13. James C. Scott, *Domination and the Arts of Resistance,* New Haven, 1990, 57. See also Pierre Bourdieu, *Outline of a Theory of Practice,* Cambridge, 1977, ch. 4, for a discussion of "symbolic capital."

14. RTsKhIDNI, f. 17, op. 2, d. 453, ll. 53–61, 70–74, 77–78, 87–92.

committed by a group of comrades, to whom I myself once belonged, mistakes which I have long ago repudiated and which I now completely disavow.

At the present plenum, which is holding session on the threshold of a new economic year, we are taking stock, to a certain extent, of the long and excruciating path of our economic development. If we place before ourselves in the most summary fashion the results of such stocktaking relative to the period that has just ended, then we deem it necessary to enumerate the following fundamental and central facts:

First, the feasibility of the "The Five Year Plan in Four Years."

Second, the surpassing of the norms outlined in the Five Year Plan for many branches of the economy, including many crucial branches of production.

Third, exceptional progress in agriculture.

Fourth, the basic resolution of the grain problem.

Fifth—and I consider this extremely important for the entire economic strategic and tactical policy for the coming economic year—the successful carrying out of state grain procurement. . . .

Sixth, the growth of the Soviet Union into a major world economic power. Consequently, we are not talking here about a political characterization of the Soviet Union but rather of the power of its technical-economic base, which, of course, also determines its political power. Then, conducting the most general summary, "a summary of summaries"—i.e., examining the whole process in terms of the class struggle—we are obliged to take note of the indisputable and obvious fact that these achievements have been attained in the course of a bitter class struggle. It was the crushing of a class enemy, of the kulak capitalist stratum, the process of a transition to total collectivization of the poor-middle peasant, petty peasant economy [*sploshnaia kollektivizatsiia bedniatsko-seredniatskogo melko-krest'ianskogo khoziaistva*], and the party's relentless and determined pursuit of the general line that gave us victory. At the same time—and it was absolutely right to do so—the party leadership had to crush [*razgromit'*] the most dangerous rightist deviation within our party.

Voroshilov: And those infected with it.

Bukharin: If you are talking about their physical destruction [*razgrom*], I leave it to those comrades who are, to one degree or another, given to bloodthirstiness. (Laughter.) . . . The contradictions of NEP, their dimensions, character, forcefulness, and significance, have proven to be greater in proportion and content than previously thought. In the first place, over a period of many years a rather solid capitalist kulak upper stratum [*golovka*] has arisen and grown in the countryside, drawing to itself certain strata of the so-called well-to-do peasantry. In the second place—and I consider this extremely important—the petty-bourgeois peasant economy has come into blatant contradiction with the colossal tempos [of production] that our socialist industry has begun to generate. For this reason, in view of our party's tactics and strategy, it has become necessary, above all, to crush the kulaks [*kulachestvo*], to undermine their foundations, to move rapidly toward a socialist consolidation of the economy. I fear that some people will reproach me for my weakness in using certain "catchwords," etc., a reproach sanctioned by party traditions, but something in the nature of a revolution against the kulak has taken place—at once from above and below.

Ordzhonikidze: If the kulaks don't want to develop in the direction of socialism, what can you do with them?! (Laughter.)

Bukharin: Nothing, of course! But I demand justice also for those who reproach me. Take, for instance, Comrade Miliutin, who always takes advantage of every opportunity to take a jab at me. Anyone who can read need only look at his article in the Great Soviet Encyclopedia entitled "Agrarian Politics" to see how he has copied everything from me, including my mistakes, everything from A to Z. But only in theory. Meanwhile, under the cover of this lord of hosts of the Communist Academy, a book was published containing a special analysis of the kolkhozy. This analysis begins—just think!—with the military settlements of Count Arakcheev: this is—speaking very, very delicately—rightist opportunism in practice. (Laughter.)

Miliutin: That's not true.

Bukharin: It is absolutely true. Allow me to conduct a "vicious struggle" not only against myself but also against all of my former allies who are now getting away with the frivolous flight of the butterfly and with smirks. Permit me to bring their actions to the light of day. I shall now pass on, however, to the essence of the matter.

In my opinion, the destruction of the kulaks constitutes, in the first place, a decisive and, if I may say frankly, painful process, a process entailing a direct break with the old structure, a process of refashioning [*peredelka*] the petty peasant economy on the basis of socialist collectivization. This is the main thing that took place, the main thing that had to take place, the main thing not understood by a group of comrades, to which your humble servant had once belonged.

Ordzhonikidze: Nikolai Ivanovich [Bukharin].

Bukharin [ironically]: Nikolai Ivanovich, indeed, if you would like to show special courtesy to your colleague on the Supreme Council for the National Economy of the USSR [VSNKh]. (Laughter.) It seems to me that there are also reasons of an international character that constitute an additional, very weighty argument for the correctness of the party's general line. I have in mind, above all, the course of the present worldwide economic crisis.

I would like to say several words about the control figures put forward here. . . . We have before us not only the quantitative growth of the indicated plan figures but also qualitative improvements in the plan, methods of planning, and compiling of control figures that, consequently, give us real guarantees against a series of mistakes that arose in the absence of this situation. . . .

First of all, this is a matter of the coordination of mutually dependent branches of the national economy . . . coordination of specific spheres of production within industry and the liquidation of disproportions therein and regulating production supplies between one branch and another. . . . The disproportion between metallurgy and metal working . . . the disproportion between light metals and electrical construction . . . the known lack of coordination between construction materials and the construction industry that now stands at the center of our attention.

Kaganovich: Bricks.

Bukharin: Comrade Kaganovich says, "bricks." I feel compelled to show my wit by recalling a certain ditty [*chastushka*], which was published in its time in the now defunct *Russian Gazette* [*Russkie Vedomosti*]: "They may beat me, they may beat me senseless, they may beat me to a pulp, but nobody is gonna kill this kid, not with a stick, a bat, or a stone." (Laughter breaks out throughout the room.) I cannot say, however, that "nobody is gonna kill me."

Kaganovich: Who, may I ask, is the kid here and who the person wielding a stone?

Bukharin: Oh, how witty you are! Obviously, it was I who was struck and beaten with a stone. And now not a single member of the plenum, I dare say, thinks that I am concealing some sort of a "stone" of resentment, not even the stone-faced Kamenev.[15]

Kaganovich: It is in vain that you think so. You must convince us.

Bukharin: Comrades, I am trying hard to convince you.

Kaganovich: Let's see how you shall convince us.

Bukharin: Of course, let's. You have acknowledged my statement as satisfactory, and whoever has doubts about it is guilty, to a certain extent, of being a left deviationist. (Laughter.) . . .

Not only is the class struggle not abating, it is becoming ever more acute. Nothing resembling the Hilferding "economic democracy" is to be found here. State capitalism is not socialism, for it does not abolish classes or the domination of the bourgeoisie, or exploitation. [State capitalism] is a forced-labor capitalism. This was proven long ago in every "left-radical" Marxist work. Here the domination of the bourgeoisie stands frankly, fundamentally, and openly opposed to the entire mass of the working class. So that one must not confuse the question of the anarchy of production with the question of the class struggle. And it is precisely the criterion of class [struggle] that is primary. Therefore, I admit in sum that in "The Economy During the Transitional Period" I overestimated the tendency toward monopolization. I admit that in my article on Bent (and this was especially damaging because it coincided with the plenum of the Executive Committee of the Communist International) I formulated my ideas in such a way that they might have given the reader

15. Two puns are involved here: (1) a pun on Kamenev's name: *kamen'* means "stone"; and (2) the expression: *derzhat' kamen' za pazukhoi*, that is, "to nurse a grievance, to harbor a grudge"—Trans.

cause to believe that I allegedly adhere to the position of the bourgeois theory of organized capitalism. Yes, I admit it. But I did not say, Comrade Molotov, that I wrote the article in the spirit of the bourgeois theory of organized capitalism (as my statement, incorrectly translated, said when published in *Inprekor*). . . .

Molotov: A little more modesty, a little more modesty and less confusion.

Bukharin: This is turning into an incoherent discussion. I am deeply sorry for this fact, but it is not my fault. I am not talking about any comparative "modesty" or "non-modesty." But I have the right to defend what I consider possible for me to defend, and I have the right to defend myself against superfluous accusations. Or do you think that I should say what I don't believe? That would mean duplicity under duress. I do not want to practice duplicity. I am responsible for what I think, though it would be odd, it seems, for you to attack me after acknowledging that I had basically given a satisfactory statement.

Molotov: A most peculiar interpretation of the resolution of the CC, very peculiar.

Bukharin: Comrade Molotov, it's your [informal *ty*] right, all power and authority are in your[16] hands, you may interpret it differently and pass a different resolution concerning this matter.

Shkiriatov: Why are you saying this?

Molotov: Hey, look here!

Bukharin: "Why, why?" you ask. If you point out specifics to me, concrete specifics—

Shkiriatov: In whose "hands" is all power and authority?

Bukharin: I have expressed myself with precision concerning all basic questions. What is it that you want? Have I ever admitted that such a thing as ultraimperialism can exist? No, I have never admitted anything of the kind! Have I ever admitted that organized capitalism can exist within the framework of a national unity? I admit here to my mistakes, I admit that I had formulated my ideas on the market in a way that could have made them susceptible of wrongful interpretation. I admit that they were politically damaging. . . .

In conclusion, I have only one thing to say: You are free to judge me as you please. On my part, let me say: whatever the circumstances, whatever the configuration of forces, whatever the political situation I am in, I shall always march in step with the party, and not only from a sense of discipline but from inner conviction. I declare to you that all doubts of the sort—"Ah! It will be too difficult. Bukharin will always be against the party leadership"—all such doubts are groundless. On the contrary, the more difficult the situation, the more solidly will we close ranks. It is absurd to suppose that a man who has worked for the party for nearly twenty-five years, who has marched an entire

16. Using the plural *vy*—addressing the entire plenum, not Molotov personally—Trans.

Document 1 *continued*

epoch in its ranks, should go against the party in its most critical moment, during the critical phase we are going through, when we are taking our struggle against the capitalist world into the international arena.

I shall permit myself to conclude with the following appeal: Long live our general line, long live the party's united front around its CC!

The interruptions by Shkiriatov and Molotov near the end of Bukharin's remarks are particularly interesting. Bukharin had accurately observed that "all power and authority are in your hands," alluding to the ruling Stalinist group. Shkiriatov and Molotov chided him for this breach of party etiquette: Bukharin's remark contradicted the party unity he was preaching and suggested a division within the nomenklatura leadership, the very situation his recantation and profession of support was supposed to end, or at least hide. Even though such passages would not be released publicly, it was necessary for the elite to maintain a unified rhetorical affirmation of power and solidarity to and for themselves. As James Scott has noted, such apologetic transcripts and rituals were not meant only for subordinates. They served to affirm unanimity within and for the elite itself, because "the audience for such displays is not only subordinates; elites are also consumers of their own performance."[17]

In spite of the generally light tone of Bukharin's confession, Kaganovich had, after all, interrupted him with the demand that the oppositionists must not only recognize their mistakes; they must sincerely convince others among their former followers. This was the real purpose of recantation. V. V. Kuibyshev, speaking for the Stalinist majority, laid down this law in no uncertain terms.

Document 2

Concluding speech by V. V. Kuibyshev at the joint plenum of the CC and CCC of the VKP(b), 19 December 1930[18]

Kuibyshev: . . . What is demanded now of a leader of the party, a leader of the Soviet state? Is it only an admission of his former mistakes, moreover in

17. Scott, *Domination*, 49, 58. For an extended examination of ritual in the Stalinist Central Committee, see J. Arch Getty, "*Samokritika* Rituals in the Stalinist Central Committee, 1933–1938," *Russian Review*, 58: 1, January 1999, 49–70.
18. RTsKhIDNI, f. 17, op. 2, d. 453, ll. 169–71, 175–86.

such an innocent form? Is it only a modest statement such as "I am doing the best I can"? This "I am doing my best" formula can even be uttered by a non-Communist. Any conscientious bureaucrat can say that he is doing the best he can. But is that all that's demanded of a leader standing at the head of the Soviet state? More than ever before, the party is entering upon the course of bitter class battles [*klassovye boi*]. The enemy has been dislodged from many of his positions, but the enemy has not given up. He has become hardened. He will resist and oppose us fiercely. Sabotage within the country, the resistance of the kulaks who are in the process of being liquidated—all of this expresses a bitter class struggle. The threats of an intervention—this is the other side of the same coin. The class enemy, sensing that its last positions are being overtaken by socialism, is becoming hardened and prepares itself for an assault on the proletarian, socialist state. And it is absolutely clear that at such a time it should be demanded of a leader of the party or Soviet state, first and foremost, that he lead the battle for the general line, that he take his place in the front ranks of this campaign. It is not enough that he should say that he "is doing the best he can" of that which is demanded of him. We demand of a leader of the party and of a leader of the Soviet state a relentless struggle against all attempts at concealing ideologically class-alien tasks from us.

Can one say that Comrade Rykov, after deviating from the party, has demonstrated the slightest effort to march in step with those who are leading the party ahead? Can one say that in his struggle with a class-alien ideology, which he [himself] once mistakenly preached, Comrade Rykov has demonstrated so much as an iota of the passion necessary for a leader? No, one cannot say any such thing. For this reason, you are forced to conclude that it is apparently hopeless at the present time to see in Comrade Rykov a steadfast comrade-in-arms in these battles.

I believe that the implementation of a plan of such exceptional difficulty as that which confronts us in 1931 demands solid unity between the top echelons of the Soviet and party leadership. Not the slightest cleft should be permitted between, on the one hand, the Soviet apparat and the comrades heading it and, on the other hand, the leadership of the party. . . . It must be clearly and firmly understood: acknowledgment of the general line is not all that is required. One must fight for the general line, and one must fight against all deviations from the general line. These, in the last analysis, conceal class-alien expectations and hopes that are hostile to us. . . .

Comrade Bukharin often says that what is demanded of him is penitence and more penitence and still more penitence and innumerable more acts of penitence. I think that it would be an affront to the Plenum of the Central Committee to think that any of us here would be guided by such a desire, that is, to watch Bukharin or Rykov once again going through the ritual of penitence from this podium: "I am guilty of this, I am guilty of that and that, too!"

That's not needed. What is needed is an admission of one's real mistakes and a correct political assessment of them. Instead, we have seen only these mistakes [defended here] in the most various ways. . . .

Kuibyshev's terms were tough. Indeed, there is reason to believe that Stalin's lieutenants took a more aggressive stance toward the opposition than he did. One month before Bukharin and Kuibyshev spoke, a Politburo meeting had considered punishments for two high-ranking Central Committee members (S. I. Syrtsov and V. V. Lominadze) who had taken a "right-opportunist" line against the excesses of collectivization. In the Politburo, Stalin proposed demoting them to the status of candidate members of the Central Committee. The majority, however, "strongly" disagreed and voted to expel them from the CC.[19]

By 1932 there was no formal organized opposition faction in the party's highest leadership. The vast majority of the leading leftist and rightist oppositionists had recanted. Although it seems that the majority of the party, both in the leadership and the rank and file, dutifully implemented the Stalin Revolution, the chaos of 1932 produced doubts, grumbling, and eventually outright opposition among some veteran Old Bolsheviks. And below the very top level, among the second- and third-rank oppositionists, resistance to Stalin's policies was still strong; in 1932 it began to coalesce. We can document three such groups: the Riutin group, a reactivated Trotskyist organization, and the Eismont-Tolmachev-Smirnov group.

M. N. Riutin had been a district secretary in the Moscow party organization in the 1920s and had supported Bukharin's challenge to Stalin's policy of collectivization. But unlike Bukharin and the other senior rightist leaders, he had refused to recant and to formally support Stalin's course. He had been stripped of his party offices and expelled from the party in 1930 "for propagandizing right-opportunist views."[20] Riutin remained in contact with fellow

19. RTsKhIDNI, f. 17, op. 163, d. 1002, l. 218 (from the "special folders" of the Politburo).
20. For information on Riutin, see Boris A. Starkov, *Martem'ian Riutin: Na koleni ne vstanu*, Moscow, 1992. See also *Izvestiia TsK KPSS*, 1989, no. 6, 103–15, and 1990, no. 3, 150–62.

opponents inside the party, and in March 1932 a secret meeting of his group produced two documents. One of these was a seven-page typewritten appeal "To All Members of the VKP(b)," which gave an abbreviated critique of Stalin and his policies and called on all party members to oppose them in any way they could.[21] At the bottom of the typewritten appeal from the "All Union Conference 'League of Marxist-Leninists'" was the request to read the document, copy it, and pass it along to others.

By far the most important document drafted at the March 1932 meeting was the so-called Riutin Platform, formally entitled "Stalin and the Crisis of the Proletarian Dictatorship." This 194-page typewritten manifesto of the League of Marxist-Leninists was a multifaceted, direct, and trenchant critique of virtually all of Stalin's policies, his methods of rule, and his personality. The Riutin Platform, drafted in March, was discussed and rewritten over the next few months. At an underground meeting of Riutin's group in a village in the Moscow suburbs on 21 August 1932, the document was put in final form by an editorial committee of the league. (Riutin, at his own request, was not formally a member of the committee because at that time he was not a party member.)[22] At a subsequent meeting, the leaders decided to circulate the platform secretly from hand to hand and by mail. Numerous copies were made and circulated in Moscow, Kharkov, and other cities.

It is not clear how widely the Riutin Platform was spread, nor do we know how many party members actually read it or even heard of it. The evidence we do have, however, suggests that the Stalin regime reacted to it in fear and panic. The document's call to "destroy Stalin's dictatorship" was taken as a call for armed revolt.

One of the contacts receiving the platform turned it in to the secret police. Arrests of league members began as early as September 1932. The entire editorial board, plus Riutin, was arrested in the fall of 1932; all were expelled from the party and sentenced to prison for membership in a "counterrevolutionary organization." Riutin himself was sentenced to ten years in prison. There is a story

21. "Ko vsem chlenam VKP(b)," in Starkov, *Martem'ian Riutin*, 252–59.
22. The committee, which was also the central leadership group of the Union, consisted of Old Bolsheviks M. S. Ivanov, V. N. Kaiurov, P. A. Galkin, and P. P. Fedorov (*Izvestiia TsK KPSS*, 1990, no. 8, 200).

that in the Politburo at the time, Stalin unsuccessfully demanded the death penalty for those connected with the Riutin Platform but was blocked by a majority of that body.[23] At any rate, by early 1937 all the central figures in the Riutin opposition group had been shot for treason.

At the end of 1932, many of the former leaders of opposition movements, including G. Ye. Zinoviev, L. B. Kamenev, Karl Radek, and others, were summoned to party disciplinary bodies and interrogated about their possible connection to the group; some were expelled anew from the party simply for knowing of the existence of the Riutin Platform, whether they had read it or not. Indeed, as we shall see, in coming years reading the platform, or even knowing about it and not reporting that knowledge to the party, came to be considered a crime. In virtually all inquisitions of former oppositionists from 1934 to 1939, this "terrorist document" would be used as evidence connecting Stalin's opponents to various treasonable conspiracies. By providing a cohesive alternative discourse around which rank-and-file party members might unite against the elite, the platform threatened nomenklatura control. It is not an exaggeration to say that the Riutin Platform began the process that would lead to terror, precisely by terrifying the ruling nomenklatura.

Document 3

The Riutin Platform [Spring–Summer 1932][24]

Stalin and the Crisis of the Proletarian Dictatorship
The Platform of "The League of Marxist-Leninists"
. . . 2. Stalin as an Unscrupulous Political Intriguer.
It is now absolutely clear to everyone that Stalin had already planned to carry out his "18th of Brumaire" in the years 1924–25. As Louis Bonaparte pledged his loyalty to the Constitution before the Chamber [of Deputies] while simultaneously preparing to proclaim himself emperor, so did Stalin in his

23. For this unsubstantiated rumor, which appears to have originated in Paris, see Boris I. Nicolaevsky, *Power and the Soviet Elite: The Letter of an Old Bolshevik and Other Essays*, New York, 1965.
24. I. V. Kurilova, N. N. Mikhailov, V. P. Naumov, eds., *Reabilitatsiia: Politicheskie protsessy 30–50-x godov*, Moscow, 1991, 334–443. Printed and published in the style and punctuation of the original.

struggle with Trotsky and then with Zinoviev and Kamenev declare that he was fighting for a collective leadership of the party, that "one cannot run the party without the collegium," that "running the party without Rykov, Bukharin, and Tomsky is impossible," that "we'll not give you Bukharin's blood," that "the politics of divisiveness is abhorrent to us"—while simultaneously preparing his "bloodless" 18th of Brumaire, carrying out his divisive policy against group after group and selecting people personally loyal to him for posts on the Central Committee and on the secretariats of city and regional committees. . . .

What is the essence of unscrupulous political intrigue? It is when a person espouses one set of convictions concerning an issue one day and (either under the same circumstances and conditions or under changed ones that nevertheless do not in reality justify change of political conduct—in the interest of a particular person or a clique) espouses exactly opposite convictions the next day. Today he will try to prove one thing and tomorrow—under similar circumstances and on a similar issue—he'll try to prove something else. All the while, the unscrupulous political intriguer considers himself consistent and right in the one case no less than in the other. He is gambling on the fact that the masses often forget today what has been said and promised to them yesterday and will forget tomorrow what is said to them today. If it happens that the masses perceive a trick in all this, the unscrupulous political intriguer will seek to justify his shift of position by claiming that the political and economic situation as well as the alignment of classes have radically changed, making necessary, therefore, a new policy, new tactics, and a new strategy. . . .

3. Stalin as a Sophist.

. . . First of all, Stalin assumes in advance as proven that which needs to be proven. On the basis of a "preordained" premise, he proceeds to draw all of his remaining conclusions. Here are [some of] his preordained premises: "Trotskyism is the vanguard of the counterrevolutionary bourgeoisie," "Right-wingers are agents of the kulak," "The middle peasants have for the most part come round to collectivization," and so on. Second, wherever he finds it profitable, he draws his conclusions on the basis of the following principle: after the fact, therefore, by reason of the fact, connected with it. Wreckers [*vrediteli*] have sought to lower the pace of industrialization. Right-wingers, as Stalin has ordained, are also opposed to quick tempos. Therefore, right-wingers are agents of the class enemy. . . .

4. Stalin as Leader and Theoretician.

. . . The party apparat and the clique of careerists and flatterers surrounding Stalin obstinately proclaim from every rooftop, day after day and month after month, that Stalin is a great theoretician and leader [*vozhd'*], a disciple of Lenin endowed with genius. His name is at the present time placed by these careerist "scholars" alongside those of Marx, Engels, and Lenin. Anyone who does not agree is held under suspicion and finds himself "under fire."

Catching hold of Marx, Engels, and Lenin, Stalin is intent on stealing his way on their backs like a scoundrel into the ranks of teachers of the working class. If history does not recognize him as a great man, then he won't recognize history, and, with the help of his careerist "scholars," he wants to fashion it anew.

If he is forever incapable of rising to the heights of theoretical and spiritual grandeur attained by Marx, Engels, and Lenin, then he is intent, on the contrary, to lower them to the level of his own insignificance. If the ruling classes, aided by the press and masses whose consciousness has been worked over, have sometimes turned people of genius into adventurists, then why couldn't the clique of an adventurist turn him into a man of genius!

To place the name of Stalin alongside the names of Marx, Engels, and Lenin means to mock Marx, Engels, and Lenin. It means to mock the proletariat. It means to lose all shame, to overstep all bounds of baseness. To place the name of Lenin alongside the name of Stalin is like placing Mount Elbrus alongside a heap of dung. To place the works of Marx, Engels, and Lenin alongside the "works" of Stalin is like placing the music of such great composers as Beethoven, Mozart, Wagner, and others alongside the music of a street organ-grinder.

Lenin was a leader [*vozhd'*] but not a dictator. Stalin, on the contrary, is a dictator but not a leader. The proletarian revolution is in need of good leaders; the proletarian Leninist party cannot do without leaders, but the proletarian revolution has no need of dictators. The party and the proletariat ought to struggle against even the "best" dictators, for the degradation of leaders into dictators signifies the degradation and degeneration of the proletarian dictatorship itself. . . .

6. Leninism and Socialist Society.

. . . Let us see now to what extent Stalin's theory is in harmony with his other pronouncements and with the decisions of the Central Committee of the All-Union Communist Party (Bolshevik) [VKP(b)] over the past three to four years. Stalin had asserted that as we progress forward along the path toward socialism, the resistance of capitalistic elements will grow and the class struggle will become more acute. Yet in the words of Stalin, along with the above, we have seen these past years (a) the carrying out of the liquidation of the kulaks as a class and the extirpation of the roots of capitalism; (b) the consolidation of the alliance between the working class and the middle peasant, which is shown, among other things, in the fact that the middle peasant has definitely come around to socialism; and (c) a rise in the material welfare, the cultural level, and the political consciousness of the middle and poor masses in the countryside.

Stalin sees no contradiction whatsoever between, on the one hand, his theory and, on the other hand, his pronouncements concerning the liquidation of the kulaks as a class, the improvement in the material conditions of the middle and poor masses, and the middle peasant's irreversible coming around to socialism. And yet, in reality, they are mutually exclusive. . . .

If the party had been pursuing a correct policy, if a real consolidation in the alliance of the working class with the middle peasant had taken place, if there were support on the part of the poor peasants, if the middle peasants were really turning toward socialism, if there were real improvement in the conditions of the toiling masses in the countryside, with growing political consciousness on the part of the broad masses of the countryside, if the kulaks were in fact being politically isolated and their economic base undermined and narrowed—then the fundamental law of class struggle for the Soviet Union ought to be formulated in the following exactly opposite way: as we progress forward along the path toward socialism, the resistance of the capitalistic elements will diminish, and the class struggle will subside and gradually fade away. . . .

The following conclusions suggest themselves from all that has been stated above in the present chapter:

1) Stalin's theory, to wit, that progress along the path toward socialism would bring about the intensified resistance of capitalistic elements and an exacerbation of the class struggle, is anti-Leninist. In its methodology, it is mechanistic and not dialectical, while, in its factual, political content, it is directed toward justifying the kindling of a civil war against the broad masses of the countryside, toward the disorganization of socialist construction, and toward the undermining of the proletarian dictatorship.

2) It is in fundamental contradiction with a host of other pronouncements and theses advanced by Stalin and his CC.

3) Stalin's slogan "the liquidation of the kulaks as a class" cannot possibly lead to any real definitive liquidation of the kulaks, since the basis for this slogan—"all-out collectivization"—is not founded on a genuine "turn among the broad masses of the countryside toward socialism." On the contrary, it is founded on direct and indirect forms of the most severe coercion, designed to force the peasants to join the kolkhozy. It is founded not on an improvement in their condition but on their direct and indirect expropriation and massive impoverishment.

4) The slogan "the liquidation of the kulaks as a class" has, during the past two to two and a half years, been applied for the most part not to the kulaks but to the middle and poor peasants.

5) At the present, the kulaks no longer exist as a specifically defined social-economic category in the countryside. There are only insignificant, dispersed elements of former kulaks. Outcries directed at the kulaks by Stalin at the present time are only a method of terrorizing the masses and concealing his own bankruptcy.

7. Simple Reproduction and Marxism.

. . . At present, one can no longer consider the top leadership of the party as people who are simply mistaken but subjectively sincere in believing in their rightness. Such a view is childish and naive.

The entire top leadership of the party, beginning with Stalin and ending with the secretaries of the regional [*oblast'*] committees are, on the whole, fully aware that they are breaking with Leninism, that they are perpetrating violence against both the party and nonparty masses, that they are killing the cause of socialism. But they have become so tangled up, have brought about such a situation, have reached such a dead end, such a vicious circle, that they themselves are incapable of breaking out of it.

The mistakes of Stalin and his clique have turned into crimes. . . .

In the struggle to destroy Stalin's dictatorship, we must in the main rely not on the old leaders but on new forces. These forces exist, these forces will quickly grow. New leaders will inevitably arise, new organizers of the masses, new authorities.

A struggle gives birth to leaders and heroes.

We must begin to take action. This struggle will call for sacrifices. It will call for gigantic efforts. Even after the overthrow of Stalin's dictatorship, many, many years will be required for the party and nation to pull out from the unprecedented quagmire into which Stalin has led them.

But to fear such difficulties is to cease to be a proletarian revolutionary. . . . Elimination of Stalin's dictatorship may be fulfilled only by the party and the working class, and they will fulfill it, whatever the difficulties to be overcome and whatever the sacrifices it will require. . . .

CERTIFIED
First Operational Commissar
SPO [Special Political Department] OGPU
[Signature: Bogan]

To those who defended the monopoly version of political reality, this text inspired fear and anger. Why did this document provoke such fury in the highest levels of the party leadership? First of all, it was a text. To those who took such pains to produce political documents, the appearance of an actual alternative text carried special significance. So anxious was the regime to bury the Riutin Platform that finding an original copy in any Russian archive has proved impossible. (The text used here is taken from a typescript copy made by the secret police in 1932.) Indeed, it seems that the words themselves were considered dangerous. Reaction to them recalls Foucault's description of the speech of a "medieval madman" whose utterances were beyond the limits of accepted speech but which at the same time had a power, perhaps a prescience and a kind of magic revealing a hidden and dangerous truth.[25] Similarly,

25. Michel Foucault, *The Archaeology of Knowledge and the Discourse on Language*, New York, 1972, 217.

Trotsky's writings in exile were sharply proscribed but were carefully read by Stalinist leaders in the 1930s.[26] To the Stalinists, the words of Riutin and Trotsky seem to have had a special kind of threatening quality, and the reaction of the elite to them seems to reflect a fear of the language itself.

Second, the Riutin Platform subjected the Stalin leadership to a sustained and withering criticism for its agricultural, industrial, and inner-party policies that remained the most damning indictment of Stalinism from inside the Soviet Union until the Gorbachev period. Even Nikita Khrushchev's 1956 "secret speech" was neither as comprehensive nor as negative in its assessment of Stalin. The language was bitter, combative, and insulting to anyone in the party leadership.

Third, the Riutin Platform could not have come at a more dangerous time for the party leadership. The industrialization drive of the first Five Year Plan had not brought economic stability, and although growth was impressive, so was the chaos and upheaval caused by mass urbanization, clogged transport, and falling real wages. The situation in the countryside was even more threatening. Collectivization and peasant resistance to it had led to the famine of 1932; eventually millions of "unnatural deaths" from starvation and repression would be recorded. Faced with this disaster, the Stalinist leadership held its cruel course and refused to abandon its forced collectivization of agriculture. On lower levels of the party, however, many in the field charged with implementation began to waver. Reluctant to consign local populations to death, many local party officials refused to push relentlessly forward and actually argued with the center about the high grain collection targets. The country and its ruling apparatus were falling apart. In such conditions, any dissident group emerging from within the besieged party was bound to provoke fear, panic, and anger from a leadership that worshiped party unity and discipline.

Finally, and politically most important, the platform threatened to carry the party leadership struggle outside the bounds of the ruling elite, the nomenklatura. The leftist opposition of the

26. In 1934 Stalin quoted from Trotsky's *Biulleten* at the 17th Party Congress: *XVII s"ezd Vsesoiuznoi Kommunisticheskoi Partii(b). 26 ianvaria–10 fevralia 1934g.: Stenograficheskii otchet.* Moscow, 1934, 32. In 1935 N. I. Yezhov quoted extensively from it to a closed meeting of the Central Committee (RTsKhIDNI, f. 17, op. 2, d. 542, ll. 73–76).

mid-1920s had attempted to do this as well by organizing public demonstrations and by agitating the rank and file of the party. The response of the leadership at that time—which included not only the Stalinists but also the moderate Bukharinists and indeed the vast majority of the party elite—had been swift and severe: expulsion from the party and even arrest. Although leaders might fight among themselves behind closed doors, no attempt to carry the struggle to the party rank and file or to the public could be tolerated.

Such a struggle not only would open the door to a split in the party between left and right but would raise the possibility of an even more dangerous rift between top and bottom. Such a danger was particularly acute in 1932 with the reluctance of some local party members to press collectivization as hard as Moscow demanded. Such a split would almost certainly destroy the Leninist generation, which saw itself as the bearer of communist ideology and as the vanguard of the less politically conscious working class and the mass of untutored new party members inducted since the civil war. But the idea of Leninism was not the only thing at stake. Isolated as they were in the midst of a sullen peasant majority— relatively few communists in a sea of peasants who wanted nothing more than private property—the Bolsheviks realized that only military discipline and party unity could keep them in power, especially during a crisis in which their survival was threatened. The nomenklatura was therefore personally threatened by opposition movements that sought to set the rank and file against the leadership. After the dangerous experience with the Trotskyist opposition, the elite at all levels understood the dangers posed by a politicization of the masses on terms other than those prescribed by the elite.

It was this understanding and group solidarity that had prevented the rightist (Bukharinist) opposition from lobbying outside the ruling stratum. The risks were too high, especially in an unstable social and political situation in which the party did not command the loyalty of a majority of the country's population. Accordingly, the sanctions invoked against the defeated rightists were much lighter than those earlier inflicted on the Trotskyists. Although some of the rightists were expelled from the party and its leaders lost their highest positions, Bukharin and his fellow leaders remained members of the Central Committee. They had, after all, played according to the terms of the unwritten gentleman's agreement not to carry the struggle outside the nomenklatura.

Although the Riutin Platform is notable for its assault on Stalin personally, it was also attacking the ruling group in the party and the stratified nomenklatura establishment that had taken shape since the 1920s. That elite regarded the platform as a call for revolution from within the party. After the Riutin incident, the ruling stratum reacted more and more sharply to any criticism of Stalin, not because its members feared him—although events would show that they should have—but because they needed him to stay in power. In this sense, Stalin's interests and those of the nomenklatura coincided.

Although the Riutin Platform originated in the right wing of the Bolshevik Party, its specific criticisms of the Stalinist regime were in the early 1930s shared by the more leftist Leon Trotsky, who also had sought to organize political opposition "from below." Trotsky had been expelled from the Bolshevik Party in 1927 and exiled from the Soviet Union in 1929. Since that time he had lived in several exile locations, writing profusely for his *Bulletin of the Opposition*. Like the Riutin group, Trotsky believed that the Soviet Union in 1932 was in a period of extreme crisis provoked by Stalin's policies. Like them, he believed that the rapid pace of forced collectivization was a disaster and that the hurried and voluntarist nature of industrial policy made rational planning impossible, resulting in a disastrous series of economic "imbalances." Along with the Riutinists, Trotsky called for a drastic change in economic course and democratization of the dictatorial regime within a party that suppressed all dissent. According to Trotsky, Stalin had brought the country to ruin.[27]

At the same time the Riutin group was forging its programmatic documents, Trotsky was attempting to activate his followers in the Soviet Union. Most of the leaders of the Trotskyist opposition had capitulated to Stalin in 1929–31, as Stalin's sharp leftist change of

27. For Trotsky's analysis of the Stalin regime see Robert H. McNeal, "Trotskyist Interpretations of Stalinism," in Robert C. Tucker, ed., *Stalinism: Essays in Historical Interpretation*, New York, 1977, 30–52.

course seemed to them consistent with the main elements of the Trotsky critique in the 1920s. Trotsky himself, however, along with a small group of "irreconcilables," had refused to accept Stalin's shift to the left and remained in opposition.

Sometime in 1932 Trotsky sent a series of secret personal letters to his former followers Karl Radek, G. I. Sokolnikov, and Ye. Preobrazhensky and others in the Soviet Union.[28] And at about the same time he sent a letter to his oppositionist colleagues in the Soviet Union by way of an English traveler: "I am not sure that you know my handwriting. If not, you will probably find someone else who does. . . . The comrades who sympathize with the Left Opposition are *obliged* to come out of their passive state at this time, maintaining, of course, all *precautions*. . . . I am certain that the menacing situation in which the party finds itself will force all the comrades devoted to the revolution to gather actively about the Left Opposition."[29]

More concretely, in late 1932 Trotsky was actively trying to forge a new opposition coalition in which former oppositionists from both left and right would participate. From Berlin, Trotsky's son Lev Sedov maintained contact with veteran Trotskyist I. N. Smirnov in the Soviet Union. Trotsky accepted Smirnov's proposal of a united oppositional bloc that would include both leftist and rightist groups in the USSR. Trotsky favored an active group: "One struggles against repression by anonymity and conspiracy, not by silence."[30] Shortly thereafter, Smirnov relayed word to Sedov that the bloc had been organized; Sedov wrote to his father that "it embraces the Zinovievists, the Sten-Lominadze group, and the Trotskyists (old '_____')."[31] Trotsky promptly announced in his newspaper that the first steps toward an illegal organization of "Bolshevik-Leninists" had been formed.[32]

Back in the Soviet Union, the authorities smashed Trotsky's bloc

---

28. The Trotsky Papers (Exile Correspondence), Houghton Library, Harvard University, 15821. The contents of these letters have not been preserved; Trotsky's archive contains only the postal receipts.

29. Trotsky Papers, 8114 (emphases in the original).

30. Trotsky Papers, 13095. See also J. Arch Getty, "Trotsky in Exile: The Founding of the Fourth International," *Soviet Studies*, 38(1), Jan. 1986, 24–35.

31. Ibid.; excision in the original document.

32. George Breitman and Bev Scott, eds., *Writings of Leon Trotsky [1932–1933]*, New York, 1972, 34.

before it got off the ground. In connection with their roundup of suspected participants in the Riutin group, nearly all the leaders of the new bloc were pulled in for questioning. Many of them were expelled from the party and sentenced to prison or exile. Sedov wrote to his father that although "the arrest of the 'ancients' is a great blow, the lower workers are safe."[33]

As with the Riutin episode, it was these "lower workers" who troubled the leadership the most, and Trotsky no doubt knew this. A few months later, Trotsky wrote a letter to the Politburo. Trotsky pointed out that he had tried to make the Stalinist leadership see the error of its ways and invite him back into the fold. This having failed, he offered Stalin one last chance to make peace and to integrate the Trotskyists back into the ruling elite. Speaking as one nomenklatura member to another, he issued the ultimate threat: if the Stalinists refused to deal with him, he would feel free to agitate for his views among rank-and-file party members.[34] Trotsky's new initiatives, like those of the Riutinists, promised to take the political struggle outside the elite and thereby strike at the heart of the nomenklatura.

The Stalinist leadership was well informed about the dissident and "conspiratorial" activities of the Riutin and Trotsky groups. It was in possession of the Riutin Platform weeks after it was written, and the Stalinists managed to neutralize the group in short order. We also know that senior leaders in Moscow read Trotsky's *Biulleten oppozitsii* and were aware of I. N. Smirnov's secret communications with Trotsky. Two years later, when Yezhov had become head of the NKVD, he disclosed that the secret police were aware at the time of Smirnov's 1932 connections with Trotsky through Sedov.[35] But what about the "lower workers," as Sedov had put it? As the preceding documents show, both Riutin and Trotsky had practically given up hope on the well-known leaders of the oppositions of the 1920s and had pinned their hopes on rank-and-file members to carry the banner against Stalin.

From the point of view of the elite, the climate "out there" gave little cause for optimism. Secret police reports on the mood of the popu-

33. Trotsky Papers, 4782.
34. Trotsky Papers, T-3522.
35. RTsKhIDNI, f. 17, op. 2, d. 577, l. 14.

lation in the larger cities showed that many common folk thought of themselves as "us" and the regime as "them."[36] Popular poems, songs and ditties (*chastushki*) expressed hostility to the regime:

Stalin stands on a coffin
Gnawing meat from a cat's bones.
Well, Soviet cows
Are such disgusting creatures.

How the collective farm village
Has become prosperous.
There used to be thirty-three farms
And now there are five.

We fulfilled the Five Year Plan
And are eating well.

We ate all the horses
And are now chasing the dogs.

Ukraine!
Breadbasket!
She sold bread to the Germans
And is now herself hungry.

O commune, O commune,
You commune of Satan.
You seized everything
All in the Soviet cause.[37]

We know very little about actual lower-level dissidence. The archives contain only sporadic evidence of such activity. We know, for example, that underground Trotskyists in the Bauman district of Moscow (the "Moscow Group of Bolshevik-Leninists") published a newsletter called "Against the Current" in 1931.[38] And as the following two documents show, we have ambiguous evidence of the existence of other groups.

Document 4

Memo from M. F. Shkiriatov to L. M. Kaganovich[39]

[Report by the chairman of the Middle Volga Territorial Control Commission (KK/RKI)]
3 September 1933
SECRET

36. See Sarah Davies, " 'Us Against Them': Social Identities in Soviet Russia, 1934–41," *The Russian Review*, 56(1), Jan. 1997, 70–89.
37. RGALI (Russian State Archive of Literature and Art), f. 1518, op. 4, d. 22, ll. 27, 28; ANSPb (St. Petersburg Archive of the Academy of Sciences), f. 717, op. 1, d. 16, l. 48. We are indebted to Gábor Rittersporn for these citations.
38. There is a copy in RTsKhIDNI, f. 17, op. 120, d. 68.
39. RTsKhIDNI, f. 17, op. 120, d. 106, ll. 56, 56ob. Shkiriatov was a high-ranking official of the Central Control Commission, the party's chief disciplinary organization. Kaganovich was a Secretary of the Central Committee.

Document 4 *continued*

Re: A COUNTERREVOLUTIONARY ORGANIZATION UNDER THE NAME OF "THE PEOPLE'S COMMUNIST PARTY"

In the last days of July 1933, a counterrevolutionary organization under the name of "The People's Communist Party" was liquidated by organs of the OGPU of the Middle Volga territory.

This organization had, in a short period of time, recruited members from students at institutions of higher education in Samara (the Communist Institute of Higher Education [*Komvuz*], the Energy Institute, the Construction Institute and Technical Colleges), as well as from institutions in the territory (the Territorial Institute for Equipment, the Treacle Trust, etc.). The organization also had members in certain districts of the territory (Stavropolsky, Mokshansky, Kashirinsky, Kinelsky, and in the city of Penza). The members of this counterrevolutionary group were organized in "fives," which operated under the leadership of the territorial center in the city of Samara. . . .

The objective of this counterrevolutionary organization was the overthrow of Soviet power, the dissolution of the kolkhozy and the restoration of individual farming [*edinolichnoye khoziaistvo*] as the predominant form of agriculture. Intent on demoralizing, the organization carried on anti-Semitic propaganda, demanding the application of fascist methods of counterrevolutionary operation—i.e., the organization of Hitlerite pogroms. It set before itself the task of infiltrating its nonparty members by means of false documents into the ranks of the VKP(b).

Here is an excerpt from the testimony of a leader of this counterrevolutionary organization:

"We have set as one of our fundamental tasks the undermining of the Communist Party by recruiting members of the party into our counterrevolutionary organization with the mission of further recruitment—i.e., of expanding the membership of the organization in order to serve as saboteurs within the party. With this objective in mind, it was decided to equip the nonparty members of the organization with false party documents so that, once having penetrated the party in this manner, they would carry on similar activity (from the testimony of L. V. Medvedev)."

. . . The organization made a number of attempts at establishing contact with White Guard–fascist organizations in Germany for the purpose of coordinating counterrevolutionary operations. Thus, not long before the liquidation of the organization, V. P. Takhaev, I. Chashkin, and A. Yegorov, students and active members, left Samara equipped with false documents in order to make their way illegally across the border into Germany. . . .

The fundamental, practical forms of activity engaged in by this organization, apart from active recruitment, were: illegal meetings, gatherings of its cadres in the country, the dissemination of leaflets, attempts to organize a printing press with the aim of publishing anti-Soviet literature on a massive scale, the theft of blank forms of party membership cards, of registration cards, and of identity cards of Soviet institutions. More than 100 blank forms of

Document 4 *continued*

documents belonging to the party and other Soviet institutions were discovered during the search of members of the organization.

36 persons were called to account for these actions. This number includes the arrest of 15 members of the VKP(b), 12 of whom have confessed to active, organized, counterrevolutionary activity. The remainder are being exposed by the testimony of the other defendants. . . .

It turns out that a number of party members who refused to participate in this counterrevolutionary organization did not report this manipulation [*obrabotka*] of them and of proposals made to them to either the OGPU or to party organs. In view of the continuing investigation and the impossibility on the part of party organs of informing the party organization, the Territorial Control Commission (KraiKK) has presented this matter to the Territorial Committee with the request that the District Committee (RK) and the District Control Commission (RKK) issue joint instructions regarding the raising of vigilance and the mobilizing of all organizations so that party members may actively repel narrow-minded gossip and counterrevolutionary agitation.

The Territorial Control Commission will provide further information at the conclusion of the investigation.

Document 5

"Counterrevolutionary" organizations in the North Caucasus, 3 September 1933[40]

[Report by Chairman Gorchaev of the North Caucasus Territorial KK/RKI]
TOP SECRET
RE: COUNTERREVOLUTIONARY ANTIPARTY ORGANIZATIONS IN THE NORTH CAUCASUS TERRITORY [SKK]

On 20 August of this year the presidium of the Control Commission and Workers'-Peasants' Inspectorate (KK/RKI) of the North Caucasus territory [SKK] examined the report by the Border Patrol (PP) of the OGPU of the North Caucasus territory (SKK) concerning a number of counterrevolutionary and antiparty organizations and groups that have been exposed in the territory.

In the city of Krasnodar there existed since Autumn 1932 a counterrevolutionary, antiparty, "Rightist-Leftist" organization headed by "a group of Bolshevik-Leninists." . . .

In order to expand its organizational operations, the "group" had worked out a draft of a [political] "platform." Attempts to discover this draft have been unsuccessful. The counterrevolutionary views of this group could be reduced to the Trotskyist theory regarding the impossibility of building socialism in one country and to the rejection of the party position that, first, "we have

40. RTsKhIDNI, f. 17, op. 120, d. 106, ll. 58–59.

already entered the era of socialism" and, second, that the question of "Who shall win?" [*Kto kogo?*] has been resolved in favor of socialism in our country.

The platform, according to testimony of members of the group, contained the assertion that the Five Year Plan has not been fulfilled in four years and that industrial production ought to be carried on at cautious and feasible annual tempos.

Concerning the present situation of agriculture, the platform states that the pace of all-out collectivization has been too rapid. Basing itself on what has allegedly already taken place—namely, the decrease in the purchasing power of the ruble—the platform draws the conclusion that the material conditions of the working class and the peasantry have deteriorated.

Concerning the situation within the party, the representatives of the group declared that a dictatorship by the party over the proletariat has come into being in the USSR, and that the principles of intraparty democracy are being violated by the party insofar as it has failed to convoke the Congress of the Party and the Congress of the Comintern at their appointed times. The group's fundamental aim is to actively struggle against the present leadership of the CC. . . .

Reports like this must of course be treated with care because they were produced as a result of secret police investigations and reports. It is possible that the organizations in question were simply inventions of zealous police investigators who rounded up some marginal people and beat false confessions out of them. As an institution, the secret police had a vested interest in periodically producing "conspiracies" to justify its position and funding. Similarly, hard-liners within the party at various levels, eager to show the need for repression, also had an interest in magnifying the importance of such "organizations," which could be portrayed as a real threat to the nomenklatura elite. Nevertheless, given the chaos and hardship that Stalin's policies provoked in the country at the time, it would be surprising if such groups were a complete figment of the police imagination.

It is clear from the preceding documents that the Stalin regime was unpopular among certain segments of the political public, and the regime knew it.[41] Among Old Bolsheviks of both left and right,

41. See Fitzpatrick, *Stalin's Peasants,* for a discussion of peasant hostility to Stalin and the regime.

rank-and-file party members, and students there was anti-Stalin grumbling. And outside the politically articulate strata, the regime was still waging virtual civil war with the majority of the peasantry. There can be no doubt that the regime was worried about the discontent and the implications for its continued rule. The fact that the highest leadership would solicit and circulate reports on clumsy groups of students (whose "platform" could not even be produced and whose criticisms had already been voiced and admitted semi-publicly) is in itself symptomatic of the nomenklatura's malaise.

Still, from the point of view of internal party self-representation, it was possible for Stalinist Bolsheviks to rationalize this opposition and reconcile it with their Leninist self-image. Thus the Trotskyist and rightist oppositions had long been categorized not as deviant tendencies within Bolshevism but as representatives of hostile class and political forces, usually the kulaks or White Guards. Along with the proposals of the Smirnov group (discussed in the next chapter), their plan to remove Stalin and change the party leadership could thus be branded un-Leninist and contrary to the Lenin-Stalin orthodoxy that was the ideological pillar of the regime.

It was more difficult to rationalize the massive discontent, resistance, and famine among the peasantry in terms of orthodoxy and regime legitimacy. Of course, the enemy class attribute was always available: acts of resistance were attributed to kulak, "bourgeois" peasant ringleaders or their "influence," just as "Trotskyist" would become an attributive category later for any form of political deviation. Despite massive evidence to the contrary, the regime maintained (and perhaps even believed) that the middle and poorer peasants were on its side. This public position allowed the Bolsheviks to claim that a majority of the country was behind them. Even within the party's secret counsels, their "hidden transcript" was the same as their public one. Mechanisms and explanations were found to rationalize peasant resistance and a widespread famine that the Bolsheviks were anxious to hide and even to deny to themselves. The mental gymnastics of rationalization—not only in public propaganda but also in the top secret documents of the regime—made it possible to avoid questioning the basic policy both out loud and to oneself. All the problems were the result of conspiracies or incompetent local officials. Even hunger was a kulak conspiracy.

Document 6

Central Control Commission circular on hunger [42]

3 September 1933
SECRET
TO THE CHAIRMEN OF REPUBLIC AND TERRITORIAL (REGIONAL) CONTROL COMMISSIONS AND WORKERS'-PEASANTS' INSPECTO-RATES (KK/RKI)

Reports of new tactics practiced by the kulaks involving the organization of hunger protests in certain places in the North Caucasus, the Ukraine, and the Lower Volga have reached the Central Control Commission from local Control Commissions and Workers'-Peasants' Inspectorates (KK/RKI).

While reports from certain localities of individual incidents of hunger among the peasants have been verified, cases of feigning hunger and starvation have been noted in spite of hidden and buried reserves of food provisions (Letter from the KK/RKI of the North Caucasus; letter from Comrade Kalinin, the chairman of the KK/RKI of the Lower Volga; dispatches of certain political sections of machine tractor stations of the North Caucasus). This represents a new maneuver on the part of the kulaks in their campaign to undermine the gathering of seeds and spring sowing.

The Central Control Commission of the VKP(b) proposes:

1) That each report of cases of hunger among kolkhoz members be investigated and that, where a case of feigning hunger is brought to light, the perpetrators are to be considered counterrevolutionary elements, and that necessary measures be taken against them.

Decisive measures are to be taken against the organizers of such protests. In addition, it is necessary that this maneuver on the part of the class enemy be exposed in the presence of the members of a given kolkhoz.

2) That, at the same time, a warning be issued against a possible bureaucratic attitude, here and there, to a real absence of food provisions in certain kolkhozy of certain districts suffering from harvest failure, and that help should be organized to provide foodstuffs from available territorial reserves to kolkhozy and kolkhoz members who are in real need.

Document 7

Circular on collective farm food supplies [c. February 1934] [43]

TOP SECRET
To All Secretaries of District Committees [Raikom] of the VKP(b) [and] All Chiefs of the Political Sections of the Machine Tractor Stations

42. RTsKhIDNI, f. 17, op. 120, d. 106, l. 17.
43. RTsKhIDNI, f. 17, op. 42, d. 90, ll. 10–11.

Materials in possession of the Territorial Committee (obtained by the OGPU, letters sent to newspaper offices, letters from certain localities) throw light on a number of incidents of starvation involving kolkhoz members in a number of districts of the Azov–Black Sea territory, including kolkhoz "shock" peasants [*udarniki*] and conscientious kolkhoz members who have put in a great number of workdays [*trudoden'*]—which especially cannot be tolerated. . . .

The Territorial Committee is of the opinion that such incidents are taking place only because at the head of these kolkhozy stand people who have lost their class outlook and their class instinct[44] and who, by treating their kolkhoz members as landowners, serve as a direct tool of the kulaks. . . .

Class-alien [*klassovo-vrazhdebnye*] elements widely exploit for their purposes all incidents of food troubles of individual kolkhoz members. These incidents take place in the majority of cases on account of the callous bureaucratic attitude toward kolkhoz members. These class-alien elements try to exacerbate the situation in the kolkhozy and to provoke the kolkhoz members to plunder the kolkhoz grain or to leave the kolkhoz without authorization and to frustrate the preparation for the spring sowing campaign. The district committees and the political sections of the machine tractor stations, however, instead of trying to find out the real situation in the district and quickly reacting to the needs and requirements of the kolkhoz members—offering help where necessary and mercilessly punishing such landowners [*barin*] and those who have completely lost their Soviet outlook—are in fact putting up and conniving with them. Otherwise, how to explain the fact that, in a situation where no kolkhozy in the territory have received less than 2 kilograms per workday, where many districts have received an enormous food assistance for the support of individual kolkhozy suffering from an insufficient per-workday food issue, and in a situation where the kolkhoz grain trade is under expansion, cases of hunger have nevertheless taken place.

The Territorial Committee proposes that all secretaries of district committees and all chiefs of the political sections of the machine tractor stations verify whether similar cases have not also taken place in other kolkhozy, in which case it proposes that such cases be eliminated. The Territorial Committee warns that at the conclusion of the investigation it will dismiss persons tolerating such incidents from work and expel them from the party.

Secretary
Azov–Black Sea Territorial Committee VKP(b)
(MALINOV)

A regime that feels it necessary to arrest groups of marginal students in small towns or that panics about a dissident program

---

44. *Chut'yo,* literally, instinct or scent, as of a dog, instead of the more expected *chuvstvo,* human feeling.—Trans.

that was narrowly circulated and never published is not a confident one. This government and its leaders were afraid of anything that might challenge their political monopoly and privilege. As former revolutionaries who had used propaganda to come to power, they feared the printed word. The attentive efforts and technical workings of Bolshevik censors to control the production of texts have been well documented.[45] What has been perhaps less well known is the extent to which the very top leadership was preoccupied with such questions. Typewritten pamphlets by student groups attracted the attention of the Politburo and found their way into that body's files.[46] The Politburo reviewed individual books and decided on their removal from libraries. Lists of such books were prepared as official orders of the Politburo.[47]

At the same time, though, their fear was not accompanied by self-doubt about policies or means. What alternatives did the Bolsheviks have for interpreting and understanding the situation in the country? One way—perhaps the most rational way—to interpret and understand the situation would have been in terms of mistaken policies. It is obvious to us today that collectivization and breakneck industrialization were ill-advised and reckless. Of course, this interpretation of events was not available to the general population or even to most layers of the party-state administration; articulation of this view brought instant repression. But in a different way it was also impossible for leading Bolsheviks within the Stalinist faction to accept that their policies were wrong. Everything in their background and intellectual baggage told them that there was a "correct" solution to every situation and that in Stalin's general line they had found the correct solution to Russia's backwardness, to class oppression, and to the problems of capitalism. Their nineteenth-century rationalist faith in scientific solutions to human problems, combined with their facile understanding of Marx's stages of historical development, told them that they were on the right track. Their victory in 1917 and dramatic rise to power seemed to validate them and their place as midwives of history.

45. See Merle Fainsod, *Smolensk Under Soviet Rule*, Cambridge, Mass., 1958, ch. 19, "Censorship: A Documented Record."

46. RTsKhIDNI, f. 17, op. 120, d. 272, ll. 10–16.

47. RTsKhIDNI, f. 17, op. 3, d. 965, ll. 30, 63–64. See also high-level concern with libraries in GARF, f. 5446, op. 22a, d. 339, ll. 5–12.

Aside from the desire to protect their privileged position, they really believed in socialism and their key importance in realizing it. It was genuinely impossible to imagine that their polices were wrong. Nevertheless, their conviction was no doubt strengthened consciously or subconsciously by the recognition that their personal positions and collective fortunes were tied to those policies.

So when things went wrong, when disasters occurred, they needed to find answers and solutions that avoided self-questioning. The most available explanation for problems, and one with resonance in Russian culture, was that conspiratorial "dark forces" were at work to sabotage the effort. If the policies were correct and if they were being implemented by the right people, there could be no other explanation. Schooled in the brutal civil war of 1918–21, when there were real conspiracies, Stalinist leaders and followers found it easy to believe that enemies of various kinds were responsible for every problem. Of course, for the top leaders, there was a convenient element of scapegoating "alien enemy forces." At the same time, reading the transcripts of closed party meetings, Central Committee sessions, and even personal letters among the senior leaders gives the strong impression that it was more than scapegoating. To a significant extent, even Politburo members seemed to have genuinely believed that myriad conspiracies existed and that they were a real threat to the regime.

The regime's fear of everything from elite platforms to gossiping students was conditioned by a silent recognition that its control was in fact weakly based in the country. The leadership's recourse to spasmodic mass violence in place of ordered administration would be another proof of weakness disguised by brute force. This fragility was combined with a fanatical lack of self-doubt, a belief in conspiracies, a traditional Russian intolerance of opposition, and a conditioned recourse to violence to produce the Stalinist mentality.

The Stalinist leadership in the coming years referred repeatedly to the "new situation" that began in 1932. In the repression of 1936–39, many party leaders were accused of involvement in the "Riutin affair." This was a key accusation against Bukharin in 1937, and even his last letter to Stalin from prison dealt with the charge. (See Document 198.) N. I. Yezhov, the head of the secret police, frequently cited the Riutin Platform and the Trotskyists' 1932 activities as evidence of a massive plot against the government. The fear that such "plots" could set the party membership and the population against the regime haunted the nomenklatura for years after the plots themselves had been smashed.

To shield itself from the perceived threat of party splits based on either ideology or status conflict, the party's leading stratum began in 1932 a series of measures to protect its monopoly on power. These measures included stiffening party discipline in the nomenklatura itself, screening the party's membership for "dubious elements" of all kinds, strengthening the repressive apparatus (both police and party organizations), reforming the judiciary in various ways, tightening ideological and cultural conformity, redefining the "enemy" in broader and broader ways, and eventually resorting to blind, mass terror.

These measures often evolved in a series of contradictory zigs and zags, moves and countermoves, rather than in a straight-line trend toward a particular goal. At the same time, however, the twisting road to terror was paved by an amazing group consensus within the nomenklatura, bordering on paranoia, on the need to tighten controls and generally to "circle the wagons" against a variety of real and imagined threats from the peasantry, the former opposition, rank-and-file members, and even its own ranks.

CHAPTER TWO

Party Discipline in 1932

One must not discuss anything behind the party's back. In view of our present situation, this is a political act, and a political act behind the party's back is manifestly an antiparty action, which could be committed only by people who have lost all connection with the party.—A. P. Smirnov, 1933

Both our internal and external situation is such that this iron discipline must not under any circumstances be relaxed. . . . That is why such factions must be hacked off without the slightest mercy, without being in the slightest troubled by any sentimental considerations concerning the past, concerning personal friendships, relationships, concerning respect for a person as such, and so forth. . . . We are currently at war, and we must exercise the strictest discipline.—N. I. Bukharin, 1933

THE CENTRAL COMMITTEE plenum of January 1933 took place in a crisis atmosphere. The famine was still raging. Because of the hunger and the rapid industrialization, population movements took on a titanic scale as millions of peasants moved about seeking food and employment. As a result of mass recruitment drives in 1929–32, the party's membership had swelled from 1.5 to 3.5 million.[1] Many of these were raw, "untested" recruits about whom the party leadership knew little. As we have seen, significant numbers of lower-level cadres had balked at the stern measures of collectivization, and the Riutin and Trotsky episodes had threatened to mobilize these lower cadres against the nomenklatura leader-

1. T. H. Rigby, *Communist Party Membership in the USSR, 1917–1967*, Princeton, 1968, 52.

ship. From the point of view of that senior leadership, things had slipped out of control in a threatening way.

Desperate to establish control, the senior party leadership took several measures. Having encouraged peasant migration to labor-short industrial areas in 1931, the Bolsheviks were faced with a loss of control of population movement as masses of peasants streamed into the cities. As a response to the famine, the regime established an internal passport system at the end of 1932 to stabilize residency.[2] To defuse the threat from its local cadres, the Central Committee in January 1933 established political departments in the rural machine tractor stations in order to purge recalcitrant local party officials. At the same time, a purge of these local cadres was under way.[3] Along the same lines, the January 1933 plenum ordered a general purge of the swollen party ranks.[4] (See Document 26.)

Given its loss of control over the country and the various threats it faced, the nomenklatura could not afford any splintering of its own ranks. The members of the Riutin and Trotskyist groups in the fall of 1932 were, from the point of view of party position, marginal figures, and it is difficult to imagine that they constituted a real threat to the regime. They had been deprived of their party posts years before, and their leaders had been expelled from the party. But at precisely this moment, in November 1932, another dissident group was "unmasked" by the police. This time its members were high-ranking members of the current party leadership.

Rites of Affirmation

In 1932 N. B. Eismont was people's commissar for supply of the RSFSR. His apartment was the scene of a series of gatherings of friends and comrades who were critical of the Stalin line on collectivization and industrialization. Among these were V. N. Tolmachev (a

2. For a discussion of this problem, see Sheila Fitzpatrick, *Stalin's Peasants: Resistance and Survival in the Russian Village After Collectivization,* New York, 1994, ch. 3.

3. For the best analysis of these developments, see Nabuo Shimotamai, "Springtime for the Politotdel: Local Party Organizations in Crisis," *Acta Slavica Iaponica,* 4, 1986, 1034.

4. See J. Arch Getty, *Origins of the Great Purges: The Soviet Communist Party Reconsidered, 1933–1938,* New York, 1991, ch. 2.

department head in one of the transport sections of the RSFSR government) and E. P. Ashukina (chief of the Personnel Planning Department of the USSR Commissariat for Agriculture), but the most influential member of the circle was A. P. Smirnov, an Old Bolshevik party member since 1898 and chairman of the Public Housing Commission of the Central Executive Committee. Smirnov had been a member of the party Central Committee since 1912 (the year Stalin became a member) and in 1932 sat on its powerful Orgburo.

At one of these gatherings, on 7 November 1932—the anniversary of the 1917 Bolshevik revolution—Eismont had a conversation with one I. V. Nikolsky, an old friend recently arrived from work in the Caucasus. As the documents below show, it is not clear exactly what Eismont said to Nikolsky, but it seems that there was considerable drinking and talk about removing or replacing Stalin as party leader. In any case, to Nikolsky the conversation had an "antiparty character," and he reported Eismont's statement to his friend M. Savelev, who in turn wrote a letter to Stalin about it.[5] The police quickly rounded up Eismont and his circle, all of whom were arrested and interrogated. A. P. Smirnov was not present at Eismont's gathering, but was on close working and personal terms with many of those present. Although he was not arrested, he was summoned to the Central Committee for an "explanation" and face-to-face confrontation with Eismont.

The participants in this affair were of sufficient rank and stature that their "case" was the subject of a debate at the next plenum of the Central Committee in January 1933. M. F. Shkiriatov and Ya. Rudzutak were the main accusers from the party's disciplinary body, the Central Control Commission. Smirnov spoke in his own defense.

Document 8

A. P. Smirnov's speech at the Central Committee plenum of 7–12 January 1933[6]

Smirnov: . . . First of all, I would like to resolutely and categorically disavow the vile, counterrevolutionary words concerning Comrade Stalin ascribed to me by Nikolsky in Eismont's words—this has to do with the question

5. See the documentary account in *Neizvestnaia Rossiia*, no. 1, 1992, 56–128.
6. RTsKhIDNI f. 17, op. 2, d. 511, ll. 137–39. Typescript with Smirnov's corrections.

of whether someone could be found—that's what he seems to have said—who could possibly remove Comrade Stalin. I think that only someone drunk out of his mind or insane could ever say such a thing.

A voice: A sober enemy could say it.

Smirnov: That's what I was going to say. Hardly anyone—an enemy, perhaps—could be found from within the ranks of the party who'd utter such a vile phrase. I doubt it. Only someone who is insane or someone who has in fact gone over completely to the enemy camp could ascribe this to me. These words are aimed at Comrade Stalin, whom I have known for many years, with whom I have worked many years, whom I have loved and love—and even if I had a falling out with him, I couldn't have, just the same, ever said such a vile thing. I don't know who fabricated such a thing against me. Even if we consider the second version of the story, which speaks of the possible replacement of Comrade Stalin, I consider it vile in the context in which it is ascribed to me—in the context of a little group discussing behind the party's back the question of replacing the general secretary—i.e., one of our finest comrades and the leader [*vozhd'*] of the party. At this time, this is simply a completely incredible, insane trick.

Ryndin: To engage in such discussions is not an insane trick, but to speak—

Smirnov: One must not discuss anything behind the party's back. In view of our present situation, this is a political act, and a political act behind the party's back is manifestly an antiparty action, which could be committed only by people who have lost all connection with the party. It's absolutely clear.

So, how did Eismont put it at the face-to-face confrontation? Unfortunately, I didn't hear the report.

Shkiriatov: But you were present at the face-to-face confrontation.

Smirnov: I don't know what they said.

Yaroslavsky: They reported what took place.

Smirnov: I too want to report what happened. When I asked Eismont when it was that I said this, he said: "I don't remember when you spoke of a possible change [*smenit'*]." When the members of the Presidium of the CCC [Central Control Committee] questioned Eismont quite reasonably as to what conclusion he had drawn from this, he said, and I quote: "Since we didn't find a better comrade, the question was no longer valid." Well, you know, don't you, one can take what Eismont says as one wishes, but he is a man with a higher education. He is not a little boy, and no one but a muddle-headed person or goodness knows who could ever so answer a question posed to him. I don't know any other way to explain the vile rubbish he gave in response.

I feel duty-bound, in addition, to declare the following: I have never denied and do not deny my faults and crimes, if indeed there are any. The fact that the plenum is discussing this matter is sufficient in itself to show—it speaks for itself—that there is something wrong with my behavior, with my actions—no doubt about it. . . .

The attacks on Smirnov at the meeting illustrate a number of aspects of the party leadership's attitude toward oppositionists in the 1930s, including guilt by association or by subjective attitude even in the absence of a specific act or violation. They also show the stricter demands that the Stalinist leadership made of former oppositionists. It was no longer enough for repentant oppositionists repeatedly to admit their mistakes, condemn their former positions, and take responsibility for the continued offenses of their former partisans. Such a position was considered too passive—"standing to one side" in the "active struggle with antiparty elements [and] for the general line of the party." The Stalinists now demanded that the former dissidents actively attack their followers, inform on those still in opposition, and work visibly to affirm the Stalinist version of reality.

As a member of the party leadership, Smirnov was obliged to oppose and to report any nefarious activities or speech to disciplinary authorities. Smirnov's "confession" was only partial. Because he wasn't present at the ill-fated drinking party, he did not think that he was personally guilty, or at least as guilty as the others. Moreover, he expressed reservations by not denying his crimes, "if indeed there are any." Subsequent remarks made it clear that this was not enough. The party leadership expected Smirnov and the others to carry out a full apology ritual: to admit their guilt, to outline the dangerous consequences of their previous actions, and thereby to affirm the truth of the charges and the right of the leadership to make them. Smirnov had not played that role completely, and his critics were quick to renew their attack.

Stalinist political practice involved considerable symbolism and ritual, and our documents provide numerous examples of ritual in action. It is well known how revolutionary regimes try to consolidate support with rituals and cults.[7] In the Soviet period, the officially sponsored cults of Lenin, Stalin, and the Great Patriotic War are well known.[8] Until the recent release of internal documenta-

7. See Sean Wilentz, ed., *Rites of Power: Symbolism, Ritual, and Politics Since the Middle Ages*, Philadelphia, 1985, 6.

8. See Nina Tumarkin, *Lenin Lives! The Lenin Cult in Soviet Russia*, Cambridge, Mass., 1983; Nina Tumarkin, *The Living and the Dead: The Rise and Fall of the Cult of World War II in Russia*, New York, 1994. On the Stalin cult, see Graeme Gill, "Personality Cult, Political Culture, and Party Structure," *Studies in Comparative Communism*, 17(2), 1984, 111–12; J. Arch Getty, "The Politics of Stalinism," in Alec Nove, ed., *The Stalin Phenomenon*, New York, 1992, 104–63.

tion, however, we have not been able to analyze elite ritual practice. Elites "justify their existence and order their actions in terms of a collection of stories, ceremonies, insignia, formalities, and appurtenances. . . . It is these—crowns and coronations, limousines and conferences—that mark the center as center and give what goes on there its aura of being not merely important but in some odd fashion connected with the way the world is built."[9]

The inseparable connection between politics and ritual can be seen in the Stalinist "apology ritual" used to censure an important official. The official, who had been either removed or merely censured, played his part by recognizing that Moscow's position was "completely correct" and reiterating Moscow's critique in the context of "self-criticism." These apologetic rituals were designed to affirm unanimity and were "a show of discursive affirmation from below" to show that the dissident "publicly accept[ed] . . . the judgment of his superior that this [was] an offense and reaffirm[ed] the rule in question."[10]

Such rituals had public versions that were performed before the general population. The most obvious examples are the show trials of the 1930s, which were crude morality plays involving apologies, confessions, and obvious scapegoating. Yet these rituals were also acted out by, and it seems for, the elite itself in private venues. In Central Committee plena and other secret texts that were never made public, we see these ritual performances being carried out in the secret confines of the elite as a kind of "fellowship of discourse" within a closed community.[11] The affirmation and validation provided by such practices seem to have been no less important for the elite than for the population it ruled.

Several of the lead critics of Smirnov, including Control Commission members Shkiriatov and Rudzutak, practically equated Smirnov's behavior with treason. Stalin's cult of personality had

---

9. Clifford Geertz, "Centers, Kings, and Charisma: Reflections on the Symbolics of Power," in Wilentz, *Rites of Power,* 15. For Geertz, the distinction between "trappings of rule and its substance become less sharp, even less real" the more closely they are examined.

10. James C. Scott, *Domination and the Arts of Resistance,* New Haven, 1990, 57. For a treatment of the function of apology as a "remedial ritual" or "remedial interchange," see Erving Goffman, *Relations in Public: Microstudies of the Public Order,* New York, 1971, 113–16.

11. See Michel Foucault, *The Archaeology of Knowledge and the Discourse on Language,* New York, 1972, 226.

already grown to such proportions that discussions about removing him from his post were regarded as calls for a counterrevolutionary coup. Several speakers referred to Stalin repeatedly as the *vozhd'*, a word that carries connotations of "chief" or "supreme leader." Because replacement of Stalin by routine electoral procedures was considered inconceivable, to remove him by other means implied illegal or treasonous acts. And, the logic went, such a removal could be successful only if it were violent. Indeed, Yan Rudzutak maintained that even talk of reelecting the general secretary was a betrayal of the party. According to the new discourse—Party = Central Committee = Stalin—criticism of one was betrayal of all.

Document 9

I. A. Akulov's speech at the Central Committee plenum of 7–12 January 1933[12]

Akulov: . . . Stalin's policy is our policy, the policy of our entire party. It is the policy of the proletarian revolution; it is the policy not only of the proletarian revolution in our country but of the proletarian revolution in the world. That's what Stalin's policy is all about. And these gentlemen will never succeed in separating us from our leader [*vozhd'*].

Smirnov's appearance today demonstrates how a man who began perhaps as a petty-bourgeois grumbler, a man of right-wing sentiments—and there is no argument about it, we have known about this a long time—can slide into open counterrevolution. To expel or not to expel Smirnov from the party? I think that Smirnov must be expelled from the party.

Voices: That's right—

Akulov: No matter how long his past party record, no matter how great his past party work, we must do it. The only thing we can agree to is to do what we did in respect of Comrade Uglanov—that is, to expel him for a certain period of time. We must say to Comrade Smirnov: "Go to a workers' district, try working in local organizations, try to prove your devotion to the party by your work." This little concession alone can we make to Smirnov.

Now as regards today's speech by Tomsky. Tomsky was always a great comedian. Even today, at this critical juncture, when the Plenum of the CC is debating the question of its attitude to Smirnov's faction, now exposed, Comrade Tomsky is making jokes, but he really shouldn't. Comrade Tomsky has

12. RTsKhIDNI f. 17, op. 2, d. 511, ll. 205–14. Typescript with Akulov's corrections.

become enamored of his own humor.[13] We have never expected nor demanded of Tomsky that he "zealously admit his mistakes." But we did expect Tomsky to tell us unequivocally his attitude toward Smirnov and the faction headed by him. Did we hear any such thing from Mikhail Pavlovich Tomsky today? No, we did not. We heard a defense of Smirnov. Even the kind of negative opinion, as expressed by Comrade Rykov toward the faction headed by Smirnov, is lacking in the case of Tomsky.

Voices: That's right.

Akulov: He took to defending Smirnov totally and fully even after the statements concerning the past factional activities of Smirnov by two party members were read here. And Tomsky wants us to trust him after all this. He wants to present the situation as if nothing out of the ordinary had happened. Concerning the fundamental questions which occupy us today, Mikhail Pavlovich Tomsky has found no answer other than that of taking to defending Smirnov. . . .

Should Tomsky, Rykov, Schmidt, and others be removed from the Central Committee? This is a serious matter—removal from the CC—all the more so since we are dealing here with people who have worked many a year on the Central Committee and were members of the Politburo. I'd give Tomsky and Rykov a final reprieve. Let them in the next several months prove by their conduct and deeds that the party can count on them as on any member of the party. This opportunity is open to them. We cannot remove responsibility from the shoulders of Tomsky and Rykov for what is happening in the party. After all, the Kozelev-Smirnov counterrevolutionary faction has used their names as cover and has followed in their footsteps. The Riutin faction has also used their names as cover. The Smirnov-Eismont faction has also used and continues to use their names as cover. Their names have become a banner for all right deviations which have arisen during this time in the party.

All that has been revealed by the history of Smirnov, Riutin, and others shows that there has been very little revolutionary vigilance in our party in recent times. The ranks of our party apparently include many comrades who may have become weary of the Revolution or who are resting on the laurels of our revolutionary achievements, who believe that if the revolutionary struggle is not over, then it is fast coming to an end. There has arisen a certain base attitude, if I may say so, among certain party members toward a whole range of fundamental questions currently under consideration by the party, a certain base attitude toward the leaders of the party. At the last plenum, when the matter of the Riutin organization was posed, already then we took note of the fact that there was insufficient revolutionary vigilance among our ranks, that proletarian and party discipline has diminished in the ranks of our party. At this plenum, we have to draw the same conclusions. We must note with all

13. Tomsky had minimized the incident by joking about one drunk innocently babbling to another; see below.

resoluteness that our former revolutionary vigilance is lacking, that our iron Leninist discipline is lacking. Only on condition that we summon the whole party to intensify its revolutionary vigilance, only on condition that we hammer our party organizations with an iron Leninist discipline, only then shall we be in a position to confront the great tasks that have been posed before us by the second Five Year Plan.

Document 10

M. F. Shkiriatov's speech at the Central Committee plenum of 7–12 January 1933[14]

Shkiriatov: Comrades, in the course of the investigation of this case by the Central Control Committee, we spoke with Comrade Smirnov twice: the first time with him alone, the second time during a face-to-face confrontation between him and Eismont. And as is evident from the materials of the case, in spite of the fact that it has been proved by the testimony of other accomplices that Smirnov, a member of the Central Committee of our party, who more than any other member of the party ought to defend the party's line, had with his factionalist aims carried on antiparty discussions, slandered the party's leaders and the party's policy of industrializing the country and collectivizing agriculture—in spite of all this, he continues to deny everything, both then at the joint session of the Politburo and the Presidium of the CCC and now in his appearance before the Plenum of the CC and the CCC. He has taken it upon himself to deny his differences of opinion with the party as regards collectivization and the pace of industrialization of our industry and to deny differences of opinion with the party, meaning speeches made against the leaders of our party and the CC headed by Comrade Stalin. Finally, he even denies his antiparty conduct in regards to Comrade Stalin, although this has been irrefutably established now on the basis of available materials and confirmed by those of his comrades who had carried on this corrupting work with him. True, during his confrontation [with Eismont] he did, in a number of specific passages, admit to a number of specific things. For example, during interrogation by the CCC (1 December), he said: "Certain differences of opinion did exist: for example, there were differences of opinion of an organizational character, differences of opinion about the pace of collectivization, the forms of collectivization, and these differences still exist today." But all this constitutes nothing but a forced, inadvertent admission.

And now, to confirm that he had never said this, what [evidence] does Comrade Smirnov adduce? Nothing but unsubstantiated assertions. This is what he said: "I consider it necessary to declare and I shall so declare at the

14. RTsKhIDNI f. 17, op. 2, d. 511, ll. 168–78. Typescript with Shkiriatov's corrections.

plenum that there is not a shred of truth to this accusation and I shall prove it with facts." Comrades, you know that Comrade Smirnov was allowed to speak before the Politburo as much as he wanted to, and then again during the interrogation by the CCC, and finally here at this podium—he could have laid out all these facts and he could have proven that all of this is not so if he were in possession of these facts. The whole point is just that: these "facts" do not exist.

I shall cite another excerpt from Comrade Smirnov's testimony. He said: "I must tell you that they have tried on many occasions to impose the label of a right-winger on me. But I have never considered myself a right-winger and do not intend to do so. I have not signed my name to any documents or acts of an opportunistic character and I do not intend to do so." And so these are all the "facts" adduced by him in justification of himself, as proof that he had not fought against the CC. Well, comrades, if Comrade Smirnov had said this elsewhere, where no one knows him, then one might believe that he was not a right-winger, but who among those present in this room, at this plenum session of the CC and the CCC does not know the sentiments of Comrade Smirnov? Is it possible that the party does not know them? There is only one thing true about his statement, and that is that he had never signed a single factional document. The CC and the CCC do not have any such document. But you see, such a statement is totally insufficient. It is well and good if Comrade Smirnov has not signed any such document, and it is well and good that, as he says, he is not a right-winger, but for a member of the CC of our party to prove that he is not a right-winger, other proofs are required. Comrade Smirnov might refresh our memory here, before this joint session of the CC and the CCC—and he could have done this earlier—by telling us where he, Comrade Smirnov, was when the right-wingers came out against the party. He might tell us whether he had ever struggled against the right-wingers, against the documents, which these right-wingers signed against the CC, whether he had ever joined the whole party in its struggle against the opportunistic, kulak platform of the right-wingers, against the right-wing, opportunistic distortions of the party line in practice. Did he wage a struggle like every member of the party, did he defend the party's Leninist line, as he especially, being a member of the Central Committee of the party, was supposed to do? Now if Smirnov were to come forward with these kinds of facts and prove where and when he had come out against the right-wingers—

Voices: That's right! That's absolutely right!

Shkiriatov: All he had to do was to come here and appear before this podium. For this, there is no need for a great memory. However, it is not only the members of the Central Committee and the members of the Central Control Commission but also all the members of the party who remember all too well that he never tried to prove the contrary by so much as a single word—that is, to prove that he is fighting on the side of the party against the rightists. He cannot adduce such facts because he has never proved it anywhere. Where was Comrade Smirnov when every member of the party, rolling up his sleeves, was battling against the active assaults of the rightist opposition? Is it not obvious from the evidence brought forward by his confederates[15] in the anti-party group that even then he was not in accord with the party line?

Taking up the question of whether or not we were dealing here with a faction, I shall respond by saying that we were. Why? Let Comrade Smirnov and others who participated with him prove that this was not so. We know the history of the struggle by the oppositionists, we know their factionalist activity against the party, their antiparty platforms; we know it all too well, comrades. But the times are changing, and the opposition is now resorting to tactics quite different from those employed against the party in the past. The fact is that this was not, formally speaking, a platform, because Smirnov's group had no written platform, but the situation is also different now. Nowadays, a direct attack on the party won't get you anywhere, a different means of attack is required, and Smirnov has chosen a different means of attack, a different way of fighting against the party. What sort of attack is it? We know from Eismont's testimony that he, Eismont, was in total harmony with the antiparty views of Smirnov. What did this total harmony consist of? It consisted of the fact that they both had a negative attitude to the party's policy in agriculture, to those measures which we are utilizing against the class enemy, against the remnants of the kulaks, now liquidated, who are furiously resisting the socialist campaign [*sotsialisticheskoe vystuplenie*]. This total harmony of views was shared by Smirnov, Eismont, and Tolmachev.

Regarding the leader of our party, Comrade Stalin—what means did they employ in their struggle against Comrade Stalin? According to Comrade Nikolsky's statement, they said that they were prepared to remove Comrade Stalin, whereas in their testimony, Eismont and others tried to replace one word with another: they had spoken not of "removing" [*ubrat'*] but of "dismissing" [*sniat'*] him. But we know what a discussion about "dismissing" the leader of the party could mean. We hold congresses, we hold plenum sessions, but as you can see, there is no question here of "dismissal" at a congress. Instead, discussions are carried on about "dismissal" in other ways. Anyone who has the slightest understanding in this matter knows by what methods Smirnov and others had planned to attempt this "dismissal." And indeed, Eismont doesn't deny in his testimony that he had spoken with Smirnov about this. He said that "he must be dismissed." We, on the other hand, consider, that all of these words—*change* [*smenit'*], *dismiss, remove*—are one and the same thing, that there is no difference whatsoever between them. In our opinion it all amounts to violent dismissal.

I consider it therefore an established fact that a faction did exist. What was the nature of this faction? Three persons would meet and talk, would meet and

---

15. *tovarishchi*, in the sense of "partners in crime"—Trans.

discuss the work of the party and our shortcomings—not at all for the purpose of helping the party but in order to change its line. But their factional activity consisted of more than that. It is enough to submit two facts to demonstrate that. Eismont recruited others, recruited a party member by the name of Nikolsky (in him we have a member of the party, a true Bolshevik, who immediately smelled a rat, who immediately saw that distinguished party members were involved in this affair, that at their head stood Comrade Smirnov, a member of the CC). Eismont did not stop at one. He went on to recruit another person—namely, Poponin—and through him he tried to wage his counterrevolutionary activity.

Now a few words concerning the characterization of this faction as given by Comrade Tomsky when he said that people had gathered "to drink wine, to get drunk." That's not the point. The point here is that people coming out actively against our party have chosen different tactics with which to do so. What tactics have they chosen with which to fight against our leadership, to fight against our decisions? "Wine and debauchery"—this is a cover behind which they intend to conceal themselves. If then they are caught, they will say: "We were just having a chat while drinking." You really couldn't find fault with that; they were just drinking vodka, they were just drinking tea. Is it not obvious that here they chose a different way of fighting against the Central Committee? I think that this has been proven by all of the testimony of Eismont and Tolmachev.

A few words about Comrade Tomsky. . . . In Nikolsky's statement, then in Eismont's testimony, it is said that Comrade Smirnov, a member of the CC and the Orgburo, was preparing, along with others, an attack on the CC, that they carried out this attack in order to replace [*smenit'*] the leadership of the party in a manner which every member of the party, every member of the CC, must resolutely fight. And what articulate thing has Comrade Tomsky said about this? Comrade Rudzutak has here quoted from a document which showed how Tomsky, rising to Smirnov's defense, tried to put the matter in a humorous light: one drunk comes over to another drunk and there, in a corner, they exchange whispers. It was in this same spirit that Comrade Tomsky—at this same plenum session—reacted to Comrade Stalin's report when [Comrade Tomsky] . . . tried to get off with a joke. What was needed here, however, was to address the issue not with a joke but openly and to the point. After all, they read all of the materials dealing with the factional, subversive work of the group headed by CC member Smirnov, and yet what did they say here? Replying to Comrade Petrovsky's inquiry as to his opinion about the Smirnov case, Tomsky said: "If you end up in a similar situation, I'll defend you." Is Comrade Tomsky's answer in the spirit of the party? He will defend all those who raise their hand against the CC. As you please, Comrade Tomsky, but I don't believe you! I think that in this case you are just mouthing words when instead you should roll up your sleeves in earnest and fight for the party line, for its leadership. Why is it that until now Comrade Tomsky had never spoken of Comrade Stalin's work as that of the leader of our party? Only now, at this plenum, did he speak of it for the first time! I do not believe your [familiar *tvoi*] speeches because in your actions against the CC, you [familiar *ty*] show that you are not fighting in earnest in defense of the CC. There is not a single Bolshevik word in what Tomsky says when he speaks from this podium. Why couldn't you [plural *vy*] say something against Smirnov? It is our opinion that there is something that you have in common with him, that you discussed something with him. It's apparently a difficult business to talk with comrades about something and then reveal what was said. It is my opinion that one ought not to believe all former oppositionists who now swear up and down that they recognize Comrade Stalin as the leader of the party, that they acknowledge the party line. . . .

I would like also to speak about other comrades. Take Comrade Bukharin, for instance. No one has said a word about him here. It seems to me, however, that Comrade Bukharin, as a Bolshevik, as a member of the CC, is duty-bound to tell us of his attitude to the Smirnov group, which carried on activities against the Central Committee, and to talk about it not the way Tomsky did but in a Bolshevik manner, like a true Bolshevik, and not from the point of view of comradely sympathy. Comrade Bukharin ought to tell us about all this and give his own assessment of this matter.

In connection with this matter it is necessary for me to pose the following question: where does this activity against the Central Committee lead? After all, Comrade Smirnov is not an ordinary member of the party. He is a member of the CC and of the Orgburo. And what does Comrade Smirnov do? The party discipline of a true Bolshevik, of a true party member, as we understand it, lies in this: that once a decision is taken by the party, one must defend it everywhere and at all times—not only at meetings but also in one's personal conversations. A party member, standing at his workbench, should explain and demonstrate the correctness of the party line to his nonparty neighbor. It is this that the true discipline of a Bolshevik consists of. If a decision has been made by the party and if you are a member of the party, a true Bolshevik, then you ought everywhere and at all times to defend this decision of the party. This is the obligation of every party member. But a far greater responsibility in this regard lies on the shoulders of a member of the Central Committee. Is the only reason for seeking the title of CC member that of seeing one's name in the papers after the election? Well, this just won't do! It is the CC member's duty to actively implement and carry out the party line, to defend the party line and its specific decisions in every way, everywhere and at all times, from attack by whosoever shall do so. And Smirnov comes and says: "Yes, certain specific expressions were incorrect and very harsh." We know, don't we, what kind of expressions these were and where these expressions lead to! If a member of the CC diverges in the slightest from the policy of the CC, then he is duty-bound to declare this openly to the CC and to propose this point for discussion by the CC rather than go discuss the decisions and policies of the CC with some underground group.[16] You will no doubt recall how things were under Ilich [Lenin]. If he found out that such and such a member of the CC tried to come out against this or that decision of the CC, he would call him to account in the most severe way. Comrade Smirnov ought to be able to remember this. How does he behave, this member of the CC, this member of the Orgburo? Here he claims that nothing out of the ordinary had taken place, while in fact he had been carrying on a battle against the party line. Eismont speaks about this, and we have no grounds for not believing it. Eismont points out that Smirnov had come out against Stalin, that he had been working against the policy of the CC. How, Comrades, are we to deal with such a member of the CC? This must be decided upon by the joint plenum.

Now we shall hear from Rykov and other members of the CC—notable figures of the former right opposition. We want to hear from them here and now about their attitudes to this group. We want to ask them whether they understand that even the words which were uttered in the Smirnov group against the CC, against Stalin, constitute a piercing weapon, that by their agitation against the CC, they placed a gun in the hands of the class enemies. Let these comrades come forward to the podium and try to prove that this is not so.

When the Riutin case was under investigation, you too got indirectly involved, Comrades Tomsky and Rykov. And what did you say about this, how did you distance yourself from this venture? Did you come forward actively in connection with this? What Smirnov and Riutin have in common is the fact that conversations have taken place in the Smirnov group concerning a possible removal or dismissal of Comrade Stalin, while in the Riutin group they spoke openly about what needed to be done with Stalin and the CC. What was common to the former and the latter was the fact that they wanted you two as leaders. They have gambled on involving both of you in their active campaign against the party. And what did you declare after all this? Did you make a resolute, Bolshevik protest against this? The party heard nothing from you about this.

Now Comrade Smirnov declares that he loves Stalin. But love has nothing to do with it.

Kosior: Much good will such love do him.

Shkiriatov: The matter has nothing to do with love. Love consists of carrying out the line pursued by the party headed by Comrade Stalin. And I ask you, members of the CC, where were you? Even if this concerned an ordinary member of the party, such a member, if he loved his party as is proper, as a Bolshevik, ought to, after reading Riutin's document—where it is said that they set their eyes on you and that you were giving them cause by your

16. *prorabotat'/prorabatyvat'*: to study in groups—Trans.

conduct—ought to protest against this in the most resolute way. You should have come forward not at this plenum but much earlier against this counter-revolutionary group, which carried on its work of wrecking. And what did you do? At the joint plenum, Comrade Rykov limited himself to saying only this, and I quote: "Comrades, this document mentions my name, nothing of the sort happened, all of this is untrue." And what he should have done was to come forward and, on the one hand, give an appropriate assessment of this counter-revolutionary group, and, on the other hand, take his stand firmly, like a Bolshevik, and speak in defense of the CC.

This is why I, for one, do not believe their words, why I do not believe them, whatever the oath Comrade Tomsky has sworn by or whatever the oath that Comrade Rykov swears by. It is necessary to show by deeds and not by words alone that you are supporting the policy of the CC. And it is not always and not in everything that one can believe you. It is impossible to believe that you are at this moment speaking the truth, since you are saying this under great pressure, under the coercive influence of the entire party. . . .

Their methods of operation are one and the same: the methods employed by the right deviationists are the same ones employed by the Trotskyists. Just what are the methods utilized by them in their struggle against the party? Well, let's take a look at the Trotskyist Krylov, who has recently been expelled from the party. How did he carry out his work against the party? He would gather certain members of the party and suggest to them that they chat for a while "not as members of the party, of course, but just so as to consider everything critically." He would carry on among them the following counterrevolutionary propaganda: "Despite the fact that Trotsky is living abroad, he still represents a great treasure to us. Everyone is touting our great achievements, but what achievements can we point to, other than the Dnieper Hydroelectric Station (Dneproges)," and so on. Two comrades unmasked this Trotskyist, but there were also others who supported these counterrevolutionary conversations (they have now been expelled). When Krylov was questioned at the Moscow Control Commission (MCC), he also pretended that he just wanted to test these party members, to see how strongly they were capable of defending the line of the Central Committee. Quite a few such facts can be adduced. This is how the antiparty manipulation [*obrabotka*] of party members is accomplished. And what about Eismont, who loved to give parties—at these parties he too conducted a "private" campaign of manipulation. He manipulated Poponin and others, and Poponin in his turn manipulated a third [party member], and so on. Antiparty "conversations" are carried on in train cars and in private residences, and this undermining work is carried out by individual members of the party who are still within our ranks. Whoever these people are, we must take decisive measures against their work. Our party must decide at this plenum to intensify its struggle against unreliable, unstable, duplicitous elements.

Our party has great achievements to its credit, enormous victories, yet we are faced with an enormous, immensely arduous work ahead of us. And this immensely arduous work can be implemented only within the framework of an iron, Bolshevik discipline in the party, when our ranks are free of any CC members who are opposed to the party, when there aren't any members in the party who are not in agreement with the party line, when within our ranks all the members implement the decisions of the party and its Central Committee in both word and deed. Before us lies work of great scope, and we cannot tolerate in our ranks those who, though few in number, go about clandestinely organizing operations against the party or interfere with our work.

I would like to speak of one other antiparty method of operation, namely, the so-called jokes [*anekdoty*]. What are these jokes? Jokes against the party constitute agitation against the party. Who among us Bolsheviks does not know how we fought against tsarism in the old days, how we told jokes in order to undermine the authority of the existing system? We know that all factional groups always resorted to such a method of malicious, hostile agitation. This has also been employed as a keen weapon against the Central Committee of the party.

Our task consists of carrying out the most resolute struggle against all those who work against the party, even if these happen to be old party members. Every party member and every nonparty worker ought to feel indignation at any conversations calling for the replacement [*smena*] of Comrade Stalin. We see how, in developing Smirnov's ideas, Ginzburg and those of his ilk are already speaking a different language. This is the same Ginzburg who, until the very last moment, did not break off his association with Tomsky. Within the milieu of these counterrevolutionary groups there are other party members who, originally members of the Mensheviks or the Bund and now members of our party, are carrying on agitation, are carrying on underground activity against the party, against Comrade Stalin.

Those who yesterday worked against Comrade Stalin are now saying of him from this rostrum that "he has now matured," "we love him"; but this is mere verbiage concealing nothing but insincerity. We see this insincerity, this refusal to tell all, to fully unmask one's incorrigible mistakes before the party, also in the conduct of those members of the CC who are former leaders of the rightist opposition.

Our task is to get rid of all this rot [*gnil'*]; our task is to work harder and harder. We ought to have in our ranks party members who will fight for the Central Committee line not in words but in deeds. In my opinion, this plenum should deal with Comrade Smirnov in the most severe way possible. You are tired, you reek with stench, you are no longer capable of working, better not interfere with our work, leave the party, let others do their work, even if you are an old member of the party, even if you have revolutionary credentials to your name!

The party will be able to cope with its problems only when its ranks are free of people who carry on activities against the party, activities manifested not only in the signing of antiparty [political] platforms, but also in words and actions, in individual conversations and talks directed against the line of our party. (Applause.)

Shkiriatov's was an extreme statement of an extremist position. Even though Smirnov had never been a member of an opposition group, Shkiriatov had shifted the burden of proof to Smirnov and demanded that he prove the history of his struggle against the opposition, that he prove that he had *not* been an adherent.

For Shkiriatov, even jokes and stories carried a dangerous counterrevolutionary character and could have no place in the prescribed loyal narrative. During NEP in the 1920s, jokes and ditties had not been sources for official obsession. But in the 1930s the onset and height of collectivization, the period following Kirov's assassination, and the terrible year 1937 each triggered dramatic increases in persecution for "anti-Soviet agitation." Jokes, songs, poems, and even conversations that in any other political system would have been ignored as innocent came to be seen as dangerous crimes. Like suicide and certain conversations, they had become "sharp weapons" against the party. The regime's agents carefully recorded jokes, poems, and the like, and these were matters for attention and concern in the country's highest political circles.[17] Osip Mandelshtam was arrested for a poem. As a prominent writer, his writings could in fact be seen as a propagandistic "weapon" against the party. But it is harder to classify as dangerously political the hundreds of thousands of utterances by ordinary citizens. Nevertheless, the regime was deeply troubled.

Yan Rudzutak, another Control Commission official, spoke for much of the elite nomenklatura, which believed that Stalin was their symbol and partner. To remove him was to remove them. As Rudzutak put it, "We as members of the Central Committee vote for Stalin because he is ours."

17. See RTsKhIDNI, f. 17, op. 120, d. 70, l. 58.

Document 11

Ya. E. Rudzutak's speech at the Central Committee plenum of 7–12 January 1933[18]

Rudzutak: . . . Smirnov has begun to admit that, indeed, discussions about the CC had in fact taken place, that differences of opinion do exist. Although even here, it is true, as regards the leadership, he continues to categorically deny it. He maintains that he never said that it was necessary to remove Stalin, while all his friends in the group assert that these discussions did take place.

What does "removal" mean if we are not speaking of reelections? How must we understand the sentence: "Is there really no one who might be capable of removing Stalin?" And such statements did take place. In the final analysis, Smirnov too did not hold out during the face-to-face confrontation. And despite the fact that Smirnov asserted that Stalin was never the object of these discussions, yet at the confrontation the following escaped Smirnov's lips: "On the whole," he said, "Stalin is not a pope, and someone else can be elected in his place." As you can see, Smirnov is not quite so innocent after all in his conversations concerning Stalin. I asked Eismont, "Well, what happens when you, a member of the CC, meet with members of the party and the conversation turns to political matters? Is it really possible that not once has anyone in your group ever come to the defense of the CC's policy?" He replied: "Not once has Aleksandr Petrovich come out against this criticism and said in defense of the Central Committee that it is acting correctly. It seemed to me that there was general agreement among us on this question"—i.e., no one was for the CC's policy, everyone was against it. . . .

Furthermore, these people did not simply blurt these things out; at least, they did not intend to merely blurt them out. This is attested to by the fact that they did not confine themselves to discussions within their three-man group but recruited supporters from elsewhere. In the materials given to you there is the testimony by Poponin, whom Eismont had tried to recruit, seeking to convince him that the present leadership is leading the party and country to ruin, that it was necessary to replace the leadership, to replace General Secretary Stalin. In this exchange of theirs, they discussed and "selected" possible candidates who might be able to replace Comrade Stalin. Moreover, Eismont asked Poponin: "Couldn't you, as a former military man, be of some use to us?" What does it mean when the question of replacing the leadership is discussed, when the question of electing candidates is discussed? What does it mean when the question "Couldn't you, as a former military man, be of some use to us?" is posed? Does this not testify to the fact that this is a real organization, openly set against the party and calculating on the use of violent measures, an organization that had been checking up on the sentiments of military officials toward Comrade Stalin? In any case, we can consider it an established fact that

18. RTsKhIDNI, f. 17, op. 2, d. 511, ll. 12–22. Typescript with Rudzutak's corrections.

the preparation for the implementation of this counterrevolutionary venture had commenced, and that Eismont had begun to seek out military officials appropriate for it. . . . And here the attitude manifested in the assessment of the matter by certain members of the CC, former leaders of the rightist opposition, is absolutely unacceptable. Here, for example, is how Comrade Tomsky characterizes this very matter (you can find it in the materials that have been distributed to you): "Eismont was drunk. Somebody, equally drunk, came over to him. Both of them, quite drunk, walked over to the corner and started babbling all sorts of incoherent rubbish." . . .

No, comrades, this is not where the matter stands. I assert that this is not an organization of idle babblers. This is an organization of persons who are, in all of their policies, in disagreement with the Central Committee of the party, in disagreement with the general line of the party, and who are carrying on a conscious campaign against our party and against the Central Committee. Their tactics have been tested over many years. It was not they who discovered the tactics of fighting the party and its leadership. Their tactics have been known to us for a long time: they make general statements to the effect that "we are for the party, we are in agreement with the party and its Central Committee, we are for the general line of the party, but we disagree with certain specific, minute details of the general party line." It is enough to remember the general declaration of the right deviationists, where they also wrote: "We are for industrialization, we are for the implementation of the Five Year Plan, we are for all of this" (you can read all of this in the party document), "but, nonetheless, we are against the party line. We are for the general party line, but we are against the pace of collectivization, we are against the pace of industrialization."

Tell me, dear comrades, in what then does your agreement with the policy of the Central Committee consist? If you throw away the main part as of no use, that is, 99 percent of our active Bolshevik work of implementing the general party line, then what will you have in common with us? Nothing but the name, nothing but a party membership card. Because on all principal points you are against the party line. If you are against the pace of collectivization and the pace of industrialization, you are against the party line. You have not taken an active role in this construction. In any case, no one has seen you working actively for it. On the contrary, over the course of many years, as Eismont has testified, you have worked actively against the party. And all that's left of you that has anything in common with us is your party card, because every party member has the same party card, and that's all.

[Here are their] methods of struggle: "We are not alone. Not just me, not just Eismont, not just Tolmachev, but think—a great many members of the CC disagree with Stalin. Just consider, for instance, Comrades Tomsky and Rykov." In just those words did Eismont declare to Nikolsky that the majority of the CC disagree with Stalin's policy, that they vote for it because they fear voting against it. Comrades, can one utter a greater slander against the members of the CC, against the Old Bolsheviks, the majority of whom served years at hard labor [*katorga*]? These, the finest people of the party, did not fear many years in prison and in exile, and now these revolutionaries, who devote themselves to the victory of the Revolution, these old revolutionary warriors, according to Smirnov, are afraid to vote against Comrade Stalin. Can it be that they vote for Stalin from a fear for authority[19] while, behind his back, they prepare—if anything comes up—to change [*meniat'*] the leadership? You are slandering the members of the party, you are slandering the members of the CC, and you are also slandering Comrade Stalin. We, as members of the CC, vote for Stalin because he is ours. (Applause.)

Exclamations: Right! (Applause.)

Rudzutak: You won't find a single instance where Stalin was not in the front rank during periods of the most active, most fierce battle for socialism and against the class enemy. You won't find a single instance where Comrade Stalin has hesitated or retreated. That is why we are with him. Yes, he vigorously chops off that which is rotten, he chops off that which is slated for destruction. If he didn't do this, he would not be a Leninist. He would not be a Communist fighter. In this lies his chief and finest and fundamental merit and quality as a leader-fighter [*rukovoditel'-boets*] who leads our party. It is not Stalin's liability but his asset that he does not seek to get around sharp angles but chops off that which needs to be chopped. He is the leader [*vozhd'*] of the most revolutionary, most militant party in the world, which implements socialism not in words but in deeds. And he would not be the leader [*vozhd'* and *rukovoditel'*] of the party if he didn't know how to chop off and destroy that which is really slated for destruction, that which is rotten, that which prevents us from moving forward. You fear Stalin because you fear that furious movement forward toward socialism, that immense work being done to build socialism, which is carried on by our party under the leadership of Comrade Stalin. . . . That's why we are all for Stalin while you are against Stalin.

And here begins the well-known tactic of fighting the party, namely, slander: "Let's slander Stalin, let's slander the Central Committee. Perhaps some of it will stick. Perhaps someone will believe it. Perhaps the leadership will weaken little by little. And where the leadership is bad, there it will be possible for us to seize it." That's your tactic. . . .

We believe that, naturally, there can be no question whatsoever of having Smirnov remain a member of the general headquarters of our Communist party.

Voices: Right!

Rudzutak: I have laid out for you the bare facts only, and I think that our joint

---

19. *ot 'strakha radi iudeiskogo'*: literally, from fear of the Jews, a distant Biblical allusion—Trans.

plenum ought to deliver its considerable opinion and pass judgment on those persons whom I have just spoken about and their actions. (Prolonged applause.)

These apology rituals had several functions. Pragmatically, from the point of view of the elite as a whole, when the accused played his role properly the scene provided a scapegoat who could be used as a negative example to those below and a symbol or signpost for a change in policy. Second, these scenes allowed Stalin to mobilize the united (and nearly always unanimous) support of the Central Committee behind him in his moves to isolate and discredit his opponents.

The unitary rituals had other effects as well. Speaker after speaker rose to join in criticism of the accused. The collective denunciations and pronouncements served to affirm and validate the organized collective (in this case, the Central Committee) as an authoritative body. Although Stalin and his circle certainly chose the accused in this case, the collective elite were being asked to validate not only his choice but their right to pass judgment on such matters. As any ritual does, these Central Committee meetings allowed the participants to make a group affirmation of their organization as a "society" or even a political subculture in the system.

Finally, like all rituals, these meetings contributed to the construction of the self-identity and self-representation of the participants as individuals. By being present as a member, by participating in what might appear to be meaningless repetitive speech, the participants implicitly made statements about who they were individually. Self-identity is, of course, a function of many complex variables, including class, kin, nationality, gender, and personal experience. Among the components of that self-identity are political status and place in the social hierarchy. Participation in apology and other rituals was to say "This is who I am: I am a revolutionary and a member of the party elite. I along with my comrades am part of the governing team of Stalinists. I insist on party discipline and stand against those who break it. In that position, I am making a contribution toward party unity and therefore toward moving the country historically toward socialism."

Former rightist oppositionists N. I. Bukharin, A. I. Rykov, and
M. P. Tomsky were also called upon to speak and make their
position clear in relation to the Smirnov group. Rykov repeated the
ritual self-criticism demanded of former oppositionists and tried to
demonstrate his lack of any connection with the group. Tomsky
took a more contrary stand. Although he also criticized his former
oppositionist positions, he pointed out that the party should not
make too much of careless and drunken conversations at evening
parties. Bukharin's speech was much more repentant, and his position was judged more acceptable; those of Rykov and Tomsky were
not, and they were roundly denounced in the discussion.

Bukharin accepted the premise that the new situation and new
threats demanded strong discipline and unconditional unity. He
understood the need for a unifying, affirming text that would make
clear his continued membership in the elite. In distinction to other
speakers, though, Bukharin did not invoke Stalin's name as *vozhd'*,
nor did he explicitly equate Stalin with the Central Committee.

Document 12

N. I. Bukharin's speech at the Central Committee plenum of 7–12 January 1933[20]

Comrades, with regard to Aleksandr Petrovich Smirnov's group, it seems to
me that no party member can be of two minds about it: if it is necessary for us,
on the whole, to indignantly repudiate a group of this sort, then it should
especially—twice and thrice—be repudiated now, and severe punishment
should be meted out. We have won dazzling victories in the building up of the
Five Year Plan. We shall win more victories in the future and go forward with
that same resoluteness. But this does not mean that all difficulties have been
taken off our agenda. There are a great many difficulties. The petty-bourgeois
forces of chaos [*stikhiia*] are still shaking up many of our districts, and sometimes these shocks are reflected here and there even in parts of the working
class that are callow, unpolished, and untempered by battle. . . .

Consequently, we can be victorious in the future—and we shall unquestionably be victorious if our party will represent a more unified amplitude
[*sic*] than it has until now—if such unity around a leadership that has come
into being historically is even more concerted, of an even more lofty kind than
it has been until now. . . .

20. RTsKhIDNI, f. 17, op. 2, d. 511, ll. 215–20. Typescript with Bukharin's
corrections.

Harsh formulations of various sorts, such as "Barracks Regime" and others, are, since they intend to bombard the regime, especially pernicious nowadays because we are currently at war and we must exercise the strictest discipline. Both our internal and external situation is such that this iron discipline must not under any circumstances be relaxed. . . . That is why such factions [*grup-pirovki*] must be hacked off without the slightest mercy, without [our] being in the slightest troubled by any sentimental considerations concerning the past, concerning personal friendships, relationships, concerning respect for a person as such, and so forth. These are all totally abstract formulations, which cannot serve the interests of an army that is storming the fortress of the enemy.

I, comrades, must tell you in all honesty, with all resoluteness, that I shall not shirk my responsibility, my personal responsibility before the party. I do not want to hide in the bushes and I shall not. If one were to analyze the source of those divergent views that have led to serious incidents within the party, and if one were to speak of the degree of guilt, then my guilt before the party, before its leaders, its Central Committee, before the working class, and before the country—this guilt of mine is heavier than that of any of my former like-minded comrades, for I was to a large extent the ideological purveyor of a host of formulations which gradually gave birth to a definite rightist-opportunistic conception. This responsibility, comrades, I shall not shirk. I shall not shift my responsibility onto someone else, and from my recent past, which I must now, without any pleasure, recall once more, I must draw—and I do in fact draw—a sound lesson. . . .

I believe that Comrades Tomsky and Rykov, my former comrades-in-arms in the leadership of the right opposition, committed an additional, extremely serious and grave political error, which they themselves admitted to, by virtue of the fact that they did not make sufficient and energetic use of the time available to them to come to the present plenum with the definite asset of their energetic work in the struggle against deviations, in the struggle to implement the general policy of the party. For this reason, I think that in the future they ought to show—through their work, by deed, not from the standpoint of formal declarations but by deed, through systematic work—that they are winning the party's trust. I personally am confident that they will regain this trust. But this is a kind of verification [*proverka*], a test, which the party ought to impose on them, and which the party in full justice imposes on them. . . .

This is how the matter stands: we must march onward, shoulder to shoulder, in battle formation, sweeping aside all vacillations with the utmost Bolshevik ruthlessness, hacking off all factions, which can only serve to reflect vacillations within the country—because our party is one and indivisible, and its various strata serve as mouthpieces for great socioeconomic processes in our country, for historic progress on a huge scale, for great processes involving the class struggle. And since, to a certain extent, all of this boils up to a concentrated form in the laboratory of our party, we must take into account in advance the fact that, however it may grieve us, certain kinds of factions will arise in our party, perhaps even worse factions.

All of this shows once again that the leaders of the party ought to issue absolutely correct slogans of vigilance, and that a loyal, wholehearted, energetic, and zealous defense of the policy that the party has charted and that it is carrying out under the iron leadership of our CC is demanded of the party's soldiers. "By this you shall conquer"—this is the banner under which we shall go forward. . . .

It may be instructive to compare these tougher demands with the relatively civil treatment of oppositionists in 1930 (see Documents 1, 2). As we have seen, Bukharin in his 1930 speech made several witty comments that were well-received with friendly laughter by his audience. His colloquies with Kaganovich and Molotov were like gentlemanly debates aimed at seeking compromise, and his critics behaved in a polite and civilized manner.

But in 1932 the mood had become tense and anxious. While Bukharin could joke about opposition in 1930, Shkiriatov in 1933 asserted that "jokes against the party are agitation against the party." The texts of Smirnov's critics were laced with nostalgic references to party discipline in Lenin's time, but they demanded much more: "iron discipline" required Central Committee members to become informers on one another. Bukharin's jest in 1930 about "physically destroying" members of the opposition elicited laughter from the Central Committee. One wonders whether it would have done so in 1933.

For their parts, several of the opposition leaders accepted the logic of the new situation. Bukharin's speech emphasized the main point: "If it is necessary for us, on the whole, to indignantly repudiate a group of this sort, then it should especially—twice and thrice—be repudiated now, and severe punishment should be meted out." Smirnov himself recognized the dangers inherent in the 1932 situation and accepted the notion that discussing Stalin's removal was " a political act, and a political act behind the party's back is manifestly an antiparty action." Smirnov found no fault with the logic of the accusation in principle; he simply denied that he had done it.

But Smirnov, Tomsky, and Rykov did not fully accept that formal guilt or innocence was not the question. For the Stalinists, on the other hand, the party made the truth. After all, Trotsky had said that one cannot be right against the party. As a party member and member of the Central Committee, Smirnov was a soldier. His duty, if so ordered, was to confess, to report on others, and to proclaim his "crimes" in order to help the party in its struggle. To disagree, or even to defend oneself against an accusation, was tantamount to insubordination, to "taking up arms against the party" in wartime, to counterrevolution. Bukharin, on the other hand, understood. Another former oppositionist, Karl Radek, also understood the new requirements and quickly did his duty:

Document 13

K. Radek's letter to Ya. Rudzutak, January 1933[21]

Dear Comrade Rudzutak—After reading Comrade A. P. Smirnov's statement, in which he rejects with great indignation the very possibility of being held in suspicion in right-wing factional work, I am hereby informing you of the following:

In 1927, sometime during the summer, G. A. Zinoviev notified those who were then the leaders of the Trotskyist opposition of a proposal made to him—i.e., to Zinoviev—by A. P. Smirnov for the formation of a bloc against Comrade Stalin. As related by Zinoviev, Smirnov complained about the regime that it was numbing the party, [that] the party had no clear policy concerning the peasantry, at times making concessions to the peasants, at times revoking them. [Smirnov] has received hundreds of letters from the countryside regarding this. [He said that] it was impossible to go on living like this, [that] the party itself ought to come to a decision, [that] if the Trotskyist opposition, fighting against his proposals, stopped branding them as kulak proposals, then a tactical agreement with him and his friends might be possible for the purpose of obtaining a freer hand in the party.

This conversation was known to all members of the opposition leadership then present in Moscow. When Comrade Stalin, referring to Trotsky's correspondence with Shatunovsky, pointed in 1928 to the existence of the idea of a Right-Left bloc and when part of the Trotskyist opposition denied the presence of such a tendency, I pointed out, in one of the articles circulating then

---

21. RTsKhIDNI, f. 17, op. 2, d. 511, ll. 117–19. Typescript.

Document 13 *continued*

among the oppositionists, Smirnov's proposal of a Right-Left block. The fact that A. P. Smirnov has denied this factional past of his in general sheds light on his statements regarding the charges brought against him today of working for the opposition.

With a Communist salute,

K. Radek

Another important element of the nomenklatura's treatment of the opposition was the distinction between personal and political factors. Bolsheviks had always separated their political and personal lives; the bitter political disputes between Lenin and Zinoviev over the question of seizing power in 1917 did not prevent them from maintaining cordial personal relations. But by 1932 the stakes were considered so high that fond personal relations and one's "goodwill" were specifically sacrificed to political needs. Consider the following speech from Commissar of Defense Voroshilov, whom no one had ever accused of subtlety or great depth of thought.

Document 14

K. Ye. Voroshilov's speech at the Central Committee plenum of 7–12 January 1933[22]

Voroshilov: Comrade Tomsky, you keep thinking that you are still a leader [*vozhd'*]. I must tell you frankly that you are anything but the leader. (Laughter, applause.) You are anything but the leader now. Mark this well, Mikhail Pavlovich.

Tomsky: I really don't think so.

Voroshilov: No, you do think so. We all know this exceedingly well. If you were to work properly, if you were to regain the party's trust, if you were a true member of the CC, carrying out its requirements fully, then it would be a different matter. In such a case, it would have been possible for you to think that you are acquiring a faint resemblance to a leader. . . . But you continue to imagine yourself a leader when, in fact, there is no one for you to "lead." And so this causes you pain and annoyance, in general, especially as it concerns your state of mind.

22. RTsKhIDNI, f. 17, op. 2, d. 511, ll. 260–66. Typescript with Voroshilov's corrections.

Tomsky: I don't think so. I have long since forgotten.

Voroshilov: And one more piece of advice, as a friend—after all, you and I were once close friends: please do not think that you are so clever. (Laughter.) You spoke before us here, and I was ashamed for your sake. You were once an intelligent person, but owing to the fact that you slept through the past four years, you poured out such rubbish here that I was simply ashamed for your sake. Even a Marxist circle of the lowest rank would be ashamed to read this. It's all elementary. All those peas pushed here and there by the nose—all of this is nothing but utter rubbish. We expected a different kind of speech from you, different words.

A word or two about Comrade Bukharin. Naturally, I believe Comrade Bukharin a hundred times more than Rykov and a thousand times more than Tomsky. Tomsky is being sly. Rykov is trying to be sincere, but, for the time being, this has been nothing but a failure. Bukharin is a sincere and honest man, but I fear for Bukharin no less than for Tomsky and Rykov. Why do I fear for Bukharin? Because he is a soft-hearted person. Whether this is good or bad I do not know, but in our present situation this soft-heartedness is not needed. It is a poor assistant and adviser in matters of policy because it, this soft-heartedness, may undermine not only the soft-hearted person himself but also the party's cause. Bukharin is a very soft-hearted person. Now, and indeed, not only now but for quite some time, he has been doing good, conscientious, honest work without chasing after glory, after the laurels of a leader. In his time, Bukharin was not a bad leader [*vozhd'*], although all sorts of quirks had from time to time cropped up in him even then. Now he doesn't imagine himself a leader but simply does his work like a good party member, and, when he works, then by necessity or owing to this very work, as a result of it, it turns out that he becomes a leader, whether over engineers or scholars—i.e., when performing the most practical work, he turns into a practical leader. (Laughter.)

This is all to the good, and it should not be ruled out that Bukharin may move on from this path to the true, broad, well-trod Bolshevik path, and that all will be well. But I have certain apprehensions. Up until now, everything has gone well, especially during the recent past. Perhaps because the Central Committee has taken certain measures in respect of his so-called school, which he has given birth to. (Laughter.) . . . And here is Nikolai Ivanovich [Bukharin], thanks to the fact that he was in his time a leader of this group but now occupies such an uncertain position.[23]

Stalin: Even now he is leading [*rukovodit*] the retreat.

Voroshilov: But very badly, just as badly as he led the attack. He is incapable of organizing his "army" so that it could retreat in an orderly fashion. It would be better if they retreated in an orderly fashion. In any case, the spectacle would be more pleasing.

I think that of the three—Bukharin, Rykov, Tomsky—Bukharin may be ruled out. In any case, we can do this now, seeing that Bukharin has recently

23. Previous sentence grammatically incoherent—Trans.

Document 14 *continued*

been doing a great deal of good and honest work on a large-scale, practical project. As for the other two—Rykov and Tomsky—they, of their own free will or otherwise, are by their conduct helping all sorts of antiparty elements to formulate their paltry antiparty ideas, their antiparty platforms, their antiparty actions, and all sorts of other things. . . .

This will also be of use in the sense that Comrade Smirnov, who had been considered one of our oldest comrades and friends, will, by being removed from the CC, be saved for our party. Although he considers himself an old man, he is not too old to receive correction and to consider his entire life from beginning to end and to walk again the path which every party member, every honest Leninist, must travel.

Finally, we shall profit from all this because all our active members, our entire party, will close ranks even more tightly, will become an even stronger, more monolithic Leninist party when it learns about this. It will unite even more around our Stalin, around our true leader, who has demonstrated and continues to demonstrate, in his life and everyday work, his devotion to Lenin's cause, his skill at governing the party, the proletariat, and its state, like Lenin, in a firm and wise manner. Apart from him there is no one else; apart from him we need no one else. Under his leadership, together, we shall go on to greater and greater victories. (Prolonged applause.)

In the end, A. P. Smirnov was expelled from the Central Committee and Orgburo but was allowed to remain in the party, with the warning that his continued membership depended on his future behavior. Eismont and those party members present at the ill-fated soiree were expelled from the party. Eismont and several others were sentenced to three years in labor camps. Technically, discussing the removal of Stalin was not a crime covered by the criminal code. But the Stalinist leadership had created an extrajudicial body, the special board (*osoboe soveshchanie*) of the OGPU, which had the right, even in the absence of a formal crime or charge, to sentence people to camps for such things as "anti-Soviet agitation" or being a "socially dangerous element." (See Document 25 for a statement of its powers.)

All of the participants still living in 1937 were arrested and shot for "counterrevolutionary activities," and thus the punishments meted out in 1933, especially to Smirnov, seem relatively light and show that some Stalinists, despite their fiery rhetoric, were undecided about how hard to push the dissidents. Repression of real or imagined opposition groups in this period was becoming more common. But the sources we have from the 1932–34 period paint an ambiguous picture of the direction of party policy. Sampling the archives from this period, we shall find a mixture of hard- and soft-line policies on matters relating to political dictatorship and dissidence.

On one hand, Stalin and his closest associates may already have been preparing for a major purge and attempting to set in place a series of decisions, personnel, and practices designed to facilitate a subsequent unleashing of terror. According to this explanation, the countervailing soft-line measures were the result of a liberal (or at least antiterror) faction within the leadership that tried to block Stalin's plans. Said to consist of S. M. Kirov, V. V. Kuibyshev, Sergo Ordzhonikidze, and others, this group would have favored a general relaxation of the dictatorship; now that capitalism and the hostile class forces had been defeated, there was no reason to maintain a high level of repression.[24]

But the documents now available make this view untenable. There is little evidence for such a plan on Stalin's part nor of the existence of a liberal faction within the Politburo. Above and beyond routine squabbles over turf or the technicalities of implementation, neither the public statements nor the documentary record shows any serious political disagreement within the Stalin group at this time. Rather, the simultaneous pursuit of both soft- and hard-line policies was the result of indecision within a leadership that did not act according to grand plans but reacted to events anxiously, and on an ad hoc basis.[25]

24. For this view see Robert Conquest, *The Great Terror: A Reassessment*, Oxford, 1990; Robert C. Tucker, *Stalin in Power: The Revolution from Above, 1928–1941*, New York, 1990; A. A. Antonov-Ovseenko, *The Time of Stalin: Portrait of Tyranny*, New York, 1980.

25. For this argument see Getty, *Origins of the Great Purges*, New York, 1991; J. Arch Getty and Roberta T. Manning, eds., *Stalinist Terror: New Perspectives*, New York, 1993; G. T. Rittersporn, *Stalinist Simplifications and Soviet Complications: Social Tensions and Political Conflicts in the USSR, 1933–1935*, Reading, England, 1991; Robert Weinberg, "Purges and Politics in the Periphery: Birobidzhan in 1937," *Slavic Review*, 52(1), Spring 1993, 13–27.

CHAPTER THREE

Repression and Legality

Anyone who feels like arresting does so, including those who have, properly speaking, no right whatsoever to make arrests. It is no wonder, therefore, that with such an orgy of arrests, the organs [of state] having the right to make arrests, including the organs of the OGPU and especially of the police, have lost all sense of proportion.—Central Committee circular, 1933

At this congress, however, there is nothing to prove and, it seems, no one to fight. Everyone sees that the line of the party has triumphed.—Stalin, 1934

LITERARY CENSORSHIP in this period provides an example both of ambiguous policies and of direct attempts to construct the regime's dominant rhetoric and narrative. Since 1917 the Bolsheviks had suppressed publication of books and newspapers by their political opponents. But during the 1920s the Stalinist leadership had often permitted the publication of statements and articles by various oppositionists within the party, at least until the moment of their defeat and expulsion. Trotsky's works were published until the mid-1920s, and Bukharin continued to publish, albeit within controlled parameters, until his arrest in 1937; he was in fact editor of the government newspaper *Izvestiia* until that time.[1]

Writing and Rewriting History

The content of historical works had always played a role in Bolshevik politics. Part of the public dispute between the Stalinists and

1. Stalin had personally nominated Bukharin to the *Izvestiia* position in 1934. See RTsKhIDNI, f. 17, op. 3, d. 939, l. 2.

the Trotskyists in the early 1920s had revolved around Trotsky's historical evaluation of the role of leading Bolsheviks in his *Lessons of October*. And in 1929 a letter to the editor of a historical journal on an apparently obscure point of party history touched off a political purge in the historical profession and a general hardening of the line on what was acceptable and what was not.[2]

By the early 1930s the Stalinists were generally more intolerant of publications from ex-oppositionists and scrutinized their writings more carefully. At the end of 1930 Bukharin could still publish statements about his position on various matters, but their content was checked word for word by the Politburo before approval. A Politburo directive of October 1930 noted that "Comrade Bukharin's statement is deemed unsatisfactory. . . . In view of the fact that the editors of *Pravda*—were Comrade Bukharin to insist on the publication of his statement in the form in which it was sent by him to the CC—would be forced to criticize it, which would be undesirable, Comrade Kaganovich is entrusted with talking to Comrade Bukharin in order to coordinate the definitive wording of the text of his statement."[3] Bukharin's statement was eventually published, but only after considerable haggling over its content.

By 1932, however, things had become harder even for veteran party litterateurs. A. S. Shliapnikov, prominent Old Bolshevik and one of the leaders of the defeated Workers' Opposition in the early 1920s, was taken to task for some of his writings on the 1917 Revolution. In this case, though, it was not a matter of prior censorship of historical works; Shliapnikov's *1917* and *On the Eve of 1917* had already been published. This time, the new situation required a formal recognition of "mistakes" and a published retraction from the author; otherwise, he would be expelled from the party. In the "new situation," the worried nomenklatura was taking command of history itself by reshaping historical texts that had

2. See John Barber, "Stalin's Letter to *Proletarskaya Revolyutsiya*," *Soviet Studies*, 28, 1976, 21–41; and George M. Enteen, "Writing Party History in the USSR: The Case of E. M. Yaroslavsky," *Journal of Contemporary History*, 21, 1986, 321–39. On the activities of Soviet censors both locally and nationally, see Merle Fainsod, *Smolensk Under Soviet Rule*, Cambridge, Mass., 1958, 365–77; and Marianna Tax Choldin and Maurice Friedberg, *The Red Pencil: Artists, Scholars, and Censors in the USSR*, Boston, 1989.

3. RTsKhIDNI, f. 17, op. 2, d. 453, ll. 169–71, 175–86.

already been promulgated. In the Stalinist system, public disquisitions—which were necessarily political—could be "repaired" and history itself could be changed along with them. Chaotic times made ideology and ideological control important because it could "render otherwise incomprehensible social situations meaningful."[4]

Document 15

Politburo decree on Comrade Shliapnikov's letter, 3 March 1932[5]

Supplement to Protocol #90 of the Politburo of the CC of the All-Union Communist Party (Bolshevik) [VKP(b)] of 3 March 1932

DECREE ISSUED BY THE ORGBURO of the CC—19 February 1932

(Confirmed by the Politburo of the CC of VKP(b)—3 March 1932)

8. Comrade Shliapnikov's letter

(Decree issued by the PB on 27 January 1932. Protocol #85, Item 3—by poll)

(Comrades Shliapnikov, Mekhlis, N. N. Popov, Stetsky, Khalatov, Belenko, Savelev, Tovstukha)

In view of the fact that Comrade Shliapnikov, in his literary work *The Year 1917*, denies the rightness of many programmatic and tactical positions of the VKP(b) and attempts to reexamine them in the spirit of a Menshevik-Trotskyist line, which is illustrated:

1) by his rejection of the slogan of Soviet power and by his attempt to impose on the party a substitute anarcho-syndicalist slogan calling for handing over power to the factory committees;

2) by his rejection of the supremacy [*gegemoniia*] of the proletariat;

3) by his rejection of the party's position in February–March 1917 concerning the development of the bourgeois-democratic revolution into a socialistic one;

4) by his rejection of the party's position concerning the transformation of the imperialistic war into a civil war throughout the period from February 1917 to the end of 1917;

5) by his unwillingness to admit his mistakes the day after the October Revolution concerning the creation of a uniform socialist government by forming a bloc with the Mensheviks and SRs and so on and so on; and seeing that Comrade Shliapnikov has not admitted his mistakes but continues to insist on his slanderous fabrications against Lenin and his party and falsely alleges that Lenin and other members of the Politburo were familiar with his books, when,

---

4. Clifford Geertz, *The Interpretation of Cultures*, New York, 1973, 219–20.

5. RTsKhIDNI, f. 17, op. 3, d. 874, l. 15.

as is evident from Comrade Shliapnikov's statement, only one of his books was known at all and that to Comrade Kamenev, who was then a member of the Politburo,

the CC decrees:

1) that the publication and dissemination of Comrade Shliapnikov's "historical" works (*The Year 1917, On the Eve of the Year 1917*) be discontinued.

2) that it be proposed[6] to Comrade Shliapnikov that he admit his mistakes and repudiate them in the press.

[The CC decrees] that, if, at the conclusion of a 5-day period, Comrade Shliapnikov has not carried out the second item, he is to be expelled from the ranks of the VKP(b).

Secretary of the CC—Postyshev

Despite the general tightening of literary "discipline," the policy of censorship in the 1932–34 period was uneven. In June 1933 a circular letter from the Central Committee formally prescribed policies for "purging of libraries." Back in 1930, during the ultraleft upsurge of the "cultural revolution," the party had insisted on removing literary and historical works by "bourgeois" and oppositionist authors from all libraries. The June 1933 circular, while approving the removal of "counterrevolutionary and religious literature," along with the works of Trotsky and Zinoviev, took a relatively moderate line on library holdings in general. Works representing "historical interest" were to remain in the libraries of the larger towns, and closed or "special" collections were forbidden, as were mass purges of libraries.

Document 16

Central Committee letter on purging of libraries, 13 June 1933[7]

A letter from the CC of the All-Union Communist Party (Bolshevik) [VKP(b)], circulated to all Departments of Culture and Propaganda of regional committees and to the CCs of the national Communist parties

6. Orders of the highest party organs conventionally followed a verbal kind of euphemism. Frequently the verb *predlagat'* (to propose or suggest) was used to describe an order that demanded compliance. For the use of euphemism to mask dominance, see James C. Scott, *Domination and the Arts of Resistance*, New Haven, 1990, 55.

7. RTsKhIDNI, f. 17, op. 120, d. 87, ll. 27–28.

Document 16 *continued*

In spite of the decision of the CC of the All-Union Communist Party (Bolshevik) [VKP(b)], categorically prohibiting mass purges of libraries, in many regions, territories, and republics, this decree is not being carried out. Departments of Culture and Propaganda [*Kul'tprop*] have not drawn the necessary lesson from those distortions which have occurred. Instances of mass purges of libraries continue to take place right to the present day: in April, the Departments of Culture and Propaganda of the Northern Caucasus Territorial Committee decided to carry out a purge of all the libraries of the region and, in line with this, an instruction was published by the Territorial Department of Public Education to the effect that along with the proposal to withdraw all counterrevolutionary monarchist literature, certain individual works by Comrades Molotov, Kaganovich, and Kalinin, classics of philosophy, of the natural sciences, imaginative literature [*khudozhestvennaya literatura*] (Orzeszkowa, Spielhagen, Haeckel, Schopenhauer, and others) are also being withdrawn. In a host of places, all books printed in the old orthography are being withdrawn.

Moreover, the widespread practice of organizing "closed stacks" in libraries has led to the situation that a significant part of the book reserves has, in fact, been withdrawn from circulation. . . .

In order to secure the most stringent control and to offer practical assistance to organs of public education in outlying areas, it is necessary for you to carry out the following measures:

. . . a) The removal of books from libraries is to be permitted only in accordance with special instructions from the Central Commission.

b) Under the leadership of the territorial commission, openly counterrevolutionary and religious literature (Gospels, lives of the saints, sermons, etc.) shall be withdrawn, while literature having a historical interest shall be permitted in the large central city libraries.

c) The books of Trotsky and Zinoviev are to be transferred from village and small district libraries to regional libraries or to the library attached to the regional committee. These books shall circulate only on an extremely restricted basis, and their circulation shall be permitted exclusively by agreement with the party organization.

d) The organization of "special" or "closed" stacks in libraries is hereby prohibited. Existing "closed" and special stacks are to be immediately abolished by entering all [works of] literature into the catalog of the libraries.

e) The directive of 1930 of the Chief Political-Education [Department] concerning the reexamination of the holdings of mass libraries is hereby annulled.

It is categorically prohibited to use the Book-Center recycling lists as a basis for withdrawing books from the libraries.

f) The responsibility for the correct utilization of book resources of libraries lies with the director of the library.

Director of the Department of Culture and Propaganda of the CC of the All-Union Communist Party (Bolshevik) [VKP(b)] A. Stetsky

13 June 1933

Even here, the Politburo had difficulty taking control of the situation. The 13 June order was ignored by hotheaded local activists, who continued to strip the libraries of books they considered counterrevolutionary. Emelian Yaroslavsky and other party leaders complained about this to the Politburo, prompting Molotov and Stalin to issue stronger strictures that characterized the purging of the libraries as "anti-Soviet" and again ordering it stopped.[8]

Beginning in 1935 the policy would harden again as Stalin assumed supervision of the Culture and Propaganda Department of the Central Committee from Andrei Zhdanov.[9] Large numbers of books would be removed from circulation and Stalinist censorship would emerge in its full form. (See Documents 44 and 45 below.) But in 1930–34, policy was still in flux.

Judiciary and Police

Similar ambiguity characterized judicial policy in this period.[10] At the beginning of the 1930s, an ultraleftist version of "socialist legality" had prevailed. A class-based justice differentiated "class-alien" defendants from the "bourgeoisie" and those from the working class or peasantry, with the former receiving much sterner treatment at the bar. Legal protections were minimal, with the secret police (OGPU until 1934) having the right to arrest, convict, and execute with only cursory judicial proceedings—or none at all. Indeed, the Collegium of the OGPU had the right to pass death sentences entirely in secret and "without the participation of the accused."

---

8. For copies of these letters and orders, see *Istochnik*, 1996, no. 4, 137–44.

9. See RTsKhIDNI, f. 17, op. 3, d. 961, l. 16.

10. For background, see Peter H. Solomon Jr., *Soviet Criminal Justice Under Stalin*, Cambridge, 1996; Robert Sharlet, "Stalinism and Soviet Legal Culture," in Robert C. Tucker, ed., *Stalinism: Essays in Historical Interpretation*, New York, 1977, 155–79; Gábor T. Rittersporn, "Soviet Officialdom and Political Evolution: Judiciary Apparatus and Penal Policy in the 1930s," *Theory and Society*, 13, no. 2, 1984, 211–36; and Eugene Huskey, "Vyshinsky, Krylenko, and the Shaping of the Soviet Legal Order," *Slavic Review*, 46(3–4), Fall–Winter 1987, 414–28.

During the period of dekulakization and collectivization, lawlessness was the rule. Squads of party officials, police, village authorities, and volunteers arrested, exiled, and even executed recalcitrant peasants without any pretense of legality.[11] As early as 2 March 1930, even Stalin recoiled from the chaos and wrote his famous "Dizziness with Success" article, in which he called for a halt to forced collectivization and ordered a reduction in the use of violence against peasants.[12] Although the article did result in a general decline in mass terror against peasants, it did not curb the powers of the police (and others) to make arrests as they chose.

Indeed, in 1932–34 the regime sent very mixed signals on the general question of judicial repression. Consider the policy toward technical specialists from the old regime. In June 1931 Stalin's "New Conditions, New Tasks" speech seemed to call a halt to the radical, class-based persecution of members of the old intelligentsia. The party's policy should be "enlisting them and taking care of them," Stalin said. "It would be stupid and unwise to regard practically every expert and engineer of the old school as an undetected criminal and wrecker."[13] The following month, the Politburo forbade arrests of specialists without high-level permission.[14] In the subsequent period, the Politburo intervened on several occasions to protect persecuted members of the intelligentsia and to rein in the activities of secret police officials persecuting them:

Document 17

Politburo order of 23 March 1932 against illegal arrests of specialists[15]

From Protocol #93 of the Politburo of the CC of the All-Union Communist Party (Bolshevik) [VKP(b)] of 23 March 1932

17/10 Re: The arrest of Professors Rossiisky and Blagovolin by organs of the OGPU

It is proposed that the OGPU Board hold the guilty parties who permitted these illegal arrests accountable for their actions.

---

11. See Solomon, *Soviet Criminal Justice,* chs. 3 and 4.

12. *Pravda,* 2 March 1930. See also his "Reply to Kolkhoz Comrades," *Pravda,* 3 April 1930.

13. I. V. Stalin, *Sochineniia,* Moscow, 1951, XIII, 72.

14. RTsKhIDNI, f. 17, op. 3, d. 840, l. 9.

15. RTsKhIDNI, f. 17, op. 3, d. 877, l. 11.

Document 18

Politburo order of 23 February 1932 against police "distortions"[16]

From Protocol #89 of the Politburo of the CC of the All-Union Communist Party (Bolshevik) [VKP(b)] of 23 February 1932

43/11 Re: The distortion of the party line in Rostov and Taganrog by party organizations and organs of the OGPU

To be submitted to the Orgburo for consideration.

An apparently contradictory "hard" signal came a few months later, when a new decree (said to have been drafted by Stalin personally) prescribed the death penalty (or long imprisonment with confiscation of one's property) for even petty thefts from collective farms. Such harsh measures testify to the climate of paranoia in the top leadership in this period. They also bespeak panic and an inability to control the countryside with anything but repression.

Document 19

Law of 7 August 1932 on theft of public property[17]

On protecting the property [*imushchestvo*] of state enterprises, kolkhozy, and cooperative societies and on consolidating public (socialist) property [*sobstvennost'*]

Decree of the Central Executive Committee and of the Council of People's Commissars of the USSR

7 August 1932

Complaints by workers and kolkhoz members about the plundering (theft) of cargo from the railroads and water transport as well as about the plundering (theft) from cooperative societies and kolkhozy by hooligan and antisocial elements have lately become more frequent. The number of complaints concerning violence and threats directed by kulak elements at kolkhoz members who do not wish to leave the kolkhozy and who are working honestly and selflessly for the consolidation of these kolkhozy has similarly increased. The Central Executive Committee and the Council of People's Commissars of the USSR consider public property (belonging to the state, to kolkhozy, or to coop-

16. RTsKhIDNI, f. 17, op. 3, d. 873, l. 8.

17. V. P. Danilov and N. A. Ivnitsky, eds., *Dokumenty svidetel'stvuiut. Iz istorii derevni nakanune i v khode kollektivizatsii 1927–1932 gg.*, Moscow, 1989, 477–78.

erative societies) as the foundation of the Soviet regime. As such, it is sacred and inviolate, and persons misappropriating public property ought to be considered enemies of the people. A resolute struggle with plunderers of public property constitutes, therefore, the primary duty of organs of Soviet power. Based on these considerations and in order to meet the demands of workers and kolkhoz members, the Central Executive Committee and the Council of People's Commissars of the USSR decree:

I.

1. To put rail and water transport cargo on a footing equal to that of state property and to reinforce with all the means at our disposal the safeguarding of this cargo.

2. To apply as a measure of judicial punishment [*repressiia*] for the plundering of rail and water transport cargo the highest measure of social protection, namely, execution with confiscation of all property, with commutation of execution under extenuating circumstances to deprivation of freedom for a term of not less than 10 years with confiscation of all property.

3. Not to grant amnesty to any criminals convicted of plunder of transport cargo.

II.

1. To put the property of kolkhozy and cooperative societies (the harvest on the field, communal reserves, livestock, cooperative warehouses and stores, etc.) on a footing equal to that of state property and to use every means at our disposal to reinforce the protection of this property from misappropriation.

2. To apply as a measure of judicial punishment for the plundering (theft) of property belonging to kolkhozy and cooperative societies the highest measure of social protection, namely, execution with confiscation of all property, with commutation of execution under extenuating circumstances to deprivation of freedom for a term of not less than 10 years with confiscation of all property.

3. Not to grant amnesty to criminals convicted of plundering property belonging to kolkhozy and cooperative societies.

III.

1. To wage a resolute struggle against those antisocial, kulak-capitalistic elements which apply violence and threats [of violence] or preach the use of violence and threats against kolkhoz members for the purpose of forcing the latter to leave the kolkhozy, for the purpose of bringing about the violent destruction of the kolkhozy. These criminal acts are to be put on a footing equal to crimes against the state.

2. To apply as a measure of judicial punishment in matters concerned with the protection of kolkhozy and kolkhoz members against violence and the threats on the part of kulak and other antisocial elements, the deprivation of freedom with imprisonment in a concentration camp for a term ranging from 5 to 10 years.

3. Not to grant amnesty to criminals convicted in cases of this nature.

Chairman of the Central Executive Committee of the USSR, M. Kalinin.

Document 19 *continued*

Chairman of the Council of People's Commissars of the USSR, V. Molotov (Skriabin)
Secretary of the Central Executive Committee of the USSR, A. Yenukidze

---

Despite the draconian nature of this law, its application was uneven and confused. The following month, September 1932, the Politburo ordered death sentences mandated by the law to be carried out immediately.[18] Nevertheless, of those convicted under the law by the end of 1933, only 4 percent received death sentences, and about one thousand persons were actually executed.[19] In Siberia, property was confiscated from only 5 percent of those convicted under the law. Although it seemed aimed at collective farm members, commentators argued that class bias should be applied and that workers and peasants should be shown leniency.[20] In 1933 the drive was reoriented away from simple peasants and against major offenders; at that time, 50 percent of all verdicts rendered under the law had been reduced. By mid-1934, most convictions for theft resulted in noncustodial sentences.[21] It is interesting to note that the Commissariat of Justice was unwilling or unable to report to higher authorities exactly how many people were convicted under its provisions, giving figures ranging from 100,000 to 180,000 as late as the spring of 1936. In spite of Stalin's strictures in the original decree against leniency, by August 1936 a secret decree had ordered the review of all sentences under the Law of 7 August 1932. Four-fifths of those convicted had their sentences reduced, and more than 40,000 of these were freed at that time.[22]

In a show trial in Moscow in April 1933, engineers "of the old school" were accused of espionage and sabotage on behalf of Great

18. RTsKhIDNI, f. 17, op. 162, d. 13, ll. 99–100.

19. See Solomon, *Soviet Criminal Justice*, 117.

20. L. A. Paparde, *Novyi etap klassovoi bor'by i revoliutsionnaia zakonnost'*, Novosibirsk, 1933, 4–26.

21. See Solomon, *Soviet Criminal Justice*, 223, 225.

22. See *Gosudarstvennyi arkhiv Rossiiskoi Federatsii* (GARF), f. 3316, op. 2, d. 1534, ll. 87, 112; d. 1754, ll. 21, 26; f. 9474, op. 16, d. 48, ll. 15, 17, 35–36, 42; d. 79, ll. 6, 16. See also the discussions in Danilov and Ivnitsky, *Dokumenty*, 41–42, and J. Arch Getty, Gábor T. Rittersporn, and V. N. Zemskov, "Victims of the Soviet Penal System in the Pre-war Years: A First Approach on the Basis of Archival Evidence," *American Historical Review*, 98(4), October 1993, 1017–49.

Britain.[23] This "Metro-Vickers" trial was the latest in a series of open proceedings against engineers and technicians of the old regime that included the Shakhty trial of 1928, and the trial of the Industrial Party in 1930. The symbolism conveyed in these proceedings, which seemed to reinforce repressive trends, was that older technical specialists from the old regime were not to be trusted and that party members and Soviet citizens must be increasingly vigilant against enemies. Even here, though, there was ambiguity. Several of the defendants were released on bail before the trial. No death sentences were handed out, and two of the defendants received no punishment at all. According to the most recent study of the trial, the proceedings seemed to signal indecision within the Soviet government, perhaps reflected in the court's hedging statement that it "was guided by the fact that the criminal wrecking activities of the aforesaid convicted persons bore a local character and did not cause serious harm to the industrial power of the USSR."[24] Nevertheless, a political trial is a political trial, and the Metro-Vickers prosecutions sent a hard signal.

Almost immediately, the regime did another volte-face in the direction of sharply relaxing repression. During the civil war and again during collectivization, the secret police had operated tribunals for the purposes of handing down drumhead sentences of death or hard labor for political enemies. The vast majority of those executed during the storm of dekulakization and collectivization were victims of police "troikas." On 7 May 1933 the Politburo ordered the troikas to stop pronouncing death sentences.[25]

The next day a document carrying the signatures of Stalin for the Central Committee and V. M. Molotov for the government ordered a drastic curtailment of arrests and a sharp reduction in the prison population. Half of all prisoners in jails (not, it should be noted, in camps or in exile) were to be released. The power to arrest

---

23. See Robert Conquest, *The Great Terror: A Reassessment,* Oxford, 1990, appendix.

24. Gordon W. Morrell, *Britain Confronts the Stalin Revolution: Anglo-Soviet Relations and the Metro-Vickers Crisis,* Waterloo, Ontario, 1995, 150.

25. RTsKhIDNI, f. 17, op. 3, d. 922, l. 16. Some exceptions were made. Troikas in the Far Eastern territory could continue passing death sentences. Moreover, in the following period, the Politburo continued to authorize death sentences by troikas on a case-by-case basis during specified periods. See, for example, RTsKhIDNI, f. 17, op. 162, d. 15, ll. 2, 27.

was sharply restricted to police organs, and all arrests had to be sanctioned by the appropriate judicial procurator. (On the question of procuratorial sanction for arrests, see Documents 21, 22, 23, 24, 25, 49, 50, 79, and 190.) The document ordered an end to "mass repression" of the peasantry.

Document 20

Central Committee/SNK decree of 8 May 1933 halting mass arrests[26]

SECRET
Not for publication
INSTRUCTIONS
To all party-soviet officials and to all organs of the OGPU, the courts, and the procuracy

The desperate resistance of the kulaks to the kolkhoz movement of the toiling peasants, already in full swing at the end of 1929 and taking the form of arson and terror against kolkhoz officials, has made it necessary for Soviet authorities to resort to mass arrests and harsh measures of repression in the form of mass expulsions of kulaks and their henchmen to northern and remote regions.

The continued resistance by kulak elements—taking the form of sabotage within the kolkhozy and sovkhozy, a fact brought to light in 1932, the mass plundering of kolkhoz and sovkhoz property—have made necessary the further intensification of repressive measures against kulak elements, against thieves and saboteurs of every stripe.

Thus the past three years of our work in the countryside have been years of struggle for the liquidation of the kulaks and for the victory of the kolkhozy.

And these three years of struggle have led to the crushing defeat of the forces of our class enemies in the countryside, to the definitive consolidation of our Soviet socialist positions in the countryside. . . .

The Central Committee and the Council of People's Commissars (SNK) [the government] are of the opinion that, as a result of our successes in the countryside, the moment has come when we are no longer in need of mass repression, which affects, as is well known, not only the kulaks but also independent peasants [edinolichniki] and some kolkhoz members as well.

True, demands for mass expulsions from the countryside and for the use of harsh forms of repression continue to come in from a number of regions, while petitions by others for the expulsions of one hundred thousand families from their regions and territories are presently in the possession of the central

26. RTsKhIDNI, f. 17, op. 3, d. 922, ll. 50–55. Printed. This document was first described by Merle Fainsod in *Smolensk Under Soviet Rule*, Cambridge Mass., 1958, 185–88, from one of the circular copies found in the Smolensk Archive.

Committee and the Council of People's Commissars.[27] Information has been received by the Central Committee and the Council of People's Commissars that makes it evident that disorderly arrests on a massive scale are still being carried out by our officials in the countryside. Arrests are being carried out by chairmen of kolkhozy, by members of the governing boards of kolkhozy, by chairmen of village soviets, by the secretaries of cells and by district and territorial commissioners. Anyone who feels like arresting does so, including those who have, properly speaking, no right whatsoever to make arrests. It is no wonder, therefore, that with such an orgy of arrests, the organs [of state] having the right to make arrests, including the organs of the OGPU and especially of the police [*militsiia*], have lost all sense of proportion. More often than not, they will arrest people for no reason at all, acting in accordance with the principle: "Arrest first, ask questions later!"

What does all this mean?

It means that not a few comrades in certain regions and territories have yet to understand the new situation. They still live in the past. . . .

It looks as if these comrades are willing to replace and are already replacing the political work conducted among the masses and designed to isolate the kulaks and antikolkhoz elements by the administrative-chekist "operations" of organs of the GPU and the regular police. They do not understand that if this kind of action took on a massive character to any extent, it could nullify the influence of our party in the countryside.

These comrades apparently do not understand that these tactics of massive deportation of the peasants outside their region has, in the new circumstances, already outlived itself, that such deportation can only be applied on an individual and partial basis and then applied only to the leaders and organizers of the struggle against the kolkhozy.

These comrades do not understand that the method of mass, disorderly arrests—if this can be considered a method—represents, in light of the new situation, only liabilities, which diminish the authority of Soviet power. They do not understand that making arrests ought to be limited and carried out under the strict control of the appropriate organs. They do not understand that the arrests must be directed solely against active enemies of Soviet power.

The Central Committee and the Council of People's Commissars do not doubt but that all these errors and deviations from the party line and others like them will be eliminated as soon as possible.

It would be wrong to assume that the new situation and the necessary transition to new methods of operation signify the elimination or even the relaxation of the class struggle in the countryside. On the contrary, the class struggle in the countryside will inevitably become more acute. It will become

27. Such demands would continue into 1935 and later. See Document 43.

more acute because the class enemy sees that the kolkhozy have triumphed, that the days of his existence are numbered, and he cannot but grasp—out of sheer desperation—at the harshest forms of struggle against Soviet power. For this reason there can be no question at all of relaxing our struggle against the class enemy. On the contrary, our struggle must be intensified with all the means at our disposal and our vigilance must be sharpened to the utmost. Therefore we are talking here about intensifying our struggle against the class enemy. The point, however, is that in the present situation it is impossible to intensify the struggle against the class enemy and to liquidate him with the aid of old methods of operation because these methods have outlived their usefulness. The point therefore is to improve the old methods of struggle, to streamline them, to make each of our blows more organized and better targeted, to politically prepare each blow in advance, to reinforce each blow with the actions of the broad masses of the peasantry. For only through such improvement in the methods of our operation can the definitive liquidation of the class enemy in the countryside be accomplished. . . .

The Central Committee of the All-Union Communist Party (Bolshevik) and the Council of People's Commissars decree:

I. ON DISCONTINUING THE MASS EXPULSIONS OF PEASANTS

All mass expulsions of peasants are to cease at once. Expulsions are to be permitted only on a case-by-case and partial basis and only with respect to those households whose heads are waging an active struggle against the kolkhozy and are organizing opposition against the sowing of crops and their purchase by the state. . . .

II. ON REGULATING THE MAKING OF ARRESTS

1) All persons who are not fully authorized by law to make arrests, namely, the chairmen of District Executive Committees (RIK), district and territorial commissioners, chairmen of village soviets, chairmen of kolkhozy and kolkhoz associations, secretaries of cells, and others, are prohibited from doing so.

Arrests may be carried out solely by organs of the procuracy, by organs of the OGPU, or by heads of police.

Investigators may make arrests only with the preliminary sanction of the procurator.

Arrests carried out by heads of police are to be sanctioned or revoked by the district commissioners of the OGPU or by the corresponding procuracy within 48 hours after said arrest.

2) The organs of the procuracy, the OGPU, and the police are prohibited from taking a person into preventive custody prior to trial for petty crimes.

Only persons accused of counterrevolution, terroristic acts, sabotage, gangsterism, robbery, espionage, border crossing and smuggling of contraband, murder, grave bodily injury, grand larceny and embezzlement, professional speculation in goods, speculation in foreign exchange, counterfeiting, malicious hooliganism, and professional recidivism may be taken into preventive custody.

3) The organs of the OGPU are to obtain the prior consent of the directorate of the procuracy when making arrests, except in cases involving terroristic acts, explosions, arson, espionage, defection, political gangsterism, and counterrevolutionary, antiparty groups. . . .

4) The procurator of the USSR and the OGPU are under obligation to guarantee the strict implementation of the instruction of 1922 pertaining to the procurator's control over the making of arrests and the maintenance in custody of persons arrested by the OGPU.

III. ON REDUCING THE POPULATION OF PLACES OF CONFINEMENT

1) The maximum number of persons that may be held in custody in places of confinement[28] attached to the People's Commissariat for Justice (NKYu), the OGPU, and the Chief Directorate of the Police, other than in camps and colonies, is not to exceed 400 thousand persons for the entire Soviet Union.

The procurator of the USSR, along with the OGPU, is to determine within the next 20 days the maximum number of prisoners for each of the republics and regions (territories), proceeding from the base figure above.

The OGPU, the People's Commissariat for Justice of each of the Union republics, and the Procuracy of the USSR are to proceed immediately to reduce the population of places of confinement. The total number of those confined is to be reduced within the next two months from the current figure of 800,000 to 400,000 persons.

The Procuracy of the USSR is charged with the responsibility for carrying out this decree to the letter.

2) A maximum number of persons kept in each given place of confinement is to be established, proceeding from the base figure of 400,000 above.

The superintendents of places of confinement are prohibited from taking prisoners in excess of the maximum number that has been established.

3) The maximum period for holding a person in custody in police lockups is to be three days. Those incarcerated are to be provided with bread rations without fail.

4) The OGPU and the People's Commissariat for Justice of each of the republics, as well as the Procuracy of the USSR, are to immediately reexamine the cases of those under arrest and under investigation, with a view to replacing their state of custody with some other preventive measure (such as release on bail, on surety, or on their own recognizance). This is to apply to all cases except those involving particularly dangerous elements.

5) The following measures are to be taken with respect to those convicted:

a) All persons convicted to a term of up to 3 years of imprisonment are to

28. "Places of confinement" [*mesta zakliucheniia*] generally refers to prisons.

have their sentences commuted to 1 year of forced labor [*prinuditel'nye raboty*], with the remaining 2 years on probation.

b) Persons convicted to a term of 3 to 5 years of imprisonment, inclusively, are to be assigned to the labor settlements of the OGPU.

c) Persons convicted to a term of over 5 years are to be assigned to OGPU camps.

6) Kulaks convicted to terms of 3 to 5 years, inclusively, are to be assigned to labor settlements along with their dependents. . . .

Chairman of the Council of People's Commissars of the USSR

V. Molotov (Skriabin)

Secretary of the Central Committee of the VKP(b)

I. Stalin

8 May 1933

Such language suggests considerable ambiguity: Although the former sharply repressive policy was correct and successful, it must end. Although the level of "class struggle" with enemy elements in the countryside will "inevitably sharpen" and the party's struggle with the class enemy "must be strengthened," it is nevertheless time for a relaxation in arrest and penal policy.

On the face of it, such language represents the usual cynical attempt to initiate a new policy by praising the discarded one and blaming local implementers who had "distorted" it. After all, the center had encouraged much of the violence now condemned in what appears to be a break with previous policy. But in another sense the document is consonant with others of the period that sought to concentrate more and more authority in Moscow's hands. In addition to admitting that blind mass repression was inefficient, the leadership wanted to get control of the situation by putting control of repression into the hands of Moscow officials rather than those of local official organs: blows against the enemy were to be "more organized" and "better targeted." In this sense the document did not in itself necessarily imply less violence but rather that violence in the future would be more tightly directed from the center.

In any case, there is evidence that this decree had concrete results. In July 1933 Stalin received a report that in the two months since the 8 May decree, the population of prisons had indeed been reduced to a figure below 400,000.[29]

29. GARF, f. 5446, op. 15a, d. 1073, l. 35.

In the next two months, the Politburo decided to make two administrative changes that also seemed to point in the direction of enhancing legality: the creation of the office of procurator of the USSR (roughly, attorney general) and of an all-Union Commissariat of Internal Affairs (NKVD). Up to this time, each constituent republic of the USSR had had its own procurator who had limited powers to supervise or interfere in the activities of central administrative, judicial, and punitive organs (including the secret police). In principle, the new procurator of the USSR was to have supervision over all courts, secret and regular police, and other procurators in the entire Soviet Union. Legally speaking, an all-Union "civilian" judicial official thus received supervisory powers over the secret police. As with procurators, each republic had previously had its own Commissariat of Internal Affairs with supervisory responsibilities over republican soviets, regular police, fire departments, and the like.

The position of procurator is an element of Continental and Russian law. Unlike Anglo-Saxon prosecutors, a procurator is not simply the representative of the people in an adversary proceeding against defense counsel. Indeed, the principal function of Russian procurators from the time of Peter the Great was administrative as much as judicial; it was to exercise supervision (variously *nadzor* or *nabliudenie*) over state bodies and over their proper and legal implementation of state measures.[30]

Document 21

Politburo decree of 1 July 1933 on establishment of USSR Procuracy[31]

Supplement to Item 14 (by poll) of Protocol #140 of the Politburo of 1 July 1933

Decree by the Central Executive Committee and by the Council of People's Commissars of the Union of the SSR

Re: The establishment of the Procuracy of the Union of the SSR

(Confirmed by the Politburo of the CC of the All-Union Communist Party (Bolshevik) [VKP(b)]—20 June 1933)

With the aim of reinforcing the socialistic legal order and the proper safeguarding of public property in the Union of the SSR from attempts on this

30. See Glenn G. Morgan, *Soviet Administrative Legality: The Role of the Attorney General's Office*, Stanford, 1962.

31. RTsKhIDNI, f. 17, op. 3, d. 925, l. 47.

public property on the part of antisocial elements, the Central Executive Committee and the Council of People's Commissars of the Union of the SSR decree:

1. The establishment of the Procuracy of the Union of the SSR.

2. That the procurator of the Union of the SSR shall carry out:

a) the supervision of the decrees and orders of individual departments [*vedomstva*] of the Union of the SSR, the Union republics, and local organs of power to assure compliance with the constitution and decrees of the government of the Union of the SSR;

b) the supervision of judicial institutions of the Union republics to assure correct and uniform application of the laws, with the right to obtain cases on demand at any stage of the judicial process, with the right to appeal the courts' sentences and decisions to courts of higher instance, and with the right to suspend the execution of said sentences and decisions;

c) the instituting of criminal proceedings and support for the prosecution in all judicial institutions in the territory of the Union of the SSR;

d) the supervision, subject to special regulations, of the legality and rightness of actions undertaken by the OGPU, by the police [*militsiia*], by the department of criminal investigation, and by corrective-labor institutions;

e) the general direction of the activity of the procuracy of the Union republics.

Chairman of the Central Executive Committee of the USSR M. Kalinin.

Chairman of the Council of People's Commissars of the USSR V. Molotov (Skriabin)

Acting Secretary of the Central Executive Committee of the USSR Medvedev.

Document 22

Appointment of USSR procurator, 1 July 1933[32]

From Protocol #140 of the Politburo of the CC of the All-Union Communist Party (Bolshevik) [VKP(b)] of 1 July 1933

33/12 Re: The procurator of the USSR

a) Com. Akulov is hereby appointed procurator of the USSR

b) Com. Vyshinsky is confirmed as deputy procurator of the USSR

3) Com. Krylenko is to remain in his post as people's commissar for justice of the RSFSR

35/14 Re: The Procuracy of the USSR

The proposed decree of the Central Executive Committee [TsIK] of the USSR and the Council of People's Commissars [SNK] of the USSR is approved [See Document 21].

32. RTsKhIDNI, f. 17, op. 3, d. 925, l. 9.

Document 23

Establishment of USSR NKVD, 20 February 1934[33]

From Protocol #1 of the Politburo of the CC of the All-Union Communist Party (Bolshevik) [VKP(b)] of 20 February 1934

4. Re: The organization of a Union People's Committee for Internal Affairs [NKVD] (Stalin)

a) The organization of a Union People's Committee for Internal Affairs [NKVD] and the incorporation within it of the reorganized OGPU are deemed necessary.

b) Comrades Yagoda, Kaganovich, and Kuibyshev are to be entrusted with the task of presenting a bill of proposals within a period of five days, which includes time already spent on this exchange of opinions.

The resulting decree announcing the formation of the NKVD USSR abolished the OGPU and incorporated its police functions into the new organization.[34] Moreover, according to the new regulations, the NKVD did not have the power to pass death sentences (as the OGPU and its predecessors the GPU and Cheka had) or to inflict extralegal "administrative" punishments of more than five years' exile. (See Documents 24 and 25.) Treason cases, formerly under the purview of the secret police, were, along with other criminal matters, referred to the regular courts or to the Supreme Court. Similarly, at this time the secret police lost the power to impose death penalties on inmates of their own camps. Special territorial courts, under the control not of the police but of the Commissariat of Justice, were established in the regions of the camps and cases of crimes (like murder) committed in the camps were now heard by those judicial bodies.[35]

Combined with the decrees on the USSR Procuracy, the formation of the NKVD seemed to herald a new era of legality, and contemporary observers were favorably impressed with what appeared to be moves in the direction of reduced repression.[36] Other decisions support the impression of a relaxation in 1933–34. As we

33. RTsKhIDNI, f. 17, op. 3, d. 939, l. 2.

34. *Izvestiia,* 11 July 1934.

35. See the documents in the Politburo's "special folders," RTsKhIDNI, f. 17, op. 163, d. 1043, ll. 33–39.

36. *Izvestiia,* 22 December 1934.

shall see, though, in 1937 and 1938 legal protections would become dead letters, as the unfettered sweeps of the police netted huge
numbers of innocent victims who were jailed, exiled, or shot without procuratorial sanction or legal proceedings or protection of any
kind. A number of key events between 1934 and 1937, including
the assassination of Politburo member S. M. Kirov, dramatically
changed and hardened the political landscape.

In June 1934 a Politburo resolution quashing the sentence received by one Seliavkin censured the OGPU for "serious shortcomings in the conduct of investigations."[37] In September a memo from
Stalin proposed the formation of a Politburo commission (chaired
by V. V. Kuibyshev and consisting of Kaganovich and State Procurator Akulov; A. A. Zhdanov was later added) to look into
OGPU abuses. Stalin called the matter "serious, in my opinion,"
and ordered the commission to "free the innocent" and "purge the
OGPU of practitioners [nositeli] of specific 'investigative tricks'
and punish them regardless of their rank." Zhdanov later bom-
barded regional party committees with admonitions and complaints about their poor compliance with the new legal regulations
on courts and procurators.

Thus, in response to Stalin's recommendation, the Kuibyshev
Commission prepared a draft resolution censuring the police for
"illegal methods of investigation" and recommending punishment
of several secret police officials. Before it could be implemented,
however, Kirov was assassinated. The mood of Stalin and the Politburo changed dramatically, and the recommendations of the
Kuibyshev Commission were shelved in a period characterized by
personnel changes in the police, scapegoating a poor harvest and
industrial failures in 1936, the rise of German fascism, and the
resurgence of spy mania in 1937.[38]

Another 1934 decree complicates the picture even further. Simultaneous with the decision to create the NKVD, the Politburo—
with Stalin and future secret police chief N. I. Yezhov taking the
leading roles—created a Special Board of the NKVD (osoboe
soveshchanie) to handle specific cases. According to the new orga-

37. RTsKhIDNI, f. 17, op. 162, d. 16, ll. 88–89.
38. B. A. Viktorov, Bez grifa "sekretno." Zapiski voennogo prokurora, Moscow, 1990, 139–40.

nization of the procuracy and the NKVD, all crimes chargeable under the criminal code were to be referred to and decided by one of the various courts in a judicial proceeding. But the special board had the right to exile "socially dangerous" persons for up to five years—to camps, abroad, or simply away from the larger cities.

Document 24

NKVD special board regulations[39]

1 April 1934

34/16 Concerning a proposed code of regulations for the NKVD and the special board

(Politburo session of 8 March 1934, Protocol #3, Item 44/24)

Comrades Stalin and Yezhov are to be included in the commission charged with working out the proposed code of regulations for the NKVD and the special board.

Document 25

NKVD special board regulations, 28 October 1934[40]

Supplement to Politburo Protocol #16, Item 19

REGULATIONS CONCERNING THE SPECIAL BOARD OF THE NKVD OF THE USSR

(Confirmed by the Politburo of the CC of the VKP(b) on 28 October 1934)

1. In the case of people recognized as socially dangerous, the NKVD is granted the right to exile them for a period of up to 5 years under direct surveillance to localities on a list established by the NKVD or to banish them from the capitals and from the major cities and industrial centers of the USSR for a period of up to 5 years under direct surveillance or to incarcerate them in corrective-labor camps for a period of up to 5 years. In the case of socially dangerous foreign nationals, the NKVD is granted the right to expel them from the USSR.

2. In order to implement the above-mentioned item, a special board is hereby established under the supervision of the NKVD and consisting of the following:

a) deputy commissar of internal affairs;

b) the plenipotentiary of the NKVD for the RSFSR;

39. RTsKhIDNI, f. 17, op. 3, d. 943, l. 10.
40. RTsKhIDNI, f. 17, op. 3, d. 954, l. 38.

Document 25 *continued*

c) the head of the chief administration of the Worker's-Peasant's Police [*militsiia*];

d) the NKVD commissar of the Union republic on whose territory the case arose.

3. In all the sessions of this special board, the procurator of the USSR or his deputy is to take part without fail. Furthermore, in case of disagreement with either the decision of the special board itself or with the fact that the case was assigned for consideration by the special board, he shall have the right to lodge a protest with the Presidium of the Central Executive Committee of the USSR.

In such cases, the decision by the special board shall be suspended until such time as the Presidium of the Central Executive Committee of the USSR shall decide on the matter.

4. A decision by the special board regarding exile and incarceration in a corrective-labor camp shall, in the case of each individual person, be accompanied by an explanation of the grounds for such measures, the district in which the exile is to be served, and the period of such exile.

5. The special board is granted the right:

a) to reduce the sentences of persons exiled or incarcerated in corrective-labor camps, depending on their conduct and on recommendations by appropriate organs of the NKVD;

b) to curtail the period served by persons serving in special labor settlements.

Certainly, compared to the former powers of the OGPU, the general trend of 1934 represented a sharp restriction on the independent punitive power of the police. On the other hand, it is important to notice that several charges of the special board ran quite contrary to legality. First, the special board consisted only of secret police officials. Aside from the "participation" ex officio of the USSR procurator, no judicial officials, judges, or attorneys were involved. Second, the "infractions" coming under the purview of the special board were not criminal offenses as defined in the criminal code; formally, it was not a crime to be a "socially dangerous" person, but under these provisions it was punishable by the police in a nonjudicial proceeding. It was therefore up to the police to define "socially dangerous" and to decide who could be punished under that category. Third, the special board passed its sentences without the participation or even presence of the accused or his or her attorney, and no appeals were envisioned. Because of the ability to punish persons who had committed no definable crime (an "advantage" later touted by Yezhov; see Document 50), these actions come under the heading of administrative, extrajudicial punishments, a category hardly consistent with formal legality.

These contradictory judicial texts lend themselves to several possible interpretations: conflicting hard and soft factions, a terrorist Stalin trying to cover his purposes with "liberal" maneuvers, or a genuine moderate trend that was later derailed. But all of them point toward regularization and centralization of police powers in the hands of fewer and fewer people.

Screening the Party Membership

Our final example of ambiguous elite policies in 1932–34 has to do with party composition. In early 1933 the party leadership decided to conduct a screening, or purge,[41] of the party's membership. Purges had been traditional events in the party's history since 1918 and had taken in a wide variety of targets. Most often, the categories of people specified for purging were not explicitly related to political opposition or dissidence; traditional purge targets included careerists, bureaucrats, and crooks of various kinds.[42] Members of oppositionist groups were not mentioned in the instructions. Still, the inclusion in a purge, announced at the same plenum that attacked A. P. Smirnov, of categories like "double-dealers," "underminers," and those who refused to "struggle against the kulak" clearly invited the expulsion of ideological opponents.

Document 26

"On Purging the Party," 28 April 1933[43]

Supplement to the protocol of the Politburo of the CC of the VKP(b) of 28 April 1933
ON PURGING THE PARTY
Decree of the CC and the CCC of the VKP(b)

41. The word is *chistka*, meaning a sweeping or cleaning.
42. See J. Arch Getty, *Origins of the Great Purges: The Soviet Communist Party Reconsidered, 1933–1938*, New York, 1991, ch. 2, for a description of party purges. See also T. H. Rigby, *Communist Party Membership in the USSR, 1910–1967*, Princeton, 1968, 204, for a discussion of these nonpolitical targets.
43. RTsKhIDNI, f. 17, op. 3, d. 922, ll. 50–55.

I. THE NECESSITY FOR A PURGE

The fulfillment of the Five Year Plan in 4 years, the triumph of industrialization in the USSR, the successes of the kolkhoz movement, and the enormous numerical growth of the working class have brought forth a new upsurge of political activity among the proletariat and peasantry.

On the basis of this upsurge, the party has increased its membership in the past 2 years by 1,400,000 persons, bringing the total to 3,200,000 (members: 2,000,000; candidate members: 1,200,000).

Nevertheless, during this mass admission into the ranks of the party, in some places frequently carried out indiscriminately and without thorough checking, certain alien elements have made their way into the party who have exploited their party membership for careerist and self-seeking interests. Duplicitous elements have entered the party who declare their loyalty to the party in word but in fact seek to undermine the execution of its policy.

On the other hand, on account of the unsatisfactory state of Marxist-Leninist education of members of the party, it turns out that the party includes a not inconsiderable number of comrades who, though honorable and ready to defend Soviet power, are either insufficiently stable, failing to understand the spirit and demands of party discipline, or else politically illiterate, ignorant of the programs, rules, and fundamental resolutions of the party and thereby incapable of actively carrying out the party's policy.

Taking into consideration these circumstances, the joint Plenum of the CC and the CCC of the VKP(b), meeting in January, has decided to carry out a purge in 1933. It has decreed that "such a party purge be organized in a manner that will ensure an iron proletarian discipline in the party and the cleansing from the ranks of the party of all unreliable, unstable, and ingrained elements."

. . . II. THE MISSION AND THE DIRECTION OF THE PURGE

The mission of the purge consists of raising the ideological level of the members of the party, of the political and organizational consolidation of the party, and of continuing to raise the level of trust toward the party by the masses, by the millions of people who are not members of the party.

This mission is to be implemented by a purge that shall include: a) open and honest self-criticism by members of the party and by party organizations; b) checking up on the work of every party cell in terms of its implementation of the decisions and instructions of the party; c) getting the working, nonparty masses to participate in the purge; d) purging the party of persons not worthy of the lofty title of party member.

The following elements shall be expelled from the party:

1) Class-alien and hostile elements who have pushed their way into the party through deception and who have remained in it for the purpose of corrupting the party ranks;

2) Duplicitous elements who live by deceiving the party, who conceal from it their real aspirations, and who, under the cover of a false oath of "loyalty" to the party, seek in fact to undermine the party's policy;

3) Open and secret violators of the iron discipline of the party and state who do not carry out the decisions of the party and government and who cast doubt on and discredit the decisions and plans set by the party by their idle talk about their "unfeasibility" and "unattainability";

4) Degenerates who, having coalesced with bourgeois elements, do not want to fight our class enemies and who do not struggle against kulak elements, self-seekers, loafers, thieves, or plunderers of public property;

5) Careerists, self-seekers, and bureaucratic elements who, isolated from the masses and scorning the material and spiritual needs of the workers and peasants, exploit their presence in the party and their official position in the Soviet state for their own personal, self-seeking ends;

6) Morally corrupt elements who, by their unseemly conduct, lower the dignity of the party and stain its banner.

. . . The administration of this purge throughout the Union is entrusted to a Central Purge Commission headed by Comrade Rudzutak (chairman). It shall also include Comrades L. M. Kaganovich, Kirov, Yaroslavsky, Shkiriatov, Yezhov, Stasova, and Piatnitsky. . . .

The Central Committee and the Central Control Commission of the party are confident that all members of the party and all honest nonparty workers will take an active part in purging the ranks of the party of unworthy and alien elements and that this purge of the party will unite the workers and kolkhoz masses ever more tightly around the party, strengthening and consolidating the party organizations and making them ever more ready to join battle in carrying out the tasks of the second Five Year Plan.

CENTRAL COMMITTEE OF THE VKP(b)
CENTRAL CONTROL COMMISSION OF THE VKP(b)
28 April 1933

It would be a mistake to regard the 1933 *chistka* as having been directed solely against members of the opposition. The largest single group expelled were "passive" party members: those carried on the rolls but not participating in party work. Next came violators of party discipline, bureaucrats, corrupt officials, and those who had hidden past crimes. Members of dissident groups did not even figure in the final tallies.[44] Stalin himself characterized the purge as a measure against bureaucratism, red tape, degenerates, and careerists, "to raise the level of organizational leadership."[45] The

44. P. N. Pospelov et al., *Istoriia Kommunisticheskoi Partii Sovetskogo Soiuza*, tom. 4, chast' 2, Moscow, 1971, 283.

45. *XVII s"ezd Vsesoiuznoi Kommunisticheskoi Partii(b). 26 ianvaria–10 fevralia 1934g.: Stenograficheskii otchet.* Moscow, 1934, 33–34.

vast majority of those expelled were fresh recruits who had entered the party since 1929, rather than Old Bolshevik oppositionists. Nevertheless, the 1933 purge expelled about 18 percent of the party's members and must be seen as a hard-line policy or signal from Moscow.

Moreover, such purges potentially affected not only ideological groups but also various strata within the party. Traditionally, purges could strike at the heart of local political machines insofar as Moscow demanded strict verification of officials. On the other hand, the sword could strike the other way. Because they were usually carried out by local party leaders or their clients, party purges could be used by them to rid the party of rank-and-file critics or people the local party "family" considered troublemakers.

The chistka can be seen in another light not directly connected with real or imagined political dissidents or possible plans for terror. If, as we have argued, the dangerous "new situation" of 1932 threatened the regime's control (that is, the nomenklatura's position), it would make sense for the elite to close ranks, prune the party, and thereby restrict the size of the politically active strata of society. The chistka served these interests by "regulating its composition" and closing off access to it by "crisis" or "unstable" elements in a time of troubles. Thus the chistka may have been seen by the leadership not as a prelude to anything but rather as a survival mechanism for the nomenklatura.

At the beginning of 1934, Stalin spoke to the Seventeenth Party Congress (dubbed the "Congress of Victors" by the party leadership). On the one hand, he noted that the oppositionist groups had been utterly defeated, their leaders forced to recant their errors. Indeed, former oppositionists Bukharin, Rykov, Tomsky, and others were allowed to speak to the congress in order to demonstrate a new party unity that Stalin proclaimed. On the other hand, however, he noted that "unhealthy moods" could still penetrate the party from outside: "The capitalist encirclement still exists, which endeavors to revive and sustain the survivals of capitalism in the economic life and in the minds of the people of the USSR, and against which we Bolsheviks must always keep our powder dry." Stalin's ambiguous (or perhaps dialectical) text thus combined the policies of stabilized legality with continued vigilance.

He criticized those who favored a weakening of state power and controls, arguing that even though the party was victorious and the class enemies were smashed, the state could not yet "wither away." Rightists and moderates had suggested that the victory of the party's general line in industry and agriculture meant that the state could relax its control and reduce the power of its repressive mechanisms. In this connection, Stalin repeated his theoretical formula that as the Soviet Union moved toward victorious socialism, its internal enemies would become more desperate, provoking a "sharper" struggle that precluded "disarming" the state. Thus, while proclaiming victory and implying the end of mass repression, Stalin left the theoretical door open for the continued use of repression on a more selective basis. (Stalin had previously ordered an end to mass repression in the countryside while simultaneously arguing that the struggle with enemies was becoming "sharper." See Document 20.) Nevertheless, the specific remedies he proposed for the remaining "problems" were in the benign areas of party education and propaganda rather than repression.

Stalin's nomenklatura listeners, beset by crises on all sides, certainly were glad to squelch any talk of "disarming." On the other hand, they must have been less pleased by the second part of his remarks, "Questions of Organizational Leadership." Here he complained about high-ranking "bureaucrats" who rested on their laurels and were lax about "fulfillment of decisions." The "incorrigible bureaucrats" he chastised were members of the nomenklatura. Rudzutak had spoken for this elite the year before when he said of Stalin, "He is ours" (Document 11). Now, however, Stalin sounded a more sour note when he implied that the nomenklatura officials must themselves obey their own party line—and that of the leader of the party. This was the beginning of diverging interests between Stalin and the elite that backed him, and although their alliance continued, signs of a rift were already present in early 1934.

Document 27

Stalin's speech to the Seventeenth Party Congress, 28 January 1934[46]

. . . I pass to the question of the party.

The present congress is taking place under the flag of the complete victory of

46. J. Stalin, "Report to the Seventeenth Party Congress on the Work of the

Leninism, under the flag of the liquidation of the remnants of the anti-Leninist groups.

The anti-Leninist group of Trotskyists has been smashed and scattered. Its organizers are now to be found in the backyards of the bourgeois parties abroad.

The anti-Leninist group of the right deviators has been smashed and scattered. Its organizers have long ago renounced their views and are now trying in every way to expiate the sins they committed against the party.

The groups of nationalist deviators have been smashed and scattered. Their organizers have either completely merged with the interventionist émigrés, or else they have recanted.

The majority of the adherents to these antirevolutionary groups had to admit that the line of the party was correct and they have capitulated to the party.

At the Fifteenth Party Congress it was still necessary to prove that the party line was correct and to wage a struggle against certain anti-Leninist groups; and at the Sixteenth Party Congress we had to deal the final blow to the last adherents of these groups. At this congress, however, there is nothing to prove and, it seems, no one to fight. Everyone sees that the line of the party has triumphed.

The policy of industrializing the country has triumphed. Its results are obvious to everyone. What arguments can be advanced against this fact?

The policy of eliminating the kulaks and of complete collectivization has triumphed. Its results are also obvious to everyone. What arguments can be advanced against this fact?

The experience of our country has shown that it is fully possible for socialism to achieve victory in one country taken separately. What arguments can be advanced against this fact?

It is evident that all these successes, and primarily the victory of the Five Year Plan, have utterly demoralized and smashed all the various anti-Leninist groups.

It must be admitted that the party today is united as it has never been before. . . .

Does this mean, however, that the fight is ended, and that the offensive of socialism is to be discontinued as superfluous?

No, it does not.

Does it mean that all is well in our party; that there will be no more deviations in the party, and that therefore we may now rest on our laurels?

No, it does not.

We have smashed the enemies of the party, the opportunists of all shades, the nationalist deviators of all kinds. But remnants of their ideology still live in the minds of individual members of the party, and not infrequently they

Central Committee of the CPSU(b)," *Selected Works*, Moscow, 1952, 392–420. This document was not translated by Benjamin Sher.

find expression. The party must not be regarded as something isolated from the people who surround it. It lives and works in its environment. It is not surprising that at times unhealthy moods penetrate into the party from outside. And the ground for such moods undoubtedly exists in our country, if only for the reason that there still exist in town and country certain intermediary strata of the population who constitute a medium which breeds such moods.

The Seventeenth Conference of our party declared that one of the fundamental political tasks in fulfilling the second Five Year Plan is to overcome the survivals of capitalism in economic life and in the minds of people. That is an absolutely correct idea. But can we say that we have already overcome all the survivals of capitalism in economic life? No, we cannot say that. Still less can we say that we have overcome the survivals of capitalism in the minds of people. We cannot say that, not only because in development the minds of people lag behind their economic position but also because the capitalist encirclement still exists, which endeavors to revive and sustain the survivals of capitalism in the economic life and in the minds of the people of the USSR, and against which we Bolsheviks must always keep our powder dry.

Naturally, these survivals cannot but be a favorable ground for a revival of the ideology of the defeated anti-Leninist groups in the minds of individual members of our party. Add to this the not very high theoretical level of the majority of our party members, the inadequate ideological work of the party bodies, and the fact that our party functionaries are overburdened with purely practical work, which deprives them of the opportunity of augmenting their theoretical knowledge, and you will understand the origin of the confusion on a number of questions of Leninism that exists in the minds of individual party members, a confusion which not infrequently penetrates into our press and helps to revive the survivals of the ideology of the defeated anti-Leninist groups.

That is why we cannot say that the fight is ended and that there is no longer any need for the policy of the socialist offensive.

It would be possible to take a number of questions of Leninism and demonstrate by means of them how tenaciously the survivals of the ideology of the defeated anti-Leninist groups continue to exist in the minds of certain party members.

Take, for example, the question of building a classless socialist society. The Seventeenth Party Conference declared that we are advancing toward the formation of a classless socialist society. Naturally, a classless society cannot come of its own accord, as it were. It has to be achieved and built by the efforts of all the working people, by strengthening the organs of the dictatorship of the proletariat, by intensifying the class struggle, by abolishing classes, by eliminating the remnants of the capitalist classes, and in battles with enemies, both internal and external.

The point is clear, one would think.

And yet, who does not know that the enunciation of this clear and elementary thesis of Leninism has given rise to not a little confusion in the minds of a section of party members and to unhealthy sentiments among them? The thesis that we are advancing toward a classless society—put forward as a slogan—was interpreted by them to mean a spontaneous process. And they began to reason in this way: if it is a classless society, then we can relax the class struggle, we can relax the dictatorship of the proletariat, and get rid of the state altogether, since it is fated to wither away soon in any case. And they fell into a state of foolish rapture, in the expectation that soon there would be no classes, and therefore no class struggle, and therefore no cares and worries, and therefore it is possible to lay down one's arms and go to bed—to sleep in expectation of the advent of a classless society.

There can be no doubt that this confusion of mind and these sentiments are exactly like the well-known views of the right deviators, who believed that the old must automatically grow into the new, and that one fine day we shall wake up and find ourselves in a socialist society.

As you see, remnants of the ideology of the defeated anti-Leninist groups are capable of revival, and are far from having lost their vitality.

Naturally, if this confusion of views and these non-Bolshevik sentiments obtained a hold over the majority of our party, the party would find itself demobilized and disarmed. . . .

There you have some of the serious and urgent problems of our ideological-political work on which there is lack of clarity, confusion, and even direct departure from Leninism in certain strata of the party. Nor are these the only questions which could serve to demonstrate the confusion in the views of certain members of the party.

After this, can it be said that all is well in the party?

Clearly, it cannot.

Our tasks in the sphere of ideological and political work are:

1) To raise the theoretical level of the party to the proper height.

2) To intensify ideological work in all the organizations of the party.

3) To carry on unceasing propaganda of Leninism in the ranks of the party.

4) To train the party organizations and the nonparty activist group [*aktiv*] which surrounds them in the spirit of Leninist internationalism.

5) Not to gloss over but boldly to criticize the deviations of certain comrades from Marxism-Leninism.

6) Systematically to expose the ideology and the remnants of the ideology of trends that are hostile to Leninism.

2. QUESTIONS OF ORGANIZATIONAL LEADERSHIP

I have spoken of our successes. I have spoken of the victory of the party line in the spheres of the national economy and of culture, and also in the sphere of overcoming anti-Leninist groups in the party. I have spoken of the historic significance of our victory. But this does not mean that we have achieved victory everywhere and in all things and that all questions have already been settled. Such successes and such victories do not occur in real life. We still have plenty of unsolved problems and defects of all sorts. Ahead of us is a host of problems demanding solution. But it does undoubtedly mean that the greater part of the urgent and immediate problems has already been successfully solved, and in this sense the very great victory of our party is beyond doubt. . . .

Some people think that it is sufficient to draw up a correct party line, proclaim it for all to hear, state it in general theses and resolutions, and have it voted for unanimously, for victory to come of itself, automatically, as it were. That, of course, is wrong. It is a gross delusion. Only incorrigible bureaucrats and red-tapists can think so. As a matter of fact, these successes and victories did not come automatically but as the result of a fierce struggle for the application of the party line. Victory never comes of itself—it is usually won by effort. Good resolutions and declarations in favor of the general line of the party are only a beginning; they merely express the desire for victory but not the victory itself. After the correct line has been laid down, after a correct solution of the problem has been found, success depends on how the work is organized; on the organization of the struggle for carrying out the party line; on the proper selection of personnel; on checking the fulfillment of the decisions of the leading bodies. Otherwise the correct line of the party and the correct solutions are in danger of being seriously prejudiced. More than that, after the correct political line has been laid down, organizational work decides everything, including the fate of the political line itself, its success or failure. . . .

We have in our party more than 2,000,000 members and candidate members. In the Young Communist League we have more than 4,000,000 members and candidate members. We have over 3,000,000 worker and peasant correspondents. The Society for the Promotion of Air and Chemical Defense has more than 12,000,000 members. The trade unions have a membership of over 17,000,000. It is to these organizations that we are indebted for our successes. And if, in spite of the existence of such organizations and of such possibilities, which facilitate the achievement of successes, we still have quite a number of shortcomings in our work and not a few failures, then it is only we ourselves, our organizational work, our bad organizational leadership, that are to blame for this.

Bureaucracy and red tape in the administrative apparatus, idle chatter about leadership in general. Instead of real and concrete leadership, the functional structure of our organizations and lack of individual responsibility; lack of personal responsibility in work, and wage equalization; the absence of a systematic check on the fulfillment of decisions; fear of self-criticism—these are the sources of our difficulties; this is where our difficulties now lie.

It would be naive to think that these difficulties can be overcome by means of resolutions and decisions. The bureaucrats and red-tapists have long been past masters in the art of demonstrating their loyalty to party and government decisions in words, and pigeonholing them in deed. In order to overcome these difficulties it was necessary to put an end to the disparity between our organizational work and the requirements of the political line of the party; it was necessary to raise the level of organizational leadership in all spheres of the national economy to the level of political leadership; it was necessary to see to it that our organizational work ensured the practical realization of the political slogans and decisions of the party.

In order to overcome these difficulties and achieve success it was necessary to organize the struggle to eliminate them; it was necessary to draw the masses of the workers and peasants into this struggle; it was necessary to mobilize the party itself; it was necessary to purge the party and the economic organizations of unreliable, unstable, and degenerate elements.

What was needed for this?

We had to organize:

1) Full development of self-criticism and exposure of shortcomings in our work.

2) The mobilization of the party, soviet, economic, trade union, and Young Communist League organizations for the struggle against difficulties. . . .

11) The exposure and expulsion from the administrative apparatus of incorrigible bureaucrats and red-tapists.

12) The removal from their posts of people who violate the decisions of the party and the government, of window-dressers and windbags, and the promotion to their place of new people—businesslike people, capable of concretely directing the work entrusted to them and of strengthening party and soviet discipline.

13) The purging of soviet and economic organizations and the reduction of their staffs.

14) Lastly, the purging of the party of unreliable and degenerate people.

These, in the main, are the measures which the party has had to adopt in order to overcome difficulties, to raise the level of our organizational work to that of political leadership, and thus ensure the application of the party line.

You know that it was precisely in this way that the Central Committee of the party carried on its organizational work during the period under review.

In this the Central Committee was guided by Lenin's brilliant thought that the chief thing in organizational work is selection of personnel and checking fulfillment.

The year 1934 evokes positive memories in the Soviet Union. It began with famine and violent class war in the countryside, but a series of reforms moved the country in the direction of a kind of legality—or, to use Gramsci's terms, hegemony rather than domination. Memoirists recall 1934 as a "good" year when the mass repression of the previous period had ended, and official statements and new judicial arrangements seemed to herald a period of relative stability and relaxation. Arrests by the secret police fell by more than half (and political convictions by more than two-thirds) from the previous year, reaching their lowest level since the storm of collectivization in 1930 (see Appendix 1).[47] The regime had made peace with the old intelligentsia and seemed to be replacing repression with political education as its main political tool. After the tumult of collectivization and hunger, the economy was improving, and the year ended with the abolition of bread rationing throughout the country.

Given the eruption of terror just a few years later, we know that the stability of 1934 was temporary. In fact, as we have seen, moderation and softening of the regime alternated and indeed coexisted with the diametrically opposed policy of repression. On the questions of treatment of dissidents, literature, and judicial policy we saw how moderate and hard-line policies were jumbled together in a contradictory way that suggested a series of zigzags more than any coherent pattern.

In one view, these zigzags represented a struggle between hard and soft factions, or at least opinions in the top leadership and a kind of jockeying for position among Stalin's lieutenants. The question, of course, is what Stalin's position was. Because he was a crafty politician always careful not to reveal too much, it is difficult to divine his thoughts and plans. Some observers view the political situation of 1932–34 as one in which different groups contended for Stalin's favor.[48] According to this line of reasoning, Stalin allowed his subordinates to contend with one another and to foster alternating initiatives and emphases. Indecision therefore made 1934 a kind of crossroads. Several alternative paths, including continued moderation, were open; terror was neither planned nor inevitable but rather a function of contingent factors that arose later.

Other analysts see the zigzags of 1932–34 as a prelude to terror.

47. Appendix 1 deals with source questions concerning the number of victims of the terror.

48. See, for example, Boris I. Nicolaevsky, *Power and the Soviet Elite: The Letter of an Old Bolshevik and Other Essays*, New York, 1965, 43, 48–50.

Indeed, many scholars believe that even then Stalin was predis-
posed toward repression and mass violence. According to this view,
the hard-line policies of the period can be associated with a Stalin
who promoted repressive policies in order to lay a groundwork for
terror. Large-scale repression was blocked, though, by a moderate
faction that favored relaxation and was often able to implement
softer policies or at least force Stalin to back down temporarily.
Opposition to Stalin thus created a stalemate and made it necessary
for him to neutralize the moderates in order to continue and indeed
expand his repressive plans. In this view 1934 was merely an illu-
sion, a temporary hiatus in which there was little potential for any
outcome other than terror.[49]

On this point it may be worthwhile to reflect briefly on what the
1932–34 period shows us about repression and Bolshevik mentality. Looking at the repressive or hard-line strand of policies, it is
easy to have the impression of a fierce regime exercising strong
totalitarian control. Without a doubt, the regime was capable of
launching bloody and violent repression, as the collectivization of
agriculture had shown.

But such repressive policies may well betray another side of the
regime and its self-image. Regimes, even those with transforma-
tional goals, need not resort to terror if they have a firm basis of
social support. They do not need messy, inefficient, out-of-control,
campaign-style politics, including mass campaigns of terror, if they
have reliable and efficient administrations that govern with any
degree of popular consensus. Governments that are sound and
firmly based do not need continued repression to survive and to
carry out their goals. The Stalinist regime clearly did need such
repression, or at least thought it did.

Given what must appear to us to be a paranoid and pathological
mentality and an institutional history of political violence, it is all
the more remarkable that moderate and legalist policies periodically surfaced among the Stalinists. How can we explain the
other, more moderate strand in Bolshevik policies in this period?
Although such initiatives, sometimes bordering on constitutionalism and legalism, lost ground to the repressive alternative after

49. See, for example, Conquest, *Great Terror*.

1935, they did not die out completely; they appeared even at the height of the terror and after.[50]

The answer is that in addition to being ideological fanatics willing to use any means, including violent "revolutionary expediency," the Stalinists were also state builders attracted to "socialist legal consciousness." USSR Procurator Andrei Vyshinsky saw no contradiction between these two goals, noting that they were compatible parts of the party's policy of "revolutionary legality."[51] Bolsheviks—including Stalin at various times—recognized that modern economies required modern states, efficient bureaucracies, predictable administration, and some measure of security for the political elite. The tension between voluntarist campaigns and arbitrary repression on the one hand and state building and orderly administration on the other marked the entire Stalin period; these two sets of policies alternated and overlapped with each other. As one scholar has noted, the Stalinist system was "two models in one," and tension between the two ran throughout the Stalin and post-Stalin periods.[52] We shall see this dynamic at work in the next period, when a political assassination raised the political temperature but provoked familiar contradictory responses.

The documents now available make it difficult to support the former hypotheses about hard-soft divisions within the Politburo or about a Stalin who resisted the impulse toward legality. Secret documents from the Politburo's "special folders" indicate a consensus in the Politburo in 1934 that the polarized situation in the country was giving way to an atmosphere of reduced conflict with the "class enemy" in which a relaxation of repression was possible. The private comments of the top leaders to one another—including those often most associated with the supposed repressive faction—show that a moderate course was in the wind. That moderate course was to be one in which peaceful means of hegemony (including constitutionalism, legality, and political education) could replace overt domination by terror and violence.

50. See J. Arch Getty, "State and Society Under Stalin: Constitutions and Elections in the 1930s," *Slavic Review*, 50(1), Spring 1991, 18–36.

51. See Solomon, *Soviet Criminal Justice*, ch. 5. For a discussion of Stalinist state building, see J. Arch Getty, "Les bureaucrates bolcheviques et l'Etat stalinien," *Revue des Etudes Slaves*, 64(1), 1991, 1–25.

52. Moshe Lewin, *The Making of the Soviet System*, New York, 1985, 281–84.

In the summer of 1934 Politburo members advocated the release of several political figures convicted of anti-Soviet crimes. In one such case, Commissar of Defense Voroshilov noted that this was possible because "the situation now has sharply changed, and I think one could free him without particular risk."[53] There was the feeling at the top that the social struggle was calming down and that the previous policy of class struggle and maximum repression was being replaced by one in which the regime could feel strong enough to grant a certain measure of democracy without fear of being overthrown. L. M. Kaganovich wrote that the reform of the secret police "means that as we are in more normal times, we can punish through the courts and not resort to extrajudicial repression as we have until now."[54]

Of course, no one in the Politburo was advocating abandonment of the party-state dictatorship. As Stalin had said at the Seventeenth Party Congress, "we cannot say that the fight is ended and that there is no longer any need for the policy of the socialist offensive." On the other hand, Stalin explicitly joined other Politburo members in proposing some kind of relaxation of that dictatorship, at least experimentally. The increased repression in later years "should not cast doubt on the intentions of Stalin and his colleagues in 1934."[55] At the beginning of 1935 he proposed a new electoral system with universal suffrage and secret ballot elections. Confident that the regime was more and more secure and that sharp repression could be tempered with legality, Stalin wrote in a note in the Politburo's special folders, "We can and should proceed with this matter to the end, without any half-measures. The situation and correlation of forces in our country at the present moment is such that we can only win politically from this."[56] Even as late as 1937, when many of these "reforms" had been abandoned, there seems to have been some kind of attempt to democratize the electoral process and to "trust" the population to support the Bolsheviks.[57]

53. RTsKhIDNI, f. 17, op. 163, d. 1033, ll. 61–62.
54. RTsKhIDNI, f. 17, op. 165, d. 47, ll. 3.
55. Solomon, *Soviet Criminal Justice*, 166.
56. RTsKhIDNI, f. 17, op. 163, d. 1052, l. 153.
57. See Getty, "State and Society Under Stalin." For another view, see Sheila Fitzpatrick, *Stalin's Peasants: Resistance and Survival in the Russian Village After Collectivization*, New York, 1994, 281.

Thus one need not necessarily find the hard and soft policies of 1932–34 to be mutually exclusive or sharply contradictory. Both were means to an end: taking and maintaining control over the country in order to further the revolutionary program. Peasant revolt and starvation, conspiracies and platforms of former party leaders, dissident youth groups, and even a lack of iron discipline among serving Central Committee members had combined to frighten the nomenklatura elite and threaten their hold on power. In response, they sought to increase party discipline, strengthen judicial and police controls, and regulate the composition of their party. In these areas, both hard and soft policies had one common aspect: they sought to increase control exercised by the Moscow center. Even the legalist policies reviewed above, including the reduction of the number of arrests and insistence on judicial procedures, had the effect of tightening Moscow's control over these activities. By regulating arrest procedures, even in the direction of legality and procuratorial control, the Stalinists were asserting their right to control the entire judicial sphere. In this light, both hard and soft initiatives were parts of a drive (a defensive drive, in the nomenklatura's view) to centralize and control many spheres in a climate that was improving but still perceived to be dangerous.

CHAPTER FOUR

Growing Tension in 1935

To execute sixty people for one Kirov means that Soviet power is showing weakness by relying on terror to put down the growing discontent. —Komsomol member Rybakova, 1935

The main reason given for the commutation of sentence from death by shooting to ten years' imprisonment was the argument that this case did not involve a fully constituted counterrevolutionary group. . . . Do these people really need the fact of a perpetrated crime in order to convict such an obvious terrorist?!—M. F. Shkiriatov, 1935

ON 1 DECEMBER 1934, Politburo member, Leningrad party secretary, and Stalin intimate Sergei Kirov was shot in the corridor outside his office in the Smolny building. Over the next four years the Stalinist leadership used the assassination as evidence of a widespread conspiracy against the Soviet state and its leaders and as a pretext for the Great Terror of the 1930s. Millions of people were arrested, imprisoned, or shot in the aftermath of the assassination, and because it provided justification for Stalinist terror, the crime has been called "the key moment which determined the development of the Soviet system, and so the future of the world."[1]

The assassin, one Leonid Nikolaev, was apprehended at the scene. Stalin and several Politburo members quickly traveled to Leningrad to investigate the circumstances. Two days after the killing, the Politburo approved an emergency decree that Stalin had drafted en route to Leningrad whereby persons accused of "terror-

1. Robert Conquest, *Stalin and the Kirov Murder,* New York, 1989, 4.

ism" could be convicted in an abbreviated procedure, denied the right of appeal, and immediately shot. This decree, the notorious Law of 1 December 1934, became the "legal" basis for thousands of summary executions over the next four years. Moreover, complicity in organizing the Kirov murder was attached to almost every high-level accusation made against Old Bolsheviks and others.

Constructing the Kirov Assassination

Stalin used the Kirov assassination as a justification for persecution of his enemies. In fact, most historians believe that he organized the assassination for this very purpose. The question is of more than antiquarian interest for two reasons. First, if Stalin was involved, one might argue convincingly that he had a long-range plan to launch a terror of the elite and, indeed, of the entire Soviet Union. If, on the other hand, the assassination was not his work, the subsequent terror must be explained outside the framework of a grand plan. Debates about Stalin's possible involvement in the Kirov murder have been fierce but inconclusive because of the lack of official documentation.

In the 1930s various writers called into question the official Stalinist story of an assassin working at the behest of an anti-Soviet criminal conspiracy. Leon Trotsky ("The Kirov Assassination," 1935), suggested that the killing may have been the accidental result of an operation by the secret police to stage an attempted assassination. *The Letter of an Old Bolshevik* (Boris Nicolaevsky, 1936) suggested that Kirov's killing was related to power struggles within the Politburo, with hard-liners standing to gain from the removal of Kirov's "liberal" influence with Stalin.

Beginning in the 1950s memoirs from some Soviet defectors began to suggest that Stalin may have arranged the crime in order to provide a justification for terror or to eliminate Kirov as a rival. In his speeches to party congresses in 1956 and 1961, Nikita Khrushchev hinted that indeed "much remained to be explained" about the assassination (although he stopped short of actually accusing Stalin.)

Working from the memoir literature, Western historians began to piece together the known events surrounding the assassination and its aftermath and elaborated a compelling case for Stalin's involvement. According to this view, in addition to creating a pretext for terror, Stalin's motives included removing a popular rival and neutralizing a liberal, conciliatory voice on the Politburo that had opposed the Stalinists' hard-line policies. Kirov was said to be the choice of a secret group of high party officials who in 1934 cast about for a possible replacement for Stalin. Many think that this group instigated a large number of delegates to the Seventeenth Party Congress in 1934 either to abstain or to vote against Stalin's candidacy to the Central Committee, and that Kaganovich personally destroyed the embarrassing anti-Stalin ballots. In this view, Stalin knew about the attempt and decided to remove the alternative candidate and, eventually, all the officials behind the plan.

The strange incompetence of the Leningrad police in failing to prevent the assassination, coupled with possible connections between them and the assassin—it seems that they had previously detained him for questioning—suggested complicity of security officers in the murder. The fact that these officers received light punishments for their failure to protect Kirov also pointed to Stalin's complicity, and their subsequent executions (along with almost everyone connected to Kirov or to the investigation of his murder) suggested a strategy of removing all witnesses. It seems possible that Stalin, working through secret police channels, engineered the assassination of Kirov.[2]

Stalin's immediate reaction to the killing also seemed suspicious. Even when the Leningrad investigation was in its initial stages, he told fellow Politburo members that the Leningrad-based Zinoviev opposition was behind the killing. He drafted the draconian Law of 1 December 1934 before he had even talked with officials on the scene. It seems, therefore, that he may have organized the assassination as an excuse to annihilate oppositionists; he quickly had culprits at hand and a mechanism in place to kill them.

In the 1980s the Politburo launched a new official investigation into the assassination. An interagency team from the Communist Party, KGB, and other bodies reexamined the evidence. But like all previous investigations, the commission failed to produce a report.

2. See Conquest, *Kirov Murder*. See also Robert C. Tucker, *Stalin in Power: The Revolution from Above, 1928–1941*, New York, 1990, ch. 12.

Their efforts dissolved into mutual recriminations among the members that leaked into the press, as some demanded a conclusion implicating Stalin while others argued that the evidence pointed the other way.[3] Proceeding from mainstream Western theories, historians associated with the official rehabilitation effort supported the idea that Stalin was involved. The official party journal in the Gorbachev years promised its readers a full historical account but never produced one. Instead, its coverage of other cases in the Stalin period obliquely suggested Stalin's involvement in the killing.[4]

As early as 1973 some historians raised doubts about the prevailing view and made the first sustained Western case against Stalin's involvement.[5] Beginning in the 1980s other Western and Soviet historians also questioned the Stalin complicity theory, the origins of the story, and Stalin's motive and opportunity, as well as investigating the circumstances surrounding the event. They noted that the sources for the theory derived originally from memoirists, mostly Cold War–era Soviet defectors, whose information was second- and thirdhand and who were in all cases far removed from the event. These writers had generated a huge and sensational literature that largely repeated and echoed itself while providing few verifiable facts, and which sometimes seemed primarily designed to enhance the status and importance of the author. Later historians noted that despite at least two official Soviet investigations and the high-level political advantages of accusing Stalin in the Khrushchev years, even the most anti-Stalin Soviet administrations had never accused Stalin of the crime, though he was directly accused of murdering many equally famous politicians.[6]

Historians have also raised questions about Kirov's supposed liberalism and resistance to Stalin.[7] The evidence for an anti-Stalin

3. "Vokrug ubiistva Kirova," *Pravda*, 4 November 1991, and A. Yakovlev, "O dekabr'skoi tragedii 1934 goda," *Pravda*, 28 January 1991.

4. See, for example, the accounts of persecution of the opposition in *Izvestiia TsK KPSS*, nos. 7 and 9, 1989.

5. Adam Ulam, *Stalin: The Man and His Era*, New York, 1973, 375–88.

6. In 1956 Khrushchev formed a commission chaired by N. Shvernik to investigate the Kirov murder. It "found nothing against Stalin. . . . Khrushchev refused to publish it—it was of no use to him." Feliks Chuev, *Sto sorok besed s Molotovym*, Moscow, 1991, 353.

7. Francesco Benvenuti, "Kirov in Soviet Politics, 1933–1934," Soviet Industrialization Project Series no. 8, University of Birmingham (England), 1977. See also

group in the leadership that backed Kirov seems weak, based on hearsay that was often contradicted by other firsthand accounts.[8] In fact, Kirov seems to have been a staunch Stalinist who did his share of persecuting Stalin's enemies. Similarly, the most recent (Gorbachev-era) official investigation into the supposed anti-Stalin votes at the Seventeenth Party Congress found that many witnesses reported the matter differently and that it was impossible to verify the story on the basis of personal testimonies or archival evidence.[9]

The question of Leningrad police complicity also seems murky. Recent evidence discounts the alleged connections between them and the assassin. One implicated NKVD official was not even in the city during the months he was supposed to have groomed the assassin.[10] It is true that many Leningrad police officials and party leaders were executed in the terror after the assassination, but so were hundreds of thousands of others. There is no compelling reason to believe that they were killed "to cover the tracks" of the Kirov assassination, as Khrushchev put it. Moreover, they were left alive (and in some cases at liberty) and free to talk for three years following the crime. Some historians have found it unlikely that Stalin would have used these agents to arrange the killing and then given them so much opportunity to betray the plot.

Shortly after the assassination, N. I. Yezhov (representing the party) and Ya. Agranov (representing the central NKVD) took the investigation out of the hands of NKVD chief Genrikh Yagoda and the Leningrad police officials. They pressed the assassin Nikolaev hard on any possible connections he may have had with the NKVD. The examination turned up nothing. More than two thousand NKVD workers in Leningrad were interrogated or investigated by Yezhov's team; three hundred were fired or transferred to other work for negligence. Yezhov reported to Stalin that although the Leningrad NKVD had in the city more than twenty-one thousand informers controlled by two thousand special informers *(rezi-*

Oleg V. Khlevniuk, *Politbiuro: Mekhanizmy politicheskoi vlasti v 1930-e gody,* Moscow, 1996, 118–25.

8. *Izvestiia TsK KPSS,* no. 7, 1989, 114–21.

9. See the analysis in *Izvestiia TsK KPSS,* no. 7, 1989, 114–21, and in J. Arch Getty and Roberta T. Manning, eds., *Stalinist Terror: New Perspectives,* New York, 1993, 44–46.

10. "Vokrug ubistva Kirova," *Pravda,* 4 November 1991.

denty), it was incompetent, careless, and incapable of operating intelligence networks that could have prevented the assassination. Bypassing Yagoda, Yezhov asked Stalin for permission to address a conference of Leningrad NKVD leaders with sharp criticism of their performance.

Yagoda (through whom Stalin presumably worked to kill Kirov) was produced in open court and in front of the world press before his execution in 1938. Knowing that he was to be shot in any event, he could have brought Stalin's entire house of cards down with a single remark about the Kirov killing. Again, such a risk would appear to be unacceptable for a complicit Stalin.

Finally, in analyzing the regime's reaction immediately after the crime, it seemed to some historians that the events surrounding the crime suggest more surprise than planning. The quickly prepared Law of 1 December 1934 (which was actually approved by the Politburo on 3 December) was a standard Bolshevik reaction to assassination of its officials. On previous occasions during and after the civil war, the Politburo had replied to such incidents with mass retaliation. Back in 1927, when Soviet diplomat Vorovsky had been shot in Warsaw, Commissar of Justice N. V. Krylenko had proposed and the Politburo approved special tribunals to exact reprisals against people not directly implicated in the assassination. The 1927 process was a model for the December 1934 law: it involved no legal prosecution or defense, no appeal, and immediate execution of sentence.

The Stalinists seemed unprepared for the assassination and panicked by it. Indeed, it took them more than eighteen months after the assassination to frame their supposed targets—members of the anti-Stalin Old Bolshevik opposition—for the killing.[11] Everyone agrees that Stalin made tremendous use of the assassination for his own purposes; it eventually enabled him to make cases against his political enemies, to settle old scores, and to launch a generalized purge. But there remains great disagreement about his involvement in arranging the crime itself.

11. See J. Arch Getty, *Origins of the Great Purges: The Soviet Communist Party Reconsidered, 1933–1938*, New York, 1985, appendix; J. Arch Getty, "The Politics of Repression Revisited," in Getty and Manning, *Stalinist Terror*, 40–62.

Many Russian scholars are less convinced of Stalin's involvement than they once were. The leading authors on opposition to Stalin in the 1930s no longer offer a judgment on the matter, and the memoirs of V. M. Molotov (perhaps unsurprisingly) observe that Kirov was never a challenger to Stalin's position.[12] The most recent scholarly work on the Kirov assassination from a Russian scholar, based on Leningrad party and police archives, concludes that Stalin had nothing to do with the killing.[13] It seems safe to say that the question is still open.

Although the instigation of the murder is still in doubt, the aftermath and results are not. Stalin used the killing for political purposes. After some initial confusion, the regime blamed the assassination (albeit indirectly) on the former oppositionists of Leningrad led by G. Ye. Zinoviev.[14] Deputy commissar of the secret police Agranov was brought in to supervise a special investigation of the crime to be aimed at Zinoviev and his associate Lev Kamenev.[15] The assassin and several former associates of Zinoviev's were quickly tried and shot, and in mid-December Zinoviev and Kamenev were arrested. After one month of questioning, Agranov reported that he was not able to prove that they had been directly involved in the assassination.[16] So in the middle of January 1935 they were tried and convicted only for "moral complicity" in the crime. That is, their opposition had created a climate in which others were incited to violence. Zinoviev was sentenced to ten years in prison, Kamenev to five.

Repression also intensified beyond the circle of party members and oppositionists. In the immediate aftermath of the killing, the

---

12. Chuev, *Sto sorok besed*, 308, 311. See also S. V. Kulashov, O. V. Volobuev, E. I. Pivovar, et al., *Nashe otechestvo. chast' II.*, Moscow, 1991, 310; Boris Starkov, "Ar'ergardnye boi staroi partiinoi gvardii," in A. V. Afanas'ev, ed., *Oni ne molchali*, Moscow, 1991, 215; Oleg V. Khlevniuk, *1937: Stalin, NKVD i sovetskoe obshchestvo*, Moscow, 1992, 46.

13. Anna Kirilina, *Rikoshet, ili skol'ko chelovek bylo ubito vystrelom v Smol'nom*, Saint Petersburg, 1993.

14. *Izvestiia TsK KPSS*, no. 7, 1989, 69, and no. 1, 1990, 39.

15. RTsKhIDNI, f. 17, op. 3, d. 955, l. 24; *Izvestiia TsK KPSS*, no. 7, 1989, 75. When the Politburo announced NKVD staff changes after the Kirov assassination, it included an unusual formulation "obligating" Yagoda to report back in three days on fulfillment of the orders. See RTsKhIDNI, f. 17, op. 3, d. 955, l. 24.

16. *Pravda*, 23 December 1934 and 16 January 1935; *Izvestiia TsK KPSS*, no. 7, 1989, 70.

regime's reaction was locally savage but spasmodic and unfocused. As it had done in the civil war, the police immediately executed groups of innocent "hostages" with no connection to the crime. Several dozen opponents, labeled "whites" and already languishing in prison, were summarily executed in cities around the Soviet Union.[17] By February 1935 Yezhov wrote to Stalin that he had rounded up about one thousand former Leningrad oppositionists. Three hundred of these had been arrested, and the remainder were exiled from the city. Yezhov's archive shows that in this period he put together elaborate card files on the Leningrad oppositionists, whom he kept under surveillance in their exile locations. Several thousand persons in Leningrad, described as "former people" (nobles, prerevolutionary industrialists, and others) were evicted from the city and forced to move elsewhere.[18]

Unfortunately, documents from the former party archive shed no direct light on high-level involvement in the Kirov assassination. They do, however, clearly support known trends in arrest statistics: the Stalin leadership chose to politicize the crime and to interpret it as a political conspiracy. Shortly after the trial, the Politburo drafted a circular letter to all party organizations about the "lessons" to be drawn from the Kirov assassination. It emphasized the danger posed by "two-faced" oppositionists who claimed to support the party but worked against it and sought to educate party members about this danger.

Document 28

Secret Central Committee letter on the Kirov assassination, 18 January 1935[19]

SECRET
SECRET LETTER OF THE CC VKP(b)
Lessons learned from the events connected with the villainous murder of Comrade KIROV
To all party organizations
Now that the nest of villainy—the Zinoviev anti-Soviet group—has been completely destroyed and the culprits of this villainy have received their just

17. See *Leningradskaia pravda*, 6, 8, 11, 12, 18 December 1934, for reports.
18. *Leningradskaia pravda*, 20 March 1935.
19. *Izvestiia TsK KPSS*, no. 8, 1989, 95–115. Printed.

punishment, the CC believes that the time has come to sum up the events connected with the murder of Comrade KIROV, to assess their political significance, and to draw the lessons that issue from an analysis of these events.

The objective of this letter of the CC VKP(b) is to make it easier for the party cadres to fulfill precisely this concluding task.

I. THE FACTS

It is necessary, first and foremost, to make note of the following indisputable facts as established by the investigation and by the trial:

1) The villainous murder was committed by the Leningrad group of Zinoviev followers calling themselves the Leningrad Center.

2) Ideologically and politically, the Leningrad Center was under the leadership of the Moscow Center of Zinoviev followers, which apparently did not know of the preparations for the murder of Comrade KIROV but which surely knew of the terroristic sentiments of the Leningrad Center and stirred up these sentiments.

3) Distinguished from each other insofar as the abettors of a crime can be distinguished from the perpetrators of a crime, these two "centers" constituted one entity, being united by one common worn-out, jaded Trotsky-Zinoviev platform and one common, unscrupulous, purely careerist goal— that of grabbing a leading role in the party and government and thereby, whatever the cost, gaining high party and government posts.

4) Having lost the trust of the working class thanks to their reactionary platform, and no longer being able to rely on any support whatsoever on the part of the party masses, Zinoviev's followers have, in order to attain their criminal goals, slid down into the mire of counterrevolutionary adventurism, into the mire of anti-Soviet individual terror, and, finally, into the mire of initiating contact with the Latvian consul in Leningrad, an agent of the German-fascist interventionists.

5) In order to conceal their criminal acts from the party and at the same time to hold onto their party cards, which gave them access to all party institutions and to all party leaders, the followers of Zinoviev adopted double-dealing as their main means of relating to the party, masking their villainous acts beneath vows and declarations of loyalty to the party and devotion to Soviet power— i.e., they took the same path customarily followed by White Guard saboteurs, intelligence officers, and provocateurs when they wish to infiltrate our camp, to worm their way into our trust and perpetrate their dirty tricks. . . .

II. POLITICAL ASSESSMENT

How could it have happened that the party failed to notice the existence of a widespread, counterrevolutionary group of Zinoviev followers, while the Leningrad party organization, and especially the organs of the Leningrad NKVD, not only overlooked the counterrevolutionary-terroristic "work" of the Leningrad Center but did not take the necessary precautionary measures even after receiving warnings from various persons about the preparations for an attempt on Comrade KIROV's life?

It ought to be borne in mind that the Zinoviev counterrevolutionary group, in the form in which it has been revealed as a result of the investigation and of the trial, represents something entirely new for which there is no precedent in the history of our party. There have been not a few factional groups in the history of our party. These groups usually made an effort to oppose their views to the party line and to defend them openly before the party. But our party has not known of a single group throughout its history which has made it its task to conceal its views and to hide its political face and which has hypocritically declared its loyalty to the party line while simultaneously preparing a terroristic attempt on the life of representatives of our party. Zinoviev's group has turned out to be the only group in the history of our party that has made double-dealing its commandment and has thereby slid down into the mire of counterrevolutionary terrorism, all the while masking its dark deeds with repeated declarations of devotion to the party in the press and at the party congress. It was difficult for the party to suppose that party veterans like Zinoviev, Kamenev, Yevdokimov, or Bakaev could fall so low and in the end get mixed up with the White Guard gang.

As for the Leningrad party organization and especially the organs of the NKVD in Leningrad, it has turned out that certain of their links [*zven'ia*] have been infected with a sense of complacency dangerous for the cause and with a negligence in matters of security unbecoming a Bolshevik. This complacency and negligence issue from an incorrect assumption that with the increase in our successes, and therefore with the increasing number of defeats inflicted on our enemies, the latter will become more and more tame and harmless, that consequently there are no longer any grounds to fear that these last enemies of our party who are on their last legs can take up terror as a "last resort." . . .

III. CONCLUSIONS

. . . The Zinoviev faction was, in essence, a White Guard organization in disguise. For this reason we have earned the right to treat its members like White Guards.

3) Under the present conditions of a complete and decisive victory for the party line, when an open struggle with the party's policy has obviously become hopeless, double-dealing has become the one evil that alone can support and conceal the existence of antiparty elements within the party. Our mission is to exterminate and extirpate this evil by the root. The double-dealer is not merely a deceiver of the party. . . .

4) We must put an end to the opportunistic complacency that issues from a mistaken assumption that as our strength increases, the enemy grows more tame and harmless. Such an assumption is fundamentally wrong. It is a throwback to the rightist deviation, which had tried to assure one and all that our enemies will crawl quietly into socialism, that in the end they will become true socialists. . . .

5) The teaching of party history to members of the party ought to be raised to a level worthy of the party. This includes the study of each and every antiparty

group in the history of our party, its methods of struggling against the party line, its tactics, and—all the more so—the study of the tactics and fighting methods of our party in its struggle against antiparty groups, tactics and methods which made it possible for our party to overcome and crush these groups. Party members ought to become familiar not only with how the party fought and overcame the Kadets, the SRs, the Mensheviks, and the anarchists, but also with how the party fought and overcame the Trotskyists, the Democratic Centralists, the Workers' Opposition, the Zinoviev group, the rightist deviationists, the rightist-leftist freaks, and so on. One ought not to forget that the knowledge and understanding of the history of our party is a most important tool, one necessary for fully securing the revolutionary vigilance of party members.

18 January 1935

Central Committee VKP(b)

Prescribed Transcripts

Although the January 1935 letter turned up the heat on present and former dissidents, it was not a call for terror. The first sentence of the letter claimed that "the nest of villainy—the Zinoviev anti-Soviet group—has been completely destroyed." By implication, in the view of the letter's authors, Kirov's assassins had been caught and punished. A party purge did not follow the letter for nearly five months, and then the screening instructions did not mention the Kirov killing. Zinoviev and Kamenev were not charged with direct organization of the Kirov killing for more than a year and a half, and then only on the basis of "new materials" unearthed in 1936 (see Document 73).

The January 1935 letter identified the "followers of Zinoviev" (but not Zinoviev himself) and other former oppositionists as counterrevolutionary enemies. This political transcript was read out at all party organization and cell meetings. Party leaders at all levels were ordered to conduct "discussions" of the letter, both in order to promulgate its conclusions and to find out what ordinary party members thought about the opposition and the assassination. These discussions also served a ritual purpose. If they went as planned, they were to be forums for rank-and-file party members and citizens to repeat and affirm the proffered political narrative.

By clear implication, the letter invited local party organizations to root out present and former dissidents. The local discussions suggest, though, that there was a shortage of real Zinovievists remaining in party organizations. Accordingly, various marginal and unpopular characters were identified and punished as oppositionists. Sometimes the discussions of the Kirov assassination and the January 1935 letter tended to be routine and ritualistic, reflecting apathy and "weak participation" in the prescribed discourse. Frequently the meetings "unmasked" some unfortunates as "enemies," but these targets tended to be defenseless marginal types. On other occasions the meetings seem to have been more emotional, either encouraging further investigations or unearthing "anti-Soviet moods."

Document 29

Discussion of CC letter on Kirov, Omsk Railroad[20]

---

19 February 1935
A POLITICAL REPORT
On the group study of the closed letter of the CC VKP(b) in party organizations attached to the railroad.

The closed letter of the CC VKP(b) was received by the Railroad Political Section (PODOR) on 20 January. On the following day it was sent to all party organizations with the demand that they immediately organize a discussion of its contents at closed party meetings involving active members with a subsequent discussion at closed meetings of primary party organizations. . . .

At the present time, party organizations are working to implement the practical measures that have been accepted regarding the closed letter. In a number of party organizations (the Conductors' Reserve at the Omsk Station, the Rudzutak Factory, the Barabinsky Depot) the existence of supporters of counterrevolutionary Zinovievist groups was brought to light during the study groups on the letter. Party members until only recently, they carried on demoralizing counterrevolutionary activity in party organizations and among the workers engaged in production. . . .

Inspection [proverka] of the party organization, in connection with the CC's letter, revealed a great deal of contamination of the Conductors' Reserve by a class-alien and counterrevolutionary element. Most prominent, among others, is Bogoliubov, a Trotskyist (chief conductor of passenger trains, expelled from the party by the Purge Commission, now dismissed from his post). He carried on openly counterrevolutionary activities, incited the Communists

20. RTsKhIDNI, f. 17, op. 120, d. 174, ll. 14, 74–75.

and nonparty workers against the party leadership, and undermined work discipline. . . .

In purging the party organization of the Conductors' Reserve, the original Purge Commission (chaired by Poliachenko) concerned itself insufficiently with the question of who was and who was not a member of Trotskyist-Zinovievist groups, while the unmasking and exposing of counterrevolutionary remnants in the party organization attached to the Conductors' Reserve should have been one of the chief tasks of the commission. This was not taken into account by the commission. . . .

BUTYRCHIK (instructor of physics). Formerly an officer in Kolchak's army, was exiled in 1930 to the Baltic–White Sea canal construction for counterrevolutionary activity in an educational institution. While teaching at a technical college, he carried on counterrevolutionary activity.

GREBENETS (instructor of German). Formerly a German officer, a war prisoner. He refuses to accept Soviet nationality. As an instructor, he has shown poor teaching abilities. At one of the meetings he declared: "I do not interfere in the everyday life of my students because present conditions are bad and you can't change them." He rejoices maliciously and laughs at certain problems and failures at the Technical College. . . .

Document 30

Discussion of CC letter on Kirov, Trans-Baikal Railroad, March 1935[21]

TOP SECRET

To Comrade Zimin, head of the political directorate of the People's Commissariat of Transport (NKPS)

To Comrade Krokhmal, head of the political section of the Trans-Baikal Railroad

POLITICAL REPORT CONCERNING THE PROGRESS AND PRELIMINARY RESULTS OF THE GROUP STUDY [*prorabotka*] OF THE SECRET LETTER OF THE CC VKP(b)

. . . On 8 February the political section of the department conducted a conference of party organizers of all departmental services. At this conference, a group study was conducted concerning the [CC] letter, including a broad discussion of the conclusions drawn from the letter and the practical tasks for our party organizations based on these conclusions. In addition, a detailed plan was formulated and an agenda established for the group study of this letter in primary party organizations.

Throughout the entire network of party educational institutions, special

21. RTsKhIDNI, f. 17, op. 120, d. 175, ll. 73, 76.

studies about the Zinoviev anti-Soviet group and its past have been conducted on a preliminary basis. Prior to undertaking the study of this subject in their respective groups [*kruzhki*], all of the party propagandists and organizers took part in the sessions of the party activists' seminar of the political section on this subject. As a result, the overwhelming majority of propagandists dealt with this theme satisfactorily in their study groups. . . .

7) QUESTIONS CONCERNING THE NKVD. A total of 32 questions was posed. Most typical were the following questions:

"How could it have happened that the NKVD did not avert the murder?"

"Why didn't the NKVD react to the warnings?"

"How do the employees of the NKVD justify their negligence?"

We need to note especially questions such as the following:

"Did the Zinoviev group have connections within the NKVD itself?"

"Did the NKVD bring available information to the attention of the CC?"

8) Six questions were raised concerning Rykov's and Bukharin's relationship to the Zinoviev group. . . .

Document 31

Discussion of CC letter on Kirov, Moscow-Donbas Railroad[22]

TOP SECRET

4 March 1935

To the Transport Department of the CC VKP(b), Comrade Yevgenev

GROUP STUDY [*prorabotka*] OF THE CLOSED LETTER OF THE CC VKP(b) CONCERNING THE LESSONS LEARNED FROM THE EVENTS CONNECTED WITH THE VILLAINOUS MURDER OF COMRADE KIROV

The closed letter from the CC VKP(b), received by the political section of the railroad on 20 January, was sent to all party organizers that same day.

The group study of the letter from the CC VKP(b) commenced with the instructional conference which the head of the political section of the railroad conducted on 20 January with the heads of the political sections, with apparat leaders of the political section of the railroad, and with the party organizers of the Moscow Center. . . .

At the party meeting, [SUSHCHINSKY] was exposed as a Trotskyist. He had been attempting to introduce Trotskyist contraband[23] into the meeting. Giving an account of the preparations for the winter, SUSHCHINSKY was challenged by a party member who demanded to know: "Why isn't the plan being ful-

---

22. RTsKhIDNI, f. 17, op. 120, d. 176, ll. 13, 125, 127, 128, 133, 135.

23. Figuratively speaking, i.e., ideas, views, etc., not materials or publications— Trans.

filled?" To which SUSHCHINSKY replied: "We have been building socialism for 18 years, but we still haven't built it." Setting himself against the political section during reelections to the soviets, he attempted to work his own people into the soviets and to worm his way into them himself. Comrade AN-NENKOV, head of the political section of this construction district, did not ascribe the appropriate political significance to this fact. It was only after much time had elapsed and at the intervention of the political section that SUSHCHINSKY was expelled from the party. The case of Comrade AN-NENKOV is now being examined by me in conjunction with the party collegium of the railroad. Evidently, he will have to be relieved of his post. . . .

3) CHUICHENKO, conductor of Okhochevka station, member of the VKP(b) since 1927, was carrying on a conversation with his associates at the controllers' office after the murder of Sergei Mironovich Kirov. Speaking about the murder, CHUICHENKO said: "It serves him [Kirov] right! He [Kirov] must have been a real swine." Here he added: "Kirov was killed by a functionary of the Workers'-Peasants' Inspectorate [RKI], who had discovered an act of injustice by Kirov. For this, Kirov dismissed him from his post, and for that reason he, Nikolaev, killed him."

. . . 8) A number of facts involving counterrevolutionary Trotskyist-Zinoviev speeches have been recently uncovered among Komsomol members: Komsomol member RYBAKOVA (Valui Construction District) said: "To execute 60 people for one KIROV means that [Soviet] power is showing weakness by relying on terror to put down the growing discontent. I am absolutely sure that among the executed were many people who were completely innocent. Where is that glorious freedom here which the Bolsheviks ranted and raved about so much and which is in fact practiced in Germany and other countries, where every citizen can join any party he wishes without the risk of being executed for it? I hate [Soviet] power, which oppresses our people. I have really begun believing in the truth of Holy Scripture, where what is written is now really being fulfilled. Now that Kirov has been killed, I have become very concerned in the past few days for the fate of my husband, who by his carelessness may come to grief. I remain in the Komsomol for the sake of appearance so that I won't lose my job." RYBAKOVA was born in 1915, completed her elementary education, and is currently working as a medical technician at a hospital outpatients department. . . .

9) At the Ozherelsky district, Komsomol member Sergei BARBOTIN tried to convince Komsomol members that "Comrade Trotsky had served as a distinguished leader of the Revolution, carrying as much authority as Lenin. Stalin was little known then and is not authoritative for the party. Criticism in the party has been clamped down, and Trotsky's literature has been banned, while Trotsky was banished from the USSR because Stalin didn't like his looks."

. . . 10) Speeches of a counterrevolutionary character took place among the students of the Yeletsky Construction Technical College. Thus, for instance, SOBOLEV, a student, said: "On the 1st [of December] they killed Kirov and on the 15th they'll kill Stalin." A similar statement was made by BOLDYREV, a student. At the Pazhensky quarry, Yeletsky Construction District, where a group of convicts is working as forced labor, one such laborer said: "They killed one of them, and the food ration cards were abolished. They'll kill another one and the price of bread will go down." . . .

SAVITSKY, a bookkeeper at the Kastorensky district, in talking to the workers, came out with a counterrevolutionary explanation of Comrade Kirov's murder: "Kirov was murdered on account of a woman. This will teach him not to run after other men's women. I know Nikolaev personally. He is honorable to a fault, an official of the RKI. If he killed Kirov, then it means that he should have." Party organizer APARIN, having received a report concerning this, carried it in his pocket for five days before handing over the [statement]. . . .

Document 32

Discussion of CC letter on Kirov, Belorussian Komsomol[24]

16 April 1935
TOP SECRET
TO: ORPO [DEPARTMENT OF LEADING PARTY ORGANS] CC VKP(b)

Preliminary results of the group study [*prorabotka*] of the CC VKP(b) letter in the Komsomol Organization of Belorussia.

With a view to organizing group studies of the [CC] letter in the primary party organizations, a number of district committees (RK) of the Leninist-Communist Youth League conducted city and district meetings of the activists (Minsk, Vitebsk, Klichev, Terekhovka, Drissa, Klimovichi, Mogilev, Borisov, Chechersk, and others). In certain districts, they also conducted the plenum sessions of the city committees and district committees of the Communist Party (Bolshevik) of Belorussia.

In the cities, group studies were conducted at the general meetings of the primary Komsomol organizations, in the villages at group meetings. In order to ensure the success of the group studies, the party organizations selected activists from the ranks of proven Communists who had been instructed by the district committees. . . .

Many organizations have openly slurred over the group study by conducting it at general district meetings where around 250–300 people participated (Drissa district, Klimovichi, Bogushev district, and others).

These meetings took place with extraordinarily feeble participation.

24. RTsKhIDNI, f. 17, op. 120, d. 174, ll. 11–13.

Document 32 *continued*

The basic method employed at the group studies in the majority of organizations amounted to a reading of the letter with a discussion afterward.

In their speeches, the secretaries of the committees of the Communist Youth League or the Komsomol organizers familiarized the meeting with the state of the organization and with the work of individual Komsomol members.

In their discussions, they yielded the floor first and foremost to Komsomol members who had never before participated in a discussion of this letter. . . .

"I don't speak up at the meetings because I was a poor student at school, and I don't know what to say. After they read out the letter and discussed it, it became obvious to me that it's not enough to know how to work well at production [*na proizvodstve*]—you also have to know your party history well. . . ."

"There are people in our kolkhoz who masked their intentions, who carried on their counterrevolutionary activities, and because of our inadequate vigilance, we have not yet been able to expose them. In our little village, there is a group consisting of 37 people who are systematically exterminating livestock. . . ."

Statistics on overall repression in the months following the Kirov assassination reveal some curious trends. In terms of police arrests, overall repression did not increase in 1935. The number of NKVD arrests in 1935 was lower than it had been even in the previous calm year (see Table 5, Appendix 1). The secret police made fewer arrests in 1935 than in any year since 1929. In fact, NKVD arrests had been declining steadily every year since 1931, and they fell even lower in 1936.

But the character of those arrests was changing. Within the lower aggregate arrest totals, arrests for political reasons were increasing: there were 10 percent more arrests for "counterrevolutionary" crimes and two and a half times as many arrests for "anti-Soviet agitation" in 1935 than in 1934.[25] The proportion of NKVD arrests for nonpolitical offenses fell correspondingly. In other words, while total arrests were down, those arrests that did take place were increasingly defined as "political" in the wake of the Kirov assassination.

In 1935 the NKVD arrested about 193,000 persons on all charges. In previous years, various proportions of those arrested

25. Anti-Soviet agitation could include anything from printing subversive leaflets to telling dangerous political jokes.

were ultimately convicted, but in 1935 convictions *exceeded* arrests by more than 74,000. In the months following the Kirov killing, thousands of people already under arrest before the assassination were apparently reconvicted under more political charges. Unfortunately, we have no information on their new sentences, but the statistics we do have do not suggest that their new politicized sentences were necessarily more harsh.

Sentencing policy in general did not harden following the Kirov assassination. In 1935, although the total number of convictions was three times higher than in 1934, the proportion of sentences to prison or labor camp fell from 75 percent to 70 percent; executions as a proportion of all sentences fell from 2.6 percent to 0.4 percent. Less severe types of sentences increased: exile (either to a specific place or as denial of right to live in major cities) rose from 7.5 percent to 12.5 percent, and other (mostly noncustodial) sentences from 14.5 percent to 17.3 percent.

Police repression of the former opposition intensified in the wake of the Kirov assassination. Aside from the January 1935 trial of Zinoviev and Kamenev, there were several less publicized judicial proceedings against former oppositionists in Leningrad, Moscow, and other cities. The trial of the "Leningrad counterrevolutionary Zinovievist group of Safarov, Zalutsky, and others" sentenced 77 defendants to camp and exile terms of four to five years.[26] Altogether in the two and a half months following the assassination, 843 former Zinovievists were arrested in Leningrad; most of them were exiled to remote regions and not sentenced to camps.[27] As one investigator told a detainee, formal guilt or innocence was not the point: "The proletariat demands the exile of everyone directly or indirectly connected with the opposition."[28]

The Nomenklatura and the Face of the Enemy

N. I. Yezhov had been a Petrograd worker who joined the Bolsheviks in the summer of 1917. Active as a political organizer and commissar during the civil war, he worked in several regional party committees in the 1920s. Yezhov had a reputation as a solid party

26. *Izvestiia TsK KPSS*, no. 1, 1990, 38–58.
27. *Izvestiia TsK KPSS*, no. 7, 1989, 85, no. 1, 1990, 39.
28. *Izvestiia TsK KPSS*, no. 1, 1990, 54.

worker.[29] Perhaps spotted by L. M. Kaganovich, who ran the Organizational-Assignment of the Central Committee in the 1920s, Yezhov was brought to Moscow to work in the central party apparatus. By 1930, at Kaganovich's suggestion, he was attending Politburo meetings.[30]

In the early 1930s he worked in the Central Committee's industrial and cadres (personnel) departments. By 1933 he had become a kind of personnel specialist. In January of that year he was heading the Central Committee's personnel assignment department. He played a leading administrative role in the 1933 party purge (*chistka*) and in a number of other bureaucratic verification operations.[31] After early 1934 his rise was meteoric; he headed the Mandate (credentials) Commission of the Seventeenth Party Congress early that year. He was elected a full member of the Central Committee (skipping over candidate member status altogether), a member of the Orgburo, and deputy chairman of the Party Control Commission.[32]

By 1934 Yezhov ranked high enough to earn the privilege of traveling abroad for rest cures, funded by hard currency from party coffers. It was common for high-ranking party leaders to go abroad for rest and relaxation in health spas. Yezhov went abroad to a spa with a disbursement of 1,200 rubles in foreign currency. He was apparently so dedicated to his work that the Politburo had to forbid him to return until the end of his rest, forwarding him an additional 1,000 gold rubles to complete his rest vacation.[33]

We now know that before the Kirov assassination, Yezhov's activities in the party Secretariat and Orgburo were connected to the secret police. In 1934 and 1935 he participated in Politburo discussions about courts and procurators and the special conference of the NKVD (see Documents 24 and 25, which he apparently helped draft).[34] In February 1935 he became a secretary of the Central Committee. The increasingly politicized atmosphere fol-

29. This, at least, was Molotov's memory of him. Chuev, *Sto sorok besed,* 438.
30. RTsKhIDNI, f. 17, op. 3, d. 805, l. 16.
31. The verification operations had to do with interagency economic agreements and investigation of customs fraud. See RTsKhIDNI, f. 17, op. 3, d. 916, l. 6; d. 913, l. 1.
32. Kaganovich, his apparent patron, was chairman of the KPK.
33. RTsKhIDNI, f. 17, op. 3, d. 948, l. 36; d. 951, l. 1.
34. RTsKhIDNI, f. 17, op. 3, d. 945, l. 5; d. 943, l. 10; d. 942, l. 2. See also, in 1935, f. 17, op. 3, d. 961, l. 62.

lowing the Kirov killing was a time for personnel "checkers," and Yezhov's career benefited from the personnel changes necessitated by Kirov's death. The following laconic Politburo protocols mark the growth of his activities, as well as other changes in the deployment of senior leaders.

Document 33

Politburo protocol: On courts and procurators[35]

From Protocol #8 of the Politburo of the CC of the All-Union Communist Party (Bolshevik) [VKP(b)] of 29 March 1934

8. On courts and procurators

(Comrades Stalin, Akulov, Krylenko, Vyshinsky)

a) To establish that the question of the existence of the Peoples' Commissariat of Justice is not under discussion.

b) To charge a commission consisting of Comrades Kuibyshev (chair), Yenukidze, Akulov, Krylenko, Vyshinsky, Yagoda, Yezhov, Bulatov, and Vinokurov to examine all the questions.

Document 34

Politburo protocol: Regulations on the NKVD assigned to Yezhov[36]

From Protocol #273 of the Politburo of the CC of the All-Union Communist Party (Bolshevik) [VKP(b)] of 31 March 1935

273.

a) Regulations pertaining to the NKVD

b) Regulations pertaining to the Chief Administration of State Security of the NKVD

Give to Comrade Yezhov for examination.

Document 35

CC Secretariat protocol: On Yezhov's secretariat[37]

From Protocol #25 of the Secretariat of the CC VKP(b) of 7 April 1935

On employees of the secretariat of Comrade Yezhov

a) The appointment of Comrades S. A. Ryzhova, V. E. Tsesarsky, and I. I.

35. RTsKhIDNI, f. 17, op. 3, d. 942, l. 2.
36. RTsKhIDNI, f. 17, op. 3, d. 961, l. 62.
37. RTsKhIDNI, f. 17, op. 114, d. 581, l. 31.

Shapiro as assistants [*referenty-dokladchiki*] of CC Secretary Comrade Yezhov is hereby approved.

b) Comrade Tsesarsky, assistant director of the Industrial Department, and Comrade Shapiro, sectional director of the Industrial Department of the CC, are to be relieved of their duties.

Document 36

Politburo protocol: Reassigning duties of CC secretaries[38]

From Protocol #32 of the meeting of the Politburo of the CC VKP(b) of 3 April 1935

#54. RE: Assigning of duties and responsibilities to secretaries of the CC*

a) Comrade A. A. Andreev is to be brought into the Orgburo of the CC.

b) Comrade Andreev is given responsibility for presiding over the sessions of the Orgburo, while Comrades Andreev and Yezhov are to be given responsibility for setting the Orgburo agenda.

c) Comrade Andreev is given responsibility for managing the industrial department of the CC and for monitoring the work of the transport section and the administrative department of the CC of the VKP(b).

d) Comrade Yezhov is to be relieved of his duties as manager of the industrial department and given responsibility for the management of the Department of Leading Party Organs.

e) Comrade Stalin is given responsibility for monitoring the work of the remaining sections of the CC, especially of the Department of Culture and Propaganda.

f) Comrade Kaganovich is given responsibility for monitoring the work of the Moscow Regional and City Party Organizations, provided that this work does not interfere with his work for the People's Commissariat for Transport and Communications (NKPS).

g) Comrade Kaganovich is to be permitted to deal with the regional and territorial committees as a secretary of the CC in seeking their help and support in matters pertaining to rail transport whenever the situation calls for it.

*OB of 9 March 1935, Protocol #24, Item #54-gs

In Moscow in early summer 1935, 110 employees of the Kremlin service administration (including Kamenev's brother) were accused in the "Kremlin Affair" of organizing a group to commit "terrorist

38. RTsKhIDNI, f. 17, op. 3, d. 961, l. 16.

acts" against the government. Two were sentenced to death; the remainder received prison or camp terms of five to ten years.[39]

The Kremlin Affair further charged the political atmosphere in mid-1935 by casting doubt for the first time on high-ranking party officials who had always sided with Stalin. The scene for this escalation of tension was the June 1935 Plenum of the Central Committee, where Avel Yenukidze, a longtime friend of Stalin's, was accused of aiding and abetting the "terrorists." Yenukidze, as secretary of the Central Executive Committee of Soviets, was responsible for administration and security of the Kremlin. The Kremlin Affair, in which dozens of Kremlin employees were arrested for conspiracy, cast suspicion on Yenukidze's supervision. The suspicion was compounded by Yenukidze's softhearted tendency to aid old revolutionaries who had run afoul of Soviet justice. Yezhov made his debut as a visible player in the Central Committee at the June plenum, where he delivered the official accusation against Yenukidze.

It was a curious text. Yezhov began not with criticism of Yenukidze but with a lengthy digression on the crimes of Zinoviev and Kamenev. To this point, they had been accused of only "moral complicity" in the death of Kirov. Now, however, Yezhov for the first time accused them of direct organization of the assassination and introduced the idea that Trotsky was also involved from his base in exile. In spite of Yezhov's claim to the contrary, this was a radical new theory and one that could give no comfort to political dissidents.

Document 37

N. I. Yezhov's speech "Concerning Comrade Yenukidze" to the CC plenum, 6 June 1935[40]

CONCERNING COMRADE YENUKIDZE AND THE APPARAT OF THE CENTRAL EXECUTIVE COMMITTEE (TsIK) OF THE USSR

Yezhov: Before turning to the immediate theme of my report concerning Comrade Yenukidze and the apparat of the Central Executive Committee (TsIK) of the USSR, as it appears on the agenda of the CC plenum, I am forced

39. *Izvestiia TsK KPSS*, no. 7, 1989, 65–93.
40. RTsKhIDNI, f. 17, op. 2, d. 542, ll. 55–86. Typed.

to touch upon a number of incidents connected with this matter that have a direct bearing on the theme under discussion.

On 1 December 1934, Sergei Mironovich KIROV, one of the finest leaders of our party, one of the staunchest and most irreconcilable of Bolsheviks, a man of deep personal charm and a favorite of the party, was treacherously murdered by the belated followers of the Zinovievist-Kamenevist-Trotskyist group.

For the party and country, the murder of Comrade Kirov is the most poignant political event of the past decade. The political poignancy and significance of this event are important because the party has suffered a grave loss, having lost one of our best Bolsheviks, as well as because this event graphically exposes the tactics of our die-hard, embittered class enemy that resorts to extreme measures in order to fight Soviet power.

The political assessment of this event and the tasks devolving upon our party organizations from this event have been given in the well-known letter by the CC of the VKP(b) concerning the murder of Comrade Kirov.

What I would like to inform you of does not alter this assessment in its essentials but only supplements it with new facts. These facts show that during the investigation of the circumstances surrounding the murder of Comrade Kirov in Leningrad, the role of Zinoviev, Kamenev, and Trotsky in the preparation of terroristic acts against the leaders of the party and Soviet state has not yet been fully revealed. The latest events show that they were not only the instigators but in fact the active organizers of the murder of Comrade Kirov, as well as of the attempt on the life of Comrade Stalin that was being prepared within the Kremlin.

Soon after the murder of Comrade Kirov, a new network of Zinovievist-Kamenevist and Trotskyist–White Guard terrorist cells was uncovered.

What makes this so grave is that several of these terrorist groups were uncovered in the Kremlin itself.

The entire country, all of us, considered the Kremlin to be the most well-defended, the most inaccessible and inviolate territory, where the protection of our leaders is properly secured. But in fact the very opposite turned out to be the case. Thanks to the total blunting of political and class vigilance of many Communists holding responsible positions in the Central Executive Committee of the USSR and, first and foremost, Comrade Yenukidze, the class enemy has succeeded in organizing terrorist cells within immediate range of the headquarters of our revolution. As you will see from the facts that shall be presented to you, this blunting of political and class vigilance nearly cost Comrade Stalin his life and borders on treason against the interests of party and country.

What are the real facts in this case?

It was discovered in the beginning of this year that many employees of the Secretariat of the Central Executive Committee of the USSR and of the Commandant's Office of the Kremlin had been systematically spreading counterrevolutionary slander with the aim of discrediting the leaders of the party: Stalin, Molotov, Kalinin, Voroshilov. The cutting edge of this slander was directed, first and foremost, at Comrade Stalin. The nature of this widespread slander leaves no doubt as to its origin: it issues from among those elements politically most hostile to us and has for its aim the creation of circumstances characterized by embitterment toward Comrade Stalin. Comrade Peterson, commandant of the Kremlin, upon receiving information concerning persons who had been spreading this slander, reported it to Comrade Yenukidze. As you know, Comrade Yenukidze was in fact responsible for all order in the Kremlin, including its security. Comrade Yenukidze failed to attribute any real significance to these reports. Instead, he dealt with them in a most criminal, thoughtless manner unbecoming a Communist.

All of this information came to the attention of the Politburo of the CC entirely by accident. The CC proposed to investigate these facts thoroughly, believing rightly that these facts conceal more serious matters.

The investigation conducted by the NKVD revealed five terroristic groups that were connected with one another yet acting independently of one another.

Two groups were organized within the Kremlin and three outside the Kremlin. They all set as their chief task the murder of Comrade Stalin. . . .

In order to be done once and for all with the matter pertaining to the organizing of the terroristic activities by the Zinovievist-Kamenevist group and by the Trotskyists, and, in particular, with the matter pertaining to the organizing of an attempt on the life of Comrade Stalin, it is necessary for us to dwell on the role played in this affair by Zinoviev, Kamenev, and Trotsky.

Utilizing their time-tested tactics of double-dealing, Zinoviev and Kamenev took all measures to evade responsibility for the murder of Comrade Kirov and for preparations of an attempt on the life of Comrade Stalin.

Only under the pressure of absolutely indisputable facts, as expressed in the depositions of dozens of their closest supporters, were they forced to acknowledge their "political and moral" responsibility for this whole affair. Nevertheless, they continue obstinately to deny their direct participation in organizing these terroristic groups. . . .

In his deposition, Kamenev says the following:

"My counterrevolutionary conversations with Zinoviev promoted the creation of an atmosphere of embitterment against Stalin. Consequently, this might have created a situation justifying terror as regards Stalin much as Kerensky created a situation for carrying out violence against Lenin. I confess that I have committed a grave crime against the party and against the Soviet state. My counterrevolutionary actions and those of Zinoviev not only created an atmosphere of malice and hatred toward Stalin. They also served to incite the counterrevolutionaries to acts of terrorism. There is no doubt now in my mind that N. B. Rozenfeld perceived our attacks and slander on Stalin as a program [*ustanovka*] of terror. I take responsibility for the fact that, as a result of the situation created by Zinoviev and me and as a result of our counterrevolutionary actions, a counterrevolutionary organization has arisen whose participants were intent on perpetrating the vilest crime of all: the murder of Stalin."

I believe that it is difficult to expect Kamenev, in his position, to confess to any more than that. But there is no need for any more confessions on his part. The investigators have at their disposal an absolutely sufficient quantity of facts that prove direct participation by Kamenev and Zinoviev in the organizing of terroristic groups, facts that follow fully from the policies of their own programs, which they issued to their supporters in their struggle against the party and government.

Trotsky, too, cannot evade responsibility for organizing the terror. He has been sufficiently unmasked by the testimony of his supporters and by his own operational pronouncements in the bulletin which he himself publishes. . . .

The direct complicity of Zinoviev, Kamenev, and Trotsky in the organizing of the terror follows also from the political positions and aims expressed by them in recent years.

These positions—gambling on intervention and terror—were already revealed during the investigation into the murder of Comrade Kirov. Now this has been confirmed by new facts and documents. . . .

This terroristic activity was taken directly under Trotsky's protection. In many of his articles concerned with the trial of the murderers of Comrade Kirov, articles published in his own *Bulletin,* Trotsky launches into diatribes against the arrest of Zinoviev and Kamenev and takes them fully under his wing. Moreover, in his most recent article, entitled "The Workers' State, Thermidor, and Bonapartism," published in issue no. 43 of *Bulletin of the Opposition* in 1935, he openly and unequivocally proposes a program of terror. In this article, presented in the form of a historical-theoretical report, Trotsky has engaged in "self-criticism." . . .

From all of these positions advocated by Trotsky certain conclusions suggest themselves. If indeed it is only the bonapartist leadership that constitutes a real threat to the workers' state and to its accomplishments and successes, then it must be removed by violent means, that is, Trotsky offers a totally perfected and fully developed program of terror, basing it "ideologically" on the interests of the Russian and international proletariat.

However, this is not enough. Trotsky's cynicism goes so far that he wants to justify in advance, both politically and morally, the terror directed at the leadership of the VKP(b). . . .

Thus Trotsky launches an appeal to all sworn enemies of Soviet power to take up the path of terror. He has now become the chief instigator and organizer of terror against leaders of our party and government, mobilizing around himself all terroristic elements within and outside the USSR.

Such are the facts concerning the organizing of terroristic activities by the Zinovievist-Kamenevist group and by the Trotskyists, as revealed during the investigation into the murder of Comrade Kirov and the preparations for an attempt on the life of Comrade Stalin.

Such are the ideological aims of these traitors of the revolution. They fully coincide with the positions taken by the most embittered and inveterate enemies of the Soviet state, the counterrevolutionary White Guards.

These facts and ideological positions show that Zinoviev, Kamenev, and Trotsky, embittered by the successes of the Revolution, have, in their hopeless attempt to make their way into the leadership of the party and country, slid down definitively into the mire of the White émigré world[41] and have advanced to the most extreme forms of struggle—namely, terror.

These facts now show that the murder of Comrade Kirov was organized by Zinoviev and Kamenev and that it constitutes only one link in a chain of terroristic plans of the Zinovievist-Kamenevist and Trotskyist groups.

These facts show that Zinoviev was the organizer of the terror in Leningrad, that he maintained personal connections with the Leningrad Trotskyists during this period, and that Kamenev was the organizer of the terror in Moscow.

These facts show that Trotsky, having openly taken under his wing Zinoviev and Kamenev and having advanced his own program of terror, is currently the chief organizer and instigator of the terror against the leaders of our party. . . .

By his un-party conduct, by his un-Bolshevik activities, Yenukidze created a situation whereby any White Guard could have easily infiltrated the Kremlin, and some did in fact infiltrate it by frequently making use of Yenukidze's direct support and high-positioned patronage. The system of selection of employees instituted by Comrade Yenukidze in the apparat of the Central Executive Committee of the USSR had nothing to do with the principles governing the Soviet system. During selection of employees, considerations relative to the affairs and interests of the state played the least important role. As a result of such a "system" of selection of employees, the apparat of the Central Executive Committee became extremely contaminated with elements alien and hostile to Soviet power. These elements, easily and freely infiltrating the apparat of the Central Executive Committee of the USSR, wove their counterrevolutionary nest in it, where they carried on their subversive work. All the while, they took refuge in their position as officials of the Central Executive Committee of the USSR. . . .

41. *beloemigrantshchina:* the most literal rendering might be "White Guard emigration," but with a derogatory connotation—Trans.

Document 37 *continued*

At the time of the purge of the party organization of the TsIK (Central Executive Committee) of the USSR, a note was handed to the chairman of the Purge Commission concerning contamination of the apparat and concerning anti-Soviet feeling on the part of TsIK personnel and, in particular, on the part of the staff employed by the government library.

The chairman of the Purge Commission, Comrade Vasiliev, brought up this matter with Yenukidze. Once again, Yenukidze took no measures to deal with it. There were many such warnings addressed to Comrade Yenukidze. Apart from these statements, Yenukidze systematically received information from the NKVD regarding anti-Soviet feelings and expressions of individual members of the TsIK of the USSR. Nevertheless, he did not act on this information either. To all of these statements and warnings Comrade Yenukidze would say: "These employees have been working in the TsIK apparat for many years, they are people of proven worth, there is no one to replace them with, nor is there any point in replacing them."

For example, the following facts characterize Yenukidze's attitude to [class]-alien persons:

The following amounts were handed out during 1934 alone from the Central Executive Committee's secret fund and credited to the government's funds: 1,500 rubles to Ramishvili, an exiled Menshevik; 600 rubles to Stepanova, one of the wives of Erdman, a writer exiled for his lampoons of Soviet power; 500 rubles to Kondrateva, the wife of a counterrevolutionary saboteur, and so on. Even after the arrest and dismissal from the apparat of the Central Executive Committee of the USSR of many [class]-alien people, Comrade Yenukidze gave them financial assistance: 1,000 rubles to former Minister Kotliarovsky; 1,000 rubles to Eliner; 1,500 rubles to Pantovich, a former Menshevik; 300 rubles to Minervina, and so on.

Such are the facts characterizing the political myopia and loss of class vigilance of Comrade Yenukidze. This is hardly a coincidence. Everyone knows that Yenukidze was never distinguished for his Bolshevik steadfastness. History knows many of his Menshevik-type vacillations. All of these facts promoted the creation in the Kremlin of a situation in which terrorists were able to prepare, with impunity, an attempt on Comrade Stalin's life. The party cannot leave this matter unpunished. Comrade Yenukidze must be punished in the most severe way because he bears responsibility for the events [*fakty*] that occurred in the Kremlin. Comrade Yenukidze is the most typical representative of the corrupt and self-complacent Communist, who not only fails to see the class enemy but in fact affiliates himself with him, becomes his involuntary accomplice [*posobnik*], opening the gates to him for his counter-revolutionary, terroristic acts.

The Central Committee places before the plenum for its consideration the matter of Comrade Yenukidze's expulsion from the Central Committee of the VKP(b).

Yezhov's speech treated the Yenukidze affair almost as a side-light, and it is tempting to see the Yenukidze accusation as a pretext for introducing a new prescribed version on Zinoviev, Kamenev, and Trotsky. If this is true, and Yezhov's speech was a kind of trial balloon (Yezhov's, or Stalin's), it was a strange and unsuccessful attempt to recast the prevailing political line on the opposition.

First of all, Stalin did not speak in support of Yezhov's theory. This in itself was not strange; Stalin often used his henchmen to make his points while remaining silent. But this time the usual chorus—Kaganovich, Rudzutak, Shkiriatov, and others—did not strongly back Yezhov. Second, despite Yezhov having posited "direct participation by Kamenev and Zinoviev in the organizing of terroristic groups" and having said that "the murder of Comrade Kirov was organized by Zinoviev and Kamenev," no new charges were brought against them. It was more than a year after Yezhov's speech that these two were brought to trial for the crime. During that period, their names almost never appeared in the press or in party speeches, even though a high-ranking party official had accused them of organizing the assassination of a Politburo member. Finally, Yezhov's failed new narrative was never published.

Why the strange delay in following up on Yezhov's thesis? No one spoke in defense of Zinoviev and Kamenev, and no one suggested moderation or delay at the plenum, at any subsequent plenum, or in any documents at our disposal. Indeed, it is hard to imagine that the nomenklatura would want to defend them. After all, by identifying these has-beens as the enemy, the new theory suggested that any and all problems could be blamed on their treason rather than on "bureaucrats" who did not "fulfill decisions."

There appear to be two possible explanations for the failure of Yezhov's initiative against Zinoviev and Kamenev in June 1935. On the one hand, there could have been quiet opposition in the Central Committee that forced Stalin to stay his hand. Or it may well have been Stalin himself who was unsure about what to do with Zinoviev and Kamenev. He might have allowed Yezhov to float his trial balloon and then left him dangling by telling him that it was possible to follow up only if Yezhov could prove the charges. It would take Yezhov a year to get the "proof" by forcing Zinoviev and Kamenev to confess.

Although Yezhov's wild denunciation of former oppositionists was met with inaction, the members of the Central Committee did discuss the Yenukidze accusation, and the discussion shows the "lessons" party members drew. As always, the target of an accusation was expected to perform an apology ritual. Yenukidze, however, refused to play his part.

Document 38

A. S. Yenukidze's speech to the CC plenum, 6 June 1935[42]

Yenukidze: Feeling that it would cause me much pain to speak before you, I even asked Comrade Yezhov to lay out the essentials of the letter which I wrote to him as a result of my conversation with him. Unfortunately, he did not do that, did not have the time for it, and therefore I shall have to state the essence of certain matters.

The matter we are discussing, comrades, is an extremely serious one, and not because it concerns my fate but because it touches upon the very serious task of safeguarding the security of our state and party organs. For this reason, we must deal with this matter with great seriousness. We must bring to light all of the circumstances of the case because in the future it shall be necessary to fully guarantee the security of one or another group of our comrades-leaders. Much that is wrong has been said here regarding the apparat of the Central Executive Committee. In the first place, the apparat has changed repeatedly during the time of its existence. It has undergone changes both as to the quality of its personnel and as to its party stratum [*prosloika*]. But the procedure for hiring workers in the Kremlin has not changed. This can be verified by consulting [the appropriate] documents. Every candidate for employment in the Kremlin would first undergo a predetermined probationary period and only then would he be enrolled on the staff. The probation was carried out with the participation of organs of the NKVD. No one was hired for work in the Kremlin without security clearance. This applies to all officials without exception.

Yagoda: That's not true.

Yenukidze: Yes, it is.

Yagoda: We gave our security report, but you insisted on hiring. We said not to hire, and you went ahead and hired.

Yenukidze: Comrade Yagoda, how could you say that? This may be the last opportunity granted to me to talk about this. I am telling you what happened, what I told Yezhov in my letter to him. I repeat: During my entire tenure at the

42. RTsKhIDNI, f. 17, op. 2, d. 542, ll. 125–41.

Kremlin as head of the [Kremlin] apparat, I never had any serious conflicts on this matter with organs of the NKVD. Yes, there were some minor arguments, but they were always resolved.

Besides, at each congress or session or whenever party congresses and conferences were organized, those employees who were recruited for that particular assignment were always once again cleared and their clearance coordinated with organs of the NKVD. I would like to say, comrades, that during all these years when our apparat held all these congresses, all these sessions, and also when it was deeply and actively involved in organizing party congresses, conferences, and plenums, everything, fortunately, turned out well in matters of security, and the main credit, as I said in my letter to Yezhov, goes to the NKVD and to the Commandant's Office of the Kremlin, which coordinated everything with us on this matter. In all matters having to do with security, the services of the NKVD have always been enlisted, and without them, naturally, nothing was ever done. . . .

I headed the [Kremlin] apparat from its very inception, and perhaps its very success has created in me a certain psychological state: there is no question that if I had been asked before these incidents whether our apparat was reliable—that is, whether it was politically trustworthy—I would have replied in all candor that our apparat is reliable. But after the revelations in the library and in the Commandant's Office of the Kremlin and right after these became known to me, I immediately declared to the comrade-members of the Politburo that it would be perfectly right to dismiss me from my post as secretary of the Central Executive Committee. In my attitude to the apparat and in my trust in it, I failed to guarantee the security of the Kremlin and therefore it was necessary to remove me.

I deeply regret the fact that far-fetched accusations of personal corruption, of cohabitation with certain women, etc., were raised against me. Comrades, I am telling you here in all candor that I have never lived with, never cohabited with any of those arrested, no matter what certain letters or depositions might say. Never. Since this has been repeated here, I feel compelled to tell you this once again. . . .

What was the most criminal thing I did? Confident of the reliability of the apparat, I did not, for instance, immediately draw the appropriate conclusion from the report given to me by the commandant of the Kremlin to the effect that a certain cleaning woman was engaged in counterrevolutionary conversations and, in particular, conversations directed against Comrade Stalin. Instead of immediately arresting the cleaning woman and handing her over to the NKVD, I said to Peterson [the commandant]: "Look into it once again." [I did this] because there have been many cases of slander, with people being informed on unjustly.

Of course, such a situation ought not to have been tolerated. Surely, immediate action ought to have been taken. These instructions of mine to the commandant of the Kremlin fell into the hands of the NKVD and then into the hands of Comrade Stalin. Comrade Stalin was the first to call attention to this, saying that this was no mere idle chatter, that it concealed very grave counterrevolutionary activity. And in fact, that is the way it turned out. . . .

Now to move on. I have been charged—and I have not concealed it; Comrade Yezhov said here that I've given him the names of certain people whom I've helped in the past and whom he didn't know—with giving help to people, to people who were our enemies in the past and perhaps also to people who are our enemies at present. But you must know that this entire system of assistance, of issuing sums of money, beginning with the first years of the Revolution, was set up within the TsIK in such a way and encompassed such dimensions that, naturally, looking back, I—more than anyone else who might try to do so—can find a host of blunders and mistakes, of money wrongly issued. These may be indignantly characterized—and [Lavrenty] Beria does so here—as treason and duplicity.

Beria: Just the same, why did you give out loans, assistance, etc.?

Yenukidze: Just wait a minute, I will tell you everything.

It has been said here that I gave help to certain outsiders. There were circumstances and cases such that I was in no condition to refuse such requests. (Commotion in the room.)

Call it what you will. My actions can be characterized only as treason and duplicity, but I am talking about it openly myself. Consider, for instance, Dumbadze—he is a deviationist. I know his present and past better than Beria.

Beria: We know his present situation now just as well as you do.

Yenukidze: I didn't help him personally.

Beria: He is a very active Trotskyist.

Stalin: He was deported [*vyslan*] by Soviet authorities.

A voice: He has been in exile [*ssylka*] for seven years.

Yenukidze: Yes, it's true. But I didn't help him. His daughter came to me when she received permission to see her father. She asked me for my help so she could go see her father in Verkhneuralsk.

As for Kondratev's wife, I am telling you in full sincerity: I do not remember, I don't know how it came about really that it is recorded that Mrs. Kondratev was given 500 rubles.[43] I cannot verify whether she had sent a written request or whether she had come in person because I don't have the documents in my possession, because they were taken from me by Comrade Belenky. I don't know her, I don't remember her. Of course, if an order issued by me does in fact exist, I shall answer for it fully.

As for help given to Ramishvili, I consider it truly criminal. I know Ramishvili, I know who he is, I know his attitude toward our Revolution, I know

43. The Russian text here is ungrammatical—Trans.

his attitude toward our party. When I was first told about the assistance given to I. Ramishvili, I thought that this was an ancient matter, but, as it turns out, it had taken place last year.

Mikoyan: You acted wrongly.

Yenukidze: I don't have the documents in my possession. I don't know what I gave him the money for.

Yezhov: How is it that there are no documents? What about the telegram sent by Isidor Ramishvili, who wrote asking you to send 1,500 rubles to a certain address?

Yenukidze: Please bear with me, Comrade Yezhov. I didn't say that these documents do not exist; I only said that I haven't seen them recently, so I can't verify what actually happened. I've forgotten what the circumstances were all about. I recall much of it. I'll go further and say that I sent Riazanov 600 rubles. I told Yezhov about it. I'm not concealing anything: His wife came to see me repeatedly, saying that she was destitute, that she was starving, and here comes Ivan Nikitich Smirnov—

Ordzhonikidze: So what if she starves to death, so what if she croaks, what does it have to do with you?

A voice: Let her get a job.

Yenukidze: It's all true. Now I am even more indignant about it than you. It's all true, comrades. I handed out a lot of money. Perhaps there were swindlers, cheats among them.

Voroshilov: Riazanov is no cheat, and you, what are you—some kind of a child? If your heart bled for someone, you could have asked any of us.

Stalin: Why ask? The man has been deported by Soviet authorities. Let him [Yenukidze] hand out money from his own pocket, if that's what he wants to do, out of his own pocket and not from state funds.

Yenukidze: That's true. That's true. . . .

It seems to me that in the future neither my years nor my health will permit me to rise to that pinnacle of trust which I had once occupied. Nevertheless, I am not in the slightest pleading with the party for leniency. Measures ought to be taken in my case that will serve as a lesson in the future for every Communist occupying this or that post in order to really strengthen our vigilance and to make it possible for our party and soviet organs to work fruitfully and peacefully.

Yenukidze did not fully understand what was required of him. Like Bukharin and A. P. Smirnov, he understood the propriety and gravity of the accusation, but he claimed that he was not guilty of anything. He refused to take his medicine and carry out the apology ritual. In his speech he claimed that his organization was no better or worse than others and blamed the NKVD and Control Commission officials for vetting the personnel who had been accused. Politically, he was still reading from a different page.

Genrikh Yagoda, head of the NKVD, had been rebuffed when he tried to interrupt Yenukidze's speech, but later had to say something in reply. According to formality and logic, his organization should have discovered the crime and reported on it. That Yezhov, from the party Secretariat, had uncovered and reported the "treason" already cast doubt on Yagoda's competence. When Yenukidze blamed the NKVD in his remarks, the commissariat was explicitly and implicitly under fire. Yagoda had to speak, and in his own defense he had to be tough and uncompromising.

Document 39

G. Yagoda's speech to the CC plenum, 6 June 1935[44]

Yagoda: I think that by his speech Yenukidze has already placed himself outside the bounds of our party.

What he said here, what he brought here to the Plenum of the Central Committee, is the pile of rubbish of a philistine. Yenukidze tried to create the impression here that he either knows nothing or that he has forgotten the facts that were presented here.

How does the matter really stand? Is the Yenukidze matter an accident?

No, it is not. It is not an accident because for a long time now Yenukidze has been the gravitational center for elements that are hostile and [class]-alien to us. I would like to remind Yenukidze of a whole series of facts which show that as early as 1928 he was degenerating and blunting his vigilance toward the enemy. If we follow the thread of facts from 1928 to the events of 1935, we are compelled to state that Yenukidze not only helped the enemy but that he, from an objective standpoint, was also an accomplice of the counterrevolutionary terrorists. There is no other conclusion to be drawn because the vicious enemy felt itself at home in the Kremlin precisely under Yenukidze's protection. . . .

Unfortunately, I am speaking without any documents, but I vouch for my words, since I have documents to substantiate every one of the facts that I shall speak of here.

I could name many people whose removal from the apparats of Kremlin institutions we proposed to Yenukidze, and yet we failed to obtain the necessary results. I could also name many people [class]-alien to us whom, with great effort, we nonetheless forced Yenukidze to banish from the Kremlin.

44. RTsKhIDNI, f. 17, op. 2, d. 542, ll. 175–78.

Document 39 *continued*

But let us assume that the NKVD really did not raise these questions with Yenukidze. Did Yenukidze show the most elementary vigilance on his side?

After all, he is not merely an ordinary member of the party. And the party demands a maximum vigilance from each of its members.

In fact, Yenukidze, having taken under his wing people whose removal we had demanded, had undermined our work and demobilized those of our officials who were engaged in the work of checking up on these people. Yenukidze did this because, as secretary of the TsIK, he enjoyed sufficient authority among us.

What is more, Yenukidze not only ignored our signals but introduced into the Kremlin his own parallel "GPU," and whenever he recognized one of our agents, he immediately banished him.

Of course, none of this removes responsibility from my shoulders.

I admit my guilt in that I did not in my time seize Yenukidze by the throat and did not force him to kick out all those swine.

Everything that Yenukidze has said here is nothing but unadulterated lies.

Yagoda proposed that Yenukidze be expelled from the party, going beyond Yezhov's recommendation only to remove him from the Central Committee. In citing Yenukidze's "parallel 'GPU,'" Yagoda revealed that as late as 1935, high-ranking members of the nomenklatura were able to thwart the secret police. In Yagoda's words, whenever Yenukidze "recognized one of our agents, he immediately banished him."

It fell to L. M. Kaganovich, as a real insider, to make the main point, provide the main "lesson" of the Yenukidze affair. Recalling one of the themes of Stalin speech to the Seventeenth Party Congress (see Document 27), Kaganovich insisted that everyone—no matter how exalted his rank—must adhere to the master narrative and to the rituals of party discipline.

Document 40

L. M. Kaganovich's speech to the CC plenum, 6 June 1935[45]

Kaganovich: . . . And you people think that the party can let a Communist holding such a responsible post go unpunished? Yenukidze here made refer-

45. RTsKhIDNI, f. 17, op. 1 d. 542, ll. 158–59.

ence to the fact that during the process of hiring personnel for the apparat of the Central Executive Committee, he would have each application endorsed by the organs of the GPU. In the first place, the officials from the NKVD declare that he paid no attention to their official stamps. But let's assume that applications were stamped "OK" by the NKVD. But then Yenukidze is a member of the CC of the party. He can't claim that GPU officials gave their seal of approval. Is that sort of talk worthy of a secretary of the Central Executive Committee? No, Comrade Yenukidze, you are responsible for the Central Executive Committee apparat. In your selection of personnel, you approached the matter in an unbusinesslike, un-party, un-Communist manner. And for us, this aspect of the matter is of foremost importance. . . .

If you are sincere, Comrade Yenukidze, about your readiness to accept punishment so that others can draw their lesson from it, then you ought to have analyzed your situation more honestly, you ought to have told us how enemies had wormed their way into the apparat, how you gave cover to good-for-nothing scoundrels. Instead, you slurred over the matter and tried to prove that nothing out of the ordinary had taken place.

Voices: That's right!

Kaganovich: We must expose, uncover, to the last detail, this whole affair, so that it can serve as a lesson to all Communists who suffer from opportunistic complacency, a subject discussed by the Central Committee in its letter concerning the murder of Comrade Kirov.

Our party is strong by virtue of the fact that it metes out its punishment equally to all members of the party, in both the upper and lower echelons. No sooner were the first facts concerning the apparat of the TsIK received than Comrade Stalin brought us all together and raised the question of removing Yenukidze from the post of secretary of the TsIK. I must add that not everyone found his bearings in this matter immediately, but Comrade Stalin at once smelled a rat.[46] He immediately perceived that the removal of Yenukidze from the post of secretary of the TsIK ought to be urgently placed on the agenda. A resolution was passed: to remove Comrade Yenukidze from his post as secretary of the TsIK. He was sent instead to the Trans-Caucasus.

Afterward, during the course of the investigation, when new facts were brought to light, Comrade Stalin proposed that Yenukidze ought not to retain a post such as that of chairman of the Trans-Caucasus TsIK. He was removed from his post as chairman of the Trans-Caucasus TsIK and given the post of commissioner of health resorts in Kislovodsk. Now when all the materials presented by Comrade Yezhov in his report have been brought to light, it is absolutely clear that Yenukidze must be severely punished. Yenukidze has disgraced and discredited himself not only as a member of the CC but also as a Communist. This is a fact. This matter, of course, is important not only as it

46. Literally, "sensed that there was something rotten here"—Trans.

pertains to Yenukidze but also because we undoubtedly have in our party people who believe that we can now "take it more easily": in view of our great victory, in view of the fact that our country is moving forward, they can now afford to rest, to take a nap. . . .

So for Kaganovich the point was not whether or not the NKVD missed the boat (although that lesson was lost on no one). The crux of the matter was not even whether or not Yenukidze was formally guilty. The point was that no one, not even those who had always been loyal Stalinists, was above party discipline. Not even highly placed members of the nomenklatura who ruled their fiefs with an iron hand were immune to control and to the demands of the party. Yenukidze's duty as a Bolshevik was to recount how enemies had stolen into the apparat, how he had protected scoundrels. The party had demanded that Yenukidze help it teach a lesson, and Yenukidze had failed to play his part.

For years, the nomenklatura had demanded that lower-ranking party functionaries play the roles assigned to them: to help provide negative examples and changes in policy by making formal apologies and posing as scapegoats. Members of opposition groups who found themselves on the losing side had been expected to do the same to win readmission to the nomenklatura. What was new in the 1930s was the expectation that the highest-ranking members of the Stalin coalition do the same when duty called. As Kaganovich said, "Our party is strong by virtue of the fact that it metes out its punishment equally to all members of the party, in both the upper and lower echelons." A. P. Smirnov in 1933 and now Yenukidze in 1935 had failed to understand that.

Kaganovich's discussion of the decision-making process on Yenukidze shows that the inner leadership, including Stalin himself, had difficulty deciding what to do with an official who didn't play the game. Various punishments had been discussed. Yezhov's personal papers contain three draft decrees on Yenukidze prepared before the meeting. The first proposed only removing him from the TsIK position and appointing him TsIK secretary in Transcaucasia. By the third draft, because of "new facts coming to light," the punishment had been escalated to "discussing Yenukidze's Central Committee membership." This was the proposal that Yezhov brought to the meeting when he moved that Yenukidze be expelled from the CC.

Speaker after speaker denounced Yenukidze's sins in a ritual display of nomenklatura unity and anger. By joining to isolate Yenukidze, the members of the Central Committee were not only supporting Stalin's charges (but not, as we shall see, Yezhov's) but implicitly affirming their individual status as well as their collective right to decide punishment. CC apology rites had a transactional component; the final sanction depended on how well the subject had played his part. In this case, Yenukidze's declining the proffered rite infuriated the group. The increasingly angry nature of the discussion at the plenum led to a second motion to expel him from the party altogether. At the end of the plenum, both proposals were put to the vote:

Document 41

CC vote on the Yenukidze affair, 7 June 1935, original version[47]

. . . Chairman: There is a proposal, explained by Comrade Yezhov, and then a second proposal, put forward by a series of comrades who spoke, as a supplement.

The first proposal on removing Comrade Yenukidze from the Central Committee: let us vote. Who is for this proposal; raise your hands. Hands down. Who is against? None. Who abstains? None.

The second proposal, to expel Comrade Yenukidze from the party. Let us vote. Who supports this proposal; raise your hands. Hands down. Who is against? Fewer. This proposal is accepted.

The split vote (itself an extreme rarity in the Central Committee) on the disposition of Yenukidze's fate was not something that the party leadership wanted to broadcast to the party rank and file. A single text had to be provided that demonstrated unity and singleness of purpose. In the version of the plenum minutes printed for distribution in the party, the event was portrayed differently. His-

---

47. RTsKhIDNI, f. 17, op. 2, d. 547, l. 69.

tory was rewritten to make it seem that there had been only one proposal and that the ultimate decision was based on Yezhov's motion. The image of a united leadership had to be maintained.

Document 42

CC vote on the Yenukidze affair, 7 June 1935, second version[48]

. . . Yezhov: I would like to propose the following resolution:

Concerning the administrative apparat of the Secretariat of the TsIK of the USSR and Comrade Yenukidze,

1. The measures adopted by the control organs responsible for the evaluation and improvement of the administrative apparat of the Secretariat of the TsIK of the USSR are to be approved.

2. A. Yenukidze is to be removed from the CC of the VKP(b) and expelled from the ranks of the VKP(b) for his political and moral corruption while serving as Secretary of the TsIK of the USSR.

Molotov (chairing): The resolution proposed by Comrade Yezhov is hereby put to a vote.

Those for the resolution, please raise your hands. You may now lower them. Those opposed? None.

The resolution carries unanimously.

Yezhov's original motion passed unanimously and the harsher proposal that superseded it passed by a majority. Yenukidze was expelled from the party.[49] It is of course possible that the second, harsher proposal came in fact from Stalin through his representatives. In this case, the strategy might have been to have Yezhov put forward a suggestion for moderate punishment of a key nomenklatura member in order not to alarm the elite, to gauge the reaction, and then to see what developed.

It is more likely, however, that the ad hoc harsher punishment came from the nomenklatura itself in the course of the plenum. In such a case, the nomenklatura was more radical in its punishment than Stalin himself. It could well be that Yenukidze's refusal to carry out the apology that elite discipline required infuriated the

---

48. RTsKhIDNI, f. 17, op. 2, d. 544, l. 22. Printed stenographic report.
49. RTsKhIDNI, f. 17, op. 2, d. 547, l. 70.

elite in the Central Committee. It may well have been that the elite went into the plenum with a quid pro quo in mind: in return for his formal apology, Yenukidze would be spared a full scapegoating and could remain in the party. His refusal or failure to comply cast doubt on the ritual and the party authority behind it. Such challenges to the rituals often led to harsher punishment.[50]

There is some reason to suspect that in the end Yenukidze was punished rather more harshly than Stalin had originally intended. At the first plausible opportunity, two plenums later in June 1936, Stalin personally proposed that Yenukidze be permitted to rejoin the party (see Document 71). At that time, Stalin explained that this was the earliest moment Yenukidze's readmission could take place: "It would have turned out then that he had been expelled at one plenum and reinstated at the next." Yenukidze's readmission in 1936 was a curious irony. For it was at that plenum that the Politburo, acting on the theory that Yezhov had put forward at the plenum that expelled Yenukidze, announced the upcoming capital trial of Zinoviev and Kamenev for the assassination of Kirov.

Central Committee members must have taken at least four lessons from the June 1935 plenum. First, they were introduced to the idea that Zinoviev's and Kamenev's guilt might be greater than previously thought. Second, Yezhov was now a visibly important player before the Central Committee: he had brought down the secretary of the Central Executive Committee and stepped forward as the herald of a modified (albeit temporarily unsuccessful) narrative. Third, Yagoda and the NKVD had been discredited. Fourth, and most uncomfortable for them, one of the highest-ranking members of the nomenklatura (and a personal friend of Stalin's) had violated discipline. For some members of the elite, this action must have been personally disquieting: if Yenukidze could fall, no one was safe. For others, however, the lesson was that the dangers and threats of the new situation had infected even the inner circle of the nomenklatura.

---

50. Many such arraignment rituals in the 1930s were "broken" or contested by the refusal of the subject to play his role. See J. Arch Getty, "*Samokritika* Rituals in the Stalinist Central Committee, 1933–1938," *The Russian Review*, 58(1), 1999, 47–70.

As was so often the case, Stalin remained in the shadows of the plenum. What did he think? What did he want? What, if any, were his plans? There would seem to be two explanations. The events of the Yenukidze plenum are consistent with a plan to escalate repression and prepare the way for terror. Incriminating Zinoviev and Kamenev (along with Trotsky) in capital crimes clearly raised the stakes in defining enemies and punishments. Similarly, casting a shadow on a serving member of the upper nomenklatura—some speakers, like the hysterical Yagoda, had practically equated Yenukidze's guilt with Zinoviev's—could open the door to persecution of the elite itself in an unfolding terror.

On the other hand, if these June 1935 events were part of a scheme to escalate terror in the wake of the Kirov assassination, it remained stillborn for so long a time that their purported lessons were lost or devalued. Yezhov's accusations against Zinoviev and Kamenev were not followed up for a year. To insiders skilled at reading the tea leaves of Central Committee plena, the unitary lesson that Yenukidze's fall apparently provided was muted by Kaganovich's admission that the Politburo had trouble deciding what to do and was erased by Yenukidze's rehabilitation by Stalin in June 1936. No ranking nomenklatura members were arrested until the end of 1936, more than a year and a half after the Yenukidze plenum.

Finally, Yezhov's debut in the role of hatchet man against "enemies" was not an unqualified success. Not only was his main "thesis" ignored, but the proposal he put forward on Yenukidze was overruled. Given that everyone must have known that his recommendation on Yenukidze must have been approved by Stalin and the Politburo beforehand, the impression created was that the radical Yezhov had been taken down a peg at the moment of his triumph. No one except the master balancer—Stalin—could have permitted that.

Other documents from June and July 1935 nevertheless suggest a more "vigilant" and repressive atmosphere on the local level. In the Azov–Black Sea territory, there was a new crackdown against rural opponents.

Document 43

Verification of kolkhoz cadres, Azov–Black Sea territory[51]

2 June 1935
STRICTLY SECRET
[SEAL] (strogo sekretno)
(FROM A SPECIAL DOSSIER)
Copying hereby prohibited
ALL-UNION COMMUNIST PARTY (Bolshevik)
AZOV–BLACK SEA TERRITORIAL COMMITTEE

To: CC VKP(b), Comrade Rudyev [partly illegible] Department of Agriculture

Extract from Protocol #46 of the buro session of the Azov–Black Sea Territorial Committee of the VKP(b), 2 June 1935

#6 Re: Verification of kolkhoz cadres

IT IS HEREBY DECREED

#6. That in view of the revelations of significant contamination by kulak and counterrevolutionary elements of the leadership and technical cadres of many kolkhozy, we must recognize the necessity for:

1) Undertaking during 1935 a verification of the leadership organs of the kolkhozy (chairmen, brigade leaders, managers of farms, members of boards, stewards, bookkeepers, accounts clerks) by means of special commissions of the territorial committee for the purpose of cleansing the cadres of alien and hostile elements.

This verification should be based on the following principles:

a) The above posts should not be held by former kulaks, counterrevolutionaries, White Army officers, members of punitive expeditions and executioners, repatriates, and those exiled for a period of over 5 years;

b) The following are to be verified on an individual basis: all leading officials of the kolkhozy who have served in the White Army, in particular, volunteers and cavalry sergeant-majors, sergeants, members of the civil service, and others holding privileged positions, [and Cossack] village chiefs [*atamany*]. With due consideration for their work and especially for their conduct during the years of sabotage, the possibility of their keeping their leading positions in the kolkhozy ought to be resolved.

2) Deporting from our territory 1,500 kulaks, counterrevolutionaries who continue to carry on their anti-Soviet, antikolkhoz activities and sabotage. The members of their families, on the other hand, may, if they so desire, remain in place.

3) Bringing this decision before the CC for its approval.

51. RTsKhIDNI, f. 17, op. 42, d. 136, l. 87.

Document 43 *continued*

4) Distributing the NKVD materials concerning the contamination of the kolkhozy to the secretaries of the district committees.

[Seal of Azov–Black Sea Territorial Committee of the VKP(b)]

Secretary

(M. Malinov) [signature]

Intensified Ideological Controls

New central decrees were also designed to tighten controls over subversive book collections in libraries, perhaps because the Kremlin Affair was said to have been hatched in the Kremlin Library.

Document 44

Orgburo resolution against wholesale purge of libraries[52]

(Orgburo of 14 June 1935, Protocol #31, Item #30 g-s)

139. Re: Removing counterrevolutionary Zinovievist-Trotskyist literature

The CC of the VKP(b) notes that during the removal of Trotskyist-Zinovievist literature from libraries an uncontrolled and ungovernable "purge" of libraries is taking place, a plundering and damaging of library resources.

The CC of the VKP(b) hereby decrees:

a) That it be recommended that party organizations, People's Commissariats for Education, the Chief Administrations for Literature and Publishing [Glavlit], and others cease their wholesale purge of libraries and indiscriminate removals of books therefrom;

b) That the Chief Administrations for Literature and Publishing, along with the NKVD, be instructed to remove from libraries and from their bookstores counterrevolutionary Trotskyist-Zinovievist literature, in accordance with the appended list (see appendix);

c) The removal of said books is to be carried out for each individual library by the district plenipotentiary [*upolnomochennyi*] of Glavlit along with the plenipotentiary [*upolnomochennyi*] of the NKVD.

An official document is drawn up concerning the removal of a book. The book is then sealed up and sent with its official document to the territorial and regional administrations of the NKVD;

d) Two copies of each withdrawn book are to remain in the special library collections of the following institutions: the CC and Moscow City Committee

52. RTsKhIDNI, f. 17, op. 3, d. 965, l. 30. Compare with Document 16.

Document 44 *continued*

of the VKP(b), the Academy of Sciences, the Marx-Engels-Lenin Institute of the CC, as well as in the Lenin Library (Moscow), the Saltykov-Shchedrin Library (Leningrad), the libraries of the Institute of Red Professors, the libraries of Communist universities in Moscow and Leningrad, the central libraries of the principal cities of the Union republics, territories, regions, and university cities, and in the governmental library attached to the Central Executive Committee of the USSR.

Document 45

List of Trotskyist-Zinovievist literature to be removed from libraries[53]

Appendix to item #139, Politburo Protocol #27
NOT FOR PUBLICATION
LIST OF TROTSKYIST-ZINOVIEVIST COUNTERREVOLUTIONARY LITERATURE SUBJECT TO REMOVAL FROM PUBLIC LIBRARIES
(Confirmed by the Politburo of the CC of the VKP(b) 16 June 1935)

1. Trotsky	All books
2. G. Zinoviev	*Philosophy of the Age,* 1925
3. G. Zinoviev	*Leninism,* 1926
4. G. Zinoviev	*Leninism and NEP,* 1926
5. G. Zinoviev	*The History of the Russian Communist Party of Bolsheviks* [no date]
6. G. Zinoviev	*The Theory of Marx and Lenin on War,* 1930
7. G. Zinoviev	*The Path of October,* 1926
8. G. Zinoviev	*We Are All Octobrists,* 1924
9. G. Zinoviev	*The Year of the Revolution (February 1917–March 1918)*
10. G. Zinoviev	*N. Lenin,* 1920
11. G. Zinoviev	*From the History of Our Party,* 1923
12. G. Zinoviev	*Our Differences of Opinion,* 1926
13. G. Zinoviev	*Of Made-up and Genuine Differences of Opinion in Our Party,* 1926
14. L. Kamenev	*Kamenev and Zinoviev on the Middle Peasant,* 1926
15. A. Shliapnikov	*The Year 1917,* 1927 and 1931, books 1, 2, 3, 4

53. RTsKhIDNI, f. 17, op. 3, d. 965, ll. 63–64.

16. A. Shliapnikov	*On the Eve of the Year 1917,* part 1, 3d edition, 1924, parts 1 and 2
17. A. Shliapnikov	*On the Eve of the Year 1917,* 1920
18. M. I. Yavorsky	*A Short History of the Ukraine,* 1927
19. M. I. Yavorsky	*Essays from the History of the Revolutionary Struggle in the Ukraine,* 1927
20. G. Gorbachev	*Two Years of a Literary Revolution,* 1926
21. Preobrazhensky	*The Twilight of Capitalism,* 1931
22. Preobrazhensky	*Economic Crises Under NEP* [no date]
23. V. Nevsky	*The History of the Russian Communist Party [RKP(b)],* 1926
24. V. Bulakh	*On Farm Laborers,* 1929
25. V. Vardin	*The Bolsheviks After October* [no date]
26. P. Zalutsky	*Questions Pertaining to Party Work and Link Organizers* [no date]
27. N. Maiorsky and N. Elvov	*Leninism and an Assessment of the October Revolution* [no date]
28. A. Lunacharsky	*Revolutionary Profiles,* 1923
29. G. Safarov	*Foundations of Leninism,* 1924
30. G. Safarov	*On the Matter of Our Stabilization,* 1925
31. Zalutsky and Safarov	*On State Capitalism and Socialism: A Reexamination,* 1926
32. G. Safarov	*Leninism as a Theory of the Development of the Proletarian Revolution,* 1925
33. G. Safarov	*The Peasant Question and Leninism* [no date]
34. G. Safarov	*Lenin's Theory of Imperialism,* 1925
35. A. Slepkov	*On the Propagation of Leninism in the Workers' Party School,* 1926
36. V. Volosevich	*Organizational Principles of Bolshevism,* 1929
37. V. Volosevich	*A Course in the History of the VKP(b),* 1930
38. V. Volosevich	*A Very Short History of the VKP(b),* 1931
39. V. Volosevich	*A Course in the History of the VKP(b),* 1931
40. V. Volosevich	*The Thirteenth Party Congress,* 1928
41. V. Volosevich	*Bolshevism During the Years of the World War* [no date]

Document 45 *continued*

42. V. Astrov   *Democracy Within the Party* [no date]
43. *The Ninth of January: A Collection [of Articles]* with a Foreword by
                    V. Friche, 1924
The list was ratified on 16 June 1935.

Increasing ideological and literary controls also extended to the members of the nomenklatura itself. Stalin, having emphasized "political education" and ideology since 1934 (see his speech to the Seventeenth Party Congress in Document 27), had personally taken control of the culture and propaganda department of the Central Committee in April 1935. His personal interest and control over ideology is reflected in the following document, in which a ranking member of the nomenklatura is brought up short. No one was to be allowed to alter the public rhetoric about the supreme leader, even in the direction of glorification, without permission.

Document 46

On editions of works of Comrade Stalin[54]

From Protocol #32 of the Politburo's meeting of 31 August 1935
#241. On editions of the works of Comrade Stalin
(a) To forbid the Trans-Caucasus *Kraikom* on Comrade Beria's personal responsibility from republishing articles and a brochure of Comrade Stalin from the period 1905–10 without [Stalin's] permission.
(b) To recognize the necessity for a full edition of Comrade Stalin's works and to charge the Institute of Marx-Engels-Lenin, together with the Department of Party Propaganda and Agitation and with the agreement of Comrade Stalin, to work out a plan for the edition.

Legal and Police Policy: Moderation vs. Legal Nihilism

Typically, however, even as things swung in the direction of harder and harder policies, there continued to be countervailing texts that suggested softer, legal tactics. The following document reflects a

54. RTsKhIDNI, f. 17, op. 3, d. 970, l. 50.

liberalization of the policy enforced on exiled "enemies." Such granting of "privileges" was uncharacteristic of either the preceding period or the subsequent terror and represents a kind of minority text in an otherwise darkening picture. The new rules permitted condemned "enemies" to work in their specialties; all memoir accounts agree that such a possibility was very important to detainees. These new regulations also removed the legal stigma from children of the regime's victims. The central leadership had not yet decided on the completely brutal and severe treatment of its victims that would follow in 1937.

Document 47

NKVD/Procuracy circular on employment of exiles, 23 December 1935[55]

SUPPLEMENT to Item #41, PB Protocol #36
CONFIRMED by SNK USSR
TOP SECRET

To all NKVD commissars and procurators of Union and autonomous republics, to all heads of territorial (regional) administrations of the NKVD and territorial (regional) procurators

In view of the inquiries coming in from various localities concerning the possible employment of persons exiled or deported administratively as well as the possible enrollment of their children in public schools, we offer the following guidelines:

1. Persons exiled or deported administratively on the basis of a decision by the Special Board of the NKVD of the USSR as, for instance, engineers, technicians, physicians, agronomists, bookkeepers, and skilled laborers, may be employed in their specialties in institutions and enterprises in those localities where they have been permitted to reside, with the exception of those persons who have been deprived, by the decision of the special board, of the right to engage in their occupation in their places of exile or deportation.

NOTE: Persons mentioned in Item #1 above may not be employed in work of a secret character or in institutions and enterprises pertaining to defense. Exceptions to this rule may be made in individual cases with the permission of the NKVD of the USSR.

2. Persons without special skills or occupations may be employed in accordance with general regulations.

3. Scientific workers may be employed in their [respective] specialties in places of exile or deportation if they were deported or exiled from capital

55. RTsKhIDNI, f. 17, op. 3, d. 374, l. 108.

cities, industrial centers, and border areas during the cleansing of these localities of socially dangerous elements.

4. The children of persons mentioned in Item #1 above, deported or exiled as dependents of their parents, are permitted to transfer to educational institutions in their places of exile or deportation.

5. In delivering the NKVD special board's decision to exiles or deportees, the organs of the NKVD are obligated to explain to them their right to work in their professional specialty in places of exile or deportation and to issue them the appropriate certificates.

6. The local organs of the NKVD and the Procuracy of the USSR are instructed to establish the strictest monitoring for the precise fulfillment of this present circular.

NKVD Commissar

G. Yagoda

Procurator of the USSR

A. Vyshinsky

23 December 1935

Document 48

Politburo decree on education of those disenfranchised, 29 December 1935[56]

Supplement to Protocol #36 of the Politburo, Item #79

ON ADMISSION TO INSTITUTIONS OF HIGHER EDUCATION AND TECHNICAL COLLEGES

Decree of the Central Executive Committee and the Council of People's Commissars of the USSR

(Approved by the Politburo of the CC VKP(b) 29 December 1935)

According to rules presently in force, admission to institutions of higher education and to technical colleges is not permitted to children of nonworking parents[57] and to children of parents deprived of voting rights.

In view of the fact that at the present time this restriction is no longer necessary, the Central Executive Committee and the Council of People's [Commissars] of the USSR decree:

1. Restrictions based on the social origin of the applicant or on the disfranchisement of the applicant's parents as they pertain to admission to institutions of higher education and technical colleges are to be abolished. . . .

---

56. RTsKhIDNI, f. 17, op. 3, d. 974, l. 137.

57. Parents from the "nonlaboring" (i.e., nonpeasant, proletarian, or "toiling intelligentsia") classes.

Document 48 *continued*

Chairman of the Central Executive Committee of the USSR, M. Kalinin
Chairman of the Council of People's Commissars of the USSR, V. Molotov
Secretary of the Central Executive Committee of the USSR, I. Akulov

In mid-June, the Central Committee produced a regulation on procedures for conducting arrests. As with all such documents (for example, Documents 20, 21, 25), it sent mixed signals. On the one hand, it seemed to tighten the requirements for arrest by insisting that all arrests without exception had to be approved by the relevant procurator. On the other hand, in spelling out the approvals necessary for detaining persons in various positions, it foreshadowed the possibility—which could not have been lost on Stalinist officials—that high-ranking persons might in the future be arrested.

Document 49

CC/SNK decree on procedures for conducting arrests, 17 June 1935[58]

Supplement to Item #157, PB Protocol #27
ON PROCEDURES FOR CONDUCTING ARRESTS
Decree by the Council of People's Commissars of the USSR and the Central Committee of the VKP(b)
Decree:

1. In modification of instructions of 8 May 1933, henceforth organs of the NKVD may make arrests only with the consent of the appropriate procurator. This applies to all cases without exception.

2. If arrests must be made at the site of the crime, officials of the NKVD authorized by law are obligated to report the arrest immediately to the appropriate procurator for his confirmation.

3. Permission to arrest members of the Central Executive Committee of the USSR and members of the Central Executive Committees of Union republics is granted to organs of the procuracy and of the NKVD only with the consent, through proper channels, of the chairman of the Central Executive Committee of the USSR or of the chairmen of the Central Executive Committees of the Union republics.

58. RTsKhIDNI, f. 17, op. 3, d. 965, l. 75.

Document 49 *continued*

Permission to arrest leading officials of the People's Commissariats of the [Soviet] Union and Union republics and of the central institutions corresponding to them (heads of administration and directors of departments, managers of trusts and their deputies, directors and deputies of industrial enterprises, sovkhozy, and so on), as well as permission to arrest engineers, agronomists, professors, and physicians employed by a variety of institutions and directors of scholarly, educational, and scientific-research institutions is granted with the consent of the appropriate people's commissars.

4. Permission to arrest members and candidate members of the VKP(b) is granted with the consent of the secretaries of the district, territorial, and regional committees of the VKP(b), the CCs of the national Communist parties, through the proper channels. Arrests of Communists occupying leading posts in the People's Commissariats of the [Soviet] Union and in central institutions of equivalent rank are to be granted upon receipt of consent by the chairman of the Commission of Party Control.

Chairman of the Council of People's Commissars of the Soviet Union
V. Molotov
Secretary of the Central Committee of the VKP(b)
I. Stalin
17 June 1935

It is also likely that this and similar decrees had another purpose: the restriction on the powers of regional party leaders to conduct their own arrests in the regions without any judicial supervision. In Belorussia, for example, party regional secretaries had sought to control railroad personnel through mass arrests. One Control Commission representative said that "Tens, hundreds were arrested by anybody and they sit in jail." In the Briansk railroad line, 75 percent of administrative-technical personnel had been sentenced to some kind of "corrective labor." In Sverdlovsk and Saratov, Control Commission inspectors sent from Moscow reported that locals had "completely baselessly [sic] arrested and convicted people and undertaken mass repressions for minor problems, sometimes for ineffective leadership, and in the majority of cases arrested and convicted workers who merely needed educational work."[59] By insisting on the procurator's permission in order to

59. See reports of Party Control Commission inspectors in TsKhSD, f. 6, op. 1, d. 5, ll. 90, 95, 98–99, 165–66; and d. 59, l. 186.

make an arrest, the Central Committee was taking unlimited arrest powers out of the hands of regional party leaders.

On the other hand, a political hardening and a kind of legal nihilism in fall 1935 contradicted many of 1934's initiatives that had seemed to augur an era of legality and rule of law. In September 1935, Yezhov gave a secret speech to a closed meeting of party personnel officials from the regions. His remarks advised party officials sharply to restrict the rights of expelled members to appeal, and not to be restrained by procurators' insistence on procedural legality (both of which contradicted written party and state texts). He also encouraged his audience to make use of extralegal bodies to convict "dangerous elements" not guilty of specific chargeable offenses.

Document 50

From N. I. Yezhov's report to a conference of regional party secretaries, 25 September 1935[60]

Yezhov: . . . Concerning the question of appeals [of those expelled from the party] and time periods for appeal: I believe that we will have to establish one general appeals time period for all party organizations. However, this does not rule out the possibility that we might set specific terms of appeal for each separate party organization. Why do we need this? Because if we permit a member of the party who has been expelled and whose party card has been taken from him to continue his appeals for six months, a year, two years, or three years and so on, it goes without saying that we shall never be rid of these appeals. What guarantee do we have that a crook may not somewhere succeed in slipping through? Besides, for all we know, a certain liberalism may have been shown in respect of individual party members, a liberalism which we have plenty of in our party collegium. . . .

In the territorial committee of the party an appeal is considered without fail in the presence of the secretary of the district committee. If someone has been rightfully expelled, then let him go to the devil; if wrongfully, then you must reinstate him. That's how I perceive the matter. And an investigation of the appeals must take place without fail in the presence of the secretary of the district committee. . . .

Levin: And in the presence of the appellant?

Yezhov: That's not absolutely necessary. Our policy up till now has gone

60. RTsKhIDNI, f. 17, op. 120, d. 179, ll. 34–77, 253–68. Uncorrected, typed text.

too far in the other direction.[61] It has been the practice of our party collegium that a case would be heard without fail in the presence of the appellant, but a case would almost never be heard in the presence of those who had expelled the appellant. The result has been a one-sided, essentially improper, case. What is needed in the first place is the presence of the person who had expelled the appellant, who is responsible for the case, and whose responsibility is to prove that he has acted properly. I think that it is desirable perhaps to hear the appeals in the presence of the secretary and the appellant. Of course, if you have no doubts whatsoever regarding the materials of the case in your possession, then you may hear the case without summoning the appellant. . . .

Now I shall discuss a group of questions directly associated with the work of cleansing the party of all hostile elements that have become ingrained in it.

The first question concerns the work of the organs of the NKVD, or rather, it concerns the mutual relation between organs of the NKVD and party organizations.

You see, comrades, I must tell you that the reproaches leveled by local party organizations against organs of the NKVD are, it seems to me, groundless. . . .

A voice: There are no directives in this line.

Yezhov: The problem here is not that of directives. We are, perhaps, a little guilty ourselves in this matter. The top brass are also human, and we haven't given attention to this matter in time. But I think that here we are dealing with people who simply do not understand what's at issue, I mean, certain officials who have gotten the NKVD involved where it is not needed, who have dumped work on the NKVD that they should have done themselves and who, on the other hand, do not permit the NKVD to concern itself with that which the NKVD should concern itself with.

I want to talk about the division of labor and about the mutual relation that ought to normally arise between [the NKVD and the party organizations].

First, I want to say that the matter comes down to this, that you conducted the verification. But in verifying a member of the party, the authenticity of his party documents—i.e., his entire past and present—you may run across a swindler, an adventurist, a scoundrel, a spy, and so on. You may have some grounds for suspicion, so you finish the case and then you hand over this person to the NKVD.

A voice: But the procurator doesn't always give his approval.

Yezhov: You are a true bureaucrat. Excuse me, but the way you are conducting your verification in Eastern Siberia shows that it is the procurator who is boss at your place and not you. Perhaps we'll entrust the verification process, then, to your procurator, if that's what you want! The territorial committee cannot make the procurator give his sanction—you are talking nonsense. And second, it is not the procurator who sanctions the arrest of a party member but the secretary of the territorial committee. The secretary of the territorial com-

---

61. *u nas byl perevorot neskol'ko na druguiu storonu*—Trans.

mittee coordinates his work with the NKVD when deciding whom to arrest. If you are afraid of taking on the responsibility, we'll reassign the task to the procurator. If you want a party member to be arrested, don't you think you can have it done yourself?[62]

We must put an end to this matter, as it concerns some of the people you are unmasking.[63] You uncover something, you hand it over to the NKVD, so that you and, in particular, the NKVD, can work over [*dorabotat'*] this person thoroughly. Now what do you do? You have gone ahead and expelled the person in question and consider the matter closed, but I think that the matter is far from closed. We would like to find out how this person has ended up in the party, under what circumstances and what wrongs has this person committed; perhaps this person is not alone, perhaps there is a whole organization behind him. This matter is for the NKVD.

In practice, there are differences of opinion here. Either you send people to the NKVD about whom there are no doubts—you just simply need to have him arrested, to have him convicted—or else you send to the NKVD people who have nothing to do with the matter in question, and often you send all of them to the NKVD.

There is a main group of people whom you haven't looked into, as to how they got their hands on a party card; perhaps we are dealing here with a petty crook with careerist aims who has gotten his party card through theft. If that's so, why send this crook [to the NKVD]?

You [the party] should organize your work with the NKVD in such a way that full daily contact is established with it, so that you can unmask a certain person [party addresses the NKVD]: "Go ahead, work on him, he is of interest to you. He'll give you a lot." Then things will move swiftly forward. . . .

There is one other deficiency: You apprehend someone, a trickster, for instance. You then hand him over to the NKVD. The NKVD strives with might and main, works him over, and so on. There are certain comrades who have been saying: Send me the biggest swindler, and I'll clear up everything. (Laughter.) They want to show that they have found the man, have exposed him, have closed the case, or rather they want to deliver a report on this case. I think that this is wrong. First of all, we do not dispose of the kind of investigative apparat possessed by organs of the NKVD. And there is no need, no purpose to arrogating their work to ourselves. What is needed is a definite identity to these [NKVD] organs. Others will work, and you will then say: "There is no need for you. We have unmasked this person." There is no need for any of this. I am talking about the mutual relation between these organizations [the NKVD and the party].

And the heart of the matter lies in this, that you establish contact with the NKVD in a way that will make possible unified work, taking into consider-

62. Compare with contradictory Document 49.
63. Syntax in original is incoherent—Trans.

ation the fact that the NKVD is the most political organization—I mean, that it is the chief department of civilian security, this political organ, which has been put to the service of the party and put so not in vain; contact with it ought to be complete. By the way—I shall return to this later—why is it important for us to establish contact and to direct the work? Because it is of some interest for us, insofar as it concerns the results of this verification, to expose fully the means utilized by the enemy. [We ought] to teach the party organization to look for the methods employed by the enemy, to look for the channels by which the enemy infiltrates the party. We may theoretically say, Lenin has said this a thousand times, Stalin has said it a thousand times, we all know the basics—that is, that the one and only ruling party in our country is the dictatorship of the proletariat, ruling justly and enjoying a colossal success, and, naturally, it draws a lot of people to it. We have become bored by this commonplace, but we must find out how these people infiltrate [the party] and how they end up in it. We, who are held answerable for such things, must find out about them. And for this reason we must maintain contact with the NKVD, who may be able to clarify such matters, who can tell us where we need to apply more pressure; this is extremely important. . . .

This is the first question relative to the verification process which may be raised at this point. I don't think that we shall write any directives. Some comrades tell us that the NKVD provides no instructions as to its policy. And here too there will be no instructions. Here we shall have to do with flexible management. Now we are even receiving fewer complaints alleging that we [the party organizations and the NKVD] are not getting along.

The second question concerns pretrial measures [*mery presecheniia*]—how to practically resolve a matter connected with the verification process when a swindler, adventurist, or trickster is brought to light, what pretrial measures should apply. Here our procuracy has, to some extent, made a mess of things. At first, it was our intention to pass a special resolution of the CC as to what we should do, how we should act when exposing a swindler, an adventurist, a thief, and so on. Such a person must be judged in accordance with the appropriate article of the law: a spy is to be tried as a spy, a thief as a thief. For this there are appropriate articles of the law. But there is a certain category of people who are not to be tried in court—for example, Trotskyists, a political category of people, former SRs, former Mensheviks, followers of Zinoviev. I am naming here the category of our political opponents. There is no point in trying them. In this case, we need to hand them over to the Special Board of the NKVD, sentence them to 3–5 years, deport them—that is, that would be much more effective and prompt and just much better. These cases must be resolved without any trials. Just look at the situation in the Ukraine. They held trials and issued quite ludicrous things [sentences]. I've read many verdicts—

Gavrilenko: It was quite a thing to see the People's Court issuing the most idiotic decision.

Document 50 *continued*

Yezhov: They tried him for having concealed his kulak origins when joining the party and gave him 5 years.[64] What the devil do we need with such things? Think about it: the kulak needs to be deported; he is nothing but a swine, deport him! As for the political groups—try them through the [NKVD] special board.

A voice: Can we try someone if he had broken into the files at the territorial committee?

Yezhov: Of course, for stealing documents. Here you need to get in touch with the NKVD. We might even pronounce a special judgment in this matter. . . .

A few weeks later, M. F. Shkiriatov, a hard-line Party Control Commission functionary, wrote to Stalin about the case of one V. A. Gagarina. His description of the case shows the Bolshevik inclination to override legal procedures and is a classic statement of party voluntarism and expediency at the expense of legality. (See Document 79 for similar complaints about excessive "legality.") It also indicates, however, that some judicial officials were willing to follow the letter of the law rather than Shkiriatov's version of political expediency. Such documents show that the "moderate" legalistic documents upholding procuratorial sanction and process, while more and more observed in the breach, did sometimes have an effect.

Document 51

Memorandum from M. F. Shkiriatov to Stalin on "crude political errors" in the Gagarina case, 27 November 1935[65]

TOP SECRET
Central Committee of the VKP(b)
To Comrade I. V. STALIN
Concerning the crude political errors committed by the RSFSR Supreme Court during its review of the case against former princess V. A. Gagarina, a counterrevolutionary and terrorist, and her accomplices.

The procurator of the Soviet Union, Comrade Vyshinsky, has notified the Commission of Party Control [KPK] of the crude political error committed by the Supreme Court of the RSFSR in wrongly commuting the sentence of death by shooting meted out to V. A. Gagarina, a flagrant counterrevolutionary and

---

64. The reference here is unclear. Evidently, Yezhov was referring to a court case known in party circles at that time.
65. RTsKhIDNI, f. 17, op. 120, d. 171, ll. 62–67ob.

terrorist, to ten years of imprisonment. The KPK examined this case thoroughly. KPK member Comrade Genkin familiarized himself with all the documents and received oral and written explanations from two members of the special collegium [*spetsial'naia kollegiia*], Comrades Sannikov and Tseller, and from assistant procurator of the RSFSR, Comrade Burmistrov. In addition, he heard oral explanations from the chairman of the Supreme Court, Comrade Bulat, from USSR Supreme Court member Comrade Krumin, and from the recently appointed chairman of the special collegium of the Supreme Court of the RSFSR, Comrade Kronberg. . . .

This case boils down essentially to the fact that, during the year 1934, along with defendants Gaziev and Gozdarov, former White Guard officers, also employed by RaiZO, V. A. Gagarina systematically carried out counterrevolutionary and terroristic agitation. The counterrevolutionary activities of this group, as well as V. A. Gagarina's terroristic agitation, were confirmed during the course of the investigation.

Gagarina herself confessed to everything at the preliminary as well as at the court investigations. Cynically and flagrantly, she told of her counterrevolutionary activities and terroristic propaganda, declaring that, should an opportunity ever present itself, she would commit any terroristic act whatsoever.

In her last statement, she declared that "she did not intend to justify her actions in any way," and after sentence was passed, she did not submit an appeal to the Supreme Court.

All this attests to the fact that V. A. Gagarina is a sworn, irreconcilable enemy of Soviet power, capable of committing any crime whatsoever.

Nevertheless, the Special Collegium of the RSFSR Supreme Court, under the chairmanship of Comrade Sannikov and with the participation of commission members, Comrades Tseller and Shakhovskoy, did, on 27 September 1935, notwithstanding the protest of Procurator Vesyolkin, commute Gagarina's sentence of death by shooting to ten years of imprisonment. It is obvious to everyone that the above-named comrades have committed a crude political error.

One might have expected that this totally extraordinary blunting of Bolshevik vigilance on the part of the special collegium would have aroused alarm on the part of members of the Presidium of the Supreme Court of the RSFSR.

However, notwithstanding a second protest by the RSFSR procuracy, the Presidium of the Supreme Court of the RSFSR, under the chairmanship of Comrade Bulat, also committed, on 14 October of this year, a crude political error by sanctioning the decision of the special collegium. Comrade Bulat's approach to the question was bureaucratic and formal, showing scorn for the substance of the case. He did not even take the trouble to familiarize himself with the relevant documents prior to making his decision. Procurator Comrade Vesyolkin lodged a second protest, both orally and in writing, at the order of the procuracy.

The main reason given for the commutation of sentence from death by shooting to ten years' imprisonment was the argument that this case did not involve a fully constituted counterrevolutionary group. Therefore, Article 58 (Item 11), calling for the supreme penalty, could not be applied in this case.

Those responsible for this decision have perverted the substance of the matter with their formal and bureaucratic arguments. Was it not obvious to them that they were dealing here with a sworn enemy, to whom no mercy should be shown?

Do these people really need the fact of a perpetrated crime in order to convict such an obvious terrorist?! Besides, the facts themselves argue against these formalists from the Supreme Court of the RSFSR.

When one familiarizes oneself with this case, one is convinced that Gagarina, Gaziev, and Gozdarov did indeed form a terrorist-minded, counterrevolutionary group, and that this group had spread its activities widely among members of the kolkhozy who visited the RaiZO and elsewhere. It is incomprehensible that the Supreme Court cannot see through this counterrevolutionary group. . . .

The question arises: How is it possible that several responsible officials of the special collegium—namely, Sannikov and Tseller—could have committed such a grave political error in a matter that is so obvious? And how could Comrade Bulat, chairman of the Supreme Court of the RSFSR, have sanctioned such an incorrect political decision at the session of the Presidium of the Supreme Court, notwithstanding the protests of the procuracy? . . .

All of this makes necessary the verification [*proverka*] of all the activities of the Supreme Court of the RSFSR, in order to change its system of operation and in order to consolidate the cadres of the Supreme Court, in particular of its special collegium.

See the decision by the Party Control Commission appended herein.

Shkiriatov

STRICTLY SECRET
(from a special dossier)
To be returned within 24 hours
COMMISSION OF PARTY CONTROL [KPK] of the CC of the VKP(b)
BKPK-32/2-g. November . . . 1935
To: Comrade STALIN

Extract from Protocol #32, Item #2(d) of the KPK buro session of 27 November 1935

2. Concerning the crude political error committed by the Supreme Court of the RSFSR in the case of the counterrevolutionary and terrorist V. A. Gagarina.

1. Severe reprimands are to be issued to Comrades S. E. Sannikov, deputy chairman of the Special Collegium of the Supreme Court of the RSFSR and member of the VKP(b) since 1918, and to Comrade G. A. Tseller, member of the

special collegium and member of the VKP(b) since 1903, for the liberalism shown in the case of the terrorist V. A. Gagarina in knowingly handing out an incorrect sentence on purely formal grounds. In addition, stern reprimands with official warnings are to be issued to them, and they are to be removed from their posts and prohibited from working in investigative-judicial organs.

2. A reprimand is to be issued to Comrade Bulat, the chairman of the Supreme Court of the RSFSR, for permitting a situation to arise in the Special Collegium of the Supreme Court of the RSFSR that fails to ensure a proper investigation of the case, as well as for manifesting a crude, bureaucratic attitude to the Gagarina case—to wit, an unwillingness, notwithstanding the two protests that had been lodged by the procuracy regarding the sentence, to familiarize himself with the essentials of the case as shown in the documents.

3. Comrade Krylenko, people's commissar for justice of the RSFSR, is duty-bound to reinforce the leadership of the apparat of the Supreme Court of the RSFSR and to systematically monitor the work of the Special Collegium.

DEPUTY CHAIRMAN OF THE COMMISSION OF PARTY CONTROL
M. Shkiriatov

CHAPTER FIVE

Screening Cadres

One thing is clear beyond dispute: it seems to me that Trotskyists undoubtedly have a center somewhere in the USSR.—N. I. Yezhov, 1935

By the time you receive this letter, I shall no longer be among the living. Why have you slandered me? What have I done to you? That which I wrote to you I now—dying—confirm, namely, that it is true that I was never a scoundrel, that for 16 years I worked honestly for the party.—V. U. Aseev, 1935

ANOTHER PARTY MEMBERSHIP screening operation, or purge, was conducted in the middle of 1935, the verification (*proverka*) of party documents. Planned even before the Kirov assassination, this purge was in the tradition of party screenings since 1921 and was designed to rid the party of "ballast": corrupt bureaucrats, those who had hidden their social origins or political pasts, those with false membership documents. The order for the operation ("On Disorders in the Registration, Distribution, and Safekeeping of Party Cards and on Measures for Regulating This Affair")[1] had characterized the verification as a housekeeping operation to bring some order to the clerical registration of party membership documents. Although the announcement of the proverka did not specifically call for the expulsion of former oppositionists, it was inevitable that many of them would be targeted in this background check.[2]

1. Smolensk Archive file 499, ll. 308–9.
2. See J. Arch Getty, *Origins of the Great Purges: The Soviet Communist Party Reconsidered, 1933–1938*, chs. 2 and 3, for background on this and other purges.

According to a report by Yezhov, who was in charge of the screenings, as of December 1935, 9.1 percent of the party's members had been expelled in the proverka, and 8.7 percent of those expelled had been arrested; he gave a corresponding figure of 15,218 arrests out of 177,000 expulsions, or a little less than 1 percent of those passing through the verification. (Oddly enough, NKVD records showed that only 2 percent of those expelled had been arrested.)[3] The level of arrests varied considerably from region to region, and there is strong evidence that relations between party and police were not always smooth. The NKVD generated documents attesting to their close cooperation with party committees, but there is evidence that some local party leaders complained about police interference in the party's political turf.

Document 52

NKVD memo on assisting party organs in the verification of party documents, 5 December 1935[4]

INFORMATION
ON ASSISTING PARTY ORGANS IN THEIR WORK OF VERIFYING PARTY DOCUMENTS
From the very first days of the verification of party documents in the Ukraine, organs of the NKVD have actively joined the operation, concentrating the efforts of all operational departments on a rapid deployment of operational and investigative and agency work in cases connected with the verification of party documents.

Along with an operational strike against active counterrevolutionary elements—Trotskyists, nationalists, spies, terrorists—who had made their way deceitfully into the ranks of the Communist Party, our [NKVD] organs have shown and continue to show maximum assistance to party organizations in unmasking anti-Soviet, class-alien, criminal, and suspicious elements.

During the period of party verification we have reported to party organs compromising materials on 17,368 members and candidate members.

These new data on NKVD participation in the proverka revise the earlier conclusions in Getty, *Origins*, where it was argued on the basis of other archives that the police played little role in the operation.

3. RTsKhIDNI, f. 17, op. 120, d. 177, ll. 20–22. This number is almost certainly incomplete. A subsequent internal Central Committee memo of February 1937 inexplicably gave a figure of 263,885 proverka expulsions (RTsKhIDNI, f. 17, op. 120, d. 278, l. 2). It was not uncommon in this period for the same agencies to give wildly varying figures for party membership, expulsion, and arrest.

4. RTsKhIDNI, f. 17, op. 120, d. 184, ll. 63–66.

Document 52 *continued*

On the basis of these materials, 6,675 persons have been expelled from the party as of 1 December.

2,095 persons expelled from the party in connection with the party verification process have been arrested.

Head of the secret political section of the Administration of State Security of the NKVD of the Ukrainian SSR

KOZELSKY

5 December 1935

Document 53

Operational work on the Ivanovo NKVD in the verification of party documents[5]

[A report from the Ivanovo regional NKVD administration to NKVD headquarters in Moscow]

COPY (23 December 1935—for Stalin)

TOP SECRET

TO: Comrade MOLCHANOV,

Head, secret political section of the Chief Administration of State Security (GUGB)

SPECIAL REPORT

Preliminary results of the operational work of the NKVD in the Ivanovo Industrial Region in connection with the verification of party documents

According to data gathered as of 1 December 1935 from 60 districts during the verification of party documents, various compromising materials concerning 3,580 persons were submitted to party organs by the Ivanovo Industrial Region [IPO] NKVD organs.

Out of this number 1,184 persons were expelled from the party.

9 counterrevolutionary groups were brought to light by the NKVD. Altogether 261 persons were arrested.

The arrested included the following:

Trotskyists, followers of Zinoviev, and others   56 persons
Under suspicion for espionage and sabotage   5
Provocateurs   5
Members of White gangs, armies, uprisings   18
Tricksters and persons deceitfully infiltrating the party   48
Persons who have concealed their social origin   95
Brought to trial without arrest   65
Total sentenced (to a variety of terms)   90

5. RTsKhIDNI, f. 17, op. 120, d. 184, ll. 60–65.

Table 1. Party Expulsions and Police Arrests, 1935

Party organization	A: NKVD files sent to party	B: Number and % of col. A suspects expelled by party organizations	C: Number and % of col. B suspects arrested by NKVD	D: % of col. A suspects ultimately arrested
Ukraine	17,368	6,675 (38%)	2,095 (31%)	12%
Ivanovo	3,580	1,184 (33%)	261 (22%)	7%
Western	3,233	1,337 (30%)	312 (23%)	10%

Sources: RTsKhIDNI, f. 17, op. 120, d. 184, ll. 63–66; f. 17, op. 120, d. 183, ll. 60–65, 92.

Such reports were meant to show unanimity to the middle party leaders. But the hidden transcript was different. Yezhov noted that cooperation between party and police organizations was not very good (see Document 50). Party organizations had been reluctant to concede a political monitoring role to the NKVD, preferring instead the former system in which the NKVD investigated state crimes not involving members of the party and left political offenses to the party organs. The information in Table 1 shows, in fact, that party and police organizations worked badly together and frequently disagreed on who was "the enemy." Yezhov gave the 1935 operation a combative stamp by calling for verifiers in the party organizations to concentrate on expelling ideological enemies of all kinds. His remarks to a closed meeting of party personnel officials emphasized the hunt for enemies.

Document 54

From N. I. Yezhov's report to a conference of regional party secretaries, 25 September 1935[6]

Yezhov: . . . Please permit me, comrades, at this time, to briefly dwell on certain matters which have become very important today. The first matter concerns the expulsion of Trotskyists.

One thing is clear beyond dispute: it seems to me that Trotskyists undoubtedly have a center somewhere in the USSR. It is impossible for a Trotskyist center from abroad, located relatively far from the USSR and poorly informed about our conditions—it is impossible, I say, for it to direct with such detail

6. RTsKhIDNI, f. 17, op. 120, d. 179, ll. 34–77.

those Trotskyist organizations which have unfortunately held out in our country and which, we believed, had been crushed.

Everywhere the same methods are practiced by Trotskyists who have held out in our party. Trotskyists try at all costs to remain in the party. They strive by every device to infiltrate the party. Their first device is to remain at all costs in the party, to give voice everywhere to the general line, to speak out everywhere in its favor while in fact carrying on their subversive work. But nevertheless, it sometimes happens that a Trotskyist slips up and is caught, is expelled from the party, in which case he takes all measures to run off with his party card. He always has in reserve a registration card, approaches another organization and is registered. Such people are expelled 3 or 4 or even 5 times each. They move from one organization to another—we have quite a few people like that. Trotskyists try at all costs to keep their party card. . . .

Their second device is not to carry out their work in the party. They do not, as a rule, carry on party work at all. They focus their attention on working among nonparty people. . . .

Above all, Trotskyists strive to infuse the nonparty people with the spirit of Trotskyism. . . .

Foreign intelligence officers, saboteurs, knew that there is no better cover for their espionage and subversive operations than a party card, and they relied on that fact. For this reason, it is necessary to hide behind a party card at whatever cost. And they utilized every means of deception in order to obtain a party card for a spy or for a saboteur. We can assert firmly that Poles, Finns, Czechs, and Germans have been openly gambling on this. . . .

For example, the Italian consul in Odessa has a party card, just in case, and whenever someone needs it, he gives it to him. Take the case of the Ukrainians. You said that they unmasked the people at the Marti factory. I must tell you that one of them obtained a party card from the Italian consul. Now it has all been cleared up and they say that he has more blank forms in reserve. I think that not only the Italian consul has a party card, just in case. Others do, too. And there are far more of these cases. They send people here and tell them: "Go and get yourself a party card."

Our party activists [*aktiv*] do not know the most basic principles of Marxism-Leninism. We encountered this in every one of our organizations. For them, you know, workers represent an inaccessible category. Look here, this veneration for the worker[7] is completely un-Bolshevik and un-Marxist. This veneration for the party member—if he is a member of the party, if he has a party card—this means that he is inviolable in his person, and so on. We must put a stop to all this, comrades.

---

7. *preklonenie*, literally, "worship" or "admiration"; *rabochii*, "factory worker"—Trans.

Table 2. Reasons for Expulsion, 1935–36 (% of all expelled)

	Yezhov 1935 report	Malenkov 1937 memo*
Spies	1.0	0.9
Trotskyists/Zinovievists	2.9	5.5
"Swindlers"	7.9	8.0
Former Whites, kulaks, etc.	19.1	27.5
Moral corruption		20.6
Incorrect documents		15.6
"Other"		17.7
Unexplained	69.1	4.2

Sources: RTsKhIDNI, f. 17, op. 20, d. 177, ll. 20–22; f. 17, op. 120, d. 278, l. 2.
*Includes persons expelled in 1936 after the completion of the *chistki*.

Despite Yezhov's concentration on Trotskyists and other enemies, the results of the verification, like previous party screenings,
struck hardest at rank-and-file party members with irregularities in
their documents, many of whom were charged with generally non-
ideological offenses having to do with malfeasance or "alien" class
background. Two reports, one from Yezhov's 1935 report and
another from an internal Central Committee memo written by
G. M. Malenkov, are summarized in Table 2 and show the categories
expelled.

Document 55

Ivanovo NKVD report on Trotskyists, 29 December 1935[8]

[A report from the Ivanovo regional NKVD administration to NKVD headquarters in Moscow]
Cases brought against SHANTYREVA, KOPOSOVA, VINOGRADOV, PUKAT,
and others (City of Kostroma)
. . . 1. In the month of November of this year, a Trotskyist terroristic group
was liquidated in the city of Kostroma. . . .
PUKAT, Karl. Born in 1898, former member of the VKP(b), Latvian, citizen
of the USSR, stevedore at a sawmill depot. Together with SHANTYREVA, he
was a member in 1927 of a Trotskyist group in Kostroma, had connections in
Moscow, traveled to the capital, [from which] he would bring illegal Trotskyist literature. . . .
Adhering to his Trotskyist convictions, PUKAT attempted to leave the So-

8. RTsKhIDNI, f. 17, op. 120, d. 184, ll. 64–65.

viet Union with the assistance of the Latvian embassy in Moscow in order to continue his struggle against the party under the direct leadership of Trotsky.

According to his own testimony, PUKAT was recruited in 1930 by the secretary of the Latvian embassy, who entrusted him on one of his visits to the embassy with gathering material of an espionage character concerning enterprises in the city of Kostroma. . . .

". . . I discussed my departure for Latvia with the secretary of the Latvian mission, who, in the course of my conversation, inquired what kind of industry was to be found in Kostroma. After my explanation, he proposed that I prove my devotion to Latvia and earn my entry permit by gathering material of an espionage character. I agreed to this and, upon returning to Kostroma, I recruited my sister Anna PUKAT, who joined me in my espionage activities at the Banner of Labor [*Znamia Truda*] factory, where she was working. I also recruited Emma MASHEN, who was working at the Lenta [machine-gun ribbon] factory as an industrial quality inspector, as well as MAROV, a metal worker at the Rabochy metallist factory. I gave information to the Latvian mission concerning: the quantity of machine gun ribbons produced by the Lenta factory, concerning the [energy] capacity of the boilers at the Znamia Truda factory, and the blueprint of the Rabochy metallist factory, which I stole from DADZE, the head of construction.

The information which I obtained was carried by my mother Anna Yanovna PUKAT to the Latvian mission. On the other hand, I myself carried the blueprint of the Rabochy metallist factory [to the Latvian mission] in May of 1935."

The investigation is still in progress.

Document 56

Report of Chief Administration of NKVD on "most important cases uncovered in the verification of party documents," 5 November 1935[9]

TRICKSTERS

1. N. T. GOSHA was arrested by the Ukrainian NKVD. He had escaped from a concentration camp and had tried to pass himself off as a member of the VKP(b). GOSHA was arrested in Berdichev while attempting to obtain money by means of a spurious money order. During the search, the following objects were found on his person: a party card and a party registration card in his name, the seal of the Kiev Regional Committee of the Ukrainian Communist Party (Bolshevik), all sorts of certificates from various institutions, as well as spurious postal money orders for the obtaining of significant sums of money. An investigation has established that he joined the party in 1930 while working in a cooperative society in Zhitomir as an unskilled laborer. In 1932, while

9. RTsKhIDNI, f. 17, op. 120, d. 181, ll. 153–55.

working near Kiev as chairman of the village soviet of Dvortsy of the Troyanovsky district, GOSHA was sentenced to 5 years of imprisonment in the Dmitrov labor camp for a whole series of acts of malfeasance. It was then that his party card was taken away from him. In May 1934, having stolen 200 rubles from the camp commissary, GOSHA escaped from the labor camp and hid for some time. Arriving in Zhitomir, he met with his relative, former party member KRAVETS, secretary of the workers' committee of the Zhitomir motor tractor station. The latter, having in his possession blank forms of party registration cards and a rubber stamp of the Troyanovsky District Committee, fabricated for GOSHA a party registration card. With this card in hand (without a party card) he showed up in June 1934 at the Berdichev City Party Committee, which put him at the disposal of the chairman of the city soviet, which, on that very day, ordered him to go to a village by the name of Bolshie Gadomtsy to assume the post of chairman of the village soviet.

Two weeks later, GOSHA was summoned to the Berdichev City Party Committee to be registered. He presented his spurious registration card. Deputy Secretary of the City Party Committee Zubareva returned it to him in view of the fact that it lacked the stamp indicating a purge and suggested, without drawing any conclusions about the identity of GOSHA, that he officially register his card with the Troyanovsky District Committee. No one at the Berdichev City Party Committee asked to see his party card. The next day, GOSHA escaped from Berdichev to Cherniakhovsky district, showed up at the district committee, presented his forged registration card to Drachinsky, the secretary of the district committee, and to Klikht, the office manager. At Drachinsky's suggestion, Klimenko, the chairman of the district executive committee, sent GOSHA to the village Zabrode to serve as chairman of the village soviet. At the Cherniakhovsky District Committee, as at the Berdichev Party District Committee, no one asked GOSHA for his party card. Two months later GOSHA reported "the loss" of his party card. Registering the loss of his party card, in accordance with Drachinsky's instructions, by putting a notice in the press, GOSHA received a party card from the Cherniakhovsky District Committee in 1934. It is characteristic that he was not even summoned to the district committee buro which was reviewing his application. In July of that year, GOSHA was removed from his post for perversion of the party line and given over to trial. In this connection, he escaped from Cherniakhovsky district, once again traveled to Zhitomir and, with the assistance of KRAVETS, made for himself a registration card for the second time and arranged for himself an official trip in the name of the Department of Cadres of the Kiev Regional Committee to the Kalinovka District Committee to be placed at their disposal. Then GOSHA and KRAVETS made three counterfeit postal money orders. With the help of a woman telegraph operator working for them, they intended to use the money orders to get their hands on up to 5,000 rubles. The investigation is still going on. KRAVETS is being sought.

Local Cadres and Family Circles

The conduct of the proverka shows some interesting aspects of the relationship between central and regional party organizations. Since the late 1920s, regional party leaders had become powerful political actors on a par with feudal barons. They controlled the police, courts, trade unions, agriculture, and industry in their territories. Responsible to Moscow for fulfillment of plans, they ran hierarchical organizations based on patronage and personal power. Stalin had referred to them in 1934 as "appanage princes," who pigeonholed Moscow's orders rather than fulfilling them, did their best to conceal the real situation from Moscow, and "thought [Moscow's] decisions were written for fools, and not for them."[10] Formally, they represented central authority in the regions, but in reality they ran powerful political machines that dominated economic, political, and social life in their territories.

The instructions locals received had been vague. On the one hand, the document instigating the verification made it out to be a clerical rectification of party files and membership cards, fully consistent with a mass screening of the rank and file (those most likely to have defective or dubious cards). On the other, Yezhov had characterized it as an operation to uncover oppositionist elements and Trotskyists-Zinovievists.

Because membership in the Trotskyist or Zinovievist organizations implied party membership dating back into the 1920s, "genuine" ex-oppositionists were likely to have worked their way up from the rank and file into leadership positions in local political machines. Yezhov's call, therefore, was implicitly a demand for local members of the nomenklatura to purge their own "families," an idea that they must have disliked. The tendency of local elites to deflect the purge downward to the rank and file was almost certainly a response to the need to find enemies somewhere without risking the loss of experienced members of their own machines, even if they had dubious backgrounds. Purge discourse was flexible.

---

10. See Stalin's speech on "fulfillment of decisions" at the Seventeenth Party Congress in early 1934: *XVII s"ezd Vsesoiuznoi Kommunisticheskoi Partii(b). 26 ianvaria–10 fevralia 1934g.: Stenograficheskii otchet*. Moscow, 1934, 23–35.

The Central Committee was not satisfied with this result. The frequent interventions from Moscow to stop local verifications and restart them, along with subsequent criticism of local administration (see Document 71), are evidence of Moscow's displeasure. Documents also show that central party officials gathered information on how many members of local political machines had been identified and expelled.[11] In response, local machines tried to show that they had screened their own people. Here we see further evidence of a rift inside the nomenklatura elite, in this case between Moscow-based party leaders and regional party officials. From Yezhov's point of view, by entrusting the purge to party organizations themselves (rather than to Control Commissions or special purge committees, as had previously been the practice), he was giving them the chance to put their own houses in order.[12] Instead, they had protected their own and displayed their "vigilance" by expelling large numbers of helpless party members outside the local nomenklaturas.

Regional party committees had begun the proverka verification in May 1935. The following month, however, many of them were brought up short by the Central Committee, which criticized them for paying only cursory attention to the process and for hastily expelling large numbers of ordinary rank-and-file members (and few leading comrades) from their own machines (see Document 71).[13] Following accepted party ritual, the local and regional committees quickly admitted that the Central Committee was right, confessed their mistakes, and tried to demonstrate their vigilance even against a few members of their own machines. Nevertheless, the overwhelming majority of those expelled were rank-and-file members with suspicious biographies ("White Guards and kulaks"). Again we have examples from the Azov–Black Sea territory:

11. For example, see RTsKhIDNI, f. 17, op. 71, d. 34, ll. 114–15.

12. He frequently noted, in 1935 but not later, that allowing party committees to purge themselves was a good idea. See RTsKhIDNI, f. 17, op. 120, d. 77, ll. 4 ff.

13. The most publicized case was the Central Committee's rebuke of the Saratov party organization. See RTsKhIDNI, f. 17, op. 114, d. 585, ll. 1–2, for the Orgburo meeting on Saratov. The resulting press campaign is in *Pravda,* 12 July 1935, *Partiinoe stroitel'stvo,* no. 13, July 1935, 44–45, and A. A. Zhdanov, *Uroki politicheskikh oshibok Saratovskogo kraikoma,* Moscow, 1935. The subject would come up again the following year.

Document 57

Orgburo protocol, "On progress in the verification of party documents in the Azov–Black Sea territory"[14]

[From Protocol #34 of the Orgburo CC VKP(b) meeting of 31 July 1935]

On progress in the verification of party documents in the Azov–Black Sea territory

(Comrades Yezhov, Malenkov, Tsekher)

1. It is to be acknowledged that the Azov–Black Sea Territorial Committee has until recently directed the verification of party documents in a thoroughly unsatisfactory manner, committing numerous crude mistakes in their implementation of the closed letter of the CC of the VKP(b) of 13 May of this year: the implementation dates specified for each district conflict with the dates specified in the CC letter; many of the first secretaries of the district committees have dodged the verification process altogether. The buro of the territorial committee has, by its decision of 15 July, failed to expose the mistakes committed by the territorial committee and by the district committees in their handling of the verification of party documents.

2. It should be noted that the Azov–Black Sea Territorial Committee, after its representative was called to account by the CC, took measures to rectify the mistakes committed by it and revoked its incorrect decisions.

The decree by the Azov–Black Sea Territorial Committee of 29 July concerning progress in the verification of party documents and concerning shortcomings in the directing of the work of verifying party documents by the territorial committee and the district committees is hereby confirmed.

3. The request by the Azov–Black Sea Territorial Committee for extension of the deadline for verifying party documents in the Azov–Black Sea territory till 1 September 1935 is hereby granted.

Document 58

Plenum of Azov–Black Sea Territorial Party Committee, "On the verification of party documents"[15]

SECRET

PROTOCOL #5

PROTOCOL OF THE PLENUM SESSION OF THE AZOV–BLACK SEA TERRITORIAL COMMITTEE OF THE VKP(b) of 15–18 December 1935

. . . Re: The verification of party documents of party members

2220

14. RTsKhIDNI, f. 17, op. 114, d. 590, l. 2.
15. RTsKhIDNI, f. 17, op. 21, d. 2194, ll. 2, 20b.

Document 58 *continued*

Decree:

1. The verification of party documents constitutes one of the most important stages in the life of the party in the past few years. The verification has played an especially important role in cleansing the ranks of the party of enemies who have deceitfully infiltrated the party, in putting the party's management in good order, and in a firm observance of the rules of the party. The verification has sharpened Bolshevik vigilance and raised the unity and implacability of the party to a higher level.

The CC letter concerning the murder of Comrade Kirov was a most important party document in mobilizing Bolshevik vigilance:

"We must put an end to the opportunistic complacency that issues from a mistaken assumption that, as our strength increases, the enemy grows more tame and harmless.

"Such an assumption is fundamentally wrong. It is a throwback to the rightist deviation, which had tried to assure one and all that our enemies will crawl quietly into socialism, that in the end they will become true socialists. It is not for Bolsheviks to rest on their laurels with their mouths wide open. It is not complacency that we need but vigilance, a genuine revolutionary, Bolshevik vigilance."

The verification of party documents has confirmed that this directive of the CC pertains in every way to the Azov–Black Sea Party organization.

Moreover, the conditions in which the Azov–Black Sea Party organization grew and operated in the past (White Guard Cossack counterrevolution, kulak sabotage in the kolkhozy) demanded special vigilance and greater efforts in the consolidation and training of the party rank and file.

The [Azov–Black Sea] Territorial Committee committed a crude political error in underestimating the significance of the verification of party documents. The territorial committee's haste, its setting of speeded-up time periods for the verification as against the periods called for by the CC has, in the first period of verification, reduced the verification process to a simple, formal check of party documents. . . .

It is to be noted that during the verification process 5,131 party members (8 percent of all party members) have been expelled:

1. Enemies who infiltrated the party apparat   35 persons
2. Spies and those suspected of espionage   50
3. Trotskyists and followers of Zinoviev   110
4. White Guard veterans and kulaks   1,333
5. Tricksters and swindlers   530

Document 59

From a speech by Sheboldaev, first secretary of the Azov–Black Sea Territorial Committee, at the plenum of the territorial committee, 17 December 1935[16]

Sheboldaev: . . . This has already been said by others, but I want to repeat it: We have to complete our thoroughgoing verification of all persons who are in any way whatsoever under suspicion by the party committee, by the basic party organization. Each and every suspicious person must be verified again and again. It was also correctly stated here that those who had recommended swindlers and enemies, those who protected and supported swindlers, also had to be verified. In one of the buro sessions, we had ordered the NKVD to verify all those who had recommended those who had been expelled from the party. Let's hope that only a few swindlers will turn up among them, but each of them must be verified. . . .

The fact that we had to a significant extent violated [party] rules, had removed, one beam at a time, the fence which had protected our party from every kind of alien element, the fact that we had impaired our organizational defense—this must be rectified immediately and in its entirety. We are dealing here with Bolshevik-Leninist-Stalinist principles pertaining to the building of our party, principles which our party had forged during its years of struggle for Bolshevism. The rules must become the foundation, the immutable law of our work pertaining to admission into the party.

Moscow party leaders were concerned that the mass expulsions could create embittered enemies among ex-party members.[17] By the end of 1935 Moscow was investigating the numbers of expelled and finding that some party organizations had as many former members as current members.[18] Moscow party officials not only kept an eye on those expelled[19] but checked into their moods as well. Sometimes these ex-members were characterized as enemies. On other occasions, Yezhov and others explicitly noted that most ex-members were not (see Document 71 [A]).

16. RTsKhIDNI, f. 17, op. 21, d. 2195, l. 790b.
17. See Yezhov's and Stalin's remarks to the June 1936 plenum of the Central Committee. RTsKhIDNI, f. 17, op. 2, d. 572, ll. 67–75.
18. RTsKhIDNI, f. 17, op. 120, d. 278, l. 7.
19. Khlevniuk has written that eventually more than 200,000 expelled party members were placed under NKVD surveillance. Oleg V. Khlevniuk, *1937: Stalin, NKVD i sovetskoe obshchestvo*, Moscow, 1992, 57. It is difficult to imagine how this was possible.

Document 60

Azov–Black Sea NKVD report on attitudes of persons expelled from the party[20]

TOP SECRET
21 November 1935
To: Comrade Molchanov,
Head, Secret Political Section of the Chief Administration of State Security (GUGB)
SPECIAL REPORT
Concerning the attitudes of persons expelled from the party in connection with the verification of party documents (in the Azov–Black Sea territory)
As of 21 November 1935
The available facts concerning the attitudes and conduct of persons expelled from the VKP(b), in connection with the verification of party documents, indicate that a significant number of persons expelled are beginning to manifest counterrevolutionary activity, committing counterrevolutionary attacks against leading party officials and threatening revenge for being unmasked and expelled from the party.

Such attitudes are expressed mainly by those who have been expelled for concealing their service with the Whites and for active counterrevolutionary actions in the past.

M. ZERNYSHKO, a metalworker working in the "OGPU" mine, expelled from the party for concealing his service with the Whites and retreating with them abroad, spread provocative, counterrevolutionary rumors on 15 November in a conversation with certain workers to the effect that "the party had reached a dead end and was conducting a systematic purge in order to pull the wool over the workers' eyes."

(ZERNYSHKO has been arrested.) . . .

Trotskyists and counterrevolutionary elements expelled from the party have openly come out after their expulsion with slanderous, counterrevolutionary statements concerning the party leadership.

LUKASHEV, a student at a professional school in the city of Shakhty. Having been expelled from the party for being a Trotskyist, he made the following statement at one of his classes:

"It was easier for Communists to work in pre-Revolutionary times than now under the Soviets."

(LUKASHEV has been arrested.) . . .

[Party member Vasiliev said:] "It's not enough to be a Communist. You have to have connections with people in power. That's how you can keep your party card. Without connections, you'll end up doing all the dirty work like an old, overworked mare."

20. RTsKhIDNI, f. 17, op. 120, d. 181, ll. 102–5.

Document 60 *continued*

(VASILIEV has been arrested.) . . .

Certain persons expelled from the party, disagreeing with the decisions of the local party organizations, attribute their expulsion to an "indiscriminate" and "unsympathetic" attitude to them on the part of party district city committees.

ROZENSHILD, a former member of the gentry in the city of Krasnodar, director of the Department of Dialectical Materialism in the Medical Institute, expelled from the party, said: "The city committee is filled with semiliterate people who do not know the first thing about questions of philosophy. I'll get reinstated in the party."

SERGEEV, a shift master at the Pervoimaisky cement factory in Novorossiisk, expelled from the party for his religious convictions and for concealing his son's service with the Whites, said in reference to Comrade Bazhayan, secretary of the City Committee: "He has no feelings, either hot or cold. He expels right and left. This is called a sympathetic attitude to party cadres. . . ."

CERTIFIED:

Operational Commissioner #12. Department of SPO of the CHIEF ADMINISTRATION OF STATE SECURITY (GUGB)

[signature:] Uemova

1935: Forms of Protest

In the months following the Kirov assassination and the party screenings, protest had become dangerous indeed. Anything resembling criticism of the regime was quickly branded "anti-Soviet agitation" or worse. Nevertheless, the secret police continued to uncover various dissident groups. One such "cell" was a group of students whose protest was against poor living standards, labor conditions, and the Stakhanov movement, which sought to speed up labor productivity.[21] In particular, their pamphlet's reference to the privations of collectivization was bound to attract the attention of nomenklatura members afraid of the "new situation," and it found its way into Central Committee files. Like the Riutin Platform, this was an alternative narrative that challenged the official one. To the fearful Stalinist elite, jealous of their monopoly on

---

21. On the Stakhanov movement, see Lewis Siegelbaum, *Stakhanovism and the Politics of Productivity in the USSR, 1935–1941*, New York, 1988.

ideology, it apparently made no difference that the challenge came from a few students. Any alternative to the master narrative, especially in the form of a written text, was a threat.

Document 61

NKVD report, anti-Stakhanovist leaflet, 29 November 1935[22]

Information supplied by the NKVD directorate of the Donetsk region concerning the discovery and unmasking of the authors of the counterrevolutionary, anti-Stakhanovist leaflets in the Rubezhansky district.

A)

On the 29th of November of this year, counterrevolutionary, anti-Stakhanovist leaflets were discovered on the premises of the Rubezhansky Institute of Chemical Technology and in the dormitory of the students of the above-mentioned institute. Moreover, one copy of the leaflet was found hanging on the wall newspaper in the institute, and a second one was found on the walls of the washroom of the dormitory. (See counterrevolutionary leaflets attached.)

An investigation conducted for the purpose of revealing the authors of the counterrevolutionary leaflet established that the author of the counterrevolutionary leaflet was a first-year student at said institute by the name of Anatoly Mikhailovich Butov.

At the same time, it has been established that Butov, holding counterrevolutionary views, organized around himself a group of students who held meetings and who, at these meetings, condemned the policy of the party and of Soviet power, saying that the party is leading the country to ruin, that the party is not following Lenin's path, that in the Soviet Union socialism is being built on the deprivations and privations [lisheniia] of the workers, that the Stakhanovist movement is a form of exploitation of the working class, etc.

On the basis of the above, we have arrested the following:

1. Butov, Anatoly Mikhailovich, son of an engineer, worked as a miner in the Gorlovsky and Yenakievsky districts prior to enrolling in the institute, a former Komsomol member.

2. Yurnin, Dmitry Semyonovich, son of a worker, first-year student, formerly worked at a factory in Yenakievo.

3. Kovshov, Leonid Nikitovich, son of an engineer. His father works at Rykovka mines 5/6 in the Stalin district. Leonid also worked there prior to enrolling in the institute.

4. Filatov, Ivan, first-year student, former party member, earlier worked at Sherbinovka mines in the Gorlovsky district.

22. RTsKhIDNI, f. 17, op. 120, d. 272, ll. 10–16.

Document 61 *continued*

5. Aliablev, Arkady Matveevich, born in 1914, worked earlier in Tambov, at the "Red Militant" factory, was formerly expelled from the Saratov Institute for anti-Soviet activities and for his attempt to poison the chief of the party organization.

6. Kikalov, Pyotr Timofeevich, son of a worker (stevedore), at the Nezhino station, has never worked in production.

7. Shumakov, Vasily, son of a kolkhoz member, former Komsomol member, prior to entering the institute worked on a kolkhoz.

8. Pleshakov, Vasily, social position not ascertained, former Komsomol member, first-year student, never worked anywhere before.

. . . We are continuing the investigation for the purpose of revealing the organized, counterrevolutionary activities on the part of the accused.

Supplement: Counterrevolutionary leaflets

Zagorsky,

acting head of the NKVD Directorate for the Donetsk region

B)

[Pamphlet, NKVD transcription]

YOU CAN'T BUILD SOCIALISM ON THE BONES OF THE PROLETARIAT

THE STAKHANOVIST MOVEMENT

What does it mean to set a record? It means to strain your physical organism to the maximum. This is characteristic of the Stakhanovist movement. Why argue about it? Why try to refute it? Students, you have all recently worked in production. You are all familiar with the "Zeal for Production" [*Proizvodstvennyi Entuziazm*]. The proletariat, trying to make ends meet, strives to keep its wages from lagging behind the galloping prices on [consumer] goods. Not sparing itself, it breaks records so as to earn more money. And imagine how cleverly this [Stakhanovist policy] has been invented. For every ton of coal that you mine in excess of the set quota, the policy of sliding-scale payment [*progressivka*] counts as double or triple. All sorts of prizes have been invented. It is true that no fines are levied, but the progressivka works exceeding well either on a plus or minus basis. If you don't fulfill the program and maintain your quota, they deduct [a certain amount] from your wages.

It is foolish to think that the Stakhanovist method raises your earnings. For the most part, this is not so. The earnings of the overwhelming majority of the engineering-technical personnel of the Donbas coal mines are below average. The newspapers are deceiving you: The Stakhanovist earnings concern isolated individuals [only].

All right, go on working! Your life may be bad, your grandchildren's lives may be bad, but at least your great-grandchildren will live a little better!

The Central Committee and Stalin are striving to build socialism for future generations at the cost of privations today.

Wretched are those who build socialism on their backs and blessed are those only who shall live in a socialist society.

FIGHT FOR A RAISE IN YOUR STIPEND!

We receive a stipend of 93 rubles [each]. If you wonder whether it is possible to live on that, the answer is: NO. Our board alone costs significantly more than that. First course—25 kop.; second course—95 kop.; bread—30 kop.; for a total of one ruble, 50 kop.; the total per month = $4.50 \times 30 = 135$ rubles. You can't survive on that. When, oh when, will our "wisest," "most brilliant," "cherished" leaders understand this truism?!

STUDENTS, FIGHT FOR REAL IMPROVEMENT IN YOUR LIFE!

Use all means possible to see to it that [our nation's] policy brings about real improvement in the life of the workers!

Do not permit socialism to be built on the bones of the proletariat!

BOLSHEVIK REALISM

Whoever said that reality [*real'nye obrazy*] alone is reflected in the literature of the Soviet Union was profoundly mistaken. Literary themes are dictated by the Central Committee of the party headed by Stalin. The CC of the party harshly punishes those who try to reflect the real situation in the country.

Is it not a fact that in 1932 each and every one of you who is reading these lines today saw people dying on the streets? The streets were strewn with people bloated from hunger and frothing at the mouth, with people in their death throes.

Is it not a fact that in 1932 entire villages died off? Were these horrors, which make our hair stand on end, depicted in our literature? No. Such a subject was placed under lock and key by the CC of the party.

Let's recall the first stages of collectivization. Recall the articles entitled "Dizzy with Success." It was around 1930 when there was an "error" in the implementation of the policy of collectivization. They were overzealous, so to speak. Peasants belonging to poorer strata came under the category of kulaks. Many, though innocent, were deported or simply executed. The peasants, seeing their bread taken from them, were forced to eat oil cakes or bread with nettles.

Where in Soviet literature will you find a reflection of these glaring facts? Is this realism?

Now we're all suffering from malnutrition: from stomach disorders, from universal anemia, from nervous disorders.

One question remains: Why are you writers camouflaging yourselves with "Bolshevik realism"? After all, you are artists! Why sell yourselves? You should reflect reality strictly and realistically!

THE MATERIAL WELFARE OF THE WORKING CLASS

We often read in the Soviet press that during the past 5–6 years there has been a significant improvement in the material welfare of the working masses. They describe it with great enthusiasm, they call Stalin "the wisest," "the most beloved," "a man of genius," "our cherished [leader]," and so on.

Document 61 *continued*

But is it true? Have the economic conditions of the working class improved? Is this so? Judge for yourselves from the information below:

I shall mention the rising prices of goods produced in the Soviet Union, and then I shall also indicate the rise in earnings of the past several years.

PRICES

Prices in 1930:

A kilogram of white bread—6 kop.

A kilogram of sugar—60 kop.

A pair of shoes—25–30 rub.

A winter coat—60–70 rub.

Prices in 1935:

Bread—1.50 rub.—an increase of 2,500%

Sugar—4.60 rub.—an increase of 800%

Shoes—100–120 rub.—an increase of 400%

A [winter] coat—250–300 rub.—an increase of 400%

WAGES

Wages or salary in 1930:

A coal hewer—100–120 rub.

Mining engineer—200–250 rub.

Unskilled labor—35–40 rub.

Wages or salary in 1935:

A coal hewer—300–350 rub.

Mining engineer—600–650 rub.

Unskilled labor—110–20 rub.

Average increase in wages or salary—300%

STUDENTS!

You represent the cultural stratum of society. You are the leaders of society. You are a politically astute group. You will read these writings critically. You will weigh their truthfulness and you will respond by analyzing the situation around you in an appropriate manner. You ought to integrate this analysis, and this analysis and synthesis ought to be reflected in your press.

Make note of all that is negative and write [about it]. Only in this way will Stalin and the "big shots" from the CC pay attention to the proletariat.

Eighteen years of privations ought to be compensated for with a new policy directed toward a real improvement in the material welfare of the working masses.

TAKE HEED! THE TIME HAS COME FOR ALL STUDENTS TO FIGHT INDIVIDUALLY AND COLLECTIVELY FOR A BETTER LIFE!

Certified by Botnarev, commissioner of the Investigative-Records Department (SPO).

1935: The Human Element

The membership screenings not only embittered those expelled. For some committed Communists, the loss of party membership meant not only a loss of privilege and elite status but a crushing psychological blow from which they could not recover. On many fronts at the end of 1935, the number of personal tragedies was increasing.

Document 62

Leningrad NKVD report on suicide of Ye. A. Zaretsky [end of 1935][23]

TOP SECRET

To: Comrade Molchanov,

Head, Secret Political Section of the Chief Administration of State Security (GUGB)

SPECIAL REPORT

CONCERNING THE SUICIDE OF YE. A. ZARETSKY, MEMBER OF THE VKP(b)

On 20 December 1935 Yevsey Abramovich ZARETSKY, a member of the VKP(b), threw himself out of the window of apartment complex #56 (Kirovsky Prospekt).

Investigation has established that until 1931 YE. A. ZARETSKY had lived in the city of Minsk. In the same year, he was taken off party registration rolls in view of his departure for Moscow, where he was to take up permanent residence. However, skipping Moscow altogether, he went instead to Leningrad, showed up at the Smolny District Party Committee (RPK), was registered on the party rolls and then sent to work in the House of Party Education [*Dom Partucheby*] as a bookkeeper (at which post ZARETSKY was working right up until his suicide).

In his letter addressed to Comrade Kasimov, secretary of the Smolny RPK, and discovered in his apartment after his suicide, ZARETSKY speaks of crimes which he had concealed from the party during the verification of party documents.

On the whole, the crimes which ZARETSKY refers to in the above letter mention:

a) Having deceitfully registered himself on the party rolls at the Smolny District Party Committee (RPK) (by substituting the word Leningrad for the word Moscow on his personal registration card [*lichnaia kartochka*] and being registered only then), and

23. RTsKhIDNI, f. 17, op. 120, d. 182, ll. 93–94.

Document 62 *continued*

b) For having passed himself off as a veteran Komsomol worker, although he most definitely was not a veteran Komsomol member.

". . . I didn't mention it," he writes in the letter addressed to Comrade Kasimov, "because I was afraid that I would be expelled from the party and deprived of my apartment. And considering the state of my health, this was tantamount to death. I had stumbled, but I had lived an honest and irreproachable life, as is fitting for a Communist-Stalinist. It is funny, of course, to end one's life with a suicide. In our country, suicide is a rare phenomenon. . . . I had no political disagreements with the party. . . . You and I are both guilty in my death. For me, the situation of distrust was becoming such that I could no longer even conceive of living and working. . . ."

The investigation is continuing.

CERTIFIED:

Operational Commissioner of Department #12 of the Investigative-Industrial Section (Special Political Department) of GUGB [NKVD]

[signature: illegible]

Document 63

Suicide note of V. U. Aseev, December 1935[24]

([?] December 1935)

[Copy]

TO THE BIISKY DISTRICT OF THE VKP(b)

from V. U. ASEEV

Forshtadskaya Street, #14.

STATEMENT

By the time you receive this letter, I shall no longer be among the living. Why have you slandered me [?] What have I done to you [?] That which I wrote to you I now—dying—confirm, namely, that it is true that I was never a scoundrel, that for 16 years I worked honestly for the party, that I devoted my whole life unreservedly to the party, that I even worked while sick with tuberculosis of the third stage, gave up everything for the party. Why have you slandered me [?]

The truth is that in 1905 I nearly burned to death. The truth is that I spent the years 1914 to 1916 in exile in Narym territory.

In 1919, while in prison, I was whipped with ramrods[25] by someone wielding the cleaning rods of a gun, as I've already told you in my letter. I was not a party member [then]. I never prided myself on this, I never boasted of it. Why did you blame me? Why did you claim that I had concocted all this? What grounds did you have for it, while I had many documents that proved it was true?

24. RTsKhIDNI, f. 17, op. 120, d. 183, l. 166.
25. A kind of punishment meted out by the White Army—Trans.

Document 63 *continued*

Why did you (. . .) destroy me? Was it not because I had worked so un-selfishly and faithfully for the party for 16 years? (. . .)

I ask you to please help Comrade NAROZHNYKH save my children. Once again, I declare to you, I swear that, though disgraced, I am innocent in every-thing. I cannot live outside the party. For me the party is as precious as air.

V. ASEEV

For the Stalinists in the 1930s, almost everything carried a threat-ening political content. Even suicide, which might be seen to repre-sent to the Stalinists a welcome self-destruction of opponents, was seen as a dangerous political "blow against the party" by a dishon-est person. As Stalin mused in 1936, "A person arrives at suicide because he is afraid that everything will be revealed and he does not want to witness his own public disgrace. . . . There you have one of the last sharp and easiest means that, before death, leaving this world, one can for the last time spit on the party, betray the party."[26]

Indeed, the most "famous" suicide of the 1930s, that of Sergo Ordzhonikidze, posed special problems for the regime. Ordzhoni-kidze had always been a staunch Stalinist, yet in February 1937 he killed himself. Unlike others, his suicide was never characterized as political betrayal. Rather, the embarrassing political fact of his suicide was hidden by the regime. His death was publicly an-nounced as heart failure, and Nikita Khrushchev, a member of the Politburo, did not learn the truth about Ordzhonikidze's death for many years.

It was not only suicides of prominent politicians that worried them; the Stalinists even feared the suicides of their opponents. During the 1930s suicides of rank-and-file party members and even ordinary citizens attracted the attention of the top leadership. Even if they involved the most minor party members, such events were routinely investigated by the Special Political Department of the NKVD and found their way into Central Committee files.[27]

26. RTsKhIDNI, f. 17, op. 2, d. 576, ll. 67–70.
27. For examples, see RTsKhIDNI, f. 17, op. 120, d. 183, l. 166; d. 181, ll. 102–5; and Gosudarstvennyi arkhiv Rossiiskoi Federatsii (GARF), f. 9415, op. 5, d. 487, ll. 90–91.

CHAPTER SIX

The Fork in the Road

We cannot . . . place the great mass of the expellees in the category of our enemies. . . . You realize that such an incorrect attitude to the expellees is dictated not by reasons of vigilance but by a striving by certain party officials to protect themselves against any eventuality.—N. I. Yezhov, 1936

DOCUMENTS FROM ROUGHLY the first half of 1936 indicate a continuing desire by the top party leadership to ease up on uncontrolled repression. The first three texts below relate to judicial policy and pertain to nonparty urban and rural victims of previous waves of repression in 1933–35. Several of these are connected to A. Vyshinsky, procurator general of the USSR, who has sometimes been seen as an advocate of procedural legalism (if not legality) and even as an opponent of indiscriminate terror (if not terror itself).[1] In February 1936 USSR Procurator Vyshinsky had complained to Stalin that NKVD officials were refusing to release prisoners whom procurators had ordered freed for lack of evidence. NKVD chief Yagoda had replied that procurators and courts were incompetent; procurators could "suggest" release of prisoners, but the decision should remain in the hands of the NKVD. On 16 February, Stalin wrote to Molotov, "Comrade Molotov: It seems to me that Vyshinsky is right." For the moment, legality had the upper hand.

1. See Eugene Huskey, "Vyshinsky, Krylenko, and the Shaping of the Soviet Legal Order," *Slavic Review,* 46(3–4), Fall–Winter 1987, 414–28; J. Arch Getty, *Origins of the Great Purges: The Soviet Communist Party Reconsidered, 1933–1938,* New York, 1991, 199–201; Robert H. McNeal, "The Decisions of the CPSU and the Great Purge," *Soviet Studies,* 23(2), October 1971, 177–85. See also Peter H. Solomon Jr., *Soviet Criminal Justice Under Stalin,* Cambridge, 1996, part 3.

Document 64

On dependents of persons deported from cities in the USSR subject to special measures[2]

From Protocol #38 of the Politburo of the CC of the VKP(b) of 20 April 1936
#48. Re: Dependents of persons deported from cities in the USSR subject to special measures
The following draft proposal of a decree by the Council of People's Commissars (SNK) of the USSR is to be confirmed:
Item #g of the instruction of the Council of People's Commissars of the USSR of 14 January 1933, Protocol #43/s, is to be rendered null and void.
Residence in localities in the USSR subject to special measures is to be permitted to dependents of persons removed from these localities: to dependents whose family is engaged in socially useful work, or to students—that is, to those people who are in no way personally to blame for anything.

Document 65

On dismissing the criminal cases against kolkhoz members[3]

From Protocol #39 of the Politburo of the CC of the VKP(b) of 20 May 1936
. . . 134. Re: Dismissing the criminal cases against kolkhoz members (memorandum by Comrade Vyshinsky)
The Procuracy and the Supreme Court of the USSR are instructed to verify the correctness of rejections of requests to dismiss criminal cases against kolkhoz members in the Ivanovo and Leningrad regions and in the Northern Caucasus region and to take all necessary measures to rectify any improper decisions made locally. . . .

Document 66

On persons deported from Leningrad in 1935 not guilty of any specific crimes[4]

From Protocol #42 of the Politburo of the CC of the VKP(b)
1 September 1936
#27. Comrade Vyshinsky's proposal
It is proposed to the Central Executive Committee of the USSR and the All-Union Central Council of Trade Unions that persons deported from Leningrad in 1935 who had not been found guilty of any specific crimes not be deprived of their voting and pension rights during their period of exile [*vysylka*].

---

2. RTsKhIDNI, f. 17, op. 3, d. 976, l. 17.
3. RTsKhIDNI, f. 17, op. 3, d. 977, ll. 32–33.
4. RTsKhIDNI, f. 17, op. 3, d. 980, l. 9.

Document 67

Formation of the USSR Commissariat for Justice[5]

---

19 July 1936

From Protocol #41 of the Politburo of the CC of the VKP(b)

VII. Re: Formation of the People's Commissariat for Justice of the USSR and of the People's Commissariat for Health of the USSR (Comrades Vyshinsky, Krylenko, Kaminsky, Molotov).

I.

1) A Union-Republic (united) People's Commissariat for Justice of the USSR is to be organized;

2) The organs of procuracy and investigation are to be removed from the system of People's Commissariats for Justice of the Union and Autonomous Republics and placed directly under the jurisdiction of the Procurator of the USSR;

3) It is to be established that criminal and civil legislation as well as laws pertaining to the judicial system and legal proceedings shall be uniform throughout the USSR;

4) Comrade N. V. Krylenko is to be appointed people's commissar for justice of the USSR;

5) Comrade N. V. Krylenko is instructed to draft within ten days a proposal entitled "The Statute Pertaining to the People's Commissariat for Justice of the USSR" for confirmation by the Presidium of the TsIK and the Council of People's Commissars (SNK) of the USSR. He is also instructed to come up with a list of [proposed] members for the council attached to the people's commissar for justice of the USSR.

Local Cadres and Family Circles: Rift in the Nomenklatura

Local party secretaries had expelled large numbers of party members in the verifications and exchanges of party documents in 1935. All elements of the nomenklatura could find political advantage in these screenings. For the nomenklatura as a whole, they made party membership more exclusive and thus restricted membership in the elite strata of political participation. By weeding out nonparticipant and nonactive members who simply used party membership for their own interests, the purges would supposedly make the party a more efficient machine.

5. RTsKhIDNI, f. 17, op. 3, d. 979, l. 3. Before mid-1936, there had been no central USSR ministry (commissariat) of justice. Courts, judges, and prosecutors had been subordinated to the various republic justice agencies.

The purges also had particular advantages for certain groups and strata, and these advantages illustrate conflicting interests within the nomenklatura elite. For Stalin and the upper circle, they held the potential to discipline local leaders by pruning their patronage "family circles" and also gave the possibility to catch a few political dissidents and conspirators in the process. For the regional and local party secretaries who actually carried out the operations on the ground, the purges were an opportunity to rid themselves of bothersome critics and individuals with political aspirations who did not belong to the local machine. Local leaders could also demonstrate their "vigilance" by expelling rather large numbers to run up the total for Moscow.

Even though we saw in the last chapter that Moscow sought to control, focus, and rein in the indiscriminate local expulsions, the screening operations remained in the hands of local leaders, who naturally used them to their own advantage. The archives for early 1936 are filled with long lists of persons whose expulsion was routinely confirmed at regional level in early 1936. Typically, they took the following form, with dozens on each page and without any personal details or individual circumstance:

> From the protocol of the meeting of the Buro of the _____ Regional Committee of the VKP(b) on [date]:
> [*Name of expelled*], party card no. _____.
> The decision of the [district] District Committee of the Party no. _____ of [date] on the expulsion from the ranks of the party of _____—is confirmed.[6]

Sometimes, though, the expulsions threatened well-connected members of local political machines. This often happened at local purge meetings when rank-and-file party members made accusations against their superiors. Such criticism from below had to be blunted and reversed by the local elite in order to protect "their people." Two documents, one perhaps more serious than the other, illustrate how the local machines closed ranks to protect their own from populist criticism:

6. For examples, see RTsKhIDNI, f. 17, op. 21, d. 2206, ll. 228–29.

Document 68

Buro session of the Azov–Black Sea Territorial Committee, on Comrade Zhuk[7]

25 April 1935
STRICTLY SECRET
(FROM A SPECIAL DOSSIER)
To be returned . . .
Copying prohibited
ALL-UNION COMMUNIST PARTY (Bolshevik)
AZOV–BLACK SEA TERRITORIAL COMMITTEE
To: CC VKP(b), Comrade Dragunsky, Comrade Zhuk—Novo-Titarov District Committee, Party Control
Extract from Protocol #44 of the buro session of the Azov–Black Sea Territorial Committee of the VKP(b)
Hearing:
#184. Re: Comrade Zhuk, secretary of the Novo-Titarov District Committee
IT IS HEREBY DECREED
That Territorial Procurator Comrade Dragunsky be entrusted with the task of instituting proceedings against persons who say compromising things about Comrade Zhuk, secretary of the Novo-Titarov District Committee—namely, that he has infected [a woman] with a venereal disease. Medical examination of Comrade Zhuk has shown that he is innocent of this accusation.
[Seal of Azov–Black Sea Territorial Committee of the VKP(b)]
Secretary
(M. Malinov)
[signature]

Document 69

Buro session of the Azov–Black Sea Territorial Committee, on Comrade Chernikov[8]

Extract from Protocol #122 of the buro of the Azov–Black Sea Territorial Committee of the VKP(b) of 27 January 1936
#22. Re: Comrade O. P. Chernikov, director of the Krapotkinsky factory
It is considered inexpedient to bring Comrade Chernikov to trial.
B. Sheboldaev,
Secretary of the Azov–Black Sea Territorial Committee of the VKP(b)

---

7. RTsKhIDNI, f. 17, op. 42, d. 136, l. 13.
8. RTsKhIDNI, f. 17, op. 42, d. 759, l. 7

The latter document shows clearly the power regional and local party leaders had over administration of justice. For the party family circle, "expedience" outweighed any consideration of formal justice, and the possible guilt or innocence of the factory director had no bearing on the political decision of his case.

Sometimes, though, friction between rank-and-file party members and their local leaders was more serious, and lower-level victims of party expulsions were able to use status differences and conflicts within the nomenklatura to fight back. Complaints and appeals from expelled members, accompanied by denunciations of the middle-level secretaries and party officials who had expelled them, reached the highest echelons of the party. There, such appeals were often ignored or routinely denied. But in some cases, Moscow-based senior party leaders took up the cause of the "little people," as such petitioners were often called. Such intervention might happen when the accused official had highly placed enemies eager to embarrass him, when the Politburo wanted to strike some balance or inflict some blow against the middle level, or when Stalin decided to make a propaganda point by publicly posturing as a defender of "little people."

Pavel Postyshev was a powerful secretary of the Ukrainian party organization. A long-time Stalin supporter, Postyshev had a reputation for "Bolshevik firmness" in dealing with "enemies" reflected in the mass expulsions that took place under his regime. (For the subsequent story of Postyshev's fall, see Documents 178, 179, 180, 181.) He also seems to have run one of the tightest party patronage machines. His machine was literally a family circle: his wife, Postolovskaya, was a senior official and chief leader of the party ideological institutions in Ukraine. The following sequence of documents, compiled by Party Control Commission official Shkiriatov, shows how Postyshev and Postolovskaya used the party screenings to rid themselves of critics and how at least some of those critics were able to fight back.

Document 70

[A]

Re: Vasilieva's connection with the remnants of the counterrevolutionary bloc of Trotskyists and nationalists

8 January 1935

In examining the matter of Vasilieva's connection with the remnants of the counterrevolutionary bloc of Trotskyists and nationalists, the party committee of the VUAMLIN [All-Ukrainian Association of Scientific-Research Marxist-Leninist Institutes] has established that:

1. Vasilieva concealed her past membership in the Trotskyist opposition from the party organization and from the Purge Commission.

2. While in the employ of VUAMLIN and the Institute of Red Professors (IKP), Vasilieva did not only fail to help the party organization expose the counterrevolutionary bloc of nationalists and the remnants of the counterrevolutionaries. Rather, using every means possible, she covered up the counterrevolutionary activities of nationalists and Trotskyists, put a brake on the struggle of the party organization of VUAMLIN against them, and protected a great many members of the counterrevolutionary bloc of nationalists and Trotskyists (Adrianov, Bervitsky, Logvin, Stepovoy, Levik, and others) and helped them in their struggle against the party.

3. Vasilieva's conduct while a member of the party organization of VUAMLIN, her undermining of the work of the Institute of Philosophy, her antiparty behavior as a leader of the seminar of philosophy and of the IKP, her antiparty speech at the session of the party committee on 7 January attest to the fact that she has not laid down her arms before the party and continues to carry on her duplicitous, antiparty activities.

On the basis of the above, the party committee has decided to expel Vasilieva from the VKP(b).

Postolovskaya,

Secretary of the Party Committee of VUAMLIN

[B]

Extract from a letter addressed by M. Garin to Comrade Stalin

17 February 1935

". . . Certain persons associated with Comrade Postyshev have, in the name of group interests having nothing in common with the party, declared my wife, A. Vasilieva, to be a Trotskyist in order thereby to get even with me. Comrade Postyshev's attitude to me, as that of other members of the Politburo,

---

9. RTsKhIDNI, f. 17, op. 120, d. 272, ll. 24–39. Quotation marks and excisions in the original.

has been most favorable. (I worked as the deputy editor of *Kommunist*. The editor is Comrade N. N. Popov.) . . .

Vasilieva was especially hard hit because she worked with them. They exploited the fact that VUAMLIN was littered with Trotskyists and nationalists in order to really pin an accusation of Trotskyism on Vasilieva. . . . Then, on 7 January, the day Comrade Postyshev returned from his vacation, Comrade Postolovskaya (by then secretary of the VUAMLIN Party Committee) assembled the committee and held a general meeting, at which she raised the question of expelling Vasilieva from the party for being a Trotskyist. As grounds for such a formulation, someone's claim was adduced that she had been an active Trotskyist while living in Sverdlovsk and that she had concealed this fact from the party. . . .

These people can perpetrate such antiparty things with impunity because Comrade Postyshev invests them with unlimited authority. Thus the matter may proceed with impunity when at the head of the party organization stands Postolovskaya, who is not distinguished either for her intellect or for her experience, and—I might add—people like Senchenko have wormed their way into her trust. . . . It is precisely this that has created an atmosphere of impunity in VUAMLIN itself, as well as an atmosphere of impunity throughout the Ukraine regarding VUAMLIN. In such a situation, even top party officials dare not openly speak of this or that mistake committed in VUAMLIN . . ."

[C]

Extract from Protocol #29 of the Politburo of the CC of the KP(b)U of 4 January 1936

Re: Vasilieva

1) The decree by the Party Committee of VUAMLIN and by the general meetings of VUAMLIN's party organization regarding the expulsion of Vasilieva from the party for her ties with Trotskyist elements and for her aiding and abetting them is hereby confirmed.

2) Vasilieva is to be removed from her post as director of the Institute of Philosophy of VUAMLIN.

S. Kosior,
Secretary of the CC of the KP(b) Ukraine

[D]

Letter by the CC of the KP(b) Ukraine to the Committee of Party Control of the CC of the VKP(b)

Re: Vasilieva

4 January 1936

In connection with your inquiry, we are sending you the decree by the Politburo of the CC of the KP(b) Ukraine of 13 January 1935 and the decree by the party committee of the All-Ukrainian Association of Scientific-Research Marxist-Leninist Institutes (VUAMLIN) concerning Vasilieva.

In the course of liquidating the Trotskyist counterrevolutionary group in the

Ukraine at the beginning of the past year, it was established that Vasilieva had close ties with many Trotskyists.

S. Kosior,
Secretary of the CC of the KP(b) Ukraine
[E]
Letter from P. P. Postyshev to N. I. Yezhov[10]
15 March 1936
How are you, Comrade Yezhov?

By virtue of the decree of the CC of the KP(b) Ukraine of 13 January 1935, Vasilieva, the former director of the Institute of Philosophy of the All-Ukrainian Association of Scientific-Research Marxist-Leninist Institutes (VUAMLIN) has been expelled from the party for her ties with and direct abetting of counterrevolutionary elements working at the Institute of Philosophy.

I know all too well that her husband is also a secret Trotskyist. His surname is Garin. You should be well acquainted with this fact. He had once worked for *Pravda*. It seems that he is now living in Irkutsk.

It looks as though right now they are planning in Moscow to restore Vasilieva to the party. You must not do that. She is undoubtedly a Trotskyist and there is no place for her in the party.

I urgently request that you instruct someone to clarify this matter and that you give the appropriate instructions to whomever is deemed necessary.

With a [comradely] greeting.
P. Postyshev
15 March 1936
[F]
Party Control Commission memorandum from Shkiriatov to Yezhov
[? June 1936]
To: Comrade Yezhov

In connection with Comrade Vasilieva's letter,[11] I am sending you information concerning her expulsion from the party.

How did this matter come about?

In November—I don't recall the exact date—Comrade Postyshev telephoned me to report that according to his information, many appeals had apparently been submitted to the Commission of Party Control by counterrevolutionary Trotskyists-nationalists (Nyrchuk and others) and that these appeals must be handled with extreme caution.

Furthermore, Comrade Postyshev told me that an appeal by Vasilieva, former director of the Institute of Philosophy in Kiev, who had been expelled from the party, had apparently also been submitted to the party collegium. Vasilieva, he said, was expelled by the Politburo of the CC of the Ukraine as a double-

10. The informal *ty* is used throughout the letter—Trans.
11. The text suggests that Vasilieva had sent an angry and accusatory letter to KPK chief Yezhov. The original of that letter has not been found in the archives.

dealing Trotskyist, and her husband Garin was also a former Trotskyist. Comrade Postyshev requested that we consider all this when investigating her case. . . .

What was Comrade Vasilieva charged with?

According to materials provided by the Party Organization of the All-Ukrainian Association of Scientific-Research Marxist-Leninist Institutes (VUAMLIN), the following two fundamental accusations were made against Vasilieva:

First, she concealed from the party organization and the Purge Commission her past membership in the Trotskyist opposition;

Second, while employed at the Institute of Philosophy, she not only failed to help in the unmasking of counterrevolutionaries, Trotskyists, and nationalists who had infiltrated into its ranks but in fact shielded and protected them in every way possible.

On 13 January 1935, the Politburo of the CC of the KP(b)U confirmed the decree by the party organization of 8 January 1935 pertaining to the expulsion of Vasilieva with the following formulation: "[expelled] for her connection with and aiding and abetting the Trotskyist counterrevolutionary group."

We received contradictory facts concerning the accusations against Vasilieva: on the one hand, charges by the party organization involving grave crimes, [such as] duplicity, the decree by the Politburo of the CC of the Ukraine, Comrade Kosior's letter, all corroborating the accusations; on the other hand, a categorical assertion by Vasilieva that she had been slandered, plus the testimony of her comrades who knew her in Moscow.

That's why I decided then to postpone the review of this case until supplementary materials had been received. Comrade Vasilieva was informed of this and we reached an understanding with her to the effect that when her case came up for review, she would be summoned from Irkutsk.

25 [*sic*] March 1936, Comrade Postyshev sent Comrade Yezhov a letter regarding the case of Vasilieva (see letter attached). In it, he confirmed the correctness of the charges brought against her for double-dealing and insisted that she be expelled from the party.

As is evident from all this, the investigation into the Vasilieva case dragged on because she was charged with being an enemy of the party, a double-dealer. And all the materials had to be gathered.

In April, Vasilieva was summoned from Irkutsk, but she reported that she could come [only] at the end of the school year in June.

When Vasilieva arrived in Moscow, I summoned her into my office on 23 June for an explanation. Comrade Vinogradov gave a report outlining the essentials of her case in her presence.

In her explanation, Vasilieva insisted on the groundlessness of the charges brought against her. . . .

Everything was done to ensure that the investigation of this complex case was carried out properly.

Shkiriatov

We do not know the outcome of this case. But the texts about Vasilieva show several things about the balance of forces within the party leadership in 1936. Vasilieva's protest and the support for her voiced by "comrades who knew her in Moscow" had embarrassed Postyshev and led to a KPK investigation of his expulsions. Shkiriatov obviously did not know which way the wind would blow: his comments on the matter were noncommittal. Moreover, although Postyshev was criticized at the time, he was not transferred to another position until the following year and even then was treated gently until 1938.

Shkiriatov's forwarding of the file to Yezhov elevated the power of this text and shows high-level interest in Postyshev's activities. Yezhov was gathering materials on Postyshev; shortly after these documents were forwarded to him, Yezhov raked Postyshev over the coals at the June 1936 plenum of the Central Committee for his high-handed and callous attitude toward rank-and-file expulsions (see Document 71). One can suspect several factors at work here: a desire by Postyshev's critics and enemies to take him down a peg, Stalin's wish to take up the cause of "little people" against the power of the regional party secretaries, and a sense in the Politburo that mass expulsions of the rank and file were becoming counterproductive. As we shall see, the Politburo was disappointed that the screenings of 1935–36 had not netted high-ranking "violators of party discipline" within the regional leading groups and was dismayed that those local leaders had so fiercely deflected the fire to lower levels. The result of this perception was a seeming "liberalization" of repression against ordinary citizens and party members, combined with intensified criticism of big shots.

The Nomenklatura Against Itself in Early 1936: Who Was to Blame?

The June 1936 plenum of the Central Committee took up the question of expulsions from the party and appeals from those expelled. The minutes of this meeting illustrate some important points about variant texts, multiple narratives, and levels of information, and about how they were used in party leadership struggles.

Minutes of the discussions of Central Committee plena exist in the archive in several versions. The raw minutes were taken down by stenographers, typed up into an "uncorrected stenogram" and distributed to the speakers, who had the right to edit and correct their remarks before preparation of the "corrected stenogram." The top party leadership (that is, Stalin and his staff in the Secretariat) then prepared and printed a "stenographic report" for formal distribution to members of the Central Committee and other important party officials charged with implementing and interpreting the decisions of the meeting. Finally, edited and sanitized versions of some of the resolutions and speeches were presented to the general public in *Pravda,* as printed speeches, summary editorials, or didactic articles.

In this sense it is instructive to think of Central Committee plena as ritualized performances intended to produce authoritative and useful texts. These meetings were not always purely scripted rituals, and even in the 1930s they were sometimes the scene of real dispute and policy decision. Nevertheless, they produced heuristic transcripts destined for particular audiences. Such variant texts fulfilled a function that one scholar has called "concealment" within the master transcript. As Scott puts it, "By controlling the public stage, the dominant can create an appearance that approximates what, ideally, they would want subordinates to see."[12] Moreover, one's role in the production and distribution of texts was a sign of power. Access to information—and, just as important, access to knowledge about what was missing from or added to the less complete transcripts *below* one's position—was an important part of the stratification of power. Knowledge of the different transcripts *was* power.

The following document illustrates these points. It represents part of Yezhov's report to the June 1936 plenum of the Central Committee, combined with what may have been a short speech by Stalin. The subject was the appeal and readmission process for those expelled in the party membership screenings of 1935–36. This was a sensitive and extremely important personal issue for the rank-and-file members who had been expelled: would it be possible to reenter the party? For the nomenklatura, assessing blame for the "mistakes" was a political issue.

Although the lowest-level, public transcript revealed very little

12. James C. Scott, *Domination and the Arts of Resistance,* New Haven, 1990, 50.

about the plenum, it was not completely devoid of information. A short notice in *Pravda* announced that a plenum of the Central Committee had taken place 1–4 June 1936. According to the laconic announcement, the meeting had discussed adoption of a new constitution, questions of rural economy, and procedures for considering appeals and readmissions of those expelled in the just-concluded verification and exchange of party documents. In connection with this latter issue, *Pravda* noted that Yezhov had given a report and that decisions were reached on the basis of his report as well as on "words from Comrade Stalin."[13] No corresponding Central Committee resolution was published, but a series of press articles in subsequent days described how lower-level party officials had taken a "heartless attitude" toward party members, had expelled many of them for simple nonparticipation in party life, and had been slow to consider appeals and readmissions of those wrongly expelled.[14]

Careful readers of even this minimal public text could discern the outlines of something a bit broader. First of all, the press formulation "on the basis of Comrade Yezhov's report and words from Comrade Stalin" was unusual. It suggested that somehow Yezhov's speech was not sufficient or completely authoritative: additional "words" from Stalin had been required. Second, by blaming low-level party officials for "mistakes," the Central Committee's formulation suggested not only the traditional blaming of subordinates but also a rift within the nomenklatura elite about who was to blame for the repression of innocent rank-and-file members. Those with access to more authoritative transcripts knew more. There were important and revealing differences among the various accounts and texts. We move now from the public version to a more private one: the printed text prepared for distribution to party insiders.

Document 71

Documents from the Plenum of the CC of the VKP(b) of 3 June 1936

[A]

[From N. I. Yezhov's report entitled "On Party Members Expelled from the Party and Their Appeals" at the Plenum of the CC of the VKP(b) of 3 June 1936,

13. *Pravda*, 5 June 1936. Apparently for security reasons, it was customary for *Pravda* to announce Central Committee plena only after they had been completed.

14. See, for example, *Pravda*, 7–10 June 1936.

from the final printed stenographic report for broad party leadership circulation][15]

Consequently, the fact that during the verification of party documents we have expelled many embittered enemies from the party places a very heavy responsibility on party organizations as it pertains to their attitude in the future toward the expellees. We ought not to think that the enemy, who yesterday was still in the party, will rest content with being expelled from the party and quietly wait for "better times."

We cannot, however, place the great mass of the expellees in the category of our enemies. They have never had and will never have anything in common with the enemies of our party. For the most part, these are people who have consciously concealed their past from the party or else have committed some other minor offenses[16] that have dishonored them as party members and have placed them outside the ranks of the VKP(b). In this category of the expellees we can also include persons who have never really been members of the party. These are people who were accepted into the party on a wholesale basis during the many mass group admissions into the VKP(b) carried out by party organizations. Often they were admitted in absentia, and often they did not consider themselves party members, did not pay their membership dues, and did not carry on any party work. Finally, we may place in this category a significant number of party members who had earlier been expelled from the VKP(b), who had never turned in their party cards, and who were still registered as members on the books of party organizations.

The majority of expellees belonging to these categories cannot and shall not be reinstated into the ranks of the VKP(b). However, a part of them shall be reinstated after their appeals have been reviewed, or they may be allowed to return to the ranks of our party after amending their conduct. Meanwhile, party organizations deal indiscriminately, mechanically, with all of the expellees from this category without looking into the reasons why they were expelled from the VKP(b).

In view of all this, however, what is especially intolerable is that many of the expellees belonging to this category of former party members are automatically dismissed from their jobs, deprived of their apartments, and expelled from universities and institutes. This practice is sometimes extended to members of their families. Such facts were especially widespread during the first period of the verification. You realize that such an incorrect attitude to the expellees is dictated not by reasons of vigilance but by a striving by certain party officials to protect themselves against any eventuality. Such vigilance has nothing to do with Bolshevik vigilance and will lead to no good.

Voices: That's right!

15. RTsKhIDNI, f. 17, op. 2, d. 572, ll. 67–73.
16. *prostupki:* i.e., "misdemeanors"—Trans.

Yezhov: Such vigilance arises from cowardice and fear of responsibility.

Voices: That's right!

Yezhov: I would like to especially single out and dwell on the matter of the so-called passive members of the party.

Out of the total number of Communists who had participated in the exchange of party documents, approximately 3.5% were not issued their party cards, and the question of their expulsion from the party has been raised. From these 3.5%, about a half fall into the category of so-called passive membership or, as they are called in many places, "ballast."

Stalin: What percent?

Yezhov: 3.5% have not been issued party cards—out of this group half fall into the passive category.

Not an insignificant percent, as you can see. Moreover, in certain specific organizations, such as the party organizations of Ivanovo, Kursk, Saratov, the Northern Caucasus, Stalingrad, Dnepropetrovsk, and Cheliabinsk, this percentage is even somewhat higher.

Such a percentage of party members and candidate members belonging to the passive category is too high and attests to the fact that somewhere the matter of determining who belongs to the category of passive members has been handled incorrectly and formally. . . .

[B]

[From Stalin's comments on N. I. Yezhov's report at the Plenum of the CC of the VKP(b) of 3 June 1936, from the final printed stenographic report for broad party leadership circulation][17]

Stalin: I would like to say a few things concerning certain points which in my opinion are especially important if we are to put the affairs of the party in good order and direct the regulating of party membership properly.

First of all, let me say something concerning the matter of appeals. Naturally, appeals must be handled in timely fashion, without dragging them out. They must not be put on the shelf. This goes without saying. But let me raise a question: Is it not possible for us to reinstate some or many of the appellants as candidate members? We do not allow, as you know, for a transitional category. Either you are a member of the party or you are not. Either you are nothing in the eyes of the party or you are a party member with full rights. But there is a middle ground.

Party rules do not provide direct instructions as to whether a party member who has been expelled may be brought back into the party at least as a candidate member. Such instructions are not mentioned in the party rules, but there are no prohibitions against it, either. Insofar as these party expellees cannot, as things stand, be reinstated as full members, why couldn't we reinstate some of the appellants into the party as candidate members? Why can't we do it?!

17. RTsKhIDNI, f. 17, op. 2, d. 572, ll. 73–75.

Document 71 *continued*

Voices: We can! We can!

Stalin: There are no prohibitions in the party rules on this account, though there are no direct instructions concerning this, either.

Voices: It is now being done.

Stalin: No, I don't think that it is being done. To this day, a certain, if I may say so, wholesale attitude toward party members has held sway among party leaders. They expel you. You appeal. If they can reinstate you as a full member of the party, fine. If they can't, then you remain outside the party. All ties with the party are severed. We have party sympathizers, party candidate members, and party members, and they are connected with each other. If party members are expelled and cannot be reinstated as full party members, then they are not reinstated as sympathizers or candidate party members. Is this practice right?

In my opinion, such a practice is not right.

For this reason, it would be a good idea if the Orgburo of the CC clarified this as soon as possible, if it explained that it doesn't follow from the party rules, from the traditions of the Bolshevik Party, that a party member who has been expelled could not be reinstated as a candidate member or a sympathizer. This, after all, will allow a man to retain certain spiritual and organizational ties with the party. This opens up real prospects for him.

Party organizations must learn well the following principle: they must establish a gradation, whereby they can determine whom to reinstate as party members—if the facts and materials available justify it—whom to reinstate as candidate members, and whom perhaps to reinstate as sympathizers, so as to give such comrades a real prospect, so as to help them rise and later become full party members.

Chairman: There is a motion on the floor, on the basis of Comrade Yezhov's report and Comrade Stalin's proposals, to instruct the Orgburo of the CC to work out draft proposals regarding the procedures for expulsion and admission to the party and regarding the review of appeals. Any objections?

Shubrikov: Comrade Stalin, 90% of all appeals have already been reviewed. Ought we then to review all appeals all over again? According to instructions issued by the CC, this work should have been completed by 20 May.

Stalin: Perhaps it was a mistake, then, to have set a deadline?

Yezhov: This is the case in your region. The decisions of the regional committee have not yet been reviewed by the Commission of Appeals of the Party Control Commission (KPK), which can rectify matters here and there.

Chairman (Molotov): There is another motion on the floor to review the matter of Comrade Yenukidze. His request to be reinstated as a party member had already been received by the CC about five months ago. At the time, as we all understand, it was too early to place this question before you.

Stalin: It would've turned out then that he had been expelled from the party at one plenum and reinstated at the next one.

Chairman: A year has passed since Comrade Yenukidze's expulsion from the party. There is a motion on the floor to submit to the Plenum of the CC the following resolution: "The plenum shall lift the ban concerning Comrade Yenukidze's [re-]admission into the party and shall leave it to the local organizations to decide this matter. Comrade Yenukidze may then submit such request for reinstatement to them."

Voroshilov: No one will take the risk of admitting him.

A voice: We will admit him at the plenum.

Chairman: It would be too solemn an occasion for a case like this.

Stalin: It would be too solemn to admit him at the plenum. There are no grounds for doing so. In the second place, we did not contact the local organization, the Kharkov organization, where he is employed, to find out its opinion. We have a report from another organization, the Kislovodsk organization, a negative report. After his work there, he was transferred to Kharkov. We don't know how he has conducted himself there, how his work has turned out. And if the plenum lifts the ban and tells the local organization where he works that it should resolve this matter by itself, that is, whether to admit him or not, that would be quite sufficient. If he has earned the right, he will be accepted into the party.

Chairman: If he is not admitted by the local organization, then he can appeal to the CC. The resolution by the Plenum of the CC proposed here predetermines the case of Comrade Yenukidze in the affirmative with a probability of 90%.

I call for a vote: Who is for the motion that I have just read? Please raise your hands. Who is opposed? The motion is adopted.

The two texts above were produced for an expanded audience of party officials below Central Committee rank whose job it was to explain the plenum to the rank-and-file members. The intended message of this "semiprivate" (party) transcript was carefully crafted: (*a*) there had been some incorrect expulsions from the party, but they were a minority, (*b*) most of those expelled were not dangerous enemies, (*c*) too many "passive" members had been expelled, (*d*) "certain party officials" had been careless about all this and were to blame, and (*e*) Stalin had taken a personal interest in these questions, adopting the position that many of those expelled—perhaps more than Yezhov had envisioned—could be readmitted to the party, with Yenukidze as a symbol of possible readmissions of those previously thrown out.[18]

18. Here Stalin seems to have changed his mind once again on Yenukidze. The previous September he had written to Kaganovich that NKVD materials suggested that Yenukidze was "not one of us [*chuzhdyi nam chelovek*]." RTsKhIDNI, f. 81, op. 3, d. 100, ll. 92–93.

But behind this text for party audiences there was sharper disagreement. The original, most private account of the meeting (a "hidden transcript") reveals at least two conclusions that the upper nomenklatura wished hidden from those outside its elite ranks: (*a*) that Stalin's position was further from Yezhov's than might otherwise be adduced and (*b*) that rather large numbers of people had been wrongly expelled, while the main targets of the screening may have been missed altogether (see Document 71 [C] and [D]).

Document 71 (cont.)

[C]

[From N. I. Yezhov's report entitled "On Party Members Expelled from the Party and Their Appeals," at the Plenum of the CC of the VKP(b) of 3 June 1936, *final* version from the printed stenographic report for broad party leadership distribution][19]

Yezhov: . . . You know, comrades, that during the verification of party documents we have expelled over 200 thousand Communists.

Stalin: That's quite a lot.

Yezhov: Yes, that is quite a lot. And this obligates all party organizations all the more so to be extremely attentive to members who have been expelled and who are now appealing. . . .

[D]

[From N. I. Yezhov's report entitled "On Party Members Expelled from the Party and Their Appeals," at the Plenum of the CC of the VKP(b) of 3 June 1936, *original* version from the uncorrected stenogram, not appearing in the final stenographic report][20]

Yezhov: . . . Comrades, as a result of the verification of party documents, we have expelled over 200 thousand party members.

Stalin: That's quite a lot.

Yezhov: Yes, quite a lot. I'll talk about it—

Stalin: If we expel 30,000—(inaudible), and if we also expel 600 former Trotskyists and Zinovievists, then we would gain even more from that.

Yezhov: We have expelled over 200 thousand party members. Some of the expellees, comrades, have been arrested.

In the final version of the plenum transcript, the upper nomenklatura was not eager to reveal that the criticism of regional party

---

19. RTsKhIDNI, f. 17, op. 2, d. 572, ll. 67.
20. RTsKhIDNI, f. 17, op. 2, d. 568, ll. 135–36.

secretaries was more severe, and that Pavel Postyshev had been a specific target, even scapegoat, for the excessive expulsions:

Document 71 (cont.)

[E]

[From N. I. Yezhov's report entitled "On Party Members Expelled from the Party and Their Appeals," at the Plenum of the CC of the VKP(b) of 3 June 1936, *original* version from the uncorrected stenogram, excised from the stenographic report][21]

Yezhov: I must tell you that no one has shown any attentiveness to the expellees. Some district committee secretary expels someone from the party and considers his role in the matter finished. What happens to this person, where he'll end up, will he find work or won't he—this concerns absolutely no one.

Moreover, comrades, a significant number of the expellees is made up of people whom we cannot include in the category of our enemies. They were expelled for having deceived the party, for instance, someone, a former White officer, may have concealed this fact from the party and not said a word about it to anyone. Yet after this, he may have conducted himself quite well without besmirching his standing as a Soviet citizen. But it goes without saying that as a party member he cannot and must not remain in the party. And along with the fact that these people have been expelled from the party and deprived of work, it is the practice among us to deprive the expellee's family of work, too. As a result, these former party members have gone without work for months at a time, have worn out the doormats of district committees and of all our institutions, and nowhere were they given work.

As you can see, it is vigilance turned upside down. Of course, that kind of vigilance isn't worth a farthing. Our party bureaucrats and all other bureaucrats simply protected themselves against any eventuality: Why should I hire someone who has been expelled from the party? Somebody will start an investigation and tell me that "there are too many party expellees on your staff; why are they working for you?" In this way, everyone has protected himself, and no one has given them any work.

Let me cite an example. A certain Bulgakov, party member since 1932, was expelled from the party for having concealed his social origin. His father was a merchant, in a word, something of this sort. After he was expelled from the party, this Bulgakov was without work for 5 months. He made the rounds of literally dozens of institutes, where people with his skills were needed. He was not accepted anywhere. And then he submitted his appeal, appearing in person at the Commission of Party Control and saying: "Either arrest me and throw me in prison or else give me some work." It was only at the intervention

21. RTsKhIDNI, f. 17, op. 2, d. 568, ll. 13, 141, 154–55.

of the Commission of Party Control that he was given work by one institute. Besides, when we insisted on his being accepted, the director of this institute was willing to go along, but the secretary of the party cell objected: "What do we need him for? He was expelled from the party."

Do you understand, comrades, what all these examples speak of? Naturally, this has nothing to do with vigilance.

Voices: That's right!

Yezhov: It is not vigilance but nonsense. It is nothing but a case of bureaucrats protecting themselves, so that no one will say that they are not vigilant. [ironically] Better not hire [the expellees]! This is a callous attitude. In reality, these people are worse than our enemies, because they drive people into the camp of our enemies. A man goes without a job for five months. In such a case, he either becomes embittered or else commits some crime. This has nothing to do with vigilance. We on the Commission of Party Control have even expelled someone for just such a callous attitude, and we intend to publish this decision in the press in order to teach people a lesson or two.

You know the procedures to be followed in the exchange of documents. In the small district organizations it is the secretary of the district committee who directly handles the exchange of documents. He is under obligation to talk to the party member whose card he is replacing. In the larger organizations, we allow the second secretary and buro members to handle the exchange of cards, but only with the proviso that the buro member talk to everyone whose card he is replacing.

Postyshev: What do you mean "talk to"?

Yezhov: You see, Pavel Petrovich [Postyshev], what I mean by "talking," there are cases in your organization, in Kiev, for instance.

Postyshev: In what district?

Yezhov: I'll tell you in a minute. I don't have it right on me, but I will send you the information. The secretary puts together a preliminary questionnaire, sends it to every party member and then says: "Here you are, go ahead and prepare yourself. I'll discuss these questions with you later." This questionnaire includes questions of the following sort: "What is the law of diminishing fertility? What is money?" etc.

Postyshev: Such a discussion is important.

Yezhov: That discussions take place is important. . . . [But] we are against [this kind of] discussion. The CC did not have such discussions in mind when it said that a party member must be summoned. What it had in mind is to find out about the party member, what he is doing, what kind of Bolshevik he is, and not to make him take a test, as was done in many places. And so, instead of bringing out, in the course of the discussion, what kind of Bolshevik the party member is, they followed the course of least resistance, prepared the lists [of questions] in advance, and the discussion either took the course of empty, formal idle chatter or else it touched on theoretical subjects. Or else they asked them the standard questions: "Do you have any suggestions perhaps on how to improve the work of the district committee?"

What do these strange texts suggest? First, the differences between the printed stenographic report and the public press version reveal that the Politburo's condemnation of party secretaries for excessive expulsions of the rank and file was harsher and more far-reaching than the nomenklatura wished to advertise. The public version, in contrast to the one for the middle level of the party, vaguely suggested that the regional secretaries, as a group, were to blame for unjust repression of the party rank and file. The secret uncorrected stenogram was harsher, labeling party secretaries with the pejorative *chinovnik* (a tsarist-era arbitrary bureaucrat), calling them "worse than our enemies," and directly accusing them of a perversion of vigilance by inflicting punishment on party members to insure themselves against being considered soft. The stenogram also specifically attacked a high-ranking official (Ukrainian party leader Pavel Postyshev) for such arbitrary punishment of innocent party members, an event missing from versions aimed at broader audiences.

Stalin interrupted Yezhov twice (on the question of total numbers expelled and the percentage of "passives" expelled). This could indicate either his disapproval of the way Yezhov had conducted the screenings or perhaps a desire to pose as the righter of wrongs against "little people" and to distance himself tactically from Yezhov's extreme measures. His sanitized interjections "How many?" and "What percent?" were printed in the stenographic report. This, along with the public transcript associating "words of Comrade Stalin" with the liberalized attitude toward appeals, broadcast the symbol of Stalin as defender of the little person. Yet his actual interruption of Yezhov's speech at the point when the numbers of expulsions was discussed suggests more than just posturing or tactics.

His interjection, recorded only in the most private transcript, that it would have been better to expel 600 "real" enemies than thousands of rank-and-file members suggests genuine dissatisfaction with the results of the membership screenings that Yezhov had administered. This remark was potentially quite incendiary. It could be interpreted to mean that those who carried out the verification and exchange of party documents (including Yezhov and the network of regional secretaries) had missed the boat, had failed to get the real targets of the operation. More seriously, it raised questions about the basic relationship between leaders and led in the party. Although Yezhov and other leaders were at pains to repeat that the expulsions had been more or less necessary, Stalin's remark could suggest the opposite to the rank-and-file victims of the screenings: that their expulsions may not have been the point of the exercise at all. The dangerous implication was that hundreds of thousands of loyal and innocent party members (whom even Yezhov had admitted were not enemies) had had their lives ruined because of nomenklatura "mistakes." Suggesting as it did questions of basic justice and the legitimacy of the party leadership, such a sentiment raised questions the nomenklatura did not want aired; it therefore had to be kept secret and was reserved for the private elite version of reality.

Accordingly, Stalin's actual remark was excised even from the printed stenographic report of the plenum, which contained a more benign version. Similarly, it seems that the plenum did in fact produce a resolution criticizing the regional secretaries for mass expulsions. But that resolution was never published, cannot be located in the archives, and was only quoted in part two years later.[22]

After the June plenum, substantial numbers of expelled rank-and-file members were readmitted on appeal. But most were not. Even if Stalin had decided that the mass screenings had not hit the right targets, it was politically impossible to admit it or openly to correct the "mistake" on a large scale. To do so would have cast doubt not only on his own leadership but on the legitimacy and prerogatives of the nomenklatura itself, which had carried out the operation against those beneath it. Those capriciously expelled therefore paid the price for saving the nomenklatura's face.

Stalin's interjections and his concluding remarks implied a generous approach to rank-and-file members and a downright liberal

22. *Pravda,* 19 June 1938.

attitude toward the readmission of Yenukidze, who only a year earlier had been denounced at a Central Committee plenum by some as an enemy. The resurrection of Yenukidze is one of a number of zigs and zags in Stalin's attitude toward "enemies." As we saw, Yenukidze had been expelled from the party in 1935 in a move that went beyond Yezhov's proposal. Now Stalin sponsored his rehabilitation. Yet in another volte face the following year, Yenukidze was arrested for treason and executed.

These concluding remarks of Stalin's are problematic for other reasons. According to the original uncorrected stenogram, Stalin's remarks to the June 1936 plenum had not been foreseen in the preplenum agenda, a document traditionally planned by the Politburo and distributed in advance to Central Committee members. His words were "not stenogramed"; this notation and a blank page appear in the original plenum version in the archives.[23] Where, then, did the remarks that appeared in the printed stenographic report (Document 71 [B]) originate? It is entirely possible that Stalin never said these words at the plenum but prepared them later for inclusion in the stenogram text.

His concluding remarks are also relevant to another puzzle of the June 1936 plenum. The most important item on the plenum's agenda was never mentioned in any of the accounts of the meeting, and discussion of it was not recorded in any of the stenograms or reports. This ultrasecret transcript concerned the upcoming show trial of Zinoviev and Kamenev for treason.[24] We know from subsequent accounts that Stalin spoke on this matter, apparently delivering a Politburo report on the question. He probably announced the upcoming trial and gave an overview of the charges against the accused, based on evidence that Yezhov had been gathering since the beginning of 1936 (see Document 73). Moreover, the original version of the minutes notes that the plenum heard a "communication" [*soobshchenie*] from NKVD chief Yagoda. Subsequent minutes from the February–March 1937 plenum refer to this Yagoda

23. RTsKhIDNI, f. 17, op. 2, d. 568, ll. 165–68.

24. *Voprosy istorii,* no. 2, 1995, 9. (Stenographic report of the February–March 1937 plenum.) No archival version of the full stenographic report of this plenum has yet become available to researchers. It is serialized in the journal *Voprosy istorii;* subsequent references to that journal are to this published plenum transcript, unless otherwise indicated.

report to the June plenum and make it clear that he spoke about the upcoming show trial of Zinoviev and Kamenev.[25] In contrast to Stalin, Yagoda was reported to have minimized Trotsky's guilt in the Zinoviev-Kamenev conspiracy; perhaps for this reason this section of the proceedings was not recorded, again to avoid the impression of interelite conflict.

The June 1936 plenum presents us with a series of contrasts and apparent contradictions. It denounced careless mass expulsions from the party and encouraged speedy appeals and readmissions. But it also announced the beginning of organized terror against former members of the opposition. The plenum launched the destruction of dissident Old Bolsheviks but rehabilitated the most senior of them who had so far been purged, Yenukidze. Stalin implicitly criticized Yezhov for excessive expulsions but would promote him to head the terror less than three months later.

There was no real contradiction between Stalin's condemnation of the party membership purges and his launching of terror against Old Bolsheviks. The purges had been carried out by members of the nomenklatura, while the terror was directed against it, even enlisting the support of the rank-and-file victims of the screenings. No one at the time thought that the recently completed screenings had anything to do with the purge trials.

Stalin once again revealed himself to be a master of compromise, balance, and political maneuver inside and outside the nomenklatura. No one knew exactly where he stood and no one (including, perhaps, Stalin himself) knew exactly where events were leading. Regional officials were criticized strongly, but the affair was hidden from the rank and file, and no one from that group was punished: Postyshev, for example, was raked over the coals but retained his position and rank. The regional secretaries' sins were deliberately hidden from rank-and-file anger, but enough was leaked to suggest to party members that all might not be quite right with their immediate superiors. The soft line on Old Bolshevik Yenukidze was balanced by the hard line against Old Bolshevik Zinoviev. Leniency toward NKVD chief Yagoda, who remained in

25. RTsKhIDNI, f. 17, op. 2. d. 562, l. 2; f. 17, op. 2, d. 598, l. 34; *Voprosy istorii*, no. 2, 1995, 18. (Stenographic report of the February–March 1937 plenum.)

office, was balanced by the more aggressive investigations of Yezhov.

The variant texts had strategic importance as well. In spite of the severe attacks on regional party leaders, when all was said and done, Stalin, Molotov, Postyshev, and the network of regional secretaries were all members of the same club, the nomenklatura. While they might thrash each other in the private confines of the Central Committee, such intragroup conflicts had to be muted or hidden from the public. A principal function of public transcripts is to foster the image of cohesion. Serious discord must be hidden so as not to disturb "the smooth surface of euphemized power."[26] Thus the public transcript only vaguely hinted that unnamed, low-level party functionaries had made "mistakes." Stalin could, in the interests of conveying an image of party unity, simply keep the entire episode out of the public view. Nevertheless, by even hinting in the public press that there was a shadow of some kind over the regional secretaries, Stalin and his circle were able to hold a kind of sword over these officials: they were not entirely immune from censure and disclosure of their sins.

These textual variations show more than mere censorship of secret party meetings. They illustrate alternative political transcripts, constructed realities, that presented different versions of politics to different audiences. The public received a hazy general picture that nevertheless communicated something significant: some unnamed individual party secretaries had made mistakes. The senior leadership was united; Stalin and Yezhov were attending to the problems. To insiders, the problem of wrongful expulsions was portrayed as being more serious. Stalin had personally intervened (textually, if not orally) and had criticized the party secretaries and, implicitly, Yezhov. To those in the senior nomenklatura and the Central Committee, Stalin had been sharply critical of the entire screening process, suggesting it had targeted the wrong people. A senior nomenklaturchik, Postyshev, had been directly attacked.

Finally, it is interesting that Stalin chose to reveal anything of the conflicts outside the top leadership. Attentive readers of even the

26. Scott, *Domination*, 55–56.

laconic public versions must have noted something in the way of disharmony. Why, for example, was Stalin's intervention necessary at all? Similarly, party members also received clues about possible discord in the top ranks. It may well be that Stalin decided to leak these tidbits as a way of chastising the nomenklatura by suggesting to its members that in the future, the solid facade of elite unity was not necessarily obligatory, and that their public image would depend on their conduct.

M. N. Riutin

Members of the left opposition, 1920s: left front, L. D. Trotsky; center, L. B.
Kamenev; center right (smiling), G. Ye. Zinoviev

Karl Radek

L. B. Kamenev

A. I. Rykov

G. Ye. Zinoviev

N. I. Bukharin

Left to right, L. M. Kaganovich, I. V. Stalin, V. M. Molotov, 1920s

A. A. Andreev

Ya. E. Rudzutak

Sergo Ordzhonikidze

I. A. Akukov

A. S. Yenukidze

N. I. Yezhov

Sergo Ordzhonikidze, left,
and N. I. Yezhov

S. M. Kirov

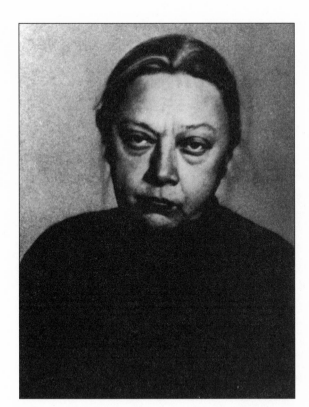

N. K. Krupskaia

A. I. Mikoyan

K. I. Voroshilov

L. M. Kaganovich

Ye. M. Yaroslavsky

A. Ya. Vyshinsky

G. M. Malenkov

A. A. Zhdanov

L. P. Beria

P. P. Postyshev

II
The Terror

The Face of the Enemy, 1936

The interests of the Revolution demand that we put an immediate end to the activities of this gang of rabid murderers, agents of fascism.—Azov–Black Sea party committee resolution, 1936

Surely, things will go smoothly with Yezhov at the helm.—L. M. Kaganovich to G. K. Ordzhonikidze, 1936

IN THE FIRST DAYS of 1936 one Valentin Olberg, a former associate of Trotsky, was arrested by the NKVD in the city of Gorky, apparently in connection with a suspicious history of foreign travel.[1] Under interrogation, he admitted to being an "emissary" of Trotsky's who had carried news to the exiled leader and "instructions" from him back into the USSR. This "information," along with scattered reports from NKVD informers about other couriers, was passed to Stalin in the Central Committee. Stalin had decided to reopen the Kirov investigation. According to Yezhov's later account, "Stalin, correctly sensing in all this something not quite right, gave instructions to continue [the investigations] and, in particular, to send me from the Central Committee to oversee the investigation."[2]

Extracting confessions, no doubt under pressure, from successive interrogations, NKVD investigators working for Yagoda but

1. Olberg may have been a double agent or police informer, secretly spying on the Trotskyist organizations on behalf of the NKVD. To date, no documents have been found to support or disprove this.

2. *Voprosy istorii*, no. 10, 1994, 21, 26. (Stenographic report of the February–March 1937 plenum.)

under Yezhov's supervision expanded the circle of the "conspiracy." By spring, they had arrested important former Trotskyists, including I. N. Smirnov. Yezhov, eager to make a case and a name for himself, used his mandate from Stalin to expand the circle of arrests. By late spring he had elaborated a conspiracy theory in which Zinoviev and Kamenev, acting under instructions from Trotsky in exile, had plotted the assassinations of Kirov, Stalin, and other members of the Politburo. Effectively, then, Stalin had reopened the investigation into the Kirov assassination more than a year after he had pronounced it closed and several months after Yezhov's failed attempt to reopen it in June 1935 (see Documents 28 and 37). Zinoviev and Kamenev, who had been in prison since early 1935, were reinterrogated.

Yagoda had been under a cloud since early 1935. After all, the "negligence" of his security officers had permitted Kirov's assassin to get close enough to fire the shot. We have also seen that the Kremlin Affair of mid-1935 was pointedly "uncovered" by Yezhov and party organs, rather than by the NKVD, whose job it should have been. Indeed, Yezhov had written to Stalin in July 1935 that the NKVD had not been "sufficiently active" in the struggle against enemies. Now, in the first half of 1936, Yagoda was being undermined by Yezhov again. Subsequent accusations in 1937 suggested that during Yezhov's 1936 "supervision" of the investigation, Yagoda and his deputy G. A. Molchanov had downplayed the importance of the Trotsky-Zinoviev connection and had tried to deflect or limit Yezhov's efforts. At one point, Yagoda had called the evidence that Trotsky was ordering terrorism in the USSR "trifles" and "nonsense" [chepukha, erunda]. At another point, Stalin telephoned Yagoda and threatened to "punch him in the nose" if he continued to drag his feet.[3]

No doubt in response to this pressure, Yagoda proposed drastic measures against Trotskyists—even those already in prison—in a 25 March 1936 memorandum to Stalin. As a means of "liquidating the Trotskyist underground," Yagoda proposed summary death sentences for any Trotskyists suspected of "terrorist activity." Sta-

3. *Voprosy istorii*, no. 2, 1995, 17. (Stenographic report of the February–March 1937 plenum.) *Izvestiia TsK KPSS*, no. 8, 1989, 85.

lin referred Yagoda's memo to Procurator Vyshinsky for a legal opinion and received the following reply.

Document 72

Letter from Vyshinsky to Stalin on Trotskyists[4]

31 March 1936

Central Committee—to I. V. Stalin

I consider that Comrade Yagoda's memo of 25 March 1936 correctly and in a timely manner poses the question of the decisive crushing [razgrom] of the Trotskyist cadres.

From my point of view, I consider it necessary to send all Trotskyists currently in exile and carrying out active work to distant labor camps by means of decrees of the Special Board of the NKVD, after examination of each concrete case. In accordance with this procedure, I consider it necessary to send to labor camps Trotskyists expelled from the party in the recent verification of party documents.

From my point of view, there is no objection to transferring the cases of Trotskyists whose guilt in terrorist activities had been established—that is, of preparing terrorist acts—to the Military Collegium of the Supreme Court, with application of the Law of 1 December 1934[5] and the highest means of punishment—shooting. . . .

A. Vyshinsky

After this, the roundup and persecution intensified. By April 1936, 508 Trotskyists were under arrest. In May the Politburo ordered all Trotskyists in exile and those formerly expelled from the party for "enemy activity" to be sent to remote camps for three to five years. Those convicted of participation in "terror" were to be retried and executed.[6] By July, Yezhov had secured confessions from a number of former Trotskyist leaders, as well as from Zinoviev and Kamenev. There are persistent rumors that Zinoviev and Kamenev agreed to confess to the scenario in return for promises that their lives would be spared, but no documentary evidence

4. *Izvestiia TsK KPSS,* no. 9, 1989, 35.

5. The so-called Kirov Law, passed immediately after Kirov's assassination, mandated abbreviated legal proceedings and immediate application of death sentences, without appeal, to those convicted of terrorism.

6. *Izvestiia TsK KPSS,* no. 8, 1989, 83.

or firsthand testimony has been found to support this. Others argue that they may have confessed out of loyalty to the party, which needed their confessions as negative examples.[7] This explanation of the confessions of Old Bolsheviks in the show trials of the 1930s is supported by Bukharin's last letter to Stalin from prison (see Document 198).

The stage was set for the first in a series of public treason trials of former oppositionists, as promised to Central Committee members at the June 1936 plenum. Now it was time to inform a broader party audience, and in July 1936 the Central Committee sent the following circular letter to party organizations.[8] Written by Yezhov and edited by Stalin, the letter had to answer questions that were bound to arise in connection with this announcement: Why did it take so long to discover the conspiracy, especially when the NKVD had closed the case in 1935? How could these Old Bolsheviks, who fought in the Revolution and civil war, have conspired with evil forces to cede part of the country? Given the 1936 volte face toward strong persecution of the opposition, it was necessary to amend the existing master narrative on the opposition leaders and to change the content of the Trotskyist trope.

Document 73

Secret Central Committee letter "Concerning the terroristic activity of the Trotskyist-Zinovievist counterrevolutionary bloc," 29 July 1936[9]

TOP SECRET

SECRET LETTER FROM THE CENTRAL COMMITTEE OF THE VKP(B)

To all regional and territorial committees, to the Central Committees of national Communist Parties, city committees, and district committees of the VKP(b).

Concerning the terroristic activity of the Trotskyist-Zinovievist counterrevolutionary bloc.

On 18 January 1935 the Central Committee of the VKP(b) directed a secret letter to all party organizations concerning the lessons to be derived from the events associated with the villainous murder of Comrade Kirov. . . .

As is well known, at that time Zinoviev and Kamenev admitted their guilt

7. See Arthur Koestler, *Darkness at Noon*, New York, 1941.
8. *Izvestiia TsK KPSS*, no. 8, 1989, 91–92, 102.
9. *Izvestiia TsK KPSS*, no. 8, 1989, 100–115. Printed.

only for having whipped up terroristic sentiments, declaring that they bear only a moral and political responsibility for the murder of S. M. Kirov.

However, as has now been revealed, the facts concerning the base counter-revolutionary White Guard terroristic activity of Zinovievists were not fully brought out during the investigation, a year and a half ago, into the murder of S. M. Kirov. The role of the Trotskyists in the murder of Comrade Kirov had similarly not been revealed.

On the basis of new materials gathered by the NKVD in 1936, it can be considered an established fact that Zinoviev and Kamenev were not only the fomenters of terroristic activity against the leaders of our party and government but also the authors of direct instructions regarding the murder of S. M. Kirov as well as preparations for attempts on the lives of other leaders of our party and, first and foremost, on the life of Comrade Stalin. . . .

Similarly, it can be considered an established fact that Zinovievists carried out their terroristic practices in a solid bloc with Trotsky and Trotskyists.

In connection with this, the Central Committee of the VKP(b) considers it necessary to inform party organizations of the new facts concerning terroristic activity by Trotskyists and Zinovievists.

What are the facts of the case, as they have recently been brought to light?

I. THE FACTS

1. During 1936, after the murder of S. M. Kirov, a host of terroristic groups made up of Trotskyists and Zinovievists has been exposed by organs of the NKVD in Moscow, Leningrad, Gorky, Minsk, Kiev, Baku, and other cities.

The overwhelming majority of members of these terroristic groups admitted under investigation that they considered the preparation of terroristic acts against the leaders of the party and government to be their fundamental task.

2. The Trotskyist and Zinovievist groups that have been exposed and all of their terroristic activity in the USSR have been led by the Trotskyist and Zinovievist bloc.

The bloc consisting of the Trotskyist group and the Zinovievist-Kamenevist group was formed at the end of 1932 after negotiations carried out among leaders of counterrevolutionary groups. As a result, a united center [*ob"edinennyi tsentr*] came into being, made up of the Zinoviev camp (Zinoviev, Kamenev, Bakaev, Yevdokimov, Kuklin) and the Trotsky camp (I. N. Smirnov, Mrachkovsky, and Ter-Vaganian). . . .

So, for instance, Zinoviev, when interrogated in connection with the exposure of terroristic groups, admitted the following at the investigation conducted on 23–25 July 1936:

"I was indeed a member of the united Trotskyist-Zinovievist center organized in 1932.

"The Trotskyist-Zinovievist center considered as its chief task the murder of leaders of the VKP(b) and, first and foremost, the murder of Stalin and Kirov. The center was connected with Trotsky through its members I. N.

Smirnov and Mrachkovsky. Direct instructions from Trotsky for the preparation of Stalin's murder were received by Smirnov."

(G. Zinoviev. Minutes of the interrogation of 23–25 July 1936.)[10] . . .

Regarding Trotsky's attitude to the creation of a united Trotskyist-Zinovievist bloc and regarding the conditions of unification, the notorious Trotskyist, S. V. Mrachkovsky, one of Trotsky's closest comrades-in-arms, testified at the investigation as follows:

"In the middle of 1932, I. N. Smirnov placed on the agenda of our ruling troika the necessity of unifying our organization with the Zinoviev-Kamenev and Shatskin-Lominadze groups. It was then that it was decided to inquire of Trotsky concerning this matter and to receive new instructions from him. Trotsky agreed to the creation of a bloc, on the condition that the united bloc consider the necessity of a violent removal [from power] of the leaders of the VKP(b) and, first and foremost, of Stalin."

(Mrachkovsky. Minutes of the interrogation of 19–20 July 1936.) . . .

3. Sergei Mironovich Kirov was killed in accordance with the decision of the united center of the Trotskyist-Zinovievist bloc.

The entire practical work of organizing the assassination attempt was placed on the shoulders of Bakaev, member of the united center. To assist Bakaev, the center assigned Karev, the notorious Zinovievist working in Leningrad, who was personally closely connected with Zinoviev.

As a result of the decision of the united center, several Trotskyist and Zinovievist terroristic groups were organized in Leningrad, including the Rumyantsev-Katalynov-Nikolaev group, which committed the murder of Kirov.

As for the fact that the murder of Kirov was committed in accordance with the decision of the united Trotskyist-Zinovievist center, this has been attested to at the investigation by the majority of the active members of the terroristic groups, including Zinoviev, Kamenev, Bakaev, Karev, and others.

Thus, for example, Zinoviev testified as follows at the investigation:

"I also confess that Bakaev and Karev, members of the organization, were entrusted by me, in the name of the united center, with the organization of terroristic acts against Stalin in Moscow and Kirov in Leningrad. These instructions by me were given in the fall of 1932."

(Zinoviev. Minutes of the interrogation of 23–25 July 1936.) . . .

4. The united center of the Trotskyist-Zinovievist counterrevolutionary bloc considered as its fundamental and primary task the murder of Comrades Stalin, Voroshilov, Kaganovich, Kirov, Ordzhonikidze, Zhdanov, Kosior, and Postyshev.[11]

10. The letter was prepared quickly. Note that many of these testimonies were recorded only a few days before the letter was written.

11. Postyshev, who had been sharply criticized for high-handed "mistakes," was nevertheless included in a place of honor as a target of the alleged assassins. Molotov, who had frequently criticized Postyshev, was left out of this pantheon of victims.

The decision to murder Comrade Stalin was taken simultaneously with the decision to murder Comrade Kirov. With this aim in mind, the center organized a number of strictly conspiratorial, terroristic groups in Moscow. In order to unify the activities of these groups, the All-Union Trotskyist-Zinovievist center created the Moscow center comprising Bakaev, Reingold, and Pikel (Zinovievists) and Mrachkovsky and Dreitser (Trotskyists). The immediate organization of the murder of Comrade Stalin was entrusted to Bakaev. At the investigation, Bakaev confessed his role as the direct organizer of terroristic acts. . . .

From abroad, Trotsky, who was directing the activities of the All-Union, united Trotskyist-Zinovievist center, has used every means at his disposal, especially after the arrest of Kamenev and Zinoviev, to speed up the murder of Comrades Stalin and Voroshilov. He has been systematically sending directives and practical instructions through his agents concerning the organizing of the murder.

E. A. Dreitser, a man close to Trotsky, formerly serving as his bodyguard, a member of the Trotskyist-Zinovievist bloc, confessed at his investigation that in 1934 he had received a written directive from Trotsky regarding the preparation of a terroristic act against Comrades Stalin and Voroshilov.

He reported the following:

"I received this directive through Stalovitskaya, my sister, a permanent resident of Warsaw, who traveled to Moscow at the end of September 1934.

"The contents of Trotsky's letter were brief. It began with the following words:

"'My dear friend! Please pass on the information that the following main tasks are on the next day's agenda:

"'First task: the removal of Stalin and Voroshilov.

"'Second task: the organization of cells in the army.

"'Third: in case of war, to make use of confusion and failure of every sort in order to seize power.'"

(Dreitser. Minutes of the interrogation of 23 July 1936.) . . .

5. Setting out on the path of individual White Guard terror, the Trotskyist-Zinovievist bloc lost all feeling of squeamishness and in order to carry out its criminal designs began to make use of the services not only of the crushed remnants of the belated followers of the White Guard oppositionism[12] but also of the services of foreign intelligence services, foreign secret police operators, spies, and provocateurs.

For example, the terroristic group headed by M. Lure, who arrived here from Germany, was in fact organized by Franz Weitz, an active German fascist and Himmler's representative (at the time leader of the fascist storm troop detachments in Berlin, currently leader of the GESTAPO, the German secret police).

When visiting Zinoviev, M. Lure informed him that the members of his

12. The derogatory *belogvardeishchina*—Trans.

terroristic group were organizationally connected with the fascist Franz Weitz and the German secret police, the GESTAPO, and asked Zinoviev for his attitude to this.

Zinoviev replied:

"What do you find so disturbing in this? After all, Moisey Ilich, you are a historian. You know the case of Lassalle and Bismarck, when Lassalle wanted to exploit Bismarck in the interests of revolution."

(M. Lure. Minutes of the interrogation of 21 July 1936.)

E. K. Konstant, a member of the terroristic group organized by M. Lure, in speaking of the motivations for his connection with Franz Weitz, the representative of the German secret police, testified as follows at the investigation:

"Being extremely embittered at the policies of the VKP(b) and being personally bitter at Stalin, I gave in with relative ease to the political working over directed at me by Franz Weitz. In his conversations with me, Franz Weitz pointed out that the differences in our political positions (I am a Trotskyist, he is a fascist) may not exclude and, on the contrary, ought to presuppose united action by Trotskyists and National Socialists in their struggle against Stalin and his supporters. After many doubts and hesitations, I agreed with Franz Weitz's conclusions and remained the whole time in constant contact with him."

(Konstant. Minutes of the interrogation of 21 July 1936.) . . .

6. In order to acquire the necessary financial resources associated with the preparation of terroristic acts, the Trotskyist-Zinovievist counterrevolutionary bloc has resorted to the theft of state funds and to direct plundering of money belonging to the people.

It was established at the investigation that at one of the sessions of the united Trotskyist-Zinovievist center it was proposed to certain active Zinovievists to make contact with secret Zinovievists working in the economic sphere in order to obtain funds. In particular, Reingold was entrusted with such a task. In accordance with a commission by Kamenev, Reingold was supposed to make contact with G. M. Arkus, a secret double-dealer, who held the post of deputy chairman of the State Bank of the USSR (Gosbank). . . .

II. CONCLUSIONS

The facts show that the Trotskyist-Zinovievist counterrevolutionary center and its leaders—Trotsky, Zinoviev, and Kamenev—have slid definitively into the mire of White Guard oppositionism, have merged with the most embittered, inveterate enemies of Soviet power, and have become transformed into an organizing force of the remnants of classes crushed in the USSR, which in their desperation are resorting to the basest tool of the struggle against the Soviet government—namely, the use of terror. . . .

The Central Committee of the VKP(b) considers it necessary to inform all party organizations of these facts regarding the terroristic activities of Trotskyists and Zinovievists and to once again focus the attention of all members of the party on the struggle against vestiges of the villainous enemies of our party and of the working class, to focus their attention on raising Bolshevik revolutionary vigilance with every means at their disposal.

The Central Committee of the VKP(b) calls upon all members of the party to take notice of the fact that even after the murder of Comrade Kirov, in certain party organizations, and, as a result of the latter's inadequate vigilance, the enemies of the party succeeded, under cover of their Communist rank, to continue their active terroristic work.

It is only the absence of proper Bolshevik vigilance that can explain the fact that Olberg, an agent of Trotsky's, who came here from Berlin in 1935, succeeded—with the help of Fedotov and Yelin, secret Trotskyists working in positions of responsibility in the apparat of the Gorky Regional Party Committee—in making himself legal and in organizing a terroristic group, which was preparing the murder of the leaders of the party.

It is only the absence of proper Bolshevik vigilance that can explain the fact that in certain district party committees in Leningrad (Vyborgsky), Trotskyists and Zinovievists, expelled from the VKP(b), had already succeeded in 1935 in being restored into the party, and in certain cases they succeeded in making their way into the party apparat and exploiting it for their own vile terroristic aims.

It is only the absence of proper Bolshevik vigilance that can explain the fact that Zinovievists had built themselves a solid nest in a host of scientific-research institutes, in the Academy of Sciences, and in certain other institutions in Moscow, Leningrad, Kiev, and Minsk.

Finally, it is only the absence of Bolshevik vigilance that can explain the fact that some of the members of terroristic groups under arrest had undergone the verification of party documents in many party organizations and had been kept in the ranks of the party.

Now, when it has been proven that the Trotskyist-Zinovievist monsters unite in their struggle against Soviet power all of the most embittered and sworn enemies of the workers of our country—spies, provocateurs, saboteurs, White Guards, kulaks, and so on, when all distinctions between these elements, on the one hand, and the Trotskyists and Zinovievists, on the other hand, have been effaced—all party organizations, all party members must come to understand that the vigilance of Communists is necessary in every area and in every situation.

The indelible mark of every Bolshevik in the current situation ought to be his ability to recognize and identify the enemies of the party, no matter how well they may have camouflaged their identity.

The Central Committee of the VKP(b), Moscow, 29 July 1936

The subsequent political trial could not have come as much of a surprise in the top party leadership. Yezhov's supervision of the investigation from the beginning of the year was widely known in the upper leadership, and he had essentially made the case against Zinoviev and Kamenev more than a year before at the June 1935 CC plenum. Stalin had discussed the upcoming repression with the Central Committee in June 1936, and the July letter was read out to all party organizations.[13]

Like other public accusations and show trials of this period, the 1936 trial scenario was based on a kernel of truth that had been embellished and exaggerated. We know that in the fall of 1932 a single bloc of oppositionists uniting Trotskyists and Zinovievists had in fact been formed at Trotsky's initiative.[14] But there is no evidence that this bloc was oriented toward organizing "terrorist acts" or anything other than political conspiracy. In the hands of the Stalinists, though, this event was magnified into a terrorist conspiracy aimed at killing the Soviet leaders.

During 19–24 August 1936, Zinoviev, Kamenev, I. N. Smirnov, and thirteen other former oppositionists were tried for treason in Moscow. With the exception of Smirnov, who retracted his confession, all of the accused admitted to having organized a "terrorist center" at Trotsky's instructions and to having planned the assassinations of Kirov, Stalin, Kaganovich, and other members of the Politburo. Although Yagoda and Vyshinsky assembled the scenario, we now know that Stalin (as with all the major show trials) played an active role in rewording the indictment, selecting the final slate of defendants, and prescribing the sentences.[15] The death sentences meted out to the defendants (as with all death sentences in political cases for years before)[16] were decided beforehand by the Politburo.[17] One hundred sixty persons were eventually ar-

---

13. This first show trial was hardly a "bolt from the blue," as some émigré commentators, far from the events they described, wrote. See Robert Conquest, *The Great Terror*, Oxford, 1968, 1973, 150, citing the apocryphal "Letter of an Old Bolshevik."

14. The Trotsky Papers (Exile Correspondence), Houghton Library, Harvard University, 13095.

15. *Izvestiia TsK KPSS*, no. 8, 1989, 92; no. 9, 1989, 42.

16. For examples of such decisions from the "special folders" [*osobye papki*] of the Politburo, see RTsKhIDNI, f. 17, op. 162, d. 16, ll. 1, 62, 64.

17. The transcript of the trial was published: *Sudebnyi otchet po delu Trotskistsko-Zinov'evskogo terroristicheskogo tsentra*, Moscow, 1936, and was translated into English as *The Case of the Trotskyist-Zinovievite Center*, New York, 1936.

rested and shot during 1936 in connection with "terrorist conspiracies" related to this trial.[18]

The first show trial of the opposition sent a strong signal through the ranks of the nomenklatura and the party in general: former leftist oppositionists could no longer be trusted to work loyally, even if they had recanted their views. Leaders of party organizations understood the signal and the required ritual. In line with directives from Moscow to mobilize support for the trial, they organized meetings of party members and ordinary citizens to produce supporting resolutions and letters. Such texts as these collective resolutions ostensibly came from below, but because of their solicitation and formulaic nature they should be considered elements of central, public rhetoric designed to affirm the desired unanimity.

Document 74

Telegram from Makhachkala party organization to the CC, August 1936[19]

Telegram of the party aktiv of the city of Makhachkala to the CC of the VKP(b)

THE PARTY AKTIV OF MAKHACHKALA, HAVING DISCUSSED THE PROGRESS OF THE TRIAL OF THE TROTSKYIST-ZINOVIEVIST GANG, DEMANDS THAT THE SUPREME COURT EXECUTE THE THREE-TIME CONTEMPTIBLE DEGENERATES, WHO HAVE SLID INTO THE MIRE OF FASCISM AND AIMED THEIR GUNS AT THE HEART OF OUR PARTY, THE GREAT STALIN. THE REPORT OF THE SUICIDE OF TOMSKY, WHO WAS MIXED UP WITH COUNTERREVOLUTIONARY TROTSKYIST-ZINOVIEVIST TERRORISTS, IS AN ATTEMPT TO COVER UP ALL TRACES OF TREASONOUS ACTIVITY BY THE RIGHTISTS' RINGLEADERS AGAINST THE PARTY. WE DEMAND THAT THE ORGANS OF THE PROLETARIAN COURT CARRY OUT THE MOST THOROUGH INVESTIGATION OF THE CASE OF BUKHARIN, PIATAKOV, UGLANOV, RYKOV, RADEK. IF THEY HAVE IN ANY WAY BETRAYED THE INTERESTS OF THE LENINIST-STALINIST CAUSE, WE DEMAND THAT THE SUPREME PENALTY OF SOCIAL JUSTICE BE APPLIED TO THEM. THE PARTY AKTIV ASSURES OUR GREAT LEADER [*vozhd'*] THAT NO MANEUVERS BY THE DOUBLE-DEALING CRIMINALS SHALL AROUSE CONFUSION OR DISMAY AMONG OUR

18. *Izvestiia TsK KPSS*, no. 8, 1989, 93.
19. RTsKhIDNI, f. 17, op. 120, d. 271, l. 21.

Document 74 *continued*

RANKS. THE DAGESTAN PARTY ORGANIZATION AND THE BROAD
WORKING MASSES OF DAGESTAN HAVE CLOSED RANKS EVER MORE
TIGHTLY AROUND THEIR STALINIST CC, AROUND THEIR BELOVED
AND DEAR STALIN. LONG LIVE THE GREAT LEADER OF ALL THE OP-
PRESSED AND ENSLAVED OF THE WORLD, OUR DEAR AND BELOVED
STALIN! DEATH TO THE MURDERERS, TO THE TERRORISTS, TO THE
VILE TRAITORS OF THE SOCIALIST MOTHERLAND!

Document 75

Letter from the Azov–Black Sea Party Committee to Stalin, 29 August 1936[20]

Letter from the Azov–Black Sea Territorial Committee of the VKP(b) to I. V.
Stalin. Adopted at the Plenum of the Territorial Committee of 26–29 August
1936.

Dear Comrade Stalin:

It is with great satisfaction that the Bolsheviks of the Azov–Black Sea region
received the news that the sentence handed down by the military collegium of
the Supreme Court in the case of Zinoviev, Kamenev, Smirnov, Mrachkovsky,
Ter-Vaganian, and others, Trotskyist-Zinovievist bandits and traitors who had
betrayed the motherland, had been carried out. These rabid dogs of fascism
ambushed and killed Sergei Mironovich Kirov, one of your best friends and
disciples. These vicious enemies of the Soviet state, hirelings and agents of the
fascist secret police, raised their hands against you, Comrade Stalin, our leader,
leader and best friend of all working people, and against your best lieutenants.
By means of this clandestine murder, Trotsky, Zinoviev, Kamenev, and their
gang of bandits attempted to force their way into power in a country whose
people, 170 million strong, hate them with a fierce hatred. They did this all in
order to restore capitalism and reenslave the workers and peasants. . . .

B. Sheboldaev,
Secretary of the Azov–Black Sea Territorial Committee of the VKP(b)

Thus the language surrounding the Zinoviev-Kamenev trial consisted of several parts. The July letter elaborated the discursive line;
the prescribed letters and telegrams provided symbolic affirmation
from below; the trial itself provided the ritual performance of the
new line. This was a classic example of the mechanism for changing
Stalinist policies: tropes were filled with new content. But the fact

20. RTsKhIDNI, f. 17, op. 21, d. 2195, ll. 114, 1140b.

that actors at the various levels played their roles does not mean that they did so insincerely or that they did not believe the new line. Obviously, the new transcript could not have been successful had it not filled particular needs or found resonance at various levels. It could not create reality; it could only adapt and redirect it.

The official face of the enemy had been reconstructed in the summer of 1936: he was a former left oppositionist who had taken the path of terror. He was an agent of Trotsky, a spy, an assassin. This version had advantages for several segments of the party. For Stalin and his circle, it provided a rationale for finally destroying personal and political enemies whose opposition went back more than a decade, and it created a climate in which future opposition obviously carried life-and-death risks. For the nomenklatura at all levels, it justified the obliteration of and final victory over a possible alternative leadership whose leaders had argued for years that the Stalinist faction should be removed. This definition—or attribution—of the enemy also benefited the ruling elite as a whole insofar as it presented a clearly defined evil and opposite "other": the groups behind Zinoviev, Kamenev, and Trotsky. They had for years stood for an alternative leadership, an alternative team to lead the country. If they won, however unlikely that might seem, the current team would be replaced in quick order. Although there seemed little chance that Zinoviev or Trotsky would return to power in the mid-1930s, the possibility always existed. Memories of nomenklatura members told them that stranger things had happened. Lenin's ascension to power in 1917 must have seemed at least as far-fetched in 1915. This evil force could be conveniently blamed for a variety of sins of the moment, including industrial failure, agricultural shortfalls, and other policy shortcomings more properly attributable to the nomenklatura itself.[21] The left opposition made perfect scapegoats.

But they were scapegoats of a particularly believable kind, given the prevailing mentalities of the time. The 1917 revolutions, civil war, and party struggles of the 1920s had created a kind of conspiracy mentality among the Bolsheviks. The vicious and violent civil

21. See Roberta T. Manning, "The Soviet Economic Crisis of 1936–1940 and the Great Purges," in J. Arch Getty and Roberta T. Manning, eds., *Stalinist Terror: New Perspectives*, New York, 1993, 116–41.

war, which was rich with real conspiracies and constant, nagging insecurity, was the formative experience for this generation of nomenklatura and party members. In their view of reality, politics *was* conspiracy, and it was not very hard for them to believe that professional revolutionaries and skilled conspirators like Zinoviev and Trotsky *had* been up to no good on some level. Similarly, for the Russian populace, with its cultural legacies of good vs. evil, belief in the machinations of dark forces of all kinds, and a traditional suspicion of educated intellectuals, it was not too difficult to accept the notion that Jewish Bolshevik intellectuals probably were involved in some sort of clandestine business.

There seem to have been no protests or questions raised in party leadership circles about executing these former oppositionists. Fear was one deterrent: knowing that police investigations were ongoing, who would question Stalin's leadership on such a serious matter and risk being regarded as a defender of enemies? Party discipline provides a further answer. In the crisis atmosphere of the times, which was perceived as a continuation of the "new situation" following the Riutin affair, there was strong incentive in the party to close ranks against the perceived threat.

The Zinoviev and Trotsky oppositions had broken the rules of the nomenklatura. In the 1920s (and as recently as the Riutin Platform) they had threatened to organize politically outside the party elite. Their strategy had been to agitate among the party's rank and file to gain support for their platforms against the ruling group. This was the unpardonable sin. By threatening to split the party—the Bolsheviks' worst nightmare since the civil war—the oppositionists threatened the survival of the regime and thus the Revolution.

They also threatened to turn the membership against the ruling stratum. This could not be tolerated. The opposition, therefore, represented a continuing menace to the corporate interests of the Stalinist nomenklatura that outweighed any nostalgia that the Old Bolshevik oppositionist comrades-in-arms may otherwise have inspired. The party elite did not regard the annihilation of Zinoviev and Kamenev as threatening to itself. It was not hard for the serving party leadership to support the final decimation of the left opposition out of political and personal self-interest. Once again, Stalin and the nomenklatura had common interests.

Cadres Issues in the Party

However convenient it may have seemed to scapegoat the opposition and to identify officially approved enemies for public consumption, the tactic carried risks for the party elite. It was in their interest to identify the former left oppositionists as enemies and to neutralize them permanently. It was convenient for regional party secretaries to use a fluid definition of Trotskyism to marginalize, expel, and even arrest troublesome people in the localities. On the other hand, an increasingly plastic definition of enemies and "Trotskyists" could be a land mine for the nomenklatura itself. The new rhetoric set a dangerous precedent.

It was not only the serving members of the nomenklatura who could use the new accusatory narrative against their opponents. Ideological fanatics, careerists, opportunists, and ordinary party members with grudges to settle adopted the new line for their own purposes. In the aftermath of the July closed letter and the first trial, denunciations had increased at all levels.

Document 76

Letter from A. Flegontov to N. I. Yezhov[22]

---

20 August 1936

To Comrade Yezhov,

Secretary of the CC of the VKP(b)

I have learned from the letter circulated by the VKP(b) and from Comrade P. P. Postyshev's report at the Kiev Regional and City Party aktiv meeting of 16 August of this year that Mrachkovsky, notwithstanding his statement during the party purge of 1934 that he acknowledges the party's general line and that he has broken with Trotskyism, still belongs to the Trotskyist, counterrevolutionary, terroristic organization.

I consider it my duty, therefore, to report that Grigory Maksimovich Krutov, chairman of the Far Eastern Territorial Executive Committee, a party member, was on exceptionally friendly terms with Mrachkovsky, with whom he was associated as a Trotskyist since 1923.

While employed as supervisor of construction of the Baikal-Amur railroad (BAM), Mrachkovsky frequently visited Khabarovsk, where he would always stay at Krutov's apartment and was considered a member of his family.

22. RTsKhIDNI, f. 17, op. 120, d. 272, l. 42.

Document 76 *continued*

The other day, I accidentally found out that while in Kharkov in 1935 on his vacation, Krutov had spent some time with the Trotskyist Vinokur-Naumov (former chairman of the Directorate of Services for the Cooperatives of the Handicrafts Council [*Ukopromsovet*]). Together, they visited the Kharkov locomotive works.

During Krutov's tenure as deputy chairman of the Territorial Executive Committee of the Far Eastern region (DVK), Vinokur-Naumov served as commissioner of the People's Forestry Committee of the Far Eastern region and maintained close and friendly ties with him.

Besides, Krutov's personal secretary before the 1934 purge was a former Trotskyist, a certain Ivan Nikitich Mikhailov. During this period, Krutov's assistant was the former Trotskyist Aizenshtat.

Now, weighing all the above-mentioned facts, I've come to the conclusion that [Krutov's] friendship with Mrachkovsky and with Vinokur-Naumov was no accident. The same may be said for the fact that he surrounded himself with Trotskyists.

A. Flegontov,
Chairman of the Council of the Handicrafts Cooperatives of the Ukraine and member of the KP(b) Ukraine since 1919
Party card no. 0700479

Denunciations like these posed a new question: aside from marginalized has-beens like Zinoviev, were Trotskyists at work among serving officials in the state and party apparatus? The testimony of the Zinoviev trial had given a signal. Almost as an aside, some of the defendants had suggested conspiratorial links with long-recanted, apparently loyal ex-Trotskyists who were currently serving in state offices. Georgy Piatakov, deputy commissar of heavy industry, and the prominent journalist Karl Radek had sided with the Trotskyist opposition in the 1920s. Although they had forsworn Trotskyism early in the 1930s, they were implicated in the trial testimony, as were rightist leaders Bukharin, Rykov, and Tomsky. Could it be that even high-ranking captains of industry with ancient Trotskyist connections were also guilty of treason? Evidently, Stalin had authorized Yezhov to root out all former active Trotskyists and Zinovievists; to follow the trail of their personal connections wherever it led. And because such people with politically compromised pasts were working for the state or the party, the path of investigations began to wind itself into the bureaucracy. Regional leaders of the nomenklatura picked up on the increasingly ambiguous definition of the enemy's face. What had seemed a useful definition of the enemy was mutating in menacing ways. If captains of industry with compromising pasts were at risk, what about their subordinates with similarly blemished political records? Although the regional secretaries were obliged to promulgate the new ideological transcript, it could have given them no pleasure to incorporate into their resolutions the notion that their own machines needed to be "checked and rechecked."

Document 77

Discussion of the August 1936 secret CC letter in the Azov–Black Sea Party Committee[23]

Extract from Protocol #183 of the buro of the Azov–Black Sea Territorial Committee of the VKP(b)

19 August 1936

2. Questions concerning the secret letter of the CC of the VKP(b)

All district and city committees are instructed to personally check all officials appointed to nomenklatura positions of the CC and territorial committee for the purposes of exposing persons connected in the past with the counterrevolutionary group of Trotsky-Zinoviev and whose devotion to the party's cause is suspect. The district committees are to complete this task within 10 days and the city committees by 1 September.

A memorandum concerning this is to be presented by secretaries of the rural district committees by 25 August and by secretaries of the city committees by 1 September.

B. Sheboldaev

Secretary of the Azov–Black Sea Territorial Committee of the VKP(b)

This checking and rechecking would by early 1937 result in the removal and sometimes arrest of a number of lower-level party officials in the regions. By that time, according to data provided by chief of the Central Committee's party registration sector G. M. Malenkov, some 3,500 party members across the USSR had been removed from office as "enemies," representing about 3.5 percent of all those checked.[24]

23. RTsKhIDNI, f. 17, op. 42, d. 759, l. 165.
24. *Voprosy istorii*, no. 10, 1995, 8.

The threat posed by these clouds over the heads of the regional party leaders is difficult to assess. Beginning in fall 1936, criticism of these officials escalated as the hunt for Trotskyists expanded. But in late 1936 through the first half of 1937, no regional party secretary was accused of disloyalty or association with "enemy conspiracies." Nearly a year passed before senior party secretaries themselves were directly tarred with the Trotskyist brush. In fall 1936 the only implication was that they had been lax in keeping their own political houses in order, and as late as the February–March 1937 Plenum of the Central Committee, Stalin went out of his way to publicly absolve them, arguing that they were by no means "bad" in this regard.[25]

On the other hand, it is possible to see in these moves the first step in a devious Stalin plan to destroy the regional party leaders and apparatus. Indeed, several months later, in the second half of 1937, he did just that. The new political line of late 1936 can thus be explained as the first tactical step in weakening the regional leaders so that they could be finished off later. The restraint Stalin showed at this point may have been a cat-and-mouse game. Or it may have been a means to threaten the regional leaders while at the same time giving them a clean bill of political health in order to secure their support in the upcoming move to destroy Bukharin, the military, or others.

Presumably, of course, Stalin could simply arrest and remove them individually or en masse at any time, and it is hard to see what he would have gained by toying with them. Stalin did not need to entice or encourage the regional secretaries to support a move against Bukharin. Experience had shown that they were perfectly willing to condemn former oppositionists without much encouragement. If Stalin planned at this time to destroy the regional party leaders, he had nothing to gain by waiting, a tactic that also carried a certain risk.

Even if Stalin was not planning to destroy the regional nomenklatura, criticism of them was a useful tool to control and discipline them. Regional party secretaries, as we have seen, were powerful satraps in their territories, dominating the legal, cultural, ideologi-

25. Voprosy istorii, no. 3, 1995, 3–15.

cal, and everyday lives of the population. Many of them were petty tyrants, operating their own regional and local personality cults. In Azerbaijan, progress in the oil industry was attributed to the wise guidance of the party first secretary in Baku. Stalin had observed that in the Caucasus there was not one real party committee but rather rule based on the will of individual party chieftains—he used the Cossack term *ataman*. In the Ukraine an authoritative text on literature noted that the development of Ukrainian and Russian literature was in considerable measure due to the opinions of the party secretary in Kiev. One issue of a local newspaper mentioned the first secretary's name sixty times. (The fact that the secretary's wife ran the ideological institute was no doubt a factor.) The first secretary of the Western oblast, whose photograph frequently adorned the regional newspaper, was "the best Bolshevik in the region." In Kazakhstan the republican party politburo even tried to rename the highest peak in the Tien Shan mountain range after the first secretary.[26]

From Moscow's point of view, this situation was profoundly troubling and required considerable subtlety. On the one hand, Stalin needed these satraps to carry out Moscow's policies in the far-flung regions of the country. It had been necessary to vest them with tremendous authority to implement collectivization and industrialization. They were Moscow's only presence in the countryside and thus indispensable to the party. On the other hand, their near-absolute powers had permitted them to use patronage to create their own political machines: miniature nomenklaturas under their personal control, complete with regional personality cults.

Often, as Yezhov admitted in 1935, Moscow did not even know the identities of many local party leaders who served in the regional machines.[27] Appointment of city and district party secretaries had been subject to Central Committee confirmation only since early 1935. Even by early 1937 the list of party officials subject to Central Committee confirmation (the list being known as the Central

26. For examples, see speeches by Malenkov, Mekhlis, Beria, and Kudriavtsev to the February–March 1937 plenum. *Voprosy istorii,* no. 5–6, 1995, 10; no. 7, 1995, 19–21; no. 10, 1995, 10–15.

27. Smolensk Archive file 116/154e, l. 88.

Committee nomenklatura) included only 5,860 officials of a national stratum of party secretaries and officials numbering well over 100 thousand.[28] In the mid-thirties, squabbles between regional leaders and the Central Committee secretariat about the appointment of this or that person were common and involved continuous negotiation. Generally, though, the regional party secretaries could prevail if they pushed the point hard enough, and they were thus able to staff their machines with "their people" more often than not.

How, then, could Moscow control the activities of the regional governors? Stalin created various parallel hierarchies and channels of information (the NKVD and Party Control Commission were examples), but experience showed that even these nominally independent institutions sooner or later came under machine control locally.[29] Another tactic that Stalin used frequently throughout his reign was "control from below," a policy he discussed at some length at the February–March Plenum of the Central Committee.[30] The often arbitrary rule of regional leaders created resentment from below, and Stalin encouraged criticism of the party apparatus from those quarters. Of course, it was in the interests of neither Stalin nor the nomenklatura to permit a full and open discussion of the problem of government, so this discourse had to be kept within strict limits. The real reasons for local misconduct, dysfunctional administration, and corresponding popular resentment could not be discussed; things could not be named by their names. A genuine analysis of administrative problems would have included discussion of the dictatorship itself and would have threatened the governing myths of the regime. Such a discussion would touch on the lack of national consensus on Bolshevik dictatorship, the undemocratic selection of leaders at all levels, the constant recourse to terror as a substitute for consensual government, and the zigzag-

28. Malenkov's speech to the February–March 1937 Plenum of the Central Committee. *Voprosy istorii*, no. 10, 1995, 7.

29. See J. Arch Getty, "Pragmatists and Puritans: The Rise and Fall of the Party Control Commission in the 1930," *The Carl Beck Papers in Russian and East European Studies*, Pittsburgh, 1997.

30. See Stalin's concluding speech in *Voprosy istorii*, no. 3, 1995, 3–15; no. 11–12, 1995, 11–22. His remarks were published as a pamphlet called *Mastering Bolshevism*, New York, 1937.

ging voluntarist policy mistakes that characterized Bolshevik rule.[31]

The trick, then, and the essence of control from below was to encourage rank-and-file criticism of the middle-level leaders on particular issues of non-fulfillment or negligence. In this way, Stalin could receive specific information that bypassed the nomenklatura's normal information filters. He could solicit grassroots reports about official misconduct, suspicious characters in high positions, and the failure to act on party and state decisions. Moreover, these informal channels allowed him to play the role of the good tsar, posing as a caring and attentive friend of the little guy against the high-handed actions of the "feudal princes," as he had called the regional secretaries at the 1934 Party Congress. It was desirable to use the rank and file as a check on the midlevel apparatus without inciting riot from below. Because of the power of the local party leaders, such criticism could not happen without high-level license and approval.

Stalin wanted to hold the regional secretaries' feet to the fire without setting the whole house ablaze. The new public rhetoric about nomenklatura "political laxity" provided a vehicle for their underlings to criticize the regional party elite around the country. As such, it emphasized the long-standing tension between leaders and led. This policy was delicate; it was designed to place blame for the sins of the regime on (and thereby exercise control over) the middle party apparatus without destroying it completely. In his speech to the February–March plenum, Stalin pointed out that although the regional party officials were not themselves bad, the rank-and-file members often knew better than they who was suspicious and who was not.[32]

A resolution of the Azov–Black Sea Territorial Party Organization during the Zinoviev trial crystallized these themes and is a representative document of the period and its discursive system. It touched on virtually all the political issues of the day: the nature of the oppositionists, the membership screenings, control of the appa-

31. For a fuller discussion of this problem, see Gábor T. Rittersporn, *Stalinist Simplifications and Soviet Complications: Social Tensions and Political Conflicts in the USSR, 1933–1953*, Reading, 1991.

32. *Voprosy istorii*, no. 5–6, 1995, 4.

ratus, and the difference between the elite and the rank and file. It also suggested that these issues, once discrete, were beginning to fuse into a dangerous new political language. The document included not only the ritual call for the execution of the defendants but also a demand for increased "vigilance" and a call to "verify the party apparatus" in the towns and districts (but not, it should be noted, in the higher territorial apparatus itself) to weed out "doubtful" people and those in any way connected "even in the past" with Trotskyists and Zinovievists. As Stalin had done at the June plenum (see Document 71), the resolution cast doubt on the efficacy of the recently completed verification and exchange of party documents (which the apparatus had itself carried out) by suggesting that those operations had not gotten the real enemies at all. The resolution also put another cloud over the workings of the secret police (nationally under Yagoda's direction but locally often under the influence of party secretaries). Finally, in its last section, it more than implied that regional leaders had ignored "signals" from below (perhaps like Document 76) about politically suspicious people in high positions.

Document 78

Results of the July 1936 secret CC letter in the Azov–Black Sea Party Committee[33]

Extract from Protocol #176 of the buro of the Azov–Black Sea Territorial Committee of the VKP(b)

3 August 1936

64. Secret letter from the CC of the VKP(b) entitled "Concerning the terroristic activity of the Trotskyist-Zinovievist counterrevolutionary bloc" of 29 July 1936

1. Having discussed the secret letter of 29 July of this year, the buro of the territorial committee considers the conclusions drawn by the CC of the VKP(b) concerning the terroristic activity of the Trotskyist-Zinovievist counterrevolutionary bloc to be totally correct.

The buro of the territorial committee considers it necessary to put an end, once and for all, to the terroristic work carried on by the leaders of the Trotskyist-Zinovievist bloc in the persons of Zinoviev, Trotsky, Kamenev, Bakaev, Smirnov, Mrachkovsky, Ter-Vaganian, and others, all of whom are directly responsible for the murder of Sergei Mironovich Kirov. In addition, they are

33. RTsKhIDNI, f. 17, op. 42, d. 759, ll. 149–50.

carrying on, viciously and spitefully, preparations for the murder of the leaders of the party, first and foremost, for the murder of STALIN.

The interests of the Revolution demand that we put an immediate end to the activities of this gang of rabid murderers, agents of fascism.

The buro of the territorial committee considers it necessary to place before the CC of the VKP(b) the matter of carrying out legal proceedings against this gang and applying to Zinoviev, Kamenev, Bakaev, I. N. Smirnov, Mrachkovsky, Ter-Vaganian, and others the supreme penalty of social justice as befitting the most embittered enemies of the people and the Revolution.

2. The first secretaries of city and district committees are instructed to personally and thoroughly evaluate [*proverit'*], from top to bottom, the party apparats of the city and district committees and of the primary party organizations [PPO] in order to purge the apparats of persons of questionable or wavering [loyalty] and in any way connected, in the present or past, with Trotskyism and Zinovievism [*zinovievshchina*].

3. It is to be established that in the future whenever a party worker is admitted into the party apparat, the first secretary shall conduct a thorough and detailed check into the political aspect of the party worker.

The first secretaries of city and district committees are to be warned that they bear personal responsibility for the slightest contamination of the party apparat.

4. The first secretaries of city and district committees are under obligation to personally and thoroughly evaluate once again the loyalty of former Trotskyists and Zinovievists to the party's cause as well as the devotion of all Communists who had wavered in the past, had undergone verification of party documents, had been kept in the party and received new party cards. The first secretaries are to do this in order that they may be able to weigh all the facts and ascertain whether the decision to keep them in the party was correct and whether their continued presence in the party is possible.

5. A commission consisting of Comrades Malinov, Dvolaitsky, Berezin, and Rud is instructed to review the personnel of the scientific-research institutions of the territory [*krai*].

6. The NKVD is instructed to carry out a second and thorough investigation pertaining to Trotskyists and Zinovievists who had been expelled from the party in the course of the verification of party documents, arrested but subsequently released without incurring punishment, in view of the fact that the buro of the territorial committee is subjecting the quality of work of the apparat of the regional directorate of the NKVD to serious doubt in this matter.

7. The buro of the territorial committee believes that a proper Bolshevik vigilance is still lacking in the territorial party organization and, being guided by the secret letter of the CC of the VKP(b), proposes to all city and district committees to raise the revolutionary vigilance of the party organization.

As a practical measure, the buro of the territorial committee proposes that

Document 78 *continued*

every statement on the part of Communists and nonparty persons and any piece of information whatsoever that casts doubt on this or that party member's devotion to the party's cause or pertaining to any ties with the counter-revolutionary, Trotskyist-Zinovievist bloc be met with a thoroughgoing response and fully investigated.

SPECIAL RESOLUTION

In view of the poor work of the Azov–Black Sea Directorate of the NKVD, we ask the CC to strengthen its leadership.

B. Sheboldaev,
Secretary of the Azov–Black Sea Territorial Committee of the VKP(b)

As it spread into the level of serving officials, the continuing hunt for Trotskyists disturbed the leaders of the party apparatus. Although, as we shall see, they gave up some of their valued assistants with dubious pasts when they had to, they also tried to limit the definition and application of the Trotskyist label and to protect their own. In this period, courts and procurators controlled by the local party machine frequently adopted a narrow definition of Trotskyism (and the criminality associated with it). Central organs often complained about the practice.

Document 79

NKVD memo "Concerning deficiencies in the work of the courts and of the procuracy of the Azov–Black Sea region"[34]

From a memorandum of the 10th Department of the Political-Secret Section of the Chief Administration of State Security concerning deficiencies in the work of the courts and of the procuracy of the Azov–Black Sea region, August 1936.

Many deficiencies of a substantive nature have taken place in the work of the judicial organs and of the procuracy of the Azov–Black Sea region. They have led to a distortion of punitive policy and to the perversion of revolutionary legality.

Among the chief deficiencies we may consider the following:

1. A formal approach during the review of cases under investigation and the practice of stripping the materials obtained during the preliminary investigation of their political essence;

34. RTsKhIDNI, f. 17, op. 120, d. 171, ll. 181, 183–85, 188–90.

Document 79 continued

2. The granting of inadmissibly light sentences (or even acquittal) to notorious criminals, notwithstanding sufficient proof to the contrary presented by the prosecution;

3. Red tape and the widespread practice of remanding investigative cases for further investigation without sufficient grounds for such action;

4. The practice of stripping and distorting the testimonies of witnesses for the prosecution when entering them into the minutes of the court sessions. . . .

The following circumstance deserves attention:

The special section of the territorial procuracy insistently demands from officials of the administration of the NKVD, notwithstanding statutory regulations [to the contrary], that, during their interrogations of witnesses and the accused, they record verbatim the counterrevolutionary, lewd, and cynical, insulting words directed at the leaders of the party and of the government. And [that], for these reasons, they remand the cases for "further investigation."

In connection with the categorical refusal by the administration of the NKVD to carry out these demands, the special section of the territorial procuracy carries out an auxiliary interrogation of individual witnesses, entering into the minutes indecent and insulting words directed at the leaders of the party and of the government. . . .

There are cases where the procuracy has refused to sanction arrests by the administration of the NKVD of obvious criminals. This is supported by the following facts:

On 16 June this year, the matter of arresting Pyotr Timofeevich Kozlov was raised before the territorial procuracy. He is a student at the Main Industrial Workers' School [rabfak] in Rostov-on-the-Don. During the discussion at the party-Komsomol meeting concerning the Trotskyist outburst by Barmbaumov—another student, during a lesson in the history of the VKP(b)—Kozlov spoke out in defense of Barmbaumov and said: "Trotsky has rendered immense service to his country. He is one of the most popular leaders of the Revolution. In fact, as early as 1905, he was the chairman of the Petersburg Soviet of Workers' Deputies," and so on.

When asked how he knew all this, Kozlov answered that he had read much by Trotsky and about him. When accused of Trotskyism, Kozlov answered: "I am not a Trotskyist. Do you mean to tell me that Trotskyists are really like me? After all, all Trotskyists are people of genius."

Considering such a speech an open counterrevolutionary Trotskyist sally (all the more so when taking into account Kozlov's many anti-Soviet pronouncements previous to this), the [chief] administration of the NKVD requested sanction for Kozlov's arrest.

Comrade Startsev, assistant procurator in the special section of the procuracy, refused to sanction such an arrest, declaring that "Kozlov's actions do not show any signs of Trotskyist activity," that he finds nothing Trotskyist in

Kozlov's behavior, and [that] "after all, Trotsky did occupy the posts which Kozlov referred to at the meeting." . . .

In this period there were several competing definitions of Trotskyism. Traditionally, Trotskyists were those who had formally or openly participated in the left opposition (from 1923 as Trotskyists or from 1926 as "united oppositionists," together with the Zinoviev group). By the early 1930s the definition was expanded to include those who might at some time have voted for a Trotskyist platform at a party meeting or defended a known Trotskyist from party punishment. Such actions were considered "incompatible with party membership" and had resulted in expulsion from the party. In many cases, active Trotskyists were sentenced by the Special Board of the NKVD to exile. Trotskyism, although a party crime, was not a punishable offense under the state's criminal code. It was therefore necessary to use extralegal bodies like the NKVD's Special Board to punish oppositionists. (See Document 25 and Document 50 for Yezhov's recommendation and authorization of this strategy.) In 1936, however, both the definition of Trotskyism and the prescribed sanctions against it became much more severe. By summer, Trotskyists suspected of "terrorism" were being executed (see Document 72). The Zinoviev trial made this new line public: some oppositionists were said to have crossed the line from political dissidence to treasonable criminal activity. But as Document 79 shows, not all elements in the party-state hierarchy were eager to apply the new standard.

At the end of September 1936 the Politburo made a firm statement on the matter. Trotskyists were no longer to be considered polemical opponents on the left; now, as a category, they were defined as fascist spies and saboteurs. This document provides an excellent example not only of attributive definition of enemies but also of explicit and self-conscious narrative construction through a prescriptive text. The political-linguistic process of attribution was quite open: a "directive" defined "our stance" on certain groups who "must now therefore be considered" in a different way. The form of the enemy was now filled with new content.

Document 80

Politburo resolution, "Our stance toward counterrevolutionary, Trotskyist-Zinovievist elements"[35]

From Protocol #43 of the Politburo of the CC of the VKP(b)
29 September 1936

Item #305. Re: Our stance toward counterrevolutionary, Trotskyist-Zinovievist elements

The following directive concerning our stance toward counterrevolutionary, Trotskyist-Zinovievist elements is to be adopted:

a) Until very recently, the CC of the VKP(b) considered the Trotskyist-Zinovievist scoundrels as the leading political and organizational detachment of the international bourgeoisie.

The latest facts tell us that these gentlemen have slid even deeper [into the mire]. They must therefore now be considered foreign agents, spies, subversives, and wreckers representing the fascist bourgeoisie of Europe.

b) In connection with this, it is necessary for us to make short work of these Trotskyist-Zinovievist scoundrels. This is to include not only those who have been arrested and whose investigation has already been completed, and not only those like Muralov, Piatakov, Beloborodov, and others, who are currently under investigation, but also those who had been exiled earlier.

The dramatic and disorienting social changes in the country since 1929, the disastrous famine of the early 1930s, the incomprehensible economic system with its unpredictable "mistakes" and lurches back and forth all cried out for simplistic explanations. From peasant to Politburo member, the language about evil conspirators served a purpose. For the plebeians, it provided a possible explanation for the daily chaos and misery of life. For the many committed enthusiasts it explained why their Herculean efforts to build socialism often produced bad results. For the nomenklatura member, it was an excuse to destroy their only challengers. For local party chiefs, it was a rationale for again expelling inconvenient people from the local machines. For the Politburo member, it provided a means to avoid self-questioning about party policy and a vehicle for

---

35. RTsKhIDNI, f. 17, op. 3, d. 981, l. 58. The Politburo did not meet to approve this resolution. See *Izvestiia TsK KPSS,* no. 5, 1989, 72. Drafted by Yezhov and later signed by Stalin (who was on vacation at the time), the Politburo resolution was approved by polling the members. Yezhov's draft originally included a third point—removed by Stalin—calling for the summary shooting of several thousand Trotskyists and the exile of thousands of others to Yakutia.

closing ranks. The image of evil, conspiring Trotskyists was convenient for everybody.[36] The question, of course, was who the evil force was.

After receipt of the July letter and before the trial itself began, local secretaries ordered the party members to be screened again for any connection in the past with Zinovievist or Trotskyist groups.[37] Over the next several months, thousands were expelled from the party for present and past suspicious activities. Meetings were held, files were scanned again, and memories racked to uncover any possible former connection to the left opposition. In the climate following the trial, the definition of Trotskyism became quite fluid; it could include a careless remark decades before, an abstention on some resolution against Trotsky in the early 1920s, or a perceived lack of faith in the party line at any time.

Table 3 shows the quantitative dimension of these expulsions in comparison with those of the recently completed party screenings. Numerically, the attrition of this round of purges was smaller than the verification and exchange of documents (*obmen*); only about one-half of one percent of the party was expelled. But whereas explicitly named Trotskyists and Zinovievists had constituted a small fraction of those expelled earlier, they made up nearly half of those removed in the later campaign. There was, however, one similarity between this round of expulsions and the previous operations. In both cases, local and regional party secretaries were able to serve their own ends. They were able to direct the fire downward: the vast majority of victims of these expulsions were again rank-and-file party members.

"Surely, things will go smoothly with Yezhov at the helm"

NKVD chief Yagoda had been under a cloud at least since the Kirov assassination, when the failure of his service to prevent the shooting had called his competence into question. Yagoda said that he had always considered the followers of Zinoviev, Kamenev, and

36. See Gábor T. Rittersporn, "The Omnipresent Conspiracy: On Soviet Imagery of Politics and Social Relations in the 1930s," in Getty and Manning, *Stalinist Terror*, 99–115.

37. For examples of such far-fetched accusations from this era, see RTsKhIDNI, f. 17, op. 71, d. 35, ll. 6–15, and d. 74, ll. 2–3.

Table 3. Expulsion of "Oppositionists," 1935–36

Time period	Expelled from party	% of party expelled	Trotskyists/ Zinovievists expelled	Trotskyists/ Zinovievists as % of expelled
1935 proverka	263,885	11.1	7,504	2.8
1936 obmen	37,891	1.8	3,324	8.8
From 1936 obmen to Feb. 1937	13,752	0.6	6,658	48.4

Source: RTsKhIDNI, f. 17. op. 120, d. 278, ll. 2–3.

Trotsky to be guilty and had participated in the trials and repressions of them until the fall of 1936.[38] But since the attack on Yenukidze in mid-1935, it always seemed to be the party, not the NKVD, that uncovered the various plots and conspiracies. Behind the scenes, Yagoda's position became much worse in 1936. Yezhov, with Stalin's support, became curator of the NKVD's investigations of the opposition, further undermining Yagoda's credibility and leadership of the secret police. Materials in Yezhov's archive show that he angled for Yagoda's job, never missing an opportunity to criticize the NKVD chief to Stalin.

Moreover, when former rightist Mikhail Tomsky committed suicide in August 1936, he left behind a letter hinting that Yagoda had been the one to recruit him into the right opposition back in 1928. Yezhov investigated the accusation, and although he reported to Stalin that Tomsky's charge against Yagoda lacked credibility, he nevertheless noted that "so many deficiencies have been uncovered in the work of the NKVD that it is impossible to tolerate them further."[39] In this light, it is perhaps surprising that Yagoda held on as long as he did.

But Yagoda's eclipse within his own bailiwick by Yezhov strongly suggests that Stalin had decided on the change sometime early in 1936 and used the first three-quarters of the year to permit Yezhov to learn the procedures of the NKVD and to sort out friend from foe within that organization. Yezhov used this time successfully to co-opt several of Yagoda's key deputies, including

38. RTsKhIDNI, f. 17, op. 2, d. 598, ll. 1–18.
39. Quoted from Yezhov's archive (without citation) in Oleg V. Khlevniuk, *Politbiuro: Mekhanizmy politicheskoi vlasti v 1930-e gody*, Moscow, 1996, 205.

M. P. Frinovsky, L. M. Zakovsky, and the brothers B. D. and M. D. Berman, against Yagoda loyalists Molchanov and G. Ye. Prokofiev. Deputy NKVD Commissar Yakov Agranov seems to have tried to play both sides against each other. (See Documents 144, 146, and 147.) Finally Yagoda was removed. From their vacation site at Sochi, Stalin and A. A. Zhdanov sent a telegram to the Politburo on 25 September calling for Yezhov to be put in charge of the NKVD, claiming that under Yagoda the commissariat was "four years behind" in investigating the left opposition.[40]

It is difficult to know the exact catalyst for this decision. Perhaps the dramatic explosions in the mines of Kemerovo three days earlier (which were soon characterized as Trotskyist sabotage) cast further doubt on Yagoda's security measures. It is also possible that the arrest of Piatakov, deputy commissar for heavy industry, was related to Yagoda's fall. The arrest of Piatakov in mid-September (see Document 88) may have further weakened Yagoda's position: Piatakov was an important sitting official whose arrest occasioned protests from Sergo Ordzhonikidze and perhaps others. The coincidence in time between Piatakov's arrest and Yagoda's removal may suggest that Yagoda had put his foot down against arrests within the office-holding bureaucracy. Or perhaps Yagoda's dismissal had been discussed by the Politburo in advance. At any rate, Stalin's proposal was approved without a Politburo meeting (by polling the members, *oprosom*), though not formally ratified until 11 October. Even then, Yagoda's fate was not clear. Transferred to the "reserve list," he was appointed commissar of communications[41] and remained at liberty—still a member of the Central Committee—for six months. When he was finally arrested at the end of March 1937, the order was couched in a sudden urgency not apparent at the time of his firing in September of 1936 (see Documents 148[a] and 148[b]).

---

40. Nikita Khrushchev, *The Secret Speech Delivered to the Closed Session of the 20th Congress of the CPSU*, London, 1956, 35–36. The "four years behind" referred to the formation of the Zinoviev-Trotsky bloc and the simultaneous appearance of the Riutin Platform in late 1932. See also the discussion of Yagoda's fall in J. Arch Getty, *Origins of the Great Purges: The Soviet Communist Party Reconsidered, 1933–1938*, New York, 1991, 119–26.

41. Replacing Rykov.

Document 81

Politburo order removing Yagoda from NKVD[42]

From Protocol #43 of the Politburo of the CC of the VKP(b)
11 October 1936
#258: Re: NKVD
a) Comrade G. G. Yagoda is to be relieved of his responsibilities as people's commissar for internal affairs of the USSR.
b) Comrade N. I. Yezhov is to be appointed people's commissar for internal affairs of the USSR. Along with this post, he is to retain the positions of secretary of the CC of the VKP(b) and chairman of the Party Control Commission on condition that he devote nine-tenths of his time to the NKVD.

Yezhov was regarded as a conscientious and loyal party worker, and his appointment did not cause any special alarm in party circles. Yagoda had not been a popular figure. Even Bukharin "got along very well" with Yezhov, considered him an "honest person," and welcomed the appointment.[43] Most Politburo members were on vacation at the time of Yezhov's appointment, and L. M. Kaganovich, who remained on duty for the Politburo in Moscow, wrote to his friend Sergo Ordzhonikidze (commissar for heavy industry) with the news. By this time, several of Ordzhonikidze's assistants, department heads, and plant managers with "suspicious" pasts were already under investigation. Kaganovich's letter sought to reassure Ordzhonikidze that the appointment was a good one.

Document 82

Letter from L. M. Kaganovich to G. K. Ordzhonikidze on Yezhov appointment[44]

30 September 1936
My dear, dear Sergo, how are you?
First of all, I hope you are not angry with me for not writing to you for so long.

42. RTsKhIDNI, f. 17, op. 36, d. 981, l. 50.
43. A. M. Larina, *Nezabyvaemoe*, Moscow, 1989, 269–70.
44. RTsKhIDNI, f. 85, op. 27, d. 93, ll. 12–13. Handwritten.

30/IX Здравствуй дорогой родной Серго.

Прежде всего прошу не сердиться, что так долго не писал.

1) Главная наша последняя новость это назначение Ежова. Это замечательное мудрое решение нашего родителя назрело и встретило ~~[зачеркнуто]~~ прекрасное отношение в партии и в стране. Ягода безусловно оказался слабым для такой роли, быть организатором строительства это одно, а быть политически зрелым и вскрывать своевремено врагов это другое.

А О.Г.П.У опоздало в этом деле на ряд лет и не предупредило подлое убийство Кирова. У Ежова наверняка

DOCUMENT 82. Letter from L. M. Kaganovich to G. K. Ordzhonikidze on Yezhov appointment, 30 September 1936

дела пойдут хорошо. По моим
сведениям ч[то] в среде чекистов
за небольшим исключением
встретили смену руководства
хорошо. Сам Ягода, видимо,
тяжело переживает его
перемещение, но это нас трогать
не может когда дело идет об интересах
государства. Что касается Любова,
то этот годе не на своем месте
мал он оказался для Союзного
наркомата.

2) В хозяйстве дела идут не плохо,
конечно в ряде районов недород
оказался большим чем вначале
предполагали. ~~[зачёркнуто]~~

Document 82 continued

1) The latest news from here concerns the appointment of Yezhov. This remarkable and wise decision of our father,[45] which had been pending for some time, had met with a splendid reception in the party and in the country. Yagoda had undoubtedly turned out to be too weak for such a role. It is one thing to organize a build-up [of the OGPU]. It is another thing to be politically mature and expose enemies in good time.

The OGPU has been years behind schedule in this matter. It failed to forestall the vile murder of Kirov. Surely, things will go smoothly with Yezhov at the helm. According to my information, the change in leadership was favorably received also, with few exceptions, among the ranks of the chekists. Yagoda himself, apparently, took his transfer quite painfully, but we cannot allow ourselves to be affected by this when the interests of the state are at stake. . . .

Yezhov's new appointment occasioned several developments. First, he set about replacing Yagoda's people in the apparatus of the NKVD with "new men." These new recruits, brought in to "strengthen" and rebuild the staff of the NKVD, were largely taken from the party apparatus and from party political training schools; the Orgburo was kept busy processing these appointments.[46] The Politburo ratified numerous lists of "mobilizations" of party workers for service in the NKVD. Yezhov later bragged that he purged 14,000 chekists from the NKVD (see Document 199).

Document 83

Résumé of Comrade Isaak Borisovich Bliakhman for appointment to NKVD[47]

Résumé from the Department of Leading Party Organs of the CC of the VKP(b) for Comrade Isaak Borisovich Bliakhman, presented for confirmation to the CC of the VKP(b) for the position of _____

February 1936 . . .

Last place of employment: Student of courses in Marxism-Leninism.

Previous work experience:

1918–20: Employed by the military commissariat of the city of Drissa.

1920: Director of the Central Press Agency.

1920–21: Political official in the Red Army, Kuban region.

45. *roditel'*: an unusual use of the obsolete word for "father" instead of the modern *otets*—Trans.

46. See *Pravda*, 20 December 1937, and *20 let VchK-OGPU-NKVD*, Moscow, 1938.

47. RTsKhIDNI, f. 17, op. 114, d. 740, ll. 2, 20b.

Document 83 *continued*

1921–24: Political official in the armies of the All-Russian Extraordinary Commission (VChK)-OGPU in Rostov-on-the-Don.

1924–25: Official of the OGPU in Rostov-on-the-Don.

1925–28: Party investigator for the Territorial Control Commission of the VKP(b) for the city of Rostov.

1928–29: Senior inspector of the regional directorate of the police.

1928–30: Official of the OGPU.

1930–35: Student of courses in Marxism-Leninism.

Conclusion reached by the Department of Leading Party Organs of the CC of the VKP(b):

The Department of Leading Party Organs (ORPO) of the CC recommends that, having completed his courses in Marxism-Leninism, Comrade I. B. Bliakhman be placed at the service of the NKVD.

Yagoda's fall and Yezhov's appointment at NKVD coincided with the extension of serious proceedings against ex-Trotskyists and other "suspicious persons" wherever they could be found. The July letter announcing the upcoming Zinoviev trial (Document 73) claimed that terrorists had been able to embezzle state funds to support their activities. As early as summer 1936, G. I. Malenkov (head of the membership registration sector of the Central Committee and a close collaborator of Yezhov's) had ordered his deputies to check the party files of several hundred responsible officials in economic administration for signs of suspicious activity in their pasts. In one such check, the files of 2,150 "leading personnel in industry and transport" turned up "compromising material" (defined not only as previous adherence to oppositional groups but also as previous party reprimands or membership in other political parties) on 526 officials. At that time, though, only 50 of them were removed from their positions.[48]

Document 84

Report to Malenkov on suspicious backgrounds of economic officials [Summer–Fall 1936][49]

Information supplied by the registration sector of leading cadres of the Department of Organization and Propaganda of the CC of the VKP(b)

48. RTsKhIDNI, f. 17, op. 71, d. 42, ll. 1–8.
49. RTsKhIDNI, f. 17, op. 71, d. 42, l. 8.

Document 84 *continued*

To Comrade Malenkov, director of the Department of Leading Party Organs

Nomenklatura officials of the CC of the VKP(b) responsible for cadres in industry and transport who have incurred penalties by the party, were members of other parties, or who belonged to antiparty groups . . .

1. Cadres in industry.

1. Shipov, Mark Oskarovich—director of the Union Office of the All-Union State Association for the Manufacture and Marketing of Automobile and Tractor Spare Parts and Components (*Vatozapchast'sbyt*), party member since 1917. From 1910 to 1917, he belonged to the Bund, son of a merchant, served as an officer in the old army. In 1924 he was expelled from the party by the Moscow Control Commission (MCC) as an alien element. In June 1924 the CCC of the VKP(b) reinstated him into the party with a severe reprimand. In 1926 he was reprimanded by the MCC for failure to pay his apartment rent during the previous two years. In January 1928 he was again expelled from the party by the MCC as an alien element, after being charged with favoritism, [with] careerism, with publicizing his connections with key officials, and with neglecting his responsibilities toward trade union and party organizations. In that same year of 1928 he was reinstated into the party for the second time by the CCC with a severe reprimand. In June 1935 the KPK reprimanded him for permitting an exceptional degree of contamination of the central and local apparat of the Vatozapchastsbyt by class-alien elements.

2. Tiurnikov, Ivan Ivanovich—deputy head of the Chief Administration of the Sugar Industry (Glavsakhar), party member since 1922, former son of a kulak [*sic*], graduated from the Petty Officers' School with the rank of corporal. Became an active Social Revolutionary in 1917, fought against the Bolsheviks, served in Kolchak's army, served in campaigns against the Red Army. In 1920 he entered the party, in 1921 he was expelled as an alien element, but in 1922 he was readmitted to the party. In 1933 the Purge Commission responsible for purging the Glavsakhar cell once again expelled him from the party as a former SR, as an active enemy of the Bolshevik Party. . . .

Starting in fall 1936, the NKVD arrested economic officials, mostly of low rank, ostensibly in connection with various incidents of industrial sabotage. By the beginning of 1937 nearly a thousand persons working in economic commissariats were under arrest.[50] The real bombshell, however, came in mid-September, when Piatakov was arrested. Piatakov, a well-known former Trotskyist, had been under a cloud at least since July, when an NKVD raid on the apartment of his ex-wife turned up compromising materials on

50. *Voprosy istorii*, no. 2, 1994, 22.

his Trotskyist activities ten years before. In August, Yezhov interviewed him and told him that he was being transferred to a position as head of a construction project. Piatakov protested his innocence, claiming that his only sin was in not seeing the counterrevolutionary activities of his wife. He offered to testify against Zinoviev and Kamenev and even volunteered to execute them (and his ex-wife) personally. (Yezhov declined the offer as "absurd.") Piatakov wrote to both Stalin and Ordzhonikidze, protesting his innocence and referring to Zinoviev, Kamenev, and Trotsky as "rotten" and "base."[51] None of this did him any good. He was expelled from the party on 11 September and arrested the next day.

As Sergo Ordzhonikidze's deputy at heavy industry, Piatakov was an important official with overall supervision over mining, chemicals, and other industrial operations. His arrest for sabotage and "terrorism" sent shock waves through the industrial establishment. Ordzhonikidze, who had been successful in protecting lower-level industrial cadres from NKVD harassment, is said to have tried to intercede with Stalin to secure Piatakov's freedom.[52] But Stalin and Yezhov forwarded to him transcripts of interrogations in which Piatakov gradually confessed to economic "wrecking," sabotage, and collaboration with Zinoviev and Trotsky in a monstrous plot to overthrow the Bolshevik regime.[53] According to Bukharin, who was present, Ordzhonikidze was invited to a "confrontation" with the arrested Piatakov, where he asked his deputy if his confessions were coerced or voluntary. Piatakov answered that they were completely voluntary.[54]

There are no documents attesting to Ordzhonikidze's protest. Aside from the account of his attendance at Piatakov's confrontation, we have only a couple of oblique references by Stalin and Molotov at the next plenum (February–March 1937) that Ordzhonikidze had been slow to recognize the guilt of some enemies. But there is no evidence that his intervention took the form of protest against the use of terror against party enemies; he was by no

51. *Izvestiia TsK KPSS*, no 9, 1989, 36; RTsKhIDNI, f. 85, op. 1, d. 136, ll. 47–48.

52. See Oleg V. Khlevniuk, *Stalin i Ordzhonikidze: Konflikty v Politbiuro v 30-e gody*, Moscow, 1993.

53. RTsKhIDNI, f. 17, op. 85, d. 186.

54. Larina, *Nezabyvaemoe*, 327–28.

means a "liberal" in such matters. Ordzhonikidze, as far as we know, never complained about the measures against Zinoviev, Kamenev, Trotsky, Bukharin, Rykov, Tomsky, or any other oppositionist. His was a bureaucrat's defense of "his people," with whom he worked and whom he needed to make his organization function. From his point of view, Yezhov's depredations were improper only when they intruded into Ordzhonikidze's bailiwick, when they threatened the smooth fulfillment of the economic plans his organization answered for, and when they infringed on his circle of clients. As a card-carrying member of the upper nomenklatura, Ordzhonikidze was not against using terror against the elite's enemies, but he did fight to protect the patronage rights that he enjoyed as a member of that stratum.

In another case, Ordzhonikidze had tried to shield another client, the former dissident Lominadze, from arrest, by promising Stalin to bring Lominadze around to a loyal position. But when Ordzhonikidze became convinced that Lominadze was a lost cause, he proposed having him shot, a solution that was at the time too radical even for Stalin.[55]

The procedure by which Piatakov was expelled from the party illustrates the themes of strong party discipline and nomenklatura solidarity. It also graphically shows the consequences of that solidarity when the elite began to commit suicide. Upon motions to expel a member of the Central Committee, members and candidates unanimously voted yes. (An occasional exception was Lenin's widow, Krupskaia, who sometimes voted "agreed" to the expulsion motion, rather than the more positive "yes" [za].)[56] There were no dissidents, no argument. Nomenklatura discipline overrode all other considerations. Piatakov voted to expel Sokolnikov, then was himself expelled. I. P. Zhukov voted (rather fiercely) to expel Piatakov, then was himself expelled a few months later.

---

55. *Voprosy istorii,* no. 11–12, 1995, 14–16.
56. For an example, see RTsKhIDNI, f. 17, op. 2, d. 614, l. 2140b.

Карточка учета рассылки и возврата ~~протокола ПБ~~ № Л3682

От ___ из 12? голосовало 12?.

КОМУ ПОСЛАН	Расписка в получении	Отметка о возврате	№№ экземп.	КОМУ ПОСЛАН	Расписка в получении	Отметка о возврате
Чл. ЦК ВКП(б)				45 Носову	за. Т-ма 729/ш	
Алексееву	за. Т-ма 811/ш		~~46~~	~~Орджоникидзе~~		
Андрееву	за. т-ма 791/ш		47	Петровскому	за. Т-ма 825/ш	
Антипову	за. Воп.		48	Постышеву	за. Т-ма 805/ш	
Бадаеву	за. Воп.		~~49~~	~~Пятакову~~		
Балицкому	за. Воп.		50	Пятницкому	за. Воп.	
Бауману	за. Воп.		51	Разумову	за. т-ма 800/ш	
Берия	за. Т-ма 787/ш		52	Рудзутаку	за. Воп.	
Бубнову	за. Воп.		53	Румянцеву	за. Воп. 784/ш	
Варейкису	за. Т-ма 813/ш		54	Рухимовичу	за. Воп.	
Ворошилову	за. Воп.		55	Рындину	за. т-ма 819/ш	
Гамарнику	за. Воп. 802/ш		56	Сталину	за. См. ориг. голос.	
Евдокимову	за. т-ма 802/ш		57	Стецкому	за. Воп.	
Ежову	за. Воп.		58	Сулимову	за. Воп.	
~~Енукидзе~~			~~59~~	~~Уханову~~		
Жданову	за. См. ориг. голос		60	Хатаевичу	за. Т-ма 817/ш	
Жукову	за. Воп.		61	Хрущеву	за. Воп.	
Зеленскому	за. Воп.		62	Чернову	за. Воп.	
Иванову	за. Воп.		63	Чубарю	за. Воп.	
Икрамову	за. Воп.		64	Чувырину	за. Т-ма 81?/ш	
~~Кабакову~~			65	Чудову	за. Воп.	
Кагановичу Л.	за. Воп.		66	Швернику	за. Воп.	
Кагановичу М.	за. Воп.		67	Шеболдаеву	за. т-ма 801/ш	
Калинину	за. См. ориг. голос		68	Эйхе	за. т-ма 793/ш	
~~Кирову~~			~~69~~	~~Ягода~~		
Кнорину	за. Воп.		70	Якиру	за. Воп.	
Кодацкому	за. Воп.		71	Яковлеву Я.	за. Воп.	
Косареву	за. Воп.					
Косиору Ст.	за. Т-ма 794/ш			**Кандидатам в ЦК**		
Косиору И.	не посылалось.		72	Багирову	за. Т-ма 814/ш	
Кржижановскому	за. Воп.		73	Благонравову	за. Воп.	
Криницкому	за. Т-ма 790/ш		74	Блюхеру	за. Т-ма 813/ш	
Крупской	Согласна. Воп.		75	Буденному	за. Воп.	
~~Куйбышеву~~			76	Булганину	за. Воп.	
Лаврентьеву	за. Т-ма 785/ш		77	Булину	за. Воп.	
Лебедю	за. Воп.		~~78~~	~~Бухарину Н. И.~~		
Литвинову	за. Воп.		79	Бройдо	за. Воп.	
Лобову	за. Воп.		80	Быкину	за. Т-ма 786/ш	
Любимову	за. Воп.		81	Вегеру	за. т-ма 796/ш	
Мануильскому	за. Воп.		82	Вейнбергу	за. Воп.	
Межлауку В.	за. Воп.		83	Гикало	за. Т-ма 812/ш	
Микояну	за. Воп.		84	Голодеду	за. Т-ма 806/ш	
Мирзояну	за. Т-ма 804/ш		85	Гринько	за. Воп.	
Молотову	за. Воп.		86	Грядинскому	за. Т-ма 793/ш	
Николаевой	за. Воп.		87	Демченко	за. Воп.	

Unanimous Central Committee vote to expel K. Ukhanov, 20 May 1937, all voting "for" *(za)*, except Lenin's widow, Krupskaia, voting "agreed" *(soglasna)*

Document 85

Piatakov telegram to CC voting to expel Sokolnikov[57]

27 July 1936
THE PROPOSAL TO EXPEL SOKOLNIKOV AS A CANDIDATE MEMBER OF THE CC AS WELL AS FROM THE VKP(B) FOR MAINTAINING CLOSE TIES WITH THE TERRORISTIC GROUP OF TROTSKYISTS AND ZINOVIEV- ISTS MEETS WITH MY FULL APPROVAL.
PIATAKOV

Document 86

Politburo resolution expelling Piatakov, 11 September 1936[58]

From the protocol of the Plenum of the CC of the VKP(b)
(Decision taken by polling of members) 10–11 September 1936
Re: Yu. L. Piatakov
On the basis of indisputable facts to the effect that Yu. L. Piatakov, a member of the CC, maintained close ties with the terrorist groups of Trotskyists and Zinovievists, the CC of the VKP(b), deeming such conduct by Piatakov incompatible with his presence on the CC and his membership in the VKP(b), decrees that Yu. L. Piatakov is to be expelled from the CC and from the VKP(b).

Document 87

Zhukov telegram to CC voting to expel Piatakov, version 1[59]

No. 29
From Nalchik to the secretariat of the CC of the VKP(b)
13 September 1936
[I vote] FOR EXPULSION [of Piatakov] FROM CC OF VKP(B) AND FOR TRYING HIM IN ACCORDANCE WITH STRICTEST STANDARDS OF OUR LAW.
Zhukov

57. RTsKhIDNI, f. 17, op. 2, d. 573, l. 23.
58. RTsKhIDNI, f. 17, op. 2, d. 573, l. 26.
59. RTsKhIDNI, f. 17, op. 2, d. 573, l. 35.

Экз. №

Народный Комиссариат Внутренних Дел Союза ССР
3-е ОТДЕЛЕНИЕ СПЕЦОТДЕЛА ГУГБ

ак **ШИФРОВКА ВХ. № 15424/1067**

Получ. "27/7" 193 6 г. 19 ч. " " м. Расшифр. "27/7" 19 ч. 30 " " м.
Из СУХУМА   Отпечатано "_____" экз.
Куда и кому СЕКРЕТАРЮ ЦК ВКП(б) тов. С Т А Л И Н У.

Предложением исключении Сокольникова состава кандида—
тов члены ЦК и из рядов ВКП(б), как поддерживавшего тес—
ную связь террористической группой троцкистов и зиновье—
вцев вполне согласен.

27/VII. П Я Т А К О В

Отп. "_____" экз. № 1 т. СТАЛИНУ   экз. № 4 т.   экз. № 7 т.
    " 2 т. " "   " № 5 т.   " № 8 т.
    " 3 т.   " № 6 т.
П/и. 3-го Отделения Спецотдела ГУГБ

DOCUMENT 85. Piatakov telegram to CC voting to expel Sokolnikov, 27 July 1936

Членам ЦК ВКП(б)

На голосование

На основании неопровержимых данных установлено, что член ЦК т. Пятаков Ю.Л. поддерживал тесные связи с террористическими группами троцкистов и зиновьевцев. П.Б., считая, что такое поведение Пятакова несовместимо с пребыванием в составе ЦК и с принадлежностью к ВКП(б), вносит на голосование членов ЦК предложение об исключении Пятакова из состава членов ЦК и из рядов ВКП(б)

За Л. Каганович

DOCUMENT 86. Politburo resolution expelling Piatakov, 11 September 1936 (Kaganovich's first draft)

ЦЕНТРАЛЬНЫЙ КОМИТЕТ Всесоюзной Коммунистической Партии (большевиков)

ПОЛИТБЮРО ПЛЕНУМ

Протокол № Пл 8/2 пункт Опросом членов ЦК ВКП(б) от 10-11.IX 1936 г.

СЛУШАЛИ:	ПОСТАНОВИЛИ:
О Пятакове Ю.Л.	На основании установленных неопровержимых данных о том, что член ЦК Пятаков Ю.Л. поддерживал тесные связи с террористическими группами троцкистов и зиновьевцев, ЦК ВКП(б), считая, что такое поведение Пятакова несовместимо с пребыванием в составе ЦК и с принадлежностью к ВКП(б), постановляет исключить Пятакова Ю.Л. из состава членов ЦК и из рядов ВКП(б).

Выписки т.т.

Ежову

Кем отправлены

(подпись)

Архив: Дело № 9 т. 4-й.

DOCUMENT 86. Politburo resolution expelling Piatakov, 11 September 1936 (final version)

Document 88

Zhukov telegram to CC voting to expel Piatakov, version 2[60]

From Nalchik to the secretariat of the CC of the VKP(b)
14 September 1936
AS SUPPLEMENT TO OUR #29, PLEASE READ AFTER WORD "EXPUL-
SION": [He is] TO BE ARRESTED IMMEDIATELY AND PUT ON TRIAL IN
ACCORDANCE WITH STRICTEST STANDARDS OF OUR LAW.
Zhukov

Even Ordzhonikidze, who privately complained about Piatakov's detention, defended the leadership's line and voted for his
expulsion and consequent arrest. Regardless of his doubts, he defended the notion of Piatakov's guilt to his deputies at heavy industry and chastised them for failing to uncover the work of saboteurs.
At the same time, he sought to reassure "his people."

Document 89

Ordzhonikidze telegram to CC voting to expel Piatakov[61]

From Piatigorsk to L. M. Kaganovich, the CC of the VKP(b)
11 September 1936
AM IN FULL AGREEMENT WITH POLITBURO'S [proposed] DECREE TO
EXPEL [Piatakov] FROM CC OF VKP(B) AND ON INCOMPATIBILITY WITH
HIS RETAINING HIS MEMBERSHIP IN VKP(B) IN THE FUTURE. I VOTE
"YES."
Ordzhonikidze

60. RTsKhIDNI, f. 17, op. 2, d. 573, l. 36.
61. RTsKhIDNI, f. 17, op. 2, d. 573, l. 33.

Народный Комиссариат Внутренних Дел Союза ССР

3-е ОТДЕЛЕНИЕ СПЕЦОТДЕЛА ГУГБ

СОВ. СЕКРЕТНО

Снятие копий воспрещается

ШИФРОВКА ВХ. № 18883/2028

Получ. „ 11 „ IX „ 193 6 г. 16 ч. „ 00 „ м. Расшифр. „ 11 „ IX „ 16 ч. „ 30 „ м.

Из ПЯТИГОРСКА   Отпечатано „ _____ „ экз.

Куда и кому ЦК ВКП(б). тов. КАГАНОВИЧУ

С постановлением Политбюро об исключении из ЦК ВКП(б) и

несовместимость дальнейшим его пребыванием в рядах ВКП(б)

полностью согласен и голосую за .

ОРДЖОНИКИДЗЕ . 11/IX

Отп. „ _____ „ экз. № 1 т. ЦК ВКП(б)   экз № 7 т. _____

        „ № 2 т. _____   „ № 8 т. _____

        „ № 3 т. _____

                                              экз. № 4 т. _____

                                                    „ № 5 т. _____

                                                    „ № 6 т. _____

П/п. 3-го Отделения Спецотдела ГУГБ

Document 90

From a speech by Ordzhonikidze at a meeting of the heads of the chief directorates of the Commissariat for Heavy Industry, 5 February 1937[62]

Ordzhonikidze: . . . In my opinion, we must do the following: all heads of chief directorates, their deputies, and the best of their officials ought to go to their factories and cheer up their directors—just think what state of mind they must be in now! Vasilkovsky told me that Alperovich had told him as a joke that as a result of the trials of the scoundrels, directors of certain factories feel themselves nowadays under attack as if they were criminals, as if they all must now answer for Piatakov and others. Nothing of the sort! They must be told frankly that they are not criminals, that they are our cadres. The criminals have been caught, they have been shot. If there are more criminals in the future, they too shall be caught. We shall shoot all the swine that we find. We are not talking about them. We are talking about the great mass of cadres, of splendid cadres trained by us. That's what they should all be told frankly. One ought not to ignore the fact that the workers at the factories are seething with rage. . . .

You think that if I had as my first deputy a man like Piatakov, who had worked in industry for the past 15 years, who had tremendous connections with all sorts of people, you think that this person couldn't possibly sneak one or two of his people in. But sneak them he did! Some of them were found out, others were not. You have, after all, heard of their tactics. Who among you has raised the question of finding out how things are going on in your chief directorate?

You think that a saboteur [*vreditel'*] is someone who walks around with a revolver in his pocket, someone who hides in some dark corner somewhere, waiting for his victim? Who could imagine that Piatakov could be a saboteur, and yet he turned out to be a saboteur, and, more still, a fine talker. He told [the investigators] how he did it. You saw the unhappy Todorsky when that scoundrel [Piatakov] named him. We kicked him out of the party, and the CC gave me a solid thrashing for daring to expel him from the party.

Look now how the CC of our party values its officials. Why should a person who has been sentenced to be shot have any apparent reason to name names? And yet, at the last minute he names Todorovsky.[63] Why should he [Piatakov] lie? Take him away, throw him in prison. Not only did the CC not do so, it even reprimanded the party organization for having expelled a person from the party. You see how attentive it is to each and every person. This obliges us all the more so to approach this matter as is proper. And what do you do? Not a thing, not a goddamn thing!

Glebov was running the show at Borisov's. Did you bother to examine what

62. RTsKhIDNI, f. 85, op. 29, d. 156, ll. 5–12. Typed text without corrections.
63. Note discrepancy in spelling: apparently Todorsky—Trans.

was going on there, did you tell me what you found there, did you tell me how to rectify the disgraceful situation there? The hell you did!

Borisov: I handed you a secret memo concerning the matter of defense.

Ordzhonikidze: You sent me nothing more than a request, surely it was a request for more money. What was the request for?

Borisov: I said in my memo that we must resolve a host of issues which had not yet been resolved, that had reached a dead end.

Ordzhonikidze: And furthermore, comrades, there is the matter that I raised just now. On the 20th of this month, the Plenum of the CC of our party will hold its session. The agenda will include the results and the lessons of this filthy business. I shall represent the People's Commissariat for Heavy Industry. Should I take the rap for all of you? If sabotage is going on at the factories, then Ordzhonikidze is to blame, and no one else. And have you given me evidence showing how you are trying to put an end to the sabotage, what sort of measures you are undertaking? No, you aren't doing a damn thing! You dump the responsibility on the chemical division, on the coal-mining division. Let them take the rap! This is of no concern to us! No, comrades, you must dig deep, surely there must be big or small cells everywhere in our organization which have committed filthy deeds. Look at Barinov. Several of his derricks collapsed. It could have happened that a scoundrel overturned several derricks by himself and said that they were overthrown by the snowstorm. Go figure!

A most interesting question keeps nagging at me: How could this have happened? You and I have been working together for so many years, we have done a fairly good job, the results have been fairly satisfactory. We even completed the Five Year Plan in four years. So how could it have happened that Piatakov was on our staff and yet no one, by God, saw through him? You'll say to me: "He was your deputy, but you didn't see through him. So what do you want from us?" It's not right. If some worker in Kemerovo had said this, he would be right, but if you are saying this, then it's not right. . . .

Why? Because many of you have worked with him for a longer period of time than with me, and many of you had an apparent liking for him. I am not saying this as a reproach. I am only saying this because here was a man who seemed to be helping us. That's what happened. Why did this take place? Could it really be that this happened because we had become so blind?

We must pose this question to ourselves. If we are not hauled into court, then we ought to present ourselves at court ourselves, that is, at the court of our conscience and raise the question as to how this could have happened. Because we evidently did not sufficiently monitor what was happening around us. Because many of us evidently had rested on our laurels, on our successes. So what happens? There is an accident at a mine and 10 or 12 people are dead. Well, so they are dead. So what? Technical defects. . . .

What does this say? It says we have a callous attitude. Whether 10 persons have perished or only one, everyone should feel his insides turning and twisting. They are, after all, not strangers, these people. They are our brothers. But is this our attitude? No, our feelings have become blunted. This is the rust that has begun to engulf us at every point. This rust is extremely dangerous. It is a clear sign of bureaucratism, when a high official or bureaucrat feels himself so cut off from the masses. I am not saying that you have failed to attend [party] meetings. It's possible to attend the meetings and still be cut off from people—that is, not to share the life of the masses.

This damned Piatakov, this damned Rataichak and others! They have played such filthy tricks on us. But their ruin, that is, the fact that they were caught, thrown into prison and forced to tell all that has happened, this fact ought to open our eyes. We could put it this way: We couldn't have guessed, no one could have guessed—why are you dumping (responsibility) on us? But now we must answer for it. That's what we shall have to reflect on very seriously. It is obvious that we are entering upon a period when it will be necessary once again to reorganize our ranks, our leadership, when it will be necessary, evidently, to govern anew. The hell with it! Unless there is a shake-up, we'll all rust. . . .

1936: The Human Element

By autumn 1936 the circle of arrests was widening. Those arrested or expelled from the party, or their relatives, frequently appealed to high-ranking leaders for help and intercession. Often these requests were ignored. Sometimes, however, a Politburo member would intercede and use his personal power to save an acquaintance. Such petitions for intercession were part of a long Russian tradition of appeal to tsars for help and are a special category of personal-political text. In the following case, the author used apologetic discourse, paying his "symbolic taxes" by confessing his errors to a powerful figure. In so doing, despite his complaints about injustice, the author implicitly affirmed the terms and rules of the system.

Document 91

Letter from I. Moiseev (Yershistyi) to V. M. Molotov[64]

2 September 1936
To Dear Comrade Viacheslav Mikhailovich Molotov
My dear and precious Viacheslav Mikhailovich!

64. RTsKhIDNI, f. 17, op. 120, d. 272, ll. 54–55.

Having suffered an exceptionally grave tragedy in my party life, I have taken the liberty to turn to you once again with a deep, heartfelt request to help me and my young children. Please don't let me sink into a life of shame and scorn.

Eleven years ago, at the 14th Party Congress, I committed in your eyes a great crime before the party by participating in the opposition (may it be a thousand times cursed!).

For this crime I was expelled from the party by the Kuibyshev District Committee in Leningrad on 28 August of this year. Once more, I've been deported from Leningrad.

My dear and precious Viacheslav Mikhailovich, you know the details of my crime better than anyone else. It began at the 22d Leningrad Regional Party Conference, which took place just before the 14th Party Congress.

Not only had I never spoken out—before the conference—at a single party or workers' meeting in favor of the oppositionists, but I also never took part in the preparations by the opposition and knew nothing about them. Not only because I was at the time on vacation but also because no one had ever considered me a supporter of the Zinovievist riffraff, who had never trusted me and never let me come near their group. And as you know, since 1919 I had repeatedly taken a most active part, along with Comrades Antipov, Lobov, Komarov, Semyonov, and Zhenya Yegorov, in attacking the stronghold of the vile Zinovievist rabble and their usurpation of the Leningrad organization.

However, at the 22d Conference itself, I was inveigled into the opposition by the lies, deception, and intrigue of these vile double-dealers. I acted criminally, naively. I believed these scoundrels when they alleged that they were doing all this on behalf of the purity of the Leninist-Stalinist line of our party's CC, that they were working against that Judas, that traitor, that bloody dog Trotsky.

When it became absolutely clear, at the 14th Party Congress, that these vile traitors, who had deceived the Leningrad organization, had been waging a campaign against the Leninist-Stalinist Central Committee, I did not find within myself sufficient strength of will to distance myself from the opposition, thinking naively and criminally that the congress, whose decisions are binding on all party members, would [soon] end, and that [after it ended] all opposition would cease. I did not see that these scum would not stop at that. That was the whole extent of my crime, which I have agonized over for eleven years, and which has caused me intolerable moral and physical pain. . . .

My dear and precious Viacheslav Mikhailovich, you [informal *ty*] know my life in the party in its entirety. I came from the lowest rank of the peasantry of the Gorky region. At the age of 14, I left the countryside for good and became a working proletarian. From 1906 to the time of the October Revolution, I came to know more than my share of want and hunger, of unemployment and the whole oppressive weight of capitalist exploitation. From my earliest years I took my stand in the ranks of the revolutionaries, the fighters for the working class, for socialism under the banner of our party, the party headed by leaders of genius, by Lenin and Stalin.

In 1914 I worked in the Moscow underground under the leadership of such splendid Bolsheviks as Comrade Shkiriatov, Sakharov, Zaslavsky, Shumkin—a favorite of Ilich [Lenin]—and others. From 1914 till the October Revolution, I worked in the Leningrad underground under your leadership, my precious Viacheslav Mikhailovich, and under the leadership of Comrades M. I. Kalinin, N. K. Antipov, and A. A. Andreev. All of you know the fearlessness, the devotion with which I gave my all to our party's cause. I was repeatedly arrested and deported. I have known more than my share of the torments of the tsar's prisons and secret police. Out of 45 years of my life, I have devoted 27 years, all of my conscious life, all of my strength and energy to the struggle for the ideals of our Great Communist Party. I had no life outside our party, nor could there ever be any other life for me, no matter what happens to me in the future or however the party may punish me. All of my life attests to the fact that I have never been nor will I ever be an enemy of the party, that I have given all of my life to the party. My crime, committed eleven years ago at the 14th Party Congress, was an inadvertent act, which I curse and shall continue to curse till my dying day. . . .

My dear, precious, beloved Viacheslav Mikhailovich, I know that our party is so great, so mighty that the purity of its Leninist-Stalinist ideas is more exalted than anything else on earth, that it is the highest law of life. For that reason, my dear, beloved Viacheslav Mikhailovich, the greatest disciple of Lenin, who was a man of genius, I swear to you, the first and greatest assistant and loyal Comrade in Arms of the Great Stalin, to You, my dear, beloved Viacheslav Mikhailovich, I swear with all that's left of my life, I swear by the young lives of my beloved children that I will never violate this exalted law of the party. I swear to you that I would gladly wipe away my crime with my own blood at the party's call at any moment. Don't punish me so harshly, don't deprive me of that which I have believed in and revered all my life. Please help me to be restored into the good graces of our party, give me the opportunity to devote to it the little that is left of my life.[65] Other than this crime, which I have written you [formal *vy*] about and which I have repented of a thousand times, I haven't been charged or accused of anything by anyone.

I implore you [informal *ty*] fervently, my Dear Viacheslav Mikhailovich, please do check all these facts, go on and verify[66] them all with the most rigorous Stalinist vigilance. You'll see that my crime is far less serious than that of many others who have been permitted to remain in the party.

Help me![67] My burden is so heavy. I am so ashamed of my crime. My

---

65. The previous two sentences beginning with "Don't punish me" refer either to Molotov personally (formal mode of address by implication) or to the party. Moiseev uses the imperative mood without a personal pronoun—Trans.

66. Formal *vy* with the imperative—Trans.

67. Formal *vy* with the imperative—Trans.

Document 91 *continued*

suffering has been so great these past two years. I shall be forever indebted to you [informal *ty*], my Precious Viacheslav Mikhailovich!

I. Moiseev (Yershistyi)

[Two sets of instructions are appended to the letter:]

To Comrade Yezhov: Moiseev-Yershistyi could hardly be troublesome to anybody in Leningrad. I doubt that he was justifiably expelled from the VKP(b).

9 September 1936. V. Molotov

Inquire with Shkiriatov. We have agreed to keep him in Leningrad and not to expel him from the party. Let [the proper authorities in Leningrad] know about this.

Yezhov

The following letter was written by Mikhail Tomsky's widow to Yezhov following her husband's suicide. No record of an answer has been found in the archives.

Document 92

Letter from M. Tomskaya to N. I. Yezhov[68]

27 October 1936

My dear Nikolai Ivanovich:

Please help me find a job. I cannot live without work. Sometimes I feel that I am going crazy. I can no longer go on living cut off from life.

I have worked for a long time in the field of public catering and was a member of the Presidium of the Committee on Public Catering. I have also done administrative-economic work. I know how to work.

My eyes are hurting me now (the blood vessels in the pupils of both my eyes have burst), and I can read and write only for short periods of time. Perhaps it will all pass.

Concerning OGIZ (Association of State Publishing Houses).

At the OGIZ, Mikhail Pavlovich [Tomsky] left behind his party card, his trade union card, his insurance papers, his bonds for exchange, his vacation permit, and his briefcases. . . .

68. RTsKhIDNI, f. 17, op. 120, d. 272, ll. 76–78.

Дорогому Вячеславу Михайловичу
Товарищу МОЛОТОВУ.

Дорогой, родной мой Вячеслав Михайлович!

Переживая исключительно тяжёлую трагедию в моей партийной жизни, я снова осмелился обратится к Вам с самой горячей, с самой сердечной просьбой помочь мне и моим юным детям. Не допуститься до жизни позора и презрения.

Одиннадцать лет тому назад, на ХІУ-м съезде нашей партии, своим участием в оппозиции, будь она тысячи раз проклята, я на Ваших глазах совершил большое преступление перед партией.

За это преступление, Куйбышевский райком в Ленинграде 28-го августа с/г. исключил меня из партии, и опять выселяют из Ленинграда.

Дорогой, родной Вячеслав Михайлович Вы как никто лучше знаете все поступки моего преступления. Оно началось с 22-й Ленинградской Губпартконференции, которая состоялась перед самым ХІУ-м партийном съездом

До конференции я не только не выступал ни на одном партийном или рабочем собрании с оппозиционными речами, но и никакого участия не принимал в подготовке к оппозиции и ничего об этом не знал. Не только потому, что я в это время был в отпуске, но и потому, что меня никто и никогда не считал приверженцем зиновьевского отребья, мне не доверяли и не подпускали близко к их кругу людей. И как Вы знаете, я с 1919 года нераз принимал самое активное участие, вместе с товарищами Антиповым, Лобовым, Комаровым, Семеновым, Женей Егоровой, в борьбе против вотчины зиновьевского подлого охвостия и их узурпаторства в Ленинградской организации. Но на самой 22-й конференции я, ложью, обманом, интриганством этих подлых двурушников был втянут в оппозицию. Наивно, преступно поверив этим негодяям, что борьба якобы идет за чистоту Ленинско-Сталинской линии ЦК нашей партии, против иуды предателя, кровавой собаки Троцкого.

На ХІУ-м съезде нашей партии, когда совершенно стало ясно, что эти подлые предатели, обманув Ленинградскую организацию, подняли борьбу против Ленинско-Сталинского Центрального Комитета, я не сумел найти тогда в себе достаточно силы воли, чтобы отмежеваться от оппозиции, наивно преступно думая, что кончится съезд, решения которого для всех членов партии обязательны и кончится всякая оппозиция. Не видел того, что эти мерзавцы не могли на этом остановится. Вот в чем вся сила моего преступления, которым я мучаюсь одиннадцать лет до нестерпимой, моральной и физической боли.

После съезда, как тебе известно Родной Вячеслав Михайлович, я ни на одном заводе, ни на одном собрании не выступал в засчиту оппозиции. В конце января 1926 года, мучаясь сознанием своего преступления, я заявил тогда незабвенному Сергею Мироновичу Кирову, и тов.Комарову, об отходе от оппозиции. После болезни и отпуска, я еще раз заявил об этом товарищу Антипову Николаю Кириловичу.

DOCUMENT 91. Letter from I. Moiseev (Yershistyi) to V. M. Molotov, 2 September 1936 (with Molotov notes to Yezhov)

Document 92 *continued*

Other things, belonging to the wives' organization, in which I used to work, were also left behind, namely: all the articles written by wives of construction workers which were given to me to prepare for the press. Also: ready-made children's dresses sewn by the wives, textiles, and lamp-shades for the dormitories of construction workers.

I am supposed to hand all of these items to those for whom they were intended. . . .

Yesterday, the 26th of the month, I called and asked when it would be possible to receive all this from the OGIZ. I also asked about the vacation pay as well as the matter of money which he wanted to clear up.

He replied: "Yes, I am trying to clear up the matter, but where it is, I won't tell you."

But why does it take so long for him to clear things up? It shouldn't take more than a minute. I decided to call myself and find out about this. I immediately called Comrade Sulimov, but fortunately his secretary answered that Comrade Sulimov was at a meeting, or else I'd have felt ashamed.

Comrade Bron called soon thereafter and said that I should call you, Nikolai Ivanovich.

Only then did I learn that Comrade Bron was not present at the opening of the safe and that there was no money in the safe.

I could not figure out why he asked me in that manner; after all, he asked me several times.

Your secretary asked me to write to you about this.

I apologize for the length of this letter, but it's difficult to write more briefly.

My greetings.

M. Tomskaya

CHAPTER EIGHT

The Tide Turns

BUKHARIN: Do you really believe that I could have anything in common with these subversives, with these saboteurs, with these scum, after thirty years in the party and after all of this? This is nothing but madness. . . . But I cannot admit, either today or tomorrow or the day after tomorrow, anything which I am not guilty of.
STALIN: I'm not saying anything personal about you.
—Central Committee plenum, December 1936

FROM THE DOCK of the August 1936 show trial, Lev Kamenev had mentioned the names of former rightist leaders Nikolai Bukharin, Aleksei Rykov, and Mikhail Tomsky in his testimony. Such allusions in a carefully scripted trial text were not accidental. At the close of the court session, Procurator Andrei Vyshinsky announced that he was opening an official investigation of their possible complicity with the accused. The next day, Tomsky committed suicide.[1] Even before this, the denunciations of the leftists had begun to rub off on Bukharin. On the eve of the trial, in the wake of the closed letter of July, denunciations of Bukharin and other rightists had begun to flow in to the Central Committee. It is not known whether they were spontaneous or solicited.

1. *Izvestiia TsK KPSS*, no. 5, 1989, 70.

Document 93

Letter from I. Kuchkin to N. I. Yezhov[2]

---

11 August 1936

Dear Comrade Yezhov:

I would like to call your attention to the following:

Comrade N. I. Bukharin has been traveling to Leningrad frequently. While there, he has been staying at the apartment of Busygin, a former Trotskyist and now a counterrevolutionary.

Comrade Bukharin has maintained a close relationship with him, both in person and by correspondence. He and Volgin were close friends of Busygin.

The fact was uncovered at a party meeting of this institute and reported by Zubkov, who was expelled from the party as a White Guard and abettor of counterrevolutionary work.

I consider it my duty to report this to you in view of the fact that a simple friendship with a sworn counterrevolutionary is hardly possible. It is my suspicion that Comrade Bukharin was aware of Busygin's work and, in particular, of his counterrevolutionary activities at the Institute of the Academy of Sciences.

With Communist greetings,

I. Kuchkin,

Official of the Vasileostrovsky Party District Committee

Address: Gavanskaya Street, Building 37, Apt. 29, Vas. Island, Leningrad, VKP(b) member since 1926. Party card no. 0626936

Bukharin had been on vacation, mountain climbing in the Pamirs, when his name was mentioned at the Zinoviev trial. He rushed back to Moscow to defend himself, quickly writing a letter to Stalin protesting his innocence and demanding a confrontation with those arrested who had given evidence against him. Yezhov had meanwhile been busy trying to build a case against Bukharin. The key was G. I. Sokolnikov, a former oppositionist who had been arrested a month before the Zinoviev trial. In the course of his interrogation, Sokolnikov apparently not only had admitted his own close connections with the Zinovievists and Trotskyists but had alleged some complicity on Bukharin's part. Following Sokolnikov's testimony, Yezhov wrote to Stalin that in his opinion the rightists were involved in conspiracy, and he asked permission to pursue the matter by reinterrogating several former right opposi-

2. RTsKhIDNI, f. 17, op. 120, d. 272, l. 41.

Тов. ЕЖОВ!

Довожу до Вашего сведения:

т.Бухарин Н.И. часто приезжал в Ленинград, останавливался на квартире троцкиста - Бусыгина в прошлом, контрреволюционера в настоящем.

Бусыгин работал в системе Академии Наук в ин-те Антропологии и этнограф. ныне арестован органами НКВД за подрывную контрреволюционную работу против партии.

т.Бухарин с ним имел тесную связь письменную и личную, вместе с Волгиным у Бусыгина были неразлучными друзьями.

Факт вскрыт на одном партсобрании этого ин-та, сообщил Зубков, которого исключали из партии как белогвардейца и пособника контрреволюционной работы.

Считаю своим долгом сообщить, т.к. простой дружбы с от"явленным контрреволюционером навряд-ли могло быть, у меня есть подозрение, что т.Бухарин был в курсе работы Бусыгина и в частности его контрреволюционной деятельности в ин-те Академии Наук.

Работник Василеостровского райкома партии И.Кучкин.

Адрес: Ленинград, Вас.остров Гаванская 37, кв.29.

чл. ВКП(б) с 1926г. п/б. 0626936.

С ком.приветом И.Кучкин.

11.УШ.36г.

В е р н о: *Филимонов*

DOCUMENT 93. Letter from I. Kuchkin to N. I. Yezhov, 11 August 1936 tionists. Stalin agreed. The results of these inquiries, combined with Sokolnikov's statement, were apparently the basis for the public mention of Bukharin at Zinoviev's trial.[3]

On 8 September, Bukharin and Rykov were granted a confrontation with the arrested Sokolnikov at Central Committee headquarters in the presence of a Politburo commission consisting of Kaganovich, Yezhov, and Vyshinsky. At that meeting, Bukharin and Rykov denied any guilt and were permitted to question Sokolnikov. Sokolnikov stated that he had no personal knowledge of Bukharin's or Rykov's guilt. His only information was that Kamenev had told him (Sokolnikov) back in 1933 or 1934 that Bukharin and Rykov knew about the 1932 united opposition bloc; he suggested that maybe that was not true and that Kamenev may only have been trying to recruit support by claiming the adherence of rightist leaders. Kaganovich immediately reported these results to Stalin, who ordered proceedings against Bukharin and Rykov stopped. Two days later, Vyshinsky's office made a statement that there was insufficient evidence to proceed against the two rightist leaders.[4]

Yezhov went back to the drawing board. Two days after Vyshinsky's statement, Piatakov was arrested, and Yezhov was occupied with the interrogations of the leftists. Nevertheless, arrests and interrogations of former rightists continued; over the next five months Yezhov forwarded to Stalin some sixty transcripts of these interrogations.[5] In October and November, Yezhov secured testimony about the complicity of Bukharin and Rykov from such people as Tomsky's personal secretary and Old Bolshevik V. I. Nevsky.[6]

The Beginning of the End for Bukharin: The December 1936 Plenum

Finally, by the first week in December, the stage was set for the arraignment of Bukharin and Rykov before the Central Commit-

3. *Izvestiia TsK KPSS*, no. 5, 1989, 72–73. Those to be reinterrogated included Nikolai Uglanov, former district party secretary in Moscow, and M. N. Riutin.
4. *Izvestiia TsK KPSS*, no. 5, 1989, 71.
5. *Izvestiia TsK KPSS*, no. 5, 1989, 74.
6. *Izvestiia TsK KPSS*, no. 5, 1989, 74, 84.

tee's plenum. Yezhov gave the main speech against them. Citing testimony from a variety of middle- and lower-level former oppositionists, he made the case that Bukharin, Rykov, and Tomsky were involved in the Zinoviev-Trotsky terrorist organization. As he would again and again, Bukharin refused to admit his party guilt and attempted to refute the charges specifically and in detail.

Document 94

Yezhov's speech to the December 1936 CC plenum, 4 December 1936[7]

Yezhov: . . . You know that already at the August trial Zinoviev testified that apart from the main center of the Zinovievist-Trotskyist bloc, there existed also a backup center. Zinoviev gave 4 surnames as members of the backup center: Piatakov, Sokolnikov, Radek, and Serebriakov. All of this has now been fully confirmed by the testimony of the defendants themselves, who are now under arrest: Piatakov, Sokolnikov, Radek, and Serebriakov. All four members of the backup center have testified that they were members of this center. . . .

I must say that this so-called backup center, despite the fact that, according to the original testimony of Piatakov, it had become active only after the collapse of the main center—that is, after the arrest of Zinoviev, Kamenev, Smirnov, and others—despite this, it had deployed its activities significantly earlier, especially Piatakov. At any rate, the activity of this center was significantly more dangerous, if one may so express oneself, or more filthy, even in comparison with the counterrevolutionary work of the previous center that had been exposed. To a certain degree, this is explained by the fact that it had the opportunity to work in a more clandestine [konspirativno] manner, that it had a more clandestine means of carrying on its work, that it had elicited greater trust to it, so it deployed its activities to a significantly greater degree. At any rate, if we look at it in terms of its connections, it enjoyed significantly greater connections with the periphery than did the center whose trial took place in 1936.

Beria: And also in terms of its connections abroad.

Yezhov: Yes, that's true.

As for the ties linking the so-called backup center and the periphery, they were strong, whether we speak of personal ties or ties with groups of people. . . .

In the Azov–Black Sea organization over 200 persons, headed by Glebov, Beloborodov, and others, were arrested. In Georgia over 300 persons

---

7. RTsKhIDNI, f. 17, op. 2, d. 575, ll. 11–19, 40–45, 49–53, 57–60, 66–67. From the uncorrected shorthand minutes.

headed by Akudzhava were arrested. In Leningrad over 400 persons and in Sverdlovsk over 100 persons were arrested.

We should add that the rather large group of Trotskyists in Sverdlovsk was in fact directed by Japanese intelligence through Kniazev, formerly head of Japanese intelligence [in Sverdlovsk]. . . .

At any rate, people not only discussed the question of terror. They also concretely prepared for it. At any rate, many attempts were made to carry out terrorist acts of assassination. In particular, the Azov–Black Sea counter-revolutionary terrorist group headed by Beloborodov assigned a group under the direction of a certain Dukat from the Trotskyists, who tried to hunt down Comrade Stalin in Sochi. Beloborodov gave instructions to Dukat so that the latter could take advantage of Comrade Stalin's stay in Sochi on his vacation, so that he could find a propitious moment to carry out his assassination. When Dukat failed in his attempt, Beloborodov vilified him in every way possible for failing to organize this business.

In Western Siberia, there were direct attempts to organize an assassination attempt against Comrade Molotov, in the Urals against Comrade Kaganovich. . . .

Here is an example of the most vivid testimony from that region, testimony given by Norkin, now under arrest, formerly the head of the Kemerovo chemical kombinat, who had once served as deputy head of the chief chemical industries under Piatakov and who had been a party member since 1918.

This is what he reports about Piatakov's attitude to the workers at the time he gave them[8] their subversive assignments: "At his last meeting, in July 1936, Piatakov said" (reads) "'So, I see you've found someone to pity, haven't you, that herd of sheep—'"

Beria: The swine! (Noise of indignation in the room.)

A voice: The brutes!

Yezhov: That's how low this vicious fascist agent, this degenerate Communist, has sunk to, God knows what else! These swine must be strangled! We cannot deal with them calmly.

So that's their attitude to the workers! So that's the cynicism with which they speak of the working class. I asked him deliberately: "Is this true?"

Molotov: You asked whom?

Yezhov: Piatakov. I asked him: "Is it true that this was your attitude toward the working class?" He laughed and said: "Yes, apparently, I said something of that sort in order to cheer them up. But perhaps I didn't say that, perhaps they didn't report precisely what I said."

A voice: That scum! (Noise, more indignation in the room.)

Yezhov: If such indeed are the kinds of directives issued by the head of the counterrevolutionary organization to its members, directives saying, "Don't

8. I.e., his confederates—Trans.

have pity on the workers, the workers are nothing but cattle," it is clear that members of this Trotskyist, counterrevolutionary center have tried in every way possible to continue this policy from their posts.

You already know, comrades, about these absolutely monstrous assaults [*izdevatel'stva*] which have cost the lives of so many workers. . . .

A voice: What about Bukharin?

Yezhov: I will now talk about Bukharin and Rykov. (Commotion in the room.) . . .

Stalin: We need to talk about them. They denied that they had any [political] platform. They had a platform, but it was awkward for them to show it. They concealed it. But there was a platform. What did it call for? For the restoration of private enterprise [*chastnaia initsiativa*] in industry, for the opening of our gates to foreign capital, especially to English capital.

Beria: There's a scoundrel for you!

Liubchenko: What swine.

Stalin: For the restoration of capital[ism], for the restoration of private enterprise in agriculture, for the curtailment of the kolkhozy, for the restoration of the kulaks, for moving the Comintern out of the USSR. That was their program. "We were afraid to say this [aloud]," they said.

Voices: What about the [tsarist] debts?

Stalin: Concerning the debts, they hinted that "perhaps we will pay the old debts if you give us a loan." Their response was: "We might give you a loan if you start paying off your debts."

A voice: What about the [foreign] concessions?

Stalin: Concerning the concessions, [their platform called for] opening up the gates to English capital and to foreign capital in general. They had connections with England, with France, with America. That was their platform.

They asked the English: "Please don't force us to openly advocate our platform. It would be awkward for us to do so. The people would be outraged. For this reason, after we come to power, we shall put our platform into effect, little by little, but please don't demand this of us all at once . . ."

Yezhov: I dragged out my report somewhat. Please permit me now to move on to the rightists.

Comrades, it is well known to you that already at his investigation Zinoviev testified that the rightists Rykov, Tomsky, Bukharin, and Uglanov, at least so far as he knew about it, shared the views of the Trotskyist-Zinovievist bloc in their entirety and were informed of it. I shall remind you of Zinoviev's testimony on this matter: "Concerning a united Trotskyist-Zinovievist center and its terroristic views I spoke to Tomsky, and he promised to inform 'his people' about this" (reads).

Rudzutak: And was this perhaps the next backup center?

Yezhov: No, it was the active center, Comrade Rudzutak. Zinoviev's testimony was corroborated by the testimonies of others under arrest and in particular by Sokolnikov. Sokolnikov referred more specifically to the fact that negotiations were conducted by him concerning a direct organizational bloc with the rightists. In his testimony he said the following: "Soon after this meeting in 1934 in the State Publishing House (Gosizdat) with Tomsky, I met with Piatakov" (reads) ". . . to which I also gave my consent."

After this came the testimonies of Piatakov, Serebriakov, and now Radek. Sokolnikov's testimony to the effect that Tomsky was nominated as a member of the backup center has been totally corroborated. In connection with the fact that the surnames of the rightists were given out at the trial, Comrade Kaganovich and I set up face-to-face confrontations between Rykov and Bukharin, on the one hand, and some of the defendants, in accordance with instructions by the CC. It is true, these testimonies at the time were not very concrete, but at any rate, they allowed us to establish the fact that, undoubtedly, the rightists were informed of all plans for terrorism, etc., by the Trotskyist-Zinovievist bloc.

Beria: And how else could they be nominated for the government?

Bukharin: (approaches the Presidium) May I please have the floor?

Yezhov: At any rate, that was the impression we were left with after we carried out the face-to-face confrontations.

Now this has been corroborated not only by the testimonies of Trotskyists and Zinovievists but also by the more concrete cases of the rightists recently arrested.

Here, for example, is what Sosnovsky tells us in his testimony, where he gives [evidence] on the basis of his conversations with Bukharin—

Beria: Who is he?

Yezhov: He is a well-known journalist. He has recently worked for *Izvestia*. By the way, *Izvestia* has had more than its share of swine on its staff. I may be a man of peace, but I seem to have arrested a good dozen of them. This Sosnovsky, in talking about Bukharin, gives the following testimony: "'Take, for instance, the Riutin Platform,' said Bukharin, 'which from first line to last'—" (reads).[9]

(Bukharin replies from his seat, but his words are inaudible.)

Yezhov: Of course, he [Bukharin] may try to justify himself.

Beria: It would be difficult for him to justify himself.

Yezhov: He is trying to prove that the word "terror" never actually appears in the Riutin Platform. But there was no real need for that. It follows logically from it (reads).

Mikoyan: When did this conversation take place?

Yezhov: In 1935 or even in 1936.

Kosior: Very, very recently, then!

Yezhov: . . . And now, comrades, I would like to remind you of the all-

9. Yezhov is apparently quoting from Sosnovsky's report of the latter's alleged conversations with Bukharin.

important, well known decision of the CC of our party concerning our attitude toward all these Trotskyist-Zinovievist, counterrevolutionary swine.[10] The decision says (reads). It seems to me that this directive applies directly to all party organizations and to all party members. We have people here who seem to have broken sharply with the past, but at any rate, these are not party people as such, but only peripheral people [*okolopartiinye*].

As for the work of the Cheka, comrades, I can only assure you that this directive of the CC of the party, written by Comrade Stalin and set down for us, shall be fully carried out, that we shall pull up this Trotskyist-Zinovievist slime by the roots and physically annihilate them.

Voices: That's right!

Prevailing party norms meant that one was supposed to confess and implicate one's confederates as a matter of party duty. Otherwise, one's position was understood as an attack on the party and the Central Committee. Bukharin and Rykov proposed a competing rhetoric, denial of guilt. If, as we have suggested, Bolshevik political reality was shaped by party discourse and ritual, their position denied not only Yezhov's charges but his authority and, because Yezhov was a CC secretary, that of the party elite to shape that dominant narrative. Their denials turned what was to be a ritual of affirmation into a contested ritual. For this, each was denounced for "acting like a lawyer" instead of a Bolshevik and for being "antiparty." And in terms of party understanding, they were. They must have known this, so we have the question of what they could possibly have hoped to gain by so stridently denying not only the charges but the affirming canons and group power assumptions that lay behind them.

Assuming that Bukharin was neither stupid nor suicidal, there is only one answer. At the June 1935 plenum on Yenukidze, Yezhov's proposal had not been authoritative. Then, in September, Stalin had saved Bukharin from the wolves by quashing the investigation against him. Now, in December, Bukharin was gambling that Stalin would again intervene to save him by contradicting Yezhov's line. It was a risky strategy.

---

10. See Document 80.

Document 95

Bukharin's speech to the December 1936 CC plenum, 4 December 1936[11]

Bukharin: Comrades, it is very difficult for me to speak here today, because this may well be the last time that I speak before you. I know that it is especially difficult for me to speak now, because, in point of fact, it is necessary for all members of the party from top to bottom to exercise extreme vigilance and to help the appropriate [NKVD] organs utterly destroy those swine who are engaged in acts of sabotage and so on.

It follows quite naturally from all this—and should serve as our point of departure—that this is the main directive, that this is the main task before our party. I am happy that this entire business has been brought to light before war breaks out and that our [NKVD] organs have been in a position to expose all of this rot before the war so that we can come out of war victorious. Because if all of this had not been revealed before the war but during it, it would have brought about absolutely extraordinary and grievous defeats for the cause of socialism.[12]

Beria: I think you ought rather to tell us what role you played in this whole affair. Tell us, what were you doing?

Bukharin: I'll tell you.

A voice: Before the war and after it, we shall not ask about it.

Bukharin: It is difficult for me now to speak because a whole lot of letters, people, tears, and gestures have passed before your eyes and before the eyes of the investigators who have scrutinized these cases, and all of this has turned out to be false.

But I shall begin with the following. I was present at the death of Vladimir Ilich Lenin, and I swear by the last breath of Vladimir Ilich—and everyone knows how much I loved him—that everything that has been spoken here today, that there is not a word of truth in it, that there is not a single word of truth in any of it. I had one and only one face-to-face confrontation, and that was with Sokolnikov. After this confrontation, Comrade Kaganovich told me that they had the impression that I had nothing to do with this matter. Two days later appeared the statement by the procuracy. Based on the above-mentioned confrontation, it said that the investigation must be discontinued. If you had the impression that I was really involved, that I had something to do with this affair, then why did you make that statement?

Kaganovich: We were referring to the juridical aspect of the matter. That's why we said [this to you at the time]. It's one thing to speak of juridical matters, quite another thing to speak of political matters—

11. RTsKhIDNI, f. 17, op. 2, d. 575, ll. 69–74, 82–86. From the uncorrected shorthand minutes.

12. In the 1970s, an unrepentant Molotov defended the terror in precisely the same terms. See Feliks Chuev, *Sto sorok besed s Molotovym*, Moscow 1991, 390, 413, 432.

Bukharin: For God's sake, don't interrupt me. After all, I asked [you] to record the fact that he [Sokolnikov] didn't speak to me about any political matters, that he got this fact from Tomsky, who was already dead at the time. Nikolai Ivanovich Yezhov asked me in particular not to allude in any way to the fact that Tomsky had already been shot, that they have all been shot.

Liubchenko: Tomsky shot himself. He was not executed.

Bukharin: But he was no longer alive. What could a confrontation with Sokolnikov yield? After all, Sokolnikov spoke to me about nothing. Not a word about politics was exchanged between me and Sokolnikov. Suddenly, this horrible, monstrous charge was brought against me. On the basis of this, the impression was created that I had participated in this affair—

A voice from the Presidium: I read to you the testimonies of Uglanov and Kulikov.

Bukharin: As it pertains to Sosnovsky, comrades, I have written several times. Why could you not have arranged a confrontation for me with Sosnovsky? I never had a single conversation about politics with him and never spoke to him about any Riutin Platform. I myself have never read the Riutin Platform because it had been shown to me once and only once at Comrade Stalin's order. I never saw it. I was never even informed of it.[13]

And suddenly this monstrous charge was brought against me. Why? And why, to make an end of it, if you say that Sosnovsky said this, why do you not arrange a confrontation for me with him? Why do I not have the opportunity to confront him?

Stalin: You were offered a confrontation with Sosnovsky, but you were ill, we were looking for you.

Bukharin: But I wrote Yezhov a letter. I really was ill, but I told him in my letter that, though I was ill, I would drag myself to the confrontation. But no one called for me.

Molotov: At any rate, this can be arranged without difficulty.

Bukharin: But this is the Plenum of the CC. Is this the way things are done at the Plenum of the CC? I must tell you, comrades, that I have never denied that in the years 1928–29 I was an oppositionist, that I fought against the party. But I don't know how I can assure you that I had not the slightest notion, not an atom, about these general views, these platforms, or about these aims. And the charge has been thrown in my face that I knew about it, that I participated in it, that all this time I was trying to worm my way into the government! Do you really believe that I am that type of person? Do you really believe that I could have anything in common with these subversives, with these saboteurs, with these scum, after 30 years in the party and after all of this? This is nothing but madness.

Molotov: Kamenev and Zinoviev also spent their entire lives in the party.

Bukharin: Kamenev and Zinoviev lusted for power, they were reaching for

13. Bukharin later qualified his denial in Document 198.

power. So you think that I too aspired to power?! Are you serious? What are you saying, comrades? After all, there are many old comrades who know me well, who not only know my platform, who know not only this or that about me but my very soul, my inner life—

Beria: It is hard to know someone's soul.

Bukharin: All right then, so it is difficult to know someone's soul. But judge me as a human being! I am saying that, before bringing charges against me, you should have settled all this business having to do with the face-to-face confrontations.

Beria: They'll be settled.

Bukharin: Very well, Comrade Beria, but I wasn't asking you. I wasn't referring to you.

. . . Stalin: Why should they be lying about you? They may be lying but why would they? Can we conceal this from the plenum? You [informal *ty*] are indignant that we raised this question at the plenum, and now you must accept this as a fait accompli.

Bukharin: I am not indignant that the matter has been raised at the plenum, but rather that Nikolai Ivanovich [Yezhov] had drawn the conclusion that I knew about the terror, that I am guilty of terrorist acts, etc.

Concerning Kulikov, it is very easy to do this, to clear up the matter—as to where and when he saw me—and it will become clear that he has not seen me since 1928–29.

Stalin: That's possible.

. . . Bukharin: In 1928–29, I don't deny that some members of the CC were at my apartment. They were. But should one deduce from this fact that I am affiliated with foreign states, that I have placed my name as a candidate for the government, that I am helping those sons of bitches to kill the workers in the mining shafts? And after all this, you [plural *vy*] brought me into the CC at the 16th Party Congress.

Molotov: Piatakov was a member of the CC. It was his business to do so.

Bukharin: Let me appeal to Comrade Sergo Ordzhonikidze. I'd like to tell you about something that happened a long time ago, at the beginning of my party work. I was at Sergo's apartment when he asked me: "What is your opinion of Piatakov?" This is literally what I told him: "My impression of him is that he is the sort of person who is so thoroughly ruined by his tactical approach to things that he doesn't know when he is speaking the truth and when he is speaking from tactical considerations."

Ordzhonikidze: That's true.

Bukharin: So here Sergo is confirming what I said. So could I have ever recommended an accomplice and leader in this way?

Beria: Well, you [formal *vy*] could have said that out of tactical considerations.

Bukharin: Well, that's quite simple. There is always a logical way out. If I say that I've met with a certain person, then it's out of tactical considerations.

If I say that I didn't meet with him, then it's because of conspiratorial considerations. There is no such dialectic that allows you to say that someone has both met and not met someone else.

Kalinin: You must simply help the investigation.

Bukharin: Well, it looks like I'm a son of a bitch, no matter what I do. That's all.

If I am to speak from a businesslike, calm—insofar as I can speak calmly—point of view, then, first of all, let's talk about the face-to-face confrontation with Sokolnikov. I assert that, by its very nature, this confrontation could not possibly have yielded anything for the simple reason that, as Sokolnikov himself has admitted, and I asked that this fact be entered by the investigators in their notebooks, he did not so much as once talk to me about politics. He spoke to me about a review of his wife's book.

Stalin: But he had talked with Tomsky, who told you, didn't he?

Beria: At any rate, he is not an enemy of yours, is he?

Bukharin: I am not speaking of Tomsky. I am speaking of myself. When I was asked about Tomsky by Comrades Yezhov and Lazar Moiseevich [Kaganovich], I told them that in my opinion he might have complained that life was going badly for him. But I could never suppose that he would engage in such matters. For me, this whole business with Tomsky remains an enigma because Sokolnikov said that Tomsky had spoken at my instructions. I know that I never talked to Tomsky about such things. I am suspicious of anything said about Tomsky.

Kaganovich: Tomsky himself admitted his connections with Zinoviev.

Bukharin: He might have admitted his connections [with Zinoviev]. I don't know anything about his connections with Zinoviev. He never said a word about them to me. . . .

Document 96

Rykov's speech to the December 1936 CC plenum, 4 December 1936[14]

Rykov: Comrades, it is even more difficult for me to speak than for Bukharin because my speech follows that of Comrade Stalin.[15] I must fully and totally acknowledge the justice of all of his instructions. Justice in the sense that we are living in an age when double-dealing and deception of the party have attained such dimensions and acquired such a keen, pathological character, that, of course, it would be totally strange if Bukharin or I were taken at our word.

If it's necessary to verify every accusation that may be advanced by someone

14. RTsKhIDNI, f. 17, op. 2, d. 575, ll. 94–97, 100–104. From the uncorrected shorthand minutes.

15. There seems to be no transcript of Stalin's speech to the plenum. The archives contain only "excerpts" and "interjections." See Document 101.

against us, against me, to verify it thoroughly and in every detail, in order that on the basis of this verification it could be established, for instance, whether I am right in asserting that all accusations against me, from beginning to end, are lies, then by all means go ahead and investigate them. I assert that all accusations against me, from beginning to end, are lies, that Kotov was lying when he said that I met with him. I never met with Kotov and never spoke to him. I never laid eyes on him.

When I spoke with Comrade Yezhov, I posed to him what, to my mind, was a very simple question: Kamenev had testified at his trial that he had met with me every year up until 1936. So I asked Comrade Yezhov to find out when and where I met with him, so that I could somehow or other refute that lie. I was told that Kamenev was not asked about it and now it is impossible to ask him about it. He has been shot. This spy and murderer told this to Reingold and to other swine. They all repeat this—that is, that I met with him every year right up until 1936. What can I do about it? If he had mentioned the time and place and circumstances of our meeting, I could prove that this was incorrect. But then we don't know when or where I was supposed to have met with him, so how can I try to prove anything about this unknown something?

Kotov's testimony was made public here. Why was I not told about this testimony earlier? This is the first time I've heard of it, and I've been living in Moscow the whole time. Why was this testimony not verified? It was not verified. I was not asked about it, and I was not even told about it. How can you do things in this way? . . .

When I sat listening to Sokolnikov, I could hardly conceive of more nightmarish things; I could hardly imagine anything like this in my dreams. Sokolnikov said, for example, that they had decided to kill many of our people in Leningrad and then that they decided to call on the troops to come in and save the Revolution. That is, they were supposed to first kill and then save. He also says that I had arranged to see that son of a bitch who allegedly is the district assistant commander. I never laid eyes on him. I don't even remember his last name. After all, this ought to be investigated.

Molotov: His story is more logical than yours. Perhaps his story is implausible, but it is more logical than the one you are telling us now.

Rykov: Perhaps I got something mixed up here, but on the whole, what he said is more or less what I've just described. This same Sokolnikov said, he accused me of [being involved] in the preparation of certain radio stations in Leningrad. Well, this is certainly a tragedy. One can easily question, verify, confront the people from these stations, find out what sort of people they are. Well, these are the kinds of nightmarish things I was talking about.

Stalin: Comrade Rykov, that means therefore that you knew nothing about it, that you suspected nothing. My apologies for interrupting. Go on, Rykov.

Rykov: I am saying that I met with Kamenev but never spoke with him about politics.

Vyshinsky: And with Tomsky?

Rykov: I belonged, along with Tomsky, to the same group of rightists.

Vyshinksy: And what about 1934?

Rykov: I've already told you about that.

Vyshinsky: You spoke to Tomsky concerning Zinoviev?

Rykov: During the course of a little more than two years I saw Tomsky three times, twice under conditions which exclude any possible political conversations of any sort, because at the time his apartment was filled with crowds of people, a number of actors and actresses. And, once, Tomsky was at my place, during the time Zinoviev was working on the editorial board of *Bolshevik*. I told Comrade Vyshinsky about this conversation, talked about it at my [party] cell meeting; I never concealed a single syllable of it . . .

Molotov: Was [Tomsky] at [Zinoviev's] dacha?

Rykov: I don't know.

Vyshinsky: And did he buy Zinoviev a dog?

Rykov: I must note that each and every meeting is an attempt to form a group. That's what I told Tomsky, and he agreed with me.

Kaganovich: This happened precisely during the year when they killed Kirov. Zinoviev invites Tomsky to his dacha. Rykov knows about it and doesn't tell a soul about it. And all of this is finally clarified only at the face-to-face confrontation with Sokolnikov.

Rykov: I told everything at my [party] cell meeting. I told everything that happened to me. My meetings with Tomsky during the past two years were very rare. With Bukharin, I don't know, it seems I saw him in 1934. I told him that it may be harmful for us to meet, and now I see that it was harmful. At any rate, as it pertains to Tomsky, I proceeded from the assumption that it would be extremely dangerous for us to continue our meetings with each other, [that it would be taken] as a continuation of our troika. We never spoke of political matters.

Beria: You didn't find other means?

Bagirov: And just why did you find such meetings dangerous?

Rykov: Just think about it. It's clear that if we had discussed political matters, talked about politics, it is clear that, one way or another, this would have been a continuation of our old group. This is absolutely clear. That is why we discontinued all these discussions. According to the testimony of Kulikov and Uglanov, the center continued to exist until that time.

Beria: Why were you nominated for the government? Why were they so concerned about you?

Rykov: In my opinion, this was my punishment for my glaring mistake, for my participation in the rightist deviation. That's the first thing. Second, there was a certain effort on their part to project onto other people what was in themselves, to look at other people as if they were looking in the mirror. It's clear that this was so. And, as far as it concerns me, there was the testimony of

Document 96 *continued*

Kamenev. And, second, as far as I know, Sokolnikov testified in my presence that Tomsky joined after his conversation with me and with Bukharin. Besides, Tomsky reported this to Piatakov.

Here the difficulty of refuting this testimony lies in the fact that Tomsky ended up committing suicide. Personally, when I learned about the suicide, I was more inclined to think that this was a result of his nervous condition, because earlier, when seriously ill, he time and again contemplated suicide. From that which has been made public here and from the fact that Tomsky had conducted himself toward me the past year in a way unlike ever before— and from the fact that I found out about his death the next afternoon—this convinces me that somehow, as far as I know, he had participated in this affair. Now from all that has been said here, it seems to be absolutely beyond doubt.

Strictly speaking, though, I came up to the podium for one reason only, namely, so that on the basis of that which has been said by Comrade Stalin and everything else said here, I would be granted the opportunity to confront [my accusers], to verify the documents, to verify the testimonies, and to defend myself. These must, perforce, always be granted, but in this case they are more mandatory than ever because this is no laughing matter, because the issue here is whether I am a traitor or not, whether I am a traitor to the state, to the party, to the Revolution, whether I am a fascist or not. Because there is no middle ground here. There can be no middle ground because if these traitors and turncoats had spoken to me about treason and I had not worked for them but only knew about it, then their fate would have been in my hands [and therefore it would have been up to me to report them].

Document 97

Molotov's speech to the December 1936 CC plenum, 4 [?] December 1936[16]

Molotov: . . . Now I shall talk about Tomsky. Comrade Rykov says that he [Tomsky] was apparently involved but that he had been suffering from nervous exhaustion. I cannot call this anything else but a typical example of underhanded scheming. (Noise in the room.)

Voices of approval: That's right, that's a fact.

Molotov: At any rate, this does not speak of an honest attitude toward the matter. And the facts, comrades, confirm this. At least, this is my understanding of the facts received by the Central Committee. Tomsky's suicide was a plot, a premeditated act. Tomsky had arranged, not with one person but with

16. RTsKhIDNI, f. 17, op. 2, d. 575, ll. 122–26. From the uncorrected shorthand minutes.

several people, to commit suicide and therefore to strike a blow once again at the Central Committee.

Comrades, it was only before 7 November 1936 that a group of rightist terrorists, headed by Slavinsky, was arrested. Slavinsky was chairman of the CC of the Union of Fine Arts Workers, a well-known personal friend of Tomsky's. This group included Tomsky's personal secretaries, Stankin and Voinov. They were members of a political group which was preparing a final act of terror on 7 November 1936 and which was arrested only toward the end of October 1936. Doesn't this say something to us about Tomsky's frame of mind? It's clear to everybody what Tomsky was, but Bukharin and Rykov don't seem to get it.

Bukharin: I heard about it.

Molotov: That's not the point. You are always acting as a lawyer, not just for others but also for yourself. You know how to make use of tears and sighs. But I personally do not believe these tears. These facts must all be verified, so much and so thoroughly has Bukharin lied through his teeth these past few years.

Bukharin: In what way have I lied through my teeth? In what way did this manifest itself?

Molotov: I shall add one more thing. Before I tell you about the political lies of the leaders of the rightists and express my own opinion, I shall dwell only on the minutes of the testimony given by Kulikov of 30 November 1936. I received these minutes yesterday and read them. Parts of them were cited here by Comrade Yezhov. I shall cite those passages of the testimony that deserve most attention and that have connection with what we are discussing here (reads). . . .

Here all the members of plenum know what the Riutin Platform was all about. And yet you[17] do not know anything about it. Why are you such a hypocrite? It isn't a question of whether you read it. You are acting as your own lawyer.

Bukharin: I have the right to defend myself.

Molotov: I agree, you have the right to defend yourself, a thousand times over. But I consider it my right not to believe your words. Because you are a political hypocrite. And we shall verify this juridically.

Bukharin: I am not a political hypocrite, not even for a second! (Noise in the room, voices of indignation.)

Molotov: That's also what Piatakov said. We shall verify all these facts, but we are not political cowards. It is rather you who are a coward.

Bukharin: I am not accusing you of political cowardice.

Molotov: Of course, now you are singing a different tune. Let me read further: "From the words of Uglanov it is known to me that such a discussion of

17. Informal *ty* to the end of document—Trans.

the platform took place in the fall of 1932 in Tomsky's apartment with the participation of Tomsky, Rykov, Shmidt, and Uglanov. As Uglanov told me, it was emphasized by all those who had gathered there that the [Riutin] platform formulates fully and correctly the views advanced by the center of the organization both as it pertains to the evaluation of the situation in the country and as it pertains to the imminent tasks of the organization, especially the task of a central[ly directed] terror. . . ."

Document 98

S. V. Kosior's speech to the December 1936 CC plenum, December 1936[18]

Kosior: . . . Take, for instance, the decree and the [Riutin] platform. You know, no matter how much you try to prove it by saying that you were shown the platform and that you didn't read it, no one will believe you.

Bukharin: I didn't read it.

Kosior: That's just talk. At the time the matter [of the Riutin Platform] came up, it was clear to all of us what was going on.

Bukharin: Comrade Kosior, I was not in Moscow at the time.

Kosior: Nothing is proven by that. This doesn't prove that he didn't read the platform. That's no argument, either. Do you want us to believe now, after all that's happened, do you want us to believe that Bukharin is such an honest, devoted party worker, that he knows nothing?

Bukharin: Yes, Comrade Kosior. I was not in Moscow at the time.

Kosior: I don't know where you were at the time.

Bukharin: I was in Asia at the time.

Kosior: That is of no importance. That only proves it once more, and it seems that all that has been spoken here must be taken into account. We must take into account all that which Nikolai Ivanovich Yezhov has spoken of here. I believe that we are obligated to raise the question as required. We shall investigate the matter.

Bukharin: How on earth could you—

Kosior: And you think that we will so easily believe you. If we were so gullible, then we would long ago have placed you in the dock. We have dozens of testimonies and facts. . . .

That is why we had to present everything here, and we had to do it in a thoroughly determined and urgent manner without paying attention to tears

18. RTsKhIDNI, f. 17, op. 2, d. 575, ll. 134–37. From the uncorrected shorthand minutes. Unlike most other speakers, Kosior addresses Bukharin throughout with the formal *vy*—Trans.

and complaints. We must discuss the matter of Bukharin and Rykov from all angles, and we must make an appropriate decision.

You yourselves are both guilty of this, from the beginning to the end, and not only in 1929 but during the whole period in question. Now you must answer for all of this and give appropriate testimony.

Document 99

Sarkisov-Bukharin exchange at the December 1936 CC plenum, 4 December 1936[19]

Sarkisov: . . . So here you are swearing by Lenin. Permit me to remind you all of one story. Here Bukharin is telling you that he swears by Lenin, but, together with the Left-SRs, he in fact wanted to arrest Lenin.

Bukharin: Rubbish!

Sarkisov: It's a historical fact. It's not rubbish. You yourself said so once.

Bukharin: I said that the SRs suggested this, but I reported this to Lenin. How shameless of you to juggle the facts!

Sarkisov: You are not denying it. That only confirms the fact.

Bukharin: I told this to Lenin, and now [ironically] I am guilty of having wanted to arrest Lenin?!!!

Sarkisov: A political worker may make a mistake. It is well known that I had committed a gross [political] error in belonging to the Trotskyists, but nonetheless, a person cannot make mistakes systematically, only sporadically. And yet that's what happened in your case. And now you are assuring us that you are swearing by Ilich. At the very least, this is a case of duplicity.

Document 100

Kaganovich's speech to the December 1936 CC plenum, 4 December 1936[20]

Kaganovich: . . . What should we consider as established fact so that we may bring a supplementary charge against Bukharin and Rykov? We may consider it as indisputably established not only on the basis of our inner conviction but also on the basis of facts, that the rightists maintained ties with the Trotskyist-Zinovievist center. Before his suicide, while he was still trying to defend himself before a meeting of a party organization in the Association of State Publishing Houses (OGIZ), Tomsky was forced to admit to many very grave facts.

19. RTsKhIDNI, f. 17, op. 2, d. 575, l. 144. From the uncorrected shorthand minutes.

20. RTsKhIDNI, f. 17, op. 2, d. 575, ll. 159–62, 165–67, 169–72. From the uncorrected shorthand minutes.

What are all these facts? Beginning in 1928, Kamenev established ties with Tomsky. Moreover, Bukharin was present at their conversations. We know all this from Tomsky's statement. This is apart from the conversations which Bukharin had with Kamenev personally. By the way, in 1931, as Rykov has testified at his face-to-face confrontation, Kamenev was at his place and proposed that all of the Old Bolsheviks meet at Kamenev's apartment. Rykov asserts that he rejected this proposal by Kamenev, but he said nothing about this to anyone right up to his confrontation with Sokolnikov.

Rykov: Kamenev was at my place in my capacity as chairman of the Council of People's Commissars [SNK]. He was giving a report in his capacity as chairman of the Main Concession Committee. (Noise.)

Kaganovich: Consequently, as chairman of the Main Concession Committee, he came to you, chairman of the Council of People's Commissars, and proposed that all of the Old Bolsheviks should meet in order to discuss the political issues of the country? (Noise in the room.)

Rykov: Let me explain: After he ended his report on the plan, that is, as chairman of the concession committee, he said to me: "Let's have a meeting of Old Bolsheviks in order to clear up all of the misunderstandings among us." I told him: "You are talking rot. What sort of misunderstandings can there be among Old Bolsheviks—there is nothing for us to clear up."

Liubchenko: Why didn't you [informal *ty*] mention this conversation to the Politburo?

Rykov: I did.

Kaganovich: Nonsense.

Rykov: I spoke about this very thing.

Kaganovich: At your confrontation you admitted that you made a mistake in not having reported this.

Rykov: No, I confessed my mistake on the question of [not reporting] conversations with Tomsky. . . .

Kaganovich: And finally, in 1934 Zinoviev invited Tomsky to his dacha to drink tea. Tomsky went. Evidently, this tea party was preceded by something else, because after drinking tea Tomsky and Zinoviev went in Tomsky's car to pick out a dog for Zinoviev. You see what friendship, what help, they went together to pick out a dog.

Stalin: What about this dog? Was it a hunting dog or a guard dog?

Kaganovich: It was not possible to establish this. After picking out the dog, Tomsky went again to Zinoviev's to drink tea. Tomsky asked Rykov about this tea party: "Zinoviev invited me to his dacha, should I go?" Rykov states that he told him, "It's not necessary to go," but Tomsky went anyway.

Stalin: Anyway, did they fetch the dog?

Kaganovich: They got it. They were searching for a four-legged companion not unlike themselves.

Stalin: Was it a good dog or a bad dog, anybody know? (Laughter in the hall.)

Kaganovich: It was hard to establish this at the confrontation. . . . And we know that he [Rykov] met with Tomsky not only in 1934–35 but even in the most recent times; even when Tomsky was being called to account, he asked you [Rykov] for advice. You yourself said this at the confrontation. Don't shake your head.

Rykov: No, excuse me, I didn't say that.

Kaganovich: Please, I will read; I am repeating what you said at the confrontation. It's completely exact.

Rykov: When I was at Tomsky's apartment in the spring of this year—

A voice: Of what year?

Rykov: Of this year, 1936—

Stalin: You were at Tomsky's place?

Rykov: In the spring of this year, but I didn't talk about Zinoviev.

Kaganovich: . . . You see, that he [Tomsky] asked Rykov [whether Tomsky should go to Zinoviev's], and Rykov said he was against it. Isn't this a political act, political relations?

Budenny: Why didn't Tomsky ask Kaganovich if he should go?

Kaganovich: . . . From all this there can be only one conclusion: Tomsky had to admit that he was associated with Zinoviev and that Zinoviev had carried on political discussions with him, that he also helped Kamenev and helped Zinoviev and even went with him to buy a dog. Tomsky was associated with Zinoviev up until 1936. It is absolutely clear that Rykov could not have failed to know about Tomsky's actions, could not have failed to know about Tomsky's conversations with Zinoviev just as Bukharin could not have failed to know about this.

Bukharin: Nothing of the sort.

Kaganovich: This was in 1928, 1932, 1933, and 1934.

Bukharin: That's not true.

Kaganovich: Let me ask you: What [articles of] the platform were you and the Zinovievists not in agreement about? You are a political leader [*deiatel'*]. You failed to give us here a full and thorough explanation. Do you think that we will believe your tears here? No. Political leaders who have gone through the Leninist-Stalinist school of fighting enemies will not believe you. You have tried to move us here to pity. Rather, you should show us where, on what political questions, you did not solidly share their views.

Bukharin: I did not share their views on anything.

Kaganovich: You were against the CC.

Bukharin: No.

Kaganovich: You are against the CC.

Bukharin: That's not true.

Kaganovich: I've adduced all the facts.

Bukharin: You've adduced facts from the year 1928. What sort of facts are these?

Document 100 *continued*

Kaganovich: They followed their own line, quite apart from this one. I think we can say this with perfect clarity. The bloc remained in place: [their purpose was] to maintain their army, to carry out their plans pertaining to terrorist acts.

Bukharin: What, Comrade Kaganovich, have you gone out of your mind?!

. . .

Document 101

Excerpts from Stalin's speech to the December 1936 CC plenum, December 1936[21]

Stalin: . . . If a person says openly that he adheres to the party line, then, in accordance with the established, widely known traditions of Lenin's party, the party considers that this person values his ideas and that he has genuinely renounced his former errors and has adopted the positions of the party. We believed in you and we were mistaken. We were mistaken, Comrade Bukharin.

Bukharin: Yes, yes.

Stalin: . . . We believed in you, we decorated you with the Order of Lenin, we moved you up the ladder and we were mistaken. Isn't it true, Comrade Bukharin?

Bukharin: It's true, it's true, I have said the same myself.

Stalin: [apparently paraphrasing and mocking Bukharin] You can go ahead and shoot me, if you like. That's your business. But I don't want my honor to be besmirched. And what testimony does he give today? That's what happens, Comrade Bukharin.

Bukharin: But I cannot admit, either today or tomorrow or the day after tomorrow, anything which I am not guilty of. (Noise in the room.)

Stalin: I'm not saying anything personal about you [informal *ty*]. . . .

Have you seen the letter Furer left behind him after his suicide?! Tears well up in your eyes as you read it. . . .

It takes little political experience to understand that here we are dealing with something else. We know about Furer. We know what he was capable of. So what do you think happened? "I am right, I love the party, I am pure, but my nerves are shot. I can't bear the thought that someone in the party may think that I, Furer, had once been associated with Trotskyists. My honor does not allow me to go on living." And what happened? What happened was worse than one could ever imagine. . . .

The man took his life because he was afraid that everything would be re-

21. RTsKhIDNI, f. 17, op. 2, d. 576, ll. 67–70. From uncorrected "excerpts" pages of the minutes.

vealed. He didn't want to be a witness to his own universal shame. This was true of Furer and Lominadze—

Mikoyan: And of Khandzhian—

Stalin: And of Khandzhian and Skrypnik and Tomsky. . . .

Here you see one of the ultimate and most cunning and easiest means by which one can spit at and deceive the party one last time before dying, before leaving the world. That, Comrade Bukharin, is the underlying reason for these last suicides. And you [formal *vy*], Comrade Bukharin, do you want us to take you at your word?

Bukharin: No, I don't.

Stalin: No, never, under any circumstances.

Bukharin: No, I don't.

Stalin: And if you don't want us to, then don't be indignant that we have raised this question before the Plenum of the CC. Perhaps you're right. It's been very hard on you. But when you consider all these facts which I have talked about, and of which there are so many, we have no choice but to look more closely into this matter. . . .

These texts from the December 1936 plenum reveal a great deal about the nature of the attack on Bukharin and his response to it. Several speakers dismissed Bukharin's factual proofs that he could not have met with other accused at particular times. For Kosior, "Nothing is proven by that." Molotov was dismissive: "That's not the point. You are always acting as a lawyer." The specific facts and charges were not the point for this party audience; Bukharin's duty was to be politically and ritually useful.

Stalin even made jokes about Kaganovich's laborious factual reconstruction of the story of Tomsky, Zinoviev, and the dog. And in his final interchange with Bukharin, Stalin made the point perfectly clear: Bukharin's position required him to provide the text that the party demanded, regardless of Bukharin's "personal honor" or, indeed, of his "legal" guilt or innocence. As an exasperated Kalinin told Bukharin at the plenum, "You must simply help the investigation." Otherwise, Bukharin would fall into the category of the party's enemies who struck a blow by committing suicide (literally or figuratively) without cooperating with the party.

Kaganovich's distinction between juridical guilt and party guilt holds the key to this matter and to much that happened in the party during the period of the terror. According to party thinking, Bukharin might well be innocent in a juridical sense of the specific charges made against him, but he nevertheless was guilty in a party sense for not supporting the party's line. That line, as was clear to all in the leading strata of the party, was the destruction of the former opposition, and as a good soldier of the party and nomenklatura, Bukharin was supposed to cooperate.

Bukharin was obliged to do everything in his power to support that policy: to join in the denunciations of his former followers, to inform on any suspicious activities on their parts, and, if necessary, to confess and publicly associate himself with their crimes, all for the good of the party. If that meant his death, so be it. Since the civil war, party members were in all cases supposed to be prepared to give their lives for the Revolution (which, as Bolsheviks, they believed to be synonymous with the party line). This was the price of iron party discipline, a standard that Bukharin himself had helped to build and to which he had held others. For the Bolsheviks, personal existence was a subset of party existence, and the life of the party took precedence over physical life. As we have seen, even suicide—that most personal of acts—had only political meaning for the Bolsheviks.

Bukharin's personal agony did not elicit sympathy or pity from his former friends on the Central Committee. (Oddly enough, Stalin's remarks to and about Bukharin were the only remotely conciliatory ones.) Quite the contrary, Bukharin's decision to contest the ritual, his elevation of personal honor above his party (and group ritual) duty, infuriated the nomenklatura. It was an attack not only on the authority of the party leadership but also on its members, and they reacted with scorn, insults, and fury at one of their own who had broken the rules and who had jeopardized party unity for personal reasons, insulting them in the process. According to the Bolshevik tradition going back to Lenin's time, Bukharin put himself outside the pale of the comrades and into the category of "enemies" that contained tsarists, counterrevolutionaries, and fascists. Bukharin had addressed the plenum as *we,* but they already thought of him as part of *them.* As we have seen, Bukharin's flat denial challenged the new Yezhov line on the rightists as enemies. By refusing to ritually confess, Bukharin was also denying the nomenklatura's right to establish the dominant narrative.

The stenogram notwithstanding, it is difficult to know exactly what happened politically at the December 1936 plenum. No one spoke up to defend Bukharin and Rykov. Nevertheless, the plenum did not expel Bukharin and Rykov from the party, nor did it order their arrest, despite specific proposals to that effect from some of the Central Committee members. This inconclusive result was not for want of trying on Yezhov's part. His speech was direct and unambiguously accusatory, repeating the charges he had been making against Bukharin for three months. Even while the plenum was meeting, he was sending to Stalin, Molotov, and Kaganovich records of the interrogation of rightist E. F. Kulikov, who testified that Bukharin had told him in 1932 of "directives" to kill Stalin.[22] The last day the plenum was meeting, Stalin apparently ordered another confrontation between the accused Kulikov and Piatakov on the one hand and Bukharin and Rykov on the other. Bukharin and Rykov denied all charges.

Then Stalin did a strange thing. Despite Yezhov's strong report, the lack of any support for Bukharin and Rykov from the plenum, and the damning testimony of Kulikov and others, Stalin moved "to consider the matter of Bukharin and Rykov unfinished" and suggested postponing a decision until the next plenum.[23] Once again Yezhov's proposals were not adopted.

We do not know the reasons for Stalin's procrastination with Bukharin. This was the second time (the first was during the Zinoviev trial) that Stalin had ordered proceedings against Bukharin quashed, suspended, or delayed. It is tempting to imagine the existence of some group within the Central Committee that was resisting the move against the rightists, forcing Stalin to retreat and prepare his position again. But there is absolutely no evidence to support this. Unlike the case of the valuable Piatakov, neither Ordzhonikidze nor any other leader interceded for Bukharin. As far as we can tell from the documents, Bukharin and Rykov were met

---

22. *Izvestiia TsK KPSS*, no. 5, 1989, 75–76.
23. *Izvestiia TsK KPSS*, no 5, 1989, 76. In the versions of the plenum available to researchers in RTsKhIDNI, this part of the transcript has been removed.

only with unrelenting hostility and even rude insults from those present at the plenum, many of whom were prepared to order his arrest on the spot. The only person dragging his feet was Stalin. As we shall see, this was not the last time Stalin resisted or delayed a move against Bukharin. Even in 1937, after the death of Ordzhonikidze, Stalin showed little enthusiasm for a quick and final liquidation of the leading rightists.

Perhaps he felt some special sympathy for his former friend Bukharin. Perhaps he feared some reaction from the party or country, should he destroy the rightist leader. Or perhaps he merely wished to keep his lieutenants uncertain of his plans. Perhaps he himself was not sure of his plans. It was clear that Bukharin had been expected to carry out the apology ritual and had pointedly refused to do so. But unlike Yenukidze's demurral in 1935, Bukharin's resulted in leniency, not harsher punishment.

One additional aspect of this mysterious meeting suggests hesitation or indecision on Stalin's part. The December plenum was a completely hidden transcript. Unlike virtually every other party plenum in Soviet history, it was kept completely secret. No announcement, however terse, appeared in the party press before or after the meeting. In fact, until very recently scholars were not sure that a plenum had taken place at that time, much less that Stalin had called off an attack on Bukharin at the last minute. Stalin hushed it up completely. The December 1936 plenum was somehow a bungled discourse, at least for Yezhov and the other lieutenants who had called for rightist blood.

On this question too, the December 1936 plenum leaves us with more questions than answers. Was Stalin afraid to announce the meeting beforehand for fear of allowing pro-Bukharin forces to prepare? Probably not. After all, such hypothetical forces could exist only in the Central Committee, and members of that body knew of the meeting beforehand; they had even received protocols of testimony against Bukharin before the meeting. And why maintain the secrecy for years after the meeting, even to the point that someone later went back into the archives and removed the text of Stalin's speech? Could it have been that once Bukharin's fate was decided in 1937, there was something embarrassing about wavering or indecision back in 1936?

We can speculate, from the documents we have, on some of the motivations for the new policy to destroy the opposition in 1936, and we can explain some of the actions of the political players. For Stalin, discrediting and annihilating alternative leaders, even has-beens of the defeated opposition, had a clear political advantage, whether personal malice or revenge for past slights played a part or not. It allowed him, by implied threat, to secure the obedience of his bureaucracy.

For the party as a whole, there were also motives for cooperation in the destruction of the opposition. Fear certainly played a part. On a very basic level, once the policy became clear no one was prepared to defend those identified as the party's enemies for fear of joining in their punishment. No one wanted to die or lose his position and privileges. But fear alone cannot explain these events and the conduct of the political actors in them. Even though serving state leaders had been arrested and condemned in autumn 1936, no one in the nomenklatura could logically fear that *he* would become a target. They must have said to themselves: "Of course it is a serious thing to execute a Zinoviev or a Piatakov, but after all they had been dissidents, and I never was anything but a loyal team player. Besides, they were clever and professional politicians and organizers, and probably were up to something unsavory. Zinoviev and Piatakov, like other party enemies (including in their time tsarist officers, Whites, and foreign powers) belong to the category of *them*, not *us*. Repression was something *we* did to *them* (and vice-versa) and it was inconceivable that *we* would repress *us*. I was never one of *them*, why should I be afraid?"

Moreover, although the political weakness of their regime meant that any threatening "new situation" was likely to inspire *political* fear, paralyzing personal fear did not come easily to such people. Before the Revolution, many of them had spent long years in prison or Siberian exile. Yan Rudzutak had spent ten years in chains in a tsarist jail. In the civil war, nearly all of them had been combatants; they had killed, ordered deaths, and seen comrades fall beside them. Some of them had been captured by Whites, tortured, and sentenced to death. These were hard men, and it took a lot to frighten them. Indeed, the accounts we have of survivors of Stalinist camps are notable for the lack of personal terror they relate during their ordeals. We need not fall back on some concept of Russian courage or fatalism to explain their mentality. Ideological fanaticism, a wartime formative experience, and Bolshevik traditions, combined with a lifetime national experience of deprivation and hard living, more than account for it.

Aside from fear, there were other reasons for the nomenklatura to support the destruction of the opposition. First, one suspects that, having read the voluminous confessions of former colleagues whom they knew well, most Central Committee members believed that Bukharin was actually guilty as charged. All of these veteran Bolsheviks were intensely political persons and professional conspirators who also functioned within a long-standing cultural matrix of patrons and clients. Their lives had largely consisted of forming blocs, conspiracies, and factions. It was impossible for them to believe that Bukharin and Rykov, who were practitioners from the same school, could have cut off all contact with their adherents and clients and given up all hope of regaining influence. It simply didn't ring true to the other members of the club who shared the same mentality. That Bukharin and Rykov did not know what their followers were doing or thinking was impossible to believe. Party circles in Moscow and Leningrad were not large; everyone knew everyone. Conversations in kitchens and dachas, social meetings, and telephone contacts took place constantly. Who could believe that all this could have been without political content, as Bukharin and Rykov claimed? As Kosior said, "Do you want us to believe now, after all that's happened, do you want us to believe that Bukharin . . . knows nothing?"

Second, for the nomenklatura, the destruction of its leaders and adherents was the final neutralization of the alternative party nomenklatura. Although the threat from the opposition seems negligible to us, the elite at the time obviously felt a continuing crisis in the wake of collectivization and with the rise of German fascism: a "new situation" in which economic and social stability was still a hope and in which the final success of the Stalinist line was by no means assured. After all, they themselves had come to power unexpectedly in the midst of a national crisis twenty years before, and even Bukharin had mentioned the necessity to clear the political decks before a war. The nomenklatura members of the Central Committee would react hysterically at the accusation that the opposition had formed a "shadow government" that awaited a crisis to seize power.

Third, those in the highest level of the elite in Stalin's immediate circle must have felt a special urgency to destroy the former dissidents. As for Stalin and the nomenklatura in general, the "liquidation" of the opposition and its leaders was a matter of preemptive self-preservation and political insurance. But the Molotovs, Kaganoviches, and Zhdanovs of the Politburo had their own particular interests. To take the present case, as long as Bukharin was alive, they lived under an implied threat. Not so long before, Stalin had embraced Bukharin as the other of the two "Himalayas" of the party, and throughout the 1920s the two had virtually been co-rulers. Bukharin had been close to Stalin, a guest at his family gatherings.[24] The fall of Bukharin and "his people" in 1929 had meant the supremacy in the inner circle of the Molotovs and Kaganoviches (and "their people"). But Stalin's maneuvers and sudden changes of political line in the 1920s meant that anything could happen at the top. So while Stalin's lieutenants probably never slept very well in the dictator's shadow, as long as Bukharin and Rykov lived an additional threat hung over them. Stalin undoubtedly knew this; it could be one explanation of his strange procrastination in destroying Bukharin.

Indeed, Stalin's surprise delay on Bukharin had very strange implications for those at the plenum. Yezhov had presented the case based on NKVD investigations undoubtedly sanctioned or instigated by the Politburo and Stalin. Senior members of the Politburo attacked Bukharin at the meeting. It was, therefore, evident party policy—the proposed new political narrative—to bring him down; the matter had been decided and the decision could not be questioned. In this sense, Bukharin's strategy would appear to have had absolutely no chance from the beginning. No member of the nomenklatura would have been prepared to join or support the line

24. Svetlana Alliluyeva, *Twenty Letters to a Friend*, New York, 1967, 31.

taken by Bukharin. The facts of the matter notwithstanding, Bukharin's stance in defending himself and questioning the accusations, in the Bolshevik understanding, automatically put him in an "antiparty" stance, in a camp populated in the Bolshevik mind by Trotsky, capitalists, Nazis, and the like. It was therefore a shock when Stalin decided that the matter was not decided. After their speeches to the plenum, Yezhov, Molotov, and the other senior leaders who had led the charge against Bukharin could have derived no pleasure from Stalin's sudden turn against their position. Stalin's move put the new political line in doubt. Bukharin's denial had been a risky gamble to challenge the nomenklatura, deny Yezhov's authority, and rely on Stalin for support. Oddly enough, it worked.

Within the party leadership, therefore, there was an identifiable politics. Stalin, his close circle, the broader Central Committee nomenklatura, the regional party secretaries, and the party rank and file all had particular interests. Above the level of the rank and file, the party's leaders were all skilled and experienced politicians and professional conspirators with the ability to calculate threats and self-interest. In the present case, the destruction of the former opposition served most interests. For the nomenklatura at large, it meant convenient scapegoating of enemies for various economic failures and the elimination of potential rivals. For Stalin, it also meant the maximization of his personal power and the possibility of keeping the Central Committee members under control by raising the question of their "laxity."

It further allowed him to keep his lieutenants guessing about whom he would in the end embrace as "his people." The Politburo lieutenants had the most to gain by the elimination of the opposition, which they saw not only as a threat from outside but as another option for Stalin. With the alternative lieutenants dead, they must have reasoned, Stalin would have to throw in his lot with them as the only game in town. It is therefore perhaps not an accident that the baiting of Bukharin and Rykov at the 1936 and 1937 plena was conducted with particular ferocity and rudeness by these lieutenants. In this instance, they may not have been acting simply as Stalin's puppets or prearranged stalking horses. His relative silence at the plena served several possible purposes. It allowed him to pose, when necessary, as a moderate, liberal, radical, or simple balancer, as the case might require. It also masked, perhaps to his closest collaborators, his true intentions, whatever they were.

It is possible to interpret the events of 1936–37 as volatile elements in a swirling crucible of political forces. If we set aside the notion of a grand Stalin plan to kill everyone—the evidence for which, aside from our knowing the end and reading backward, is quite weak—it is possible to understand the politics of the 1930s as an evolving political history in which self-interested persons and groups jockeyed for position. Stalin was desperate to achieve supreme power and to be able to discipline the apparatus. The lieutenants wanted to remain lieutenants. The nomenklatura wanted to eliminate rivals and control those beneath them. It may have been that at any given moment, all the players were maneuvering for advantage, using the available political tools, issues, and discourses, without any of them, including Stalin, knowing where everything was headed. This fluid situation was described fifty years later by Molotov, who admitted his role in the terror and still believed it to have been necessary. For Molotov, the developing events were "not simply tactics. Gradually things came to light in a sharp struggle in various areas."[25]

25. Chuev, *Sto sorok besed,* 463.

CHAPTER NINE

The Sky Darkens

If you knew someone, you'd give him your full trust. Everything was based on these connections and on trust. How can one do such things?!—A. A. Andreev, 1937

I consider the criticism and the party sanctions levied against me personally by the Central Committee to be, in my opinion, very lenient—because of the enormous harm caused by me as a result of the activities of these Trotskyists.—B. P. Sheboldaev, 1937

IN JANUARY 1937 Moscow decided to press the point about the dangers of "carelessness" among the regional nomenklatura by making examples of two of the most prominent regional leaders, Pavel Postyshev (secretary in the Ukraine) and Boris Sheboldaev (first secretary of the Azov–Black Sea Territorial Party Committee). Recent arrests of alleged Trotskyist terrorists in both regions provided an issue and a setting for criticizing the practices of the regional satraps without delving too much into the real workings of the system and without weakening the regional party apparatus as an institution, both points that no central party leaders wanted to discuss. The new Moscow political transcript went as follows: the arrests of terrorists under the noses of trusted, veteran party leaders revealed deficiencies in leadership. The leading secretaries had been too trusting, too "politically blind," and too involved in economic administration to pay the necessary attention to "party work." Their laxity had allowed the enemy to work unmolested, and the bureaucratism and "familyness" of their machines made them deaf to "signals from below" about enemies.

It is clear that this new line was carefully thought out and presented by the Stalinist center. By criticizing the regional leaders and making examples of two of the most prominent, Stalin could have been serving several purposes. These actions first of all allowed Stalin to root out former oppositionists down to the local level. Local party leaders were no longer able to shield such people, regardless of their talents and usefulness to local economic and administrative agencies. The new policy thus weakened local patronage control and made it clear that Moscow would have a say in hirings and firings and would intrude itself into cadres policy. The new line also showed territorial party leaders who was boss and put them on notice that they must toe the current Moscow political line. By encouraging rank-and-file criticism, within limits, Stalin also attempted to open up new lines of information (or denunciation) that bypassed the middle-level leadership, which before this had been able to squelch discontent and filter information coming from below.

At the same time, the tsar could not govern without his boyars, or at least without a boyar class. The new critical line against the party apparatus was carefully circumscribed. Although the leaders were criticized, they were not denounced as enemies, conscious protectors of enemies, swindlers, or even poor Bolsheviks. Stalin made this very clear in his speech to the upcoming February–March plenum, which was prominently published in party newspapers.[1] The two leading secretaries who lost their jobs were given new posts as heads of other regions. Grassroots criticism was to be kept under control and channeled against particular leaders and their faults rather than against the regime itself.

These Stalinist tactics were risky for the nomenklatura, whose smooth functioning at all levels was based on patronage control, on maintaining its grip over the rank-and-file members (as well as the population at large), and on a unified narrative at all levels of the nomenklatura. Stalin's tactic of encouraging party democracy in the form of criticism from below risked a split in the party elite by turning the top against the middle and by inciting the rank and file against their heretofore legitimate leaders. Although at this time the regional leaders were not branded as enemies or their loyalty questioned, the new political transcript from the top represented the

1. *Pravda,* 29 March and 1 April 1937.

beginning of Stalin's offensive against the nomenklatura. Iron-
ically, it had been this very idea—organizing the lower levels of the
party against their leaders—that had so terrorized and infuriated
the nomenklatura as a whole when Riutin had suggested it.

Making Examples of Some Regional Chiefs

In the first week of January, Stalinist emissary A. A. Andreev traveled to Rostov to promulgate the new line on careless regional
secretaries by organizing the removal of Boris Sheboldaev, first
secretary of the Azov–Black Sea Territorial Party Organization. In
autumn 1936 arrests of former Trotskyists had reached into Sheboldaev's region, and he had been summoned to the Politburo for a
dressing down about the tolerance he had shown for them. On 2
January the Politburo passed a resolution removing him from his
position, and it was this text that Andreev carried with him to
Rostov-on-Don, the capital of the territory, to validate the new
line. First convening the narrow leadership circle (the buro of the
territorial committee) and then the broader regional elite (the
plenum of the territorial committee), Andreev laid out the Politburo's decision, chastised the Sheboldaev team and encouraged
lower-level party members to help root out incompetent leaders
and traitors. As usual, the procedure by which a party leader was
disciplined was a kind of performance ritual with its own internal
set of rules. An emissary from the "center" arrived and arraigned
the local leader. That leader then provided the required apologetic
"tax payment" by confessing his error and pointedly affirming the
justice of the charges (usually by saying that they were "completely
correct"). Then, those in attendance affirmed the accusations by
providing additional details and charges. Finally, a resolution was
adopted that transformed the new discourse into a formal text.

Document 102

Resolution of the Azov–Black Sea Territorial Committee on removal of Comrade Sheboldaev 5 January 1937[2]

From Protocol #216 of the buro of the Azov–Black Sea Territorial Committee of the VKP(b)

2. RTsKhIDNI, f. 17, op. 21, d. 2214, l. 5

Document 102 *continued*

5 January 1937

A report by Comrade A. A. Andreev, secretary of the CC.

1) Having heard the report by Comrade Andreev, secretary of the CC, concerning the decision by the CC of the VKP(b) of 2 January 1937 entitled "On the Mistakes Committed by Comrade Sheboldaev, Secretary of the Azov–Black Sea Territorial Committee and on the Unsatisfactory Political Leadership of the Territorial Committee of the VKP(b)," the decision by the CC is to be recognized as fully and totally right.

2) Comrade Sheboldaev is to be relieved of his duties as first secretary of the territorial committee.

3) Comrade Yevdokimov is to be elected as first secretary of the territorial committee.

4) Proposals are to be placed before the plenum of the territorial committee. The plenum of the territorial committee is to be convened for 6 January at 11 A.M. and is to include the participation of the secretaries of the city committees and district committees.

5) A meeting is called for 7 January at 5 P.M. of the aktiv of the Rostov party organization, summoning the aktiv of Taganrog, Shakhty, Krasnodar, Sula, Novocherkassk, and Novorossiisk party organizations to take part in it.

M. Malinov,

Secretary of the Azov–Black Sea Territorial Committee of the VKP(b)

Document 103

A. A. Andreev's speech to the plenum of the Azov–Black Sea Territorial Committee, 6 January 1937[3]

Malinov (chairman): Comrades, I declare this session of the plenum of the Azov–Black Sea Territorial Committee of the VKP(b), the secretaries attending, open. There is only one item on the agenda, namely, a report by Comrade Andreev, secretary of the CC of the VKP(b), concerning the mistakes committed by Comrade Sheboldaev, secretary of the Azov–Black Sea Territorial Committee of the VKP(b), and concerning the political leadership of the territorial committee.

Andreev: Comrades, in connection with the arrests of the Trotskyists who had worked in the Azov–Black Sea region, the CC of the party has obtained substantial materials relative to the poor situation existing in the party leadership of the region which led to the rather active and brazen activities by the Trotskyists in the Azov–Black Sea region. In connection with this, Comrade Stalin proposed that the CC of the VKP(b) discuss the situation in the Azov–

3. RTsKhIDNI, f. 17, op. 21, d. 2196, ll. 10–13, 16–17, 22–23, 32–40. Typed, without corrections.

Black Sea Territorial Committee of the VKP(b) and that it summon Comrade Sheboldaev, first secretary of the territorial committee of the VKP(b), to appear and explain the situation before the CC of the VKP(b).

This discussion took place on 31 December, at the Politburo of the CC in the presence of Comrade Sheboldaev. A day or two later, a decision was made by the Central Committee of the party. I was instructed by the CC of the VKP(b) to make this decision known to you and to explain it. Please permit me to make public the decision of the CC. (He reads the decree by the CC of the VKP(b) concerning the mistakes committed by Comrade Sheboldaev, secretary of the Azov–Black Sea Territorial Committee and the unsatisfactory political leadership of the territorial committee of the VKP(b).)

Here is the decision adopted by the CC of the VKP(b). As you can see, this is a stern decision. Yet it is also a correct one, and it shall have enormous significance, not only for the work of the Azov–Black Sea party organization. No, it shall have far greater significance. Why has the Central Committee adopted such a stern decision? Because the CC was in possession of the following very grave facts:

1) The Trotskyist center carried out its activities in Rostov with impunity for a fairly long period of time. This center, to which belonged traitors to the motherland, Trotskyists, saboteurs, had been in operation for a fairly long period of time, and it felt itself quite free to operate.

Yet far from acting alone, it seized the main economic-political posts of the region. It placed its people in key economic-political positions. In Rostov it seized the city committee in its entirety and appointed the first and second secretaries of the city committee. . . .

In Taganrog, too, it [the Trotskyist center] had at its disposal the city committee of Taganrog in the person of Vardanian, first secretary of the city committee. It also had at its disposal the district committee of SELMASH,[4] where Gogoberidze was one of the center's active members. There are grounds for believing that in this respect, the situation was no better in the Shakhty party organization. I believe that materials concerning this will be presented at this plenum. There are grounds for supposing that things were no better in this respect with the Krasnodar party organization. Apart from seizing posts in the party, the Trotskyists seized the post of leader of the Komsomol in the person of Yerofitsky, first secretary of the territorial committee of the Komsomol.

The post of chairman of the city soviet of Rostov, a major and critical city in the region, was seized [by Trotskyists] in the person of Ovchinnikov, chairman of the city soviet. Two economic posts of vital importance were seized: the post of director of the factory of agricultural machinery (SELMASH), which not only manufactures products for agriculture but is also involved in major defense works; this post was seized by Glebov-Avilov, a sworn enemy of

4. [Rost]Sel'mash—the Rostov factory of agricultural machinery—Trans.

the party. A second factory—the metallurgical factory in Taganrog—was headed by Kolesnikov, a well-known enemy of the party, who also succeeded in causing great harm to Soviet power there.

We may add to this the fact that a very important post in the territorial committee itself was seized by the enemies of the party. It is true that, at first glance, it seems to be a secondary post, but it is an extremely important post which gave access to all secret documents, to the entire work of the territorial committee. This is the post of assistant to the first secretary of the territorial committee. The assistant to the first secretary turned out to be an enemy of the party, who [had access to] all documents which were sent by the CC of the territorial committee c/o the first secretary. All of these documents came into the possession of enemies of the party. All of these documents came into the possession of the Trotskyist center operating in the Azov–Black Sea region.

If we also add the fact that, as a result of all this, three members of the buro of the territorial committee were arrested and that fifteen members of the plenum of the territorial committee were also arrested, then, comrades, you may come to understand the condition which the territorial committee is in at present and the circumstances in which it finds itself.

What has remained of it, of the territorial committee, one may wonder? What has remained of it, when the leading posts have turned out to be in the hands of enemies? What is there left?

In the city of Rostov, the capital of the region, the leadership of the party and soviet and economic operations at a major factory was seized from right under your noses. The same thing happened in Taganrog, the second-largest city of the region. Party, soviet, and economic leadership posts turned out to be in the hands of enemies. Consequently, the territorial committee turned out to be surrounded by enemies of the party. . . .

There, where we are not active, the enemy is always active. . . .

Perhaps you will say that this is an exaggeration. No, comrades, this is not an exaggeration. How else are we to explain the following fact: A purge took place before the verification of 1934–35, approximately twelve people from around the region were expelled at the beginning of 1935, and yet the enemy, the true enemy remained within the ranks of the party. The purge was followed by the verification. I don't know if you are acquainted with all of this. . . .

The verification proceeded haltingly, by fits and starts, with corrections introduced by the CC during the verification process. The verification was carried out. What happened? A significant number of party members were expelled during the verification. Nevertheless, the enemies dug in, the enemies kept their posts in the party and continued their operations. The verification was followed by the exchange of party documents. Did the territorial committee put its affairs in order during the exchange? No, the exchange took place, 45 Trotskyists, all apparently small fry, were expelled, but the enemies remained in the party. They remained unnoticed during the exchange. After all, it should be borne in mind that the verification and the exchange were instituted first and foremost so as to purge our party ranks of enemies of the party, and here we saw a succession of purge, verification, and exchange, and yet the enemies remained in our midst. The same was true of the exchange. 45 persons were expelled during the exchange, yet over 400 persons—and now in accordance with the calculations of the territorial committee itself, over 500 enemies of the party—were expelled after the exchange of party documents, after the CC wrote another scathing political letter after the trial in August, after investigation into the activities of the Trotskyists was initiated. Is this not clear confirmation of a careless attitude to the directing of such a critical matter as party work and the verification and exchange of party documents? . . .

This then is the principal reason why the enemy was afforded such a broad opportunity to carry out its activities.

The second reason is the extremely uncritical, credulous attitude—inadmissible for a Bolshevik—on the part of people such as Comrade Sheboldaev, a member of the CC, a credulous attitude to people such as Kolotilin, Karpov, Ovchinnikov, and Gogoberidze. It is evident that the leaders of the territorial committee had forgotten the main precondition [for a Bolshevik], about which Lenin spoke very often and about which Comrade Stalin has spoken—namely, that it is not enough for a Bolshevik leader to assign tasks correctly at any given moment, to select and appoint people to their appropriate posts for the implementation of these tasks. This is not enough. The chief duty of a Bolshevik leader is to check and evaluate his people in the course of practical [party] work, to study them. This main precondition was lacking in the case of the leaders of the territorial committee in their capacity as political leaders. Everything in your territorial committee was based on having connections. If you knew someone, you'd give him your full trust. Everything was based on these connections and on trust. How can one do such things?! . . .

Take, for instance, Kolotilin. It is clear now that he was an enemy, a sworn enemy of the party. And the fact that he committed suicide—he was given this opportunity to kill himself by the officials of the territorial committee—we let him out of our hands; he could have given us much valuable testimony which would have helped us to expose our enemies, which could have helped us to solve a thing here or there. The officials of the territorial committee, who had tolerated his presence at this very post for many years, decided that they could not wait for two days and decided to remove him from his post as secretary. And an hour later he blew his brains out. In doing this, in committing suicide, he fully confirmed his guilt. Because there is no reason for an innocent person to shoot himself. An innocent person, a Bolshevik, if he is innocent, will receive justice, he ought to receive justice, he will receive justice. The circumstances here [in our society] are not such that he could not receive justice. He will receive justice. A scoundrel who has no place to turn to shoots himself.

This is a peculiar tactic. It is now clear that this is a peculiar means of evading an investigation and avoiding shame. We have several such examples.

Lominadze shot himself to death. At first, certain people felt sorry for him, but he turned out to be a scoundrel of scoundrels. He shot himself because there was no place for him to turn to. Either way, he would have been exposed. Tomsky shot himself to death, left behind a letter to the effect that he was innocent, that he had been unjustly slandered, that he couldn't go on living, and so on. And yet, according to the testimonies, he has now turned out to be an organizer of rightist terrorists. Now these testimonies have been brought to light, fully and clearly. He committed suicide because he decided to avoid shame, public shame, and to evade the investigation. We would have surely convicted him. Furer, an official of the Moscow committee, shot himself to death and left behind a letter nearly fifteen pages long. When you read the letter, you feel as if you are hearing the heart-rending cry of a sincere person. Yet what actually happened? It turned out that he was one of the active members of a center of terrorists in the Ukraine, that he participated in terrorist acts. You can see what these suicides are really worth. We shall from now on consider them only as confirmation of these testimonies. We shall consider each and every suicide a confirmation of only one thing: it is the enemy who has shot himself and no one else.

Kolotilin turned out to be an enemy. And were there really so few warnings in the territorial committee pertaining to the poor situation that existed in the Rostov party organization? Were there really so few warnings? Did the territorial committee really have no grounds for a critical assessment of Kolotilin and Karpov? Did it really have so few grounds for checking up on these people in practice, for tracking down their activities? But that is the point, that in spite of warnings by the CC of poor work, the territorial committee obstinately clung to this Kolotilin, supported and trusted him in every way. And this credulousness, comrades, is especially unacceptable and criminal, I would say, after all the organizations of our party had received a rather severe warning by virtue of Comrade Kirov's murder, by virtue of the political letter sent by the CC to all party organizations, by virtue of the June Plenum of the CC, at which Comrade Stalin spoke, and at which he spoke very sternly about our need to draw the lessons of political vigilance. Representatives of the Azov–Black Sea Territorial Committee were present at the plenum. This was followed in August by yet another political letter by the CC. This letter also cautioned the party organization. After that came the trial of the Trotskyists-Zinovievists. However, these political warnings were not heeded or made use of by the territorial committee. I ought to add that the territorial committee received special warnings apart from those above. It seems that in the course of 1936, there were around 4 such warnings connected with the verification, with the exchange of party documents, and with a special review of the affairs of the Rostov organization. These all related specifically to the Azov–Black Sea organization. Comrade Stalin spoke to Comrade Sheboldaev concerning these people— didn't he?—he warned him many times. In my opinion, the territorial committee's guilt is aggravated by the fact that, having received these warnings, it did not make use of them to rectify its course. On the other hand, they remained deaf and blind to every sort of warning that came from below. One must say that self-criticism in Rostov was almost totally suppressed. The Central Committee verified that self-criticism was almost totally suppressed. I have already said that we have facts to show that people were expelled from the party as Trotskyists for self-criticism. Yesterday, these facts were brought up at the meeting of the buro. We cannot know everything and the territorial committee cannot know everything by intuition, but it can be prompted by reports from party members below as to what it should turn its attention to, and it is in this that self-criticism is of the utmost importance. Nevertheless, the territorial committee reacted to these warnings with indifference and this served to set up the situation that followed.

These, comrades, are the organizational mistakes of the territorial committee, becoming essentially political mistakes, which led to the fact that the territorial committee itself was surrounded by enemies of the party and to the fact that the enemy operated with relative freedom as it carried out its espionage, sabotage, and terrorist operations. I must tell you, comrades, that such a shameful situation is not to be found in any other region or in any other organization. For that reason, the Central Committee has been compelled to adopt this stern decision. . . .

All the more so because you were supposed to be on your utmost guard, because your region is of utmost importance in every respect. It is important in the economic sphere because it is one of the grain-producing regions. It is important in the industrial sphere because major factories, coal mines, and oil [wells] are concentrated in it. It is important in the political sphere because it is the region that is inhabited by the Cossacks and therefore demands special attention, special attention on the part of the political leadership, and this should have put you in a state of ultra-Bolshevik vigilance, but this was not so.

That is why the CC has adopted such a stern decision. This decision, as you can see, affects Comrade Sheboldaev more than anyone else. But then, he is the first secretary, he is the chief leader of the territorial committee, he is a member of the CC, the man entrusted most by the CC with its activities in the region. By virtue of his position he ought to be able to see farther than others. He ought to be able to see and notice things much sooner than others. That is why the CC has adopted such a stern decision toward him.

But take note, he does not bear responsibility for this state of affairs alone. So do other members of the territorial committee, especially the members of the buro of the territorial committee. Does Comrade Malinov not bear a certain responsibility? Comrade Malinov, as is known, is second secretary. Comrade Malinov was entrusted with party work. And how did Comrade Malinov deal with this task? He shifted responsibility onto someone else's shoulders. In all of his work for the territorial committee, Comrade Malinov appears at best as an economic planner and not as a party leader. Comrade Berezin stood at the helm of the territorial committee's [department] especially adapted for the practical leadership of the party organizations. It was his responsibility to check on the work of the party organizations. And how did he acquit himself? How well did he check on the party organizations? How did he, practically speaking, lead the people in the party organizations? Unfortunately, I must say that he hardly resembled a party leader. Hardly indeed, to put it mildly. For some reason or other, he was slow to understand this and came to understand this only yesterday at the meeting of the buro of the territorial committee, where he so very passionately spoke about the decision by the CC. . . .

But one thing is clear: the matter will not end with the arrests that have been made or with the expulsion from the party of the enemies of the party. You must, as is called for by the decision of the CC of the VKP(b), go through your party organization properly like true Bolsheviks, cleanse your party organization of all traces of Trotskyists, Zinovievists, and others. It is clear that they would not betray their cadres. We are now convinced of this because there was a trial and we passed judgment on Zinoviev, Kamenev—and yet they did not betray their main people. After this we seized many important people. It is clear that Trotskyists under arrest do not betray all of their cadres, either. Some of their cadres continue to exist. And we must expose them in the party organization. We must root them out of the economic, soviet, and Komsomol organizations. In this consists our mission.

You must draw lessons from this decision of the CC which I have made public to you. You must do this like true Bolsheviks in order to decisively correct the situation in all of the party organizations of the region. This is what is demanded of you by the CC of the VKP(b). (Everyone rises. Stormy, prolonged applause.)

Unlike Yenukidze and Bukharin, Sheboldaev understood the need for an apologetic performance and recognized that he did not have the stature or influence to avoid it. Such a speech was necessary both to affirm the unity and "correctness" of the party leadership and to reinforce Sheboldaev's implicit claim to continued membership in the elite. Playing the role expected of him as a loyal member of the nomenklatura, Sheboldaev bowed before the Central Committee's will and took his medicine by making a ritualized affirmation of the new dominant line.

Document 104

B. P. Sheboldaev's speech to the plenum of the Azov–Black Sea Territorial Committee, 6 January 1937[5]

Comrades, I have come up to the podium for only one reason—namely, to say that I consider the decision by the Central Committee of the VKP(b) concerning my mistakes and the work of the territorial committee of the VKP(b), of which I was the leader, to be absolutely right, absolutely just, because no other decision by the CC of the VKP(b) is possible. This is so for the following reason: if many of our leaders, if the practical leadership of the Rostov organization, our main, the pivotal one, and of that of Taganrog, as it concerns the Komsomol, if all these double-dealing enemies, these Trotskyists—that is, Kolotilin, Karpov, Vardanian, Yerofitsky, and others—had managed to work side by side with us, had managed to weave their nests right under our eyes and carried out their counterrevolutionary activity over the course of many years, then it can only mean that I was surrounded by enemies, that the territorial committee of the VKP(b) was surrounded by the vilest of enemies, and we, blind and credulous in a manner unworthy of Bolsheviks, did not see it.

Comrades, I consider it to be absolutely correct that the chief and main responsibility for this state of affairs should be placed on my shoulders. I am saying this not only because I am a member of the CC of the VKP(b) and because I am the first secretary of the territorial committee of the VKP(b), and not only because I have served in this region for the past 6 years, but also because I had earlier been acquainted with a great number of the people who had turned out to be enemies. Despite this, trusting these people criminally, I could not see their counterrevolutionary activities.

Besides, comrades, it is absolutely clear that this mistake, which basically amounts to the fact that we did not see these enemies—and I didn't see them either—is to some extent a repetition of the mistake committed in 1932 when none of us, including myself, saw the enemies of the kolkhozy. Moreover, my responsibility and guilt are aggravated by the fact that we, myself included, know that the activities carried out by the Trotskyists were widespread in our region—of this Andrei Andreevich [Andreev] has already spoken. These activities are especially dangerous for a number of reasons. It seems to me, comrades, that I bear special responsibility above all for the group which worked earlier in Saratov, where I served as secretary of the Lower Volga Territorial Committee of the VKP(b) in the years 1928–30. Of course, comrades, I was also acquainted with Kolotilin. I knew him as early as 1923–24 in Tashkent while working in that organization. He also came to work with us in 1932. And I trusted him, and I trusted Ovchinnikov, secretary of the Volsk Okrug Committee of the Lower Volga region, and I trusted Yerofitsky, secre-

5. RTsKhIDNI, f. 17, op. 21, d. 2196, ll. 5–9. Typed text, unsigned and uncorrected.

tary of the Lower Volga Komsomol Territorial Committee—I trusted them, believing them to be honest people, and now it has been brought to light and it is clear that in 1929 they were members of a Trotskyist organization in Saratov on the Lower Volga. This organization was headed by Shatskin, Pavlov, and other enemies, who carried out underground activities at that time. And as we can see now, this criminal trust on my part has led to the fact that it gave these people the opportunity to carry out their activities here.

Concerning Gogoberidze and Vardanian. I knew Gogoberidze when I was in the underground in Baku in 1918. As for Vardanian, I didn't know him at all. Gogoberidze arrived here in 1934 to serve in the region. He came to Yeisk, to the territorial committee, and I—we—gave him the opportunity to carry on his activities. It is absolutely true that we failed to take measures to expose the former Trotskyists—for instance, Glebov, Kolesnikov, Beloborodov. And we failed to recognize as Trotskyists those who were not known as Trotskyists but who turned out to be the most vicious of enemies. Meanwhile, there is no doubt that they carried out these activities (this has now been proven with absolute clarity). There is no doubt that, had we exercised Bolshevik vigilance, had we checked on our people, we could have exposed them much, much earlier. Time and again we received warnings of their activity, warnings to which we, because of our blindness, did not ascribe any significance. And we made no effort to dig beneath the surface to discover the meaning of these warnings. Proceeding from trust, from credulity, we essentially covered up their activities and helped carry them out. And this was reflected in our decisions. There were many such incorrect decisions: the decision concerning Ovchinnikov, the decision concerning the car accident involving Gogoberidze, who killed someone because he feared him, the decision concerning Limarev in Shakhty, who criticized Liubarsky—these and a host of many other decisions about which, no doubt, you will be hearing, all of this, comrades, speaks of gross, totally unacceptable errors which I, as a leader, had committed and which, objectively speaking, have slowed down the unmasking of those enemies whom we, in effect, by virtue of our authority, shielded from the [party] organization and the Central Committee of our party.

I thought—and this was literally days before Kolotilin's suicide—I hoped and believed that so long as there was no clear evidence of his participation in a Trotskyist organization, that he could work in the Rostov organization. Had it not been for my intolerable trust [in him]—I ought to have made a decision concerning this matter much earlier, immediately, and thereby drawn the conclusions from the decisions of the Central Committee.

Comrades, I am especially to blame because the Central Committee gave us many instructions which ought to have put us on our guard and forced us to evaluate them all. And like a [true] Bolshevik to draw conclusions concerning the leadership of Rostov and Taganrog.

Concerning Vardanian, Comrade Stalin has openly stated that this man had committed a host of gross mistakes in Armenia, and nevertheless, we, I and others, failed to draw any conclusions from this.

Concerning Ovchinnikov and others, Andrei Andreevich has already spoken about them. And yet now, when it is absolutely clear that this entire gang, linked closely to one another and connected with the Trotskyist-Beloborodovist center, was carrying out its counterrevolutionary activities over many years, when they carried out their sabotage in party organizations, sabotage now brought to light and also revealed in many of their testimonies and in the speeches delivered at the latest meeting of the city aktiv, at the primary [party] organizations—6 At that time too, comrades, we had assessed the situation incorrectly. We spoke of Kolotilin's bureaucratism, and no more than a few days ago, Kolotilin gave a report at the plenum concerning the decision of the Central Committee. This happened because we trusted him then, because we were blind, and, to be frank, because we supported him.

Comrades, I consider the decision of the Central Committee to be absolutely correct. I consider the criticism and the party sanctions levied against me personally by the Central Committee to be, in my opinion, very lenient— because of the enormous harm caused by me as a result of the activities of these Trotskyists, who occupied the most critical posts, because of the undermining of trust toward the territorial committee of the party brought on by this entire affair. All of this has caused enormous damage to the party organization.

Comrades, I know of course, that far from everyone has as yet been unmasked. I know that this is the way it must be since the Rostov organization was headed by Kolotilin, an enemy. It is impossible that there should be no more enemies in Taganrog and in many other places. Comrades, I believe that the decision of the Central Committee, a correct and just decision, shall have, in this respect, the effect, first and foremost, of totally eradicating the Trotskyist underground in our organization. It shall also have the effect of bringing about a change in party work, for the negligence and ruin of which we, above all, carry responsibility, the territorial committee and I myself.

Comrade Stalin was absolutely right when he said at the Politburo session that I have degenerated from a political leader of the party into an economic planner [*khoziaistvennik*]. That, comrades, is, in fact, the case. We, and I first and foremost, were preoccupied with agriculture, first and foremost with all sorts of economic matters. Matters concerned with party work, with leadership of the party organization, with liaison with the party organization, with the daily implementation of leadership of intraparty work—all of this was abandoned. And as it has already been pointed out here, the result was that very negligence on account of which—in view of our credulity—it was especially easy for the Trotskyists to organize and carry on their activities.

Comrades, I am fully cognizant of my responsibility in this matter, both before the party organization and before the Central Committee of the party. I

6. Incomplete sentence in original text—Trans.

shall draw the conclusions from this decision for myself, I shall draw these conclusions concerning my grave deficiencies both as a party member and, all the more so, as a member of the Central Committee. I shall draw these conclusions wherever and however I may have to work, wherever they give me work, wherever the Central Committee may direct me to work. Everywhere, comrades, I shall draw these lessons for myself concerning the last period of my work in the Azov–Black Sea organization in order that I may prove by my work that I have understood these mistakes, so intolerable for a Bolshevik, and that I have rectified them.

For loyally participating in the required apology ritual, Sheboldaev was not severely punished. Although he was removed from Rostov, he immediately received another important posting in another party organization.

Encouraged by the new line and freed from Sheboldaev's control, party members then ran with the new line and unleashed heretofore impossible criticism of the former regional party leadership. No less than Sheboldaev himself, they were playing roles contributing to party unity and affirming their status.

Document 105

Ivnitsky's speech to the plenum of the Azov–Black Sea Territorial Committee, 6 January 1937[7]

Ivnitsky: Comrades, I, who have been a member of the Azov–Black Sea organization for 21 years, have felt with special keenness the vile, ugly situation which we have come to at the present time.

Voices: Don't get too upset!

Ivnitsky: What do you mean not get upset? There is so much to get upset about! Naturally, like the entire plenum of the territorial committee, I bear responsibility for what has taken place in our organization, I bear full responsibility for it, and I consider the decision of the Central Committee to apply to me fully.

In the final analysis, we are guilty, all of the members of the territorial committee are guilty of not having stopped in time the totally incorrect policy of Comrade Boris Petrovich Sheboldaev. It is our fault. We tried to do this now and then, but we were harshly silenced, and, in certain specific cases, we found ourselves crushed as if in a vise, we gave in, we were incapable of

7. RTsKhIDNI, f. 17, op. 21, d. 2196, ll. 48–49.

unmasking this incorrect policy which was harmful to the party and the working class and which was carried on here with obstinate insistence.

Let us mention several facts. What does Boris Petrovich Sheboldaev's guilt consist of as our former leader? His guilt lies not only in the fact, as has been pointed out here, that he was surrounded by counterrevolutionary Trotskyists. He was guilty not only of that—his guilt lies in the fact that these people were appointed by him, that's the first thing, and his guilt lies in the fact that he defended them to the bitter end like no one else when we exposed them. That's what he is guilty of. In this way, he appointed them to their positions himself and when we tried to expose them, he defended them and cruelly punished those who tried to say anything about them. It was I and other comrades of the North Don organization who, at [a caucus of] our delegation at the last Azov–Black Sea Territorial Party Conference, voted down Ovchinnikov for membership on the territorial committee. We were not in possession of evidence that he was a Trotskyist, but we voted against him because he was a provocateur.

Voices: What's the difference?

Ivnitsky: Please, let me go on! We voted against him because he had discredited the party by his provocative actions at the Veshensk district. When we made this decision, and when Boris Petrovich Sheboldaev found out about it, he summoned me and Gurevich, former secretary of the regional committee, and declared: "What kind of leaders are you to have allowed Ovchinnikov to be voted down?" I told him that perhaps it wasn't necessary to elect him, but I didn't say it strongly enough. I didn't say it forcefully enough. After this, the delegation was called into session. The delegation was hurriedly transported in cars because the conference was supposed to take place very soon thereafter. Boris Petrovich Sheboldaev personally appeared at the meeting of our delegation and defended Ovchinnikov for well over an hour.

Sheboldaev: Yes.

Ivnitsky: Our delegation turned down Ovchinnikov for membership on the territorial committee in this case, too. Boris Petrovich did not place this matter before the delegation for a vote because he perceived that even if the matter were voted upon, he [Ovchinnikov] would be rejected.

Sheboldaev: It was then that we removed his name as a candidate. . . .

Document 106

Berezin's speech to the plenum of the Azov–Black Sea Territorial Committee, 6 January 1937[8]

. . . I would like to bring up one piece of information, about which Comrade Andreev spoke, namely, the number of Trotskyists who were expelled at

8. RTsKhIDNI, f. 17, op. 21, d. 2196, l. 133.

Document 106 *continued*

different times for each given city. Let's take Rostov, for instance. 51 Trotskyists were expelled during the verification of party documents, another 38 during the exchange of party documents, and another 134 during the distribution of new documents. In Novorossiisk, 9 were expelled during the verification, 2 during the exchange, and 33 after the exchange of party documents. In Taganrog, 5 were expelled during the verification, 10 during the exchange, and 44 after the exchange. In Shakhty, 4 were expelled during the verification, 3 during the exchange, and 43 during the distribution of new party documents.

The total for the region as a whole is: 155 Trotskyists during the verification of party documents, 111 during the exchange, and 509 after the exchange. . . .

Document 107

Amatuni's speech to the plenum of the Azov–Black Sea Territorial Committee, 6 January 1937[9]

Amatuni: . . . All of the facts now speak of and confirm that the decision by the CC of the party regarding the territorial committee, and in particular regarding Comrade Sheboldaev, is totally correct. I must say, comrades, that the decision by the CC is extremely timely because the continued presence of Comrade Sheboldaev at his post would undoubtedly be harmful. Harmful because a certain group of people has formed around the leadership of the territorial committee, around Comrade Sheboldaev, part of whom were brought here, imported into our organization from Saratov, and part of whom had formed and grown here from favoritism. The political character of this group is absolutely clear: the majority of them have turned out to be Trotskyists or people of rotten character or else people of no use to the organization. Boris Petrovich Sheboldaev delegated [tasks] to these people and permitted them to operate without inspection or control. This would constitute an extremely grave and gross political error for any Bolshevik, all the more so for a leader of an entire region. . . .

I would like, comrades, to speak about the conditions that existed at the buro of the territorial committee. The buro, comrades, was run by three main figures, who had essentially determined the course of all the work at the buro: Sheboldaev, Brike, and Malinov. As for Sheboldaev, the CC has adopted a specific decision concerning him. The opinion of the territorial committee seems to be expressed with absolute clarity in the speeches of the comrades. Comrade Sheboldaev, you ought to think about one thing—that is, that the people you surrounded yourself with, who considered you to be the first Bol-

9. RTsKhIDNI, f. 17, op. 21, d. 2196, ll. 248–51.

shevik in the region, who rose to their feet to applaud you whenever you entered the room—you ought to consider the fact that these same people are criticizing you severely. That's no accident because you were apparently totally ignorant of the true sentiments of these people, and you apparently poorly understand them now.

As for Comrade Brike [KPK representative], let me say the following: He ought to have known, of course, that our inspection organs have certain traditions when it comes to fighting the Trotskyists. These rich traditions were not utilized here. Comrade Brike, you must admit that when the documents were placed right under your nose, it should not have been too difficult to read them. Being in possession of these documents, you ought to have waged a real campaign [against the Trotskyists].

Voices: You are also a member of the buro. . . .

G. M. Malenkov, head of the personnel registration sector of the Central Committee, had accompanied Andreev to Rostov. Whereas Andreev had emphasized the vigilance against enemies theme, Malenkov concentrated on the lack of democracy and input from below that had characterized Sheboldaev's leadership.

Document 108

G. M. Malenkov's speech to the plenum of the Azov–Black Sea Territorial Committee, 6 January 1937[10]

Malenkov: . . . First of all, comrades, I'd like to bring up the following matter in order to explain the present situation. Undoubtedly many of you here have underestimated the strength of the enemy. Yes, the enemy has been crushed, there is no need to overestimate his strength. Yet an overly simplistic view of the enemy is also not recommended. . . .

Second, the Bolshevik apparat has ceased to operate in a true Bolshevik manner in certain of its links in the Azov–Black Sea region. Consider well, comrades, the facts which have been introduced here by many of the speakers. Here is the first fact. The members of the territorial committee, members of a Bolshevik committee that is at the head of an organization consisting of 75,000 members, spoke here before us. What did they speak about? They said that the leadership was isolated from them and that they were not being used. Production workers appeared before us along with many comrades and said: "We

10. RTsKhIDNI, f. 17, op. 21, d. 2196, ll. 266–70.

want to work. After all, we were elected by the party organization, and yet we are cut off from the leadership. No one wants to use us." Is this the way the Bolsheviks operate? Is this a Bolshevik apparat? Many secretaries of district committees spoke before us, and it has become indisputable here that many secretaries of district committees, many secretaries of our Bolshevik committees found it impossible to talk to their superiors for a full 3 or 4 years. Is this the way a Bolshevik apparat works? I shall permit myself to ask Comrade Sheboldaev how he would feel if he as the chief representative of the party in the region, if he, upon arriving at the Central Committee, could not talk to someone, could not resolve the problems which stand before him. And here there are people who have been trying hard to talk to somebody for 3 or 4 years and they can't.

A voice: 5 or 6 years!

Malenkov: What has remained of Bolshevism here in this Bolshevik apparat? After all, the secretary of the district committee is a chief representative in the district of the Central Committee and the territorial committee of the party; he ought to have the right to come here into the territorial committee and resolve all problems that trouble him. If the problems are bad, if the problems have been unsuccessfully dealt with, that can only mean that the leader is bad. This too must be looked into. After all, anything which troubles the secretary of the district committee ought also to trouble the Bolshevik apparat.

Third, comrades, many have stated here, many have complained, that they have not received information from their headquarters, from the territorial committee, concerning the most important events taking place in their organization.

Voices: That's true. We know that from members of the kolkhozy.

Malenkov: What is there left of Bolshevism, comrades, in this apparat? What does all this indicate? . . .

In the discussion, there was criticism of several members of Sheboldaev's former leadership team. One special target was the territorial chief of the party control commission, the party's disciplinary body that was supposed to have been more vigilant against the recently uncovered Trotskyists. Comrade Brike of the KPK was frequently denounced from the floor. Here we have an example of the central nomenklatura's carefully trying to shape the language in order to keep the criticism within manageable limits. Brike, as KPK representative, answered to the party's KPK in Moscow. That body was headed in early 1937 by N. I. Yezhov. As someone with such a powerful potential protector, Brike was rescued by Malenkov.

Document 109

From discussion at the plenum of the Azov–Black Sea Territorial Committee, 6 January 1937[11]

. . . The resolution of the plenum is read aloud.

Malinov: There is a motion on the floor to adopt the main points of the resolution. The motion is carried unanimously.

Kamensky: . . . We must say openly before the Central Committee of the party that Comrade Brike has failed to secure things, that he must also be relieved of his duties, and that the apparat of the plenipotentiary of party control must be strengthened.

Malenkov: Comrades, the draft resolution includes an assessment of the activities of the plenipotentiary of the KPK. The Central Committee shall concern itself with this matter, and this matter shall henceforth become the Central Committee's concern.

Voices: But may we ask for this? (Laughter.)

In the wake of Andreev's visit, district party meetings around the region removed members of the Sheboldaev team. In accordance with party tradition, larger meetings of party activists were organized to promulgate and discuss Moscow's decision to remove Sheboldaev.[12] These meetings dutifully adopted resolutions in favor of the change and sent corresponding affirmations to the center.

Document 110

Letter by the aktiv of the Rostov party organization to I. V. Stalin, 10 January 1937[13]

Dear Iosif Vissarionovich!

The aktiv of the Rostov party organization sends you its warm Bolshevik greeting.

The aktiv has discussed Comrade Sheboldaev's mistakes and the unsatisfactory political leadership of the territorial committee, deploying Bolshevik self-criticism without regard as to who may be affected.

The CC of the VKP(b) has been tremendously helpful to the Azov–Black Sea party organization in eradicating once and for all the counterrevolutionary Trotskyists-Zinovievists.

The Bolsheviks of the Rostov party organization and of the entire region

11. RTsKhIDNI, f. 17, op. 21, d. 2196, l. 279.
12. RTsKhIDNI, f. 17, op. 21, d. 2214, l. 9.
13. RTsKhIDNI, f. 17, op. 3, d. 981, l. 58.

assure you, Comrade Stalin, that they will in short order and resolutely rectify the gross political errors that have taken place as a result of the political blindness manifested toward the enemies of the party by the leaders of the territorial committee of the VKP(b) and by the Rostov City Committee of the party, and that they shall, harshly and mercilessly, punish Trotskyists, Zinovievists, and their vile rightist accomplices, all these sworn enemies of the party—terrorists, saboteurs, wreckers, and spies.

Boldly deploying Bolshevik self-criticism, we shall eliminate negligence from party work and achieve a real uplift [*pod"em*] in our party work.

Closing ranks ever more tightly around the Stalinist Central Committee, the Bolsheviks of the Azov–Black Sea region shall lead the territorial party organization into the ranks of the leading organizations of our party.

Long live our unshakable, united, and great Leninist-Stalinist party!

Long live the wise, cherished, and beloved leader of the workers, Comrade STALIN!

The presidium of the aktiv meeting

These discursive rituals were the vehicles by which policies were implemented. Everyone played his part. But it is again important to remember that these were not hollow ceremonies or events invented a priori. They responded to and at the same time influenced real political events in the localities. In the present case, for example, the new rhetoric prompted calls in these party organizations to speed up the reexamination of cases of rank-and-file members who had been expelled in the previous year's verification and exchange of party documents. Sheboldaev's team had carried out these expulsions; the implication was that if they had so misread the danger of Trotskyism, they might well have expelled the wrong people. Stalin had said as much at the June 1936 plenum (see Document 71 [D]).

Document 111

Results of the plenum of the Shakhty City Party Committee, 16–17 January 1937[14]

From Protocol #223 of the Buro of the Azov-Black Sea Territorial Committee of the VKP(b). 9 February 1937

#5. Re: Results of the plenum of the Shakhty City Committee of the VKP(b) of 16–17 January 1937 (Comrade Shatsky)

14. RTsKhIDNI, f. 17, op. 21, d. 2214, ll. 970b, 98.

Document 111 *continued*

. . . With the aim of strengthening the party leadership of the district and with aim of totally eradicating sabotage in the party and economic work, the buro of the territorial committee of the VKP(b) decrees:

1. To nullify [the results of] the exchange of party documents carried out in the Shakhty party organization by Liubarsky and Sagoian, enemies of the party and the people.

The buro shall request the CC of the VKP(b) for permission to carry out a second exchange of party documents.

2. In view of the fact that the present plenum of the Shakhty City Committee was elected on the eve of the 17th Party Congress, that more than half of the members of the plenum had left the party organization, and that the plenum included 9 enemies of the party and the people, the buro has called for the convening of a city party conference for the reelection of the city committee. The Department of Leading Party Organs (ORPO) is instructed to set a date for the convening of the conference.

3. The decision to break up the Shakhty City Committee into smaller units is postponed.

4. Sagoian (former 2d secretary of the city committee) is to be expelled from the plenum as an enemy of the party and the people.

5. To submit to the next plenum of the territorial committee for their decision the matter of removing Gorbatenko, manager of the Artem mines, and Gabelev, former secretary of the party committee (PK) of the Artem mines, from the plenum of the territorial committee for having worked for a long time with Kolotilin and Liubarsky, enemies of the party and counterrevolutionary Trotskyists, and for having shown themselves incapable of exposing them.

6. The decision of the plenum of the city committee concerning the removal of Kotliarov, deputy manager of the Department of Party Cadres, and of Sorokin, director of the Department of Culture and Propaganda, from their posts is to be confirmed.

7. The ORPO of the territorial committee is instructed to come up with measures for a decisive buildup [*pod"em*] of the entire party work of the Shakhty party organization.

The party group of the territorial executive committee and the Department of Industry of the territorial committee are instructed to come up with concrete measures for the preparation of all mines and the Artem hydroelectric station for the fulfillment of the plan as it pertains to the mining of coal and to the operation of the Artem hydroelectric station.

The Territorial Trade Union Council is instructed to come up with concrete measures for providing cultural services at workers' mines, especially for the night shifts ([in] offices for work assignments, in baths, in dormitories and so on).

8. The CC is requested to expedite the nomination of a candidate for first secretary of the Shakhty City Committee.

Document 112

Azov–Black Sea Territorial Party Committee resolution, "Procedures to be followed in reviewing the appeals of persons expelled from the party"[15]

From Protocol #224 of the buro of the Azov–Black Sea Territorial Committee of the VKP(b)

16 February 1937

#5. Re: Procedures to be followed in reviewing the appeals of persons expelled from the party (Comrades Shatsky and Semiakin)

The buro of the territorial committee has established that the review of appeals in the territorial committee was conducted incorrectly, with a crude violation of the procedure established by the CC of the VKP(b): The appellants were not summoned to appear before the buro of the territorial committee during the review of their cases and the cases were reviewed in their absence. The preparation of the cases for hearing before the buro of the territorial committee was conducted carelessly. The technical work in the appeals group was neglected, the appellants' cases were not registered, there was a great delay in the handling of their cases, answers to the appellants were held back, a statistical registering of appeals received was not established, and so on.

To prepare the files for the appeals, persons were brought in who were incapable of carrying out this serious work, who carried out the preparations formally without seriously reviewing the essence of the case of each person expelled and without verifying in essence the charges brought against the expellee.

A great number of the appeals were prepared for the buro's review by persons now unmasked as enemies of the people: Glebov-Avilov, Bortnikov, Mogilenko, Brailovsky, Gutman, and Amatuni.

The territorial committee has in its possession 1,200 appeals which have never been prepared for review by the buro of the territorial committee of the VKP(b).

A very great number of complaints are received by the territorial committee concerning improper expulsion from the party with requests for review of the expulsion.

Ye. Yevdokimov,
Secretary, Azov–Black Sea Territorial Committee of the VKP(b)

Shortly after Sheboldaev's removal, the powerful Pavel Postyshev, who was second secretary of the Ukrainian party organization and first secretary of the Kiev party committee, was also reprimanded and deprived of one of his posts. Seven weeks later, he was fired from his position as Ukrainian party secretary and transferred to the position of first secretary of the Kuibyshev Regional Party Organization.

15. RTsKhIDNI, f. 17, op. 21, d. 2214, l. 1140b.

Document 113

Stalin telegram removing Postyshev from Kiev, 13 January 1937[16]

"On the unsatisfactory party leadership of the Kiev Regional Committee of the KP(b)U [Communist Party of the Ukraine] and on deficiencies in the work of the CC of the KP(b)U."

Telegram

Tiraspol [Moldavia], regional committee of the party

To Sidersky, first secretary of the Moldavian Regional Committee, for the Moldavian Regional Committee (Telegram conveyed through the Baudot telegraph)

Decree issued by the CC of the VKP(b) of January 13, 1937:

The CC of the VKP(b) has determined that an extraordinarily great level of contamination by Trotskyists has taken place in the apparat of the Kiev Regional Committee of the KP(b)U. The following traitors and wreckers have been unmasked as of the present:

Radkov, director of the Department of Industrial Transport of the regional committee;

Karpov, director of the Department of Party Propaganda and Agitation;

Kantorovich, director of the Department of Leading Party Organs of the regional committee;

Zak, Radkov's wife, acting director of the Department of Trade;

Vasilkov, secretary of the Kaganovich District Party Committee;

Starovoy, regional procurator;

Todor, deputy chairman of the regional executive committee;

Kushnir, counterrevolutionary, right deviationist, deputy chairman of the regional executive committee.

Occupying the majority of leading posts in the apparat of the regional committee, these Trotskyists selected for the apparat either their own people, traitors just like themselves, or else people who, keeping silent, wouldn't dare to say anything bad about their bosses. Whenever an official from the lower ranks of the party organization complained about Radkov or any of the other members of the Trotskyist group, he was transferred to another job.

Comrades Postyshev and Ilin, leaders of the regional committee, trusted Radkov with such blindness that they turned over to him the verification of declarations entered into the record against Trotskyists, while he in turn investigated them in such a manner that it was those who submitted the declarations who turned out to be guilty.

In the absence of the most basic party vigilance in the regional committee, Radkov and his Trotskyist gang had the opportunity of organizing sabotage at enterprises—in particular, at enterprises of military significance, to place their

16. RTsKhIDNI, f. 558, op 1, d. 5023, ll. 1–17. Manuscript, apparently in Stalin's hand.

people in enterprises and organizations. They even found an opportunity to co-opt [*kooptirovat'*] their own Trotskyist sympathizers onto the staff of the regional committee of the party. Taking advantage of the fact that *a*) Comrade Postyshev, first secretary of the regional committee, being occupied with the affairs of the CC of the KP(b)U, had not devoted the necessary time to the regional committee, and that *b*) Comrade Ilin, the second secretary, turned out to be too credulous an official, and besides politically blind, Radkov, a Trotskyist wrecker, served in effect as the secretary of the Kiev Regional Committee.

The CC of VKP(b) believes that responsibility for the present situation in the organization of the Kiev Regional Committee lies, first and foremost, with the first secretary of the regional committee—namely, with Comrade Postyshev.

After the villainous murder of S. M. Kirov, the CC of the VKP(b), in secret letters addressed to all party organizations, demanded from the first secretaries of all regional committees and from the CCs of national Communist parties, above all, to concentrate to the utmost on raising and improving [the quality of] party political work. The CC of the VKP(b) demanded of them that they avoid becoming mere economic functionaries, that, indeed, they act as regional and republic party leaders and make general observations [*obobshchat'*] concerning the work of Soviet economic and other organizations on all fronts of socialist construction. These all-important directives of the CC of the VKP(b) were violated by Comrade Postyshev. Instead of exercising direct leadership of practical party political work, Comrade Postyshev turned all his energies to waging economic campaigns, thereby turning over regional party leadership to the Trotskyists Radkov and Kantorovich.

Having attained certain accomplishments in the economic sphere, the leadership of the Kiev Regional Committee rested on its laurels and let its concern for the improvement of party political work slacken.

Furthermore, the CC of the VKP(b) believes that the Kiev Regional Committee and its secretaries, Comrades Postyshev and Ilin, violated the party rules by which the elective policy relative to party organs has been prescribed. The inadmissible co-opting of people onto posts in the regional committee has been widely practiced in the Kiev Regional Committee. This fundamentally contradicts the spirit and letter of the [party] rules.

The CC of the VKP(b) points to the fact that un-party customs in the selection of party workers have taken root in the Ukraine and, in particular, in Kiev, where persons, both men and women, who were not invested with the necessary authority—that is, who were not holding the appropriate positions—have in fact influenced and at times predetermined the appointment of officials here and there for the appropriate posts. As a consequence of this un-party approach, unreliable and Trotskyist elements have been appointed to posts.

The CC of the VKP(b) has established the fact that such cases of contamination took place not only in the Kiev Regional Committee but also in the Kharkov, Dnepropetrovsk, Donetsk, and Odessa Regional Committees. It has established the fact that Trotskyists-wreckers, now under arrest, have been holding posts of leadership in the apparat itself of the CC of the KP(b)U and in All-Ukrainian scientific-cultural organizations. Among them are, for example, Killorog, director of the Department of Propaganda and Agitation of the CC of the KP(b)U; after his removal, Ashrafyan; the Trotskyist Krovitsky, director of the Department of Science of the CC of the KP(b)U; Dzenis, a Trotskyist, director of the All-Ukrainian Association of Marxist-Leninist Scientific-Research Institutes; Senchenko, chairman of the Union of Writers, and so on.

The CC of the VKP(b) believes that responsibility for contamination both in the Kiev Regional Committee and in other regional committees, in the apparat of the CC of the KP(b)U, and in the scientific-cultural organizations of the Ukraine, lies on the Politburo of the CC of the KP(b)U and on Kosior, the first secretary of the CC of the KP(b)U, and that such contamination is also the result of the blunting of party vigilance.

The CC of the VKP(b) decrees that:

First, Comrade Kosior, first secretary of the CC of the KP(b)U, is to be admonished for lack of vigilance, for slackened attention paid to party work, and for failure to take measures against contamination of the apparat of the CC of the KP(b)U, the apparats of the regional committees, and the leading cadres of scientific-cultural organizations.

Second, Comrade Postyshev, first secretary of the Kiev Regional Committee, is to be reprimanded and furthermore is to be warned that in case such slackening of party vigilance and failure to pay attention to party work are repeated, harsher penalties will be taken against him. In view of the fact that it is impossible for Comrade Postyshev to hold both posts—namely, the post of second secretary of the CC of the KP(b)U and the post of first secretary of the Kiev Regional Committee—he is to be relieved of his duties as first secretary of the Kiev Regional Committee.

Third, Comrade Ilin is to be reprimanded and removed from his post as second secretary of the Kiev Regional Committee. Furthermore, he is to remain at the disposal of the CC of the KP(b)U.

Fourth, to recommend Comrade Kudriavtsev for the post of first secretary of the Kiev Regional Committee after relieving him of his duties in the Kharkov organization.

Fifth, to obligate the CC of the KP(b)U and the Kiev Regional Committee and, personally, Comrades Kosior and Postyshev:

a) To eliminate the practice of co-opting people onto party organs and to require a strict implementation of party rules concerning the selection of officials to party organs;

b) To eliminate the totally un-Bolshevik custom whereby officials responsible for leading party work turn over party work to second-level officials not invested with leadership responsibilities;

c) To work out practical measures for the removal of all deficiencies established in this decree;

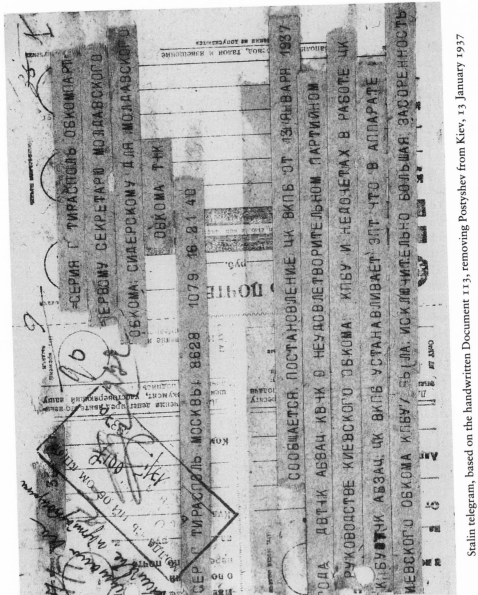

Stalin telegram, based on the handwritten Document 113, removing Postyshev from Kiev, 13 January 1937

Document 113 *continued*

d) To present a special report to the CC of the VKP(b) after a month regarding the implementation of the present decree.

Sixth, to send Comrade Kaganovich, secretary of the CC of the VKP(b), to Kiev in order to explain the present decree to Kiev's party aktiv.

I. Stalin, Secretary of the CC

Document 114

Politburo order removing Postyshev as second secretary of KP(b)U, 7 March 1937[17]

From Protocol #46 of the Politburo CC VKP(b) meeting of 7 March 1937

85. On the second secretary of the CC KP(b)U and first secretary of the Dnepropetrovsk Regional Committee KP(b)U.

1. To relieve Comrade P. P. Postyshev from duties as second secretary of the KP(b)U, placing him at the disposal of the CC of the VKP(b).

2. To recommend as second secretary of the KP(b)U Comrade M. M. Khataevich, relieving him from duties as first secretary of the Dnepropetrovsk Regional Committee.

3. To recommend to the Dnepropetrovsk Regional Committee KP(b)U as first secretary of the Dnepropetrovsk Regional Committee, Comrade N. V. Margolin, relieving him from duties as second secretary of the Moscow Regional Committee.

The demotions of Sheboldaev and Postyshev were significant events. These were powerful men who had acted practically as independent princes of their territories. Their censures were accompanied by a visible political campaign against "suppression of criticism" and "violations of party democracy." At the February–March 1937 Plenum of the Central Committee, A. A. Zhdanov would give a fiery speech on these themes, decrying the practice of "co-optation," by which regional party leaders had refused to call party elections, instead appointing their favorites to high positions in their machines. Zhdanov called for mandatory party elections to be held in May of 1937 in which party leaders at all levels were to face reelection in unprecedented secret-ballot elections by the party rank and file. Several Central Committee members greeted Zhdanov's electoral proposal with lukewarm enthusiasm; some even openly

17. RTsKhIDNI, f. 17, op. 3, d. 984, ll. 18–19.

suggested postponing the voting for various reasons.[18] But Stalin defended Zhdanov's proposal for new party elections.[19]

The new emphasis on "party democracy" authorized lower-level party members to criticize their superiors for poor work and suppression of criticism. Before the plenum such criticism was dangerous; it almost always led to retaliation by the regional machines that controlled the fates of party members in their regions. Postyshev was taken to task before and during the February–March plenum for persecuting (and allowing his wife to persecute) "inconvenient" rank-and-file critics (see Documents 70 and 71). In other regions, the February–March plenum unleashed serious insurrections within the party. In one district of the Western region, for example, a membership meeting expelled the local district party secretary against the wishes of the regional committee. Representing the regional party machine, the local NKVD chief tried to defend the district secretary, to no avail. Protecting one of their own, the regional leadership gave the ejected leader a job in the regional party committee.[20]

The criticism of regional party chiefs in early 1937 also revisited the issue of who had been wrongly expelled in the recently completed membership screenings of 1935–36: the verification and exchange of party documents. As we have seen, those operations had been under the control of the regional chiefs themselves and had resulted in mass expulsions of rank-and-file party members; only rarely were any full-time party officials expelled in these screenings.

In June 1936, Stalin and others complained about this practice and ordered the territorial leaders to "correct mistakes" by speeding up appeals and readmissions of those who had been expelled for no good reason. At that time, Stalin interrupted Yezhov's speech to note that the screenings were being directed against the wrong targets. In early March 1937, top-level Moscow leaders again denounced the "heartless and bureaucratic" repression of "little

18. *Pravda*, 6 March 1937. For the stenographic report of Zhdanov's speech and the discussion of it, see RTsKhIDNI, f. 17, op. 2, d. 612, ll. 3–42. For unenthusiastic comments from CC members, see the remarks of Kosior (l. 19), Khataevich (l. 21), and Mirzoian (ll. 27–29). See also *Voprosy istorii*, no. 10, 1995, 21.

19. RTsKhIDNI, f. 17, op. 2, d. 612, l. 42.

20. Smolensk Archive, f. 111, ll. 2–66; f. 321, ll. 87–96. See also the discussion in J. Arch Getty, *Origins of the Great Purges: The Soviet Communist Party Reconsidered, 1933–1938*, New York, 1991, 151–53.

people." Malenkov noted that more than 100,000 of those expelled had been kicked out for little or no reason, while Trotskyists who occupied party leadership posts had passed through the screenings with little difficulty.[21]

Stalin echoed the theme in one of his speeches to the February–March 1937 plenum. According to him, by the most extravagant count the numbers of Trotskyists, Zinovievists, and rightists could be no more than 30,000 persons. Yet in the membership screenings, more than 300,000 had been expelled; some factories now contained more ex-members than members. Stalin worried that this was creating large numbers of embittered former party members, and he blamed the territorial chiefs for the problem: "All these outrages that you have committed are water for the enemy's mill."[22] In the case of Postyshev's removal, Stalin and others had taken up the cause of one Nikolaenko, a party member expelled by Postyshev's wife Postolovskaya in Kiev. "Signals" from "little people" like Nikolaenko about enemies had been ignored by Postyshev, who had instead persecuted those sending the warnings.[23]

Certainly, much of this rhetoric was demagogic posturing. For Stalin and other central leaders it made good political capital to pose as the defenders of the rank and file against the depredations of evil boyars. Indeed, although appeals and reconsiderations continued throughout the 1930s, many of these little people were never readmitted. Moreover, it was time-honored practice for higher leaders to blame their subordinates for unpopular or mistaken policies and for the subordinates dutifully to admit their mistakes.

On the other hand, even in the darkest days of the hysterical hunt for enemies in 1937 and 1938, most of those expelled back in 1935 and 1936 who appealed to Moscow were reinstated. Virtually all those expelled for "passivity" were readmitted, and appellants charged with more serious party offenses who appealed to the party control commission in Moscow (run by Yezhov and later by the equally fierce Shkiriatov) were usually readmitted, the proportion of successful appeals reaching 63 percent by 1938.[24]

21. *Voprosy istorii*, no. 10, 1995, 3–4.

22. *Voprosy istorii*, no. 11–12, 1995, 21.

23. For a discussion of the Nikolaenko affair, see Oleg V. Khlevniuk, *1937: Stalin, NKVD i sovetskoe obshchestvo*, Moscow, 1992, 102–9.

24. Tsentr khraneniia sovremennoi dokumentatsii (hereafter TsKhSD), f. 6, op. 6, d. 23, ll. 1–2, files of the party control commission.

Further, a good bit of Stalin's criticism was hidden behind closed doors to the Central Committee and never intended for public consumption, thus reducing any demagogic impact. More important, statistical data presented by Malenkov and never released to the public showed vast differences between regional officials' and Moscow leaders' versions of membership verification. Table 3 showed how the screenings had targeted masses of rank-and-file party members in 1935 and 1936, when checking was done by territorial officials. But after the completion of the screenings, verification of party members was under the direct control of the Central Committee, and the results were different (see Table 4). When "checking" was done by central, rather than territorial, authorities, the attrition was heavier at the top than at the bottom. Moscow was less interested in (and even hostile to) mass expulsions of the rank and file; their targets were former Trotskyists with rank. Clearly, Moscow and the regional secretaries had different ideas about what the screenings should accomplish.

At the February–March 1937 plenum, Stalin criticized the undemocratic practices of party officials in the regions but drew a sharp line between their "mistakes" and the crimes of the "enemies," who needed to be "smashed." "Is it that our party comrades have become worse than they were before, have become less conscientious and disciplined? No, of course not. Is it that they have begun to degenerate? Again, no. Such a supposition is completely unfounded. Then what is the matter? . . . The fact is that our party comrades, carried away by economic campaigns and by enormous successes on the front of economic construction, simply forgot some very important facts."[25]

The Politburo was at pains to show that Sheboldaev and Postyshev were not to be considered enemies themselves; they had simply been negligent, even though Sheboldaev's personal secretary and most of Postyshev's lieutenants in Kiev had been arrested as Trotskyists. While criticizing Sheboldaev, Postyshev, and others, several speakers at the plenum cited mitigating circumstances: such leaders were, in fact, burdened with economic work and were not completely at fault. Significantly, both secretaries were transferred to lesser but important posts: Postyshev became first secretary of

25. *Pravda*, 1 April 1937; *Voprosy istorii*, no. 3, 1995, 5.

Table 4. Verification and Expulsion of Party Cadres, 1935–37

	Checked by CC	Expelled (%)
Obkom dept. heads	398	35 (8.8%)
Gorkom dept. heads	2,031	111 (5.5%)
Instructors	1,620	63 (3.9%)
Gorkom/raikom secretaries	5,275	184 (3.5%)
Cell secretaries	94,145	3,212 (3.4%)
Totals	103,469	3,605 (3.5%)

Source: Malenkov speech to February–March plenum, *Voprosy istorii*, no. 10, 1995, 7–8.

Kuibyshev oblast, and Sheboldaev was sent to head the Kursk party organization. A. A. Andreev, who had led the sacking of Sheboldaev, had prepared a resolution for the February–March plenum linking Sheboldaev and Postyshev and denouncing them in rather strong language.[26] Apparently, though, Stalin decided not to allow such a strong statement, and the resolution was never introduced.

Similarly, in the weeks that followed the transfers of these two, the Central Committee intervened on several occasions to protect them from those who sought to characterize their demotions more negatively. In one case, a newspaper editor in the Azov–Black Sea territory had allowed an article saying that Sheboldaev had been fired.[27]

Document 115

Azov–Black Sea Territorial Party Committee resolution, "A second exchange of party documents"[28]

From Protocol #220 of the buro of the Azov–Black Sea Territorial Committee of the VKP(b), 25 January 1937.

. . . #36. Re: A second exchange of party documents (Comrade Shatsky)

A second exchange of party documents is to be carried out throughout the Rostov, Krasnodar, Taganrog, Sochi, Sula, Novocherkassk, Shakhty, Chernoerkov, and Voloshino party organizations.

The CC of the party is requested to give its approval for such a decision. The Department of Leading Party Organs (ORPO) is instructed to prepare a memorandum concerning this question for the CC of the party.

26. RTsKhIDNI, f. 73, op. 2, d. 4.

27. *sniat'*: removal with negative connotations, instead of the official characterization, *osvobozhdat'*, freed from responsibilities, as in a transfer to a new job.— Trans.

28. RTsKhIDNI, f. 17, op. 21, d. 2214, ll. 16–18, 26.

Document 115 *continued*

#66. Re: The gross perversion by the editorial board of the district newspaper *Kolkhoznaia Tribuna* (organ of the Mechetin District Committee of the VKP(b)) of the decision of the CC of the VKP(b) "Concerning the mistakes committed by Comrade Sheboldaev and the unsatisfactory political leadership of the Azov–Black Sea Territorial Committee of the VKP(b)." (Comrades Shvartsberg, Babeshko, Shatsky.)*

After hearing the explanation by Comrade P. V. Shvartsberg, second secretary of the Mechetin District Committee, and by Comrade G. I. Babeshko, deputy to the editor-in-chief of the Mechetin district newspaper *Kolkhoznaia Tribuna,* the territorial committee deems that a crude political error was committed in the report concerning the plenum of the district committee in the 13 January 1937 issue of *Kolkhoznaia Tribuna.* In this report, it was pointed out that the plenum of the district committee fully approved the decision of the CC of the VKP(b) pertaining to the removal of Comrade Sheboldaev from his post as secretary of the territorial committee, when, in fact, the plenum of the district committee had not adopted such a decision. The deputy editor of *Kolkhoznaia Tribuna,* Comrade G. I. Babeshko, published this report without coordinating it with the district committee of the VKP(b).

On 14 January 1937, having learned about this gross political error committed by the *Kolkhoznaia Tribuna,* Comrade P. V. Shvartsberg, second secretary of the district committee, went only so far as to orally reprimand Comrade G. I. Babeshko, the deputy editor, and to publish a correction on page 3, at the very bottom, in the 15 January issue of *Kolkhoznaia Tribuna.* In his correction, he mentioned that the plenum of the district committee had fully approved the decision of the CC of the VKP(b). However, in its approval, the district committee did not speak of Comrade Sheboldaev's "removal" from his post as secretary of the Azov–Black Sea Territorial Committee of the VKP(b). Instead, it referred to his "being relieved of his duties."[29]

The buro of the territorial committee has decreed:

1. To reprimand Comrade P. V. Shvartsberg, second secretary of the Mechetin Territorial Committee of the VKP(b), for not having submitted this matter to the buro of the Mechetin District Committee for discussion.

2. To remove Comrade G. I. Babeshko, deputy editor of the district newspaper *Kolkhoznaia Tribuna,* from his post as deputy editor of *Kolkhoznaia Tribuna* for having committed a gross political error.

*Decision by polling of members, 20 January 1937.

In another instance, Stalin intervened personally as late as July 1937, to order a "campaign against Comrade Postyshev" stopped.

29. Quotation marks added by the translator.

As always, such carefully crafted language had to be followed precisely.

Document 116

Politburo resolution on Gubelman and Postyshev, 14 July 1937[30]

From Politburo Protocol #51 of the meetings 20 June–31 July 1937

39. Statement of Comrade Gubelman about Comrade Postyshev

1. The Politburo of the CC has established the fact of Comrade Postyshev's sending a degrading petition in 1910 to the commander of the Moscow Military District requesting mitigation of judicial sentence on the grounds of his youth and lack of [political] consciousness.

2. The Politburo of the CC considers it wrong that Comrade Postyshev did not inform the Central Committee about this petition, and therefore issues a reprimand to Comrade Postyshev.

3. By this resolution, the Politburo considers this matter closed and suggests to Comrade Gubelman that he stop the behind-the-scenes campaign against Comrade Postyshev which he is conducting by means of these materials on Comrade Postyshev.

. . . 14 July 1937

---

30. RTsKhIDNI, f. 17, op. 3. d. 989 (Protocol no. 51 of the Politburo, 20 June–31 July 1937, no. 39).

CHAPTER TEN

Party Discipline and the
Fall of Bukharin

I won't shoot myself because then people will say that I killed myself so as to harm the party. But if I die, as it were, from an illness, then what will you lose by it? . . . Look, if I am a saboteur, a son of a bitch, then why spare me? I make no claims to anything. I am just describing what's on my mind, what I am going through. If this in any way entails any political damage, however minute, then, no question about it, I'll do whatever you say. (Laughter.) Why are you laughing? There is absolutely nothing funny about any of this.—N. I. Bukharin, 1937

Well, go on, throw me in prison. So you think the fact that you are yelling: "Throw him in prison!" will make me talk differently? No, it won't. —N. I. Bukharin, 1937

ALTHOUGH THERE WAS A critical but generally conciliatory attitude toward the regional secretaries at the February–March plenum, the official rhetoric on former oppositionists was increasingly severe. Two months earlier, at Stalin's suggestion, the previous plenum had not condemned Bukharin and Rykov and had postponed consideration to the next meeting. In the interim, Yezhov had been busy. He continued to interrogate former oppositionists in order to get "evidence" incriminating the rightist leaders. On January 13, 1937, Bukharin participated in a "confrontation" with V. N. Astrov, a former pupil of Bukharin's now arrested for treason. In the presence of Stalin and other Politburo members, Astrov angrily accused Bukharin of active participation in subversive conspiracies. Astrov alleged that Bukharin had used his former students in the Institute of Red Professors (the "Bukharin School") as the basis for an underground organization. Bukharin denied everything.[1]

Between 23 and 30 January, Moscow was the site of the second of the famous show trials. This time, Deputy Commissar of Heavy Industry Piatakov, journalist Karl Radek, former diplomat G. Sokolnikov, and fourteen other defendants were charged with industrial wrecking and espionage at the behest of Trotsky and the German government. As before, all the defendants confessed.

The Fall of Bukharin: The February–March Plenum of the Central Committee

The stage was now set for Bukharin's next arraignment at the upcoming Plenum of the Central Committee, scheduled for 19 February 1937. The meeting had to be postponed, however, because of the sudden death of Heavy Industry Commissar Sergo Ordzhonikidze on the eighteenth. Officially announced as heart failure, his death now seems clearly to have been a suicide. Subsequent testimony from those around him suggests that he had been despondent for some time, and there is information that he had arguments with Stalin, perhaps about those from his agency who had been arrested.[2]

The plenum was rescheduled to open 23 February, but the drama began three days earlier when Bukharin sent two documents to the Central Committee. The first was a letter again protesting his innocence and announcing that he was beginning a hunger strike on 21 February to protest the accusations against him. He wrote, "I cannot live like this any more. I have written an answer to the slanderers. I am in no physical or moral condition to come to the

---

1. *Izvestiia TsK KPSS*, no. 4, 1989, 76, 84. Six months later, at Stalin's order, Astrov was released from prison and given an apartment and a job in historical research. Later, in the Khrushchev period, Astrov stated that Yezhov himself had "confirmed" to Astrov that the rightists were in fact terrorists. As Astrov said in 1957, "This confirmation removed my moral impetus to resist the demands of the investigators." I. V. Kurilova, N. N. Mikhailov, V. P. Naumov, eds., *Reabilitatsiia: Politicheskie protsessy 30–50-x godov*, Moscow, 1991, 259.

2. See the account in Oleg V. Khlevniuk, *Stalin i Ordzhonikidze: Konflikty v Politbiuro v 30-e gody*, Moscow, 1993, 111–29.

plenum, my legs will not go, I cannot endure the existing atmosphere, I am in no condition to speak. . . . In this extraordinary situation, from tomorrow I will begin a total hunger strike until the accusations of betrayal, wrecking, and terrorism are dropped."[3]

Along with this letter, which Bukharin asked the Politburo not to circulate to the full Central Committee, he forwarded a statement to that body of more than one hundred pages in which he attempted to refute, point by point, the charges made against him. With careful detail he showed the inconsistencies among the various confessions and statements implicating him, and in many cases he proved that he could not have been where his accusers placed him. He maintained his complete loyalty to Stalin's party line since 1930. He again denied the charges of terrorism and treason and expressed outrage that such accusations could even have been made. Moreover, in a very subtle way, he questioned the honesty of the secret police by alluding to the fact that confessions could be supplied by defendants according to the demands of the police.

It would seem that Bukharin's only chance to survive—and it was a slim one—was to "come clean" and confess to all charges, then throw himself on the mercy of the Central Committee. Only by capitulating could Bukharin "disarm" completely before the party, "clean himself of the filth he had fallen into," as Stalin was to say, and provide the service—as a public counterexample—that the party demanded. After all, that was the standard that Bukharin had demanded of the Trotskyists back in the 1920s, and for him to resist it now with a legalistic defense would make him look self-serving and hypocritical to his comrades. He decided to do just that and again to challenge the ritual. His hunger strike and initial refusal to attend the plenum (both of which he retracted almost immediately) were taken as vivid examples of antiparty offenses—or, as Mikoyan would call them, "demonstrations" against the party—no less insulting or threatening than an actual street rally against Bolshevism. Discipline and Leninist traditions of democratic centralism required Bukharin either to obey or to be considered an enemy.

In this light, how could Bukharin have hoped to prevail or even

3. *Voprosy istorii,* no. 2–3, 1992, 6.

survive by continuing to deny the charges? Perhaps he based his position on the ambiguous outcome of the previous plenum, when he had challenged Yezhov's sally and Stalin had blocked Bukharin's demise. If he counted on that in February, however, he was wrong.

Document 117

Bukharin's statement to the Politburo[4]

Workers of the world, unite!
STRICTLY SECRET
The Central Committee of the All-Union Communist Party (Bolshevik)
No. P46/35 22 February 1937
Extract from Protocol #46 of the Politburo of the CC of__193_
By polling the Politburo of the CC of the VKP(b) on 22 February 1937
Comrade Bukharin's statement to the Politburo of the CC of the VKP(b)
#25. The following decision of the Politburo of the CC of the VKP(b) is to be sent to members and candidate members of the CC of the VKP(b):
In connection with Comrade Bukharin's statement in which he declared that he would "go on a hunger strike until accusations of betrayal, wrecking, and terrorism brought against him had been dropped," and also in connection with his refusal to come before the Plenum of the CC of the VKP(b) to give an account of his actions, the Politburo of the CC of VKP(b) considers it necessary to declare the following:
1) The Politburo rejects Comrade Bukharin's proposal not to inform the Plenum of the CC of his "hunger strike" statement and sends his statement to all members of the CC of the VKP(b) because it believes that the Politburo cannot and must not hold secrets from the CC of the VKP(b);
2) The Politburo considers itself duty-bound to transmit all questions concerned with the case of Comrades Bukharin and Rykov—including all questions concerned with [Comrade Bukharin's] "hunger strike" and his refusal to come to the plenum—for consideration to the plenum, which opens its session tomorrow, 23 February.
Secretary of the CC

The plenum opened on 23 February with the formal report by Yezhov on the charges against Bukharin and Rykov. In the days before the plenum, members of the Central Committee had re-

4. *Voprosy istorii*, no. 2–3, 1992, 43.

ceived voluminous materials on these charges, including lengthy transcripts of the confessions of Bukharin's former associates. Yezhov's speech therefore contained few examples or quotations but rather summarized the accusations. Beginning with a long survey of the history of the right opposition, he said that the former rightists, like the Trotskyists, had formed underground terrorist cells with the goal of carrying out espionage and assassinations against the Soviet government. This conspiracy had as its founding document the Riutin Platform, the dangerous competing discourse of 1932, which Yezhov now said that Bukharin had at least commissioned, if not written.

Yezhov went on to say that "incontrovertible documentary materials" established that Bukharin and Rykov had at least known of preparations for the Kirov assassination and had conspired to kill other party leaders as part of a planned "palace revolution" to overthrow the party. With members shouting assent, Yezhov declared, "It seems to me that all this raises—in connection with Bukharin and Rykov, people who are fully responsible for the whole activity of the right opposition in general and for their anti-soviet activity in particular—raises the question of their continuation not only in the Central Committee [A voice: 'Right!'] but also as members of the party. [A voice: 'Right.' A voice: 'It is too little.']."[5]

Yezhov was followed by A. I. Mikoyan, who was no less severe in his castigation of Bukharin and Rykov as traitors and assassins. Mikoyan noted that Trotsky's tactics since the late 1920s had been to organize various declarations, protests, and demonstrations against the party leadership. "Bukharin, following in enemy of the people Trotsky's footsteps, turned his arms against the Central Committee. It was Trotsky who was always putting forth ultimatums, Trotsky always hurled written statements at us. . . . Trotsky even organized demonstrations against the party on the street, but Bukharin does not have the possibility to organize a demonstration; now he has no masses, it is another time. . . . When there are no masses, no other means of protest, then Bukharin resorts to a hunger strike as a form of protest."[6]

5. *Voprosy istorii*, no. 4–5, 1992, 16.
6. *Voprosy istorii*, no. 4–5, 1992, 16.

Even, Mikoyan said, if for the sake of argument one accepted Bukharin's claim that he did not order any assassinations, it was clear from the testimonies of his former associates that at a minimum Bukharin must have known the evil deeds they were planning. To know about such things and not to inform the party made Bukharin as guilty as if he had in fact given the order. In Mikoyan's words,

> One thing nobody can argue with. To know of terror against the leadership of the party, of wrecking in our factories, of espionage, of Gestapo agents, and to say nothing about it to the party—what is this?! He is a member of the Central Committee and a member of the party. This is proved incontrovertibly, it is proved by the confrontations [with those confessing]; the materials in the presence of Politburo members proved that the rightist terroristic activities were known to the pupils of Bukharin, the partisans of Bukharin. They were known to Bukharin, he knew that they were preparing terrorist acts against the leadership of the party, he knew and he did not tell the Central Committee. Is this permissible for a member of the Central Committee and a member of the party?! It is proved and clear even to a blind man.[7]

Finally, it was Bukharin's turn to speak. He was not to have an easy time of it.

Document 118

From Bukharin's speech to the February–March 1937 Plenum of the Central Committee, 23 February 1937[8]

Bukharin: . . . I should say, first of all, that I know the Central Committee well enough to say that the CC can never be intimidated.

Khlopliankin: But why did you write that you won't end your hunger strike until charges against you have been dropped?

Bukharin: Comrades, I implore you not to interrupt me because it is difficult for me, it is simply physically hard for me to speak. I'll answer any question posed to me, but please do not interrupt me just now. In my letters, I described my personal psychological state.

A voice: Why did you write that [you won't end your hunger strike] until the charges are dropped? . . .

7. *Voprosy istorii*, no. 4–5, 1992, 22.
8. *Voprosy istorii*, no. 4–5, 1992, 24, 32–34.

Bukharin: I won't shoot myself because then people will say that I killed myself so as to harm the party. But if I die, as it were, from an illness, then what will you lose by it? (Laughter.)

Voices: Blackmailer!

Voroshilov: You scoundrel! Keep your trap shut! How vile! How dare you speak like that!

Bukharin: But you must understand—it's very hard for me to go on living.

Stalin: And it's easy for us?!

Voroshilov: Did you hear that: "I won't shoot myself, but I will die"?!

Bukharin: It's easy for you to talk about me. What will you lose, after all? Look, if I am a saboteur, a son of a bitch, then why spare me? I make no claims to anything. I am just describing what's on my mind, what I am going through. If this in any way entails any political damage, however minute, then, no question about it, I'll do whatever you say. (Laughter.) Why are you laughing? There is absolutely nothing funny about any of this. . . .

Stalin: Why should Astrov be lying?

Bukharin: Why should Astrov be lying? Well, I think—

Stalin: Why should Slepkov be lying? After all, that won't do them any good.

Bukharin: I don't know.

Stalin: No good whatsoever.

Bukharin: After Astrov testified, you yourself said that he could be released.

Stalin: You wouldn't say he is a swindler, would you?

Bukharin: I don't know. (Laughter.) Try to understand now the psychology of people. You have just declared me a terrorist, a wrecker, along with Radek and so on—

Stalin: No, no, no! I'm sorry, but may I reestablish the facts? You were at the face-to-face confrontation on the premises of the Orgburo, and so were we, members of the Politburo. Astrov was there and some of the others who were arrested. Piatakov was there, so were Radek and Sosnovsky and Kulikov and others. When I or someone else asked each of these: "Tell me honestly, have you given your testimony freely or was it squeezed out of you?" Radek even burst out in tears when asked this question: "Squeezed out of me? Are you kidding! Freely, completely freely." Astrov gave us all an impression of an honest man, so we took pity on him. Astrov is an honest man, who does not want to lie. He was indignant. He turned to you several times and said: "You organized us, in your hostility you turned us against the party, and now you want to wriggle your way out of an answer. You should be ashamed of yourself!"

Bukharin: Whom did he turn to?

Stalin: To you.

Bukharin: And what was my answer, Comrade Stalin?

Stalin: What was your answer? Your answers were of two kinds: the first kind concerning the Trotskyists was: "You are lying, you scoundrels." You said the same concerning the others.

Document 118 *continued*

Bukharin: Absolutely not.

Stalin: And what did our attempt show? Even you, I think, were affected by the testimony of Astrov and Kulikov when we confronted you both with them.

Bukharin: Nothing of the sort! Absolutely not! Radek is an archscoundrel.

Stalin: I am not talking about Radek.

Bukharin: You are dividing everybody into Trotskyists and rightists.

Stalin: I am not concerned with the Trotskyists.

Bukharin: They are all born rascals. Kulikov is, first and foremost, a worker. That's why I treated him differently.

Stalin: Astrov is not a worker.

Bukharin: Astrov is not a worker, but when the Trotskyists spoke at the face-to-face confrontation, I scolded them for it, and when they brazenly lied, I interrupted them. On the contrary, I spoke gently to Kulikov, although I too yelled several times: "You are lying shamelessly." So there are gradations and nuances also in my fulmination against the testimony of these people who are nothing but born scoundrels. I behaved most gently in my dealings with Kulikov and Astrov. In fact, I told Astrov that I was guilty before them, that I had once led them astray from the true path.

Stalin: You treated Astrov very gently, yet Astrov was trying to ruin you.

Bukharin: I don't know why he tried to ruin me, but he did try to ruin me, they are all trying to ruin me, and perhaps they will end up ruining me.

Shkiriatov: They are telling the truth.

Bukharin: As for the truth, you, Shkiriatov, are in a better position to know whether they are speaking the truth or not.

Stalin: I don't understand why Astrov should be lying about you. Or why Slepkov should be lying about you. After all, it won't do them any good. Tsetlin is not here—don't defend him, don't shield him. But Astrov is a more honest person. No one should call him a liar. Slepkov was the man closest to you, so why should he lie about you? I am well aware of Slepkov's moral nature. It leaves much to be desired. As for Astrov, I have the impression that he is an honest person. Voroshilov and I took pity on him. He is a ruined man. He could have become a real Marxist.

Bukharin: I believe that all of these young folks are lying about me for a simple reason.

Yezhov: Why are they doing you in?

Bukharin: First of all, everyone who has been arrested thinks that I am the cause of their arrest.

Shkiriatov: But they are all testifying against themselves.

Bukharin: It's not that I informed on them, but rather that they were arraigned because I am under investigation.

Voroshilov: They were arrested before you were.

Stalin: On the contrary, at the last face-to-face confrontation, we included not only Bukharin but also Pugachev, the well-known military official, whose testimony we wanted to check. After all, a face-to-face confrontation is notable for the fact that the accused—when they show up at the confrontation—feel as follows: how wonderful, the members of the Politburo have arrived, now I can tell them everything in my defense. That's the psychological state which arises during a confrontation in the minds of those under arrest. I admit that the chekists do exaggerate here and there—it's in the nature of their work to allow for certain exaggerations—but I do not in any way doubt the sincerity of their work. Still, they could get carried away. But at the last confrontation, where the old minutes fully coincided with the testimony taken in our presence, I became convinced that the chekists were working properly and honestly.

Petrovsky: Honestly?

Stalin: Honestly. After all, Radek and the others had the opportunity to tell the truth. We pleaded with them: in all honesty, tell the truth. I'm telling you the truth, even his eyes, the tone of his story. I am an old man, I know people, I have come to know many of them. I may be wrong, but my impression here is that he is a sincere man.

Bukharin: If you think that he told the truth, that I issued terroristic instructions while out hunting, then I won't be able to change your mind. I consider this a monstrous lie, which I can't take seriously.

Stalin: You and he babbled on and on, and then you forgot.

Bukharin: I didn't say a word. Really!

Stalin: You really babble a lot.

Bukharin: I agree, I babble a lot, but I do not agree that I babbled about terrorism. That's absolute nonsense. Just think, comrades, how could you ascribe to me a plan for a palace coup?! Tomsky was to become secretary of the Central Committee and the entire CC apparat was to be manned by Slepkovists! Bukharin was allegedly always opposed to Lenin, he is an opportunist and so on, but is it conceivable that the entire CC apparat was to be taken over by Slepkovists? . . .

Kaganovich: You didn't deny at the confrontation that you nurtured that "school" [*shkola*] of yours in such a way that all of you were supposed to grow as leaders of the party, as members of the Politburo. And here Astrov spoke the truth.

Bukharin: I didn't talk about anything of the sort, but I want to remind you that I said something to the effect. . . . When the comrades nominated two or three persons as members for the Central Committee, I spoke out against it.

Stetsky: Tomsky was being prepared to become secretary of the CC. I talked about that as early as 1928. You didn't dare to deny it then.

Bukharin: And what post were you supposed to occupy?

Stetsky: I don't know what post I was supposed to occupy, but I said in 1928 at the July plenum that Tomsky was being prepared to become secretary of the CC.

Bukharin: There is nothing funny about the notion that Tomsky was being prepared for the post of secretary of the CC, but there is something funny about

Document 118 *continued*

the idea that the entire apparat was to be occupied by Slepkovists. It was a question of a palace coup in 1929–30. . . .

Molotov: And what's your assessment of the testimonies of your former friends from that school of yours—the testimonies of Astrov, Zaitsev, Tsetlin, and others concerning themselves, concerning their participation in terroristic activities?

Voroshilov: What reason would they have to slander themselves?

Bukharin: My assessment? As far as Tsetlin is concerned, I do not believe that he was engaged in terror.

Molotov: You mean he lied about himself? And Astrov? Why would he do so?

Stalin: Rozit stood at the head of a kombinat. Why would someone slander himself?

Bukharin: If I knew who believed what in connection with this, why they were testifying against themselves, I would have told you. But I don't know. . . .

Bukharin was followed to the podium by his fellow rightist leader Aleksei Rykov.

Document 119

From Rykov's speech to the February–March 1937 Plenum of the Central Committee, 24 February 1937[9]

Rykov: . . . A little discussion took place here yesterday concerning the conduct of this investigation [of the rightists' activities], the quality of the materials obtained therefrom. I must say that this investigation was conducted swiftly and, in my opinion, in good form. In fact, the investigation was conducted so well that one could not have grounds or occasion for saying of those people who participated in it that it was to their advantage to lodge a false accusation against me or Bukharin. It seems to me that there is absolutely no doubt about it. Absolutely no doubt about it. The very fact that three sessions have been devoted to the discussion of this question also speaks in and of itself for it. And as for the [party] cadres, those people who are conducting this investigation, in view of the attention paid to it by the Central Committee, in view of the precautions taken by the apparat, which had recently been completely overhauled, the same may also be said of it, of course, namely that it strives, of course, with all means available to it, to tell the Central Committee

9. *Voprosy istorii*, no. 6–7, 1992, 4, 16–17.

only the truth, only that which accords with their conscience. Still, when it comes to revealing the truth, even the investigative apparat, which is totally honest, would meet with considerable difficulties. It seems to me that there are serious obstacles here. . . .

Can a political leader disavow responsibility for the fact that many traitors, criminals, and wreckers model themselves on him and think that he is their instigator? I do not disavow responsibility for this. I had also made other mistakes. If I had been more vigilant—

A voice: How naive. (Laughter in the room.)

Rykov: If I had been more persistent, I could probably have found out and done something about these two matters having to do with Radek and Zinoviev; of course, if I had informed the CC of the party about it at the time, then the whole matter could have turned out differently, if all of these acts of sabotage had been discovered much earlier than they were in fact. And, yes, it is a fact that in my work I confined myself to the narrow sphere of the People's Commissariat and withdrew.[10] Essentially, in steering back in the direction of the party, I went only so far as to make a break, which led later on to the termination, in the literal sense of the word, of those meetings with Bukharin and the others. I was guilty of pure pragmatic narrow-mindedness [*deliachestvo*]. I call it pragmatic narrow-mindedness. It was completely wrong. Some political measures, some political influence, could be demanded of me in this case, a certain number of political unmaskings, some political responsibility for this and for those people whom I called upon in my time to struggle for the rightist deviation, some responsibility for that which they did. I bear responsibility for this, I do not disavow it, an enormous responsibility, because that which has happened just now in the party and in the country is of no small importance. And there is no disgrace greater than the fact that many people perpetrated these revolting deeds by modeling themselves on me— this is a horrible thing.

But it does not at all follow from this, it seems to me, that on the basis of this one ought to accuse me of knowing that Trotskyists talked to Hess, that they conceded the Ukraine to Germany, that they handed over the Baltic region[11] to the Japanese, that they systematically practiced spying and sabotage on the widest possible scale. And if you think that I knew about this, then it's clear that such people ought to be annihilated.

A voice: You are right!

Rykov: Such people ought to be annihilated. But I am innocent in this. I was never either a saboteur, a wrecker, a terrorist, or a Trotskyist. I fought against Trotsky along with the others and have never been sorry for it. The fact that I fought on your side against Trotsky and Zinoviev is not found in the testimony

10. From political work, i.e., and thus lowered my political vigilance—Trans.
11. Rykov apparently means Primorsky Krai on the Pacific Ocean—Trans.

of those people who have been writing about me for the past 8 years. At any rate, I didn't find it in these cases. I am innocent of this. . . .

After Bukharin and Rykov spoke, the plenum saw one Central Committee member after another go to the podium and denounce the two in the strongest possible terms. This arraignment lasted more than two days.

Document 120

From Shkiriatov's speech to the February–March 1937 Plenum of the Central Committee, 24 February 1937[12]

Shkiriatov: . . . Enough, we must put an end to this, we must make a decision. Not only is there no place for these people in the CC and in the party. Their place is at a court of law; their place—i.e., the place of these state criminals—is in the dock.

Kosior: Let them prove it at a court of law.

Shkiriatov: Yes, at a court of law. What makes you think, Bukharin and Rykov, that leniency will be shown to you? Why? When such feverish work is carried out against our party, when these people are organizing conspiratorial, terroristic cells against the party in order, by their terroristic actions, "to put the members of the Politburo out of their way"? We cannot limit ourselves to merely expelling them [Bukharin and Rykov] from the party. This must not be! The law established by the socialist state must be applied to the enemy. They must not only be expelled from the CC and from the party. They must be prosecuted.

Document 121

From K. Voroshilov's speech to the February–March 1937 Plenum of the Central Committee, 24 February 1937[13]

Voroshilov: Comrades, a very serious accusation has been brought against Bukharin, Rykov, and Tomsky, who made up the former general staff of the resurgent right-wing renegades in our party, an accusation corroborated by the innumerable testimonies of eyewitnesses, who along with them participated

12. *Voprosy istorii,* no. 6–7, 1992, 23.
13. *Voprosy istorii,* no. 6–7, 1992, 23–24, 30.

directly in various groups and organizations directed on the whole against our party, against the party leadership, against our state. Naturally, this accusation must be refuted, and it was this that the two representatives, still living, of the so-called general staff of the rightists—crushed in its own time and then secretly reconstituted—namely Bukharin and Rykov, were engaged in during the course of a rather long period of time. As for the third comember—he solved the problem with relative ease. This doesn't mean that [Tomsky's suicide] isn't vile, this doesn't mean that it is permissible for an honest person, not to mention for a member of the party. Although he, like Bukharin and Rykov, left a note claiming innocence. In dying, he left a note claiming that he was not implicated in that of which he could be accused, since no charge had ever been brought against him during his lifetime. . . .

In the pages circulated by him [Bukharin], he casts suspicion on organs of the NKVD and even on the CC, because the organs of the NKVD work, naturally, under the immediate direction of the CC in the person of the secretary of the CC. All of his equivocations, all of his, you know, innuendoes and insinuations to the effect that not everything here is on the up and up, that, you know, he finds himself now in the position of a persecuted man, that an atmosphere has been created in which he feels himself at a dead end and so on—all this is nothing but an accusation directed at the CC. This is Bukharin's method. This method has been known to us for a long time. Bukharin is a very peculiar person. He is capable of many things. Vile, you know, as a mischievous cat and at once he starts covering his tracks, he starts confusing things, he starts carrying out all kinds of pranks, in order to come out of this filthy business clean, and he had succeeded in this often thanks to the kindness of the Central Committee. He had often succeeded in extricating himself with relative success from very unpleasant incidents. And he is trying to do the same thing this time around.

A voice: He won't get away with it!

Voroshilov: He must not get away with it. The Central Committee is not a tribunal. We do not represent a court of law. The Central Committee is a political organ. Its members are duty-bound to discuss such a grave matter, taking into consideration not only the facts as a whole available at present to the investigative organs, not only all the testimony presented by the accomplices of these monstrous organizations replicated in great numbers by them, and whose instigator and organizer was Bukharin. Its members are also duty-bound to examine the personality of the people they know, with whom they worked, and also the personality of those who accuse him. . . .

I believe that the guilt of this group, of Bukharin, of Rykov, and especially of Tomsky, has been completely proven. I admit that beginning at a certain point in time these persons began meeting less and less, perhaps beginning in 1934 and 1935, then they began to issue fewer directives, and that certain of them even simply ceased altogether to issue directives to the organizations under their command. Perhaps at a certain period of time, these people wanted deep down all that which had been oppressing them to come to an end. I admit all this. It's all possible. But I am absolutely convinced that all of these people who have been arrested now and who have undergone interrogation, are telling the truth. All of this relates to the year 1932, perhaps to 1930, 1931, mainly 1932, to what were very difficult years, when our party exerted all its efforts in order to consolidate all that which is salutary in our country so as to escape from its predicament. And all of these comrades—unfortunately, we must consider them comrades until such time as a decision is taken—these comrades carried out a vile, counterrevolutionary line opposed to the people. They are now reaping the consequences of their actions, which, for the time being, are verbal but will later, I think, be real.

A. A. Andreev noted Stalin's "patience" in the matter of prosecuting Bukharin and the others:

Document 122

From A. A. Andreev's speech to the February–March 1937 Plenum of the Central Committee, 25 February 1937[14]

Andreev: Comrades, we have heard two lengthy speeches by Comrades Bukharin and Rykov. We have read the lengthy written explanations of Bukharin. What conclusion suggests itself as a result of all this? It seems to me that, despite new evidence, which fully exposes Comrades Rykov and Bukharin, despite face-to-face confrontations, they maintain, in my opinion, the same positions which they held at the last plenum, positions denying any participation. It is only thus that we can understand the explanations which they made to the Central Committee at its plenum. The second conclusion suggested by these explanations is, in my opinion, that Comrades Bukharin and Rykov have even avoided acknowledging the existence of anti-Soviet activity by rightist elements. They avoid acknowledging this fact and avoid giving a [political] assessment of these anti-Soviet activities by the rightists. Look at the document sent by Comrade Bukharin to members of the plenum. Is there the slightest attempt in it to give a [political] assessment of all of these anti-Soviet activities, of unmasked activities by rightist elements? No, we find no such attempts. This is especially true of Bukharin. Meanwhile, what do the investigative materials afforded to plenum members speak of? It seems to me that, first of all, they decisively unmask the rightists, they unmask them in the sense that there was never any—now it is clear—there was never any difference between Trotskyists and rightists. Such a difference never existed. These

14. *Voprosy istorii*, no. 8–9, 1992, 3, 8–9.

investigative materials point out the obvious fact that during the course of several years the rightists and Trotskyists walked the same path. There was no difference between Trotskyists and rightists in that both the Trotskyists and the rightists maintained their full cadres. They possessed a full system of conspiratorial organizations led by its center and with local organizations in the regions. There is no difference between the Trotskyists and the rightists also in regard to their programs. There never was any difference. They all agreed about one thing: an irreconcilable attitude to the party's socialist policy with respect to both agriculture and industry. . . .

All comparisons of the basic facts, of the testimony and of their [Bukharin's and Rykov's] personal conduct has led me to the firm conviction that Bukharin and Rykov knew of the treasonous work by the Trotskyists.

Postyshev: Absolutely.

Andreev: They knew about it. They were linked with them. My conviction is that Bukharin and Rykov not only knew of the activities of rightist elements, but rather they continued, very cautiously and subtly, to serve as leaders of these rightist elements; to the very last moment they served as their leaders and maintained their link with them. They encouraged them in their anti-Soviet activities and abetted their crimes, goaded these people to commit their crimes—I am convinced of this, no matter how much Bukharin and Rykov might deny it. What, we may wonder, is the value of statements and intimations by Bukharin and Rykov—namely, "that we are not allowed to prove our innocence, that they do not believe our vows and so on"?

Eikhe: We have stopped believing you [Bukharin and Rykov], we believed you for too long.

Andreev: No, no, as far as you are concerned, the party and the Central Committee have given you sufficient time, more than enough time and means to disarm yourselves and prove yourselves innocent. No one else from the ranks of the oppositionists and enemies has been afforded such a period of time, the party has not afforded such a period of time to anyone other than you. The party did the maximum to keep you in its ranks. How much effort has been expended, how much patience has been shown to you by the party and especially, I must say, by Comrade Stalin.

A voice: That's right.

Andreev: Yes, precisely, by Comrade Stalin, who always urged us, who constantly warned us, whenever comrades here or there, whenever local organizations here or there raised the issue "point-blank," as it is said, in reference to the rightists, and whenever the question would arise in the CC, Comrade Stalin would caution them against excessive haste; he always warned us. Nevertheless, you abused the party's trust.

A voice: What insolence!

Andreev: You completely abused the party's trust in you. Instead of disarming yourself and burning your bridges behind you, instead of helping the party to expose Zinovievists—

Document 122 *continued*

Budenny: And yourselves.

Andreev: You used methods of duplicity and deception in dealing with the party. You have shielded rightist counterrevolutionaries. You were associated with these enemies of Soviet power and of the party. . . .

In conclusion, I think, comrades, that the CC of the party has at its disposal sufficient facts not only to remove Comrades Bukharin and Rykov from the register of the CC and to expel them from the party, but also to hand the case over to investigative organs.

Voices: Right! Absolutely right! . . .

Document 123

From Kabakov's speech to the February–March 1937 Plenum of the Central Committee, 25 February 1937[15]

Kabakov: . . . You have said here that "we had nothing, we never contemplated carrying out terror," yet every terroristic group created under your leadership was familiar with and felt your daily influence and said that "we were preparing to carry out terror, we were engaged in sabotage, we were fulfilling the will of Rykov, Bukharin, and Tomsky." . . .

Exclamations from many corners: That's right!

Kabakov: The conclusion, comrades, appears to me obvious: We must remove Bukharin and Rykov from the register of the CC, we must expel them from the party and put them on trial just as we put Trotskyists on trial.

Exclamations from many corners: Right, Comrade Kabakov! . . .

Document 124

From Makarov's speech to the February–March 1937 Plenum of the Central Committee, 25 February 1937[16]

Makarov: . . . The materials reported by Comrade Yezhov are characterized by the fact that not only do the numerous persons corroborate the fact that the leaders of the rightist opposition knew about the existence of a Trotskyist-Zinovievist center, the fact that they themselves had direct contact with it, but also that they took part in it. What characterizes the numerous persons who testified is the fact that, while residing all over our Union, they each gave his or her own distinct testimony, yet the essence of their testimony remains the same, their reply to these two questions is in the affirmative, that they knew of the existence of a Trotskyist-Zinovievist center and that they themselves were

15. *Voprosy istorii*, no. 8–9, 1992, 11.
16. *Voprosy istorii*, no. 8–9, 1992, 11–14.

directly involved in all the counterrevolutionary activities which had been carried out both by so-called leftists and rightists and by the Trotskyist-Zinovievist center. In addition to what the testimonies here tell us, the face-to-face confrontation is characterized by the fact that Rykov and Bukharin do not in any way claim that there is any discrepancy whatsoever between the confrontation and the testimonies given by eyewitnesses. This is a fact of great importance. At the last plenum, when Bukharin and Rykov demanded a face-to-face confrontation, I had the impression that, clearly, at this confrontation, new details would be brought to light. And what has this confrontation now confirmed? It has confirmed fully and totally that which eyewitnesses had previously testified to. . . .

I personally believe, comrades, that it would be absolutely proper for us to make the following decision. First and foremost, Bukharin and Rykov must be removed from the register of the plenum and expelled from the ranks of the party. We are dealing here with extraordinary crimes such as the history of our party has never known. We must treat these people just as we would treat enemies of the people, just as we would treat Trotskyist-Zinovievist bandits. Then we must submit the matter to investigative agencies and submit them to judgment in accordance with the principles of revolutionary legality.

Voices: That's right! That's right!

Document 125

From A. Kosarev's speech to the February–March 1937 Plenum of the Central Committee, 25 February 1937[17]

Kosarev: . . . Comrades, we have heard the calm, may I say, restrained report by Comrade Yezhov concerning the materials presented by the investigation. After this patient, objective and thorough investigation, all of us expected Bukharin and Rykov—assuming that a drop of Bolshevism still flowed through their veins—to admit their grave crimes against the party. In their speeches, Bukharin and Rykov have conducted themselves like enemies.

Gamarnik: That's right.

Kosarev: In their speeches, they have burned all bridges behind them that lead to the Leninist-Stalinist party. . . . Like Trotsky, they sought to slam the door behind them. We cannot even call Bukharin's speech an ambiguous one. This is the speech of an embittered enemy, who, being surrounded on all sides by the incontrovertible facts of his vile crimes, will stop at nothing, will, as a last resort, slander the investigation and our investigative organs. Bukharin wants to create the impression that the CC seeks his innocent blood and that he

17. *Voprosy istorii*, no. 8–9, 1992, 17–19.

Document 125 *continued*

is prepared to give it. Only an enemy could speak like this—an enemy, more-over, caught red-handed and refusing to acknowledge his crimes. . . .

It seems to me that the time has come for us to stop calling Rykov, Bukharin, and other rightists comrades. People who have laid their hands on our party, on the leadership of our party—people who have lifted their hands against Comrade Stalin—cannot be our comrades. They are enemies, and we must deal with them as we would with any enemy. Bukharin and Rykov must be expelled from the register of the Central Committee and from the party. They must be arrested at once and brought to trial for working as enemies against our socialist country.

Exclamations from many sides: Right! Right!

Molotov noted that the real point was Bukharin's and Rykov's duty to set an example to others by "disarming." By refuting the charges, they were giving aid and comfort to the enemy and sending dangerous signals to others.

Document 126

From V. M. Molotov's speech to the February–March 1937 Plenum of the Central Committee, 25 February 1937[18]

Molotov: . . . However, comrades, when it comes to Bukharin and Rykov, we are discussing a very important question. Along with this, we understand that Bukharin and Rykov are both—in their present state—nothing but good-for-nothings.

Mezhlauk: That's right!

Molotov: All they can do is what everyone does from behind a corner, on the sly, like a double-dealer, like a person who conceals his face while he does what he does.

A voice: Coward!

Molotov: But we must consider the fact that there are enemies in our midst. When they give a signal such as: "Hold on, keep on struggling, don't give up, deny the truth, deny the evidence, dodge, duck"—this still leaves some people in the position of enemies, of people who have not disarmed themselves. It's not Rykov and Bukharin—they have other people, they have been in our party, and they are still in it now. We cannot close our eyes to this. They call out not only to their supporters in our party but also to those who are outside the party. They give them their signal. It is clear from the policies of

18. *Voprosy istorii*, no. 8–9, 1992, 20, 25, 29.

Bukharin and Rykov at the present time that they have strayed much farther along the path of doubts and errors, that they have strayed far, that they are straying more and more, that they are continuing their worse traditions of struggling against the party. . . .

Already at the last plenum we had sufficient evidence, and yet we postponed this case once again. We decided to give this man the opportunity to extricate himself if he is in trouble. If he is guilty, we'll give him time to admit his mistakes, to turn aside from it, to repent of it, to put an end to it. We have sought to bring this about in every way possible. And what does he say? Do you think Bukharin doesn't have a copy of his letter[19] on him? Don't you think he will make use of it when necessary?

Beria: If he hadn't already made use of it.

Stalin: What was Voroshilov's reply?

Molotov: Voroshilov's reply was a good one. I must read Voroshilov's reply to you:

"3 September

"To Comrade Bukharin: I am returning your letter, in which you [familiar *ty*] have permitted yourself to make vile attacks on our party leadership. If your wish was to convince me by this letter of your complete innocence, then you have succeeded in convincing me of only one thing—namely, that in the future I should place an even greater distance between us, regardless of the results of the investigation into your case. And if you do not recant your vile epithets against the party leadership, then I shall consider you, in addition, a scoundrel."

Voices: That's right!

Postyshev: It's as clear as can be!

Molotov: . . . However, if rightists and Trotskyists now say to us—not all, but many: "Yes, we have committed sabotage, yes, we were engaged in terrorism, yes, we have contaminated the workers' water, we have poisoned the workers with gas in their workshops . . . " Such cases do exist. They are now talking about this. This means that they are people who have completely broken with the working class, with our party, with Marxism and Leninism. It means that they are in another camp. Whenever someone would break away from that camp, whenever someone would find courage within himself to remember what he could still do for the workers, we bore it patiently and took measures to deal with it. But if, on the other hand, you start fighting against the party and then turn to open counterrevolutionary action, we will deal with you as is proper for us to deal with such gentlemen.

Voices: Right! (Applause.)

---

19. A letter from Bukharin to Kliment Voroshilov on the eve of the plenum. The original text of the letter has not been found.

Document 127

From Bykin's speech to the February–March 1937 Plenum of the Central Committee, 25 February 1937[20]

. . . In order to exterminate the evil of duplicity which they, along with Trotsky and Zinoviev, succeeded in implanting in our ranks and for which they have been greatly honored by international counterrevolution, by Hitler, in order to extirpate duplicity from the ranks of our party, it is necessary to do away finally and once and for all with these people. It is necessary that they receive the same punishment meted out to their accomplices and friends at the first and second trial of the Trotskyists and Zinovievists. It is necessary that the rightists be exterminated just as the Trotskyists were. . . .

Document 128

From M. I. Kalinin's speech to the February–March 1937 Plenum of the Central Committee, 25 February 1937[21]

Kalinin: . . . And when some people shouted at Bukharin during his speech that, namely, you are acting like a lawyer, Bukharin replied: "Well, what of it? My situation is such that I must defend myself." I think, and those comrades who shouted at him also probably think, when they speak of "acting like a lawyer," that it doesn't mean that Bukharin should not defend himself. That's not the point. What it means, instead, is that, in defending himself, he is employing the methods of a lawyer who wants, at whatever cost, to defend the accused, even when the latter's case is completely hopeless—

Voices: That's right!

Kalinin: Who employs all methods, all means, who, caring little a priori whether the accused is guilty or not, believes that he ought to be acquitted— for this reason he employs all sorts of artifice and methods to influence the case. . . . It means that he assumed a priori that there were two camps here, namely the CC and Bukharin. In fact, though, to tell the truth, in this case all of the members of the CC have come out vehemently [against him], you wouldn't find a single member of the CC who would not have come out with unbelievable vehemence against Bukharin. But isn't it true that every member of the CC wants Bukharin to be cleared?

A voice: How can he clear himself?

Postyshev: It's a little too late for that.

Kalinin: . . . Personally, I would not want such "supporters" in the ranks of the party. It is a disgrace for the party. I want you to understand this. But as

20. *Voprosy istorii*, no. 10, 1992, 5.
21. *Voprosy istorii*, no. 10, 1992, 6–7.

they say: a fact is a fact and you can't escape from such facts. You will now pose the question: what should we do? I believe that facts speak for themselves as to what the Central Committee must do.

Shkiriatov: Well, what should we do?

Kalinin: There is no way out.

Shkiriatov: You have evaded an answer. You yourself posed the question, but you haven't answered it.

Kalinin: There is no need to answer it. It is Comrade Vyshinsky who must answer such questions.

Document 129

From G. Yagoda's speech to the February–March 1937 Plenum of the Central Committee, 25 February 1937[22]

. . . I am convinced, comrades, that they are here trying to deny their indisputable guilt, thinking that their maneuver would not be exposed. Comrade Molotov revealed and exposed their maneuvers, which come down to this: that they seek to give a signal to those of their confederates in counterrevolutionary action still at large to continue their struggle against the party. Bukharin and Rykov, no more than two minutes remain to you to come to understand that you have been exposed. You are to understand that the only way out for you is, here and now, at this plenum, to give the full particulars of your criminal terroristic activity against the party. But that's impossible because even now you are still enemies of the party, even now you are still carrying on your struggle.

Document 130

From Vlas Chubar's speech to the February–March 1937 Plenum of the Central Committee, 25 February 1937[23]

Chubar: Comrades, the Central Committee of our party has time and again done all it can to help those members of our party who have made mistakes to correct them. The Central Committee has done all it can to correct the rightists who have been so obstinate in their errors, making use of all the means at the disposal of the party. But this policy on the part of the Central Committee, this kindheartedness of our party, as our experience with our struggle with the Trotskyists and rightists has shown, has not always been crowned with success. In our battle against the right deviationists, the party crushed the theoretical positions of this deviation. It crushed the organization of the right devia-

22. *Voprosy istorii*, no. 10, 1992, 8.
23. *Voprosy istorii*, no. 10, 1992, 8–12.

tionists, yet after a certain interval of time, Rykov, Bukharin, and Tomsky, the leaders of the rightist deviation, took over the position, which can no longer be characterized as a deviation but as open counterrevolution, not as errors but as criminal, counterrevolutionary acts. . . .

When at the present plenum, a little more than two months after the previous Plenum of the CC of the VKP(b), Rykov and Bukharin had the opportunity to honestly, not just like a Bolshevik but like a human being, with minimal human honesty, to recount what they did, recount how they carried out their undermining, counterrevolutionary activity, we got an entirely topsy-turvy answer: a denial of the numerous testimonies contained in our investigative dossiers. . . .

When I read Bukharin's note concerning the charges brought against him, I felt such disgust, as if you saw before you a snake, a viper. I'm sure everyone of you felt the same. From first word to last, this note is steeped in vile insinuations and assaults on the CC. It is steeped in a spirit of confrontation, in which he perceives himself as offended or oppressed by somebody. Calling all those who recounted his vile deeds slanderers, he asserted that "a million people may testify against me, but I still won't confess." . . .

Bukharin composed the entire note in the style of a lawyer, in the worst sense of that word. In his speech to the plenum, he presented an explanation of the concept of a lawyer—namely, that "lawyer" means counsel for the defense. Who needs such an explanation here? What kind of lawyer Bukharin is and what he is defending—this every party member will come to know. It is hopeless for someone caught red-handed, whose guilt in counterrevolutionary activity has been established by eyewitnesses, to try to defend himself. And yet Bukharin considers it an act of heroism, an act worthy of himself, to fill nearly one hundred pages with casuistic comparisons of every sort, all in order to deceive the party once again, in order to extricate himself and emerge clean as a whistle. There is no extricating oneself this time. He will not succeed. Bukharin began by [imploring us] "to understand my condition humanely." He is calculating that someone here might be moved like a philistine by his hypocritical tears and by his casuistic, duplicitous twists and turns. . . .

They must now pay for all this vile counterrevolutionary activity.

Shkiriatov: And they deserve it!

Chubar: And here the comrades have said rightly that there is only one conclusion possible—namely, that not only can they not be considered party members but that in the battle to disarm and neutralize [them], the investigation must continue and they must be brought to justice.

Voices: That's right!

Chubar: For the tactics employed by Rykov and Bukharin at the previous plenum and at this plenum plainly attest to the fact that they do not want to disarm, that they do not want to reveal their tentacles, to help the party and Soviet power to eradicate the remnants of counterrevolutionary groups. Without the eradication of these espionage-saboteur tentacles in the immediate future, our country stands to lose much in time of military attack by fascism, and we do not wish to suffer such a loss. The fact that fascism has found loyal agents among Trotskyists, Zinovievists, and rightists, that it has found accomplices in its struggle against the USSR, demands the liquidation as soon as possible of all these remnants of duplicity. All measures must be utilized to expose the roots of the rightists' counterrevolutionary organizations.

Document 131

From A. I. Ugarov's speech to the February–March 1937 Plenum of the Central Committee, 25 February 1937[24]

Ugarov: . . . At the Plenum of the CC of the VKP(b), Bukharin expressed the following opinion: "Is my guilt established in everything? And do all the facts coincide in time, place, details, and so on?" Suppose that not all of the facts coincide. The main thing is obvious: The cadres of terrorists and wreckers from the ranks of the rightists looked upon Bukharin as their leader [*vozhd'*] and organizer—one of the leaders [*rukovoditel'*]—directing all of the center's work. Now Bukharin is trying to convince us that since the troika leading the rightist deviation has never been named as a center in the history of our intraparty struggle, the allusions of rightists under arrest to the existence of a rightist, counterrevolutionary organizational center are not true. Their assertions[, he insists,] go too far. It is all rubbish, comrades. We cannot take these things seriously because the question is not what they were called and whether or not they were noted as such in the minutes. One thing is absolutely clear, namely, that Bukharin, Rykov, Tomsky, Uglanov, and Shmidt formed the leading group of rightists, a real center, which directed all the counterrevolutionary activity of the rightists, a center—even if not designated as such, because the question of outward designation, the question of who was closest to the center, who farther away from it, whether Rykov should be considered more in the background and Bukharin more in the foreground—all of these are tactical questions, questions having no significance whatsoever within the present context of the plenum's discussion and assessment. . . .

After the publication of a report that said that there were no juridical grounds for bringing charges against Bukharin, he, Bukharin—instead of coming to his party and telling it all he knows of the counterrevolutionary activity of former members of the rightist group—began with a slanderous assault against the party leadership, against the party. It is obvious to all of us that Bukharin and Rykov are waging a struggle against the party, against the Soviet state, that they have gone over to the camp of our worst enemies, that they have broken off completely with the party. They are the instigators of the counterrevolutionary activity of the rightists, of acts of terror and sabotage unmasked

24. *Voprosy istorii*, no. 10, 1992, 12–16.

Document 131 continued

by the organs of the NKVD. They are responsible for the counterrevolutionary activity of the rightists, and we must treat them as our party treats all other enemies of the people.

Molotov [Chair]: I call upon Comrade Zhukov.[25]

Kosior: And what, is not Osinsky scheduled to speak?

Voices: Will Osinsky speak?

Kosior: Comrade Molotov, the people want to know. Will Osinsky speak?

Molotov: He has not as yet put his name on the list.

Postyshev: He has been silent a long time.

Kosior: He has been silent for many years now.

Document 132

From Zhukov's speech to the February–March 1937 Plenum of the Central Committee, 25 February 1937[26]

. . . In vain do we bother with this counterrevolutionary gang. In vain do we try to persuade them. It's hopeless. You will never succeed in persuading them. They will be able to [repudiate it] not only here but in any place, wherever they will be given opportunity to speak. They will repudiate it a hundred times. Lying and swindling has entered their blood and accompanies them at every step. They carried out their counterrevolutionary acts to the best of their ability. For this reason I am not sure there is any need for us to go on debating this matter. In my opinion, the matter is so clear after all of these incredible, murderous testimonies against them. . . . (Laughter, noise.) . . .

I end this by saying that these people need to be judged in accordance with all the principles of our legality. These people must be shot just as [other] scoundrels were shot.

Document 133

From V. Mezhlauk's speech to the February–March 1937 Plenum of the Central Committee, 25 February 1937[27]

Mezhlauk: . . . I ought to tell you that we are not tormenting you. On the contrary, you are tormenting us in the basest, most impermissible way.

Voices: That's right! That's right!

Mezhlauk: You have been tormenting the party over many, many years, and it is only thanks to the angelic patience of Comrade Stalin that we have not

25. Deputy Commissar of Communications I. P. Zhukov, not to be confused with the famous general G. K. Zhukov.

26. *Voprosy istorii,* no. 10, 1992, 18–19.

27. *Voprosy istorii,* no. 10, 1992, 21–23.

torn you politically to pieces for your vile, terroristic work. We would have done this long ago, two months ago, were it not for Comrade Stalin, were it not that policy dictated by the interests of the working class predominates in Stalin over his just sense of indignation, were it not that he can see farther and better than any of us. . . .

Finally, comrades, what conclusion should we draw from all of this? We have heard the speeches of lawyers, real bourgeois lawyers, as Bukharin himself put it. What is a bourgeois lawyer? A lawyer is a person who in no way seeks to establish the truth, as they ought to have done at the plenum. A lawyer of a bourgeois country is a person who seeks to defend his client at any cost—and if he can whitewash a guilty client, that makes him a better lawyer. Recall, if you will, the practices of the past. Did the lawyers who defended the revolutionaries really speak at court with the purpose of establishing the truth and saying that such and such a defendant really belonged to the secret criminal society [*soobshchestvo*] that went by the name of the Russian Social Democratic Party? Such a lawyer would be strange indeed. You spoke like a bourgeois lawyer. In your letter to Voroshilov, you have dared to refer to the CC of the VKP(b) as "cowards." It's not the members of the CC who are cowards but you. You are both cowards.

A voice: Pitiful cowards.

Mezhlauk: Pitiful cowards, base cowards. There is no place for you either on the Central Committee or in the party. The only place for you is in the hands of the investigative organs, where you will no doubt talk differently, because here at the plenum you've lacked the most basic courage which one of your own disciples, Zaitsev by name—perverted by you—had when he said, speaking about both himself and you: "I am a viper and I ask Soviet power to exterminate me like a viper."

A voice: That's right!

Document 134

From L. M. Kaganovich's speech to the February–March 1937 Plenum of the Central Committee, 25 February 1937[28]

Kaganovich: Comrades, although around two months had passed since the last plenum of the party CC, Bukharin and Rykov found themselves incapable of adducing serious arguments in their defense at this plenum. Once more, they repeated their barefaced denials, their barefaced declarations—namely, "believe us"—or else they attempted to fish out chance contradictions of a formal nature here and there in order to build their defense on them, instead of going to the plenum—if you think that you are right, that you are innocent— instead of going to the plenum and disclosing, first and foremost, the facts, I mean, your positive activity and your positive, principled political line, the

28. *Voprosy istorii*, no. 10, 1992, 23–25, 35–36.

facts as they truly emerged during your lifelong struggle. This is the most convincing argument. Instead of this, they keep on repeating the old proverb: "Never laid eyes on them!"[29] And this is no accident. . . .

I asked Kulikov [when the latter was under arrest]: "You were at my place in 1932 and apologized then. Does that mean that you were already engaging in duplicity then?" "Yes, I was, I was even guilty of duplicity in my relations with you," said Kulikov. Voroshilov then asked him: "And why did you want to kill Kaganovich?" Kulikov replied: "[We] wanted to kill him for the same reason we wanted to kill Stalin—namely, in order to decapitate the leadership." What's left? As you can see, the minutes and the face-to-face confrontation confirmed one and the same thing. There are no discrepancies in Kulikov's testimony, as Bukharin claims. Bukharin alleges that in the minutes Kulikov said that he had wanted to commit a terroristic act against Stalin, whereas at the face-to-face confrontation he said that he had wanted to commit a terroristic act only against Kaganovich. I could cite several other passages where Kulikov repeatedly confirms that he had conversations with Bukharin. Bukharin himself has tried to admit to some of them, called them a mistake. Here is what he says. . . . (reads) "and I believe what he [Kulikov] now says."

Mikoyan: Bukharin said that?

Kaganovich: Yes, after the face-to-face confrontation. "But I categorically protest—" (reads).

Today, in 1936, we have uncovered despicable acts, such as we could never have imagined. We never imagined before 1936 to what depths Zinoviev and Kamenev, who we had expelled several times from the party, could have sunk, nor to what depths Piatakov, Livshits, and others could sink. To what depths they are capable of sinking—we see this in 1936 in a different light. This is why we must no longer, in my opinion, continue this magnanimous [policy] of ours. Our party must be purged of these people. We must proceed even further with our investigation in order to have done, in order to have done with these people who, though lacking support, may be enemies. We must do away with these people in order to keep them from harming us. (Applause.)

Document 135

From V. Osinsky's speech to the February–March 1937 Plenum of the Central Committee, 26 February 1937[30]

Osinsky: On this question, comrades, I had not thought to speak for the following two reasons—(Voices from the floor.) . . .

29. Kaganovich uses the expression "Ya ne ya, i loshad' ne moya," literally, "I am not me, the horse is not mine," a traditional peasant expression indicating denial of guilt.

30. *Voprosy istorii*, nos. 11–12, 1992, 3, 4, 10.

Document 135 *continued*

From the very start you begin to interrupt me.

Shkiriatov: No, can't one ask a simple question?

Kosior: We so rarely hear you.

Osinsky: And if you rarely hear me, then permit me to say that the third reason I had not wished to speak consists in the following: at the last plenum I signed up thirteenth on the list to speak on agricultural questions which interest me. Thirty people spoke but they never called on me.

A voice: He's insulted. They shut him up. (Laughter.)

Osinsky: . . . But I have been summoned, so to speak, to the rostrum at the initiative of Comrades Beria, Postyshev, and others, and, being flattered by the Central Committee's attention, I have decided to speak. Perhaps I'll be of some use.

Why, strictly speaking, did they suddenly remember me after Zhukov's speech? Why did they propose me as speaker?

Kosior: We have long been interested in you.

Shkiriatov: We even remember you, we have long been interested in you.

Osinsky: Apparently, that is my understanding of it, because if Zhukov was Rykov's deputy, then my name is undoubtedly associated with Bukharin's name, because we were once the two leaders of left communism, then we worked together as editors on *Izvestiia,* and both of us were members of the Academy of Sciences, and we are still members—both Bukharin and I.

A voice: Still members of the party!

. . . Osinsky: I heard Mikoyan, Voroshilov and fully agree with them. I heard Kaganovich and must say that he took the words right out of my mouth in the area of conclusions I might have made. Everything that could be said on this question would be more or less repetition. Anyone looking at this business is struck by how, with their "alibis" (that is, the classic legal device "I was somewhere else at the moment of the crime") and proffered contradictions [in the testimony], Bukharin and Rykov refute essentially secondary points. They do not refute the essentials, and the basic accusations against them still stand. They talk only about how the testimony contradicts itself, not about how it goes together. And there are many more points of convergence than contradiction, and these points of contradiction are the most essential and decisive.

In its entirety, their defense makes the impression of an absence of a common line and of a coherent explanation of all the facts. Kaganovich spoke the truth here, and I shall repeat that they said nothing positive in the sense of an essential explanation, whatever their point of view or their activity in the corresponding years. On the whole, all of their defense is completely inconsistent, poorly constructed and spineless. And it is spineless not because Bukharin and Rykov lack capability but because on all main points they have nothing to say. In sum, it behooves us to establish the fact that the situation is extremely clear. The conclusions are also very clear. Like many other comrades who feel this, I too am baffled why we, in fact, are continuing this

Document 135 *continued*

discussion. Perhaps in their final words, if indeed there are any, Bukharin and Rykov will say something new. In that case, they should be afforded an immediate opportunity to do so. But I believe that the chances that we will hear something new from them are nil. And the resulting conclusion—and there is no chance that it will change, either—is to be formulated as follows: if the August trial was followed by a report that "there are no juridical facts that would justify bringing charges against Bukharin and Rykov," then the formula at the present time has been changed to read: "All logical and juridical facts exist to justify bringing Bukharin and Rykov to trial."

Document 136

From Ye. Yaroslavsky's speech to the February–March 1937 Plenum of the Central Committee, 26 February 1937[31]

Comrades, let's hope that this is the last time that we'll discuss the question of treasonous members and candidates of the CC in the Central Committee of our party. The charge that Bukharin and Rykov have betrayed our Bolshevik Party is, in my opinion, totally proven. It has been proven by the investigative materials. . . .

Let them not gamble on the idea that new trials are as unprofitable to us as they no doubt are to them. Of course, it would have been preferable for us to manage without this whole business. That's true. But we must not hide our head in the sand, we must not carry on an ostrich policy. Of course, to make an omelet, you have to break a few eggs. It is much more dangerous when during the course of several months people ask us: "Well, tell us, are Bukharin and Rykov, in the final analysis, guilty or not guilty? Why can't you establish this fact?" That is much more dangerous. Any further postponement of this case can only cause us great harm because, otherwise, the younger members of the party will begin wondering whether we have solid facts against Bukharin and Rykov. And we do have very solid facts, incontrovertible facts, fully proving their guilt. We should keep in mind the upbringing of our younger generation.

Document 137

From Ikramov's speech to the February–March 1937 Plenum of the Central Committee, 26 February 1937[32]

. . . Now concerning the conclusions. I think that we ought to first say what this is all about. It seems to me that this can be called an uprising against the

31. *Voprosy istorii,* nos. 11–12, 1992, 10–11, 14.
32. *Voprosy istorii,* nos. 11–12, 1992, 14, 19.

party, against Soviet power. And every uprising must be crushed. I remember that, as early as 1926, Dzerzhinsky said the following concerning Zinoviev: "You rose up against the party, and we shall crush you." I think that these words of Dzerzhinsky apply fully to these renegades. There is only one conclusion possible concerning them: They must be put on trial and isolated, especially their leaders, so that they can never again carry on their anti-Soviet, counterrevolutionary conversations.

After this litany of denunciations from Central Committee members, Bukharin and Rykov were given another chance to speak. Allowing those accused of party crimes to speak a second time in rebuttal was a fairly unusual procedure and was cited by some speakers as proof that the Central Committee was willing to give the two accused every fair chance to defend themselves. As before, however, they were not allowed to speak unmolested. Rykov was so rattled by the attacks that he allowed himself to be tripped up in a most damaging fashion.

Document 138

From N. I. Bukharin's second speech to the February–March 1937 Plenum of the Central Committee, 26 February 1937[33]

Bukharin: Comrades, first and foremost, I must tell you that I shall disregard all sorts of attacks bearing, to a significant extent, on my personal character, attacks which depicted me either as a buffoon or as a subtle hypocrite. I cannot dwell on the unworthy aspect of these speeches, and I consider this entirely superfluous. . . .

They told me that I was using some sort of cunning maneuver, that I was writing to the Politburo, then that I wrote personally to Comrade Stalin in order to influence his goodwill.

Stalin: I am not complaining.

Bukharin: I am talking about this because they touched upon this subject, and also because I have been reproached and scolded for having written to Stalin in a manner different from that in which I wrote to the Politburo. But comrades, I do not believe that such a reproach is sound nor that I should be suspected here of special cunning. It is perfectly natural that when one writes a letter to an official party organ, he writes in one way, and when he writes to

33. *Voprosy istorii*, no. 2, 1993, 3–10, 17.

Comrade Stalin—that is, the highest authority in the country and in the party—he would express a host of waverings, pose a host of questions, and would write about things he would never mention in an official document. Here there is a certain difference, a certain nuance. And it seems to me that such a thing had already become established under Lenin. Whenever one of us wrote to Ilich [Lenin], he would pose the kind of questions which he would not present to the Politburo. He would write to him concerning his doubts and waverings and so on. And no one saw subtle cunning in any of this. The same holds true now: it is one thing to write to the Politburo, another thing to write to Comrade Stalin. There is nothing reprehensible in posing a host of questions to Comrade Stalin in a way different than in posing questions in official letters. I see nothing reprehensible in this. They tell me that I want to play on Comrade Stalin's goodwill. I don't think Comrade Stalin is the kind of person whose goodwill you can play on. He would swiftly see through any such play. . . .

The second question associated with these matters is the question of my alleged assault on the NKVD. Well, comrades, I would like to say that, without exception, all those who spoke here, all of the comrades who criticized me and came down on me with terrifying vehemence—all of them have based their speeches on the same thesis, namely, that the testimonies of eyewitnesses are the truth, and that the only untruth consists in this, that they have not told the whole truth. This is the main thesis developed in the speeches of the comrades who have spoken against me, who have criticized my method of critiquing the testimonies directed against me. I absolutely refuse to agree with this thesis. . . .

Personally, I am not of the opinion that I should consider the testimonies [against me] correct in advance—that is, a priori—and insofar as I feel myself completely innocent in such and such matters, permit me to refute[34] these testimonies instead of defending them. The task of a defense consists in refuting testimonies that it considers wrong.

A voice: You won't get away with it, Nikolai Ivanovich!

Bukharin: Is refuting these testimonies an attack on the NKVD? I think that refuting such testimony, any testimony, does not constitute an attack on the NKVD because the NKVD does not give testimony [*sub"ekt pokazanii*] but gathers it. It is not obligated to answer 100% for its truth. It digs up the testimonies, it receives them, it seeks to obtain them. It assists in formulating these testimonies, but it is in no way obligated to answer for the truth of each and every testimony. [These] testimonies are investigative materials subject to further verification, to rectification [*ochistka*], filtration [*fil'tratsiia*], etc. . . .

Molotov: Well, the point is that there were two trials of Trotskyists, and they confessed their guilt. Can we believe their testimonies when they have testified against themselves, when they have testified that they are terrorists, wreckers, and so on?

34. *razrushat'*: to crush—Trans.

Bukharin: Yes, we can.

Mikoyan: Why?

Molotov: If in accordance with your logic, it follows from my speech that the confession of guilt has been made only out of personal interests, how can we explain the conduct of the Trotskyists? We have appealed to you as we appealed to Piatakov and the others. Why do you, really—The plenum ought to be able to expect more or less the same from you.

Bukharin: Viacheslav Mikhailovich [Molotov], personally, I am in no way discrediting the trial of the Trotskyists.

A voice: How is it that you are not discrediting it?

Molotov: Your friends followed the same pattern. They also denied everything, then they said: it's true.

Bukharin: You can't say that. Because only guilty persons deny at first and then confess, while certain innocent people may not confess, may deny, and then sometimes confess from a variety of reasons based on calculations.

Mikoyan: You know Radek well. Why has he confessed?

Bukharin: You see, Anastas Ivanovich [Mikoyan], I thought that I knew Radek quite well, but I now think that I didn't know him all that well—

A voice: He is giving us the slip!

Molotov: Is the Trotskyists' testimony plausible?

Bukharin: Of course.

Molotov: And is the testimony given by your followers not plausible?

Bukharin: But no, what Trotskyists?

Molotov: Radek, Sokolnikov, Livshits, and others.

Bukharin: Let me develop my arguments one at a time—

Molotov: My question is easy to answer.

Bukharin: . . . My answer is: You can't apply one and the same standard or norm to everything. We must differentiate here each case, we must deal with each case individually.

Molotov: In that case, the testimony of the Trotskyists is plausible.

Bukharin: The testimony of what Trotskyists?

Molotov: Sokolnikov, Piatakov, Radek.

Bukharin: Whatever they are testifying against me is not true. (Laughter, noise in the room.) Why are you laughing? There is nothing funny in all this.

Molotov: And is their testimony against themselves plausible?

Bukharin: Yes, it's plausible.

Molotov: And is the testimony concerning Astrov and others plausible?

Bukharin: I've already said yesterday that I do not believe that Rozit was engaged in terrorism, that Tsetlin was engaged in terrorism. I don't believe it. As for Astrov—I don't know.

Molotov: How could that be? After all, Astrov gave his testimony.

Bukharin: I am speaking of what he says in his testimony: There are plausible and implausible things here.

Molotov: Is there at least one rightist who gives plausible testimony or are there no such rightists?

Bukharin: Perhaps there are. But permit me to distinctly formulate the following to you. Why am I so guarded in my speech? Because I am not accustomed to accusing other people just like that, I am not accustomed to declaring that I consider this to be "plausible," that I consider this person or that person to have been engaged in terrorism. It's already almost an accusation. To do that, you must have at least some facts. And these people, whom Viacheslav Mikhailovich asked about—

A voice: Testimony which you yourself read—

Bukharin: I have not seen these people—as you [Molotov] well know—since 1932.

Molotov: Have you seen Astrov?

Bukharin: I saw him at the face-to-face confrontation. But I really don't know his evolution, his evolution the past few years. I don't know the changes which may have taken place with him and in him since the time I first knew him and saw him. I assert that I lost contact with these people over the course of the past several years.

Molotov: But is their testimony plausible or not?

Bukharin: I can't say anything about them. Theoretically speaking, nothing is excluded. But I cannot say yes or no about people who are essentially unknown to me at the present time because they are strangers to me, because I no longer know them. I cannot solve one equation with many unknowns. In continuing to struggle against the party, they could have resorted to anything. But what does all this have to do with me?

Postyshev: Let me pose to him the following question: when Rykov, together with unknown members of the CC of the trade unions, heard the reading of the Riutin Platform, did he tell you about it?

Bukharin. No, he didn't tell me about it.

A voice: You're lying!

Bukharin: You can say "You're lying!" all you want.

Mikoyan: And when Rykov, speaking about your note, says that where there is smoke, there is fire—is he telling the truth?

Bukharin: Generally speaking, it seems that there can be no smoke without fire. (Laughter.)

Mikoyan: Well, that's precisely what we are talking about.

Bukharin: But that brings up another question: To what extent can you call my note "smoke"?

Mikoyan: Is Rykov telling the truth or not?

Bukharin: What he says is his business. He says that Tomsky was guilty. That's his opinion. As for myself, I don't know. I cannot say that someone is guilty just because that person is dead.

Postyshev: Then tell us about the living. Rykov is not dead. Tell us about him.

Bukharin: About the living I can say only the following: even if we do not go back further than 1935 or 1936, then in those years I did not once see Rykov or Tomsky or Uglanov, and Uglanov was not even a member of the troika.

Molotov: A troika can only have three members.

Bukharin: Viacheslav Mikhailovich, you may consider such a witticism to be a refutation of me. In fact, though, it is a refutation of yourself because "troika" was the current term then and no one spoke of a "center." So this troika was in fact a troika.

Molotov: And you think this is really witty?

Bukharin: I don't know, but in any case, I think it is quite convincing.

Khrushchev: And Tsetlin said that in essence you had a second CC.

(Bukharin is silent.)

Shkiriatov: You are saying what you said in the beginning. You are continuing along the same path.

Bukharin: How is that? I am here answering Comrade Voroshilov's speech. I could not have known "in the beginning" what he would say.

A voice: You are speaking today as a lawyer for all the defendants.

Bukharin: If you say that I wanted to discredit the new personnel of the NKVD, then I must declare that I had absolutely no intention of doing so.

Lozovsky: You wrote that it is demand that produces supply.

Bukharin: Demand produces supply—that means that those who give testimony know the nature of the general atmosphere. (Laughter, noise in the room.)

Postyshev: What kind of atmosphere are you talking about?

. . . Bukharin: There is one other remark, repeated by a host of comrades. They put it as follows. In connection with the fact that I developed a detailed argumentation, which Comrade Chubar wanted to characterize as casuistry, they say: "This is not a tribunal. It would be another matter if this place were a tribunal. We weigh everything here from a political standpoint." To be honest, I don't know, I cannot understand this position. What does it mean to say that this is not a tribunal? What are the grounds for this assertion? Is this not a place where individual facts are judged? Have not the testimonies of eyewitness, the factual evidence, been circulated to you? Yes, they have. Does this factual evidence not weigh heavily on the minds of comrades summoned to judge and draw conclusions? It does.

A voice: This is not a tribunal. This is the CC of the party.

Bukharin: I know that this is the CC of the party and not a Revolutionary Tribunal. If the difference lay in the name, then this would be simply a tautology. Where does the difference lie? The matter has to do with the relationship between the Soviet and party institutions. The question is first resolved within the party [*v partiinom poriadke*] in full detail, then implemented by the Soviet state [*v sovetskom poriadke*]. First, the question is considered by weighing all the details, even at times the most minute ones, with a full knowledge of the case, and then the decision is carried out by the Soviet state. So here, I believe, the same applies. Is the matter to be decided here intuitively? No, it is to be decided by weighing the facts. Here we have, in fact, a party trial. And since this is so, I ask you: how can you refute the many facts of this case? I believe that these facts break down into two large categories. The first category includes separate, individual face-to-face conversations [*razgovory s glazu na glaz*]—that's the first category. The second category includes all the remaining facts. Now comrades, I ask you simply to consider carefully what the situation looks like from the point of view of the defense. If you are in possession of individual facts which speak of a face-to-face conversation, how can one refute them? There is nothing [for me] to do in this case other than to say to the person in question: no.

Postyshev: You held whole sessions, speak of these sessions.

Bukharin: Comrade Postyshev, please wait, I'll get around to the sessions yet. I have to answer a whole array of matters touched upon by Kaganovich, Molotov. (Noise.)

A voice: Concerning a time limit. Should we not set a time limit for him? Are we obligated to listen to everything?

Molotov: Comrades, don't interfere!

Bukharin: If you don't have to listen to me, then I shall not speak.

Stalin: You don't want to speak?

Bukharin: Yes, I do want to speak. Now, to move on to the second [category] of facts. What is required here is a thorough analysis, a comparison of facts and contradictions, establishing the fact that you could not have been present at such a time and at such a place and so on. And that is what I am doing. Who objects to this? Comrade Chubar calls this casuistry.

Chubar: Absolutely.

A voice: That's right.

Budenny: That's the way the Jesuits talk.

Bukharin: I don't know, Comrade Budenny, perhaps you are familiar with the history of the Jesuits—

Budenny: I, at least, know my party, and you are lying to your party.

Postyshev [to Budenny]: Tell him that you learned about the Jesuits by studying them.[35]

Bukharin: So, comrades, is it necessary for me to carry on this analysis? Yes, it is necessary. Only in this way can I refute the facts. True or not true? Yes, I think that this is true. And for this reason I've come under such fire from you.

A voice: You are refuting this?!

Bukharin: I will dwell on Comrade Kaganovich's speech. First, concerning the matter of Sokolnikov and Kulikov. No one has bothered to consider Radek and Piatakov, about whom I spoke in detail in my written answer. I believe

35. Bukharin, Rykov, etc.—Trans.

that the analysis of the testimony by Tsetlin, once my closest friend, has been demolished by me. (Noise, laughter.)

Shkiriatov: You have demolished it?!

Postyshev: Demolished indeed! You are demolished!

Bukharin: OK, then why has no one really mentioned it? That's no answer.

Kaganovich: We spoke of your main argument, that Tsetlin is offended at you, that you didn't defend him.

Bukharin: But that is not at all my main argument. I have compared facts, many chronological dates. Armed with this comparison, I've refuted everything right down to the single assertion by Tsetlin.

Molotov: Nothing of the sort. Your refutation is not worth a farthing, because we have enough facts.

Bukharin: I would be grateful if someone, anyone were to mention it, but not a single person has mentioned it, no one has said a word about it.

Molotov: By God! Everybody is talking about it.

Petrovsky: Tsetlin has come around to Communist self-consciousness, and you want to discredit him.

Kosior: As for Communist self-consciousness—this is a rather doubtful matter.

A voice: He has begun to acknowledge it.

Bukharin: . . . The matter proceeds on to the "strongest argument" advanced against me: why are they testifying against themselves? I have already answered this question some time ago. Concerning one part of them, it may be said that, theoretically speaking, they could have been engaged in whatever you please, since they continued their struggle. Concerning the other part, as I have already said here before—I consider it highly improbable. But I ask you to look closely at the following fact. Their situation is an extremely difficult one. Consider only—this is what I think—that since they are told that "you have been unmasked, you are a liar, you are a hypocrite," then they may well calculate that if they only confess to something and slander themselves, then they would be better off. This is meant for those cases involving slander. And there, where someone is really guilty and has been caught in the act, there the evidence and the consciousness of their own guilt weigh heavily on them, not to mention the fear that the whole truth will come out anyway and that then they would be worse off.

Kalygina: And what about the face-to-face confrontation with Kulikov? After all, this is a matter of provocation, of slander.

Bukharin: I consider it a case of conjecture when I speak of slander against oneself; I am saying that this is a hypothesis, but I am also saying that I cannot fully answer this question. If I knew the rules governing interrogation, if I knew all of the questions put to the accused, all of their testimonies, if I knew what has been presented to them from others' testimonies, and if I knew the order of these testimonies and so on, I could and would know how to fully answer this question, but right now I cannot do so.

A voice: And is Kuzmin's testimony true or not?

Kalygina: Are they engaging in slander?

Bukharin: . . . I repeat once more: you are judging my activities not from the standpoint of party history but, mainly, from the standpoint of the present moment. [To understand the present moment] one must also, of course, know party history and coordinate it with the case in hand. . . .

My sins before the party have been very grave. My sins were especially grave during the period of the decisive onslaught of socialism, when, in fact, our group, serving as an enormous brake to the socialist offensive, caused it great harm. I've confessed to these sins. I confessed that from 1930 to 1932 I committed many political sins. I have come to understand this. But with the same forcefulness with which I confess my real guilt, with that same forcefulness I deny the guilt which is thrust upon me, and I shall deny it forever. And not because it has only personal significance, but because I believe that no one should under any circumstances take upon himself anything superfluous, especially when the party doesn't need it, when the country doesn't need it, when I don't need it. (Noise in the room, laughter.)

In spite of the fact that I cannot explain a host of things, fair questions posed to me, [in spite of the fact that] I cannot explain fully or even half-fully many questions posed to me concerning the conduct of people testifying against me.[36] However, this circumstance—namely, that I cannot explain everything—is not in my eyes an argument for my guilt. I repeat, I've been guilty of many things, but I protest with all the strength of my soul against being charged with such things as treason to my homeland, sabotage, terrorism, and so on, because any person possessing such qualities would be my deadly enemy. I am ready and willing to do anything against such a person. (Noise, voices.) . . .

The whole tragedy of my situation lies in this, that this Piatakov and others like him so poisoned the atmosphere, such an atmosphere arose that no one believes human feelings—not emotions, not the impulses of the heart, not tears. (Laughter.) Many manifestations of human feeling, which had earlier represented a form of proof—and there was nothing shameful in this—have today lost their validity and force.

Kaganovich: You practiced too much duplicity!

Bukharin: Comrades, let me say the following concerning what happened—

Khlopliankin: It's time to throw you in prison!

Bukharin: What?

Khlopliankin: You should have been thrown in prison a long time ago!

Bukharin: Well, go on, throw me in prison. So you think the fact that you are yelling: "Throw him in prison!" will make me talk differently? No, it won't.

---

36. Sentence incomplete—Trans.

Document 139

From A. I. Rykov's second speech to the February–March 1937 Plenum of the Central Committee, 26 February 1937[37]

Rykov: First, comrades, I must apologize if I cannot give a detailed answer to everything that has been said, because I did not have the strength to listen to everything and was absent part of the time from the room during the discussion of this question. The plenum is making what is for me, strictly speaking, the last decision. This meeting will be the last, the very last party meeting of my life. From what I have heard here, this is absolutely and completely clear. But since I have been a party member for over 36 years, this has meaning for my entire life. Accusations of the widest scope have been brought against me—i.e., criminal accusations which dwarf anything possible. And all of these accusations are considered proven facts. Many speakers have cited testimonies against me. In my first speech I tried to characterize these eyewitness testimonies. Not one testimony alone but five or six have been brought against me, and I wanted to prove that among these people some—for instance, Radin—slandered me maliciously; certain others, perhaps, slandered me without malice, but, just the same, here I'm dealing with slander. . . .

I cannot say what I said. But I assure you that if everything that people say is recorded with precision, if minutes have been kept over the course of the past 5–6 years, then I must tell you that they are lying. We ought not to believe that they can remember all this. There is no doubt in my mind that if they had retained anything in their memory, if anything had been stamped on their memory 8 years ago, if, in the ensuing 8 years, new layers had accumulated in their minds concerning this question, then everything would be forgotten and shrouded in confusion. I am not a jurist or a lawyer, but you will probably find a zillion examples in our legal proceedings of cases where a crime comes to light after several years and where innumerable major discrepancies, crucial discrepancies appear in the testimonies relative to them.

Postyshev: There are no particular discrepancies.

Rykov: On the other hand, any discrepancy as to whether I was or was not a Trotskyist-murderer is no trifle for me.

Postyshev: There is no discrepancy here.

Shkiriatov: He was only talking about rabbits.[38]

Stalin: There are those who give truthful, though horrifying, testimony but with the aim of shaking off completely the filth that sticks to them. And there are also those who don't give truthful testimony because they have come to love the filth which sticks to them and don't want to part with it.

Rykov: In moments such as these, under the conditions that I find myself

---

37. *Voprosy istorii*, no. 2, 1993, 17, 20–21, 26.
38. In other words, a large number of small, unimportant matters.

now, you find yourself saying something that never was—just to get out of the dead end you are in.

Stalin: You have lost your head. What profit is there in it?

Rykov: What, what?

Voroshilov: Where is the advantage?

Stalin: What have we to gain?

Rykov: I am saying that here, in spite of oneself, one says something that never was.

Stalin: Mrachkovsky, Shestov, Piatakov—they wanted to pull themselves out of the filth they landed in, at whatever cost. Such people ought not to be chastised as harshly as those who give untruthful testimony because they have become accustomed to the filth that sticks to them.

Rykov: That's true. It is now absolutely clear to me that I will be better treated if I confess. This is absolutely clear to me—and many of my torments will also come to an end, at whatever price, just so long as it comes to some end.

Postyshev: What's clear? What torments? He is painting himself as a martyr.

Rykov: I'm sorry, I shouldn't have mentioned that. . . .

I would like to say something about the Riutin Platform. That which I know about it I already said. . . . I again confirm that it was a chance trip, that I found many people there, that some of them went into the room, that they sent for me and said that the leaflet which had been circulated at the factory had been brought in. We listened to it. I lashed out at it.

A voice: Who read it?

Rykov: I don't remember. They stood as a group. I was sitting at a distance from them, but near enough to hear them. I lashed out at this platform. But to think that a meeting could possibly be taking place there, to consider me the kind of person who would sit down with unknown people—

Beria: You know them.

Rykov: I am telling you what I know, Comrade Beria. You can say whatever you know.

Postyshev: Why didn't you tell this to the CC? What did you have in mind?

Rykov: I didn't have anything in mind.

Voroshilov: Ugh! How naive you are.

Rykov: Tomsky was there. The document was brought in from the factory. The Central Committee is informed of it. It was made public there.

Voroshilov: Why did you have to acquaint yourself with this program for the second time?

Rykov: I knew of its existence, that it had been circulated, that arrests had been made.

Voroshilov: Did you go there to acquaint yourself with it?

Rykov: I didn't know that it would be there.

Yaroslavsky: Why did you say at the plenum that you hadn't heard it?

Voroshilov: But if it had luckily fallen into your hands, then you should have put it in your pocket and taken it to the Central Committee.

Rykov: That's all that happened there. No one discussed it there. No one ratified it there.

Postyshev: Why didn't you report it during the session of the Central Committee?

Rykov: First of all, I didn't ascribe any significance to it, since it was not approved by anyone. I didn't hear anyone express approval of it.

A voice: Why circulate counterrevolutionary documents?

Postyshev: And if they had approved it, would you have brought the matter to the attention of the CC?

Rykov: Everybody lashed out at it, and so did I.

Liubchenko: Why didn't you say at the Central Committee plenum that it had already been read at Tomsky's?

Khrushchev: Our candidate members of the party—if an antiparty document falls into their hands, they bring it to their cell, and you are a candidate member of the CC.

Rykov: It was a perfectly obvious mistake, but my attitude toward the Riutin program has always been, now and forever, a negative one.

Postyshev: Why are you being evasive?

Rykov: If I had supported this program . . . I am being slandered for what never was. I would like to say only one thing—

Postyshev: Why didn't you bring the matter to the attention of the CC? . . .

Molotov: And so how did it come about? After the reading of the Riutin Platform at Tomsky's dacha, the Central Committee held a plenum where this platform was discussed. You spoke at this plenum and said that if you had known that someone had such a program, you would have dragged such a person to the GPU. You did say this, didn't you? Yes, you did.

Rykov: Yes, in this matter I am guilty, and I fully admit my guilt.

Molotov: It is an indisputable fact, Comrade Rykov, you got all confused on this point.

Rykov: On what point?

Molotov: On what point? At the plenum you said the following: if you had ever seen such a program, this White Guard program, you would have dragged such a person to the GPU. And yet you didn't say a word at the plenum to the effect that you had already read this program. How did this come about?

Rykov: I said that I didn't remember whether this was before or after the plenum. (General noise, laughter.)

Exclamation: You are lying through and through!

Rykov: Perhaps before the plenum. I'm telling you everything that I know, everything that I remember about it. In all of this there is, of course, something bad, not only something good. I in no way asserted that I would tell lies about myself, but only that which would save me. For this I am being rebuked. I ought to be punished for that which I did, but I shouldn't be punished for that which I didn't do.

Molotov: We are talking here only about one thing: did you or did you not lie with deliberate intent?

Rykov: . . . I don't know, of course, you can go ahead and mock me. I am now finished. There is no question about it, but why must you mock me like this to no purpose?

Postyshev: We are not mocking you. It's just that we must establish the facts.

Rykov: This is absurd.

Postyshev: There is no point in mocking you. You have only yourself to blame.

Rykov: I am finishing my speech. I understand all too well that this is my last speech both at a CC plenum and possibly for the rest of my life. But I repeat once more that to confess to that which I did not do, to make myself a scoundrel for the sake of my own comfort or someone else's, as I am depicted here, this I will never do.

Stalin: And who demands that you do this?

Rykov: Oh, my Lord, be it your will, it's all too clear. I was never a part of any bloc, I never belonged to any rightist center, I never engaged in any wrecking, espionage, sabotage, terrorism, or any other vile deeds. And I will continue to assert this as long as I am alive.

In accordance with party traditions, the rapporteur on the agenda question was given a chance to give a concluding speech. In this case, Yezhov summed up the case against Bukharin and Rykov. Although his original report had called only for expelling them from the party, the final sentence in his concluding remarks suggested that they should be arrested.

Document 140

From Yezhov's concluding speech on the Bukharin-Rykov question to the February–March 1937 Plenum of the Central Committee, 26 February 1937[39]

Yezhov: Comrades, this is the fourth day in which the CC plenum of our party has been discussing the matter of Bukharin and Rykov. When the matter was placed before the Plenum of the CC of the party, it was done with a view to having these two candidate members of the CC of the party hold themselves

39. *Voprosy istorii*, no. 2, 1993, 26, 27, 33.

politically accountable before the Plenum of the CC of the party, before the entire party, for the entire sum of those political actions in word or deed [*vystupleniia*] against the party and Soviet power which they made during a period of time spanning many, many years.

Three main charges were brought against them. First, it has been charged that Bukharin and Rykov, after giving a statement in which they declared their full submission to the party and their recantation of their rightist-opportunistic views, deceived the party and engaged in duplicity and camouflage. In renouncing their rightist-opportunistic views, they maintained their faction, the members of which went underground, continued to adhere to their old political platform without ceasing their struggle against the party, and submitting only to their intrafactional discipline. In order to govern this faction, a center was created as early as 1928, and it continued to exist up until very recently. The most active participants, members, of this center were Bukharin and Rykov.

Second, it has been charged that Bukharin and Rykov did not renounce their political convictions, so hostile to our country, and favored a platform of capitalistic restoration in the USSR.

Third, it has been charged that, in order to attain their aim of overthrowing the Leninist-Stalinist leadership, Bukharin and Rykov have formed an open bloc with Trotskyists, Zinovievists, "leftists," SRs, Mensheviks, and with all the remaining factional groups, which have long since been crushed. Forming a bloc with all the enemies of the Soviet Union, they moved on to adopt terroristic methods, organizing an armed uprising, and resorting to methods of sabotage. These are the political charges brought against Bukharin and Rykov.

However, neither Bukharin nor Rykov answered these political charges. Here everyone rightly called them bourgeois lawyers. There is nothing accidental whatsoever about the fact that, in their speeches and statements, they completely avoided a [political] assessment of all this vile gang of Trotskyist-Zinovievist scum, which we have recently executed. There is nothing accidental whatsoever about the fact that, in pursuing their defense, Bukharin and Rykov sought mainly to uncover contradictions and discrepancies in the testimonies of like-minded friends, of accomplices under arrest.

If they have adopted such a policy, then, as a result of this discussion and with full right, we may bring one further political charge against them— namely, that they have remained enemies who haven't put down their arms, who give their signal to all enemy forces, both here in the USSR and abroad.

Voices: That's true.

Yezhov: This, comrades, is the fourth charge we can, with full right, bring against Bukharin and Rykov as a result of this discussion of the matter. They give their signals to their like-minded friends, namely: Work in greater secrecy [*konspirirovat'sia*]. If you are caught, don't confess. That's their policy. Not only have they cast doubt on the investigation in pursuing their defense. In defending themselves, they have also necessarily cast doubt on the Trotskyist-Zinovievist trial, both the first one and the second one.

At any rate, Bukharin mentions this unambiguously in his statement.

Bukharin: Where did I say that?

Yezhov: Read it carefully. You say it everywhere. You defend everyone belonging to this vile gang—

Bukharin: What is this? This is outrageous!

Yezhov: Yes, you defend everyone belonging to this vile gang. You attempt to discredit all of the trials that had already taken place.

Shkiriatov: You're right, Nikolai Ivanovich [Yezhov]! You're speaking the truth.

Yezhov: . . . You see, Bukharin is seeking out isolated contradictions and discrepancies in the testimony of this or that person under arrest and draws from there the following conclusion, namely: "You see, the investigation is carried out in such a manner that people are prompted to say what they say. They are being prompted to say inaccurate things." You see, comrades, if we wanted to contrive all this evidence against Bukharin, it's quite evident that such evidence would have been smoothed over and made orderly—

Postyshev: The discrepancies would have been removed.

Yezhov: Yes, the discrepancies would have been removed. Everyone said what he had to say. This fact speaks for the correct carrying out of the investigation. Dozens of people under arrest are queried in different places—

Beria: And at different times.

Yezhov: Persons under arrest are not told what the evidence against them is, and each reports, in his own way, the facts as they are. . . . I think that if it [the evidence] all agreed, then Bukharin would have shouted from all the rooftops that it was contrived.

Beria: He would have gambled on it.

Yezhov: Absolutely. He would have gambled on it. . . .

Besides, comrades, let me add the following concerning the Trotskyists. Bukharin attempted to give himself credit by saying that he could not have formed a bloc with the Trotskyists because, as he says, he had once fought against Trotsky, had once fought on the side of the party. It's true, he had fought against him, but how? He waged his battle from his own positions.

Postyshev: And with what aims!

Yezhov: . . . Comrades, I now conclude. This has dragged on a little longer than it should. You see, I think that they did not give a political answer but, instead, referred to discrepancies in the investigation. I think that the plenum will afford Bukharin and Rykov the opportunity to convince themselves of the objectivity of the investigation and to see how the investigation is being carried out.

Voices: That's right!

Document 140 *continued*

Andreev: Comrades, there is a motion to ask the plenum to elect a commission whose responsibility would be to make a decision concerning the case of Rykov and Bukharin, which has just been discussed.

Voices: That's right.

Andreev: Any objections?

Voices: No.

Andreev: It is proposed that a commission be elected consisting of the following persons: Mikoyan, chairman, Andreev, Stalin, Molotov . . . (Reads.) Here is the commission which has been proposed. Any objections?

Voices: No.

Stalin: Add Antipov, [and] Gamarnik.

Voices: That's right, let's add the names.

Andreev: With these amendments, the formation of the commission is therefore approved. It is proposed that the evening session of the plenum begin at 8 P.M.

Voices: That's right!

From the speeches to the plenum, it seemed that there was little disagreement on the question. "Clear, one would think," as Stalin often said. None of the speakers even came close to defending Bukharin or opposing arrests of traitors. They were furious with Bukharin and Rykov not only for their alleged "treason" to the party, but for their refusal to serve the party and the ritual by playing the prescribed roles. Once again, the senior nomenklatura had closed ranks against those perceived as violating their rules. What was meant to be a ceremony of group affirmation and discipline was transformed into contested ritual space.

Even though we have a version of the entire text concerning Bukharin and Rykov, however, the plenum's proceedings to a great extent remain mysterious. Indeed, the documents themselves raise strange questions. Since Lenin's time, it had always been a party tradition that the main reporter on an agenda question offered a draft resolution beforehand. More recently, it had become the responsibility of the Politburo—that is, of Stalin himself—to prepare such a preliminary resolution in advance of the plenum. These drafts were circulated to the Central Committee members before the report and speeches were ever given. In the present case, Bukharin's letter to the plenum referred to such a draft resolution to be adopted on the basis of Yezhov's main report. The draft has not been located in the archives; presumably it followed the outlines of Yezhov's recommendation and called for expelling Bukharin and Rykov from the party.

In the vast majority of cases in the 1930s, discussion of the main report was perfunctory, and although minor corrections and amendments might be offered and even accepted from the floor, the Central Committee almost always voted unanimously to adopt the draft resolution. In rare cases when there was disagreement or when the drift of the meeting went beyond the draft proposals, an ad hoc commission of Central Committee members would retire during the meeting to work out a new text for the final resolution. (This had happened at the Seventeenth Party Congress in 1934, when Ordzhonikidze and Molotov had proposed different industrial targets for the second Five Year Plan.)[40]

In this case, in light of Bukharin's refusal to accept his role in the apology ritual, thereby contesting the entire ritual space, several of the speakers had gone beyond Yezhov's formal recommendation for expulsion. Some of them—including Yezhov— had called for arresting Bukharin and Rykov. Others had flatly suggested that they be shot. Formally, then, it would seem to be necessary for a commission to edit the draft resolution in favor of stronger measures. But the matter was more complicated than that. There is evidence that some, perhaps including Stalin himself, may have argued for a different approach altogether. The resolution subsequently produced by the commission and approved by the plenum did, in fact, consign Bukharin and Rykov to the not-so-tender mercies of the NKVD. But it contained language suggesting a difference in approach between them and the thoroughly evil Trotskyists, and indicating indecision at the top.

40. See *XVII s"ezd Vsesoiuznoi Kommunisticheskoi Partii(b). 26 ianvaria–10 fevralia 1934g.: Stenograficheskii otchet.* Moscow, 1934, 435–36, 648–50, and the accounts in Kendall E. Bailes, *Technology and Society Under Lenin and Stalin: Origins of the Soviet Technical Intelligentsia, 1917–1941,* Princeton, 1978, 302, and in Eugene Zaleski, *Stalinist Planning for Economic Growth, 1933–1953,* Chapel Hill, 1980, 115–29.

Document 141

Resolution of the February–March 1937 CC plenum on the affair of Bukharin and Rykov[41]

Resolution of the Plenum of the CC of the VKP(b), "The case of Comrades Bukharin and Rykov"

3 March 1937

1. On the basis of investigative materials furnished by the NKVD, on the basis of the face-to-face confrontation between Comrade Bukharin and Radek, Piatakov, Sosnovsky, and Sokolnikov, as well as on the basis of a thorough and detailed discussion of the matter at the plenum, the Plenum of the CC of the VKP(b) has established that, at a minimum, Comrades Bukharin and Rykov knew of the criminal, terrorist, espionage, and sabotage-wrecking activities of the Trotskyist center, and that they not only did not combat these activities but in fact helped these activities along by concealing them from the party and not reporting them to the CC of the VKP(b).

2. On the basis of investigative materials furnished by the NKVD, on the basis of Comrade Bukharin's face-to-face confrontation with the rightists—with Kulikov and Astrov—in the presence of members of the Politburo of the CC of the VKP(b) and Comrade Rykov's face-to-face confrontation with Kotov, Shmidt, Nesterov, and Radin, as well as on the basis of a detailed and thorough discussion of the matter at the Plenum of the CC, the Plenum of the CC of the VKP(b) has established that Comrades Bukharin and Rykov, at a minimum, knew from their followers and supporters, that is, from Slepkov, Tsetlin, Astrov, Maretsky, Nesterov, Radin, Kulikov, Kotov, Uglanov, Zaitsev, Kuzmin, Sapozhnikov, and others, that criminal terrorist groups had been organized, and they not only did not resist them but in fact encouraged them.

3. The Plenum of the CC of the VKP(b) has established that Comrade Bukharin's note to the CC of the VKP(b), where he seeks to refute the evidence of the above-mentioned Trotskyists and right terrorists, is, by virtue of its contents, a slanderous document. It not only reveals Comrade Bukharin's total inability to refute the evidence of the Trotskyists and right terrorists against him but, under the guise of a "legalistic" challenge[42] of this evidence, is carrying out slanderous assaults against the NKVD. Furthermore, he is mounting an attack, unworthy of a Communist, on the party and its CC—in view of which Comrade Bukharin's note ought not to be considered as anything other than as a document without substance and deserving no credibility whatsoever.

Bearing in mind the above and taking into account the fact that even while Lenin was alive Comrade Bukharin waged a campaign against the party and against Lenin himself both before the October Revolution (concerning the dictatorship of the proletariat) and after the October Revolution (concerning

41. RTsKhIDNI, f. 17, op. 2, d. 577, l. 4.
42. *advokatskoe osparivanie*, literally, "challenge by a lawyer"—Trans.

the Brest-Litovsk peace treaty, the party's program, the nationalities question, and the role of the trade unions) and the fact that Comrade Rykov also waged a campaign against the party and against Lenin himself both before the October Revolution and at the time of the October uprising (he was against the October Revolution), as well as after the October coup d'état (he demanded a coalition with the Mensheviks and SRs, and, as a sign of protest, he quit his post of commissar for foreign affairs, for which he received from Lenin the nickname of "strikebreaker"), and that all this speaks indubitably of the fact that the political fall of Comrades Bukharin and Rykov is not merely fortuitous or unexpected—taking into account all this, the Plenum of the CC of the VKP(b) considers that Comrades Bukharin and Rykov deserve to be immediately expelled from the party and brought to trial before the military tribunal.

However, taking into consideration the fact that Comrades Bukharin and Rykov, in contrast to the Trotskyists and Zinovievists, had not incurred serious party penalties until now (they had not been expelled from the party), the Plenum of the CC of the VKP(b) decrees that it shall be satisfied with the following:

1) That Comrades Bukharin and Rykov shall be expelled from candidate membership in the CC of the VKP(b) and from the VKP(b).

2) That the case of Bukharin and Rykov be handed over to the NKVD.

Such documents are carefully worded because they are used to propagate the exact party line to those at lower levels. In this case, Bukharin and Rykov were not labeled enemies; they were not explicitly consigned to prosecution or trial. There seems to be a distinction behind the difference here, because as we shall see, such measures were earlier proposed and explicitly rejected by the commission. More ambiguity arises from Stalin's report to the plenum on the deliberations of the ad hoc commission.

Document 142

Stalin's report to the February–March 1937 CC plenum on the commission on the affair of Bukharin and Rykov, 27 February 1937[43]

Stalin: Comrades, the commission of the CC plenum has entrusted me with the task of reporting to you the results of its work. Permit me to read you the report. The members of the commission were all in accord that, at a minimum,

43. *Voprosy istorii*, no. 1, 1994, 12–13.

Bukharin and Rykov should be punished by being expelled from the list of candidate members of the CC and from the ranks of the VKP(b). There was not a single person on the commission who expressed himself against this proposal. There were differences of opinion as to whether they should be handed over for trial or not handed over for trial, and if not, then as to what we should confine ourselves to. Part of the commission expressed itself in favor of handing them over to a military tribunal and having them executed. Another part of the commission expressed itself in favor of handing them over for trial and having them receive a sentence of 10 years in prison. A third part expressed itself in favor of having them handed over for trial without a preliminary decision as to what should be their sentence. And, finally, a fourth part of the commission expressed itself in favor of not handing them over for trial but instead referring the matter of Bukharin and Rykov to the NKVD. The last-named proposal won out.

As a result, the commission unanimously decided to expel them from the list of candidate members of the CC and from the ranks of the VKP(b) and to refer the matter of Bukharin and Rykov to the NKVD.

And now for the commission's motives. Naturally, the feeling of indignation at both the antiparty and anti-Soviet activities of Bukharin and Rykov, as well as at their conduct here at the plenum during the discussion concerning them, was very great, as much so among members of the commission as at the plenum. But the commission is of the opinion that it cannot and should not be governed by a feeling of indignation. There were some on the commission, a rather substantial number, as well as here at the CC plenum, who felt that there was apparently no difference between Bukharin and Rykov, on the one hand, and those Trotskyists and Zinovievists, on the other hand, who were brought to trial and punished accordingly. The commission does not agree with such a position and believes that one ought not to lump Bukharin and Rykov in with the group of Trotskyists and Zinovievists, since there is a difference between them, a difference that speaks in favor of Bukharin and Rykov.

If we look at the Trotskyists and Zinovievists, we see that they were expelled from the party, then restored, then expelled again. If we look at Bukharin and Rykov, we see that they had never been expelled. We should not equate the Trotskyists and Zinovievists, who once, as you well know, staged an anti-Soviet demonstration in 1927, with Rykov and Bukharin. There are no such sins in their past.

The commission could not fail but take into account that there are no such sins in the past actions of Bukharin and Rykov and that, until very recently, they gave no cause or grounds for expelling them from the party. Consequently, the commission had to take into account that until recently neither Bukharin nor Rykov had incurred serious party penalties, unless we consider their removal from the Politburo a serious penalty, and, besides, Rykov was removed from his post as chairman of the Council of People's Commissars. As a result, the commission has passed the following resolution. May I read it to you?

Voices: Please go ahead.

Stalin: (reading) "Resolution of the Plenum of the CC of the VKP(b) regarding the case of Comrades Bukharin and Rykov. On the basis of investigative materials submitted by the NKVD, by face-to-face confrontation . . . (reads) . . . to transfer the case of Bukharin and Rykov to the NKVD." . . .

This resolution is passed unanimously by the commission.

Andreev: Does anyone wish to speak? No. Are there any other proposals besides the one made by Comrade Stalin? No. Are there any amendments to the proposal made by Comrade Stalin in the name of the commission? No. Should we all vote on it? Let's vote. I must notify you, comrades, that, in accordance with the rules, members of the Commission of Party Control will also be voting, along with members of the CC and candidate members of the CC. All those in favor of adopting the resolution, please raise your hands. You may now lower them. All those against. None. Any abstentions? Two. So, the resolution carries with two abstentions—Bukharin and Rykov. The session will adjourn till tomorrow at 12 noon.

It was quite unusual for Stalin himself to give such reports; this is the first and only time in party history that he did so. This text was truly a hidden transcript: it was never published with any of the versions of the stenographic report and was never transferred to the party archives with other materials of the plenum. Aside from Bukharin's refusal to play his role and confess, something strange had happened that would prevent the full use of the February–March plenum text. The transcript of this ambiguous and contradictory decision on Bukharin never even found its way into the heavily edited and limited-circulation stenographic report, which showed the plenum beginning on 27 February—four days after it actually started.[44]

Equally peculiar are the editorial changes made to the skeletal protocol of the commission's deliberations on which Stalin reported. An original typed draft was edited by an unknown hand between the meeting of the commission and Stalin's report to the plenum. Document 143 shows the parts that were ~~struck from~~ and highlights the parts that were **added to** the original document.

44. RTsKhIDNI, f. 17, op. 2, d. 612, volumes 1 and 2.

Document 143

Protocol of the meeting of the Commission of the Central Committee on the matter of Bukharin and Rykov[45]

27 February 1937

Present:

Comrade Mikoyan, chairman

Members of the commission: Comrades Andreev, Stalin, Molotov, Kaganovich L. M., Voroshilov, Kalinin, Yezhov, Shkiriatov, Krupskaia, Kosior, Yaroslavsky, Zhdanov, Khrushchev, Ulianova, Manuilsky, Litvinov, Yakir, Kabakov, Beria, Mirzoyan, Eikhe, Bagirov, Ikramov, Vareikis, Budenny, Yakovlev, Chubar, Kosarev, Postyshev, Petrovsky, Nikolaeva, Shvernik, Ugarov, Antipov, Gamarnik.

Discussion: of the suggestions of members of the commission.

~~The proposal of~~ 1. Comrade Yezhov—to expel Bukharin and Rykov as candidate members of the Central Committee and members of the VKP(b) and to transfer them to the military tribunal with application of the highest measure of punishment—shooting.

~~THE SUGGESTIONS OF MEMBERS OF THE COMMISSION:~~

~~1.~~ 2. Postyshev—to expel from the ranks of candidate members of the Central Committee and as members of the VKP(b), to transfer them to court without application of the death penalty.

~~2.~~ 3. Budenny—to expel from the ranks of candidate members of the Central Committee and as members of the VKP(b), to transfer them to court with application of the death penalty.

~~3.~~ 4. Stalin—to expel from the ranks of candidate members of the Central Committee and as members of the VKP(b), not to send them to court but rather to ~~exile them.~~ **transfer their case to the NKVD.**

~~4.~~ 5. Manuilsky—to expel from the ranks of candidate members of the Central Committee and as members of the VKP(b), to transfer them to court with application of the death penalty.

5. Shkiriatov—to expel from the ranks of candidate members of the Central Committee and as members of the VKP(b), to transfer them to court without application of the death penalty.

6. Antipov—same as above.

7. Khrushchev—same as above.

8. Nikolaeva—same as above.

9. Ulianova—for the suggestion of Comrade Stalin.

10. Shvernik—to expel from the ranks of candidate members of the Central Committee and as members of the VKP(b), to transfer them to court with application of the death penalty.

45. RTsKhIDNI, f. 17, op. 2, d. 577, ll. 30–33. Typed, with handwritten edits, deletions, and additions.

11. Kosior—to expel from the ranks of candidate members of the Central Committee and as members of the VKP(b), to transfer them to court without application of the death penalty.

12. Petrovsky—to expel from the ranks of candidate members of the Central Committee and as members of the VKP(b), to transfer them to court without application of the death penalty.

13. Litvinov—same as above.

14. Krupskaia—for the suggestion of Comrade Stalin.

15. Kosarev—to expel from the ranks of candidate members of the Central Committee and as members of the VKP(b), to transfer them to court with application of the death penalty.

16. Yakir—same as above.

17. Vareikis—for the suggestion of Comrade Stalin.

18. Molotov—for the suggestion of Comrade Stalin.

19. Voroshilov—for the suggestion of Comrade Stalin.

DECISION:

1. To expel from the ranks of candidate members of the Central Committee and as members of the VKP(b), not to send them to court but rather ~~transfer them to the NKVD~~**transfer the case of Bukharin and Rykov to the NKVD** (adopted unanimously).

2. To instruct a commission composed of Comrades Stalin, Molotov, Voroshilov, Kaganovich, Mikoyan, and Yezhov to work out on the basis of this decision an acceptable resolution.

[Signed] A. Mikoyan, chairman

The editorial revisions made to this document raise more questions than they answer. First, in the original version, Yezhov was the main reporter who proposed handing Bukharin and Rykov over to the courts and executing them. However, because this was not the final result and because party discursive tradition prohibited even a private admission that a formal report was rejected, the document was doctored to make it appear that there had been no main report or proposal from Yezhov, but rather a round-table with numbered "exchange of opinions" among the members of the commission.

Second, in the original polling, while expulsion from the party was a foregone conclusion, not a single member proposed or voted for what would become the final decision: turning the matter of Bukharin and Rykov over to the NKVD for further investigation.

П Р О Т О К О Л

заседания комиссии Пленума ЦК ВКП(б) по делу

Бухарина и Рыкова

27 февраля 1937 года.

ПРИСУТСТВОВАЛИ:

тов.МИКОЯН – председатель.

Члены комиссии: т.т. Андреев,Сталин,Молотов,Каганович Л.М.,
Ворошилов,Калинин,Ежов,Шкирятов,Крупская
Косиор,Ярославский,Жданов,Хрущев,Улья-
нова,Мануильский,Литвинов, Якир, Каба-
ков,Берия,Мирзоян,Эйхе,Багиров,Икрамов,
Варейкис,Буденный,Яковлев Я., Чубарь,
Косарев,Постышев,Петровский,Николаева,
Шверник,Угаров,Антипов,Гамарник.

Слушали: предложению члену Комиссии:

Предложение т.Ежова-об исключении Бухарина и Рыкова из состава
кандидатов ЦК ВКП(б) и членов ВКП(б) и предании их суду Военного
Трибунала с применением высшей меры наказания – расстрела.

Членами комиссии были внесены следующие предложения:

2. т.Постышева – исключить из состава кандидатов ЦК ВКП(б)
и членов ВКП(б) и предать суду, без примене-
ния расстрела.

3. т.Буденный – исключить из состава кандидатов ЦК ВКП(б) и
членов ВКП(б) и предать суду с применением
расстрела.

4. т.Сталина – исключить из состава кандидатов ЦК ВКП(б) и
членов ВКП(б), суду не предавать, а внелать.

5. т.Мануильский – исключить из состава кандидатов ЦК ВКП(б) и
членов ВКП(б), предать суду и расстрелять.

5. т.Шкирятов – исключить из состава кандидатов ЦК ВКП(б) и
членов ВКП(б), предать суду, без применения
расстрела.

6. т.Антипов – То же.

7. т.Хрущев – То же.

8. т.Николаев – То же.

9. т.Ульянов М. – За предложение т.Сталина.

10. т.Шверник – Исключить из состава кандидатов ЦК ВКП(б) и
членов ВКП(б), предать суду и расстрелять.

11. т.Косиор С. – Исключить из состава кандидатов ЦК ВКП(б)
и членов ВКП(б), предать суду, без применения
расстрела.

DOCUMENT 143. Protocol of the meeting of the Commission of the Central Committee on the matter of Bukharin and Rykov, 27 February 1937 (with edits)

12. т.Петровский   — Исключить из состава кандидатов ЦК ВКП(б) и членов ВКП(б), предать суду, без применения расстрела.

13. т.Литвинов   —   Т о   ж е.

14. т.Крупская   — За предложение т.Сталина.

15. Косарев   — исключить из состава кандидатов ЦК ВКП(б) и членов ВКП(б), предать суду и расстрелять.

16. т.Якир   —   Т о   ж е.

17. т.Варейкис   — за предложение т.Сталина.

18. т.Молотов   — за предложение т.Сталина.

19. т.Ворошилов   — за предложение т.Сталина.

П о с т а н о в и л и:

1) Исключить из состава кандидатов ЦК ВКП(б) и членов ВКП(б) Бухарина и Рыкова; суду их не предавать, а ~~передать НКВД~~ *направить дело будет в НКВД*

(Принято единогласно).

2) Поручить комиссии в составе т.т.Сталина, Молотова, Ворошилова, Кагановича, Микояна и Ежова выработать на основе принятого решения проект мотивированной резолюции.

ПРЕДСЕДАТЕЛЬ

In the initial polling of thirty-six members of the commission, six spoke for executing Bukharin and Rykov. Eight, including the particularly vituperative Postyshev and Shkiriatov, were for arresting and trying Bukharin and Rykov but for sentencing them to prison rather than to death. Sixteen members either expressed no opinion or their votes were not recorded.

It is the remaining group that is especially intriguing. As the first draft indicates, five members were "for the suggestion of Comrade Stalin." But what was that suggestion? In the original document, Stalin spoke against the death penalty, a prison sentence, or even a trial, and for the relatively lenient punishment of internal exile. In the final version, Stalin's modified "suggestion" had become the final decision not to send them to trial but to turn the matter of Bukharin and Rykov over to the NKVD for further investigation.

Following Bukharin's exoneration in September 1936 and Stalin's move to delay proceedings against him at the December 1936 plenum, this was the third time that Stalin had personally intervened to avoid unambiguously condemning Bukharin. It was the second time Bukharin had pointedly refused to play his scapegoat role in the Central Committee ritual.

We can now finally rule out the notion, so often found in the literature, that Stalin in this period was backing down before an antiterror "liberal" coalition of senior Bolsheviks. Of those often mentioned in such a role (Kuibyshev, Kirov, Ordzhonikidze, and others), none were alive at the time of the plenum. On the contrary, according to the documents, once again only Stalin was resisting application of either a prison or death sentence. Why?

It may have been that he was holding back, proposing a light punishment in order to see what the others said, thereby identifying those with "soft" views on the opposition and marking them for later retaliation. In this way, he would be able to test the level of support for his plan to kill off the former opposition. This could explain why his most intimate collaborators (Molotov, Voroshilov, Andreev, Kalinin, Mikoyan, and Kaganovich), aware of the game, simply expressed themselves in favor of Stalin's proposal or kept silent. Militating against this explanation, however, is the lack of any correlation between the penalties proposed by those present and their fates. Thus Shkiriatov, Khrushchev, Nikolaeva, Petrovsky, and Litvinov voted against the sternest punishment, execution, but all survived the purges. Kosarev, Yakir, and Yezhov voted for execution and were themselves arrested and shot.

On the other hand, Stalin's original suggestion of "exile" may not have been entirely disingenuous. Going into the plenum, Stalin may not have decided exactly how far to proceed against Bukharin and Rykov. As the final resolution showed, it had not been "proved" that they had in fact joined the Trotskyist "terror organization." Rather, "at a minimum" they knew about the Trotskyists' plans, which is not the same thing. Yezhov had been the one closest to the investigations and interrogations of the rightists. Back in the fall of 1936, he had written to Stalin to express "doubt that the rightists had concluded a direct organizational bloc with the Trotskyists and Zinovievists." At that time, Yezhov recommended a "minimum punishment" of exile to a far region for Bukharin and Rykov.[46] Yezhov's 1936 formulation was precisely the one voiced by Stalin at the February–March 1937 plenum: that "at a minimum" Bukharin and Rykov knew about the terrorist plans of others and failed to report them. A distinction was made between them and the Trotskyists, and Stalin's first proposed punishment was exile. He used the same word, *vysylka,* that Yezhov had used in his letter the previous autumn. When Stalin reported the several contending points of view at the meeting and related how a compromise had been reached, he may have been telling the truth.

Perhaps Stalin proceeded with caution against Bukharin because, unlike Zinoviev, Kamenev, Piatakov, or any of the other previously persecuted oppositionists, Bukharin was a relatively big fish. Lenin had called him the "favorite of the party," and he had been virtual coruler of the regime with Stalin in the second half of the 1920s. It may well have been that before publicly committing himself to Bukharin's destruction he wanted to prepare the ground as much as possible.

Maybe Stalin decided that he needed a public trial and confession from Bukharin to justify the move against the rightists. Before he had that in hand, it would have perhaps been inadvisable for him to endorse killing Bukharin. More than a year would pass before Bukharin's trial. As late as June 1937, after Bukharin had been in prison three months, Stalin told a meeting of military officers that although Bukharin and Rykov had "connections" to enemies, "we have no information [*dannye*] that he himself was an informer."[47] Even after Bukharin began to "confess" to the charges against him (later in June), it would be half a year before Stalin brought him to the dock.

Could it have been that Stalin put off destroying him for personal reasons? Although personal affection seems unlikely from such a calculating political monster, certainly treatment of no other repressed oppositionist was moderated so many times at Stalin's initiative. Even after Bukharin's arrest, his wife was allowed to live in her apartment in the Kremlin for several months. Stalin personally intervened to prevent her eviction. About the time Bukharin began to confess in summer 1937, his wife was given the option to live in any of five cities outside Moscow; she picked Astrakhan. Although Yezhov wanted to have her shot along with other "wives of enemies of the people" (according to Beria), Stalin refused.[48] Ultimately, however, she spent many years in exile.

There is no doubt that Stalin had instigated or authorized Yezhov's campaign against the rightists. Things could never have gone this far without his continued support. But when and how mercilessly would Bukharin be destroyed? It is possible that Stalin himself had not decided exactly what to do with Bukharin and Rykov. As we have seen, as long as these former lieutenants lived, Stalin's political options remained open and the futures of his present lieutenants remained in doubt. By once again postponing a final decision on Bukharin, Stalin maintained the mystery about his true intentions, or even whether he had decided them.

Stalin's position also maintained maximum flexibility. He had not publicly or wholeheartedly associated himself with Yezhov's charges and had taken an almost neutral stance at the plenum; he gave Bukharin and Rykov unprecedented time to answer the charges and in comparison with the other speakers his demeanor

47. *Istochnik*, no. 3, 1994, 75.
48. Beria told this to Bukharin's widow. A. M. Larina, *Nezabyvaemoe*, Moscow, 1989, 178.

seemed balanced and evenhanded. The minutes of the plenum's deliberations on Bukharin and Rykov were never circulated, even to senior regional party officials. Only those present knew what had been said, and given Stalin's reticence and ambiguous stance, not even they were sure what he wanted. Even now, his proposal implied that the matter was not proved and needed to be checked further.

As in December 1936, Stalin's move to postpone implicitly cast doubt on Yezhov's investigation to date and left open the possibility of a changed course at any time. Indeed, at the end of 1938 Stalin removed Yezhov, disavowed the latter's excesses, ordered the arrest of the purgers, and released a number of those "falsely arrested." As long as Bukharin's death did not have Stalin's official stamp, as long as he postponed a decision, such a reversal was possible. Bukharin could be released and Yezhov and the purgers arrested. Stranger things could and did happen in this period.

Bukharin and Rykov were arrested at the plenum and sent to prison, yet it was more than a year before they were brought to trial, in March 1938. For whatever reason, the Bukharin affair resembled the Yenukidze and Postyshev cases. In all three instances, the victims were personal friends of Stalin's who were ultimately executed. But in each of these cases, the road to the execution cellar zigged and zagged and was characterized by hesitation and false starts directly attributable to Stalin. Even today, when we have a mass of revealing documents, the story remains unclear. Like any highly skilled politician, his maneuvers, his personal and political motives remain hidden.

CHAPTER ELEVEN

The Storm of 1937:
The Party Commits Suicide

All kulaks, criminals, and other anti-Soviet elements subject to punitive measures are broken down into two categories. . . . To the first category belong all the most active of the above-mentioned elements. They are subject to immediate arrest and, after consideration of their case by the troikas, to be shot.—NKVD operational order, 1937

We did not trust; that's the thing.—V. M. Molotov

THE FEBRUARY–MARCH 1937 plenum was also the stage for an incipient purge of the police. Although Yezhov had taken over leadership of the NKVD from Yagoda the previous September, most of Yagoda's senior deputies and appointees were still in place. These NKVD officials were professional chekists, having served in the police since the civil war, and removing such people unceremoniously would be disruptive and politically difficult. Not only were they entrenched political players of the nomenklatura, but their removal could raise inconvenient questions: if Yagoda and company were to be directly branded as longtime incompetents (or worse), as was becoming the fashion, the long series of political persecutions and prosecutions (against Mensheviks, Trotskyists, kulaks, and other opponents) could be challenged. When Yagoda had been replaced, therefore, his political loyalty had not been disputed, and he had been given the position of commissar of communications. Removing such people was a delicate and high-level political procedure requiring considerable preparation and "political education."

"Strengthening" the NKVD, Again

Stalin and Yezhov chose the February–March plenum as the venue for attack. The agenda contained the item "Lessons learned from the wrecking, sabotage, and espionage activities of the Japanese-German-Trotskyist agents," for which Yezhov was slated to give the main report, a denunciation of Yagoda's management of the NKVD. Since the middle of 1936, when Yezhov had summoned NKVD Deputy Commissar Yakov Agranov to a "conspiratorial meeting," Yezhov had been trying to turn Yagoda's deputies against him.[1] By early 1937 he had succeeded in "turning" several central and regional NKVD officials. In preparation for the attack he was to give at the plenum, he issued special invitations to this new "Yezhov group" within the police.

Document 144

Yezhov's request for NKVD presence at the February–March 1937 CC plenum[2]

From Protocol #66 of the meeting of the Secretariat of the Central Committee, VKP(b) of 16 February 1937

94. Request of Comrade Yezhov to permit 19 workers of the NKVD to be present at the Plenum of the Central Committee

To permit the presence of NKVD officials at the CC plenum: from the central staff: Comrades Belsky, M. Berman, Frinovsky, Mironov, Kursky, Leplevsky, Deich, Litvinov, B. Berman, Roshal; regional chiefs of the NKVD: Comrades Zakovsky (Leningrad oblast), Liushkov (Azov–Black Sea territory), Mironov (Western Siberia), Minaev (Stalingrad oblast), Dagin (Northern Caucasus), Dmitriev (Sverdlovsk oblast), Zalin (Kazakhstan); Comrade Goglidze, NKVD Georgia, and Comrade Sumbatov, NKVD Azerbaijan.

Yezhov's report attacked Yagoda's leadership indirectly by focusing on the sins of his deputy Molchanov, former chief of the Secret Political Section of the NKVD. The plenum unanimously approved a resolution closely based on Yezhov's report.

1. *Izvestiia TsK KPSS*, no. 9, 1989, 36. See also Robert Conquest, *Inside Stalin's Secret Police: NKVD Politics, 1936–39*, Stanford, 1985.
2. RTsKhIDNI, f. 17, op. 114, d. 622, l. 13.

Document 145

Resolution of the February–March 1937 CC plenum on "Lessons of the wrecking, diversionary, and espionage activities of the Japanese-German-Trotskyist agents"[3]

Approved 3 March 1937

Resolution of the Plenum of the CC of the VKP(b), "Lessons learned from the wrecking, diversionary, and espionage activities of the Japanese-German-Trotskyist agents." Adopted 3 March 1937.

The Plenum of the CC of the VKP(b) believes that all the facts brought out during the course of the investigation pertaining to the cases of the anti-Soviet Trotskyist center and its local supporters show that the NKVD was at least 4 years late in unmasking these vicious enemies of the people.

The traitors to the motherland—Trotskyists and other double-dealers in league with the German and Japanese counterintelligence services—succeeded in deploying their wrecking, sabotage, espionage, and terrorist activities with relative impunity. They succeeded in inflicting damage to the cause of socialist construction in many branches of industry and transport not only because of deficiencies in the work of party and economic organizations but also because of the feeble work in the organs of state security of the NKVD of the USSR.

Despite the repeated warnings of the CC of the VKP(b) concerning the total restructuring [*perestroika*] of chekist operations toward a more organized and more focused battle with counterrevolution (the directive of the CC of the VKP(b) and of the Council of People's Commissars [SNK] of the USSR of 8 May 1933, the secret letter by the CC of the VKP(b) concerning the lessons to be drawn from the events connected with the villainous murder of Comrade Kirov and from other events), the NKVD of the USSR did not carry out these directives of the party and government and showed itself to be incapable of unmasking the anti-Soviet Trotskyist gang in time.

As the main deficiencies in the work of state security, which have had a decisive influence on delaying the unmasking of the Trotskyist anti-Soviet organization, and which persist to this very day, we may name the following:

A) The NKVD of the USSR did not ascribe a sufficiently high priority to the work of agents. This work constitutes one of the chief levers in combating counterrevolution. Agents were recruited haphazardly and at random. As a rule, crucial districts where a network of agents ought to have been well laid out received scant attention. The network of agents was especially weak among Trotskyists, Zinovievists, and rightists, even in places of their greatest concentration. In addition, there was hardly a network of agents in any of the anti-Soviet organizations abroad, including Trotskyist organizations. The chief operational officials of the NKVD did not as a rule concern themselves with agents. Meetings with agents and the obtaining of information from them were carried out by poorly qualified low-rank officials of the NKVD.

B) In all of its operations, the NKVD of the USSR carried out an incorrect punitive policy, particularly as it pertains to Trotskyists and other enemies of the Soviet system [*stroi*].

An analysis of the arrests carried out in the years 1935–36 demonstrates that the main thrust of the operations of state security was directed not against organized counterrevolutionary organizations but chiefly against isolated incidents of anti-Soviet agitation, against every sort of malfeasance in office, hooliganism, ordinary crimes [*bytovye prestupleniia*], and so on.[4] Around 80% of those arrested and subjected to punitive measures in the years 1935–36 fall into the category of petty crimes of every sort, a category belonging essentially within the jurisdiction of the [regular] police and not that of the organs of state security.

C) Even more intolerable are the prison procedures established by the NKVD of the USSR as it pertains to Trotskyists, Zinovievists, rightists, SRs, and other thoroughly vicious enemies of Soviet power who have been convicted.

All of these enemies of the people were as a rule assigned to so-called political isolation prisons,[5] which were placed under the command of the NKVD of the USSR. Conditions in these political isolation prisons were particularly favorable. The prisons resembled forced vacation homes more than prisons.

In these political isolation prisons, inmates were afforded the opportunity of associating closely with each other, of discussing all political matters taking place in the country, of working out plans for anti-Soviet operations to be carried out by their organizations, and of maintaining relationships with people on the outside. The convicts were granted the right to unrestricted use of literature, paper, and writing instruments, the right to receive an unlimited number of letters and telegrams, to acquire their own personal effects [*inventar'*] and keep them in their cells, and to receive, along with their official rations, packages from the outside in any number and containing any type of goods.

However, the dilatory character with which the anti-Soviet activities of the Trotskyist bandits were unmasked is explained not only by these general deficiencies in the work of state security but also by the concrete criminal activities of individual officials in key positions of the Cheka, and in particular by the criminal activities of Molchanov, former head of the Secret Political Section of the Chief Administration of State Security (GUGB) of the NKVD of the USSR.

This criminal activity manifested itself above all in the fact that the Secret

---

4. Reference here is to the reluctance of local and regional NKVD chiefs to investigate or arrest members of party machines and the corresponding tendency to direct the heat toward ordinary and unprotected people.

5. *izoliator*, special prison for political detainees—Trans.

Political Section already had in its possession, as early as the years 1932–33, all the information necessary for fully exposing the monstrous conspiracy by the Trotskyists against Soviet power. In 1932 the Secret Political Section of the Chief Administration of State Security of the NKVD had at its disposal sufficient materials submitted by agents which contained direct references to the existence of a Trotskyist center headed by I. N. Smirnov and sufficient materials concerning Smirnov's connections with Trotsky and his son Sedov and concerning the terrorist intentions of many important Trotskyists.[6] It was clear from these materials that the Trotskyist center was establishing organizational ties with local groups of Trotskyists and that it was carrying out the directive calling for the formation of a bloc with Zinovievists and rightists.

It was on the basis of these materials submitted by agents that the Trotskyist group headed by Smirnov was arrested at the beginning of 1933. Having at its disposal such materials as those submitted by agents, the investigation was afforded the full opportunity of thoroughly exposing all of the organizational ties and all of the criminal terrorist activities of the Trotskyists and Zinovievists. Nonetheless, the investigation was carried out with such criminal negligence that the principal materials of the case, supplied by agents, were not utilized. The head of the Trotskyist center, I. N. Smirnov, was interrogated only concerning his attitude toward collectivization; Safonova, a very active member of the Trotskyist center, was asked only whether she had read Trotsky's *My Life;* as for Ter-Vaganian, the [interrogators] were only interested in his disagreements with the party line; Pereverzev, a terrorist and an emissary of Trotsky, was never interrogated at all. As a result of conducting the investigation in such a criminal way, the accused were able to get away with mild punishment and were sent to the political isolation prisons and into exile [*ssylka*], where they were granted the widest opportunities for the continuation of their anti-Soviet criminal activities.

Totally without parallel is the case of a secret agent of the NKVD board for the Moscow region by the name of Z-n.[7] Beginning in November 1933, agent Z-n gave warning in a number of his reports of anti-Soviet operations deployed by Trotskyists, of the existence of a leading Trotskyist center, and of the participation of Dreitser, Muralov, Piatakov, Radek, and others in the active work of the center. The materials submitted by agent Z-n speak openly of the terroristic views of Trotskyists and point to the close ties between Trotskyists [here] and abroad and to the ties between imprisoned Trotskyists and the world outside. On the basis of materials submitted by Z-n, Khrustalev and Zilberman, active Trotskyists-terrorists, were arrested. Nevertheless, Molchanov, the former head of the Secret Political Section, redirected the investigation in such a way that as a result these active Trotskyists, Khrustalev and

6. For details on the Trotskyist secret bloc of 1932, see J. Arch Getty, "Trotsky in Exile: The Founding of the Fourth International," *Soviet Studies,* 38(1), January 1986, 24–35.
7. Thus abbreviated in the original—Trans.

Document 145 *continued*

Zilberman, were released, while agent Z-n was exiled [*soslan*] for 5 years on a charge of provocation. Meanwhile, in the person of Khrustalev we saw released one of the most ferocious enemies of Soviet power, the owner of an apartment that served as a secret rendezvous for the Moscow Trotskyist terrorist center, and from which Comrade Stalin's itineraries were watched and observed. . . .

Moreover, Molchanov, being personally connected with the Trotskyist Furer, systematically told him about the secret facts available in the Secret Political Section concerning the anti-Soviet activities of the Trotskyists. As it has now been established by the investigation, Furer, acting on the direct instructions of Livshits, head of the entire Trotskyist sabotage-espionage terrorist organization in the field of transport, inquired about it from Molchanov.

These are examples of criminal activities of certain officials of the NKVD and in particular of Molchanov, former head of the Secret Political Section of the Chief Administration of State Security.

These are the main reasons why the NKVD failed to unmask in time the monstrous anti-Soviet conspiracy by Trotskyist agents of the German-Japanese counterintelligence services. . . .

The Plenum of the Central Committee of the VKP(b) expresses its firm conviction that all chekists will thoroughly learn the lessons of mistakes connected with the unmasking of the anti-Soviet, Zinovievist, and Trotskyist conspiracy, that, as true Bolsheviks, they will correct their mistakes as soon as possible and justify in their deeds their lofty title as the leading armed detachment of the party of Lenin and Stalin.

Yagoda had attempted to defend himself by refuting the charges of lax leadership and by claiming that he had in fact taken the lead in investigating and arresting Trotskyists. One of Yezhov's new followers, Leningrad NKVD chief Leonid Zakovsky, took the lead in attacking Yagoda and Molchanov. His speech, and that of Agranov that followed, provides a rare glimpse inside NKVD politics and party-police relations.

Document 146

From L. M. Zakovsky's speech to the February–March 1937 CC plenum[8]

I) L. M. Zakovsky's appearance before the Plenum of the CC of the VKP(b) 3 March 1937

8. RTsKhIDNI, f. 17, op. 2, d. 598, ll. 2–4, 12–15, 17–18. Typed, corrected minutes.

Document 146 *continued*

Zakovsky: Comrades, yesterday we heard Comrade Yezhov's report concerning treason and betrayal in the apparat of state security. Comrade Yezhov revealed the causes for this phenomenon and analyzed that which has caused our party a great deal of sorrow and inflicted damage on the economy of our country.

We heard what I would consider a very incoherent speech by Comrade Yagoda, our former commissar for internal affairs, and I believe that the Plenum of the Central Committee of the party cannot be satisfied with it. First of all, Comrade Yagoda's speech contained many errors, very incorrect, inexact [assertions], and, I would add, no political [assessment]. It is not true that Yagoda's hands were tied and that he could not manage the apparat of state security.

Yagoda: I didn't say that.

Zakovsky: That's exactly what you said.

Yagoda: I said that operational leadership was not concentrated in my hands.

Zakovsky: This operational leadership was in your hands. We all know too well that Comrade Frinovsky controls the armies of the NKVD better than you or I; we all know that Comrade Belsky has been engaged in [controlling] the [regular] police, that Comrade Prokofiev has been in charge of administrative matters, while Berman has done a pretty good job in building the canal—and so, operational leadership was in fact in your hands.

Yagoda: And what was Agranov doing?

Andreev: Comrade Yagoda, do not interfere, I'll put your name on the list [of speakers].

Zakovsky: . . . But it must be said openly that what has been happening in our apparat for some time now has had little to do with party spirit [*partiinost'*]. Party spirit and Bolshevik principles have been lacking in our apparat for the past several years. It was this that gave rise to intrigues, squabbles, and favoritism in personnel [*podbor svoikh liudei*].

Yagoda: What squabbles, what favoritism? Tell me, what intrigues?

Zakovsky: Didn't you kick out Comrade Yevdokimov and Comrade Akulov?

Yagoda: I didn't kick him out. He was removed in accordance with a directive of the CC.

Zakovsky: In your directives, Comrade Yagoda, you frequently made reference to the directives of the CC.

Yagoda: Not without good reasons.

Zakovsky: Sometimes without any good reason. In carrying out your directives, you've always reinforced them by stating that they have been coordinated with the Central Committee. And for that reason, Comrade Yagoda, you succeeded, little by little, in gradually creating [your own] apparat, in putting your own people on the staff of the [Chief] Administration of State Security, people who, in essence, lacked self-criticism, so that even the forms of management under the conditions of such an apparat were not entirely in the party spirit. . . .

I would like, comrades, to bring up a certain directive dated August 1934. It is a report by Comrade Yagoda made at the operational conference of officials of the Chief Administration of State Security. Certain views pertaining to our work are proposed in this report, and our campaign against counterrevolution is given a certain direction. . . .

There is not a word in this directive about Trotskyists, or Zinovievists, not to mention the right deviationists, apart from a passage from Comrade Stalin's report at the January plenum,[9] where reference is made to the tactics employed by the class enemy.

I believe that the policy represented by this directive, and not only by this one, was to divert necessary attention from materials pertaining to Zinovievists and Trotskyists which were in our possession. It was this that constituted our main political mistake and, if you will, our crime.

I believe that such an operational policy is a cover, in essence, for terror, sabotage, and espionage. . . .

I would now like to talk about the political line after the murder of S. M. Kirov. We all thought that we were through with the Zinovievists—so thought the central apparat under the leadership of Comrade Yagoda.

Day in and day out and in all of our conversations after the murder of Comrade Kirov, Comrade Zhdanov directed the apparat of the Leningrad NKVD against the Trotskyist-Zinovievist underground. And I must say that it took a long time, but, step by step, by utilizing the resources of our agents, we gradually reached the core of the Trotskyist-Zinovievist underground. At the beginning of 1936, Comrade Yagoda announced at last that the party's Central Committee gave permission to strike a blow at the Trotskyist underground. This blow was aimed only at the Trotskyists. It had been decided beforehand that Trotskyists who had been involved in counterrevolutionary actions would be deported [*vyslat'*] to Kolyma. When the operation, prompted by [NKVD] agents, was launched in Leningrad, we were convinced once again that we were dealing here not only with Trotskyists but also with Zinovievists and that our materials concerning a bloc [of Trotskyists and Zinovievists] were essentially confirmed. I myself—when I examined these materials—found myself in a difficult position. There were not only Trotskyists here but both Trotskyists and Zinovievists. (Laughter.) Both Trotskyists and Zinovievists were united in one counterrevolutionary underground [bloc]. . . .

One other circumstance: when Yakovlev and Zaidel first testified against Zinoviev and Kamenev in the case involving the academician,[10] the central

9. Probably a reference to the January 1933 plenum.
10. Reference unknown.

apparat fell into a state of confusion and dismay as if the apparat were not in possession of facts furnished by agents that would allow it to verify this case. How are we to explain this?

Yagoda: It was you, Zakovsky, who were in a state of confusion.

Zakovsky: It was not I who was confused and dismayed. I will tell you about it. I didn't conceal any materials. There was no reason [for me] to be confused. There was also the time when Karev gave testimony against Bukharin and against the right deviationists in general. I reported to Yagoda that Karev gave testimony against Bukharin. Yagoda replied: "What testimony, what right deviationists?! What are you talking about?!"

Yagoda: That's not true! I considered Kamenev and Zinoviev guilty of the murder the whole time.

Zakovsky: I don't know what you thought. I'm just telling it the way it was. You asked "What right deviationists?" I answered: "Bukharin." You then said: "You always come up with things like that."

I should add that Karev gave very convincing evidence concerning the counterrevolutionary activities of the right deviationists. There was no confusion or dismay whatever [in our agency] in Leningrad. When Prigozhin first gave testimony against Radek, everybody was also thrown into confusion. Didn't you believe it?

Yagoda: I summoned Prigozhin to Moscow.

Zakovsky: When did you summon him to Moscow? You summoned me to Moscow and asked: "How could there be such horrifying documents in your department?!" Yes, the documents were horrifying, but they proved to be true. Who was confused here, you or me?

Now about sabotage: materials concerning sabotage were being received at the very beginning of the investigation, but you said that this was a case not of sabotage but only of terror. . . .

In my opinion, comrades, it is not Molchanov who is the issue here. Our system does not allow for one person to run the apparat, to take possession of all operational materials and to conceal them from the party, from the leadership of the NKVD and from the country. Isn't that true? We were dealing here with a whole succession of counterrevolutionary actions.

A voice: That's true.

Yakov Agranov had been named Yezhov's deputy commissar of the NKVD in the same 1936 Politburo resolution under which Yezhov was appointed, and Yezhov had used Agranov to undermine Yagoda for some time. Although the evidence is slim, it seems that Agranov had tried to play both sides of the fence by imple-

menting Yezhov's directives in such a way as not to offend Yagoda.
He now came under attack for this ambiguity.[11]

Document 147

From Ya. S. Agranov's speech to the February–March 1937 CC plenum, 3 March 1937[12]

Agranov: Under the cover of the exclusive secrecy surrounding chekist
work, an antiparty idea has been insistently drummed in veiled form into the
heads of chekists to the effect that it is absolutely shameful to point out to the
party organization deficiencies existing in the organs of the NKVD, that it
would be a gross violation of chekist discipline and chekist secrecy to do so,
and that it would inflict damage to departmental "honor." . . .

The organs of the Cheka were being artificially transformed into a closed
world, where it frequently was the practice, crudely and at times under direct
threat, to silence every manifestation of political and operational initiative on
the part of chekists who dare to point out to their superiors the necessity for
taking measures against this or that counterrevolutionary formation. . . .

Zhukov: Whom did Molchanov answer to?

Agranov: I'll talk about it later. I want to emphasize in particular the fact that
the chekists, including the Cheka's leading personnel, had been constantly
inculcated with the idea that the Cheka was its own boss, a house unto itself,
and which consequently could not admit so much as a ray of party light.

Here is an instructive example: In the summer of 1936, I happened to be
holding discussions with Comrade Yagoda concerning the convening of a
certain interdepartmental commission consisting of representatives of the
procuracy and the courts. When I pointed out to Comrade Yagoda that this
matter had to be coordinated with Comrade Yezhov, secretary of the CC of the
VKP(b), he replied curtly: "If you're not the boss in your own house, then go
ahead and coordinate your work with him."

It goes without saying that I coordinated this matter with Comrade Yezhov
and told him about this.

A voice: So you are not the boss, are you?!

Agranov: I must admit that such an openly "bossy" declaration by Comrade
Yagoda shocked me. I understood it as the expression of a certain irritation on
the part of Comrade Yagoda against the party monitoring [*kontrol'*] of the
NKVD implemented by Comrade Yezhov in the course of the past 2 or 3 years.

---

11. Agranov was not arrested until mid-1937. Three weeks after the plenum, he
addressed an NKVD conference on the sins of Molchanov. See *Izvestiia TsK KPSS*,
no. 8, 1989, 84.

12. RTsKhIDNI, f. 17, op. 2, d. 598, ll. 23–26, 29–35, 41, 42. Typed, corrected
minutes.

I was shocked because, as far as I'm concerned, there's no such thing as one's own house or one's own department, not in my case or in that of the overwhelming majority of Bolshevik chekists, nor can there be such a thing because we would never place our departmental interests before the interests of the party. . . .

It shall become evident from what follows as to how this came about. Let me tell you about it. In his extensive report, Comrade Yezhov adduced a great many facts attesting to the criminal disregard by Molchanov of direct warnings by agents concerning terrorist activities carried out by Trotskyists and right deviationists. As an illustration of this, I would like to bring up Molchanov's resistance to the offensive carried out against the Trotskyists in 1935.

In the middle of 1935 Comrade Yezhov told me that in his opinion and in the opinion of the party's Central Committee, there was in our country a Trotskyist center that had not yet been exposed. Comrade Yezhov gave me official sanction to carry out an operation against Trotskyists in Moscow. I ordered Comrade Molchanov to prepare for such an operation and informed Comrade Yagoda about it.

Utilizing every kind of pretext and pointing out that preparatory measures for such an operation were not yet complete, Molchanov did not so much as begin to carry out this order.

I then instructed Comrade Redens of the NKVD board for Moscow region to provide me with information about the existence of underground Trotskyist groups in Moscow. I received a detailed report from the NKVD board for Moscow region, which made it clear that there existed in Moscow several dozen active conspiratorial Trotskyist groups, including the Dreitser group.

In view of the fact that my oral instructions (it is customary for us, for the sake of speed, to give oral instructions) were not carried out, I gave a written order [*prikazanie*] to Molchanov immediately to present to me a plan of operations for the liquidation of all counterrevolutionary Trotskyist nests. . . .

Molchanov tried to prove that the number of Trotskyists operating actively in Moscow was not so great. Nevertheless, in spite of this, I urgently proposed to carry out this operation. Unfortunately, I was absent for a long time afterward due to illness, and it was not until June 1936 that I found out that the operation against the Trotskyists had never been carried out, that, subsequent to my written order, Molchanov summoned the chief operational officials of the NKVD board for Moscow region and scolded them crudely for having provided me with the [above-mentioned] information. He tried to prove to them that no serious Trotskyist underground existed in Moscow. If we add to this the conscious disregard by Molchanov of all warnings by agents concerning the terrorist activities of Trotskyists and right deviationists, then it becomes clear why the apparat of the Investigative-Judicial Department (SPO) turned out to be incapable of exposing the Trotskyist plot in time.

Beria: But you shouldn't have given orders, you should have organized it yourself.

Agranov: The apparat was in the hands of Molchanov.

Gamarnik: So it turns out that Molchanov was more powerful than the people's commissar and the deputy people's commissar?

Beria: You should have sat down with Molchanov and taken care of the whole business.

Agranov: I ought to say, comrades, that we were invariably saved from failures and mistakes by the concrete assistance shown by the Central Committee of our party to organs of state security and that it was this assistance that led us onto the true path of fighting the enemy.

In this connection, I ought to tell the plenum how, with the help and thanks to the instructions of the CC of our party, we succeeded in putting the investigation into the Trotskyist-Zinovievist terrorist plot back on the right track. We did this in spite of the wrong policy pursued in this case by Comrades Yagoda and Molchanov.

Most assuredly, Molchanov tried to wind up the case and complete the investigation as early as 1936. He tried to prove that the unmasked Shemelev-Olberg-Safonova terrorist group associated with I. N. Smirnov did in fact constitute the all-Union Trotskyist center and that, with the exposure of this center, the active members of the Trotskyist leadership [*aktiv*] had been liquidated. Comrade Yagoda—and Molchanov after him—asserted, moreover, that, without question, Trotsky himself had had no direct contact with representatives of the Trotskyist center in the USSR. Comrade Yagoda also made this categorical assertion in his report at the June Plenum of the CC in 1936. . . . In such a state of affairs, the full unmasking and liquidation of the Trotskyist gang would surely have been disrupted, had not the Central Committee of the party intervened.

In June of last year, upon my return after my illness, Comrade Yezhov, secretary of the CC of the VKP(b), conveyed to me Comrade Stalin's remarks to the effect that mistakes were committed by the investigation into the Trotskyists' case and commissioned me to take measures to expose the real Trotskyist center, to reveal to the very last detail the terrorist gang which had clearly not yet been unmasked and Trotsky's personal role in all of this. . . .

I must say, comrades, that ours is not the usual apparat; it is a secret apparat. If Comrade Yagoda gave instructions to Molchanov, he could have concealed this from me, and I would have found out about it a year later.

A voice: You have the right to check up on all operations.

Agranov: Comrade Yagoda declared here that his mistake lay in the fact that the leadership of the Main Administration for State Security (GUGB) was not concentrated in his hands. That's not true! One need only point out the operational conferences of department heads held daily by Comrade Yagoda during the course of 1935–36. These conferences constituted an ersatz leadership of the Main Administration for State Security. They took up an immense amount of time, deprived us of our individual responsibility and brought nothing but disorder into our work. Leading operational officials spent several hours each day preparing for these meetings, squandering their efforts to no purpose. . . .

Comrades! It is absolutely clear that the old leadership of the NKVD has turned out to be incapable of managing state security.

The Central Committee of our party acted wisely in placing Comrade Yezhov, secretary of the CC of our party, at the head of the NKVD.

The person to head the militant organ of the proletarian dictatorship ought to be someone invested with the full trust of the party of Lenin and Stalin.

The appointment of Comrade Yezhov has cleared the air with its strong, bracing party spirit.

Four months at most have passed since Comrade Yezhov has taken over leadership. And the organs of state security have begun to swiftly consolidate, made compact by a powerful party-Bolshevik cement. Once again we have become capable of taking the offensive, once again we are mobilized to crush all enemies of Communism.

There is no doubt that under the leadership and with the help of the Central Committee of our party and of our leader, Comrade Stalin, and under the militant Stalinist leadership of Comrade Yezhov, we shall succeed in short order like true Bolsheviks in correcting all of our mistakes, in raising the fighting efficiency of our people to its appropriate heights. We shall succeed in learning to unmask the enemy skillfully and promptly. We shall succeed in learning, as Comrade Stalin has repeatedly taught us, to carry out our actions to the end, to carry out to the last detail the full extermination of Trotskyist agents and other agents of fascism and to root out, without vestiges, all enemies of Soviet power.

Molotov: And, above all, in deeds and not merely in words.

The attack on Yagoda had been strong, but inexplicable delays surround his downfall. At the end of the discussion, an especially aggressive member, I. P. Zhukov, called directly for Yagoda's arrest. Zhukov was always trying to display his vigilance, and his attacks on Bukharin had been so wild as to elicit laughter from the plenum. Now he went beyond the script and had to be restrained:

ZHUKOV: Because this business needs to be investigated, and in order to investigate it, it is necessary to give instructions to the NKVD, to Comrade Yezhov. He will conduct the matter perfectly—(Noise in the hall.)

A VOICE: I don't understand. What is the proposal?

Yezhov: Everybody is arrested.

Zhukov: Why not arrest Yagoda? (Noise in the hall.) Yes, yes. I am convinced that the matter will come to that.

Kosior: What is your proposal? (Movement and noise in the hall.)

A voice: What is the proposal? It's not necessary to agree to anything.[13]

Yagoda was neither expelled from the party nor arrested by the plenum. Yet one month later, the Politburo ordered exactly those penalties. When that decree was promulgated, the text contained a note of unusual urgency about arresting the former NKVD chief that seemed to contradict the plenum's hesitation to take the step just a few weeks before. It is likely that in the intervening weeks, Molchanov and others from Yagoda's circle were arrested and forced to give testimony implicating Yagoda in "criminal activities."

Even after the decision was taken to expel and arrest Yagoda, there seems to have been some indecision. The order exists in two variants, the second (signed by Stalin) expressing the urgent need for the arrest. Even then, Yagoda was not dismissed from his position as commissar for communications for another week.[14]

Document 148(a)

Politburo order to arrest Yagoda, 31 March to 1 April 1937, version 1[15]

Decree of the Plenum of the CC of the VKP(b) (by polling members of the CC of the VKP(b))

31 March to 1 April 1937

Re: Yagoda

The following proposal by the Politburo of the CC is to be confirmed [by the CC]:

In view of the antistate and criminal acts—now brought to light—committed by Yagoda, the people's commissar for communications, during his tenure as people's commissar for internal affairs as well as after his transfer to the

---

13. *Voprosy istorii,* no. 2, 1995, 21.

14. RTsKhIDNI, f. 17, op. 3, d. 985, ll. 3, 34.

15. RTsKhIDNI, f. 17, op. 2, d. 614, l. 94. This is a Politburo document. Although the Central Committee was not in session at this time, the Politburo frequently took decisions in the CC's name, subject to formal confirmation at the next plenum.

ОПРОСОМ ЧЛЕНОВ ЦК ВКП

от 31.Ш-1.1У.37г.

<u>О Ягода.</u>

Утвердить следующее предложение Политбюро ЦК:

Ввиду обнаруженных антигосударственных и уголовных преступлений Наркома Связи Ягода, совершенных в бытность его Наркомом Внутренних Дел, а также после его перехода в Наркомат Связи, считать необходимым исключение его из партии и ЦК и ~~немедленный~~ его арест.

санкционировка

СЕКРЕТАРЬ ЦК

Оригинал сдан в архив.

DOCUMENT 148(A). Politburo order to arrest Yagoda, 31 March to
1 April 1937 (first version, with Stalin's initials)

Document 148(a) *continued*

People's Commissariat for Communications, it is considered necessary to expel him from the party and from the CC and to sanction his arrest.

Secretary of the CC [No signature]

[marginal notes in handscript:]
1. Send copy to Yezhov. 2. The original has been sent to the archives.

Document 148(b)

Politburo order to arrest Yagoda, 31 March, 17, 20 May 1937, version 2[16]

Excerpts-decision[17] from the protocol of the Plenum of the CC VKP(b)
31 March, 17, 20 May 1937
(a) On Yagoda. 31 March 1937

In view of the antistate and criminal acts—now brought to light—committed by Yagoda, the people's commissar for communications, during his tenure as people's commissar for internal affairs as well as after his transfer to the People's Commissariat for Communications, the Politburo considers it necessary to expel him from the party and from the CC and to order his immediate arrest.

The Politburo of the CC of the VKP(b) undertakes to inform the members of the CC of the VKP that, in view of the danger of leaving Yagoda at liberty for so much as one day, it is compelled to order his immediate arrest. The Politburo of the CC of the VKP(b) asks the members of the CC of the VKP(b) to sanction Yagoda's expulsion from the party and from the CC and to sanction his arrest.

Acting under the instructions of the Politburo of the CC of the VKP(b)
I. Stalin,
Secretary of the CC of the VKP

[Autograph votes of certain members of the CC]:
I vote for!! And I am especially pleased that the scoundrel was unmasked. Zhukov. 31 March.
I vote for. Rudzutak.
STRICTLY SECRET.
Workers of the world, unite!
ALL-UNION COMMUNIST PARTY (Bolshevik)
CENTRAL COMMITTEE

---

16. RTsKhIDNI, f. 17, op. 2, d. 614, ll. 103, 119.

17. All such excerpt-decisions, forwarded to all members and candidate members of the CC, were printed on special forms stamped: "Subject to return at the Second Division of the Special Sector of the CC of the VKP(b)."

In the days following Yagoda's arrest, Yezhov began shifting around regional and central NKVD personnel in order to put his loyal followers into key positions. He also began a series of "mobilizations" of dependable cadres to staff the NKVD, drawing them from the ideological party schools.

Document 149

Politburo decision on chiefs of the NKVD[18]

From Protocol #48 of the Politburo meeting of 16 April 1937

57. On the chiefs [nachal'niki] of the NKVD

1. To appoint Comrade Dagin chief of the NKVD in Gorky region, relieving him from work as chief of the NKVD in Ordzhonikidzevsky territory.

2. To appoint Comrade Bulakh chief of the NKVD in Ordzhonikidzevsky territory.

3. To relieve Comrade Gendin from work as chief of the NKVD in the Western region in connection with his appointment as deputy chief of the Fourth Department of the Chief Administration of State Security of the NKVD USSR.

4. To appoint Comrade Karutsky as chief of the NKVD in the Western oblast, relieving him from his position as deputy commissar of NKVD Belorussia.

5. To relieve Comrade Zalpeter from work as chief of the NKVD of Krasnoiarsk territory in connection with his appointment as deputy chief of the Second Department of the Chief Administration of State Security of the NKVD USSR.

6. To appoint Comrade Leoniuk as chief of the NKVD for Krasnoiarsk territory.

Document 150

Orgburo order on NKVD recruitment[19]

From Protocol #71 of the Orgburo meeting of 29 April 1937

89. On workers for the NKVD USSR (Politburo order of 17 April 1937, Protocol #49.)

To put at the disposal of the NKVD USSR the following comrades, relieving them from study at the Higher School of Party Organizers Attached to the CC VKP(b): Amosov, Azmolinsky, [here follow the names of 43 persons]

18. RTsKhIDNI, f. 17, op. 3, d. 986, ll. 16–17.
19. RTsKhIDNI, f. 17, op. 114, d. 627, ll. 17, 76, 86, 104.

And the jails began to fill up to the point that the system began to strain.

Document 151
Politburo order on maintaining those arrested in preliminary detention cells[20]

From Protocol #47 of the Politburo meeting
7 April 1937
109. On maintaining those arrested in preliminary detention cells of the militia [regular police].

Comrade Yezhov's proposal for the establishment in remote districts of a policy whereby persons under arrest are to be held for 10 days in the temporary custody of the [regular] police is to be agreed to. Furthermore, in such cases persons under arrest are to be provided with hot meals.

Cadres in Trouble: After the February Plenum

The February–March plenum had written a new political transcript for the party. It had raised the level of "vigilance" against oppositionists and enemies to new heights and established the principle that the enemy was everywhere. It had also criticized the regional nomenklatura for not being vigilant enough to prevent infiltration by those enemies. These regional bosses were taken to task for bureaucratism, suppression of criticism, undemocratic practices, and paying too much attention to economic management.

In the precise texts of the plenum, these themes were discrete: The opposition was the enemy, but the cadres were just careless. The enemy had to be destroyed, but poor cadres should be retrained and indoctrinated. In the wake of the plenum, however, these themes began to blur together. Partly as a result of the new "criticism from below" campaign, incompetent, abusive, or unpopular party leaders in the provinces were more and more often branded as enemies themselves. Carelessly tolerating the enemy became protecting the enemy. Suppression of the rank and file gradually became Trotskyist sabotage of party norms. Not catch-

20. RTsKhIDNI, f. 17, op. 3, d. 985, l. 3.

ing a wrecker became wrecking. Reports on the February 1937 plenum to local organizations show increasing paranoia and vigilance. The stated differences between Trotskyists and rightists and among various foreign enemies ran together in the popular mind.

Document 152

Azov–Black Sea party organization information on the February–March 1937 CC plenum[21]

Protocol #8 of the eighth plenum of the Azov–Black Sea Territorial Committee of the VKP(b)

14–16 March 1937

1. Information pertaining to the decisions of the Plenum of the CC (Comrade Yevdokimov).

a) The plenum of the Azov–Black Sea Territorial Committee of the VKP(b) fully and wholeheartedly approves the decisions of the Plenum of the CC of the VKP(b) and obliges all party organizations to immediately proceed in a true Bolshevik manner to their practical implementation.

The plenum welcomes the expulsion of Bukharin and Rykov from the party as double-dealers and as ringleaders of right deviationists and accomplices of Japanese-German-Trotskyist agents of fascism.

The plenum obliges all party organizations to make every party worker and every party member aware of the decisions of the Plenum of the CC.

Implementing Comrade Stalin's slogan on mastering Bolshevism, the Azov–Black Sea party organization resolves to raise the level of party political work to meet the demands placed upon it by the turn of events in the political life of the country represented by the introduction of the Stalin constitution, and it resolves to stand at the head of the working masses of the region during the elections to be conducted in accordance with the new electoral system.

Document 153

Ye. Yevdokimov's report to the Azov–Black Sea Territorial Party Committee on the February–March 1937 CC Plenum[22]

From Ye. Yevdokimov's report to the eighth plenum of the Azov–Black Sea Territorial Committee VKP(b) summarizing the Plenum of the Central Committee VKP(b)

14 March 1937

21. RTsKhIDNI, f. 17, op. 21, d. 2196, l. 309.
22. RTsKhIDNI, f. 17, op. 21, d. 2197, ll. 78, 36, 44–46, 66, 93, 96–98.

. . . Meanwhile the enemy is wide awake. The facts in our possession show that counterrevolutionary clergymen and sectarians are very actively preparing for the elections, agitating in their communities and preparing to submit their candidacies for the secret ballot. And we must not forget that our region included, in its time—as is well known—important church and sectarian centers of old tsarist Russia. These centers continued to exist right up until very recently. The underground counterrevolutionary activities of clergymen and sectarians in our region are still significant, and antireligious work in our region has been abandoned by everyone. As has been established by our evaluation of the situation, our party organizations take no interest in these matters. . . .

Let me now speak about the lessons to be learned from wrecking, sabotage, and espionage activities of Japanese-German-Trotskyist agents. . . .

The first warning was the villainous murder of Comrade Kirov. In its secret letter of 18 January 1935, the CC warned the entire party and all party organizations of the duplicitous activities of enemies of the party. The CC pointed out that "the stronger the USSR becomes and the more hopeless the position of our enemies, the sooner will our enemies, precisely because of their hopeless situation, slide down into the mire of terror, in view of which it is necessary for us, with all the means at our disposal, to raise the vigilance of our officials."

The Central Committee has issued a stern warning in its letter against repetition of the errors committed in the Leningrad party organization and by organs of the Leningrad NKVD.

At the plenum, Comrade Stalin said that the case of the villainous murder of Comrade Kirov speaks loudly for itself.

We received a second warning from the Central Committee in connection with the uncovering of terrorist activities perpetrated by the Trotskyist-Zinovievist bloc. . . .

Even after this grave warning, the comrades in the local organizations got busy only with difficulty. They did not ascribe sufficient importance to the development in oneself of the qualities of a Bolshevik—namely, the ability to recognize the enemy.

The party organizations and their leaders did not put into effect the necessary policy change which would have led to the intensification of party and political work. They did not fully utilize the verification of party documents and the overhauling of party machinery for the purpose of purging the party of its enemies.

And not only that—if we take our Azov–Black Sea party organization as an example, vile double-dealers, having wormed their way deceitfully into the leadership of party organizations, used the verification of party documents and the exchange [of party documents] for their counterrevolutionary aims. . . .

Sergo [G. K. Ordzhonikidze] suffered from a certain amount of excessive trust. Comrade Stalin said that Sergo was one of the best members of the Politburo, a man who had helped thousands of outstanding people grow to maturity. However, when it came to trusting people, he was weak, on account of which bad things had been overlooked. Comrade Stalin said that we all love Sergo, but the truth and the party are more precious to us than he is.

People often allege that the fulfillment of the economic plan in this or that sphere of the economy is a guarantee that this sphere is free of sabotage. But this is not true. This theory is not true and we must combat it. We must not forget that our plans are minimalist. They have been set excessively low in many places, and our enemies have taken advantage of this in order to conceal their activities. . . .

And now a few words about the right deviationists. As early as the last Plenum of the CC of the VKP(b), it had been clearly and completely proven that Bukharin and Rykov knew of the activities of the Trotskyist-Zinovievist bloc. They themselves espoused these positions. A thorough investigation into their case was conducted after the last plenum. Nearly all of the followers of the so-called "school" of Bukharin already under arrest were interrogated. This includes the man closest to Bukharin, his secretary Tseitlin,[23] some of Rykov's people (i.e., the economic managers) who were associated with him, his secretary Radin, then Uglanov. All of this testimony has established the direct complicity of the right deviationists—that is, of Bukharin and Rykov, in counterrevolutionary activities against Soviet power, against socialism, and for capitalism. In drawing up their indictment, we could use the same formula that had been applied to the Trotskyists-fascists. . . .

How did they conduct themselves at the plenum? Disgustingly. The testimony was circulated to all members of the CC. Bukharin addressed the CC and members of the plenum. He called his speech "Against the slanderers" and accused all of his friends and all of his underlings [*lychniki*] of slander. Moreover, he analyzed his case in a manner that made it appear that all of this had been contrived by the NKVD, and he attacked the CC. The following legitimate question was posed to him: "All right. You have been slandered, but why then has the man closest to you, Yefim Tseitlin, your secretary, slandered you; why have your followers, whom you have trained and brought up, why have they slandered you?" Bukharin explained that he had had a quarrel with Yefim Tseitlin. But what about the others? The others—he doesn't know why. If they had slandered you, then why are they slandering themselves by confessing to their own counterrevolutionary actions, such as preparations for terror, etc.? Why? He is at a loss. Bukharin had had many meetings with Trotskyists, Zinovievists, and his confederates. The record shows that. He had to acknowledge all these meetings and conversations, but he tried to describe them in a

---

23. Spelled Tsetlin in Documents 118, 138, and 141—Trans.

way that made it look as if he had had these conversations for purposes of edification, in order to lead his confederates away from the path of counter-revolution. . . .

Why did the Plenum of the CC spend nearly three days hearing and investigating every aspect of this case? [Because] these people have done the party certain services. The party undertook every measure to correct them, to put them on the right path. [The case of] Bukharin and Rykov is self-evident in and of itself. Their case was placed before the plenum and discussed for so long because there are enemies among us. Enemies remain not only outside the party but also within it. The speeches of Bukharin and Rykov are speeches by people who have not laid down their arms. They are appealing to those who have not as yet been unmasked, who have not as yet laid down their arms, saying: "Follow in our path, do not confess, do not lay down your arms." The meaning of all this lies in the fact that capitalism and communism are at war with each other.[24] And this is one form in which the class struggle manifests itself.

Document 154

Comrade Balashova's report on the February–March 1937 CC plenum[25]

Extract from protocol #8 of the meeting of the Azov–Black Sea Territorial Party Committee VKP(b)

16 March 1937

3. Comrade Balashova's statement

The plenum has established that Dvolaitsky, former director of the Department of Party Propaganda and Agitation of the territorial committee, has, during his tenure at this post, allowed glaring deficiencies and a loss of all party vigilance to occur in his work. This has led to the fact that enemies of the party and the people have seized the Institute of Marxism-Leninism (IML) [of the region], an institute of supreme importance for the preparation of party cadres.

In discussing the historic decisions of the Plenum of the CC of 22 February–5 March, the plenum of the territorial committee could not pass over these glaring facts in silence, and since Dvolaitsky, in his appearance at the plenum, did not critique his own mistakes, the plenum demanded an explanation from Dvolaitsky concerning the essence of the matter. Nonetheless, Dvolaitsky attempted to shift responsibility and blame for this onto other officials, assert-

24. . . . *chto idet bor'ba kapitalizma i kommunizma;* the word *bor'ba* has a very wide range of meanings, including wrestling, a fight, a struggle as in "class struggle," combat, or campaign. My use of *war* is more figurative than literal—Trans.

25. RTsKhIDNI, f. 17, op. 21, d. 2196, ll. 313–14.

ing, without any grounds for doing so, that he (Dvolaitsky) had been the object of insensitive treatment.

Beginning with an attempt to evade [self-]criticism of his mistakes, Dvolaitsky has slid onto an antiparty path by trying to commit suicide.

The plenum hereby decrees:

1) To recognize Comrade Dvolaitsky's attempted suicide—after being rightfully criticized at the plenum of the territorial committee for his poor work as the director of the Department of Propaganda and Agitation, for a host of grave political errors, and for the loss of revolutionary Bolshevik vigilance—as an antiparty act unworthy of a party member, all the more so of a member of the territorial committee of the party.

The plenum resolutely condemns such action inasmuch as all of our experience in fighting and crushing Trotskyists and other double-dealers has demonstrated that suicide is a weapon utilized by [our] enemies, who resort to it in order to evade responsibility and avoid being unmasked and in order to obstruct the cause of unmasking and crushing of counterrevolutionary, subversive activities.

2) To consider Dvolaitsky's explanation for his antiparty act unsatisfactory, insofar as the matter of Dvolaitsky has essentially not yet been investigated and insofar as he has been granted full opportunity to speak before the plenum and offer explanations and present information on any subject.

3) To recognize that Dvolaitsky's action as well as his appearance before the plenum not only does not help us draw lessons from the mistakes of the Azov–Black Sea Territorial Committee of the VKP(b) but in fact constitutes a hostile act against the decision of the Central Committee and the deployment of self-criticism.

4) To remove Dvolaitsky from the plenum of the territorial committee.

5) To instruct the buro to consider the matter of Dvolaitsky's party membership [*partiinost'*].

Ye. Yevdokimov,
Secretary of the Azov–Black Sea Territorial Committee of the VKP(b)

That the regional party leaders were coming more and more under a cloud following the February–March 1937 plenum is clear from several events. First, on the basis of a speech by A. A. Zhdanov, the Central Committee ordered regional party leaders to stand for reelection in May. Heretofore, such elections had been purely a formality; they were not secret, and the regional nomenklatura was able to keep its people in power because no one below was willing openly to oppose the leadership's candidates. This time, though, the rules were different. The elections were to be held by secret ballot, and it seems to have been the intention of the Moscow leaders to take advantage of rank-and-file party hostility to local chiefs in order to control those chiefs "from below" with an election. If the party elections of May 1937 were meant to dethrone territorial party leaders, they were a failure. Although there was significant turnover in district and cell committees, the upper reaches of the regional party elite remained in office through spring 1937.[26]

A second, less publicized event was just as important. Another of the mechanisms that regional "family circles" had used to protect themselves was the inclusion of the local NKVD chief in the machine. Although nominally it reported to Moscow, the regional NKVD was more often than not part of the local party group. As long as the long-serving NKVD chiefs remained in place, they tended to defend party leaders who were being criticized from below.[27] Few prominent local party machine members were arrested, and police persecution fell on ordinary people for minor offenses (see Document 145). In spring 1937 this situation began to change, as Yezhov quietly replaced the regional NKVD leaders (see Documents 149 and 150). At the same time, party organizations inside the security services were transferred from the control of the territorial party committees to the police themselves, thereby detaching local NKVD officials from those committees.

Document 155

Orgburo order transferring NKVD party cells from party committees to the NKVD[28]

From Protocol #67 of the Orgburo of the CC of the VKP(b)
25 March 1937
11. Re: Request by the NKVD for the transfer of party organizations of the main and district boards for the border and for internal security of the NKVD

---

26. See J. Arch Getty, *Origins of the Great Purges: The Soviet Communist Party Reconsidered, 1933–1938,* New York, 1991, chapter 6, for an analysis of the 1937 party elections.

27. See, for example, Roberta T. Manning, "The Great Purges in a Rural District: Belyi Raion Revisited," in J. Arch Getty and Roberta T. Manning, eds., *Stalinist Terror: New Perspectives,* New York, 1993, 168–97.

28. RTsKhIDNI, f. 17, op. 114, d. 623, l. 5.

from city committees and district committees of the VKP(b) to the political organs for the border and for internal security of the NKVD (Comrades Roshal, Malenkov, and Yezhov).

a) Primary party organizations, operating on the basis of "Instructions to the organizations of the VKP(b) in the Red Army," are to be organized in the main and district boards for the border and for internal security of the NKVD.

b) The leadership of the party organizations of the main and district boards for the border and for internal security of the NKVD is to be transferred to the political organs for the border and for internal security.

12. Re: Dispatching of officials of the CC of the VKP(b) to various localities for the duration of the elections of party organs (Comrades Malenkov, L. M. Kaganovich, Andreev).

Comrade Malenkov is instructed to compile a list of persons who are to be sent temporarily to various localities, including officials of the CC apparat as well as students [*slushateli*] of institutions of higher learning, in particular, of the Higher School of Party Organizers.

This list is to be submitted to the Secretariat of the CC for its approval.

The Explosion

On 11 June 1937 the world was shocked at the Soviet press announcement that eight of the most senior officers of the Red Army had been arrested and indicted for treason and espionage on behalf of the Germans and Japanese. The list included the most well-known field commanders in the Soviet military: Marshal M. N. Tukhachevsky (deputy commissar of defense) and Generals S. I. Kork (commandant of the Frunze Military Academy), I. E. Yakir (commander of the Kiev Military District), and I. P. Uborevich (commander of the Belorussian Military District), among others. Arrested the last week of May, the generals were brutally interrogated by the NKVD and "confessed" by the beginning of June. On 2 June a meeting of 116 high-ranking officers heard reports by Defense Commissar Voroshilov and Stalin on the case. At that meeting, Stalin said that "without a doubt a military-political conspiracy against Soviet power had taken place, stimulated and financed by German fascists."[29] On 12 June, at an expanded session of the Military Collegium of the Supreme Court, all were convicted.

29. *Istochnik*, no. 3, 1994, 73.

They were shot on the same day.[30] Yan Gamarnik, chief of the political administration of the Red Army, had committed suicide before he could be arrested.

We still do not know why Stalin decided to decapitate the Red Army in 1937. Several possible elements may have contributed to the decision. First, Tukhachevsky and the others accused had frequently disagreed with Stalin's loyal but incompetent minister of defense, K. I. Voroshilov, and on at least one occasion Tukhachevsky had openly insulted him. Second, rumors had reached Stalin from Europe (apparently along with disinformation documents from the German secret police) to the effect that Tukhachevsky and his group were disloyal. Third, relations between party and army in the Soviet system had always been rocky. From time to time, the party had appointed "political commissars" to watch over the officer corps; such political watchdogs had been installed just before the arrest of the generals.[31] The Tukhachevsky group were not "party first, army second" personalities like Voroshilov, Semyon Budenny, and others who had fought alongside Stalin in the civil war. Finally, of course, the army was an armed, organized force that could conceivably challenge Stalin and the party regime for control of the country.

The officers had been under suspicion for some time. Both Stalin and Molotov had mentioned at the February–March plenum that it would be necessary to verify [*proverit'*] the military in order to weed out any enemies. The previous year Yezhov had arrested a few military officers who had been active Trotskyists at some time in the past, and the NKVD had been questioning them for months. In spring 1937 the investigators had focused on securing testimony against Tukhachevsky and his circle. It seems that several things came together in April and May: the possible receipt of the disinformation documents from Germany and the confessions of V. M. Primakov and other Trotskyist officers directly implicating Tukhachevsky.

Considerable evidence suggests that the top leadership may have

30. The most authoritative account of the "military conspiracy" based on still secret archives is in *Izvestiia TsK KPSS*, no. 4, 1989, 42–80.

31. See V. A. Zolotarev, ed., *Prikazy narodnogo komissara oborony SSSR, 1937–21 iiunia 1941g.*, Moscow, 1994, 11–13.

believed the military plot was real. In 1971 and 1975 V. M. Molotov admitted that many "mistakes" had been made in the repressions of the 1930s. But he doggedly insisted that of all the cases, that of Tukhachevsky and the generals had been clear: they were guilty of preparing a coup against Stalin. "Beginning in the second half of 1936 or maybe from the end of 1936 he was hurrying with a coup. . . . And it is understandable. He was afraid that he would be arrested. . . . We even knew the date of the coup."[32]

In 1937, in private conversation with Georgi Dimitrov, head of the Communist International, Stalin said of the oppositionists, "We knew something even last year and were getting ready to deal with them, but we waited in order to gather more clues.[33] They were getting ready at the beginning of this year to take action. But they couldn't decide. They prepared in June to seize the Politburo in the Kremlin. But they were afraid—they said 'Stalin is beginning executions and this will cause a scandal.' I said to our people—they can't make up their minds to act, and we laughed at their plans."[34]

Indeed, given the iron discipline of the nomenklatura behind Stalin, the army had been the last force capable of stopping the arrests. Bukharin, under arrest since March, may have realized this. Just before his arrest, he apparently told his wife that the current leadership wanted to destroy the Old Bolshevik oppositionists for fear that if they came to power, they would destroy the Stalinist faction. He advised her that in the event of his arrest, she should flee the country with the help of the American diplomat William Bullit, who had promised to help.[35] Later, his wife was taunted by an NKVD interrogator: "You thought that Yakir and Tukhachevsky would save your Bukharin. But we work well. That's why it didn't happen."[36] Nine days after the

32. Feliks Chuev, *Sto sorok besed*, Moscow, 1991, 418, 442.

33. *niti*: literally, threads—Trans.

34. Diary of Georgi Dimitrov, Nov. 11, 1937. Hereafter cited as Dimitrov diary, this material comes from the personal archive of the Comintern specialist F. I. Firsov, based on his archival notes from the still secret Dimitrov's diary. The author is deeply grateful to Professor Firsov for sharing his encyclopedic knowledge of repression in the Comintern.

35. RTsKhIDNI, f. 39, op. 2, d. 45, ll. 105–7. This was relayed to Stalin in March 1937 from the NKVD.

36. A. M. Larina, *Nezabyvaemoe*, Moscow, 1989, 27.

arrest of Tukhachevsky and Yakir, Bukharin wrote to Yezhov from prison and began to confess.[37]

The arrests of the generals and of several powerful civilian figures in May 1937 represent a major watershed: the first repression of large numbers of people who had never been overt oppositionists and had always sided with Stalin in the various party disputes. The new policy in the second half of 1937 was, essentially, to destroy anyone suspected of present or potential disloyalty to the ruling Stalin group. As Molotov put it,

> 1937 was necessary. . . . We were obligated in 1937 [to ensure] that in time of war there would be no fifth column. Really among Bolsheviks there were and are those who are good and faithful when everything is good, when the country and the party are not in danger. But if anything happens, they shiver and desert. I don't think that the rehabilitation [by Khrushchev] of many military men, repressed in 1937, was correct. The documents are hidden now, but with time there will be clarity. It is doubtful that these people were spies, but they were connected with spies, and the main thing is that in the decisive moment there was no relying on them. . . . If Tukhachevsky and Yakir and Rykov and Zinoviev in time of war went into opposition, it would cause such a sharp struggle, there would be a colossal number of victims. Colossal. And on the other hand, it would mean doom. It would be impossible to surrender, it [the internal struggle] would go to the end. We would begin to destroy everyone mercilessly. Somebody would, of course, win in the end, but on both sides there would be huge casualties.[38]

There is no evidence that the accused officers were involved in any plot against Stalin, despite rumors to the contrary.[39] Yet the leaders of the regime acted as if they believed that there was a plot, or at least as if they feared retaliation from some corner. All the officers were arrested in transit, secretly, away from their commands. Tolerating no delay, Yezhov's investigators tortured the officers mercilessly until they confessed. Analysis many years later showed that there were bloodstains on the confession signed by

---

37. Boris A. Starkov, "Narkom Yezhov," in Getty and Manning, *Stalinist Terror,* 35, based on documents in the KGB archive.

38. Chuev, *Sto sorok besed,* 390, 413.

39. See, for example, A. Svetlanin (pseud. V. Likhachev), *Dal'nevostochnyi zagovor,* Frankfurt, 1953; Walter Krivitsky, *I Was Stalin's Agent,* New York, 1939.

Tukhachevsky.[40] On the day of the trial, investigators were still beating confessions out of the accused, who were shot immediately after sentencing. In contrast with the long delays in the cases of Bukharin and some others, this was a Stalin-Yezhov coup that was presented to the country as a fait accompli.

The laconic party documents marking the party expulsion of the officers do not capture the drama and brutality of the event.

Document 156

Politburo resolution to expel Rudzutak and Tukhachevsky[41]

No. 3690
24 May 1937
To the members and candidate members of the CC VKP(b)
The Central Committee has received information implicating CC member Rudzutak and CC candidate member Tukhachevsky in participation in an anti-Soviet, Trotskyist-rightist conspiratorial bloc and in espionage work against the USSR on behalf of fascist Germany. In connection with this, the Politburo of the CC VKP(b) puts to a vote to members and candidate members of the CC VKP(b) the proposal to expel Rudzutak and Tukhachevsky from the party and transfer their cases to the NKVD.
Secretary of the CC VKP(b)
I. Stalin

[marginal notes, in handscript:]
Unconditionally yes. It's necessary to finish off this scum. S. Budenny, 25.5.37 11:20
I vote for the motion of the Politburo. 25 May 1937. Unshlikht.

---

40. *Izvestiia TsK KPSS*, no. 4, 1989, 50.
41. RTsKhIDNI, f. 17, op. 2, d. 615, l. 68.

ВСЕСОЮЗНАЯ КОММУНИСТИЧЕСКАЯ ПАРТИЯ (большевиков).
ЦЕНТРАЛЬНЫЙ КОМИТЕТ.

№ П3690   24 мая 1937 г.

ЧЛЕНАМ И КАНДИДАТАМ ЦК ВКП.

Тов. *Буденному.*

ЦК ВКП получил данные, изобличающие члена ЦК ВКП Рудзутака и кандидата ЦК ВКП Тухачевского в участии в антисоветском троцкистско-правом заговорщическом блоке и шпионской работе против СССР в пользу фашистской Германии. В связи с этим Политбюро ЦК ВКП ставит на голосование членов и кандидатов ЦК ВКП предложение об исключении из партии Рудзутака и Тухачевского и передаче их дела в Наркомвнудел.

СЕКРЕТАРЬ ЦК ВКП   *И. Стали-*

Омн

DOCUMENT 156. Politburo resolution to expel Rudzutak and Tukhachevsky, 24 May 1937 (Budenny's copy, with manuscript comment: "Unconditionally yes. It's necessary to finish off this scum.")

Document 157

Politburo proposal to expel Gamarnik and Aronshtam[42]

From Protocol #49 of the meeting of the Politburo VKP(b)
(b) 30 May 1937
390. On Comrades Gamarnik and Aronshtam
Comrades Gamarnik and Aronshtam are to be dismissed from their positions in the People's Commissariat of Defense and expelled from the military council. They have been found to be closely associated as a group with Yakir, who has been expelled from the party for taking part in a military, fascist plot.

The archives are filled with such documents, each legally required in order to expel a Central Committee member from the party before arrest. Clearly, though, it is legalism at work here and not legality. First, Rudzutak and Tukhachevsky were no longer referred to as "comrade" in the document proposing their expulsion. Procedures required that they be called comrades until their official expulsion from the party. Second, this action was taken before any trial or formal accusation or even before the "information" could be evaluated. In the atmosphere of 1937, simply "receiving information" was enough for the Politburo to seal one's fate. As was always the case in 1937, every member and candidate member of the Central Committee once again held to nomenklatura discipline and voted in favor of the resolution. Even Lenin's widow Krupskaia, who sometimes qualified her vote by answering "agreed" rather than "for," voted "for" in this case.[43]

In the ten days following the death of Tukhachevsky, 980 senior commanders were arrested. Many were tortured and shot. In the months that followed, the Soviet military establishment was devastated by arrests and executions. In 1937, 7.7 percent of the officer corps were dismissed for political reasons and never reinstated; in 1938 another 3.7 percent were removed. In that two-year period more than 33,000 military officers were discharged for political reasons; 9,941 were arrested, and 23,434 were discharged but not arrested. Of these, 11,596 were reinstated by 1940, leaving 21,779

42. RTsKhIDNI, f. 17, op. 3, d. 987, ll. 3, 94, 100.
43. RTsKhIDNI, f. 17, op. 2, d. 615, ll. 79–790b.

permanent victims either arrested or fired in the military purge.[44]
In the wake of Stalin's coup against the military, special service was
duly rewarded.

Document 158

Politburo resolution awarding the Order of Lenin to Yezhov[45]

Resolution of the Politburo
24 July 1937
Item #300. Re: Decorating Comrade N. I. Yezhov with the Order of Lenin.
The following draft decree by the Central Executive Committee of the USSR
is to be approved.
The Central Executive Committee of the USSR hereby decrees:
Comrade N. I. Yezhov is to be awarded the Order of Lenin for his outstanding success in leading the organs of the NKVD in their implementation of
governmental assignments.

The fall of the generals triggered a nationwide explosion of terror
directed at leading cadres in all fields and at all levels. In the second
half of 1937, most peoples' commissars (ministers), nearly all regional first party secretaries, and thousands of other officials were
branded traitors and arrested. The majority of these high-ranking
officials seem to have been shot in 1937–40.[46]

The first wave included a large number of members and candidate members of the Central Committee. If there had been high-
level indecision in the previous period, zigs and zags about repression of some leaders, there was none now. And if Stalin had seemed
neutral or unenthusiastic about repressing certain people, after the
fall of the generals his name is all over the horrible documents
authorizing the terror. As usual, the remaining members of the CC
voted unanimously for the proposed expulsions from the party.

---

44. Roger Reese, "The Red Army and the Great Purges," in Getty and Manning,
Stalinist Terror, 198–214; "M. N. Tukhachevskii i 'voenno-fashistskii zagovor,'
martirolog RKKA," *Voenno-Istoricheskii Arkhiv*, vypusk 2, Moscow, 1997, 105–
17.

45. RTsKhIDNI, f. 17, op. 3, d. 989, l. 60.

46. See RTsKhIDNI, f. 17, op. 2, d. 614 for numerous Politburo orders to arrest
Central Committee members and other high-ranking party leaders.

Document 159

CC resolution "On Comrades P. Alekseev, Liubimov, Sulimov, . . . "[47]

From Protocol #10, of the Plenum of the CC of the VKP(b), 23–29 June 1937

A) 23 June 1937

1. Re: Comrades P. Alekseev, Liubimov, Sulimov, Kuritsyn, Musabekov, Osinsky, and Sedelnikov.

The CC of the VKP(b) declares its lack of political confidence in Comrades Alekseev, Liubimov, and Sulimov, members of the CC of the VKP(b), and in Comrades Kuritsyn, Musabekov, Osinsky, and Sedelnikov, candidate members of the CC of the VKP(b), and hereby decrees:

That Comrades P. Alekseev, Liubimov, and Sulimov be expelled from membership in the CC of the VKP(b) and that Comrades Kuritsyn, Musabekov, Osinsky, and Sedelnikov be expelled from candidate membership in the CC of the VKP(b).

2. Re: Antipov, Balitsky, Zhukov, Knorin, Lavrentev, Lobov, Razumov, Rumiantsev, Sheboldaev, Blagonravov, Veger, Goloded, Kalmanovich, Komarov, Kubiak, V. Mikhailov, Polonsky, N. N. Popov, Unshlikht, Aronshtam, Krutov.

The following motion by the Politburo of the CC is to be confirmed.

The following persons are to be expelled for treason to the party and motherland and for active counterrevolutionary activities:

[a] Antipov, Balitsky, Zhukov, Knorin, Lavrentev, Lobov, Razumov, Rumiantsev, and Sheboldaev are to be expelled from membership in the CC of the VKP(b) and from the party;

[b] Blagonravov, Veger, Goloded, Kalmanovich, Komarov, Kubiak, V. Mikhailov, Polonsky, N. N. Popov, and Unshlikht are to be expelled from candidate membership in the CC of the VKP(b) and from the party;

[c] Aronshtam and Krutov are to be expelled from membership in the Central Inspection Commission and from the party.

[d] The cases of the above-mentioned persons are to be referred to the NKVD.

9. Re: Kodatsky, Chudov, Pavlunovsky, and Struppe.

In view of incontrovertible facts concerning their belonging to a counterrevolutionary group, Chudov and Kodatsky are to be expelled from membership in the CC of the VKP(b) and from the party, and Pavlunovsky and Struppe are to be expelled from candidate membership in the CC of the VKP(b) and from the party.

This first list of Central Committee expulsions in June had included several leading regional party secretaries, including Rumiantsev from Smolensk, Sheboldaev from Kursk, and Chudov

47. RTsKhIDNI, f. 17, op. 2, d. 614, ll. 1–4.

and Kodatsky from Leningrad. By the end of 1937, nearly all of the eighty regional party leaders had been replaced, including the party leaders of the union republics. Frequently they were blamed for economic and agricultural failures that appeared in 1936–37.[48] Negligence had become treason.

Document 160

Politburo resolution "On the leadership of the Central Committee of the KP(b) Belorussia"[49]

Resolution of the Politburo

401. On the leadership of the Central Committee of the KP(b) Belorussia
27 July 1937

More than 2 months ago, the CC of the VKP(b) instructed the new leadership of the CC of the KP(b) of Belorussia (Sharangovich) to liquidate the effects of sabotage committed by Polish spies—namely, Cherviakov, Goloded, Benek, and their fascist-espionage gang.

In particular, the CC of the VKP(b) instructed the new leadership to liquidate the sovkhozy created by the wreckers on peasant lands at the order of Polish intelligence and to grant to the kolkhoz members the personal plots [priusadebnye uchastki] due to them by law [prinadlezhashchie im po zakonu].

Sharangovich, first secretary of the CC of the KP(b) of Belorussia; Deniskevich, second secretary; and Nizovtsev, people's commissar for agriculture of Belorussia, not only failed to carry out this assignment of the CC of the VKP(b) but did not even set out to do so. Furthermore, by their acts of sabotage, Sharangovich and Deniskevich artificially created breadlines throughout Belorussia. Instead of turning to the CC of the VKP(b) for help, they concealed this fact from the CC of the VKP(b), even though the CC of the VKP(b) had never refused such help to Belorussia in the past.

The Central Committee of the VKP(b) considers the actions of Sharangovich, Deniskevich, and Nizovtsev as sabotage, as hostile acts toward Soviet power and the people of Belorussia. The CC hereby decrees:

1. That Sharangovich, first secretary of the CC of the KP(b) of Belorussia, be dismissed from his post as an enemy of the people and that his case, like that of Deniskevich and Nizovtsev, [also] enemies of the people, be referred to the NKVD.

2. That leadership of the Belorussian party organization be handed over temporarily to Comrade Ya. A. Yakovlev, member of the CC of the VKP(b), until the situation is cleared up.

---

48. See Roberta T. Manning, "The Soviet Economic Crisis of 1936–1940 and the Great Purges," in Getty and Manning, *Stalinist Terror*, 116–41.

49. RTsKhIDNI, f. 17, op. 3, d. 989, l. 76.

Because expelling and removing a regional party secretary formally required a vote from his party organization, and because Stalin wished to mobilize rank-and-file party members against the midlevel leadership, these removals were conducted in a specific way. A high-ranking Politburo emissary was dispatched from Moscow to the regional capital with instructions to "verify" the party leadership. A plenum of the regional party committee was called, with the emissary putting forward the charges against the regional leader and "his people." Typically, the local first secretary would speak (if he was still at liberty), and then members of the local party committee would denounce their leader, who would then be removed.[50]

Between June and September 1937, for example, A. A. Andreev traveled to Voronezh, Cheliabinsk, Sverdlovsk, Kursk, Saratov, Kuibyshev, Tashkent, Rostov, and Krasnodar to remove the territorial leaderships.[51] At each stop, he was in telegraphic communication with Stalin, relaying to him the results of the plena and the opinions of the local party members. Frequently, Andreev recommended expelling and arresting the local leadership, and Stalin always approved these requests. The language used in both the report and the reply strongly indicate that both Andreev and Stalin actually believed they were uprooting real treason. In some cases, the matter was more doubtful and Stalin proposed simply removing the regional secretary and sending him to Moscow, where, in almost all cases, he would be arrested.[52]

Document 161

Telegram from Stalin to Andreev on execution of MTS workers[53]

Telegram from I. V. Stalin to A. A. Andreev in Saratov
The Central Committee agrees with your proposal to bring to court and shoot the former workers of the machine tractor stations.
Stalin
28 July 1937

---

50. For an example of such an incident based on transcripts of local party documents when Kaganovich visited Smolensk, see RTsKhIDNI, f. 17, op. 21, dd. 3966–4092.
51. RTsKhIDNI, f. 73, op. 2, d. 19, ll. 1–106.
52. RTsKhIDNI, f. 73, op. 2, d. 19, ll. 6, 44.
53. TsKhSD, f. 89, op. 48, d. 9, l. 1.

The campaign for vigilance was now out of control, with officials at all levels denouncing each other and encouraging arrests to protect themselves. Purges and counterpurges were initiated by various leadership factions around the country. On several occasions, Andreev was accompanied by a central NKVD official to carry out the necessary arrests. In several places, Andreev told Stalin that the former local party leadership, through its control of the local NKVD, had arrested large numbers of innocent people. In Saratov, Andreev reported that the former ruling group had dictated false testimony for the signatures of those arrested, and he blamed it on the "Agranov gang" within the NKVD. In Voronezh, Andreev complained that "masses" of innocent people had been expelled and arrested. With Stalin's approval, Andreev organized special troikas to review these cases—600 in Voronezh alone—and release those arrested by the now-condemned former leadership.[54]

The archives currently available to us provide very little in the way of personal correspondence between key leaders. Such private, hidden transcripts would provide important clues about the correlation between what the Stalinists said in public and what they confided to each other. It is, of course, difficult to know the inner thoughts of the top leaders about the degree of guilt of those they destroyed. But if the following rare example of their private correspondence is typical, there apparently was little difference between the Stalinist leaders' private thoughts and their public positions. They seem really to have believed in the existence of a far-flung conspiracy.

Document 162

Letter from A. S. Shcherbakov to A. A. Zhdanov, 18 June 1937[55]

Irkutsk 18 June 1937

Andrei Aleksandrovich!

I consider it necessary to inform you of the following fact: Having become familiar with the testimony given by saboteurs belonging to the Trotskyist-"rightist" gang who are under arrest, I came across a passage in the testimony

54. RTsKhIDNI, f. 73, op. 2, d. 19, ll. 6–7, 27, 106.
55. RTsKhIDNI, f. 88, op. 1, d. 1045, ll. 1–5. Handwritten.

of Lerman, who served as a representative of the East Siberian Regional Executive Committee in Moscow. Earlier, he had worked for a long time in Irkutsk. To the interrogator's question "Name all of the members of the counterrevolutionary, Trotskyist organization," Lerman named, among others: "Snegov—former secretary of the Irkutsk City Committee of the VKP(b). I know him personally to be a member of the counterrevolutionary organization, in view of the fact that I was assigned tasks by him in 1933 relative to the undermining and wrecking of the construction association." Snegov is currently working as a supervisor of the political section of the Murmansk Fish Products. I instructed the NKVD to check this evidence once more and whatever supplementary information I discover I shall report to you. However, I must now tell you that persons who worked earlier in East Siberia ought not to be trusted. The united Trotskyist-"rightist," counterrevolutionary organization has been in existence here since 1930–31. At first, this organization was led by Leonov, then by Razumov, so that, notwithstanding further materials, Snegov ought to be removed from his post because Murmansk is too crucial an area. The situation in East Siberia appears to be the same as in Sverdlovsk or in Rostov or perhaps even worse. The party and soviet leadership was entirely in the hands of enemies. All leaders of regional soviet departments have been arrested, also all directors of regional committee departments and their deputies (except for, at the present, two) and also instructors, many secretaries of district committees, managers of economic organizations, directors of enterprises, and so on. Thus there are no officials left to work in either the party or soviet apparat. It was difficult even to imagine it. Now we are beginning to dig into the army and the NKVD. However, not only am I not dejected. I am more confident than ever that we shall sweep everything before us, that we shall pull out everything by root and branch and crush everything and eliminate the effects of sabotage. I have even forgotten my illness and fatigue, especially after visiting Comrades Stalin and Molotov. I ask you urgently: Please help by sending us more cadres from Leningrad. Send a group of officials at your discretion. I have sent Malenkov a priority list of posts which must be filled.

With comradely greetings,
A. Shcherbakov

Stalin and Molotov took a personal hand in whipping up the hysteria. On several occasions they not only signed long lists of people to be shot, but also encouraged terror in the provinces.

Document 163

Stalin letter on agricultural trials, 3 August 1937[56]

Directive letter from the Central Committee, VKP(b)
8:40 P.M.

Directive letter from the CC of the VKP(b) to secretaries of regional committees, territorial committees of the VKP(b), and to CCs of national Communist parties.

Sabotage perpetrated by enemies of the people in the agriculture of regions and republics has recently been brought to light. It has as its aim the undermining of the economy of the kolkhozy and the fomenting of discontent against Soviet power among members of the kolkhozy by systematic derision and mockery directed at them.

The CC considers the way in which the campaign of annihilating the saboteurs in agriculture has been conducted to suffer from a major deficiency insofar as the elimination of the sabotage [vreditel'stvo] has been carried out in secret only by organs of the NKVD, while the members of the kolkhozy have not been mobilized against the sabotage and its perpetrators.

I consider it absolutely necessary to politically mobilize members of the kolkhozy for a campaign aimed at inflicting a crushing defeat on enemies of the people in agriculture. The CC of the VKP(b) orders the regional committees, the territorial committees, and the CCs of the national Communist parties to organize, in each district of each region, two or three public show trials of enemies of the people–agricultural saboteurs who have wormed their way into district party, soviet, and agricultural organs (officials of machinery and tractor stations [MTS] and district land departments [RaiZO], chairmen of district executive committees, secretaries of district committees, etc.). These trials should be covered in their entirety by the local press.[57]

Stalin
Secretary of the CC of the VKP [sic]
3 August 1937

56. TsKhSD, f. 89, op. 48, d. 12, l. 1–2.
57. For such local press coverage see *Rabochii put'* (Smolensk), 29 August; 6–8, 20–24, 25–27 September; 2, 27 October; 17–18 November 1937. See also Sheila Fitzpatrick, "How the Mice Buried the Cat: Scenes from the Great Purges of 1937 in the Russian Provinces," *The Russian Review*, 52(3), July 1993, 299–320.

СЕКРЕТАРЯМ ОБКОМОВ, КРАЙКОМОВ ВКП(б) и ЦК
НАЦКОМПАРТИЙ.

За последнее время в ~~многих~~ краях, областях и респуб-
ликах вскрыта вредительская ~~~~ работа врагов народа
в области сельского хозяйства, направленная на подрыв хозяйства колхозов и на провоцирование колхозников путем це-
лой системы издевок и глумлений над ~~колхозниками~~,

ЦК считает существенным недостатком руководства ~~мест-
ных организаций~~ делом разгрома и ~~выкорчевывания~~ вредителей
в сельском хозяйстве тот факт, что ликвидация вредителей
проводится лишь закрытым порядком по линии органов НКВД, а
колхозники не мобилизуются на борьбу с вредительством и его
носителями.

Считая совершенно необходимой политическую мобилизацию
колхозников вокруг работы, проводящейся ~~партией и Советской
властью~~ по разгрому вредителей в сельском хозяйстве, – ЦК
ВКП(б) обязывает ~~ЦК~~ Нацкомпартий организовать в
каждой области по районам 2 – 3 открытых показательных процесса над вредителями сельского хозяйства, пробравшимися в
районные партийные, советские и земельные органы (~~директо-
ра~~ МТС, ~~заведующие~~ райЗО, предРИК'и, секретари РК и т.п.),
широко осветив ход судебных процессов в местной печати.

№ 11/с   № 1178/ш

Секретарь ЦК ВКП
Сталин.

(4.7)

DOCUMENT 163. Stalin letter on agricultural trials, 3 August 1937

Document 164

Politburo decision on sabotage of livestock[58]

Decision by the Politburo of the CC of the VKP(b) of 2 October 1937

On the basis of investigative materials furnished by the NKVD of the USSR, it has been established that the subversive actions of enemies of the people in regions have taken an especially vicious form of sabotage and wrecking as it pertains to the development of animal husbandry. These actions have taken the form:

a) Of carrying on acts of bacteriological subversion by infecting cattle, horses, herds of sheep, and swine with plague, foot-and-mouth disease, anthrax, brucellosis, anemia, and other epidemic diseases.

b) Of undermining the work of supplying districts afflicted by epizootic with medications and disinfectants and by sabotage of biological factories producing serum.

c) Of sabotaging by contracting the sowing acreage of fodder cultures with the aim of narrowing the food base.

A significant number of veterinarians, zoological technicians, laboratory assistants of biological factories have been arrested for sabotage in the field of animal husbandry. As a matter of fact, it was they who organized the dissemination of infectious diseases leading to the death en masse of the livestock.

As a result of sabotage carried out in the sphere of animal husbandry, members of kolkhozy lost several hundred thousand head of cattle and horses this past year, not to mention small livestock.

With the aim of protecting the kolkhozy and sovkhozy from the sabotage of enemies of the people, the Council of People's Commissars of the USSR and the CC of the VKP(b) have decided to crush and annihilate the cadres of wreckers in the field of animal husbandry.

The Council of People's Commissars of the USSR and the CC of the VKP(b) place all secretaries of regional committees, the CCs of the national Communist parties, all republic chairmen of councils of people's commissars, and all chairmen of executive committees of regions under the obligation of organizing forthwith show trials for saboteurs in the sphere of animal husbandry, keeping in mind both unmasked veterinarians, zoological technicians, and laboratory assistants of biological factories, as well as officials of local land and sovkhoz departments.

With this aim in mind, the Council of People's Commissars of the USSR and the CC of the VKP(b) propose that 3 to 6 open show trials be organized in each republic and region, that the broad masses of peasants be involved in them, and that the trials be widely covered in the press.

58. TsKhSD, f. 89, op. 48, d. 20, ll. 1–2.

[рукописный текст сверху]

На основании следственных материалов НКВД СССР установлено, что в ~~большинстве~~ краев и областей подрывная работа врагов народа особо злостную форму вредительства и диверсий приняла в области развития животноводства. Эта подрывная работа выразилась:

а) В проведении актов бактериологической диверсии путем заражения крупного рогатого скота, конского поголовья, овечьего и свиного стада чумой, ящуром, сибирской язвой, бруцеллозом, анемией и др. эпидемическими заболеваниями;

б) в срыве снабжения препаратами и дезинфецирующими средствами районов, пораженных эпизоотией и вредительством при изготовлении сыворотки на биофабриках;

в) во вредительском ~~планировании массо~~ва площадей кормовых культур, с целью сужения кормовой базы.

По вредительству в области животноводства арестовано значительное количество ветеринаров, зоотехников, лаборантов биофабрик, которые, собственно, и являлись организаторами распространения заразных болезней, ведущих к массовой гибели скота.

За последний год, в результате вредительства в области животноводства, колхозники лишились сотен тысяч крупного рогатого скота и лошадей, не говоря уже о гибели мелкого скота.

В целях ограждения колхозов и совхозов от вредительской деятельности врагов народа, СНК СССР и ЦК ВКП(б) решили разгромить и уничтожить кадры вредителей в области животноводства.

Пошло на места шифром
2.X.37г. № 1622/ш —см.
папку решений ПБ.

2565

DOCUMENT 164. Politburo decision on sabotage of livestock, 2 October 1937

СНК СССР и ЦК ВКП(б) обязывают всех секретарей обкомов, крайкомов, ЦК нацкомпартий, всех председателей совнаркомов республик и председателей исполкомов областей и краев организовать незамедлительно показательные суды над вредителями по животноводству, имея в виду как изобличенных ветеринаров, зоот᠎чиков, лаборантов биофабрик, так и работников местных земельных и совхозных органов.

В этих целях ш Совнарком СССР и ЦК ВКП(б) предлагают организовать по каждой республик, краю и области от 3 до 6 открытых показательных процессов с привлечением крестьянских масс и широким освещением процесса в печати.

Изобличенных во вредительстве приговаривать к расстрелу, об исполнении приговоров публиковать в местной печати.

Председатель СНК Союза ССР
В. Молотов.

Секретарь ЦК ВКП(б)
И. Сталин

2565

All persons convicted of sabotage are to be sentenced to death by execution, and reports of these executions are to be published in the local press.
Chairman of the Council of Ministers of the USSR
V. Molotov
Secretary of the Central Committee, VKP(b)
I. Stalin

In fall 1937 the decimation of the Central Committee continued, with Stalin showing no hesitation or indecision.

Document 165

Politburo resolution on replacements for the CC, 11–12 October 1937[59]

. . . II. On the Composition of the Central Committee, VKP(b) (Comrade Stalin)
From Protocol #11 of the Plenum of the CC of the VKP(b)
11–12 October 1937
II. Re: Membership in the CC of the VKP(b) (Comrade Stalin).
The following motion by the Politburo of the CC of the VKP(b) is approved.
The following persons are to be removed from membership in the CC of the VKP(b) as enemies of the people: Zelensky, Lebed, Nosov, Piatnitsky, Khataevich, Ikramov, Krinitsky, Vareikis.
The following persons are to be removed from candidate membership in the CC of the VKP(b) as enemies of the people: Grinko, Liubchenko, Yeremin, Deribas, Demchenko, Kalygina, Semyonov, Serebrovsky, Shubrikov, Griadinsky, Sarkisov, Bykin, Rozengolts, Lepa, Gikalo, Ptukha. (Adopted unanimously.)
III. Re: Replenishing the membership of the CC of the VKP(b).
The following candidate members of the CC of the VKP(b), elected by the 17th Congress of the VKP(b), are to be promoted to [full] membership in the CC of the VKP(b):
Comrades N. I. Pakhomov, U. D. Isaev, P. I. Smorodin, V. K. Bliukher, N. K. Bulganin, A. S. Bulin, M. M. Kulkov, S. A. Lozovsky, M. D. Bagirov, I. G. Makarov, M. E. Mikhailov, M. Z. Mekhlis, A. I. Ugarov, and Ye. K. Pramnek. (Adopted unanimously.)
IV. Re: Replenishing the membership of the Politburo of the CC of the VKP(b).

---

59. RTsKhIDNI, f. 17, op. 2, d. 624, ll. 1–2.

Comrade N. I. Yezhov, secretary of the CC of the VKP(b), is to be promoted to candidate membership in the Politburo of the CC of the VKP(b). (Adopted unanimously.)

Document 166

Stalin's speech on replacements for the CC, 11–12 October 1937[60]

From the stenogram of the plenary session of the Central Committee, VKP(b)

11–12 October 1937

Andreev: Let us now move on to the second question on the agenda. Comrade Stalin has the floor.

Stalin: At the suggestion of the Politburo, I'd like to place, as the second item on the agenda, several matters for discussion before the Plenum of the CC and to offer proposals for dealing with them.

The first question concerns membership in the CC. During the period between the June plenum and the present plenum several members of the CC were removed from the CC and arrested: Zelensky, who turned out to be a tsarist secret police agent [*okhrannik*], Lebed, Nosov, Piatnitsky, Khataevich, Ikramov, Krinitsky, Vareikis—altogether 8 persons. Examination and verification of all available materials have shown that these people are all enemies.

If there are no questions, I would like the plenum to take this information under advisement.

Voices: That's right. We have taken it under advisement.

Stalin: In addition, during this same period 16 persons were removed from the CC as candidate members and arrested: Grinko, Liubchenko—who shot himself to death; Yeremin, Deribas—who turned out to be a Japanese spy; Demchenko, Kalygina, Semyonov, Serebrovsky—who turned out to be a spy; Shubrikov, Griadinsky, Sarkisov, Bykin, Rozengolts—who turned out to be a German-English-Japanese spy—

Voices: Wow!

Stalin: Lepa, Gikalo, and Ptukha—altogether 16 persons. An investigation and verification of materials available showed that these [16] people were also enemies of the people. If there are no questions or objections, I would like for the plenum to take this information also under advisement.

Voices: Let's approve it.

Andreev: There is a motion on the floor to approve the Politburo's proposal. Any objections?

Voices: None.

60. RTsKhIDNI, f. 17, op. 2, d. 628, ll. 115–19.

Document 166 *continued*

Andreev: (voting) Adopted unanimously.

Stalin: It is the usual practice of our party when someone leaves the CC, whether through death or expulsion, to replace the members of the CC with candidate members. That is how we have done until now. And the Politburo considers it advisable to act similarly in this case. Our list of candidate members for the CC, compiled at the congress, is, as you know, not arranged in alphabetic order but in accordance with the number of votes cast—not in alphabetic order.

The Politburo of the CC considers it advisable to promote the first ten candidate members to [full] membership in the CC. Who are they?

Pakhomov, the people's commissar for water transport, received the greatest number of votes. After him, in order of votes cast at the congress, came Isaev, chairman of the Council of People's Commissars of Kazakhstan; Smorodin, first secretary of the Stalingrad Regional Committee; Bliukher—you all know him well; Bulganin—you know him well, too; Bulin—who works in the military department; Kulkov—you must know him well, too; Lozovsky—you know him well, too; Bagirov—first secretary of the Azerbaijan CC; Makarov—who works in the steel division of the People's Commissariat for Heavy Industry: 10 persons.

Voices: That's right.

Stalin: The Politburo proposes that the plenum decide to promote these candidate members to membership in the CC on the basis of their having received the greatest number of votes cast at the 17th Party Congress.

Andreev: Are there any other motions on the floor?

Khrushchev: I would like to propose a supplement to Comrade Stalin's motion. I would propose comrades not included on the list that Comrade Stalin spoke of, that is, on the list compiled in accordance with the number of votes cast, but comrades who are known to the party's Central Committee, comrades who are carrying out works of great scope—these comrades, I think, ought to be promoted from candidate membership to membership in the CC. Pramnek is the secretary of the Donetsk Regional Committee, a regional committee of major importance, and everybody knows this comrade. Mekhlis is editor in chief of *Pravda* and is a candidate member of the CC. Mikhailov is the secretary of the Voronezh Regional Committee of the party—this comrade also holds a most important post. Ugarov is the second secretary of the Leningrad Regional Party Committee. He has shown himself for a long time to be a hard-working Bolshevik working in such a major organization. I move that these comrades also be promoted from candidate membership to membership in the CC.

Andreev: The plenum will act as it sees fit.

Voices: Let's take a vote on it.

Andreev: Should we vote separately on the motion proposed by the Politburo and on the motion proposed by Comrade Khrushchev?

Document 166 *continued*

Voices: [Khrushchev's motion] is not a motion but a supplement.

Andreev: Or should we vote on them both together by attaching an amendment, a supplement, to the Politburo's motion?

Voices: On both of them together.

Andreev: So, let's take a vote on the Politburo's motion along with the supplement offered by Comrade Khrushchev. Those in favor of the motion, please raise your hands. Please lower them. Those opposed? None. Any abstentions? None. Motion carried unanimously.

Stalin: We could promote all candidate members to membership in the CC—yes, we have the right to do so—but first of all, we have no need for this, and, second, we cannot leave the CC without reserves, without candidate members. Therefore we should confine ourselves to the decision which had already been taken.

A second question concerns membership in the Politburo. The Politburo proposes that Comrade Yezhov be promoted to candidate member of the Politburo and that this candidate membership be confirmed [by the plenum].

Voices: That's right.

Andreev: Is there a motion on the floor?

Voices: Let's take a vote.

Andreev: Those for the Politburo's motion to promote Comrade Yezhov to candidate membership of the Politburo—please raise your hands. Those opposed? None. Any abstentions? None. Motion carried unanimously.

Document 167

Politburo proposal "Concerning Bauman, Bubnov, Bulin, . . ."[61]

To members and candidate members of the Central Committee VKP(b)
4 December 1937
Excerpts from the protocol of the December Plenum of the CC of the VKP(b) pertaining to the following decision: "Concerning Bauman, Bubnov, Bulin, Mezhlauk, Rukhimovich, Chernov, Ivanov, Yakovlev, Mikhailov, Ryndin."

On the basis of incontrovertible facts, the Politburo of the CC of the VKP(b) deems it necessary to remove the following persons from membership in the CC of the VKP(b) and to arrest them as enemies of the people: Bauman, Bubnov, Bulin, V. Mezhlauk, Rukhimovich, and Chernov, who have turned out to be German spies, V. Ivanov and Ya. Yakovlev, who have turned out to be German spies and agents of the tsarist secret police, M. Mikhailov, a counter-revolutionary confederate of Yakovlev, and Ryndin, a counterrevolutionary confederate of Rykov and Sulimov. All of these persons have admitted their

61. RTsKhIDNI, f. 17, op. 2, d. 630, ll. 38, 56, 57.

Подлежит возврату во
II часть ОС ЦК ВКП(б).

Пролетарии всех стран, соединяйтесь! СТРОГО СЕКРЕТНО.

ВСЕСОЮЗНАЯ КОММУНИСТИЧЕСКАЯ ПАРТИЯ(большевиков)

ЦЕНТРАЛЬНЫЙ КОМИТЕТ.

№ П4128.   4 декабря 1937 г.

ЧЛЕНАМ И КАНДИДАТАМ ЦК ВКП(б)

тов. *Мануильскому*

На основании неопровержимых данных Политбюро ЦК ВКП(б) признало необходимым вывести из состава членов ЦК ВКП(б) и подвергнуть аресту, как врагов народа : Баумана, Бубнова, Булина, Межлаука В., Рухимовича и Чернова, оказавшихся немецкими шпионами, Иванова В. и Яковлева Я., оказавшихся немецкими шпионами и агентами царской охранки, Михайлова М., связанного по контрреволюционной работе с Яковлевым, и Рындина, связанного по контрреволюционной работе с Рыковым, Сулимовым. Все эти лица признали себя виновными. Политбюро ЦК просит санкционировать вывод из ЦК ВКП(б) и арест поименованных лиц.

СЕКРЕТАРЬ ЦК ВКП(б)   *И. Стали*

*голосую за постановление
Политбюро*

Д. Мануильский

30/ac

DOCUMENT 167. Politburo proposal "Concerning Bauman, Bubnov, Bulin, . . . " 4 December 1937 (with Stalin signature)

Document 167 *continued*

guilt. The Politburo requests that their removal from the CC of the VKP(b) and the arrest of the above-mentioned persons be hereby sanctioned.

I. Stalin,
Secretary of the CC of the VKP(b)

[marginal notes:]
I vote for the Politburo's decree—D. Manuilsky.
All of these scoundrels ought to be wiped off the face of the earth as the most loathsome reptiles and repulsive filth—V. I. Yegorov. 8 December 1937.

One wonders how the above people had confessed if their arrest had not yet been sanctioned.

As had always been the case, the members of the Central Committee voted quickly and unanimously to expel those designated as enemies. Partly, no doubt, they did this out of fear of being branded enemies themselves if they protested.[62] It is also important that these arrests of Central Committee members proceeded over more than a year's time. At no point was it clear to anyone how far the process would go; each member at a given moment probably thought that despite the spreading arrests, he was not an enemy and was therefore safe. Molotov explained the process in 1975:

> MOLOTOV: In the first place, on democratic centralism—Listen, it did not happen that a minority expelled a majority. It happened gradually. Seventy expelled 10–15 people, then 60 expelled another 15. All in line with majority and minority.
>
> CHUEV: This indicates an excellent tactic, but it doesn't indicate rectitude.
>
> MOLOTOV: But permit me to say that it corresponds with the factual development of events, and not simply tactics. Gradually things were disclosed in a sharp struggle in various areas. Someplace it was possible to tolerate: to be restrained even though we didn't trust [someone]. Someplace it was impossible to wait. And gradually, all was done in the order of democratic centralism, without formal violation. Essentially, it happened that a minority

---

62. The only two members said to have protested were G. Kamensky and O. Piatnitsky, at either the June 1937 or the June 1938 Central Committee plenum. See V. I. Piatnitskii, *Zagovor protiv Stalina,* Moscow, 1998. Unfortunately, no record of their remarks can be found in available archives.

of the composition of the TsK remained of this majority, but without formal violation. Thus there was no violation of democratic centralism, it happened gradually although in a fairly rapid process of clearing the road.[63]

Finally, there was the strong pull of party tradition and democratic centralism, the feeling that the nomenklatura had to remain unified, to hang together even as they were hanging separately. In the name of party unity and with a desperate feeling of corporate self-preservation, the nomenklatura committed suicide.

A Blind, Mass Terror

The terror of 1937–38 was not limited to the party's elite. We have seen how various leaders tried to protect themselves by ordering mass expulsions and arrests of rank-and-file party members. In turn, the rank and file denounced their bosses as enemies. It was a war of all against all. As an unrepentant Molotov later recalled, "Party careerism played its role—each looked after his own interests. And then, in our system, if you conducted some kind of campaign, you conducted it to the end. And all kinds of things can happen when everything is on such a scale."[64]

But in the second half of 1937 the terror spread beyond the bounds of the Communist Party, as the Moscow leadership became afraid of other threats in the countryside. In 1936 the USSR had adopted a new constitution that envisioned the election of a new legislature, the Supreme Soviet. In June 1937 the Central Committee prescribed electoral procedures that would enfranchise the entire adult population, including groups like former White officers, tsarist policemen, and kulaks in a system of secret-ballot elections. These elections, according to the June 1937 decree, would be for contested seats, with multiple candidates campaigning for each. During 1937 local party leaders complained to Moscow that the proposed Supreme Soviet elections were giving new hope and life to various anti-Bolshevik "class

63. Chuev, *Sto sorok besed*, 463.
64. Chuev, *Sto sorok besed*, 393.

enemies," who sought to use the electoral campaign to organize legally (see Document 153).[65]

The dangerous plan for contested elections would remain in force until October 1937. But two weeks after the fall of the military leaders and as the arrests began to consume the middle and upper ranks of the party leadership, members of the Politburo became worried about losing whatever control of the countryside they enjoyed to mysterious, hidden, "anti-Soviet elements." The same day the press published the regulations on the upcoming contested elections, Stalin sent a telegram to all party organizations calling for mass executions of "anti-Soviet elements."

Document 168

Politburo decision "On the discovery of counterrevolutionary insurrectionist organizations among exiled kulaks in Western Siberia"[66]

Protocol #51 of the meeting of the Politburo VKP(b)

66. On the discovery of counterrevolutionary insurrectionist organizations among exiled kulaks in Western Siberia

(Decision of 28 June 1937)

Item #66. Re: The uncovering of a counterrevolutionary, insurrectionary organization among deported kulaks in Western Siberia.

1. We consider it necessary to apply the supreme penalty to all activists belonging to this insurrectionary organization of deported kulaks.

2. In order to speed up the review of cases, a troika is to be formed consisting of Comrade Mironov (chairman), head of the NKVD for Western Siberia, Comrade Barkov, procurator for Western Siberia, and Comrade Eikhe, secretary of the Western-Siberian Territorial Committee.

Secretary of the CC.

Troikas, or three-person tribunals, had existed during the civil war to provide drumhead justice to enemies of the regime on an

65. See J. Arch Getty, "State and Society Under Stalin: Constitutions and Elections in the 1930s," *Slavic Review*, 50(1), Spring 1991, 18–36; Sheila Fitzpatrick, *Stalin's Peasants: Resistance and Survival in the Russian Village After Collectivization*, Oxford, 1994, 212–13, 282–85.

66. TsKhSD, f. 89, op. 43, d. 48, l. 1.

expedited basis without usual judicial procedure. They had been revived during collectivization to deal out mass sentences of exile or death to opponents of the collective farms. Their reestablishment in 1937 reflected what the regime thought was a crisis atmosphere in the country.[67] The new troikas of 1937–38, composed of the territorial party first secretary, procurator, and NKVD chief, would be the main agents for terror across the USSR in these years. In 1937 the troikas would hand down 688,000 sentences, 87 percent of all criminal sentences in the USSR; the figure for 1938 was 75 percent. According to official figures released by the Russian government in 1995, of the 681,692 people sentenced to be shot in 1937–38, 92.6 percent were sentenced by troikas.[68]

Document 169

Stalin telegram on anti-Soviet elements, 3 July 1937[69]

Extract from Protocol #51 of the Politburo of the CC resolution of 2 July 1937 STRICTLY SECRET Central Committee All-Union Communist Party (Bolshevik)

No. P51/94 3 July 1937

To: Comrade Yezhov, secretaries of regional and territorial committees, CCs of the national Communist parties

#94. On anti-Soviet elements.

The following telegram is to be sent to secretaries of regional and territorial committees and to the CCs of national Communist parties:

"IT HAS BEEN OBSERVED THAT A LARGE NUMBER OF FORMER KULAKS AND CRIMINALS DEPORTED AT A CERTAIN TIME FROM VARIOUS REGIONS TO THE NORTH AND TO SIBERIAN DISTRICTS AND THEN HAVING RETURNED TO THEIR REGIONS AT THE EXPIRATION OF THEIR PERIOD OF EXILE ARE THE CHIEF INSTIGATORS OF ALL SORTS OF ANTI-SOVIET CRIMES, INCLUDING SABOTAGE, BOTH IN THE KOLKHOZY AND SOVKHOZY AS WELL AS IN THE FIELD OF TRANSPORT AND IN CERTAIN BRANCHES OF INDUSTRY. THE CC OF THE VKP(B) RECOMMENDS TO ALL SECRETARIES OF REGIONAL AND TERRITORIAL ORGANIZATIONS AND TO ALL REGIONAL, TERRITORIAL, AND REPUB-

---

67. For a survey of the history of extrajudicial organs, including troikas, in Soviet history see *Izvestiia TsK KPSS*, no. 10, 1989, 80–82.

68. "Vestnik Arkhiva Prezidenta Rossiiskoi Federatsii: I.1995," *Istochnik*, no. 1, 1995, 120.

69. *Trud*, no. 88, June 4, 1992, 1.

LIC REPRESENTATIVES OF THE NKVD THAT THEY REGISTER ALL
KULAKS AND CRIMINALS WHO HAVE RETURNED HOME IN ORDER
THAT THE MOST HOSTILE AMONG THEM BE FORTHWITH ADMINIS-
TRATIVELY ARRESTED AND EXECUTED BY MEANS OF A 3-MAN COM-
MISSION [*troika*] AND THAT THE REMAINING, LESS ACTIVE BUT NEV-
ERTHELESS HOSTILE ELEMENTS BE LISTED AND EXILED TO DISTRICTS
[*raiony*] AS INDICATED BY THE NKVD. THE CC OF THE VKP(B) RECOM-
MENDS THAT THE NAMES OF THOSE COMPRISING THE 3-MAN COM-
MISSIONS BE PRESENTED TO THE CC WITHIN FIVE DAYS, AS WELL AS
THE NUMBER OF THOSE SUBJECT TO EXECUTION AND THE NUMBER
OF THOSE SUBJECT TO EXILE."
Secretary of the CC I. Stalin

Over the next two weeks, troikas were established in several
regions and territories across the USSR.[70] On a region-by-region
basis, their compositions were proposed by regional leaders and
individually approved by the Politburo. The regional authorities
also responded to Stalin's telegram by proposing precise numbers
of "anti-Soviet elements" in their regions who were to be shot or
exiled; apparently they had lists ready to hand.[71] One month later,
in the first days of July, the Politburo and NKVD decided to regularize and centralize the process by establishing quotas centrally. As
had often been the case in the past, local repression outdistanced
that envisioned by the center. It is interesting that in nearly all
regions, the precise local numbers proposed to be shot after Stalin's
telegram at the beginning of July were higher than the round-number quotas later approved by Moscow (in Document 170) at the
end of the month.

Nevertheless, the text that follows is surely one of the most chill-
ing documents in modern history. It prescribed the summary execution of more than 72,000 people who had committed no capital
crime and were to be "swiftly" judged by extralegal organs without
benefit of counsel or even formal charge. Their "trials" were to be
purely formal; these victims were "after consideration of their case
by the troikas, to be shot." An extract of the troika's minutes would
form the only "legal" basis for the execution.

70. TsKhSD, f. 89, op. 43, d. 41, ll. 3–4.
71. See, for example, TsKhSD, f. 89, op. 73, d. 49, ll. 1–2.

Almost anyone could fall under one of the categories of victims: not only criminals but also those committing "anti-Soviet activities," those in camps and prisons carrying out "sabotage," people whose cases were "not yet considered by the judicial organs," family members "capable of active anti-Soviet actions." It is also significant that round-number quotas were established, with victims to be chosen by local party, police, and judicial officials according to their own lights. These quotas do not correlate exactly with population; they rather seem to reflect a focus on sensitive economic areas where the regime believed the concentration of "enemies" to be the greatest, or where in previous trials and campaigns the greatest number of oppositionists had been unmasked. Thus the Azov–Black Sea (Donbas) and Western Siberian territories had large quotas, perhaps reflecting the larger numbers of people there accused of industrial sabotage. The regime was lashing out blindly at suspected concentrations of enemies.

This "operation," which extended into the next year, represented a reversion to the combative methods of the civil war, when groups of hostages were taken and shot prophylactically or in blind retaliation. It also recalled the storm of dekulakization in 1929, when the regime was also unable to specify exactly who was the enemy and lashed out with round-number quotas for deportation.[72] The new Red Terror of 1937, like its predecessors, reflected a deep-seated insecurity and fear of enemies on the part of the regime, as well as an inability to say exactly who was the enemy. Stalin and his associates knew that there was opposition to the regime, feared that opposition (as well as their own inability to identify or specify it concretely), and decided to lash out brutally and wholesale. In this sense, the new Red Terror was an admission of the regime's inability to govern the countryside efficiently or predictably, or even to control it with anything other than periodic bursts of unfocused violence.

At first glance, it is perhaps surprising that the authors of this massacre would commit their plans to writing and would preserve the document in archives for future historians to find. On the other hand, the Bolshevik leaders believed that they were right to "clean" the country of "alien elements." Although, as in the similarly

72. Fitzpatrick, *Stalin's Peasants*, 55.

worded documents on the mass executions of Polish officers in 1940, they never publicly stated what they had done, they were not afraid to create a text about their decision. They were not ashamed of what they were doing. In true bureaucratic fashion, a text, albeit a secret one, was produced: personnel, budgetary appropriations, and transportation were specified. The supplement to this document shows how this terror was administered according to the Bolsheviks' vision of economic rationality.

Document 170

NKVD operational order "Concerning the punishment of former kulaks, criminals, and other anti-Soviet elements," 30 July 1937[73]

To Comrade Poskrebyshev[74]

I am sending you operational order No. 00447 concerning the punishment of former kulaks, criminals, and other anti-Soviet elements. In addition, I am sending you the decree. I ask that you send the decree to members of the Politburo for their vote, and please send an extract of relevant items to Comrade Yezhov.

Frinovsky[75]

30 July 1937 . . .

[TOP SECRET] Copy no. 1.

OPERATIONAL ORDER

of the people's commissar for internal affairs of the USSR. No. 00447 concerning the punishment of former kulaks, criminals, and other anti-Soviet elements.

30 July 1937. City of Moscow

It has been established by investigative materials relative to the cases of anti-Soviet formations that a significant number of former kulaks who had earlier been subjected to punitive measures and who had evaded them, who had escaped from camps, exile, and labor settlements, have settled in the countryside. This also includes many church officials and sectarians who had been formerly put down, former active participants of anti-Soviet armed campaigns. Significant cadres of anti-Soviet political parties (SRs, Georgian Mensheviks, Dashnaks, Mussavatists, Ittihadists, etc.), as well as cadres of former active members of bandit uprisings, Whites, members of punitive expeditions, repatriates, and so on remain nearly untouched in the countryside. Some of the above-mentioned elements, leaving the countryside for the cities,

73. *Trud,* no. 88, June 4, 1992, 1, 4.
74. A. N. Poskrebyshev was Stalin's personal secretary.
75. M. P. Frinovsky was deputy commissar of the USSR NKVD.

have infiltrated enterprises of industry, transport, and construction. Besides, significant cadres of criminals are still entrenched in both countryside and city. These include horse and cattle thieves, recidivist thieves, robbers, and others who had been serving their sentences and who had escaped and are now in hiding. Inadequate efforts to combat these criminal bands have created a state of impunity promoting their criminal activities. As has been established, all of these anti-Soviet elements constitute the chief instigators of every kind of anti-Soviet crimes and sabotage in the kolkhozy and sovkhozy as well as in the field of transport and in certain spheres of industry. The organs of state security are faced with the task of mercilessly crushing this entire gang of anti-Soviet elements, of defending the working Soviet people from their counterrevolutionary machinations, and, finally, of putting an end, once and for all, to their base undermining of the foundations of the Soviet state. Accordingly, I therefore ORDER THAT AS OF 5 AUGUST 1937, ALL REPUBLICS AND REGIONS LAUNCH A CAMPAIGN OF PUNITIVE MEASURES AGAINST FORMER KULAKS, ACTIVE ANTI-SOVIET ELEMENTS, AND CRIMINALS. . . .

The organization and execution of this campaign should be guided by the following:

I. GROUPS SUBJECT TO PUNITIVE MEASURES.

1. Former kulaks who have returned home after having served their sentences and who continue to carry out active, anti-Soviet sabotage.

2. Former kulaks who have escaped from camps or from labor settlements, as well as kulaks who have been in hiding from dekulakization, who carry out anti-Soviet activities.

3. Former kulaks and socially dangerous elements who were members of insurrectionary, fascist, terroristic, and bandit formations, who have served their sentences, who have been in hiding from punishment, or who have escaped from places of confinement and renewed their anti-Soviet, criminal activities.

4. Members of anti-Soviet parties (SRs, Georgian Mensheviks, Dashnaks, Mussavatists, Ittihadists, etc.), former Whites, gendarmes, bureaucrats, members of punitive expeditions, bandits, gang abettors, transferees, re-émigrés, who are in hiding from punishment, who have escaped from places of confinement, and who continue to carry out active anti-Soviet activities.

5. Persons unmasked by investigators and whose evidence is verified by materials obtained by investigative agencies and who are the most hostile and active members of Cossack–White Guard insurrectionary organizations slated for liquidation and fascist, terroristic, and espionage-saboteur counterrevolutionary formations. In addition, punitive measures are to be taken against elements of this category who are kept at the present under guard, whose cases have been fully investigated but not yet considered by the judicial organs.

6. The most active anti-Soviet elements from former kulaks, members of punitive expeditions, bandits, Whites, sectarian activists, church officials,

and others, who are presently held in prisons, camps, labor settlements, and colonies and who continue to carry out in those places their active anti-Soviet sabotage.

7. Criminals (bandits, robbers, recidivist thieves, professional contraband smugglers, recidivist swindlers, cattle and horse thieves) who are carrying out criminal activities and who are associated with the criminal underworld. In addition, punitive measures are to be taken against elements of this category who are kept at the present under guard, whose cases have been fully investigated but not yet considered by the judicial organs.

8. Criminal elements in camps and labor settlements who are carrying out criminal activities in them.

9. All of the groups enumerated above, to be found at present in the countryside—i.e., in kolkhozy, sovkhozy, on agricultural enterprises—as well as in the city—i.e., at industrial and trade enterprises, in transport, in Soviet institutions, and in construction—are subject to punitive measures.

II. CONCERNING THE PUNISHMENT TO BE IMPOSED ON THOSE SUBJECT TO PUNITIVE MEASURES AND THE NUMBER OF PERSONS SUBJECT TO PUNITIVE MEASURES.

1. All kulaks, criminals, and other anti-Soviet elements subject to punitive measures are broken down into two categories:

a) To the first category belong all the most active of the above-mentioned elements. They are subject to immediate arrest and, after consideration of their case by the troikas, to be shot.

b) To the second category belong all the remaining less active but nonetheless hostile elements. They are subject to arrest and to confinement in concentration camps for a term ranging from 8 to 10 years, while the most vicious and socially dangerous among them are subject to confinement for similar terms in prisons as determined by the troikas.

2. In accordance with the registration data presented by the people's commissars of the republic NKVD and by the heads of territorial and regional boards of the NKVD, the following number of persons subject to punitive measures is hereby established:

	First Category	Second Category	Total
Azerbaijan SSR	1,500	3,750	5,250
Armenian SSR	500	1,000	1,500
Belorussian SSR	2,000	10,000	12,000
Georgian SSR	2,000	3,000	5,000
Kirghiz SSR	250	500	750
Tadzhik SSR	500	1,300	1,800
Turkmen SSR	500	1,500	2,000

(continued)

Document 170 *continued*

	First Category	Second Category	Total
Uzbek SSR	750	4,000	4,750
Bashkir ASSR	500	1,500	2,000
Buryat-Mongolian ASSR	350	1,500	1,850
Dagestan ASSR	500	2,500	3,000
Karelian ASSR	300	700	1,000
Kabardino-Balkar ASSR	300	700	1,000
Crimean ASSR	300	1,200	1,500
Komi ASSR	100	300	400
Kalmyk ASSR	100	300	400
Mari ASSR	300	1,500	1,800
Mordvinian ASSR	300	1,500	1,800
German-Povolzhia ASSR	200	700	900
Northern Ossetian ASSR	200	500	700
Tatar ASSR	500	1,500	2,000
Udmurt ASSR	200	500	700
Chechen-Ingush ASSR	500	1,500	2,000
Chuvash ASSR	300	1,500	1,800
Azov–Black Sea territory	5,000	8,000	13,000
Far Eastern territory	2,000	4,000	6,000
Western Siberia territory	5,000	12,000	17,000
Krasnoyarsk territory	750	2,500	3,250
Ordzhonikidze territory	1,000	4,000	5,000
Eastern Siberia territory	1,000	4,000	5,000
Voronezh region	1,000	3,500	4,500
Gorky region	1,000	3,500	4,500
Western region	1,000	5,000	6,000
Ivanovo region	750	2,000	2,750
Kalinin region	1,000	3,000	4,000
Kursk region	1,000	3,000	4,000
Kuibyshev region	1,000	4,000	5,000
Kirov region	500	1,500	2,000
Leningrad region	4,000	10,000	14,000
Moscow region	5,000	30,000	35,000
Omsk region	1,000	2,500	3,500
Orenburg region	1,500	3,000	4,500
Saratov region	1,000	2,000	3,000
Stalingrad region	1,000	3,000	4,000
Sverdlovsk region	4,000	6,000	10,000
Northern region	750	2,000	2,750
Cheliabinsk region	1,500	4,500	6,000
Yaroslavl region	750	1,250	2,000

Document 170 *continued*

. . . 4. The families of those sentenced in accordance with the first or second category are not as a rule subject to punitive measures. Exceptions to this include:

a) Families, members of which are capable of active anti-Soviet actions. Pursuant to the special decree by the three-man commission, members of such families are subject to being transferred to camps or labor settlements.

b) The families of persons punished in accordance with the first category, who live in border areas, are subject to expulsion beyond the border area within the republics or regions.

c) The families of those punished in accordance with the first category who live in Moscow, Leningrad, Kiev, Tbilisi, Baku, Rostov-on-the-Don, Taganrog, and in the districts of Sochi, Gagry, and Sukhumi, are subject to expulsion from these centers to other regions of their choice, except for districts near the border.

5. All families of persons punished in accordance with the first and second categories are to be registered and placed under systematic observation. . . .

IV. ORDER FOR CONDUCTING THE INVESTIGATION.

1. Investigation shall be conducted into the case of each person or group of persons arrested. The investigation shall be carried out in a swift and simplified manner. During the course of the trial, all criminal connections of persons arrested are to be disclosed.

2. At the conclusion of the investigation, the case is to be submitted for consideration to the troika. . . .

VI. ORDER OF IMPLEMENTATION OF SENTENCES.

1. The sentences are to be carried out by persons in accordance with instructions by the chairmen of the three-man commissions—i.e., by the people's commissars of the republic NKVDs, by the heads of governing boards, or by the regional departments of the NKVD. . . . The basis for the implementation of the sentence shall be the certified extract from the minutes of the troika session containing an account of the sentence regarding each convicted person and a special directive bearing the signature of the chairman of the troika, which are to be handed to the person who carries out the sentence.

2. The sentences included under the first category are to be carried out in places and in the order as instructed by the people's commissars of internal affairs, by the heads of governing boards, or by the regional departments of the NKVD. . . . Documents concerning the implementation of the sentence are attached in a separate envelope to the investigative dossier of each convicted person.

3. The assignment to camps of persons condemned under the second category is to be carried out on the basis of warrants communicated by the GULAG of the NKVD of the USSR.

VII. ORGANIZING THE OPERATIONAL LEADERSHIP AND MAINTENANCE OF RECORDS.

1. I lay the responsibility for the general directing of the implementation of the operations on the shoulders of my deputy, i.e., Comrade Frinovsky, Corps Commander, head of the main board of state security. A special group is to be formed under him in order to implement the tasks associated with the direction of these operations. . . .

Thoroughgoing measures are to be taken during the organization and implementation of the operations in order to prevent persons subject to punitive measures from going underground, in order to prevent their escape from their places of residence, and especially beyond the border, in order to prevent their forming groups of bandits and robbers, and to prevent any excesses. Any attempts to commit counterrevolutionary actions are to be brought to light promptly and quickly nipped in the bud.

PEOPLE'S COMMISSAR FOR INTERNAL AFFAIRS OF THE USSR AND GENERAL COMMISSAR FOR STATE SECURITY,

[N. YEZHOV]

Certified: M. Frinovsky

Strictly secret, All-Union Communist Party (Bolshevik) Central Committee No. P-51/442 31 July 1937.

To Comrade Yezhov: all items; To Comrade L. Kaganovich: #6; To Comrade Ivanov: #8, #9, #10, #15; To Comrade G. Smirnov: #10; To Comrade Arbuzov: #5, #10, #11; To Comrade Voroshilov: #13; To Comrade Propper-Grashchenkov: #14.

Extract from Protocol #51 of the Politburo of the CC, DECISION of 31 July 1937.

442- Re: THE NKVD.

1. To confirm the plan presented by the NKVD of an operational order concerning the imposition of punitive measures on former kulaks, criminals, and other anti-Soviet elements.

2. To commence operations in all regions of the USSR on 5 August 1937; in the Far Eastern territory, in Eastern Siberia region, and in Krasnoyarsk territory as of 15 August 1937; in Turkmen, Uzbek, Tadzhik, and Kirghiz republics as of 10 August 1937. The entire operation is to be completed within a period of 4 months. . . .

5. To issue to the NKVD 75 million rubles from the reserve fund of the Council of People's Commissars (SNK) to cover operational expenses associated with the implementation of the operation, of which 25 million rubles is to be earmarked for payment of rail transport fees.

6. To require the NKPS [People's Commissariat for Transport and Communications]to grant the NKVD rolling stock in accordance with its demands for the purpose of transporting the condemned within the regions and to the camps.

7. To utilize as follows all of the kulaks, criminals, and other anti-Soviet

elements condemned under the second category to confinement in camps for periods of time:

a) on construction projects currently under way in the GULAG of the NKVD of the USSR;

b) on constructing new camps in the remote areas of Kazakhstan;

c) on the construction of new camps especially organized for timber works undertaken by convict labor.

8. To propose to the People's Commissariat for Forestry that it forthwith transfer to the GULAG of the NKVD the following forest tracts for the purpose of organizing camps for forest works. [List follows] . . .

9. To propose to the People's Commissariat for Forestry and to the GULAG of the NKVD of the USSR to determine within a period of ten days which additional forest tracts, other than those enumerated above, ought to be transferred to the GULAG for the purpose of organizing new camps.

10. To commission the State Planning Commission (Gosplan) of the USSR, the GULAG of the NKVD, and the People's Commissariat for Forestry to work out within a period of 20 days and to present for confirmation to the Council of People's Commissars (SNK) of the USSR:

a) plans for the organization of timber cuttings, the labor force needed for this purpose, the necessary material resources, the funds and the cadres of specialists;

b) to define the program of timber cuttings of these camps for the year 1938. . . .

11. To issue to the GULAG of the NKVD an advance of 10 million rubles from the reserve fund of the Council of People's Commissars (SNK) of the USSR for the purpose of organizing camps and for the carrying out of preliminary works. To consider that in the 3d and 4th quarters of 1937 convicts will be utilized for the production of preparatory works for the fulfillment of the program for the year 1938.

12. To propose to the regional and territorial committees of the VKP(b) and of the All-Union Leninist Communist Union of Youth (VLKSM) in regions where camps are being organized, to assign to the NKVD the necessary number of Communists and Komsomol members in order to bring the administrative and camp security apparat to full strength (as demanded by the NKVD).

13. To require the People's Commissariat for Defense to summon from the RKKA [Workers' and Peasants' Red Army] reserves 240 commanding officers and political workers in order to bring the cadres of the supervisory personnel of the military security forces of newly organized camps to full strength.

14. To require the People's Commissariat for Health to issue to the GULAG of the NKVD 150 physicians and 400 medical attendants for service in the newly organized camps.

15. To require the People's Commissariat for Forestry to issue to the GULAG

10 eminent specialists in forestry and to transfer 50 graduates of the Leningrad Academy of Forest Technology to the GULAG.
  Secretary of the CC

These documents mark a drastic change in the pattern of Stalinist discourse. Certainly, because it is a text, any document is a form of transcript or narrative. But the ensuing period, that of "blind terror," marks the temporary eclipse of the discursive strategy. It is as if the Stalinists, prisoners of their fears and iron discipline, had decided that they could not rule any longer by rhetorical means.

These texts on mass shootings (including also Documents 182, 183, 184) were completely hidden transcripts; they were not designed for circulation, discussion, or compliance in the party, state, or society. Unlike other party documents, they were not normative and did not prescribe forms of behavior. They were in no sense an implicit conversation designed to negotiate compliance. They involved no variant texts or emphases tailored to specific groups. Unlike other discursive texts there was no affirmation involved, either of unanimity or of power relations. Nor were there suggestions of, or invitations to, established rituals or similar linguistic practices. Aside from those directly charged with the killings, no one was to know. In one sense, the outbreak of this blind terror was not the culmination of previous rhetoric; it was the end or negation of discourse altogether.

Unlike previous identifications of enemies, for which various symbols (Trotskyist, rightist) were often invested with new content, this operation was simply a mass killing with numerical quotas of vaguely specified opponents. Without negotiating or defining who was to be involved, the operation sought to remove statistical slices of the population.

Hysteria, spy-mania, and xenophobia reached new heights. In late 1937 and 1938 NKVD orders approved by the Politburo targeted Germans, Poles, Koreans, Chinese, Latvians, Greeks, Estonians, Finns, Bulgarians, Macedonians, Rumanians, Iranians, Afghanis, and other nationalities living in the Soviet Union, ordering mass operations against "anti-Soviet elements" among them. The police combed old records of tsarist-era foreign firms working in Russia and arrested their surviving employees. NKVD orders specified the arrests of stamp collectors with foreign correspondents and of Soviet citizens studying Esperanto. In September 1937 the Politburo even approved a request from Deputy Commissar of the NKVD Frinovsky to organize special troikas "to examine the cases of Mongolian lamas." This was not a targeting of enemies, but blind rage and panic. It reflected not control of events but a recognition that the regime lacked regularized control mechanisms. It was not policy but the failure of policy. It was a sign of failure to rule with anything but force.

1937: The Human Element

The terror of 1937 destroyed countless lives of victims and their families. Many of those victimized wrote letters to people in positions of authority asking them to intercede on their behalf to correct injustices or otherwise alleviate their situation. Such letters were in a long Russian peasant tradition of appealing to powerful persons for help. Sometimes they were addressed to official bodies, particularly to the Presidium of the Central Executive Committee of Soviets. More often they were directed to particular persons: to Stalin or to M. I. Kalinin (chairman of the Presidium of the CEC and titular head of state). As the only one in the top leadership of peasant origins, Kalinin was nicknamed the All-Union village elder and, as such, received a huge number of letters of appeal. As far as we can tell, the vast majority of these letters went unanswered during the 1937–38 terror.

Nevertheless, their appeals are interesting because they illustrate how people used various rhetorical strategies to mitigate their (or others') situation. In the first letter below, from GULAG prisoners, the appeal is for elementary and customary rights due to revolutionary prisoners. The prisoners attempt to exploit resonant traditions of the Stalinists themselves, many of whom had themselves been revolutionary exiles. But the GULAG petitioners go beyond this anticipated resonance by denying the basic validity of the official reality: They claim that "not one sensible person can believe any of the preposterous, slanderous charges which judges have brought against the accused." The other three letters, however, are appeals "within official discourse of dominance"[76] insofar as they

76. James C. Scott, *Domination and the Arts of Resistance*, New Haven, 1990, 95.

affirm the existing order. In the second letter, Tkachenko launches a different strategy. He does not deny the officially prescribed representation whereby "alien origins" or "connection to aliens" was incompatible with party membership. Instead, Tkachenko makes use of constitutional and legal norms enunciated by the regime, plus factual evidence, to deny culpability. The third letter, from Trofimov, illustrates a third strategy. Like Tkachenko, Trofimov does not question the dominant language about enemies and traitors. Unlike him, however, Trofimov highlights the problem of slander and how unfair allegations pervert the process.

Document 171

GULAG prisoners' letter of protest, 31 March 1937[77]

To the Central Executive Committee and the Council of People's Commissars of the USSR, city of Moscow

Having learned of the verdict returned by the section of the territorial court for the Far Eastern territory in Magadan involving the cases of Comrades Krol, Baranovsky, Maidenberg, Besitsky, and Bolotnikov, who, as Communist political prisoners, have been sentenced to death, as well as the cases of 12 other people sentenced to 10 years in prison, we, Communist political prisoners, cannot but protest this punishment directed against Communists. The charges brought against them are shocking because of their absurdity and total groundlessness (preparation for the seizure of power in Kolyma, sabotage and poisoning of the workers, and so on).

Not one sensible person can believe any of the preposterous, slanderous charges which judges have brought against the accused. We are forced therefore to look for other motives by which the court might have been guided in passing its sentences. We know that the condemned comrades participated in prolonged hunger strikes, that they did not show up for work in order to protest against the harsh camp conditions in which they were placed from the very beginning by the commanding officers of the Northeastern camp (Sevostlag). Comrades Krol, Baranovsky, Maidenberg, and others were guilty only of resisting the attempt by the NKVD to make the regime of camp slavery a permanent one for Communist political prisoners, a regime of physical and moral annihilation. They sought the granting of a political regime—i.e., of conditions of imprisonment which generations of revolutionaries had sought in tsarist prisons and which political prisoners had already enjoyed in Soviet prisons and camps. They would rather perish from prolonged hunger strikes, as had been the case of their comrades G. Ter-Oganesov, M. Korkhina,

---

77. RTsKhIDNI, f. 78, op. 1, d. 592, ll. 89–90.

M. Kurits, E. Solntsev, than relinquish their political dignity and become slaves. The NKVD adopted extraordinarily harsh measures to repress the hunger strikes, yet they were forced to partially satisfy the demands of the prisoners on hunger strike. This the jailers could not forgive and waited for the opportune moment to mete out their vindictive punishment against them.

We protest the illegal judicial procedures employed against unyielding proletarian revolutionaries, whom the Stalinist court had for the first time dared put on trial. Commencing on 8 February 1937, the court examination, carried on openly, was abruptly halted, evidently in view of the total groundlessness of the charges. A month later, the trial was renewed in camera. This made it possible for the judges to conceal the groundlessness of the charges from public opinion and to pass their vindictive sentence.

We ask the highest organs of Soviet power to take note of the fact that, in connection with the trial of the political prisoners in Magadan, a systematic incitement of pogroms [*pogromnaia agitatsiia*] and persecution of political prisoners have taken place in Kolyma, with the direct participation of many officials, owing to which, acts of physical violence perpetrated by criminal inmates against political prisoners have become more frequent. As an example of this, we may cite the attack by bandits on the barracks occupied by political prisoners at our "Five Year Plan" camp on the night of 27 March 1937, which ended with the severe beating of three persons. In addition, a custodian coming to the aid of the political prisoners sustained a grave injury inflicted by a dagger. The bandits carried out their pogrom under the slogan: "For every ten dead Trotskyists, they'll add only one year to our sentence."

We place responsibility for the deaths of the citizens-Communists and for the future victims of arbitrary rule by the repressive organs and for future victims of pogroms carried out by bandits entirely on the shoulders of the government. We demand an end to the pogroms and persecutions.

We demand the creation of normal living conditions for political prisoners. The first step in this direction ought to be the nullification of the sentences handed down by the Magadan court pertaining to the cases of Comrades Krol, Maidenberg, Baranovsky, and others.

Sh. Gocholashkvili, P. Sviridov, N. Makhi, political prisoners.
31 March 1937

Document 172

Letter from Tkachenko to Kalinin [June 1937][78]

To: Mikhail I. Kalinin, chairman of the Central Executive Committee: Mikhail Ivanovich!

78. RTsKhIDNI, f. 78, op. 1, d. 592, l. 25.

Cruel injustice has compelled me to turn to you for help in elucidating an item in the constitution.

Article 127 of the Stalin constitution states: "The citizens of the USSR shall be guaranteed inviolability of their person." My brothers and I have been the victims of a wholly undeserved cruel affront, which goes far beyond the limits of a moral slap in the face.

During the verification of party documents, I was told that I had been concealing my socially alien origin and that my four brothers had served in the Basmach Army [an anti-Soviet movement in Central Asia], and I was expelled from the party. In reality, not one of my brothers has ever served a single day with the Basmachi. On the contrary, my brothers served in the Red Partisan detachments and in the Workers' and Peasants' Red Army (RKKA). Besides, one of them was killed by the Basmachi.

No one at the KPK [Commission of Party Control] believed my documents when I presented them. They also did not believe what the documents said about my father, namely, that he was a middle peasant. On the contrary, they added that my father had been dekulakized. (My father died in 1913!) In brief, I have been expelled from the party at all levels "for concealing my socially alien origin and on account of my four brothers' service with the Basmachi."

And so I would like to know—does the constitution, pursuant to Soviet policy, give me the right to demand the surname of my slanderer for the purpose of instituting proceedings against him for slander? Do I have the right, in accordance with Soviet laws, to remove this dark blot smeared on me and my family by the slanderer and because of which my family and I are everywhere met with distrust, suspicion, and insults? I would like to know how far does the fundamental law under Soviet conditions guarantee a sound position and inviolability of person to an honest citizen like myself as well as to the slanderer.

In other words, I would like to know precisely what the following words from the fundamental law of our country mean in reference to me, an honest citizen: "The citizens of the USSR shall be guaranteed inviolability of their person."

I ask you, Mikhail Ivanovich, to elucidate this matter in the pages of *Izvestia*. Tkachenko.

My address: Moscow, 144, 2d Izvoznaia St., House no. 29, St. kor #2, Building 7, apartment 27.

[Handwritten notes across top of document:]

To Comrade Markov. Clear this up and find out precisely what this is all about. MK [Kalinin] 4 June 1937.

I summoned Tkachenko personally to give an explanation. 13 June 1937. N. Markov.

Document 173

Letter from V. Trofimov to Kalinin[79]

Trofimov, Vlad.

Moscow, 23 August 1937

Dear Mikhail Ivanovich!

During a visit to the Akulov family today, I found out that Ivan was arrested.[80] I cannot get rid of this nightmarish shock. But at the same time, I cannot accept the idea that Ivan is a traitor to the party and the motherland. I have known him now for 30 years, and I have always known him as a staunch Leninist-Stalinist as well as a man of honesty. What happened? Perhaps he has become a victim of slander? This thought gives me no peace.

I myself have twice experienced the full measure of slander. In 1921 I was put on trial by the Revolutionary tribunal due to the efforts of a scoundrel by the name of Moiseev (not the forestry specialist [Moiseev] but a certain journalist). Due to his slander, a certain not unknown Lominadze, who was at the time secretary of the district committee, demanded at the district party meeting that people like me (he didn't mention my name) be put up against the wall! The second case of slander occurred about a year ago when I allegedly tried to praise Trotsky, that monster! And, well, all four persons who had either slandered me or had dealt with me heartlessly and bureaucratically—all four, independently of my case—were, at different times, expelled from the party.

I am writing all of this under the fresh impression of the news of Akulov. My dear Mikhail Ivanovich, deep in my conscience, I cannot reconcile myself to the idea that he is a traitor. Please forgive me for troubling you.

Vlad. Trofimov

Document 174

Letter of Ye. D. Stasova to the party control commission[81]

9 November 1937

From: The CC of the International Organization for Rendering Assistance to Fighters for the Revolution (MOPR) of the USSR

N. 0717/14-s

[TOP] SECRET

To: Comrade Shkiriatov, Commission of Party Control attached to the CC of the VKP(b)

79. RTsKhIDNI, f. 78, op. 1, d. 592, ll. 125–250b. Handwritten.
80. Ivan Akulov was a former procurator of the USSR and secretary of the Central Executive Committee.
81. RTsKhIDNI, f. 356, op. 2, d. 30, ll. 1–3, 5.

Document 174 *continued*

Dear Comrade Shkiriatov:

The Central Committee of the International Organization for Rendering Assistance to Fighters for the Revolution (MOPR) of the USSR has lately had to deal with a certain matter which calls for your instructions as to how we should proceed.

As is well known, a large number of political émigrés, who were on our books, have recently been arrested. They left their families behind them.

With the arrest of the men, we have naturally ceased to issue stipends to their families, and they remain without any funds. For this reason, we have recommended that local chapters of our organization help these wives find work. But when they began helping them to find work, the local Soviet organizations told them that the International Organization for Rendering Assistance to Fighters for the Revolution (MOPR) had no business getting involved.

I would like to request your instructions as to whether the chapters of our organization should be involved in helping the wives of political émigrés under arrest find work.

Enclosed for your information is a copy of the correspondence on this matter with the Kherson City Committee of the International Organization for Rendering Assistance to Fighters for the Revolution (MOPR).

Stasova

Part of the human tragedy of this terror was its effect on families. Not only did fathers and mothers who were branded as enemies disappear, but frequently—as in the case of Alexander Tivel, with which this book began—the relatives of those repressed were themselves arrested. We know, for example, that Stalin, Molotov, and the other Politburo members routinely approved arrest lists of wives and/or children of "enemies of the people." As a native of the Caucasus, where traditions of vendetta and family vengeance were culturally rooted, Stalin perhaps naturally thought in terms of punishing kin groups as much as individuals. At a dinner on the anniversary of the October Revolution in 1937, Stalin mentioned this in a lengthy toast that was transcribed by Georgi Dimitrov: "So anyone who tries to destroy the unity of the socialist state, who hopes to separate from her a specific part or nationality, he is an enemy, a sworn enemy of the state and peoples of the USSR. And we will destroy each such enemy, be he Old Bolshevik or not, we will destroy his kin, his family. Anyone who by his actions and thoughts—yes, his thoughts—encroaches on the unity of the socialist state we will destroy. To the destruction of all enemies to the very end, them and their kin!"[82]

On the other hand, retribution against family members also had more calculating political utility. The threat of retribution against one's relatives might have a deterrent effect on possible traitors. In this atmosphere, promises that one's family would not be repressed may also have encouraged those under arrest to provide the required confessions. Finally, as Molotov noted, it was necessary to remove arrested persons' family members from society to avoid the spread of negative political sentiments. Indeed, when asked by Feliks Chuev in 1986 why family members had been repressed, Molotov at first did not even seem to understand the point of the question.

> CHUEV: Why did repression fall on wives, children?
> MOLOTOV: What does it mean, "why?" They had to be isolated to some degree. Otherwise, they would have spread all kinds of complaints . . . and degeneration[83] to a certain degree. Factually, yes [they were repressed].[84]

Once again, innocent people were victimized because of what they *might* do.

Why?

We will probably never know all the reasons for the eruption of wild terror in the middle of 1937. Nomenklatura fear of opposition, Stalin's personal vengeance and fear of alternative leaders, the top leadership's mistrust of those around them, and preparations for war all played a part.

It is clear that early in 1936 Stalin had become suspicious of the former opposition. Investigations and repression against them proceeded by degrees, with delays, indecision, and various twists and turns, zigs and zags. Back in 1935 the opposition had been accused only of moral complicity in indirectly encouraging minor figures in their dangerous opposition and assassination conspiracies. At that time the matter was declared closed. Later, "on the basis of new materials received in 1936," it was said that Zinoviev and Kamenev, at Trotsky's behest, had themselves been assassins, but that Bukharin and the Right had not been involved. Then, at the begin-

---

82. "Dimitrov Diary," Nov. 7, 1937.
83. *razlozheniia:* literally, corruption, infection—Trans.
84. Chuev, *Sto sorok besed,* 415.

ning of 1937—and not without considerable hesitation and ambiguity—the new political line began to implicate the rightists as well, though it was some time yet before this policy took its final shape. All the while, the nomenklatura cadres themselves, though criticized for a lack of vigilance and for being petty tyrants, were given clean bills of political health.

By the middle of 1937, however, and coinciding with Stalin's coup against the "military plot," suspicions hardened, political transcripts changed again, and the careful texts separating this and that group into enemies, comrades, and well-meaning bunglers blurred. There were now two distinct representations of reality. For the public, the enemy could be a party leader who was a German-Japanese spy and assassin, who for years—even as far back as Lenin's time—had betrayed socialism and carried out secret conspiracies against the party. This construction of reality was the one found in the press and in the proceedings of the show trials. It masked personal and policy conflicts within the elite and attempted to rally the population by giving it negative examples and stark, simple depictions of common enemies. As Stalin explained to Dimitrov in a particularly revealing moment, it was necessary to blacken the reputations of those repressed as much as possible for public consumption: "Workers think that everything is happening because of a fight between me and Trotsky, from the bad character of Stalin. It is necessary to point out that these people fought against Lenin, against the party during Lenin's lifetime."[85] From the minutes of closed Central Committee meetings that we have seen, it is also more than likely that many members of the nomenklatura believed in the guilt of those arrested, though perhaps not in the accusation that they had been foreign spies for twenty years.

The construction of reality in the innermost circle was a bit different. In the Politburo there were few illusions about the victims having been spies or Nazi collaborators. Here it was a matter of personal trust and loyalty. The Stalin faction, consisting of fewer than ten Politburo leaders, had by the middle of 1937 decided to destroy anyone whom they considered unreliable or potentially unreliable. The level of fear and paranoia among these leaders had reached such proportions that it led them to strike even against

85. "Dimitrov Diary," Feb. 11, 1937.

longtime friends and comrades—people who had supported the
Stalin line without fail for years—if there was the slightest reason
to believe that they had been or would in the future be disloyal.
Possible future reality became present danger. Suspicion became
guilt. A party leader could be arrested for having uttered "a liberal
phrase somewhere."[86] For this insider's view of reality, we once
again rely on the unrepentant Molotov of the 1970s and 1980s, in
this case remembering the interrogation of Yan Rudzutak:

> MOLOTOV: Rudzutak—he never confessed! He was shot. Member of
> the Politburo. I think that consciously he was not a participant [in
> a conspiracy], but he was liberal with that fraternity [of conspira-
> tors] and thought that everything about it [the investigation] was
> a trifle. But it was impossible to excuse it. He did not understand
> the danger of it. Up to a certain time he was not a bad com-
> rade. . . .
>
> He complained about the secret police, that they applied to him
> intolerable methods. But he never gave any confession: "I don't
> admit to anything that they write about me." It was at the
> NKVD. . . . They worked him over pretty hard. Evidently they
> tortured him severely.
>
> CHUEV: Couldn't you intercede for him, if you knew him well?
> MOLOTOV: It is impossible to do anything according to personal
> impressions. We had evidence.
> CHUEV: If you believed it—
> MOLOTOV: I was not 100 percent convinced. How could you be 100
> percent convinced if they say that. . . . I was not that close to
> him. . . . He said, "No, all this is wrong. I strongly deny it. They
> are tormenting me here. They are forcing me. I will not sign
> anything."
> CHUEV: And you reported this to Stalin?
> MOLOTOV: We reported it. It was impossible to acquit him. Stalin
> said, "Do whatever you decide to do there."
> CHUEV: And he was shot?
> MOLOTOV: He was shot.[87]

Molotov had a similar recollection about Politburo member Vlas
Chubar:

> MOLOTOV: Here is another example. . . .

86. According to Molotov: Chuev, *Sto sorok besed,* 423.
87. Chuev, *Sto sorok besed,* 410–12.

I was in Beria's office, we were questioning Chubar. . . . He was with the rightists, we all knew it, we sensed it, was personally connected with Rykov. . . . Antipov testified against him. . . . Antipov was a personal friend of Chubar. My dacha was in the same place as theirs; I saw that Antipov and his wife visited Chubar at his dacha.

Antipov said, and maybe he was lying, "I tell you and you told me so-on and so-forth . . . "

Chubar to him: "I cherished this snake next to my heart! Snake to my heart, provocateur!"

CHUEV: But you didn't believe him?

MOLOTOV: We didn't believe him.

CHUEV: You believed Antipov?

MOLOTOV: Not so much and not in everything; I already sensed that he could be lying. . . . Stalin could not rely on Chubar, none of us could.

CHUEV: Thus, it happened that Stalin did not pity[88] anyone?

MOLOTOV: What does it mean, to pity? He received information and had to verify it.

CHUEV: People denounced each other—

MOLOTOV: If we did not understand that, we would have been idiots. We were not idiots. [But] we could not entrust these people with such work. At any moment they could turn. . . .

There were mistakes here. But we could have had a great number more victims in time of war and even come to defeat if the leadership had trembled, if in it had been cracks and fissures, the appearance of disagreement. If the top leadership had broken in the thirties, we would be in a more difficult position, many times more difficult, than it turned out. . . .

If we did not take stern measures, the devil knows how these troubles would have ended up. Cadres, people in the state apparatus . . . such a leading composition—how it conducts itself, not firmly, staggering, doubting. Many very difficult questions which one had to solve, to take on oneself. In this I am confident. And we did not trust; that's the thing."[89]

88. *zhalet'*: to pity or to save.
89. Chuev, *Sto sorok besed*, 413–14, 393.

CHAPTER TWELVE

Ending the Terror, 1938

There were deficiencies. . . . I am not saying that Yezhov was spotless, but he was a good party worker. There should have been more supervision. . . . There was some, but not enough.—V. M. Molotov, 1973

It is interesting that before the events of the thirties, we lived all the time with oppositionists, with oppositionist groups. After the war, there were no opposition groups; it was such a relief that it made it easier to give a correct, better direction, but if a majority of these people had remained alive, I don't know if we would be standing solidly on our feet. Here Stalin took upon himself chiefly all this difficult business, but we helped properly. . . . Especially in the period of the war. All around—one against another, what good is that?—V. M. Molotov, 1982

THE WILD AND VICIOUS terror of 1937 is sometimes known as the *Yezhovshchina*: the "time of Yezhov." This is a misnomer for several reasons. First, it puts excessive emphasis on N. I. Yezhov, who, though he was the head of the secret police that carried out much of the terror, was only one of the important political actors and forces involved. He had a certain amount of freedom in identifying and arresting various "enemies," but he almost certainly took his orders from Stalin and the Politburo.

Second, *Yezhovshchina* is a misleading epithet because the terror consisted of a number of discrete movements, offensives, measures, and countermeasures. Party membership screenings were not the same as police arrests. Various groups and constituencies played changing roles; at different times, one group might be sponsoring the persecution of another, but a few months later their roles were reversed. Regional party secretaries, midlevel officials of the party apparatus, rank-and-file party members, economic managers, former members of the left and right oppositions, Politburo and Central Committee members, and ordinary citizens interacted with and against each other in the 1930s in a bewildering series of combinations and alliances.

Because all these groups were in some measure and at some time victims of the terror, it is tempting to see the events as part of a single event or grand plan directed by Stalin. Although there is no doubt that he was the organizer of much of what we call the Great Terror of the 1930s (another inexact shorthand for the disparate events of that decade), we have seen how on many occasions his policies were marked by contradiction, zigs and zags. More than once, documents reflecting his private remarks to the elite had to be altered or sanitized because they did not fit the prevailing policies or because they sharply contradicted subsequent events.

Under whatever name one chooses, terror continued throughout 1938. More than 638,000 people were arrested in that year (compared with more than 936,000 in 1937), the vast majority accused of "counterrevolutionary" crimes. At least 328,000 persons were executed in 1938, and the population of the GULAG labor camps increased that year by roughly the same number.[1] Moreover, another of the Moscow show trials was staged that year, this time of Bukharin, Rykov, Yagoda, and others, and more Central Committee and Politburo members were arrested.

The terror of 1938 hit some groups much harder than others. Indeed, unlike the wholesale slaughter of 1937, the victims and processes of 1938 lend themselves to more discrete analysis and breakdown. Unlike the maelstrom of the second half of 1937, the terror of 1938 can be broken down into identifiable targets, beneficiaries, and initiatives. Consistent with the emphasis of our study, we focus first on the party apparatus.

---

1. J. Arch Getty, Gábor T. Rittersporn, and V. N. Zemskov, "Victims of the Soviet Penal System in the Pre-war Years: A First Approach on the Basis of Archival Evidence," *American Historical Review*, 98(4), October 1993, 1022–23, based on NKVD archives found in GARF.

Cadres and Purges: The January 1938 Resolution

In January 1938 a Central Committee plenum produced a published resolution that criticized mass expulsions from the party based on "false" or excessive "vigilance." This document has been interpreted in two radically different ways, both of them wrong. On the one hand, it has been seen as an early signal that the terror was to be slowed down or stopped, or at least that some in the leadership were pushing such a relaxation.[2] Others have seen the document as another bit of Stalinist misdirection, as a cynical attempt by Stalin and his circle to pose as the guardians against a terrible and unjust phenomenon.[3] Both these views are questionable because the terror continued for many months after the promulgation of the January 1938 condemnation of excessive vigilance.

Actually, this document had little to do directly with the mass terror that was sweeping the country. It was rather part of the continuing renegotiation of the status of the nomenklatura party secretaries that had been ongoing since at least 1934. Rather than some kind of signal (false or otherwise) about terror in general, it was really part of the multifaceted and multigroup politics that we have seen in the Stalinist 1930s.

The ongoing conflict between the Politburo and the regional nomenklatura had been discursively played out in terms of a constantly shifting attempt by various groups to identify scapegoats and to divert attention from real problems and real culprits: "Who was the enemy?" or "Who was to blame?" Since 1934 Stalin had criticized the regional secretaries as "feudal princes" who had tried to make their territorial machines independent of Moscow. When the enemy had been redefined in August 1936 as has-beens of the Zinoviev and Trotskyist oppositions, the nomenklatura jumped on board this bandwagon—not a peep was raised in defense of their old revolutionary comrades—as long as suspicion did not fall on members of their own regional machines with suspicious pasts. But

---

2. Robert H. McNeal, *Stalin: Man and Ruler,* New York, 1988, 210–11.
3. Robert Conquest, *The Great Terror: A Reassessment,* New York, 1990, 248–49.

in the fall of 1936 that identification was made and party machines were combed for disloyal officials, now labeled with the flexible Trotskyist epithet. The situation took yet another course at the February–March plenum, when the focus returned to former oppositionist leaders like Bukharin and Rykov. Although Stalin's and Zhdanov's remarks at the plenum served notice on the nomenklatura that they must be obedient, the focus was elsewhere, and the secretaries quickly backed the new line on enemies.

This dynamic between Stalin and the nomenklatura was not a simple one. In a larger sense, this tension had to do with the very foundations of the regime. For Stalin to attack the nomenklatura head-on risked discrediting the entire regime: the nomenklatura *was* the Bolshevik Party, and to smash it—as he did in mid-1937—risked smashing the legitimacy of Bolshevik rule. On the other hand, unconditional Politburo support of the nomenklatura also risked discrediting the regime by endorsing elite pretensions and thereby alienating the rank-and-file party membership and ordinary citizens who were the targets of the secretaries' control and arbitrary rule. This dilemma helps to explain the Aesopian language of official proclamations, the need to manufacture different Central Committee texts for different audiences, the abstract Kabuki plays with images of traitorous Trotskyists, and the high-level waffling on the fates of Yenukidze, Bukharin, and Yagoda. Each of these contradictory maneuvers, texts, and pronouncements carried strong symbolic content.

This long-standing game came to an abrupt end in the second half of 1937, when Stalin used the power of the NKVD to destroy the regional secretaries both politically and physically. Even in this fiery chaos, as the rules of the game were obliterated by arrests and executions of the nomenklatura, there were certain nuances at work. Stalin tried to have it both ways: to destroy the independent-minded officials without casting doubt on the institutions they represented. First, the mass shootings that began in the summer of 1937 (see Documents 169 and 170) actually increased the authority of regional secretaries as a corporate group. Each regional troika included the local first secretary as a member, and the requests from these troikas to confirm and increase the number of victims were inevitably signed by the first secretary.[4] It was a grim irony that first secretaries were thus deploying unprecedented powers of life and death over their subjects at the very moment their own fates were being decided in Moscow. But even after the decimation of these nomenklatura leaders, their replacements—that is, the new regional nomenklatura elite—continued to decide who would live and who would die in the "mass operations." Second, Stalin's annihilation of the regional secretaries was publicly characterized as the removal of "Trotskyist-Bukharinist" traitors, not as a calling to account of misbehaving or high-handed officials. Although the administrative "mistakes" of the arrested secretaries were discussed (now as treason), the main public lesson that their fall was supposed to teach was one having to do with traitors and conspirators rather than with a miscreant stratum of the regime's bureaucrats. Thus the central leadership sought to destroy officeholders without weakening the institution of office holding.

This, however, was a difficult job. The mass removal of regional secretaries and their leadership machines inevitably weakened the authority of leadership in general. Memoir accounts testify to the breakdown of authority in factories and other institutions in this period, as bosses were afraid to issue any orders that might later be interpreted as sabotage and as their underlings took advantage of the situation to disobey, threaten, and denounce their chiefs. Factory workers defied managers amid a general breakdown of authority.[5] In frantic attempts to protect themselves, party secretaries continued to expel large numbers of rank-and-file members as "enemies." Especially in the party committees, many of which simply disappeared or ceased to function, the foundations of the regime were in peril.

The terror was destroying the party. The documents of the January 1938 plenum show that the Politburo, and Stalin personally, were concerned about the decay. The party had to be "rehabilitated": mass expulsions had to be stopped; admissions of new

4. *Moskovskie novosti,* 21 June 1992, 19; *Trud,* 4 June 1992, 1.

5. See Sheila Fitzpatrick, "Workers Against Bosses: The Impact of the Great Purges on Labor-Management Relations," in Lewis H. Siegelbaum and Ronald Grigor Suny, eds., *Making Workers Soviet: Power, Class, and Identity,* Ithaca, N.Y., 1994, 311–40.

members and readmissions of those expelled had to be speeded up. The Moscow leadership realized that it could not govern without a nomenklatura. The party, now cured of disease, had to be given a clean bill of health. The trick was finding a symbolic formula for that pronouncement.

In the course of the terror and in the wake of the removal of party officials, newly promoted secretaries were being installed. The new nomenklatura now needed protection, reassurance, and authority. The new, younger party officials had to have the authority to govern. At the same time, however, Stalin and his circle wanted to continue weeding out officials they considered disloyal. They wanted to continue the "mass operations" against kulaks, criminals, and others in the general population. It was necessary to find a formulation that would consolidate and restore the party: to stop the terror in the party without weakening it elsewhere. Formulating such a text would be difficult in that it had to take a position against certain kinds of "excesses" and not others.

The Central Committee resolution of January 1938 provided such a formulation. It attacked the "false vigilance" of "certain careerist Communists who are striving to . . . insure themselves against possible charges of inadequate vigilance through the indiscriminate repression of party members." Such a leader "indiscriminately spreads panic about enemies of the people" and "is willing to expel dozens of members from the party on false grounds just to appear vigilant himself."

"It is time to understand," the resolution asserted, "that Bolshevik vigilance consists essentially in the ability to unmask an enemy regardless of how clever and artful he may be, regardless of how he decks himself out, and not in indiscriminate or 'on the off-chance' expulsions, by the tens and thousands, of everyone who comes within reach."[6]

Thus the mass depredations in the party were to be blamed (not without some justification) on former party secretaries who for the most part had already been removed. The "serious mistakes" and "false vigilance" of certain party leaders, however, were not to be

6. *Pravda,* Jan. 19, 1938. A partial English version can be found in Robert H. McNeal, *Resolutions and Decisions of the CPSU,* Toronto, 1974, vol. 3, 188–95. This resolution quoted the June 1936 CC resolution on excessive expulsions.

taken as signs of a slackening of the hunt for enemies. "On the contrary," the resolution said, vigilance against enemies was not to weaken. (The upcoming show trial of Bukharin and Rykov proved that.) In fact, the NKVD was in no way criticized in the January 1938 resolution. The police—the archetypal agents of vigilance— were given credit for righting various wrongs: "Large numbers of Communists have been expelled from the party on the grounds that they are enemies of the people. But the organs of the NKVD found no grounds for arrest." Indeed, the January resolution called on the party to increase vigilance against enemies of the people.

Although the resolution had identified certain party secretaries as the cause for the crisis in the party, it nevertheless had the effect of stabilizing the party nomenklatura as a group. By locating the problem with "certain" secretaries of the previous period, it implic- itly gave approval to the actions of the new regional officials in general. In its final passages, the resolution gave responsibility for rectifying the situation (admitting more members, dramatically speeding up appeals and readmissions, and halting the expulsion of rank-and-file members) to party secretaries themselves. That is, the sins of the past were relegated to certain discredited members of the secretarial nomenklatura, but the group as a whole was not only exonerated but given the job of rebuilding the party, with the au- thority and credibility to do it. In the months that followed, mass expulsions from the party ceased, large numbers of expelled mem- bers were readmitted, and recruitment of new members began for the first time since 1933.[7]

As usual, the means chosen was the symbolism of a Central Committee plenum and resulting carefully worded texts. Symbolic policy messages were conveyed to the party and public through examples, case studies, or scapegoats on the agenda for discussion. Plenum attacks in the past on Yenukidze, Bukharin, Yagoda, and others were meant to promulgate policy by metaphor. Decrees and resolutions that followed such personal examples were important, but just as important was the lesson to be learned from the illustra- tion of a problem by personal attack. The negative example pro-

---

7. *Pravda,* Aug. 7, 1938. See also T. H. Rigby, *Communist Party Membership in the USSR, 1917–1967,* Princeton, 1968, 214–18. Rigby called the January 1938 plenum "the turning of the tide" in party expulsions.

vided by the personal target functioned as a scapegoat for all manner of regime mistakes and social problems in the country at large. Everyone in the Bolshevik leadership implicitly understood this practice, and party discipline required all to cooperate, even the person singled out as the symbol of the negative. This political culture had always served the interests of the nomenklatura and was an integral part of its survival mechanism. The nomenklatura thus became especially furious when one of its members contested the ritual and refused to play the role assigned to him for the corporate good, Bukharin's recalcitrance at the February–March 1937 plenum being a case in point.

The Fall of Postyshev

In early 1938 the needs of the Politburo and the nomenklatura in general required a scapegoat upon whom the sins of the preceding period could be heaped and whose admission of mistakes and downfall could thus put a final punctuation mark on the terror. It was Postyshev who was to play this role.

Pavel Postyshev had long been known as a territorial party secretary who favored mass expulsions of party members. Since 1935 there had been numerous complaints against him and his circle from those expelled. At the June 1936 plenum he had been criticized for a "light-minded" attitude toward the rank and file. On those occasions, however, even though he was called on the carpet, the matter was concealed from the party generally. In January 1937 Postyshev had been fired from his position in Kiev and transferred to Kuibyshev; even then the Politburo had gone out of its way to shield him from any serious attacks (see Documents 70, 71, 113, 114, and 116). Postyshev was tough. He had recently requested the arrest of his own regional NKVD chief for expressing oblique private doubts about the terror.[8] Even though he had his enemies and attracted criticism, Postyshev enjoyed high-level protection through 1937.

But given the need for a new party discourse at the beginning of 1938, Postyshev became a negative symbol. Sometime around the

8. TsKhSD, f. 89, op. 48, d. 19, l. 1.

beginning of the year, Politburo member A. A. Andreev was assigned the task of gathering compromising material on Postyshev's party expulsions in Kuibyshev.[9] These documents, which became the basis not only for the January 1938 plenum attack on Postyshev but also for the resolution of the plenum, included documentation of mass party expulsions from the Kuibyshev soviet, from the ranks of party district committee secretaries, and from other organizations.[10] One report from the Bazarno-Syzgansky district noted that large numbers had been expelled as enemies by order of Postyshev's men, though the NKVD subsequently found reason to arrest very few of them.

Document 175

Information on Bazarny Syzgan district (Kuibyshev region) [late 1937][11]

REPORT

TOP SECRET

In the Bazarny Syzgan district, 64 persons out of 200 (or 32% of the entire party organization) were expelled from the party organization under the rubric [*formulirovka*] of "enemies of the people and their accomplices." Out of 64 persons thus expelled, 27 persons were expelled under the rubric of "enemies of the people," and 37 were expelled under the rubric of "accomplices of enemies of the people." From these 37 persons classified as "accomplices of enemies of the people," the NKVD and the procuracy were able to arrest only 5 persons, while materials were lacking in the case of the remaining 32 persons in order to carry out punitive measures against them. These persons are as follows: . . .

Expulsion from the party was conducted mostly at party meetings without a preliminary evaluation [*proverka*] and on the basis of speeches made by individual members of the VKP(b).

Such a wholesale and massive expulsion from the party was carried out in the main by Tiuftin, former secretary of the district committee of the VKP(b) (who is currently under arrest). Tiuftin at first worked as second secretary of the district committee, along with Sevian, secretary of the district committee. After the latter's expulsion from the party and arrest, he was elected first

9. See the files in RTsKhIDNI, f. 17, op. 120, d. 327–29, which bear Andreev's name, on Postyshev.

10. RTsKhIDNI, f. 17, op. 120, d. 327, ll. 1, 2, 23–27; d. 329, ll. 31–36.

11. RTsKhIDNI, f. 17, op. 120, d. 329, ll. 43–45.

Document 175 *continued*

secretary of the district committee and, in order to mask [his intentions], he began to expel from the party all those persons who were the subject of un-verified allegations [*zaiavleniia*] concerning their connections with enemies of the people. During his tenure as first secretary of the district committee, 37 persons were expelled. These expulsions were justified by alleging that these persons were "enemies of the people and their accomplices." There were no grounds whatsoever, in the majority of cases, for these expulsions. . . .

Document 176

Expulsions from the Kuibyshev City Soviet[12]

Order of the meeting of the 32d plenum of the Kuibyshev City Soviet

5 January 1938

On removal from the composition of members and candidate members of the plenum of the Kuibyshev City Soviet, 16th convocation

To remove from the composition of members and candidate members of the plenum of the Kuibyshev City Soviet, 16th convocation:

I. As enemies of the people: [list of names]

II. For associating with enemies of the people and for giving aid and comfort to the enemy: [list of names]

III. For disorganizing the voter registration rolls, for sabotage, for failing to carry out the instructions of the district soviet pertaining to preparations for elections to the Supreme Soviet of the USSR: [list of names]

IV. For a callous attitude to working mothers of the telegraph office, for shielding enemies of the people, for contamination of the apparat by [class-] alien and hostile [elements]: [list of names]

V. For counterrevolutionary actions committed in 1905 which helped crush peasant uprisings in the village of Gerasimovka, for the death of Marchenko, leader of the peasant uprising, for counterrevolutionary actions in 1933 while employed by the Association of State Publishing Houses (OGIZ): [list of names]

VI. To place before the voters the matter of removing from the list of deputies persons expelled from membership and candidate membership in the plenums of the city soviet.

Kovalenko,
Acting Chairman of the City Soviet
Zubkov,
Acting Secretary of the City Soviet

12. RTsKhIDNI, f. 17, op. 120, d. 327, l. 27.

As with other events we have studied, the decision to call a Plenum of the Central Committee (and to make an example of Postyshev) showed few signs of long-range planning. The two documents above were procured weeks or even days before the plenum opened. Indeed, based on the materials Andreev compiled, the Politburo decided only on 7 January to use the occasion of a Supreme Soviet meeting to convene a plenum for 11 January, a lead time of only four days. By 9 January, G. M. Malenkov had drafted a resolution for approval at the plenum, as well as a "secret letter" to all party organizations, explaining the new line. But no secret letter was sent. Upon Stalin's suggestion at the subsequent plenum, it was redrafted into a published resolution.[13]

Document 177

Politburo announcement of January 1938 CC plenum 7–9 January 1938[14]

From record #56 of the Politburo of the CC of the VKP(b)

A) 7 January 1938

Item #250. Re: The Plenum of the CC of the VKP(b)

The CC of the VKP(b) has decided to convene a Plenum of the CC of the VKP(b) on 11 January 1938 in order to take advantage of the attendance by members of the CC of the VKP(b) at the [upcoming] session of the Supreme Soviet of the USSR.

The agenda for the plenum:

1) Questions relating to the session of the Supreme Soviet.

2) [a] Errors committed by party organizations during the expulsion of Communists from the party;

[b] Formal-bureaucratic attitude toward appeals made by persons expelled from the VKP(b);

[c] Measures to be undertaken for the removal of these deficiencies.

Attendance by members and candidate members of the CC of the VKP(b) is obligatory.

B) 9 January 1938

Item #265. Re: Politically erroneous decisions committed by the Kuibyshev Regional Committee of the VKP(b)

The CC of the VKP(b) is of the opinion that the Kuibyshev Regional Committee of the VKP(b) has been guilty of arbitrary conduct and disarray in its dealings with district party organizations. Its opinion is based on the fact that

13. RTsKhIDNI, f. 17, op. 2, d. 782, l. 3.
14. RTsKhIDNI, f. 17, op. 3, d. 994, ll. 51, 55.

during the past three months the Kuibyshev Regional Committee has disbanded 30 district committees of the party without the knowledge of the CC of the VKP(b) and merely on the grounds that certain members of these district committees had been expelled from the party.

The CC of the VKP(b) hereby decrees:

1) That the decisions of the Kuibyshev Regional Committee of the VKP(b) of 19 September, 26 September, 7 October, 19 October, 20 October, 22 October, 29 October, 3 November, 4 November, 11 November, 14 November, 19 November, 26 November, 29 November, 9 December, 14 December, 17 December, 23 December, 28 December 1937 pertaining to the disbanding of 30 district committees of the party be recognized as politically damaging and, in their consequences, manifestly provocatory.

The buro of the Kuibyshev Regional Committee of the VKP(b) and its first secretary, Comrade Postyshev, are to be severely reprimanded for indiscriminately and unwarrantedly resorting, without the knowledge of the CC, to the extraordinary measure of disbanding party committees.

2) Comrade Postyshev is to be relieved of his duties as first secretary of the Kuibyshev Regional Committee and is to be placed at the disposal of the CC of the VKP(b).

3) Comrade Andreev, secretary of the CC of the VKP(b), is to be entrusted with the task of carrying out this decree of the CC of the VKP(b).

In Malenkov's original draft resolution, which he wrote after discussing the matter with Stalin, he recommended only a censure for Postyshev and the Kuibyshev Regional Committee. At the last minute Stalin changed the recommendation to include removing Postyshev from his Kuibyshev post and the Politburo and placing him "at the disposal of the Central Committee."[15] Although Postyshev was to be sacked from his Kuibyshev position, he was not expelled from the party, nor was he denounced as an enemy.

It was necessary at the plenum itself to carry out the all-important ritual of presenting Postyshev as the "negative other." The traditional forms were followed. Evidence was gathered showing how Postyshev had ignored "signals." A decision was taken in the form of a draft resolution to be formally adopted in a plenum ritual, at which the accused leader was to confirm the charges as "completely correct" and pay his symbolic taxes by confession. Thus lessons would be taught, new signals sent, and unanimity affirmed.

15. RTsKhIDNI, f. 17, op. 163, d. 1180, l. 57–59.

As had been the case with Smirnov, Yenukidze, Bukharin, and Rykov, speaker after speaker rose to attack the accused in a kind of ritual, self-affirming ceremony of the nomenklatura elite. They closed ranks against one of their own who was now to become a symbol. These rituals had several purposes. They permitted Stalin to set the agenda for politics. They provided forums for creation of authoritative, variant texts for various audiences. They also implicitly served as vehicles for corporate construction of elite identity through the prescribed ceremony. In this case, however, Postyshev seems either not to have understood or to have rejected what was required of him. From his point of view, he had not done anything wrong. Postyshev was propagating a text that had been proper in 1937 but that was now outdated. He evidently forgot that right and wrong, correct and incorrect policy were what the party defined them to be at a given ritual moment. So important was the ritual, the creation of a correct text, that Kaganovich and other speakers even prompted Postyshev when he misspoke. Because of the semi-public nature of this ritual scapegoating, the following transcript was printed for distribution in the stenographic report.

Document 178

Postyshev's speech to the January 1938 CC plenum[16]

Excerpts from the January 1938 Plenum of the CC of the VKP(b)
A) Session of 14 January (day session).
Postyshev: . . . And now concerning the disbanding of the 30 party district committees. I must say something, comrades, concerning my mistake. My situation at the time was also a very grave one. In what sense? The soviet and party leaderships were in enemy hands, from the regional leadership at the top to the district leadership at the bottom.
Mikoyan: All of it? From top to bottom?
Postyshev: The entire district leadership. What's so amazing about it? First, Khataevich was chairman [of the regional party committee] for several years, then he was replaced by Shubrikov, then came Levin. According to my count, [the regional leadership] was riddled with enemies for twelve years. The same holds true for the soviet leadership—it too was in enemy hands. These leaders

16. RTsKhIDNI, f. 17, op. 2, d. 639, ll. 14–16, 20–22, 32–33. From the printed stenographic report.

selected their own cadres. For example, our regional executive committee was infiltrated right down to the level of technicians by the most inveterate enemies, who had confessed their sabotage and who conduct themselves [even now] in a brazen manner. Everyone, from the chairman of the regional executive committee down, including his deputy, his consultants, and his secretaries—all of them are enemies. All of the departments of the executive committee were contaminated by enemies. Now take the organization of the Regional Consumers Union: one of its members was the enemy Vermul, a relative of Khatasevich.[17] Now look at the departments having to do with trade: There were enemies there, too, who promoted their supporters, who appointed them to positions everywhere.

Bulganin: Weren't there any honest people there?!

Postyshev: Of course there were.

Bulganin: It looks like there wasn't a single honest person there.

Postyshev: I'm speaking of the top leadership. There was hardly a single honest man, as it turned out, among the top leaders, which includes the secretaries of the district committees and the chairmen of the district executive committees. What's so amazing about it?

Molotov: Aren't you [formal *vy*] exaggerating, Comrade Postyshev?

Postyshev: No, I'm not exaggerating. Take, for example, the leadership of the regional executive committee. The evidence [*materialy*] is there, these people are under arrest, and they have confessed. They themselves have given testimony of their activities as spies and enemies.

Molotov: This evidence must be checked and verified.

Mikoyan: It turns out that there are enemies even in the lower echelons, in all of the district committees.

Postyshev: This happened quite simply as follows: Shubrikov and Levin planted many of the enemy cadres from the center. Just look around you and see how many of our people turned out to be enemies. Levin promoted all of the heads of the political sections to the positions of secretaries. And the majority of them turned out to be enemies. Take the secretary of the Ulianovsk City Committee, a Red professor, an inveterate enemy. The same for the secretary of the Syzran City Committee, a Red professor, also an inveterate enemy.

Kaganovich: But there were errors. Why do you keep talking only about objective conditions?

Postyshev: I shall talk about my personal mistakes.

Kaganovich: You shouldn't justify yourself by saying that they were all scoundrels.

Postyshev: I never said all of them; I'm not so completely insane as to call everyone an enemy of the people. I never said that, I spoke only of the leadership of many of the district committees.

17. Probable misprint for Khataevich—Trans.

Bagirov: When you disband the leadership of a district committee, the organization itself is placed in doubt.

Postyshev: You [informal *ty*] yourself were just being questioned concerning your affairs. (General laughter.)

Bagirov: I didn't disband a single district committee or its leadership.

Postyshev: Good for you! I listened to you and now don't you interfere.

Bagirov: And why can't I comment on what you are saying?

Postyshev: You may comment. But why can't I answer? It's just that my time is limited and you have already finished your talk.

I repeat, I'm speaking of the leadership. The regional leadership turned out to be all in enemy hands—both the soviet and party leadership.

Molotov: Not a single honest man remained in the leadership?

Postyshev: Viacheslav Mikhailovich [Molotov], I'll be glad to enumerate them to you [formal *vy*].

Molotov: I'm [only] asking a question. I have doubts about what you are saying.

Beria: Of the members of the plenum of the regional committee—how many are left?

Postyshev: Of the members of the plenum of the regional committee—out of 61 people, 25 are left.

Beria: 25 persons—that's a fair number of people.

Postyshev: We have not disbanded it. (Commotion in the room.)

Beria: You [informal *ty*] said that no one from the party and soviet leadership was left.

Postyshev: What do you want?

Beria: I want you to tell the truth and not to distort the facts.

A voice: Nonetheless, tell [informal *ty*] us how you [plural *vy*] disbanded the district committees.

Postyshev: How we disbanded them? Comrade Beria, I ask you to please hear how we disbanded them. In this case we committed an error. In what way? A district committee usually consists of 7 to 11 persons—

Yezhov: And so it turns out that you [informal *ty*] only committed a formal mistake. But you know that the CC has characterized your mistake as not a formal one but as a major political error in substance. So are you trying to say that the decision of the CC is not correct?

Beria: Comrade Postyshev, go on, tell the plenum why you disbanded the plenums of the district committees. After all, there were honest people left in the plenums of the district committees. Why did you disband them?

Postyshev: The district committee consists of 11 party members. Seven of them were enemies, and 4 remained. What should have been done?

Molotov: The party is discredited, Comrade Postyshev, when the leaders of the regional committee turn out to be bunglers.

Postyshev: Why should I reduce the whole affair to a formal mistake?

Kaganovich: But you [informal *ty*] yourself said that your mistake lies in the fact that you should have placed the matter before the CC. But here we are discussing the substance of the matter. The CC has rendered its decision in accordance with the substance and not the form of the matter.

Postyshev: Please permit me to finish and explain this whole business to the best of my ability.

Kaganovich: You are not very good at explaining it—that's the whole point.

Postyshev: Whether I explain it well or poorly, I am speaking sincerely, my thoughts are sincere.

Kaganovich: Not every act of sincerity is correct.

Postyshev: In any case, I'm speaking sincerely.

Molotov: And we too are criticizing you sincerely.

Kaganovich: You are speaking mistakenly. If you got confused at first, then at least, correct your mistake by the time you finish your speech.

Postyshev: For instance, the secretary of the district committee is expelled from the party—does that mean that I have not been judicious in my choice? Or if the chairman of a district executive committee is expelled from the party—have I therefore not been judicious in my choice? I ask you to check and verify whether the secretaries of the district committees were rightly or wrongly expelled. It is possible that there are mistakes here, but it seemed to us that they were rightfully expelled. The majority of them turned out to be enemies. This can be verified. They have confessed.

Concerning voting by polling: the buro of the regional committee did not exist.

Beria: How many people were there?

Postyshev: Toward the end, there were only two people left, and they took away Yefremov, too.

Beria: Why weren't those that remained called into session?

Postyshev: The two of us held sessions.

Beria: And whom did you [plural *vy*] poll then?

Postyshev: There was a second secretary as a member of the buro, and a head of the NKVD as a member of the buro, but the buro as such did not exist.

Beria: And that is why [the buro] did not meet?

Postyshev: What do you mean we didn't meet? Couldn't you consider that a buro?

Beria: So then why did you conduct polling?

Postyshev: There were decisions requiring polling. I believe that my mistake consists of the fact that we permitted the disbanding of the district committees, although here my mistake is mitigated by certain considerations. I had to take upon my shoulders the responsibility for economic operations. We didn't have any managers of departments [of economic affairs]. We do not have a chairman of the regional executive committee.

A voice: And who of us does not carry this burden on his shoulders?

Postyshev: Everyone carries this burden on their shoulders. But in the absence of a chairman of the regional executive committee, I had to do this work each and every day myself, and for that reason my attention to party matters diminished.

Bagirov: And don't we deal with these matters?

Postyshev: I don't have a chairman, I had no deputy, there were no managers of the departments of the executive committee, and I had to deal with this business. You know we had a harvest and we sowed grain, there was a budget to draft, and I had no one—

Khrushchev: So it turns out that you [informal *ty*] didn't have a single capable person on hand. It turns out that there is no one to promote. What you are saying is wrong.

Postyshev: We have promoted an engineer, an honest man.

Khrushchev: So put him to work.

Postyshev: We'll certainly put him to work, but at first he can't work as he needs to. He has not yet adapted himself to soviet and economic work. He needs at the very least around 3 months for that.

Andreev (chairman): Comrade Postyshev, you [formal *vy*] have already been talking for a half hour.

Postyshev: I think that we have committed a very serious mistake.

Yezhov: And not a formal one, as you said at first.

Postyshev: You [informal *ty*] didn't understand me correctly, Nikolai Ivanovich [Yezhov].

Yezhov: And what is there to understand incorrectly? You don't even know how many of your district committees have been disbanded.

Postyshev: Comrade Malenkov wasn't talking about me here. Comrade Malenkov didn't question me about this matter even once, and I didn't answer him even once. Isn't that true?

Malenkov: Concerning what matter?

Postyshev: Concerning the number of district committees that have been disbanded.

Molotov: Comrade Postyshev might himself figure out that such matters must be reported to the CC.

Stalin: We could have calculated the number on the basis of the minutes.

Postyshev: I admit that we have committed a serious mistake. I consider the decision of the CC relative to me to be a correct one, one that I deserve, but I ask that you take into consideration the one fact that I was forced to take care of economic affairs. Our executive committee was without leadership. I asked Comrade Malenkov to send us a chairman.

Malenkov: I wanted to send you someone from Yakutia.

Postyshev: I don't know where you wanted to send someone from, but one candidate for the post was rejected.

Malenkov: You [formal *vy*] rejected him, too.

Postyshev: That's true.

B) Session of 14 January (evening session).

Document 178 *continued*

Ignatov: Yes, you went around everywhere with a magnifying glass, looking for enemies. Yes, Comrade Postyshev, all you [formal *vy*] ever did was walk around in your study with a magnifying glass in your hand. This news spread throughout the city and, in essence, you created panic among the populace. We categorically objected to such conduct by Comrade Postyshev.

Sometime after that, the Central Committee issued a directive, signed by Comrade Zhdanov, pertaining to the wrongful removal of literature under every sort of pretext. You, Comrade Postyshev, kept this directive for three weeks.

Postyshev: What directive?

Ignatov: Pertaining to the subversive removal of literature. Don't you remember?

Postyshev: That's not true.

Ignatov: Yes, it is true.

Postyshev: Everything you have said is untrue.

Ignatov: You better try to prove that it is not true.

Comrade Postyshev has stated here that we are surrounded by enemies. I would like to know how it was possible for us to promote to leadership positions on the city and district committees of the party completely new people, people chosen out of the ranks of workers, members of kolkhozy, leaders of tractor brigades—how could we have done this if we were surrounded everywhere by enemies? During this period, Comrade Malenkov, we promoted a mass of people for such positions. You know that we asked very little of you. When party organizations were exposing secretaries of district committees as bankrupt persons, as enemies, they found on their staff worthy Bolsheviks who assumed leadership positions and acquitted themselves quite well.

You, Comrade Postyshev, ran to another extreme and drew no lessons whatsoever from the instructions of the party CC. Your leadership style was an old one. Here is an example: we had no buro despite the fact that we urged you several times to place before the CC the matter of confirming a buro—

Andreev (chairman): Comrade Postyshev, take your seat. This is no place for strolling about.

Ignatov:—so that we could have a collective leadership. Our buro had only one member left. You are amazed that all of our decisions were conducted by polling.

Stalin: And how many officials do you have in your organization at the top? Do you have a second secretary?

Ignatov: I am an acting second secretary. We have only one buro member.

Stalin: Does your Department of Leading Party Organs (ORPO) have a director?

Ignatov: Yes, they sent us a director.

Stalin: Does your regional executive committee have a chairman?

Ignatov: We have a deputy chairman.

Stalin: Are there 7 or 8 people on your staff, then?

Ignatov: Yes, there are. We even discussed the question of whom to register.

A voice: Are there 25 members on your regional committee? He [Postyshev] said that there were.

Ignatov: He doesn't know how many there are. He said that there were 6 or 7 people on our district committees when in fact there were no fewer than 17. And on our rural district committees there were just as many.

That's the kind of style, comrades, [which characterized Comrade Postyshev's leadership] despite the instructions of the party's Central Committee.

Andreev: But why did you then make decisions by polling?

Ignatov: [Because] we didn't have a buro.

Beria: Whom did you poll?

Ignatov: Are you kidding? What polling?

Beria: How did you conduct a poll when there was only one person on the buro?

Ignatov: Decrees were issued.

Postyshev: But I didn't write any decrees, not a single one. You wrote all these decrees. It's all your doing.

Ignatov: I shall also talk about myself.

Postyshev: All of those decrees were yours, not mine.

Voroshilov: Oh, the poor thing, and you [informal *ty*] just signed them. Isn't that right?

Ignatov: I'll tell you how I signed them and what I signed. I think that the CC plenum will understand me. I was transferred from the post of secretary of the party committee to that of secretary of the regional committee, and I must tell you that for me, the region is one huge cumbersome organization [*makhina*]. I thought, Comrade Postyshev, that I would learn a great deal from you. But if you recall, I told you that your style was inappropriate.

Postyshev: You didn't say so.

Ignatov: Those meetings of yours, those sessions. Comrades, please believe me. He is capable of talking nonstop for eight hours and we all had to listen to him.

Postyshev: I never spoke nonstop for eight hours.

Ignatov: He would begin with the harvest, the grain procurement, the seeds, the horses, the cows, and say whatever came to mind.

Postyshev: It's not true.

Ignatov: I told you frankly that this way of working was not appropriate. When will we teach people to be answerable for the tasks assigned to them?

Postyshev: I don't remember.

Ignatov: I have witnesses. Let me tell you frankly, you thought you were a big shot and didn't consider others.

Postyshev: No, it's just not true.

Ignatov: Yes, it is true. When Andrei Andreevich [Andreev] of the Central

Committee came to visit us, you dared to do everything in your power to place yourself above everybody else.

Postyshev: Above whom?

Ignatov: As soon as you would walk into our meetings, everybody would get up and shout.

Postyshev: It's just not true.

Ignatov: It's a fact. When you tell district committee secretaries about this, they say: "That's how [the Communist Party] trains us [*vospitanie*]."

Postyshev: I spent too little time there to be able to provide any training.

Ignatov: There! You see, comrades, that's Comrade Postyshev's leadership style. I arrived in Kuibyshev only recently.

Postyshev: I arrived there 4 months before you did.

Ignatov: At the meeting, he mixes everything up, then as a result of his 8-hour talk on 32 different subjects, he at last declares: "Please let me write up the proposals."

Postyshev: That's not true.

. . . Postyshev: I ask you to please give me the floor.

Andreev: I will put your name down on the list of speakers.

Postyshev: Comrade Stalin, I ask that I be given the floor.

Stalin: Why should we let you speak out of turn?

Postyshev: I ask you just once to make an exception for me.

Andreev: We'll ask the plenum right now.

Postyshev: Comrades, please permit me to speak right now. Otherwise, I'll forget everything.

A voice: Wait your turn.

Postyshev: Please, please let me speak.

Andreev: Take your seat! I'll put it to a vote right now. Who is for letting Comrade Postyshev speak out of turn? One, two. Who is opposed to putting Comrade Postyshev's name on the list ahead of everybody else? A majority . . .

[Later] Andreev: There is a motion on the floor to give Comrade Postyshev the floor so that he can make a statement, after which discussions will cease and Comrade Malenkov will deliver the concluding speech. Any objections to this motion? None. Comrade Postyshev has the floor and he will make a statement.

Postyshev: I can only say one thing, comrades, and that is that I recognize the speech which I gave earlier to be fully and totally incorrect and incompatible with the party spirit. I do not understand myself how I could have made that speech. I ask the CC plenum to forgive me. Not only have I never associated with enemies, but I have always fought against them. I have always fought on the side of the party against enemies of the people with all my Bolshevik soul, and I shall fight the enemies of the people with all my Bolshevik soul.

I have made many mistakes. I did not understand them. Perhaps even now I have not fully understood them. I shall say only one thing, that is, that the speech I gave was incorrect and un-party in spirit and I ask the Plenum of the CC to forgive me for making this speech.

Andreev: Comrade Malenkov shall have the final word.

Malenkov: I believe that all of the comrades who have participated in these discussions, with the exception of Comrade Postyshev, fully supported the proposals which had been submitted for consideration to the Plenum of the CC of the VKP(b).

Postyshev: I, too, support them. I have already said so earlier.

Malenkov: I assert that these statements by Comrade Postyshev are untrue. And although Comrade Postyshev spoke of sincerity in his address to the Plenum of the CC of the VKP(b), nonetheless, either he has no idea at all of the true state of affairs in the region, or else he is consciously misleading the Central Committee.

A voice: Both the one and the other.

Malenkov: The majority of the members of the district committees in the 30 disbanded district committees of the party are not enemies. The total number of persons elected as members of district committees in these 30 district committees is 669. The documents themselves, carrying the signature of Comrade Postyshev, pertaining to the disbanding of the district committees, show a total of 91 enemies.

What right did you [formal *vy*] have, Comrade Postyshev, to place the entire membership of the district committees of the party under the shadow of suspicion and political doubt?

Comrade Postyshev, the Politburo deems your actions to be politically damaging and, in their consequences, manifestly provocatory. It is this matter which you ought to have addressed in your speech to the plenum. . . .

Postyshev: I consider the decision of the Central Committee concerning me to be correct. I simply underestimated the situation. Do you really think I did this deliberately?

Malenkov: You did not say this when you were speaking from the podium, when you were given the right to make a statement, and the shorthand record contains only your purely formal statement.

Postyshev: I shall correct my speech and shall record in it admission of my mistake.

Andreev: There is a motion on the floor to adopt this as a secret letter by the CC.

Beria: Concerning the time limit if at all possible, it would be desirable to increase the deadline for the review of the appeals.

Stalin: Three months.

Andreev: Fine. Any more amendments? Then this will be a secret letter by the CC. Who is for confirming it [as a secret letter]? Who is opposed? Adopted unanimously.

Document 178 *continued*

Stalin: I propose that this secret letter be recognized as a decision by the Plenum of the CC and that it be published. What is there to conceal in it?

Voices: That's right. That's right.

Stalin: Instead of being a secret letter by the CC, it will become a decree by the Plenum of the CC and will be published.

Andreev: Who is for Comrade Stalin's proposal? The proposal is adopted unanimously.

Comrade Stalin has the floor.

Stalin: It is the opinion of the Presidium of the CC, the Politburo if you will, that, after all that has happened, certain measures must be taken regarding Comrade Postyshev. In our opinion, he ought to be removed from his position as candidate member of the Politburo and remain as a member of the CC.

Voices: That's true.

Andreev: I call for a vote. Who is for adopting Comrade Stalin's proposal? A majority. Opposed? None. Any abstentions? None. The proposal is adopted.

Stalin: There is a second proposal—a motion to include Comrade Khrushchev as a candidate member of the Politburo.

Andreev: Who is for the motion? Please raise your hand. A majority. Who is opposed? None. The motion is adopted.

Many of those speaking up forcefully against Postyshev were representatives of the younger generation, the new nomenklatura: Bulganin, Khrushchev, Malenkov, and Ignatov had rarely spoken at plenums before, and certainly not against someone so senior to them as Postyshev. Postyshev's replacement as candidate Politburo member by Khrushchev was sharply symbolic of the old and new secretaries. Even though Postyshev had enjoyed strong high-level protection in the past, it was now necessary to grind him down completely in order to reassure the younger generation of its ascendancy as well as to warn them of what could happen even to a powerful party secretary. Further depositions against Postyshev were solicited and his case moved toward a conclusion.

Document 179

Explanatory statement of Kuibyshev Regional Committee instructor Laptev[18]

Explanatory note by Laptev, instructor at the Kuibyshev Regional Committee of the VKP(b), to Comrade Naidis, instructor of the CC of the VKP(b)

18. RTsKhIDNI, f. 17, op. 120, d. 329, l. 188.

Document 179 *continued*

26 January 1938

I was employed as an instructor at the Department of Leading Party Organs (ORPO) for the Kuibyshev Regional Committee of the VKP(b), responsible for reviewing appeals.

Beginning with June 1937, the buro of the regional committee of the VKP(b) completely stopped reviewing the appeals of persons expelled from the party. As an instructor responsible for reviewing appeals, I apprised the secretaries of the regional committee of the VKP(b) every two or three weeks by means of memorandums of the fact that a great number of unreviewed appeals was piling up.

It was on the basis of this that Comrade Postyshev scheduled on several occasions a session of the buro of the regional committee for the review of appeals. As the date for such sessions approached, the appellants would be summoned to the regional committee of the party, [but] several hours prior to the beginning of the session, it would be announced that the session was postponed for an indefinite period of time. The appellants would leave. This was repeated several times. . . .

It was then that Comrade Postyshev, secretary of the regional committee, suggested that I prepare for review by the buro of the regional committee all cases pertaining to those who were admitted into the party in accordance with the first and second categories but who were at the time in question expelled from the party as enemies of the people and arrested, as well as pertaining to those who ought not to be summoned to the buro. On the basis of this I prepared up to 150 cases. The decision of the buro of the regional committee of the VKP(b) was arrived at in these cases by polling extending from 1 to 8 October 1937. They confirmed the decision[s] of the district committees and city committees of the VKP(b) to expel these persons from the party.

Laptev,
Instructor for the Regional Committee of the VKP(b)

At the January 1938 plenum, Stalin had proposed removing Postyshev from the Politburo but leaving him on the Central Committee. But a month later, this decision was changed, and Postyshev was now charged not only with party malfeasance and "principled mistakes" but with knowing of the enemy's machinations. His refusal immediately to carry out the apology ritual hurt him in the end.

The documents show that Postyshev had enemies and critics in the party for years. Shkiriatov had assembled a file on him in early 1936 (Document 70). Postyshev had been attacked at the June 1936 plenum (Document 71 [E]), and fired from his Kiev job in January 1937 (Document 113). But it is hard to avoid the impression that Stalin was not among Postyshev's longtime enemies. Shkiriatov's 1936 complaint file was never pursued. The sharp personal attack on Postyshev at the June 1936 plenum was edited out of the final version of the minutes, and when Postyshev was removed from Kiev, he was given a new job running the Kuibyshev party organization.

Stalin himself had said that Postyshev's Kiev entourage had been full of enemies. Later, in May 1937, the KPK complained about Postyshev's leadership in Kuibyshev. Postyshev warned his subordinates that he gave the orders and that they should not complain about him to Moscow: "You can write [to Moscow] if you want, but I do not recommend it. It is very high there and you might fall and break your legs."

Stalin was informed of these complaints but continued to condemn Postyshev's critics (Document 116). Even in January 1938 Stalin proposed that Postyshev remain in the party and even on the Central Committee. But it seems that Postyshev's enemies finally won the war when a month later Postyshev was expelled from the party on the basis of charges not mentioned at the previous plenum. The dates of this and the preceding document are curious. Postyshev was expelled from the party by vote between 17 and 20 February, but the date on the document sending his case to the control commission (for expulsion) is 23 February.[19]

Document 180

CC decision "On Comrade Postyshev," 17–20 February 1938[20]

Protocol #13. Decisions by the Plenum of the CC of the VKP(b)
17–20 February 1938, 28 February–2 March 1938
Item #1. Re: Comrade Postyshev.
The following decree issued by the Commission of Party Control and adopted by the Politburo of the CC is to be confirmed:
Having familiarized itself with the materials concerning the work of Comrade P. P. Postyshev as first secretary of the Kuibyshev Regional Committee of the VKP(b) and having heard his explanations, the Commission of Party Control attached to the CC of the VKP(b) has established that:

---

19. RTsKhIDNI, f. 17, op. 2, d. 640, ll. 1–2, and f. 17, op. 3, d. 996, l. 4.
20. RTsKhIDNI, f. 17, op. 2, d. 640, ll. 1–2.

1) In accordance with instructions by Postyshev, and without any grounds for doing so, 35 party district committees were disbanded (out of 62 in the region). This was accompanied by unjustified expulsions from the party and repression against some of the members of the district committee plenums that had been disbanded. By his provocatory methods of leadership, Postyshev pushed the leaders of the district primary party organizations to undertake a massive expulsion of party members, listing honest and loyal Communists in the camp of enemies slated for expulsion, in consequence of which 3,300 persons in the Kuibyshev region were expelled from the party during the last five months of 1937 alone.

2) Such provocatory methods were also utilized by Postyshev toward officials of soviet organizations. Many deputies of city and district soviets were automatically expelled from the soviet only on the basis of individual, isolated statements and without any preliminary verification of such statements. So, for example, in accordance with direct instructions of Postyshev and in his presence, at one of the sessions 34 deputies were unjustifiably expelled from the Kuibyshev City Soviet.

3) Postyshev personally issued manifestly subversive and provocatory directives to district committees pertaining to the bringing of cows owned by kolkhoz members to the fields during sowing and harvest time, pertaining to the dismantling of the communal buildings of the kolkhozy, to the mowing and threshing of stubble at the height of the gathering-in of the harvest and to authorization for the practice of wide-dispersal sowing [*razbroshennyi sev*], and then he saw to it that district and kolkhoz officials were put on trial for practicing wide-dispersal sowing.

4) During his tenure in Kuibyshev, Postyshev in essence not only did not unmask any enemies of the people but, on the contrary, made it difficult, by his antiparty actions, for party organizations and the NKVD to unmask such enemies. Declaring that "he was surrounded everywhere by enemies," he struck a blow against honest Communists loyal to the party.

5) Postyshev's assistants, selected by him, both in the Ukraine and in Kuibyshev, turned out to be enemies of the people (spies). Notwithstanding repeated warnings by the CC of the VKP(b), Postyshev showed exceptional trust in his associates, supporting them, carrying them with him from one organization to another and offering them access to highly secret materials and documents of the Central Committee of the VKP(b), access which was then used by them for purposes hostile to the party.

6) Testimonies by certain enemies of the people, now under arrest, have established the fact that Postyshev, at the very least, had learned from them about the existence of a counterrevolutionary rightist-Trotskyist organization, that he had been informed of the participation of his closest associates in it and of the subversive and provocatory activities carried out by them.

The Commission of Party Control attached to the CC of the VKP(b) therefore decrees:

a) That all of the above-mentioned actions by Comrade Postyshev be recognized as antiparty in nature and as serving to benefit enemies of the people.
b) That P. P. Postyshev be expelled from the VKP(b).

The final chapter of Postyshev's public career saw the renaming of Postyshevsky district in Donetsk region.[21]

The sacking of Postyshev was accompanied by a large-scale reshuffling of the NKVD in the Ukraine. It is possible to see in this a sorting out of Ukrainian NKVD chiefs according to their membership in Postyshev's circle (see Document 181). Some of the replaced officials were probably removed ("put at the disposal of the NKVD") for their closeness to Postyshev. Others, however, were given equivalent or higher-ranking posts; perhaps they had helped gather evidence against him.

Document 181

Politburo decisions on Postyshev and on NKVD personnel[22]

Protocol #58 of the Politburo of the CC of the VKP(b)
23 February 1938
Item #4. Re: Comrade Postyshev.*
In view of the compromising materials furnished by the NKVD and the Kuibyshev party organization, the case of Comrade Postyshev is to be submitted for review to the Commission of Party Control attached to the CC of the VKP(b).
Item #140. Re: Heads of the NKVD regional and territorial boards.**
The following proposal by the NKVD of the USSR is to be adopted:
A. Appointments:
1. Comrade N. N. Fedorov is to be relieved of his duties as head of the NKVD board for the Odessa region and appointed head of the NKVD board for the Kiev region.
2. Comrade D. D. Grechukhir is to be relieved of his duties as head of the NKVD board for the Krasnoyarsk region and appointed head of the NKVD board for the Odessa region.
3. Comrade A. P. Alekseenko is to be appointed head of the NKVD board for the Krasnoyarsk region.
4. Comrade A. I. Zhabrev is to be appointed head of the NKVD board for the Kamenets-Podolsky region.

21. RTsKhIDNI, f. 17, op.114, d. 642, ll. 10.
22. RTsKhIDNI, f. 17, op. 3, d. 996, l. 34–35.

5. Comrade G. M. Viatkin is to be appointed head of the NKVD board for the Zhitomir region.

6. Comrade A. A. Volkov is to be appointed head of the NKVD board for the Poltava region.

7. Comrade A. I. Yegorov is to be appointed head of the NKVD board for the Chernigov region.

8. Comrade Chistov is to be relieved of his duties as head of the NKVD board for the Cheliabinsk region and appointed head of the NKVD board for the Donetsk region.

9. Comrade Zhuravlev is to be relieved of his duties as head of the NKVD board for the Kuibyshev region and appointed head of the NKVD board for the Ivanovo region.

10. Comrade Bocharov is to be appointed head of the NKVD board for the Kuibyshev region.

11. Comrade Korkin is to be relieved of his duties as head of the NKVD board for the Voronezh region and appointed head of the NKVD board for the Dnepropetrovsk region.

12. Comrade K. E. Denisov is to be appointed head of the NKVD board for the Voronezh region.

13. Comrade Krivets is to be relieved of his duties as head of the NKVD board for the Dnepropetrovsk region and appointed head of the NKVD board for the Ordzhonikidze region.

14. Comrade Sokolinsky is to be appointed head of the NKVD board for the Cheliabinsk region.

B. The following persons are to be relieved of their duties:

1. Comrade Radzivilovsky, head of the NKVD board for the Ivanovo region, with a recommendation that he be put at the disposal of the NKVD of the USSR.

2. Comrade Bulakh, head of the NKVD board for the Ordzhonikidze region, with a recommendation that he be put at the disposal of the NKVD of the USSR.

C. The following persons currently employed in the Ukraine as heads of regional boards of the NKVD are to be placed at the disposal of the NKVD of the USSR:

Comrades I. I. Morozov, N. T. Prikhodko, L. I. Reikhman, I. Ya. Babich, Korenev, Fisher, and L. T. Yakushev.

*Decision adopted 11 February 1938.
** Decision adopted 21 February 1938.

The Violence Continues

Even as the overvigilant Postyshev was being sacrificed for the sake of ending mass expulsions in the party, the terror continued unabated on other fronts. The same week that Postyshev was expelled from the party for his excess zeal, the Politburo formally extended the time period for work of the murderous troikas; they were supposed to have finished their "mass operations" by the end of 1937. At the same time, the Politburo raised execution and exile limits established in the original order (see Document 170). The Politburo considered and approved higher limits for various regions on a weekly basis, and sometimes more often. These decisions would eventually prolong troika operations until nearly the end of 1938. According to the following example (one of many), an additional 48,000 people ("first category") were to be shot.[23]

Document 182

Politburo decision "On anti-Soviet elements"[24]

STRICTLY SECRET
All-Union Communist Party (Bolshevik) Central Committee
31 January 1938
To Comrade Yezhov, the regional and territorial committees, and the CCs of the national Communist parties
Extract from Protocol #57 of the Politburo of the CC
#48. Re: Anti-Soviet elements.
a) The proposal by the NKVD of the USSR regarding the imposition of punitive measures on additional numbers of former kulaks, criminals, and actively anti-Soviet elements is to be approved, corresponding to the following regions, territories, and republics:

	First Category	Second Category
Armenian SSR	1,000	1,000
Belorussian SSR	1,500	[blank]
Ukrainian SSR	6,000	[blank]
Georgian SSR	1,500	[blank]
Azerbaijan SSR	2,000	[blank]
Turkmen SSR	1,000	[blank]
Kirghiz SSR	500	[blank]
Tadzhik SSR	1,000	500
Uzbek SSR	2,000	500
		(continued)

23. See TsKhSD, f. 89, op 73, d. 41, ll. 4–11.
24. *Moskovskie novosti*, no. 25, June 21, 1992, 19.

Document 182 *continued*

	First Category	Second Category
Far Eastern territory	8,000	2,000
Chita region	1,500	500
Buryat-Mongolian ASSR	500	[blank]
Irkutsk region	3,000	500
Krasnoyarsk territory	1,500	500
Novosibirsk region	1,000	[blank]
Omsk region	3,000	2,000
Altai territory	2,000	1,000
Leningrad region	3,000	[blank]
Karelian ASSR	500	200
Kalinin region	1,500	500
Moscow region	4,000	[blank]
Sverdlovsk region	2,000	[blank]

b) It is proposed that the NKVD of the USSR complete all of its operations in the above-mentioned regions, territories, and republics no later than 15 March 1938 and in the Far Eastern territory no later than 1 April 1938.

c) It is proposed that the work of the troikas be extended in accordance with the present decree. . . .

Secretary of the CC

Document 183

Politburo decision on increasing "limits" on repression in the Ukraine[25]

STRICTLY SECRET, All-Union Communist Party (Bolshevik) Central Committee

17 February 1938

To Comrade Frinovsky:

Extract from Protocol #58 of the Politburo of the CC of the VKP(b)

#67. Re: THE NKVD.

To permit the NKVD of the Ukraine to carry out supplementary arrests of kulak and other anti-Soviet elements and to submit the cases for consideration by the troikas, having increased the quota for the NKVD of the Ukrainian SSR by THIRTY THOUSAND.

Secretary of the CC

---

25. *Moskovskie novosti*, no. 25, June 21, 1992, 19.

The mass operations were particularly violent in the Far East, where they were influenced by the regime's paranoia about sealing the country's borders.

Document 184

Politburo decision on the NKVD in the Far East[26]

Extract from Protocol #57 of the Politburo of the CC of the VKP(b)
Decision of 1 February 1938
Item #61. Re: Problems of the NKVD in the Far East.
(Decree by the CC of the VKP(b) and by the Council of People's Commissars of the USSR.)
The following decision is to be adopted (see Supplement).
From the Supplement.
1. Re: The forbidden border zone and border procedures.
In order to strengthen the security of the border areas of the USSR with Japan, Korea, Manchuria, and the Mongolian People's Republic and in order to establish strict operating procedures on the territory of the USSR adjacent to the above borders, the CC of the VKP(b) and the Council of People's Commissars hereby decree:

5) That the NKVD of the USSR be instructed to evict all foreigners possessing neither Soviet nor foreign passports from the Far Eastern region, from Chita region, and from the Buryat-Mongolian ASSR and to arrest all those suspected of espionage, subversive, or other anti-Soviet activities and, utilizing current nonjudicial procedures, to refer their cases for review to troikas, regardless of the nationality declared by those subject to this punitive action. . . .

IV. Measures to be taken to reduce the inmate population of the Far Eastern camps.

18) The proposal by the NKVD of the USSR to approve punitive measures in the Far Eastern camps against an additional 12 thousand prisoners convicted of espionage, terror, subversion, treason, insurgency, and banditry, as well as career criminals, is to be adopted. The cases of these categories of prisoners are to be reviewed by 1 April 1938 by troikas established for the review of cases of former kulaks, criminals, and anti-Soviet elements. All 12 thousand persons are to receive punishment of the first category.

19) The NKVD of the USSR is ordered henceforth not to send any persons convicted of espionage, terror, subversion, treason, insurgency, and banditry, as well as career criminals, to the camps in the Far East. Similarly, the NKVD of the USSR is ordered not to send to the camps of the Far East persons of Japanese, Chinese, Korean, German, Polish, Latvian, Estonian, and Finnish nationality, as well as [Russian] residents of Harbin [China], regardless of the crime for which they had been convicted.

26. TsKhSD, f. 89, op. 73, d. 124, ll. 1–2.

Document 184 *continued*

Chairman of the Council of People's Commissars of the USSR
Secretary of the CC

The limit for the Far Eastern territory would be increased again to 20,000 (15,000 to be shot; 5,000 to the camps) in July 1938.[27]

As these large-scale repressions continued, so did the removals and arrests of high-level officials whom Stalin and the Politburo decided they could not trust. In 1938 there was a second purge of the military high command, as those officers who had sat on Tukhachevsky's court-martial were themselves purged. In the fall, the Far Eastern Red Army was purged. Its commander, Marshal Bliukher, was arrested and beaten to death without confessing.[28]

Document 185

Politburo decision "On Comrade Yegorov"[29]

From Protocol #57 of the Politburo of the CC of the VKP(b)
9 February 1938
Item #2. Re: Comrade Yegorov.* (Decree of the Council of People's Commissars (SNK) of the USSR and of the CC of the VKP(b).)

The SNK of the USSR and the CC of the VKP(b) have established that:

a) Comrade A. I. Yegorov, first deputy of the people's commissar for defense of the USSR had acquitted himself very unsatisfactorily during his tenure as chief of staff of the Workers'-Peasants' Red Army (RKKA), throwing the work of the general staff into disarray by delegating power to Levichev and Mezheninov, inveterate spies working for the Polish, German, and Italian Intelligence agencies.

The SNK of the USSR and the CC of the VKP(b) consider it suspicious that Comrade Yegorov not only did not try to monitor the activities [kontrolirovat'] of Levichev and Mezhininov[30] but placed unbounded trust in them and formed friendly relations with them.

b) As is evident from the testimonies of Belov, Grinko, Orlov, and others, all spies now under arrest, Comrade Yegorov obviously knew something concerning the existence of an army plot headed by the spies Tukhachevsky, Gamarnik, and other scoundrels who were formerly Trotskyists, right SRs, White officers, and so on.

27. TsKhSD, f. 89, op. 73, d. 149, l. 1.
28. *Izvestiia TsK KPSS,* No. 12, 1989, 100.
29. RTsKhIDNI, f. 17, op. 3, d. 995, ll. 5,6.
30. Spelled Mezheninov above—Trans.

Document 185 *continued*

Judging by these materials, Comrade Yegorov attempted to establish contact with conspirators through Tukhachevsky, a fact mentioned by the spy Bepov, a former SR, in his testimony.

c) Comrade Yegorov, unjustifiably dissatisfied with his position in the Red Army and knowing something concerning the existence of conspiratorial groups in the army, decided to organize his own antiparty group, into which he inveigled Comrade Dybenko and tried to inveigle Comrade Budenny.

On the basis of all the above, the SNK of the USSR and the CC of the VKP(b) hereby decree:

1. That the continued presence of Comrade A. I. Yegorov at the helm of the central apparat of the People's Commissariat for Defense is unacceptable in view of the fact that he cannot enjoy the full political confidence of the CC of the VKP(b) and of the SNK of the USSR.

2. That Comrade Yegorov be relieved of his duties as deputy people's commissar for defense.

3. That Comrade Yegorov be granted the opportunity, as a final test, to take over the command of one of the lesser military districts.

It is proposed that Comrade Voroshilov offer to the CC of the VKP(b) and the SNK of the USSR his suggestions for a position for Comrade Yegorov.

4. That the question of Comrade Yegorov's continued enrollment as a candidate member of the CC of the VKP(b) be submitted for discussion to the next Plenum of the CC of the VKP(b).

5. That the present decree be circulated to all members of the CC of the VKP(b) and to all commanders of military districts.

Item #3. Re: Comrade Dybenko. (Decree of the SNK of the USSR and of the CC of the VKP(b).)

The SNK of the USSR and the CC of the VKP(b) consider it an established fact that:

a) Comrade Dybenko had suspicious ties with certain Americans who turned out to be intelligence agents and that he took advantage of these ties, in a manner inadmissible for an honest Soviet citizen, in order to obtain financial assistance for his sister, who lives in America.

b) The SNK of the USSR and the CC of the VKP(b) also call serious attention to the publication in the press abroad of a report that Comrade Dybenko is a German agent. Although this report was published in the enemy White Guard press, nonetheless we ought not to overlook this since one such report concerning Sheboldaev's work as a provocateur in the past turned out to be true when subjected to verification.

c) Instead of carrying out his duties conscientiously as the commander of his district, Comrade Dybenko systematically took to heavy drinking. He fell into moral turpitude and thereby served as a very bad example to his subordinates.

In view of all the above, the SNK of the USSR and the CC of the VKP(b) hereby decree:

Document 185 continued

1. That the continued presence of Comrade Dybenko in the Red Army is unacceptable.

2. That Comrade Dybenko be dismissed from his post as commander of the Leningrad military district and be placed at the disposal of the CC of the VKP(b).

3. That Comrade Malenkov suggest possible work for Comrade Dybenko outside the military field.

4. That the present decree be circulated to all members of the CC of the VKP(b) and to all commanders of military districts.

*Decision adopted 25 January 1938.

At the same time, there are signs in the first half of 1938 that the terror was getting out of the control of the center. In February and March 1938 a series of decrees sought to reestablish centralized direction of the violence. As with the January 1938 plenum, the goal seems to have been to restore order and centralized control of parts of the terror without sending signals that might restrain "vigilance" altogether. The following two documents show that lower-level party secretaries and procurators had to be restrained from excessive purging. Whether from conviction or from a self-defensive desire to display their vigilance, their zeal had exceeded their authority. Texts were produced restricting repression of Red Army officers and re-straining zealous local prosecutors. Once again, the emphasis was on restraining uncontrolled repression "from below."

Document 186

Red Army circular on party expulsions[31]

Supplement to #160 of Protocol #58 of the Politburo.
CONFIRMED BY THE CC OF THE VKP(b) 23 February 1938.
NOT FOR PUBLICATION
TO ALL HEADS OF MILITARY DISTRICT POLITICAL DIRECTORATES, HEADS OF ARMY POLITICAL DIRECTORATES, HEADS OF POLITICAL SECTIONS OF DIVISIONS AND OF OTHER UNITS EQUAL TO THEM, HEADS OF POLITICAL SECTIONS OF ACADEMIES, MILITARY SCHOOLS, AND CENTRAL DIRECTORATES OF THE WORKERS' AND PEASANTS' RED ARMY (RKKA).

31. RTsKhIDNI, f. 17, op. 3, d. 996, l. 60.

Document 186 *continued*

Many party organizations have recently expelled from the party, often wrongly, commanding officers and commissars of regiments, brigades, divisions, and other units equal to them, whereas the question of their party membership [*partiinost'*] should be handled with the knowledge and consent of the Political Directorate of the Workers' and Peasants' Red Army (RKKA), working on an equal basis with the military department of the CC of the VKP(b). On the basis of instructions by the Central Committee of the VKP(b), the Political Directorate of the RKKA has explained that such a practice is wrong. In all cases, when the primary party organizations within the RKKA possess materials that cast doubt on the advisability of party membership of commanding officers and commissars of regiments, brigades, divisions, and higher, it is necessary to send copies of all these materials to the Political Directorate of the RKKA and only with its consent to consider the question of the party membership of this or that official. This directive is to be brought to the attention of all commissars, political officials, party commissions, and primary party organizations of units of the RKKA.

Head of the political administration of the RKKA

L. Mekhlis, Army commissar, second rank.

160/as

Certified by: Khriapkina

Document 187

Orgburo decision on district procurators[32]

From Protocol #84 of the Orgburo of the CC of the VKP(b)

26 March 1938

Item #2. Re: District procurators. (Comrades Andreev, Vyshinsky, Drynshev, Malenkov, Zhdanov, Shkiriatov.)

1. Procedures are to be established according to which the appointment and transfer of district procurators are to be carried out only with the permission of the CC of the VKP(b).

2. A commission consisting of Comrades Vyshinsky, Andreev, and Malenkov is instructed to evaluate district procurators and to implement and to carry out the necessary selection of new people in order to strengthen the district procuracies within a period of two months.

3. Comrade Vyshinsky is instructed to prepare a decree pertaining to improvement in the work of local organs of the procuracy and to present this decree to the CC.

4. Comrade Vyshinsky is instructed to work out and to present to the Org-

32. RTsKhIDNI, f. 17, op. 114, d. 642, l. 3.187

Document 187 *continued*

buro of the CC proposals for the creation of a system for the preparation of cadres for the procuracy.

5. Cognizance should be taken of Comrade Vyshinsky's report to the effect that in abolishing the procedure in existence until recently, the procurator of the USSR has on 25 February 1938 issued a decree to all district procurators prohibiting them from instituting criminal prosecutions in cases pertaining to counterrevolutionary crimes without the preliminary sanction of the procuracies of the Union and autonomous republics and of the regions, and that furthermore, in accordance with the same decree, the district procurators are prohibited from making arrests without the preliminary sanction of the procuracies of the Union and autonomous republics and of the regions, in all cases under investigation by the district procurators. . . .

On 2 March 1938 the third and last of the Moscow show trials opened. In the dock were Bukharin, Rykov, Yagoda, four former USSR commissars, and several other former officials, sixteen in all. The first show trial (of Zinoviev, Kamenev, and others in 1936) had centered around accusations of political assassination. The second (of Piatakov, Sokolnikov, Radek, and others in January 1937) had incorporated the former Trotskyist opposition and broadened the accusations to include industrial sabotage. This third spectacle tied together the previous sets of charges and associated the former right opposition with what was now called a right-Trotskyist bloc. According to this final scenario, the Trotskyists and rightists had since 1932 organized a series of underground cells for the purpose of assassinating Soviet leaders, sabotaging the economy, and carrying out espionage at the behest of Germany, Japan, and Poland. They were accused of conspiring with foreign powers to cede to them, should they come to power, parts of the USSR. The inclusion of Yagoda allegedly showed secret police collusion, thereby explaining why it had taken so long to uncover the plot.

As with the two previous trials, the event received wide publicity in the press, and a lengthy transcript of the proceedings was published in a large press run.[33] The intended lessons of the event are clear: that all oppositionists are traitors, that one must be con-

---

33. An English edition appeared as *Report of the Court Proceedings in the Case of the Anti-Soviet "Bloc of Rights and Trotskyists,"* Moscow, 1938.

stantly on guard against all kinds of sabotage, and that foreign enemies were everywhere.

Although one defendant (Krestinsky) initially balked, eventually all the accused pleaded guilty. Because Radek and Sokolnikov in the previous trial had not received death sentences, the accused in the third trial may have believed that cooperation could save their lives. On the other hand, Molotov later said they could have entertained no such hopes: "What, do you think they were fools?" he said in reply to a question on the subject.[34]

This "Bukharin trial" has been analyzed numerous times in scholarly studies.[35] One of the more interesting aspects of it was Bukharin's testimony: he again contested the ritual. While pleading guilty and admitting to the overall validity of the fantastic charges made against him, he nevertheless refused to confirm specific details of the supposed conspiracy and argued with prosecutor Vyshinsky over numerous details. Although Bukharin's real purpose will probably never be known, he may have been trying to fulfill his party duty (and perhaps prevent retaliation against his family)[36] by simultaneously confessing and defending his personal honor. As he had done at the December 1936 and February 1937 Central Committee plena, he refused to sully his reputation by admitting to monstrous accusations. In this way, his rhetoric might have been trying to send an Aesopian message to the party, the country, and the world: the accusations behind these trials are completely false, and we are being made to confess.

On the other hand, he may have been making a subtle attempt to save his life. It was possible for him to believe that his tactics could have led to a commutation of the inevitable death sentence. Bukharin in the weeks preceding the trial seems to have believed in the possibility in a letter he wrote to Stalin (see Document 198). Had he confessed fully and without reservation, there would have been no grounds to spare him; he would have been an admitted spy. But by suggesting that at least some of the charges were not true, he

34. Feliks Chuev, *Sto sorok besed s Molotovym,* Moscow 1991, 404.

35. See Conquest, *Great Terror,* ch. 11; Robert C. Tucker and Stephen F. Cohen, eds. *The Great Purge Trial,* New York, 1965.

36. After a lengthy delay, Bukharin's wife was arrested. She spent years in exile and in labor camps.

may have believed that he was leaving the door open for Stalin to spare his life; it would not have been the first time. Whatever his thinking, the decision had already been made, and Bukharin, Rykov, and the others were executed the day after the trial.

Bukharin's trial demonstrates what Karl Radek had once called the "algebra" of confession.[37] According to Stalin's formula, criticism was the same as opposition; opposition inevitably implied conspiracy; conspiracy meant treason. Algebraically, therefore, the slightest opposition to the regime, or failure to report such opposition, was tantamount to terrorism. This was the a priori formula behind the show trials, one of whose purposes was to fill in the facts—to assign values to the equation's variables—with the desired concrete testimony. Although Bukharin refused to provide the details, he admitted to the logic and truth of the algebra.

Bukharin's strategy took on an odd resonance years later in Molotov's reminiscences. When asked about Bukharin's guilt in 1973, Molotov said, "I do not admit that Rykov agreed, that Bukharin agreed, even that Trotsky agreed—to give away the Far East, Ukraine, the Caucasus—I do not exclude that some conversations about that took place and then the [NKVD] investigators simplified it." But just a few pages later, in response to a question about the lack of any concrete evidence except the testimony of the accused, Molotov retorted, "What more proof do you need of their guilt, when we knew that they were guilty, that they were enemies!" When asked, "Then there can be no question that they were guilty?" Molotov replied, "Absolutely."[38] The algebra was compelling.

Ending the Terror

Our knowledge of events in 1938 is limited. We know that arrests and executions continued, although perhaps not at the hysterical pace of 1937. According to NKVD archives, 593,326 people were arrested for "counterrevolutionary crimes" in 1938, compared

37. For a discussion of Radek's interesting testimony, see Robert Tucker, *Stalin in Power*, 394–409.
38. Chuev, *Sto sorok besed*, 401, 404.

with 779,056 in 1937. In 1938, fewer than half as many people (205,509) were sentenced to labor camps as in 1937 (429,311). Although the numbers executed in the "mass operations" in 1938 (328,618) were roughly comparable to those in 1937 (353,074), many of those shot in 1938 had doubtless been arrested the year before.[39]

There are signs that already by spring 1938 the winds were shifting in the high leadership. In March, Stalin declined Yezhov's proposal to stage a show trial of "Polish spies." In April, Yezhov was named commissar of water transport, while retaining his leadership of the NKVD and the party control commission. On the face of it, the appointment seemed to be a promotion. He now headed three important agencies: NKVD, the Commissariat for Water Transport, and the party control commission. Moreover, the appointment to water transport was not an illogical post for a chief of the secret police. The NKVD (and OGPU before it) had always been heavily involved in purging transport agencies and building canals with forced labor, and Yezhov brought a number of NKVD officials with him to water transport.[40] Still, it could not have escaped notice that Yezhov's predecessor Yagoda had been eased out of his police position by first appointing him to a similar post.

It is possible that several members of the Politburo (the names A. A. Zhdanov, A. A. Andreev, and K. Ye. Voroshilov are sometimes mentioned) had begun to complain that the arrests were weakening the state by promoting too many new and inexperienced leaders to high positions. It seems also that some officials of the NKVD had complained to party officials about Yezhov's administration of the police. These complaints are said to relate to misuse of government funds and Yezhov-authorized executions of some officials without investigation or trial.[41]

In the summer of 1938, several signals pointed to a decline in

39. GARF, f. 9401, op. 1, d. 4157, ll. 201–5.

40. RTsKhIDNI, f. 17, op. 3, d. 998, ll. 21, 37, 40–41.

41. Boris A. Starkov, "Narkom Yezhov," in J. Arch Getty and Roberta T. Manning, eds., *Stalinist Terror: New Perspectives,* New York, 1993, 36, based on NKVD documents not currently available to researchers. For an earlier view of Zhdanov as a Yezhov opponent, see J. Arch Getty, *Origins of the Great Purges: The Soviet Communist Party Reconsidered, 1933–1938,* New York, 1991, 111–19, 199–201.

Yezhov's status. In June, G. Liushkov, NKVD chief in the Far East territory, fled across the Manchurian border and defected to Japan. A close Yezhov intimate and assistant, Liushkov had participated in key police investigations from the Kirov assassination through the purge trials. His defection represented not only a serious security breach but a black mark against his chief.

Second, at the end of August, Lavrenty Beria was brought from Georgia to be Yezhov's deputy at NKVD. Like Yezhov's handpicked assistants, Beria was a career police official, but he was an outsider to the central NKVD circles, and his appointment represented Stalin placing his own man inside Yezhov's administration.[42] Yezhov sensed the threat. Archival materials show that in familiar Soviet self-defense style Yezhov began assembling files of "compromising materials" against Beria and other Politburo members.

Third, in the summer of 1938, Yezhov had had a violent disagreement with V. M. Molotov in a cabinet meeting, apparently threatening him with arrest. Stalin had forced Yezhov to apologize.[43] But Yezhov's fall and the ending of the terror were gradual processes. Even as Yezhov's personal prestige was declining, executions and arrests continued under his direction. In July a large number of arrested officials, including Yan Rudzutak, were shot. In the summer, Politburo candidate members Kosior, Chubar, and Eikhe were arrested.

By the fall of 1938, however, the Politburo was changing course. A Politburo resolution of 8 October formed a special commission to study arrest procedures and the apparent lack of judicial supervision over police activities.

Document 188

Politburo appointment of commission on arrests and investigations[44]

From Protocol #64 of the Politburo of the CC of the VKP(b)
8 October 1938

42. For the preceding few years he had been first secretary of the Transcaucasus Party Committee, but in the civil war and 1920s he was a professional chekist.

43. Boris A. Starkov, "Narkom Yezhov," in Getty and Manning, *Stalinist Terror*, 37–38.

44. RTsKhIDNI, f. 17, op. 3, d. 1002, l. 37.

Document 188 *continued*

Item #141. Re: The making of arrests, supervision by the procuracy, and the conducting of investigations.

A commission consisting of Comrades Yezhov (chairman), Beria, Rychkov, and Malenkov is instructed, within a 10-day period, to work out a draft decree by the CC, the SNK, and the NKVD pertaining to a new policy on the making of arrests, on the supervision by the procuracy, and on the conducting of investigations.

Although Yezhov chaired the commission, it is significant that the other members were from outside his circle: Beria was an outside appointment as Yezhov's deputy; Nikolai Rychkov was from the office of the state procurator, and Malenkov was from the Central Committee personnel department. To have a committee looking into arrest procedures was bad enough for Yezhov, but to have it staffed by high-ranking people from other agencies was a real danger to him.

The threat was real. The following month, the Politburo approved and distributed a decree on arrest procedures and strengthening judicial supervision. On 15 November the Politburo suspended "until further notice" the work of the murderous NKVD troikas.[45] Two days later the Politburo issued a more comprehensive decree sharply criticizing the work of the NKVD and completely "liquidating" the troikas. The 17 November decree was characteristic of Stalinist shifts in the 1930s. Discursive rules in the party forbade any admission that previous policy had been in error, so the decrees blamed the executors, not the policy makers, and praised the preceding policy while abolishing it.

As we have seen, there is clear documentary evidence that the sins now attributed to the NKVD had been encouraged, if not ordered, by the Politburo. The "mass operations," slipshod procuratorial controls, forced confessions, and the rest were part of high policy that did not originate with the NKVD. There is, however, reason to believe that Yezhov had taken rather too much initiative upon himself, in Stalin's view. We have already mentioned the rumors of Yezhov ordering executions without investigations, on his own

45. The old policy continued in the Far East. *Moskovskie novosti,* 21 June 1992, 19.

authority. The leading expert on Yezhov has concluded that "Yezhov's primary crime, however, consisted in the fact that he had not informed Stalin of his actions."[46] Without the opening of KGB archives, the exact relationship between Stalin and Yezhov, the level of independent authority the latter exercised, and the corresponding level of scapegoating in November cannot at present be established.

On another level, more than cynical scapegoating was at work here—though there was plenty of that in the text. But as had been the case in the decrees of May 1933, June 1935, and March 1937 (which the 17 November decree cited explicitly), the present order went out of its way to applaud repression while apparently seeming to limit it. As with those earlier decrees, the point was to centralize its administration in fewer hands. The 1933 and 1935 decrees had not ended arrests; they had simply limited the number of people and agencies authorized to carry them out. The clear meaning of this decree, without saying so openly, was that the NKVD (and Yezhov) were responsible for *disorderly* repression. Terror was still the order of the day, but now it was to be controlled completely by the Politburo. Yezhov and the NKVD were not blamed for terror; they were blamed for disorder. The transcript thus offered a political declaration to the readers of the decree that enemies were still dangerous, but they were to be destroyed carefully and selectively.

Document 189

Politburo decision halting work of troikas[47]

Extract from Protocol #65 of the Politburo of the CC. #110. Re: PROCURACY OF THE USSR
STRICTLY SECRET
CC of the All-Union Communist Party (Bolshevik)
15 November 1938
To confirm the following directives by the Council of People's Commissars (SNK) of the USSR and of the CC of the VKP(b) . . . I ORDER IN THE STRONGEST POSSIBLE TERMS:

46. Starkov, "Narkom Yezhov," 38.
47. *Moskovskie novosti*, 21 June 1992, 19.

Document 189 *continued*

1. Until further notice, a halt as of 16 November of this year to examination of all cases by the troikas. . . .

V. Molotov, Chairman of the Council of People's Commissars (SNK)

I. Stalin, Secretary of the CC of the VKP(b)

Document 190

Politburo decision on arrests, procuratorial supervision, and the conduct of investigations, 17 November 1938[48]

Supplement to Protocol #65 (Item #116) of the Politburo of the CC of the VKP(b)

27 October–25 November 1938

TOP SECRET

To the people's commissars for internal affairs of the Union and autonomous republics, to the heads of territorial and regional boards of the NKVD, to the heads of the military district, city, and district departments of the NKVD;

To procurators of the Union and autonomous republics, to procurators of regions, military districts, cities, and districts;

To the secretaries of the CCs of the national Communist parties, the territorial committees, the regional committees, the military district, city, and district committees of the VKP(b).

Re: The making of arrests, supervision by the procuracy, and the conducting of investigations.

A decree by the Council of People's Commissars of the USSR and the Central Committee of the VKP(b).

The Council of People's Commissars (SNK) of the USSR and the CC of the VKP(b) take note of the fact that the NKVD, under the leadership of the party, has accomplished much during 1937–38 in inflicting a crushing defeat [*razgrom*] on enemies of the people and in purging the USSR of numerous espionage, terrorist, subversive, and saboteur cadres consisting of Trotskyists, Bukharinists, SR's, Mensheviks, bourgeois nationalists, White Guards, fugitive kulaks, and criminal elements—all providing crucial support to foreign intelligence agencies in the USSR and, in particular, to the intelligence agencies of Japan, Germany, Poland, England, and France.

At the same time, the NKVD has also accomplished much in inflicting a crushing defeat on espionage-subversive agents of foreign intelligence services transferred to the USSR in great numbers from abroad under the guise of so-called political émigrés and deserters: Poles, Romanians, Finns, Germans, Latvians, Estonians, [Russian] residents of Harbin [China], and others.

48. RTsKhIDNI, f. 17, op. 3, d. 1003, ll. 85–87. Printed.

This purging of the country of subversive, insurrectionary, and espionage cadres has played a positive role in securing the further success of socialist construction.

Nonetheless, one ought not to think that the purging of the USSR of spies, wreckers, terrorists, and saboteurs is at an end.

In continuing to wage a merciless campaign against all enemies of the USSR, our task now consists of organizing this campaign by making use of more perfected and reliable methods.

This is all the more necessary insofar as the mass operations engaged in crushing and eradicating hostile elements, carried out by organs of the NKVD during 1937–38 and involving a simplified procedure of conducting investigations and trials, could not help but lead to a host of major deficiencies and distortions in the work of the NKVD and the procuracy. Moreover, enemies of the people and spies employed by foreign intelligence agencies, having wormed their way into both the central and local organs of the NKVD and continuing their subversive activities, sought in every way possible to hamper the work of investigators and agents. They sought to consciously pervert Soviet laws by carrying out mass, unjustified arrests while at the same time rescuing their confederates (especially those who had joined the NKVD) from destruction.

The chief deficiencies, brought to light recently, in the work of the NKVD and the procuracy are as follows:

First of all, officials of the NKVD had totally abandoned the work with agents and informers in favor of the much simpler method of making mass arrests without concerning themselves with the completeness or with the high quality of the investigation.

Officials of the NKVD had become unaccustomed to a meticulous, systematic work with agents and informers and had come to adopt a simplified method for conducting the investigation of cases, to such an extent that right up until the last moment they were raising questions concerning the so-called "quotas" [*limity*] imposed on the carrying out of mass arrests.

This has led to a situation where work with agents, weak enough as it was, has regressed even further. Worst of all, many officials of the NKVD have lost all inclination for agent procedures that play an exceptionally important role in the work of a chekist.

This has finally led to a situation where, in the absence of properly organized work, the investigative organs have, as a rule, been unsuccessful in fully unmasking the spies and saboteurs under arrest who were in the employ of foreign intelligence agencies and in fully exposing all of their criminal ties.

Such a failure to sufficiently appreciate the significance of work with agents and the unacceptable, thoughtless attitude to the making of arrests are all the more intolerable in view of the fact that the Council of People's Commissars

(Sovnarkom) of the USSR and the CC of the VKP(b), in their decrees of 8 May 1933, of 17 June 1935, and, finally, of 3 March 1937, had issued categorical instructions on the necessity of correctly organizing work with agents, on placing limitations on arrests and improving the work of the investigative organs.

Second, a major deficiency in the work of the NKVD has been the deeply entrenched simplified procedures for investigation, during which, as a rule, the investigator is satisfied with obtaining from the accused a confession of guilt and totally fails to concern himself with corroborating this confession with the necessary documents (testimonies of witnesses, the testimony of experts, material evidence, etc.).

The arrestee is often not interrogated until a full month after his arrest, sometimes even longer. Records are not always kept during these interrogations. Not infrequently, the testimony of the arrestee is recorded by the investigator in the form of notes and then, after much time has elapsed (after ten days, a month, or even longer), a general record of the interrogation is compiled, in which Article 138 of the Criminal Trial Code (UPK) [*ugolovno-protsessualnye kodeksy*], calling for, insofar as possible, a verbatim record of the arrestee's testimony, is not implemented at all. Very often, the minutes of the interrogation are not compiled until the arrestee has confessed to his crimes. Not infrequently, testimony by the accused which refutes this or that fact of the indictment is not recorded at all in the minutes of the interrogation.

The documents pertaining to the investigative cases are drawn up carelessly. Drafts of testimonies, written in pencil, corrected and crossed out by unknown hands, are entered into the record. Records of testimonies, unsigned by the person under interrogation and uncertified by the investigator, are entered into the record, along with unsigned and unconfirmed conclusions by the prosecution, etc.

The procuracy, for its part, has not taken the measures necessary for the removal of these deficiencies, as a rule, reducing its participation in the investigation to a simple registration and stamping of investigative materials. The organs of the procuracy not only have not removed these violations of revolutionary legality but have in fact legitimized them.

Such an irresponsible attitude to investigative work and such a crude violation of procedural rules established by law have not infrequently been cleverly utilized by enemies of the people who have wormed their way into the NKVD and into the procuracy, both in the center and in outlying localities. They have consciously perverted Soviet laws, committed forgeries, falsified investigatory documents, instituted criminal proceedings and subjected people to arrest on trivial grounds and even without any grounds whatsoever, instituted criminal cases against innocent people, while at the same time taking every possible measure to conceal and save their confederates—involved with them in criminal anti-Soviet activities—from destruction. Such things took place both in the central and in the local apparats of the NKVD.

All of these intolerable deficiencies observed in the work of the NKVD and the procuracy were possible only because enemies of the people who had wormed their way into the NKVD and into the procuracy attempted with every means at their disposal to cut off the NKVD and the procuracy from party organs, to evade the party's control and leadership and thereby to make it easier for themselves and their confederates to continue their anti-Soviet, subversive activities.

With the aim of resolutely removing the deficiencies set out above and with the aim of organizing properly the investigative work of the NKVD and the procuracy, the Council of People's Commissars of the USSR and the CC of the VKP(b) hereby decree:

1. That the NKVD and the procuracy be prohibited from carrying out any mass arrests or mass deportations [*vyselenie*].

In accordance with Article 127 of the Constitution of the USSR, arrests are to be carried out only by a writ from the court [*postanovlenie*] or with the sanction of the procurator.

Deportation from border areas is permissible in individual cases only with the permission of the Council of People's Commissars of the USSR and of the CC of the VKP(b) in accordance with a special petition by the appropriate regional committee, territorial committee, or CCs of the national Communist parties, a petition coordinated with the NKVD of the USSR.

2. The judicial troikas, created by the special decrees of the NKVD of the USSR, are to be abolished, along with the judicial troikas attached to regional, territorial, and republic boards of the Workers'-Peasants' [regular] Police.

3. During the making of arrests, the NKVD and the procuracy are to be guided by the following:

a) Coordination of arrests in strict compliance with the decree of the Council of People's Commissars of the USSR and the CC of the VKP(b) of 17 July 1935;

b) When demanding sanction for arrest from procurators, the NKVD is duty-bound to present a writ with full grounds for such an arrest as well as all materials justifying the necessity of such an arrest;

c) The procuracy is duty-bound to verify, thoroughly and substantively, the justification for the NKVD's writs of arrest, demanding, if necessary, supplementary investigative actions or the presentation of supplementary investigative materials;

d) The procuracy is duty-bound not to permit the making of arrests without sufficient grounds for such action.

It shall be established as a rule that, in the case of wrongful arrest, the procurator sanctioning such arrest shall, along with the officials of the NKVD, also bear responsibility for the arrest.

4. In carrying out their investigation, the organs of the NKVD are duty-bound to observe precisely all the requirements of the Criminal Trial Code.

In particular:

a) All investigations are to be completed within the time period established by law;

. b) Interrogations of arrestees are to be conducted no later than 24 hours following their arrest. A record of each interrogation is to be compiled immediately thereafter in accordance with Article 138 of the Criminal Trial Code (UPK) with precise details as to the beginning and end of the interrogation.

In familiarizing himself with the record of the interrogation, the procurator is duty-bound to indicate this fact in writing, making note of the hour, day, month, and year;

c) Documents, letters, and other objects removed during the house search are to be sealed immediately at the place where the search is conducted, in accordance with Article 184 of the Criminal Trial Code (UPK), and a detailed written inventory is to be made of all materials thus sealed.

5. The procuracy is duty-bound to observe precisely the demands of the Criminal Trial Code in implementing the supervision by the procuracy over the investigations conducted by the NKVD.

Procurators are accordingly duty-bound to systematically verify the implementation by investigative organs of all rules and regulations established by law for the carrying out of investigations and to immediately eliminate violations of these rules. Measures are to be undertaken to secure for the accused the procedural rights accorded him by the law, and so on.

6. In connection with the growing role of the supervision by the procurators and the responsibility placed on the procuracy for the making of arrests and the carrying out of investigations by the NKVD, the following points are to be recognized:

a) To establish the fact that all procurators implementing the supervision of the investigations carried out by the NKVD, and whose candidacies have been submitted by the appropriate regional committees, territorial committees, CCs of the national Communist parties, and the procurator of the USSR, be confirmed by the CC of the VKP(b).

b) The district committees, territorial committees, and CCs of the national Communist parties are to verify and present for confirmation to the CC of the VKP(b), within a 2-month period, the candidacies of all procurators engaged in supervising investigations by the NKVD;

c) Comrade Vyshinsky, the procurator of the USSR, is to appoint officials of the central apparat who are politically verified and professionally skilled procurators for the purpose of [utilizing them] in the supervision of investigations conducted by the central apparat of the NKVD of the USSR. He is to present them for confirmation to the CC of the VKP(b) within 20 days.

7. The measures proposed by the NKVD of the USSR for putting in order the investigative work of the NKVD, as set out in a decree of 23 October 1938, are to be confirmed. In particular, the decision by the NKVD to organize special investigative bodies in the operational departments is hereby approved.

Ascribing special significance to a proper organization of investigative work by the NKVD, the NKVD of the USSR is duty-bound to secure the appointment for the positions of investigators for the center and for outlying localities of the very finest party members enjoying the highest political trust and possessing the highest professional qualifications as demonstrated by their work.

It is established as a rule that all investigators for the NKVD, in the center and in the localities, are to be appointed only by order of the people's commissar for internal affairs of the USSR.

8. The NKVD of the USSR and the procurator of the USSR are duty-bound to give their local organs instructions for the precise implementation of the present decree. . . .

The Council of People's Commissars of the USSR and the CC of the VKP(b) call the attention of all officials of the NKVD and the procuracy to the need for a resolute elimination of the aforementioned deficiencies in the work of the NKVD and the procuracy and to the extraordinary significance attached to the reorganization of the work of the investigative organs and the procuracy.

The Council of People's Commissars of the USSR and the CC of the VKP(b) warn all officials of the NKVD and the procuracy that the slightest violation of Soviet laws and of the directives of the party and the government by any official of the NKVD and the procuracy, regardless of who the person is, shall be met with severe judicial penalties.

V. Molotov,
Chairman of the Council of People's Commissars
I. Stalin,
Secretary of the Central Committee of the VKP(b)
17 November 1938

Two days later, the Politburo again discussed the work of the NKVD, based on a report from one of Yezhov's lieutenants, Ivanovo NKVD chief V. P. Zhuravlev.[49] That report evidently was an attack on several Yezhov lieutenants, and Yezhov was blamed for not "unmasking" them himself. It is not too difficult to see the hands of Beria and Stalin in this familiar Stalinist bureaucratic tactic of attacking someone through his underlings; only they could have condemned these lieutenants and put Zhuravlev up to making his report. Four days later, after a four-hour meeting with Stalin, Molotov, and Voroshilov, Yezhov sent a letter to Stalin resigning from his post at NKVD.[50] His text was formulaic, recognizing and taking the blame for the "mistakes" of the NKVD in espionage and

49. Zhuravlev's report has not been found in the archives. His report against Yezhov was rewarded the following month when he was promoted to NKVD chief for Moscow region.

50. See *Istoricheskii arkhiv,* 1995, nos. 5–6, p. 25, for Stalin's calendar showing the meeting with Yezhov.

investigatory work. The same day, the Politburo accepted his resignation and two days later named Beria to head the NKVD. The removal of Yezhov's deputies proceeded quickly. Yezhov last appeared in public on 21 January 1939, atop Lenin's mausoleum with the rest of the Politburo.[51] He was arrested personally by Beria on 10 April in Malenkov's office in the Central Committee building. His name was in good repute until April 1939, when Sverdlovsk Obkom "requested" that one of their districts be renamed from Yezhovsk to Molotovsk.[52]

Document 191

Yezhov's letter of resignation to Stalin[53]

---

23 November 1938
To Comrade Stalin,
Politburo of the CC of the VKP(b)
I ask the CC of the VKP(b) to relieve me of my duties as people's commissar for internal affairs of the USSR for the following reasons:

1. During the discussions held at the Politburo on 19 November 1938 pertaining to the statement by Comrade Zhuravlev, head of the NKVD board for the Ivanovo region, the facts stated in it were fully confirmed. I bear chief responsibility for the fact that Comrade Zhuravlev, as is evident from his statement, warned me of the suspicious conduct of Litvin, Radzivilovsky [see Document 181], and other officials of the NKVD, who tried to put a stop to the cases of certain enemies of the people while they themselves were involved with them in conspiratorial, anti-Soviet activities.

In particular, Comrade Zhuravlev's note pertaining to the suspicious behavior of Litvin was very serious indeed. Litvin tried in every way possible to hinder the unmasking of Postyshev, with whom he himself was involved in conspiratorial activities.

It is clear that had I shown proper Bolshevik attention and heeded the warnings by Comrade Zhuravlev, Litvin, an enemy of the people, and other scoundrels would have been exposed long ago and would not have occupied leading posts in the NKVD.

2. In connection with the discussion of Comrade Zhuravlev's note at the session of the Politburo, other, totally intolerable deficiencies in the operations of the NKVD were also brought to light.

The linchpin of intelligence work, the gathering of information by agents, was, as it turned out, very poorly organized. Our intelligence operations

51. *Pravda*, 22 January, 1939
52. RTsKhIDNI, f. 17, op. 3, d. 1008, l. 59.
53. RTsKhIDNI, f. 17, op. 3, d. 1003, ll. 82–84.

abroad will essentially have to be rebuilt from scratch since the Department of Foreign Operations (INO) [a department of the NKVD] was contaminated with spies, many of whom had been in charge of networks of agents abroad who had been put in place by foreign intelligence agencies.

Investigative work has also suffered from a host of major deficiencies. The main thing is that investigations of the most important detainees were conducted by conspirators in the NKVD who had not as yet been unmasked and who succeeded thereby in putting a stop to the development of the investigative case, in strangling it at the outset, and, most importantly, in concealing their coconspirators in the Cheka.

The area in the NKVD that was most neglected turned out to be that dealing with the cadres. Instead of taking into consideration that the conspirators in the NKVD and the foreign intelligence agencies connected with them had succeeded in recruiting during the past decade—at a minimum—not only the upper echelons of the Cheka but also the middle echelons and often also officials on the lower echelons, I was content with the fact that I had crushed the upper echelons and some of the most compromised officials of the middle echelons. Many of those who were recently promoted, as has now become clear, are also secret agents and conspirators.

It is clear that I must bear responsibility for all this.

3. My most serious neglect had to do with a situation, now brought to light, in the department responsible for the security of members of the CC and the Politburo.

First of all, a significant number of as yet unmasked conspirators and vile people who had worked under [K. V.] Pauker are still there.

Second, [V. M.] Kursky, who replaced Pauker and who shot himself to death afterward, and [I. Ya.] Dagin, who is now under arrest, have also turned out to be conspirators and have planted more than a few of their own people in the security service. I believed in the last two chiefs of the security service. I believed that they were honest people. I was mistaken and I must bear responsibility for this.

Such is the general situation in the operational-chekist work in the People's Commissariat [for Internal Affairs], not to mention a host of other deficiencies.

Without touching upon the objective facts which might somehow at best explain the poor work [of the NKVD], I would like to dwell only on that which I am personally to blame for as director of the people's commissariat.

First of all, it is fully evident that I did not cope successfully with the operations of such a crucial people's commissariat, of a commissariat of such enormous scope, and that I did not succeed in managing all its highly complex intelligence activities.

I am to blame for the fact that I did not raise this question in time and keenly enough and with sufficient clarity, like a true Bolshevik, before the CC of the VKP(b).

Second, seeing a host of major deficiencies in our operations, even critiquing these deficiencies within the confines of my commissariat, I am to blame for the fact that I did not place these questions before the CC of the VKP(b). Being satisfied with isolated successes, and slurring over the deficiencies, I tried in desperation to put my house in order all by myself. Order was being established but with much difficulty. It was then that I would get anxious.

Third, I am to blame for the fact that I often dealt with the placing of cadres in a narrow-minded way [*deliacheski*]. In many cases, becoming politically suspicious of an employee [NKVD official], I dragged out the matter of arresting him and waited until someone else was picked up. For these narrow-minded reasons, I was often mistaken in [my choice of] many employees. I recommended them to important posts, and now they have been exposed as spies.

Fourth, I am to blame for the fact that I manifested a careless attitude, totally unacceptable for a chekist, in the way I pursued the task of resolutely purging the department responsible for the security of members of the CC and the Politburo. This carelessness is especially unforgivable as it applies to my dragging out the arrest of the conspirators in the Kremlin (Briukhanov and others).

Fifth, I am to blame for the fact that, being suspicious of the political integrity of such people as that traitor Liushkov, former head of the NKVD board for the Far Eastern region, and, recently, the traitor Uspensky, the people's commissar of the Ukrainian SSR, I did not take sufficient, chekist preventive measures. I thereby made it possible for Liushkov to escape to Japan and for Uspensky to escape who knows where, and the search for him is still going on.

Taken together, all of this makes it impossible for me to continue my work in the NKVD.

Once more I ask that I be relieved of my duties as people's commissar for internal affairs of the USSR.

Yet, despite all of these great deficiencies and blunders in my work, I must say that, thanks to the leadership exercised daily by the CC, the NKVD inflicted a crushing blow on its enemies.

I give my Bolshevik word and I pledge myself before the CC of the VKP(b) and before Comrade Stalin to take into consideration all of these lessons in my future work, to take into consideration my mistakes, to make amends, and to justify the trust of the CC in whatever area the CC considers it fitting to utilize me.

Yezhov

23 November 1938

Приложение
к п.№.пр.ПБ № 65

Копия

Сов.секретно

В ПОЛИТБЮРО ЦК ВКП(б)

тов.СТАЛИНУ.

Прошу ЦК ВКП(б) освободить меня от работы Наркома Внутренних Дел СССР по следующим мотивам:

1. При обсуждении на Политбюро 19-го ноября 1938 г. заявления начальника УНКВД Ивановской области т.Журавлева целиком подтвердились изложенные в нем факты. Главное за что я несу ответственность – это то, что т.Журавлев, как это видно из заявления, сигнализировал мне о подозрительном поведении Литвина, Радзивиловского и других ответственных работников НКВД, которые пытались замять дела некоторых врагов народа, будучи сами связаны с ними по заговорщической антисоветской деятельности.

В частности особо серьезной была записка т.Журавлева о подозрительном поведении Литвина, всячески тормозившего разоблачение Постышева, с которым он сам был связан по заговорщической работе.

Ясно, что если бы я проявил должное большевистское внимание и остроту к сигналам т.Журавлева, враг народа Литвин и другие мерзавцы были бы разоблачены давным давно и не занимали бы ответственнейших постов в НКВД.

2. В связи с обсуждением записки т.Журавлева на заседании Политбюро были вскрыты и другие, совершенно нетерпимые недостатки в оперативной работе органов НКВД.

Главный рычаг разведки - агентурно-осведомительная работа оказалась поставленной из рук вон плохо. Иностранную разведку по существу придется создавать заново, так как ИНО было засорено шпионами, многие из которых были резидентами за границей и работали с подставленной иностранными разведками агентурой.

DOCUMENT 191. First page of Yezhov's letter of resignation to Stalin,
23 November 1938

Document 192

Removal of Yezhov and appointment of Beria as chief of NKVD[54]

From Protocol #65A of the Politburo of the CC of the VKP(b)

27 October–25 November 1938

23 November 1938

Item #160. Statement by Comrade N. I. Yezhov.

Having considered Comrade Yezhov's statement requesting that he be relieved of his duties as people's commissar for internal affairs of the USSR and taking into consideration both the reasons set out in this statement as well as his state of ill health, which makes it impossible for him to simultaneously direct two major people's commissariats, the CC of the VKP(b) hereby decrees:

1. To grant Comrade Yezhov's request to be relieved of his duties as people's commissar for internal affairs of the USSR.

2. To maintain Comrade Yezhov in his position as secretary of the CC of the VKP(b), as chairman of the Commission of Party Control, and as people's commissar for water transport.

25 November 1938

Item #161. Re: People's commissar for internal affairs of the USSR.

Comrade L. P. Beria is to be appointed people's commissar for internal affairs of the USSR.

Document 193

Installation of Beria at NKVD[55]

Protocol #66 of the Politburo of the CC of the VKP(b)

26 November 1938–4 December 1939

5 December 1938

Item #47. Re: Transfer of authority for the NKVD (Decree of the CC of the VKP(b) and of the Council of People's Commissars of the USSR).

Comrade Yezhov is to hand over his post as people's commissar for internal affairs.

Comrade Beria is to assume the post of people's commissar for internal affairs.

This transfer of authority is to take place in the presence of Comrade Andreev, secretary of the CC of the VKP(b), and Comrade Malenkov, director of the Department of Leading Party Organs (ORPO) of the CC.

The transfer of authority is to begin on 7 December and is to be completed within a week.

54. RTsKhIDNI, f. 17, op. 3, d. 1003, ll. 34–35.
55. RTsKhIDNI, f. 17, op. 3, d. 1004, l. 11.

Document 193 *continued*

7 December 1938

Item #50. Re: Officials of the NKVD.

a) I. Z. Ressin is to be dismissed from his post as people's commissar for internal affairs of the Autonomous SSR of the Germans of the Volga.

The appointment of A. M. Astakhov as acting people's commissar for internal affairs of the ASSR of the Germans of the Volga is hereby confirmed.

b) The appointment of Comrade A. S. Blinov as acting head of the NKVD board for the Ivanovo region is hereby confirmed. He is to be relieved of his duties as deputy head of the Investigative Section of the 3d Department of the Chief Administration of State Security of the NKVD.

It may seem odd that Yezhov's letter did not refer to the "excesses" or failures in control over the NKVD that had been spelled out in the 17 November resolution (see Document 190). At his trial more than a year later, Yezhov did not admit to any excesses and rather seemed genuinely to believe that his only sin was in not purging his own apparatus (see Document 199). Or he may have been encouraged not to mention the mistakes of the NKVD in general.

The texts of fall 1938 (especially Documents 188, 189, and 190) not only ordered an end to the wild terror. They signaled a return to politics as usual. In this regard, it is less important to ascertain the degree to which procuratorial sanction would be rigorously enforced (although it seems to have been) than to recognize the return of a system of discursive politics aimed at achieving central control over politics and society. November 1938 thus represented not only an end to the terror but a return to the attempt to control events with "legal" hegemony and a systemic and systematic governing narrative.

Yezhov's removal thus again presented the question of variant "transcripts" for different audiences. For whatever reasons, Stalin had become convinced that Yezhov had to go. The real causes for making the change at this particular time probably involved a combination of factors, some of which will never be known. The question then, as it always was with the Bolsheviks, was finding the best way to use the decision (and information about it) in the service of the party leadership. The question of truth was always subservient to rhetorical control; more precisely, discourse control became truth. The real reasons for policy changes never had anything to do with the subsequent utility of information that was released to various audiences.

The general public could only read the terse *Pravda* announcement that Yezhov had resigned for reasons of health and had been replaced by Beria. It was not useful to tell them more: the mass operations had been secret (or at any rate never mentioned publicly), and in the interests of maintaining the facade of party-state unity it was inexpedient to discuss "mistakes" of the NKVD and failures of the judicial system, or to hint at conflicts in the leadership. Moreover, any criticism of excessive vigilance or NKVD mistakes would have cast doubt on the entire vigilance campaign, as well as on party control over the police, and could lead (as it did in 1956) to questions about whether victims had been unjustly condemned.

The broader party and bureaucratic audience (down to the level of district party secretary) was told something different; according to their transcript, the problem was one of "excesses" in the terror (see Document 190). Whatever the real reasons for Yezhov's fall, it was at that moment useful to the leadership to reassure the new nomenklatura that although things had been out of control, all was now in hand and there would be no more excesses. For this broader elite, it was necessary for the Politburo to portray the problem as a rogue NKVD that had somehow escaped party supervision. In this version of reality, it would have been inconvenient to discuss the attack on Yezhov's deputies, because to the nomenklatura audience it would have been clear that those deputies had in fact been vetted by the Politburo in the first place.

The more restricted privileged circle of the top leadership, however, read from yet another script, that of Zhuravlev's report and Yezhov's resulting letter. Here, the reasons for the replacement were different. Yezhov's letter mentioned the defects in the work of the NKVD (underestimating intelligence work) only in passing and never referred to the problems of excesses, lack of judicial supervision, forced confession, faked interrogation protocols, and the like. For Yezhov, his mistakes consisted only in the fact that his deputies turned out to be enemies. It might seem ironic that this least believable version was the most secret. On the other hand, as we have seen, the information power of those on high consisted largely in knowing the transcripts of those below them, not in a particular version prepared for them. They knew the real story, or at least the possible stories about Yezhov's removal. They understood the dangers of telling the masses too much and the necessity to reassure the new nomenklatura about the previous excesses.

In 1973 Molotov was vague about Yezhov's relations with Stalin and his fall from power. At times, Molotov seemed to be trying to disassociate Stalin from Yezhov:

> MOLOTOV: Yezhov was accused because he began to name
> quantities [of arrests] by regions, and in the regions numbers by
> district. In some regions they had to liquidate not less than two
> thousand, in some districts not less than fifty people. . . . That is
> what he was shot for. There was no monitoring over it. . . .
>
> CHUEV: Was it the Politburo's mistake that they trusted the organs
> [of the NKVD] too much?
>
> MOLOTOV: No. There were deficiencies. . . . I am not saying that
> Yezhov was spotless, but he was a good party worker. There
> should have been more supervision. . . . There was some, but not
> enough.[56]

Of course, Yezhov was not shot for establishing limits by region. We have seen that these limits were in each case approved by Stalin and the Politburo (see Documents 169, 170, 182).[57] The question of Stalin's "supervision" is more ambiguous. Above, Molotov suggested that there had not been enough supervision over Yezhov. Elsewhere, Molotov gave a different evaluation, and his attempts to shield Stalin from criminal responsibility were hopelessly contradictory. Finally, he admitted that whatever Stalin's role, in the final analysis the terror had been justified.

> CHUEV: If Stalin knew everything, if he did not rely on stupid advice,
> then it means that he bears direct responsibility for the repression
> of innocent people.
>
> MOLOTOV: Not quite. It is one thing to put forward an idea, and
> another thing to carry it out. It was necessary to beat the Rights,
> necessary to beat the Trotskyists, to give the order to punish them

56. Chuev, *Sto sorok besed,* 399.

57. A copy of a memorandum in Stalin's hand approving an increase in limits for execution appeared in *Moskovskie novosti,* 21 June 1992, 19.

decisively. For this [repression of innocent people], Yezhov was shot.[58]

... CHUEV: Did even Stalin have doubts in 1937 that things had gone too far?

MOLOTOV: Of course. Not only doubts. Yezhov, the chief of security, was shot.

CHUEV: But didn't Stalin make him a scapegoat in order to blame everything on him?

MOLOTOV: It is an oversimplification. Those who think so don't understand the situation in the country at that time. Of course, demands came from Stalin, of course things went too far, but I think that everything was permitted thanks to one thing: only to hold on to power![59]

The Aftermath

Yezhov's fall meant an end to the mass operations and executions, but not to the terror or its effects. Mass arrests hit the Komsomol at the end of 1938 as that organization's leadership was purged. In early 1939 several leading officials who had been arrested in 1938 were shot, including Kosior, Chubar, and Postyshev. Moreover, the new NKVD chief Beria purged the NKVD and arrested all of Yezhov's deputies and department heads.

The 17 November 1938 resolution about judicial controls and procuratorial supervision over the NKVD represented a victory for USSR Procurator Vyshinsky. For a long time he had favored maintaining procedural norms: procurators had to agree to arrests, specific charges had to be leveled, and some semblance of procedural regularity was to be followed. This approach did not necessarily mean less terror; it meant rather that the bureaucratic t's were to be crossed and the i's dotted. In April 1938 Vyshinsky had warned his procurators not to interfere in the illegal "mass operations," telling them to make legal protests "only in exceptional cases" and advising them that troika decisions were "final." Nevertheless, after Yezhov's fall, Vyshinsky's legalism became more visible in Politburo documents. While never criticizing the terror administration,

58. Chuev, *Sto sorok besed,* 437.
59. Chuev, *Sto sorok besed,* 401.

he did make suggestions aimed at controlling, regularizing, and even limiting it.

Document 194

Vyshinsky letter to Stalin on Special Board of NKVD, 10 April 1939[60]

TOP SECRET

From the procurator of the Union of Soviet Socialist Republics to Comrade Stalin, CC of the VKP(b), and to Comrade Molotov, Council of People's Commissars of the USSR.

Recently a great number of cases have been heard by the special board attached to the people's commissar for internal affairs of the USSR. 200 to 300 cases have been reviewed at each session of the special board.

Under such circumstances it is not to be ruled out that wrong decisions may have been made.

For this reason I presented my observations on the matter to Comrade Beria with a proposal to establish procedures for the work of the special board which would allow its sessions to be held more often, making it possible for fewer cases to be heard at each session.

I would consider it useful if the People's Commissariat for Internal Affairs received special instructions on this from the CC of the VKP(b) and from the Council of People's Commissars of the USSR.

A. Vyshinsky

Sent on 10 April 1939

From the end of 1938 numerous NKVD cases were reopened. We have little evidence on the scale of these reconsiderations; rumor places the number of people released in the tens of thousands. Anecdotal evidence suggests that not having signed a confession increased one's chances to be freed in the post-Yezhov period. Still, the numbers exonerated were small compared to the numbers repressed, executed, and sent to camps in the preceding two years. Releasing large numbers of the falsely accused would have raised inconvenient questions about the honesty and competence of the party and police, Stalin's role, and the need for repression in the first place. And many in the leadership really believed that huge numbers were guilty. In response to a question in 1971 about why

60. TsKhSD, f. 89, op. 18, d. 2, l. 1.

the huge numbers of innocent people were not freed, Molotov answered, "But many were correctly arrested. They checked it out, some were freed."[61] Although some were freed and "mistakes" were admitted, at least within the party circles, the fall of Yezhov did not mean a significant relaxation in state repression. In the long run, the numbers of camp victims continued to increase (although with ups and downs) until Stalin's death.[62] In the short run, a series of memoranda in 1939 shows that the mechanism of repression was still in good repair and that the leadership had no intention of relaxing it. The camp regime was not to be modified and legal barriers to rehabilitation were strengthened.

Document 195

V. Ulrikh letter to Stalin[63]

Letter by V. Ulrikh from the Military Collegium of the Supreme Court of the USSR of 14 June 1939

To:

Comrade I. V. Stalin,

Central Committee of the VKP(b)

To:

Comrade V. M. Molotov,

Council of People's Commissars of the USSR

During the past several months a great number of cases concerning members of rightist-Trotskyist, bourgeois-nationalist, and espionage organizations have been received for judicial review by the military tribunals of districts from regional boards of the NKVD.[64]

An especially large number of such cases have been received by the military tribunal of the Moscow Military District (300), by the military tribunal of the North Caucasus Military District (700), by the military tribunal of the Kharkov Military District (300), and by the military tribunal of the Siberian Military District (400).

In many cases, the defendants and their relatives have petitioned [the authorities] to allow attorneys for the defense access [to court records] so that the

---

61. Chuev, *Sto sorok besed,* 437.

62. Getty, Rittersporn, Zemskov, "Victims of the Soviet Penal System," 1048–49.

63. TsKhSD, f. 89, op. 73, d. 3, ll. 3–4. No response has been found in the archives.

64. Such judicial review could be initiated only by the procurator of the USSR; that is, by Vyshinsky.

latter may familiarize themselves with the materials of the case and speak on their behalf at court.

Taking into consideration the fact 1) that the majority of the defendants, citing the harsh conditions under which the investigations were carried out, have recanted their testimony at the judicial hearings and 2) that in many cases the minutes of the interrogations contain the surnames of persons who—for this or that reason—have not yet been arrested, allowing attorneys for the defense, a significant number of whom have yet to be politically evaluated, access may have the effect of divulging the methods employed in [our] preliminary investigations as well as of divulging the surnames of persons mentioned in testimonies.

To avoid divulging the methods employed in preliminary investigations and divulging the names of people involved in the case but who have not yet been arrested, I consider it advisable, as a rule, not to allow attorneys for the defense access in cases under review by the military tribunals of districts and involving members of rightist-Trotskyist, nationalist, and espionage organizations. After the main body of these cases has been reviewed by the military tribunals, that is, after 2 to 3 months, then, I think, it would be all right to allow attorneys for the defense access on equal terms if either the defendants or their relatives petitioned for it, except for cases having to do with materials involving a military, diplomatic, or other state secret.

Please instruct me in this matter.

V. Ulrikh

Document 196

Politburo decision on NKVD camps[65]

STRICTLY SECRET [*Strogo secretno*]
Extract from Protocol #3 of the Politburo of the CC of the VKP(b) of 10 June 1939

Item #164. Re: Camps of the NKVD.

The following proposal by the NKVD for the implementation of the measures listed below is to be confirmed:

1. The system whereby camp inmates are released on probation before the expiration of their terms is to be revoked. A convict ought to serve out the full term of his sentence, as imposed by the court, in camp.

The Procuracy of the USSR and the courts are instructed to cease and desist reviewing cases involving probationary release from the camps, and the People's Commissariat for Internal Affairs is to cease the practice of recording one day of work as two days of sentence served.

65. TsKhSD, f. 89, op. 73, d. 3, ll. 1–2.

Document 196 *continued*

2. The main incentives for increasing productivity in the camps shall be an improvement in provisions and nutrition for good production workers who demonstrate high productivity, financial bonuses for this category of prisoners, and a lightened camp regime, with general improvement in their living conditions.

Probationary release may be granted by the Collegium of the NKVD or the Special Board of the NKVD at the special petition of the camp supervisor and the supervisor of the political department of the camp to certain prisoners who have proven themselves to be exemplary workers and who have shown, over a long period of time, a high level of work.

3. Harsh coercive measures are to be applied to truant inmates, to those who refuse to work or who disrupt production: namely, a harsher camp regime, confinement to a cell, a worsening in the material living conditions and other disciplinary measures.

More severe, judicial punitive measures are to be applied to those who are most guilty of vicious disruption of camp life and production, including in some cases the supreme penalty [of death].

The camp inmates are to be fully informed of all cases where authorities have resorted to coercive measures.

4. The work force at camp should be equipped with foodstuffs and work clothes calculated in such a way that the physical strength of the camp work force may be utilized to the maximum at any productive task.

The Council of People's Commissars of the USSR should review and confirm the food and clothing norms established for the camp workforce of the NKVD.

Secretary of the CC

After the fall of Yezhov and the turn toward legality, Chairman of the USSR Supreme Court I. T. Goliakov took the lead in the legal rectification of the "mistakes" of the terror. Joined by Procurator General Mikhail Pankratiev and Commissar of Justice Rychkov, Goliakov attempted to streamline the procedure whereby procuratorial protests could result in successful appeals of those wrongly convicted. On 3 December 1939, Goliakov wrote to Stalin and Molotov proposing such an expedited procedure. Stalin referred the matter to Beria, who gave the following opinion. Molotov concurred with Beria and the idea was dropped.[66]

66. Peter H. Solomon Jr., *Soviet Criminal Justice Under Stalin*, Cambridge, 1996, 261–63.

Document 197

Beria letter to Molotov[67]

TOP SECRET

7 December 1939

To: Comrade Molotov,

Council of People's Commissars

cc: Comrade Stalin,

CC of the VKP(b)

In reference to your inquiry concerning the substance of the letter by the Supreme Court of the USSR of 3 December 1939 pertaining to #301133ss, bearing the signatures of Comrades Rychkov, Pankratiev, and Goliakov, concerning the simplification of procedures for the review of protests in cases involving counterrevolutionary crimes reviewed by the Military Collegium of the Supreme Court of the USSR, the NKVD of the USSR reports:

1. The aforementioned cases were reviewed by the Military Collegium of the Supreme Court of the USSR during the period of 1937–38 on the basis of the Law of 1 December 1934, by which the review of cases is called for without the summoning of witnesses.

2. In accordance with the law pertaining to the judicial system, if the procurator of the USSR or the chairman of the Supreme Court of the USSR finds reasons to lodge a protest, the aforementioned cases may be reconsidered only at the plenum of the Supreme Court of the USSR.

The NKVD of the USSR considers it inadvisable to violate this procedure, established by the law, for the review of protests pertaining to cases decided on by the Military Collegium of the Supreme Court of the USSR.

L. Beria,

People's commissar for internal affairs of the USSR

We conclude with another remarkable passage from Molotov in 1982 about the salutary effects of the terror on the subsequent period.

"It is interesting that before the events of the thirties, we lived all the time with oppositionists, with oppositionist groups. After the war, there were no opposition groups; it was such a relief that it made it easier to give a correct, better direction, but if a majority of these people had remained alive, I don't know if we would be standing solidly on our feet. Here Stalin took upon himself chiefly

---

67. TsKhSD, f. 89, op. 73, d. 6, l. 1.

all this difficult business, but we helped properly. Correctly. And without such a person as Stalin, it would have been very difficult. Very. Especially in the period of the war. All around—one against another, what good is that?"[68]

68. Chuev, *Sto sorok besed*, 395.

CHAPTER THIRTEEN

Two Bolsheviks

I know all too well that *great* plans, *great* ideas, and *great* interests take precedence over everything, and I know that it would be petty for me to place the question of my own person *on a par* with the *universal-historical* tasks resting, first and foremost, on your shoulders.—N. I. Bukharin, letter to Stalin, 1937

I request that Stalin be informed that I am a victim of circumstances and nothing more, yet here enemies I have overlooked may have also had a hand in this. Tell Stalin that I shall die with his name on my lips.—N. I. Yezhov, 1940

NIKOLAI IVANOVICH BUKHARIN and Nikolai Ivanovich Yezhov had both joined the party before the 1917 revolutions and therefore belonged to the exclusive group of "Old Bolsheviks."

Bukharin was of the Lenin type: a highly educated intellectual who spoke and wrote several languages. Like Lenin, Bukharin was a theoretician who produced an impressive corpus of published works within the Marxist tradition. Even as he languished in a Stalinist prison awaiting trial, he wrote several extensive philosophical and economic works, as well as a novel.[1] His theoretical writings had been cornerstones of Bolshevik politics. They were widely read and discussed by the leadership and had formed the theoretical basis for the New Economic Policy in the 1920s.

Yezhov, on the other hand, belonged to the Stalin type of practical

---

1. Gennadii Bordiugov, ed., *Tiuremnye rukopisi N. I. Bukharina,* 2 vols., Moscow, 1966.

Bolshevik organizer and administrator. A factory worker by profession, Yezhov never finished primary school. (Bukharin graduated from Moscow University.) In the civil war and through the 1920s, while Bukharin edited newspapers, Yezhov served on party committees in the provinces, working his way up the ladder to a post in a provincial party administration. Bukharin, like Lenin, was an *intelligent*. Yezhov, like Stalin, was an organizer and committeeman.

Both had sided with Stalin in the 1920s in the struggle against Trotsky, Zinoviev, and the "left opposition." Bukharin, from his lofty seat in the Politburo, brought the weight of his wit (and the controlled press) to bear on Stalin's enemies, while in the provinces numerous Yezhovs organized and purged the party committees. Their paths diverged in 1929, when Stalin veered to the left and launched the collectivization and industrialization campaigns. Bukharin protested and defended the mixed, gradualist approach of the New Economic Policy. Yezhov supported Stalin and was brought to Moscow to vet party personnel in the radical new USSR Commissariat of Agriculture, then in industry, and finally in the party personnel department itself. Yezhov thus helped to remove Bukharin's supporters from key positions.

The two knew each other. Their written correspondence was cordial and comradely. Back in March 1936, Yezhov as CC secretary in charge of such matters had broken a strict Soviet rule and approved Bukharin's request to allow his wife to join him in Paris on a business trip. For his part, Bukharin had greeted Yezhov's appointment as head of the NKVD with relief. Bukharin had blamed Yagoda for various frame-ups against the opposition, and he told his wife that Yezhov was an "honest person," who "won't falsify things."[2] Yezhov had originally taken a soft line on Bukharin when the latter was under suspicion for "organizing terror." Yezhov wrote to Stalin in 1936 that the Bukharinists were not as guilty as the Trotskyists. The latter, he thought, should be shot, but he recommended milder punishment for the rightists.[3]

The two had much in common. As Old Bolsheviks, both believed absolutely in the party dictatorship. Both believed that dangerous

---

2. A. M. Larina, *Nezabyvaemoe,* Moscow, 1989, 269–70.

3. Oleg V. Khlevniuk, *Politbiuro: Mekhanizmy politicheskoi vlasti v 1930-e gody,* Moscow, 1996, 206, quoting uncited text from Yezhov's archive.

enemies existed, that they had to be mercilessly crushed. Both believed in the discipline of democratic centralism and, as Trotsky had said, that it was impossible to be right against the party. Both believed that the truth was whatever the party said it was. Both, in their separate ways, were ready to die for the party and for the revolution. Ultimately, both had occasion to do so.

We present below the last known appeals of each of them to Stalin. Bukharin had been arrested immediately after his expulsion from the party in March 1937. He had begun to confess to the charges made against him in June, and by December of 1937 his participation in the scenario of the third show trial was confirmed. It was at that time that he wrote personally to Stalin (see Document 198).

Yezhov fell from power at the end of 1938 and was arrested in April 1939. After a lengthy interrogation at which he was accused of being a spy for Poland and England, he was confessing by the beginning of 1940. It is not known whether he wrote personally to Stalin as Bukharin did. Document 199 represents part of his final statement at his secret trial in February 1940.

These two documents are surrounded with irony. Bukharin had been glad when Yezhov came to head the NKVD in 1936, believing him to be an honest man. But soon Yezhov became Bukharin's chief tormentor at the December 1936 and February 1937 plena of the Central Committee. Although they became bitter enemies, both praised Stalin and invoked his name even while both must have known that he was the author of their downfalls. For both Bukharin and Yezhov, as their statements show, it was desperately important that Stalin know of their innocence and loyalty.

The two texts are vastly different in style. Bukharin's rambling letter is full of theoretical, historical, and literary references. Yezhov's statement, reflecting his different background, is direct and angry. But both texts suggest a similar psychological twist in their attitudes toward Stalin. On one level, of course, both knew that Stalin had ordered their arrests and would decide their fates. At the same time, in their texts both maintained a kind of separation between the process and its author. For Bukharin, his "case" was impersonally "moving" as if pushed along by some machine or process. For Yezhov, the fault was enemies within the NKVD who had done him in. Neither blamed Stalin. Was this simple etiquette or perhaps a deliberately false and flattering exoneration aimed at winning Stalin's pardon? Or could they really have believed on some level that the process and Stalin were two different things?

Document 198

Bukharin's letter to Stalin, 10 December 1937[4]

VERY SECRET [*ves'ma sekretno*]
PERSONAL
Request no one be allowed to *read* this letter without the express permission of I. V. Stalin.
To: I. V. Stalin. 7 pages + 7 pages of memoranda.[5]
Iosif Vissarionovich:
This is perhaps the last letter I shall write to you before my death. That's why, though I am a prisoner, I ask you to permit me to write this letter without resorting to officialese [*ofitsial'shchina*], all the more so since I am writing this letter to you alone: the very fact of its existence or nonexistence will remain entirely in your hands.

I've come to the last page of my drama and perhaps of my very life. I agonized over whether I should pick up pen and paper—as I write this, I am shuddering all over from disquiet and from a thousand emotions stirring within me, and I can hardly control myself. But precisely because I have so little time left, I want to *take my leave* of you in advance, before it's too late, before my hand ceases to write, before my eyes close, while my brain somehow still functions.

In order to avoid any misunderstandings, I will say to you from the outset that, as far as the *world at large* (society) is concerned: a) I have no intention of recanting anything I've written down [confessed]; b) In *this* sense (or in connection with this), I have no intention of asking you or of pleading with you for anything that might derail my case from the direction in which it is heading. But I am writing to you for your *personal* information. I cannot leave this life without writing to you these last lines because I am in the grip of torments which you should know about.

1) Standing on the edge of a precipice, from which there is no return, I tell you on my word of honor, as I await my death, that I am innocent of those crimes which I admitted to at the investigation.

---

4. *Istochnik*, 1993/0, 23–25. All text in italics was underlined by Bukharin. Bukharin addresses Stalin throughout by the familiar *ty*—Trans.
5. The memoranda have not been found in the archives.

2) Reviewing everything in my mind—insofar as I can—I can only add the following observations to what I have already said at the plenum:

a) I once heard someone say that someone had yelled out something. It seems to me that it was Kuzmin, but I had never ascribed any real significance to it—it had never even entered my mind;

b) Aikhenvald told me in passing, *post factum* as we walked on the street, about the conference which I *knew nothing* about (nor did I know anything about the Riutin Platform) ("the gang has met, and a report was read")—or something of the sort. And, yes, I concealed this fact, feeling pity for the "gang."

c) I was also guilty of engaging in duplicity in 1932 in my relations with my "followers," believing sincerely that I would thereby *win them back wholly to the party*. Otherwise, I'd have alienated them from the party. That was all there was to it. In saying this, I am clearing my conscience *totally. All the rest either never took place or, if it did, then I had no inkling of it whatsoever.*

So at the plenum I spoke the truth and *nothing but the truth*, but no one believed me. And here and now I speak the absolute truth: all these past years, I have been honestly and sincerely carrying out the party line and have learned to cherish and love you wisely.

3) I had no "way out" other than that of confirming the accusations and testimonies of others and of elaborating on them. Otherwise, it would have turned out that I had not "disarmed."

4) Apart from extraneous factors and apart from argument #3 above, I have formed, more or less, the following conception of what is going on in our country:

There is something *great and bold about the political idea* of a general purge. It is a) connected with the prewar situation and b) connected with the transition to democracy. This purge encompasses 1) the guilty; 2) persons under suspicion; and 3) persons potentially under suspicion. This business could not have been managed without me. Some are neutralized one way, others in another way, and a third group in yet another way. What serves as a guarantee for all this is the fact that people inescapably talk about each other and in doing so arouse an *everlasting* distrust in each other. (I'm judging from my own experience. How I raged against Radek, who had smeared me, and then I myself followed in his wake. . . .) In this way, the leadership is bringing about a *full guarantee* for itself.

For God's sake, don't think that I am engaging here in reproaches, even in my inner thoughts. I wasn't born yesterday. I know all too well that *great* plans, *great* ideas, and *great* interests take precedence over everything, and I know that it would be petty for me to place the question of my own person *on a par* with the *universal-historical* tasks resting, first and foremost, on your shoulders. But it is here that I feel my *deepest* agony and find myself facing my chief, agonizing paradox.

5) *If* I were absolutely sure that your thoughts ran precisely along this path, then I would feel so much more at peace with myself. Well, so what! If it must be so, then so be it! But believe me, my heart boils over when I think that you might *believe* that I am guilty of these crimes and that in your heart of hearts you *yourself* think that I am really guilty of all of these horrors. *In that case,* what would it mean? Would it turn out that I have been helping to deprive [the party] of many people (beginning with myself!)—that is, that I am wittingly committing an *evil?!* In that case, such action could never be justified. My head is giddy with confusion, and I feel like yelling at the top of my voice. I feel like pounding my head against the wall: for, *in that case,* I have become a cause for the death of others. What am I to do? What am I to do?

6) I bear not one iota of malice toward anyone, nor am I bitter. I am not a Christian. But I do have my quirks. I believe that I am suffering retribution for those years when I really waged a campaign.[6] And if you really want to know, more than anything else I am oppressed by one fact, which you have perhaps forgotten: Once, most likely during the summer of 1928, I was at your place, and you said to me: "Do you know why I consider you my friend? After all, you are not capable of intrigues, are you?" And I said: "No, I am not." At that time, I was hanging around with Kamenev ("first encounter").[7] Believe it or not, but it is *this* fact that stands out in my mind as original sin does for a Jew [*sic*]. Oh, God, what a child I was! What a fool! And now I'm paying for this with my honor and with my life. For *this* forgive me, Koba. I weep as I write. I no longer need anything, and you yourself know that I am probably making my situation worse by allowing myself to write all this. But I just can't, I simply can't keep silent. I must give you my final "farewell."[8] It is for this reason that I bear no malice toward anyone, not toward the [party-state] leadership nor the investigators nor anyone in between. I ask you for forgiveness, though I have already been punished to such an extent that everything has grown dim around me, and darkness has descended upon me.

7) When I was hallucinating, I saw you several times and once I saw Nadezhda Sergeevna.[9] She approached me and said: "What have they done with you, Nikolai Ivanovich? I'll tell Iosif to bail you out." This was so real that I was about to jump and write a letter to you and ask you to . . . bail me out! Reality had become totally mixed up in my mind with delusion. I know that Nadezhda Sergeevna would never believe that I had harbored any evil thoughts against you, and not for nothing did the subconscious of my wretched self cause this delusion in me. We talked for hours, you and I. . . . Oh, Lord, if only there were some device which would have made it possible for you to see my soul flayed and ripped open! If only you could see how I am attached to you, body and soul, quite unlike certain people like Stetsky or

6. Against the party line?—Trans.
7. Alluding metaphorically to a political romance—Trans.
8. *Prosti* can mean both "farewell" and "forgive me"—Trans.
9. Stalin's late wife.

Tal.[10] Well, so much for "psychology"—forgive me. No angel will appear now to snatch Abraham's sword from his hand. My fatal destiny shall be fulfilled.

8) Permit me, finally, to move on to my last, minor, requests.

a) It would be a thousand times easier for me *to die* than to go through the coming trial: I simply don't know how I'll be able to control myself—you know my nature: I am not an enemy either of the party or of the USSR, and I'll do all within my powers [to serve the party's cause], but, under such circumstances, my powers are minimal, and heavy emotions rise up in my soul. I'd get on my knees, forgetting shame and pride, and plead with you not to make me go through with it [the trial]. But this is probably already impossible. I'd ask you, if it were possible, to let me die before the trial. Of course, I know how harshly you look upon such matters.

b) If I'm to receive the death sentence, then I implore you beforehand, I entreat you, by all that you hold dear, not to have me shot. Let me drink poison in my cell instead. (Let me have morphine so that I can fall asleep and never wake up.) For me, this point is extremely important. I don't know what words I should summon up in order to entreat you to grant me this as an act of charity. After all, politically, it won't really matter, and, besides, no one will know a thing about it. But let me spend my last moments as I wish. Have pity on me! Surely you'll understand—knowing me as well as you do. Sometimes I look death openly in the face, just as I know very well that I am capable of brave deeds. At other times, I, ever the same person, find myself in such disarray that I am drained of all strength. So if the verdict is death, let me have a cup of morphine. I *implore* you. . . .

c) I ask you to allow me to bid farewell to my wife and son. No need for me to say good-bye to my daughter. I feel sorry for her. It will be too painful for her. It will also be too painful to Nadya[11] and my father. Anyuta,[12] on the other hand, is young. She will survive. I would like to exchange a few last words with her. I would like permission to meet her *before* the trial. My argument is as follows: If my family sees what I *confessed* to, they might commit suicide from sheer unexpectedness. I must somehow prepare them for it. It seems to me that this is in the interests of the case and its official interpretation.

d) If,[13] contrary to expectation, my life is to be spared, I would like to request (though I would first have to discuss it with my wife) the following:

*) That I be exiled to America for x number of years. My arguments are: I would myself wage a campaign [in favor] of the trials, I would wage a mortal war against Trotsky, I would win over large segments of the wavering intelligentsia, I would in effect become Anti-Trotsky and would carry out this

10. Officials of the party press department who gave evidence against Bukharin when he headed *Izvestiia.*

11. Bukharin's first wife.

12. Bukharin's current wife.

13. After the introductory "If," Bukharin has crossed out the words "you have decided in advance." From Yu. Murin's accompanying notes—Trans.

mission in a big way and, indeed, with much zeal. You could send an expert security officer [chekist] with me and, as added insurance, you could detain my wife here for six months until I have proven that I am really punching Trotsky and Company in the nose, etc.

**) But if there is the slightest doubt in your mind, then exile me to a camp in *Pechora* or *Kolyma,* even for 25 years. I could set up there the following: a university, a museum of local culture, technical stations, and so on, institutes, a painting gallery, an ethnographic museum, a zoological and botanical museum, a camp newspaper and journal.

In short, settling there with my family to the end of my days, I would carry out pioneering, enterprising, cultural work.

In any case, I declare that I would work like a dynamo wherever I am sent.

However, to tell the truth, I do not place much hope in this since the very fact of a change in the directive of the February plenum speaks for itself (and I see all too well that things point to a trial taking place any day now).

And so these, it seems, are my last requests (one more thing: my *philosophical work,* remaining after me—I have done a lot of useful work in it).

Iosif Vissarionovich! In me you have lost one of your most capable generals, one who is genuinely devoted to you. But that is all past. I remember that Marx wrote that Alexander the First lost a great helper to no purpose in Barclay de Tolly after the latter was charged with treason. It is bitter to reflect on all this. But I am preparing myself mentally to depart from this vale of tears, and there is nothing in me toward all of you, toward the party and the cause, but a great and boundless love. I am doing everything that is humanly possible and impossible. I have written to you about all this. I have crossed all the t's and dotted all the i's. I have done all this *in advance,* since I have no idea at all what condition I shall be in tomorrow and the day after tomorrow, etc. Being a neurasthenic, I shall perhaps feel such universal apathy that I won't be able even so much as to move my finger.

But now, in spite of a headache and with tears in my eyes, I am writing. My conscience is clear before you now, Koba. I ask you one final time for your forgiveness (only in your heart, not otherwise). For that reason I embrace you in my mind. Farewell forever and remember kindly your wretched

N. Bukharin   10 December 1937

Document 199

Yezhov's statement before the USSR Supreme Court[14]

A statement made before a secret judicial session of the Military Collegium of the Supreme Court of the USSR. 3 February 1940.

14. *Moskovskie novosti,* no. 5, 30 January 1994.

For a long time I have thought about what it will feel like to go to trial, how I should behave at the trial, and I have come to the conclusion that the only way I could hang on to life is by telling everything honestly and truthfully. Only yesterday, in a conversation with me, Beria said to me: "Don't assume that you will necessarily be executed. If you will confess and tell everything honestly, your life will be spared." After this conversation with Beria I decided: it is better to die, it is better to leave this earth as an honorable man and to tell nothing but the truth at the trial. At the preliminary investigation I said that I was not a spy, that I was not a terrorist, but they didn't believe me and beat me up horribly. During the 25 years of my party work I have fought honorably against enemies and have exterminated them. I have committed crimes for which I might well be executed. I will talk about them later. But I have not committed and am innocent of the crimes which have been imputed to me by the prosecution in its bill of indictment. . . .

I did not organize any conspiracy against the party and the government. On the contrary, I used everything at my disposal to expose conspiracies. In 1934, when I began conducting the case of the "Kirov affair," I was not afraid to report Yagoda and other traitors on the Extraordinary Commission (ChK) [Cheka] to the Central Committee. Sitting on the Cheka, enemies such as Agranov and others led us by the nose, claiming that this was the work of the Latvian Intelligence Service. We did not believe these chekists and forced them to reveal to us the truth [about] the participation of the rightist-Trotskyist organization. Having been in Leningrad at the time of the investigation into the murder of S. M. Kirov, I saw how the chekists tried to mess up the whole case. Upon my arrival in Moscow, I wrote a detailed report concerning all this in the name of Stalin, who immediately after this called for a meeting. . . .

One may wonder why I would repeatedly place the question of the Cheka's sloppy work before Stalin if I was a part of an anti-Soviet conspiracy. . . .

Coming to the NKVD, I found myself at first alone. I didn't have an assistant. At first, I acquainted myself with the work, and only then did I begin my work by crushing the Polish spies who had infiltrated all departments of the organs of the Cheka. Soviet intelligence was in their hands. In this way, I, "a Polish spy," began my work by crushing Polish spies. After crushing the Polish spies, I immediately set out to purge the group of turncoats. That's how I began my work for the NKVD. I personally exposed Molchanov and, along with him, also other enemies of the people, who had infiltrated the organs of the NKVD and who had occupied important positions in it. I had intended to arrest Liushkov, but he slipped out of my hands and fled abroad. I purged 14,000 chekists. But my great guilt lies in the fact that I purged so few of them. My practice was as follows: I would hand over the task of interrogating the person under arrest to one or another department head while thinking to myself: "Go on, interrogate him today—tomorrow I will arrest you." All around me were enemies of the people, my enemies. I purged chekists everywhere. It was only in Moscow, Leningrad, and the Northern Caucasus that I did not purge them. I thought they were honest, but it turned out, in fact, that I had been harboring under my wing saboteurs, wreckers, spies, and enemies of the people of other stripes. . . .

I have never taken part in an anti-Soviet conspiracy. If all the testimonies of the members of the conspiracy are carefully read, it will become apparent that they were slandering not only me but also the CC and the government. . . .

I am charged with corruption as pertaining to my morals and my private life [*moral'no-bytovoe razlozhenie*]. But where are the facts? I have been in the public eye of the party for 25 years. During these 25 years everyone saw me, everyone loved me for my modesty and honesty. I do not deny that I drank heavily, but I worked like a horse. Where is my corruption? I understand and honestly declare that the only cause for sparing my life would be for me to admit that I am guilty of the charges brought against me, to repent before the party and to implore it to spare my life. Perhaps the party will spare my life when taking my services into account. But the party has never had any need of lies, and I am once again declaring to you, that I was not a Polish spy, and I do not want to admit guilt to that charge because such an admission would only be a gift to the Polish landowners, just as admitting guilt to espionage activity for England and Japan would only be a gift to the English lords and Japanese samurai. I refuse to give such gifts to those gentlemen. . . .

I'll now finish my final address. I ask the military collegium to grant me the following requests: 1. My fate is obvious. My life, naturally, will not be spared since I myself have contributed to this at my preliminary investigation. I ask only one thing: shoot me quietly, without putting me through any agony.[15] 2. Neither the court nor the CC will believe in my innocence. If my mother is alive, I ask that she be provided for in her old age, and that my daughter be taken care of. 3. I ask that my relatives-nephews not be subjected to punitive measures because they are not guilty of anything. 4. I ask that the court investigate thoroughly the case of Zhurbenko,[16] whom I considered and still consider to be an honest man devoted to the Leninist-Stalinist cause. 5. I request that Stalin be informed that I have never in my political life deceived the party, a fact known to thousands of persons who know my honesty and modesty. I request that Stalin be informed that I am a victim of circumstances and nothing more, yet here enemies I have overlooked may have also had a hand in this. Tell Stalin that I shall die with his name on my lips.

Both Yezhov and Bukharin knew with near certainty that they would be shot. Yet both pleaded for their lives: Bukharin on the basis of a mostly blameless past and potential usefulness in the

15. *mucheniia;* the word does not necessarily imply physical torture—Trans.
16. Identity unknown.

future; Yezhov on the basis of past meritorious service and honesty even in the face of death. Both therefore clung, or wanted to cling, to some small chance that Stalin would spare them. Bukharin in particular displayed an amazing naïveté when he suggested that Stalin exile him to America, but warned that he would have to discuss it first with his wife!

Each, in his separate way, defended his personal honor. Bukharin, as he had done at his trial, made it clear that although he was prepared to admit to the overall charges against him, he was innocent of the specifics and had always been a loyal Bolshevik. Yezhov took a stronger line in his statement by repudiating the confession he had given to the NKVD interrogators and finally insisting on his complete innocence and constant loyalty to the cause.

That difference tells us a great deal about two Bolshevik attitudes toward the party and terror. Yezhov admitted to nothing in connection with the charges against him. In his statement, however, Bukharin admitted to a bit more than he had at the February 1937 Central Committee plenum. There he had denied any knowledge of the activities, conspiratorial or otherwise, of his former followers after 1930. In this letter, however, he admitted to knowing that they were up to something as late as 1932 and not telling Stalin about it out of pity or a belief that he could reform them: "I once heard someone say that someone had yelled out something. . . . Aikhenvald told me in passing . . . ('the gang has met, and a report was read')—or something of the sort. And, yes, I concealed this fact, feeling pity for the 'gang.' . . . I was also guilty of engaging in duplicity in 1932 in my relations with my 'followers,' believing sincerely that I would thereby *win them back wholly to the party.*"

It is difficult to see how such an admission could have done anything other than destroy any credibility Bukharin may have still had. Along with his testimony at the last two plena he attended, it represented another in a series of incremental concessions, each more damning than the last. Stalin might thus have legitimately wondered at what point Bukharin was telling (or would tell) the whole truth about his connections and knowledge of others' activities.

Although both Bukharin and Yezhov acknowledged in their

texts that they would probably be executed, each nevertheless pursued a different discursive strategy to try to save his life. Each, while intimating that his death was probably politically necessary, tried to give Stalin a reason to spare him. Each offered Stalin a possible public narrative and construction of reality that could explain letting him live. The documents can therefore be seen as dialogues, although their interlocutor, Stalin, remained silent.

Bukharin's letter was that of a fellow insider and longtime comrade writing to another. By surmising Stalin's "great and bold" idea for a purge, Bukharin spoke to Stalin as a fellow senior leader, as one of the top group that since before 1917 had originated and implemented great and bold ideas. Bukharin assured Stalin that he would confess at his trial and participate in the required apology-scapegoating ritual, but by drawing a distinction between that performance and the truth, Bukharin's text explicitly recognized that the campaign against enemies was constructed and not reflective of political reality.

By mentioning Stalin's late wife, drawing on the long personal relationship between Stalin and Bukharin, and mentioning his physical ailments, Bukharin was trying to evoke personal intimacy as well as political loyalty. Essentially, Bukharin was saying to Stalin, "You and I have been insiders together for a long time. I want you to know that I understand the symbolic rituals and am willing to play along to show my loyalty. But we have been friends for so long; can't you help me in my misery and at the same time find some use for me?" Given that at the last show trial Radek and Sokolnikov had not received the death penalty—and given Stalin's history of sparing Bukharin at the last minute—Bukharin must have thought he had a reasonable chance to save himself.

Yezhov took a different tack, and although he too recognized the likelihood of his own death, he may also have been pursuing a strategy to save his life. Even though his text was technically a statement to the court, it clearly was addressed to Stalin. Because of his position and different relationship to Stalin, as subordinate rather than one-time equal and friend, Yezhov's position was more complicated, and he could not draw on the same discursive strategies. He did not have the long personal connection to Stalin that Bukharin, as a fellow member of Lenin's guard, enjoyed. Aside

from the fact that he probably really believed that spies were everywhere, Yezhov could not "nod and wink" at the falsity and political construction of the hunt for enemies as Bukharin had, because,
as a subordinate, it would have been presumptuous for him to guess
at the plans of the gods. Stalin would not be likely to let him live and
tell the tale about how he carried out an essentially false campaign
of terror. Nor could he follow what might have seemed an obvious
strategy to the court: to argue that he was innocent of everything
because "Stalin told me to do it" would have been suicidal. Unlike
Bukharin, Yezhov apparently calculated that to confess to the espionage charges against him at his trial would not only help the
enemy but would deprive Stalin of a reason to save him. So
Yezhov's text followed the only rhetorical strategy really available
to him: to say to Stalin, "Unlike others, I accept as truth the basic
premise that enemies are everywhere. See? They even smeared me.
It's not necessary to scapegoat me for excesses. One could say that
what happened was not false and there were no excesses; I [we] did
what was necessary and it is defensible. I do not and will not refer to
your role in this in any way and as a loyal executor of a correct
policy could still be useful to you."

Both Bukharin and Yezhov were shaped by the texts and language of Stalinism, but in different ways. Yezhov, the compara-
tively simple party man, really believed that the victims of the terror
were enemies and that they were guilty. He bragged about the
number of enemies he had destroyed and said that his mistake
consisted in not destroying more of them. He accepted at face value
that all his assistants had turned out to be spies. The idea that the
country had been riddled with literally millions of traitors and
agents did not seem outlandish or absurd to him. He believed it to
the end. (This was also the belief of Yan Rudzutak, who from his
NKVD prison wrote to Stalin that the NKVD was infiltrated with
"enemies" who were fabricating cases against honest people.) At
his trial Yezhov refused to confess to the scenario provided him.
Instead, he told the "truth" as he understood it. He was not lying or
being coy in his statement when he feared that confessing to being a
Polish spy would give comfort to the enemy. In Yezhov's black-
and-white mentality, the enemy without really consisted of Polish
nobles, English lords, and Japanese samurai. For the Yezhovs, with

no knowledge of the outside world, these were not shorthands or caricatures but real foes: the master public narrative was true on the face of it. For him, discourse merely described reality.

Bukharin, on the other hand, perhaps because he had sat in the highest councils for so long and understood the Bolshevik utilitarian attitude toward "truth," could understand "something great and bold about the political idea of a general purge" of the guilty, the potentially guilty, and the merely suspicious. Truth, guilt, and innocence were defined by the party as whatever furthered the cause. Bukharin was prepared to give his life for that cause, telling Stalin, "*If* I were absolutely sure that your thoughts ran precisely along this path, then I would feel so much more at peace with myself." For Bukharin, the official public narrative and accompanying ritual were instruments. For him, discourse was designed to create a reality, and he understood that his death was to be a symbolic act to further the party's goals of unity. For Yezhov, on the other hand, party discourse reflected an objective reality.

Which was the more authentic Stalinist? On one level, Bukharin was. He understood what was being asked of him; in his time he had demanded similar sacrifices from other Bolsheviks. He believed in the party's need for his ritual confession as part of its "universal-historical tasks," understood his party duty, and, within his personal limits, did it. Like Arthur Koestler's protagonist Rubashov in the novel *Darkness at Noon*, Bukharin was caught in a kind of Bolshevik intellectual trap. His education and Western logic told him that he was innocent and that he did not deserve to die. But his whole political life in the Bolshevik milieu told him otherwise and forced him to play out the political sequence he himself had helped to create: everything is justified for the party. As with Rubashov, part of Bukharin's tragedy was that he had devoted his life to the Revolution, and now the Revolution was destroying him.

On another level, however, Yezhov's statement also reflected genuine Bolshevism. Its uncompromising tone, lack of personal emotion, and true belief in the need to crush all enemies spoke more to the traditional iron-willed Bolshevik than did Bukharin's intensely personal pleading. There is no reason to think that Yezhov understood anything of Bukharin's dilemma. For him, things were much simpler, and political utility or epistemological relativism did not enter into the matter. His situation was as clear-cut as a battle-field. Enemies were numerous and dangerous; his civil war experi-ence, social background, and party leadership told him so. The counterrevolutionaries had to be destroyed. He just did not happen to be one of them.

Part of the difference between the two was, of course, class back-ground. Workers like Yezhov had never been part of the theoretical world of Bolshevik politics, and intellectuals like Bukharin could relate to their plebeian followers only with great difficulty. But another difference had to do with their different positions in the party. Yezhov's belief in the "correctness" of the leadership was absolute. He was a soldier who marched, understood, and indeed shot when, what, and whom the party dictated. Bukharin, on the other hand, had long been a general. He was a founding member of the senior nomenklatura. Membership in this group cut across class and cultural lines. There were simple workers in that elite and educated party intellectuals outside it. As we have seen, the no-menklatura's position put it above not only the general population but also the several layers of the party masses and administration.

The nomenklatura was accustomed to interpreting the world for the party (and population) and presenting various layers of the party with texts, transcripts, and discourses deemed suitable for them. These decisions about suitability and interpretation were functions both of their corporate self-image as midwives of history and a basic desire to protect their status and power. The nomen-klatura's self-representation was plagued by a political paranoia about the party's position in society, which easily translated itself into defensive fear about its own corporate ability to retain power. This led to maintaining a dictatorship thrown together twenty years before as an emergency civil war measure, reserving partici-patory politics within its narrow circle, constantly regulating the composition of the party and its elite, and cultivating an unshak-able belief in iron military discipline in the party and especially within the elite layer.

Yezhov, though vicious and probably unbalanced, died simply, even honestly. He doubtless saw his end as a martyr's death, believ-ing that what he had done was right and that he had been dragged down by the omnipresent evil enemies he had tried to destroy. Bukharin also understood his execution as a martyr's fate. But he died the death of an intellectual plagued at the end by self-doubt, a death he saw as the result of a web of defensive political language, symbols, and rituals self-consciously built up to keep a certain idea (and group) in power, even if it required that the members of the group volunteer to die one by one. Conditioned as it was by elite party discipline, the constructed reality that the Bukharins had built eventually dictated their deaths. Bukharin died in a reality he helped create. Yezhov died in a reality he inherited and never really understood.

Conclusion

SERIOUS STUDY of the Soviet Union began after World War II, when the "Free World" faced the "Masters of Deceit," and when the line between good and evil seemed stark.[1] This was also a time of academic model building, hypothesis testing, and variable analysis, and these methods made important initial contributions to a new field of study. But they also sometimes facilitated the creation of straight-line causal thinking and politicized conclusions. Such chains of determinism as "Lenin → communism → Stalinism/totalitarianism → terror" were popular, and it was easy to conclude that socialism always led to terror, or that Stalinism was the inevitable product of Leninism. Yet as Stephen Cohen pointed out in a seminal essay twenty years ago, the circumstances of the Russian Revolution and Bolshevism could have produced many different outcomes. There were other possible lines of development, and Stalinism (or the terror) was not foreordained by Leninism.[2]

---

1. *Masters of Deceit* was the title of a popular book about communism, written in the 1950s by J. Edgar Hoover.

2. Stephen F. Cohen, "Bolshevism and Stalinism," in Robert C. Tucker, ed., *Stalinism: Essays in Historical Interpretation*, New York, 1977, 3–29.

Stalinist Politics as History

Historians revel in complex explanations, and therefore often seem a contumacious and exasperating lot. Some approaches look backward from an event in search of a model of causality with discrete component variables. The historical approach, in contrast, dissects elements of the phenomenon from the past forward, as it took shape, to find out what it was and how its complexity developed. This does not mean that good history is not analytical or theoretical or is simply composed of narrative details. Rather, it means that historians often prefer to analyze complexities without constant reference to simplifying or aggregating data against which predictive theories can be tested. Historical analyses are designed not to produce abecedarian answers but rather to show convoluted and intricate structures and relationships. Simple statements about what caused an event are lucky but rare products of such analysis. History, like life, is not so simple.

In our study we have not asked the question: What caused the terror? Questions like What caused the Thirty Years' War? or What caused the Great Depression? similarly invite easy answers to extremely complex problems. To identify a single main "cause" would also introduce notions of inevitability or determinism: the existence of the causal factor appears to make the result seem preordained.

The main causal element in the literature has always been Stalin's personality and culpability. In most accounts there were no other authoritative actors, no limits on his power, no politics, no discussion of society or social climate, no confusion or indecision. Stalin gave and everyone else received. The actions of others, or the environment within which he worked, were largely irrelevant or impotent. As a result, these accounts came perilously close to falling into the literary genre of fairy tales, complete with an evil and all-powerful sorcerer working against virtuous but powerless victims. Many existing historical treatments of the terror—including some quite recent ones—followed simple linguistic conventions and structures in order to illustrate their only point. Given the narrow focus, it was difficult to say more than "At this time Stalin decided to destroy. . . ."

(Western variant) or "On this date I. V. Stalin signed an order . . ." (Soviet and post-Soviet variant).

It is not necessary to look for the "main cause" of the terror elsewhere in order to give this picture nuance. Even with Stalin in the role of master conductor, orchestrating from a prepared score, a more complete explanation of the terror must include other factors, and we have tried to place these factors in the equation—to acknowledge that other powerful persons and groups had an interest in repression, that the social and political climate may have facilitated terror, that the road to terror may have been crooked and roundabout. As we noted in the Introduction, even a terrorist Stalin would have needed fertile soil to spread the violence, and it is our contention that the environment was as important as the agent in explaining the phenomenon as a whole.

We have posed different queries: What made this all possible? and What did they think they were doing? We have provided evidence of numerous factors and elements of the phenomenon, including the tradition of party discipline, corporate mentality and self-interest of the nomenklatura elite, political relations and struggles among numerous groups within the party, elite anxiety and perceptions of state-society relations, and, last but not least, the "Stalin factor." It is our view that each of these elements, and others as well—foreign relations, social identities, and Russian cultural perceptions, for example—was necessary but insufficient to explain the terror. For the terror was more than a top-down police operation; it involved people denouncing their bosses, their underlings, their comrades. Stalin played a major role in starting the violence, but we can begin to understand it as a historical phenomenon only by considering him among many factors.

Our study has concentrated on the Bolshevik elite at the top of the political pyramid. In broadest terms, the story has been about Stalin and the senior elite trying to come to terms with and shape the political and social environment they had inherited from the past and had shaped by their own policies. That environment forms the background, the preconditions for the terror.

In schematic terms, our story is one in which the Bolshevik elite, including Stalin, reacted with fear and anxiety to a disorderly and confused situation produced by the Stalin Revolution of 1929–32. Their fears of losing control, even of losing power, led them into a series of steps to protect their position and manage the situation: sanctioning and building a unifying cult around Stalin, stifling even the hint of dissent within the elite by closing ranks around a rigid notion of party discipline, and embarking on a program of centralization in everything from administration to culture. State building, with uniform laws, alternated with voluntaristic terror, but both had the same goal: asserting the control of Stalin and the Moscow elite.

But despite what appear to be successes in these steps, Stalin and the elite were not able to overcome their insecurity. Stalin's suspicious nature and the elite's fears for their position combined to form a natural partnership between them in favor of centralization. His drive for personal power and the elite's drive for corporate status and authority made the two natural allies for several years. They supported and endorsed each other to the outside world; the audience included not only the Soviet population but also the party rank and file. Although Stalin's suspicion and the elite's corporate anxiety fed upon each other, their joint action from 1932 to 1937 calmed and satisfied neither. Although they were generally united until 1937, as early as 1934 cracks had begun to appear in the alliance between Stalin and the nomenklatura elite.

As they closed ranks against a variety of real and imaginary threats, the Central Committee with its rituals and mores began to develop and affirm a sense of corporate identity. Its members saw themselves as the victorious builders of socialism and the country's new ruling stratum. As Rudzutak said, they saw Stalin as "theirs." Stalin, for his part, could not have found much pleasure in this elite consolidation. His personal tendency to see enemies and threats everywhere and to be suspicious of everyone and everything covered not only the traditional "class enemy" but now extended to "enemies with party cards."

Everything came apart in the summer of 1937. After a series of failed attempts to control the nomenklatura elite and bend them to his will, Stalin turned against that elite, that elite turned against itself, and both struck out at a variety of "enemies" in the country. Characteristically, those enemies could not be identified very precisely. Alliances fractured and re-formed; in 1937 and 1938 normal politics was replaced by a hysterical and paranoiac war of all against all.

The documents and analyses here have presented the details of this schematic view of the coming of the terror. At this point, it is possible to weave these strange stories and initiatives into an overall sketch of an answer to our original question: How was it all possible?

Reacting to Their Environment: Stalin and the Elite Struggle for Control

In 1932 the country was in chaos. The collectivization and industrialization policies of the Stalin Revolution had uprooted society, destroyed formerly prominent social groups and classes, and abolished private property and markets in favor of a new, untested, and constantly changing form of socialism. Millions of peasants and urban proprietors were angry and confused; millions of others had been killed or had died of starvation. Nobody really understood how the economy was working or should work, not even its new directors. Nobody had a solid grasp of the shifting and reactive structure of state institutions, not even their new administrators. Nobody, including those specializing in intelligence gathering, had a very clear idea of what the population was thinking or who was organizing subversive activities. Across the country, political directives, juridical norms, and even ideology were being interpreted in a wide variety of ways that sometimes bore little relation to what Moscow was saying.

Even though in 1932 the Stalinists had "won," insofar as they had in fact implemented collectivization, their victory was in many ways unsatisfying. Famine still stalked the land, and the regime had little doubt that despite its brave proclamations of victory and party unity, there was desperate opposition to it at many levels. Peasants sang about Stalin chewing bones on top of a coffin. Student groups cranked out incendiary pamphlets, and well-known party members gathered in the night to write platforms calling for the overthrow of the leadership. Even within that leadership, some Central Committee members knew about and sympathized with these nefarious activities. With hindsight it is perhaps easy to minimize the real threats, but there is little doubt that the Stalinist leadership was worried. Once again they had what seemed to be a precarious victory. As they had been at the end of the civil war, the Bolsheviks were insecure at precisely the time of their apparent ascendancy.

They were worried about personal meetings and conversations, not only among former oppositionists but even among CC members. More and more often, party leaders spoke and wrote about a "new situation" or "predicament" confronting the party in the early 1930s. That new situation was variously defined, but generally it meant the political crisis atmosphere following the storm of collectivization, the rise of fascism, and suspicions in the party about particularly threatening opposition groups.

That there seem to have been few dangerous "Riutinists" or "Trotskyists" is beside the point. We have no evidence that, aside from some small discussion circles, there was any significant organized political opposition after 1932. If there was, it certainly never reached the scale attributed to it in official propaganda. Of course, there were personal and institutional incentives to magnify the threat. The secret police had a vested interest in "uncovering" conspiracies, and both Stalin and the elite could use threats of political conspiracy as excuses to tighten their control on many fronts. Still, the ways they spoke in public and in private and the ways they wrote to each other leave the strong impression that they believed much of their own propaganda about dangerous enemies. These Bolsheviks were professional conspirators whose formative experiences involved secrecy and treachery on many levels. In the chaos and threatening environments of national breakdown and international threat, it is not so difficult to believe that they were worried.

Although potentially conspiratorial meetings between former contenders for power might somehow indeed seem threatening, this regime was worried about even the smallest political or pseudopolitical groups, whose activities by any stretch of rationality posed no threat to the regime. In the new paranoid view of the leadership, meetings at which politics was discussed were "illegal," and attempts by students to travel abroad became "attempts at establishing contact with White Guard–fascist organizations in

Germany for the purpose of coordinating counterrevolutionary operations."

The Stalinists were chronically anxious about a multitude of political and social threats and responded to all of them, great and small, without distinguishing real dangers from trifles. They tried to micromanage their entire political environment. They realized, even subconsciously, how little real day-to-day influence they had out in the countryside. Aware that they had failed to create a predictable and obedient administration, the Stalinists tried to govern by campaign, by creating ideological discourse and rituals, by the use of special plenipotentiaries, by creating parallel bureaucratic channels of information and control, by various "extraordinary situations." All of these failed.

Our story started with the calamity of 1932. We traced the Stalinists' reactions to this "new situation" through a sequential examination of their public and private texts and saw what seemed to be a kind of schizophrenic discourse. Whether we call it soft vs. hard, moderate vs. radical, or legalistic vs. repressive, there seemed to be two policies, two currents that alternated in rapid sequence.

It is tempting to see here a "moderate alternative" or "moderate opposition" that argued for a relaxation of the "class struggle" and an attenuation of repression. Others have suggested that a "moderate" and "radical" faction contended for Stalin's favor, with the dictator favoring first one side and then the other. It is reasonable to assume that from Politburo to party cell, different politicians had preferences or predilections for one emphasis or the other. It is highly suggestive, for example, that Vyshinsky and Zhdanov rarely proposed repressive solutions, while Yezhov and Shkiriatov rarely proposed anything else. Were they leaders of factions or clusters in the leadership that came together on the basis of policy alternatives? Or were they simply speaking as their roles required them to as leaders of bureaucratic organs with different responsibilities?

At this point, we cannot know for certain. Yet we found no documentary evidence of the existence of anything like stable elite factions or groups in the available archives. Given the Stalinist penchant for party discipline and unity, it is perhaps not surprising that such competing nomenklatura discourses, if they existed, never found their way into the documentary record. We did find alternating and contending policy discourses coming from the same people, including Stalin. The dichotomy between legalism and repression may at first seem sharp, and the two tendencies may seem contradictory. But the policies themselves are not incompatible if we conceive of them as complementary tactics in the campaign to achieve control.

Clearly, until the middle of 1937 Stalin and the nomenklatura were undecided or unwilling finally and completely to choose one tactic over the other. We see first one and then the other until 1937–38, when it seems that panic overwhelmed the Politburo and legalistic gestures were suspended. But the two variants were really two sides of the same coin. That coin was ending chaos, getting control, centralizing authority. The nomenklatura wanted to control printed discourse: sometimes that meant restraining locals and sometimes it meant purging libraries. In both cases the point was that such decisions were to be made centrally. The elite wanted to control the judiciary: sometimes they chose to reinforce procuratorial sanction, and sometimes they pushed the extralegal special board. Sometimes the Politburo called for more arrests; other times it seemed to be narrowly circumscribing them. In either case, Moscow, not local authorities, was to decide what was criminal and who should be arrested. The state leaders wanted to regulate the composition of the party: sometimes that meant political education and sometimes purges. (Stalin advocated both in one speech in 1934.) In either case, the goal was Moscow control of the party ranks. Thus the dichotomy was not really "hard" vs. "soft," but rather hard or soft roads to centralization and enforcing "fulfillment of decisions." Both the terror and its opposite, the Stalin constitution, were thus about the same thing.

Terror Without Planning: Stalin Against the Elite

The nomenklatura and Stalin were united in forcing the trend toward control and obedience. They agreed on the need to "clean" or purge party and society of "dangerous" or "unreliable" elements among the rank-and-file members or former oppositionists. Eventually it became clear that there could be only one boss, and Stalin meant to be it. Yet this was a gradual process.

The growing self-affirmation and group identity of the nomen-klatura was a problem for Stalin. There were hints as early as 1934 that the interests of Stalin and the senior elite had begun to diverge. Stalin's speech to the Seventeenth Party Congress that year complained about the "feudal princes" of the party apparatus who thought that party directives "were not written for them but for fools." It is possible, as we have seen, that a considerable number of delegates to that meeting may have abstained or simply not voted for Stalin's leadership. The nomenklatura's members were for discipline and obedience—among those below them. They were for using terror to root out opposition—but not in their own machines. They were for legality—as long as they controlled the courts and decided who would be arrested in their territories. Stalin and the Politburo insisted that *everyone* obey, follow discipline, and bow to central controls.

Stalin and his Moscow intimates tried a variety of tactics in the 1930s to control their own far-flung machine. Membership purges, political jawboning about "fulfillment of decisions," delicate manipulation of texts to form or adjust alliances, investigations by police and control commissions,[3] and various other tactics all failed to produce the results Stalin wanted. As we have suggested, it was a delicate game in which Stalin and the other political actors jockeyed for power and advantage. The game had rules: nothing could be allowed to jeopardize the public image of Bolshevik unity or the regime's control over the country.

The production of variant party texts in the 1930s illustrates the shifting political combinations and the constraints under which even Stalin functioned. The multiple narratives of Central Committee meetings in 1935 and 1936 were aimed at creating specific political spheres for specific groups. As we have seen, the complex of texts allowed Stalin to demonstrate his concern for "little people," a certain separation from Yezhov, and his displeasure with the elite without ever threatening party control by denouncing them too severely to lower audiences. He took a risk when he leaked to the public a hint of suspicion about the elite, and when he

---

3. For the use of the party control commission, see J. Arch Getty, "Pragmatists and Puritans: The Rise and Fall of the Party Control Commission," *The Carl Beck Papers*, 1208, October 1997, 1–45.

did it he tried to avoid damaging their prestige, for the credibility of the regime as a whole rested in part on their continued functioning. In turn, the texts allowed the nomenklatura as a whole to display a unity that did not exist and to hide criticism of certain of its members by presenting split votes as unanimous decisions.

Language also played a delicate and subtle role in crystallizing and changing politics. The evolution from "class enemy" to "the enemy with a party card" transformed a party united against the bourgeoisie into a party whose rank and file were suspicious of highly placed enemies in the elite. The "Trotskyist" trope was filled and refilled with meaning according to changing political circumstances and alignments. In the beginning, all segments of the party found it easy to marginalize, scapegoat, and attack former oppositionists as outsiders disloyal to the party. But in the autumn of 1936, after the first Moscow show trial, the definition changed, as suspicion shifted from the former dissidents per se to currently serving members of the economic apparatus who, as it happened, had suspicious pasts. The transformation was completed in the disaster of 1937, when language slipped from everyone's control, and anyone could be labeled a "Trotskyist" or "Bukharinist" and thus be isolated and destroyed. The tuning of language to influence politics led to the destruction of the political system.

The result of his insistence on control of the nomenklatura and the failure of previous efforts was the Stalin-assisted suicide of the party elite in 1937–38. Stalin and his closest associates, in a panic that still echoes in Molotov's and Kaganovich's memoirs, about the possibility of not controlling the country in time of war, threw the entire political system into the air.

Yet it is a mistake to see in this some sort of grand plan for terror. Without a doubt, at every juncture Stalin acted in ways that would increase his personal power; in this he seems to have had a clear goal. But the road to centralized power was not necessarily the road to terror. Just as there was no iron determinism that led from Lenin to Stalin, there was no inevitability from control to violence. We saw in a multitude of cases how repression moved in zigzags and circles. The cases of Zinoviev, Kamenev, Smirnov, Yenukidze, Postyshev, Yagoda, and especially Bukharin were hardly handled in such a way as to suggest a plan. In each of these cases, there were false starts and abrupt "soft" but apparently "final" resolutions that had to be contradicted later when the defendents' fates were otherwise decided. Had there been a plan, it would have been much easier and more convincing not to have let them off the hook so repeatedly and publicly.

In each case the final fatal texts had to explain previous embarrassing contrary decisions. An authoritative 1935 text exonerated Zinoviev and Kamenev of Kirov's murder; the next year's discourse maintained that, after all, they were guilty. Yenukidze was expelled and then readmitted, both apparently on Stalin's initiative and amid considerable confusion, then finally arrested a year later. The Politburo criticized Postyshev, fired him, rehired him, denounced his critics, fired him again. In January 1938 it decided to keep him in the party and then days later expelled him. Yagoda was kept on at the NKVD long after he had been discredited, then removed but casually kept on the CC. After several months he was kicked off the Central Committee and arrested in a sudden panic about his being at liberty "even one day." Bukharin was denounced at the 1936 trial and then publicly cleared in the press. He was denounced again in December but saved by Stalin at a plenum that remained secret for decades. Finally, in February 1937 he was expelled and arrested in a flurry of paperwork that raises enormous doubts about who wanted what. He was brought to trial an entire year later, and more than six months after he began to confess to the monstrous charges brought against him. Why all this delay and confusion?

One plausible answer is that no one, including Stalin, could foresee the outcome of these events. This would also help explain why there was no resistance from the nomenklatura to a process that we know eventually led to their destruction. Our reading of the Central Committee plena from the 1930s, along with other documents, has convinced us that the usual explanations for support for the terror—that Stalin secured cooperation from his senior officials through fear, cunning, intimidation, and blackmail, and by forcing them to become accomplices—are in themselves inadequate. Not only are there no signs that Stalin was feared in the early phase when the terror was engendered, but there is no evidence of any reluctance or protest among senior party leaders about the terror at any point. Instead, there seems to have been a broad consensus at various stages on the need for repression of particular groups and on cleansing the party of unreliable elements. At several key junctures Central Committee members advocated repressive measures that defied and went beyond those prescribed by Stalin's closest henchmen.[4] There seem to have been various personal and corporate interests involved. Until the middle of 1937 no high-ranking party leader who had not been an oppositionist had reason to fear repression. Subjectively, everyone thought that he was innocent and not at risk. An obsequious desire to impress the dictator seems perhaps a relevant but insufficient answer.

In order to explain some of these zigzags it is also sometimes suggested that Stalin liked to play a sadistic cat-and-mouse game with his victims. Aside from the fact that there are no sources supporting this conjecture, the basic notion is nonsense. It arose as a kind of post hoc explanation of contradictory initiatives that did not fit scholars' assumptions about Stalin's plans. No one can read the discourse of the Stalinists throughout the 1930s without sensing their nervousness, even frequent panic. This was not a time for play; these were serious matters in which lives were sacrificed to save a regime its leaders felt was hanging by a thread. Stalin evidently distrusted the NKVD until late 1936 and the army until mid-1937. It would have been insufferably stupid of him to play with elite lives in such circumstances, and no one has ever accused him of being stupid.

Alternatively, it is suggested that there was a group within the Stalinist elite who attempted to block Stalin's plans for terror. This group is variously said to have included Kirov, Kuibyshev, Ordzhonikidze, and Postyshev, and it has been claimed that their resistance to Stalin's plan for terror forced the dictator to zig and zag to appease or fool them. We have already noted the lack of any documentary evidence for such a group. Rather we have seen time and again how the nomenklatura "we" closed ranks against "them" as soon as doubts arose about potential enemies. They voted as a unit

4. See RTsKhIDNI, f. 17, op. 2, d. 547, l. 69 and d. 544, l. 22 (on Yenukidze); *Voprosy istorii,* no. 2, 1995, 21 (on Yagoda); RTsKhIDNI, f. 17, op. 2, d. 577, ll. 30–33, and *Voprosy istorii,* no. 1, 1994, 12–13 (Stalin's remarks on Bukharin).

without dissent. Kirov was certainly no softy in Leningrad, and we have texts from Kuibyshev that are equally firm against the opposition. Now that we have considerable evidence on Postyshev's conduct and discourse, he becomes practically the last candidate for "rotten liberalism." According to the leading expert, the rumored attempts by Ordzhonikidze to save his deputy Piatakov still lack documentary support.[5] There was no moderate bloc.

By accepting a priori that Stalin planned everything and that social and political relations played no role in the 1930s, even scholars who work very closely with documents have no choice but to explain zigzags as Stalinist game playing. Such an explanation is based on no documentary evidence and is weakened by the inability to find any traces of an anti-Stalin moderate faction. This view holds all other social and political "variables" constant and rests on the improbable assumption that Stalin's tactics in 1930 were the same as those in 1937.[6]

Following the principle of Ockham's razor, the simplest explanation is usually the best. There was a joint project of a power-hungry Stalin and an insecure elite to centralize power, protect the regime, and clean up the party. Stalin certainly had a drive constantly to prepare his positions and to increase his personal power and authority. But there is precious little evidence for a plan for terror. The zigzags and contradictory discourses we have seen are best understood as twists and turns in an environment of growing but unplanned fear and suspicion. We have seen several instances in which Stalin does not seem to have had the most radical or harsh attitude toward persecuting oppositionists. It is of course possible that his stances in such cases were tactical, designed to let him lie back and verify his subordinates' vigilance and loyalty. On the other hand, Stalin's "angelic patience" with the opposition (to use Andreev's words) can be explained in other ways. It could reflect genuine indecision at various points about how far and when to move against his purported opponents and threats. Although Stalin was a master of tactics, it may be only hindsight and knowledge of the terrible results that

5. Oleg V. Khlevniuk, *Politbiuro: Mekhanizmy politicheskoi vlasti v 1930-e gody*, Moscow, 1996, 177, and Oleg V. Khlevniuk, *Stalin i Ordzhonikidze: Konflikty v Politbiuro v 30-e gody*, Moscow, 1993, 71–73.
6. See, for example, Khlevniuk, *Politbiuro*.

make us see a long-term Byzantine strategy in his actions. His interventions to defer or delay repression would have been embarrassing later, in 1937 and for years thereafter, when the official line praised the complete destruction of the "traitors." This may explain why several of Stalin's speeches to the Central Committee in 1935–37 either were not transcribed or were later removed from the archives, and it could account for the fact that the December 1936 plenum, where he displayed his most ambiguous attitude, was hushed up completely during his lifetime.

It is also likely, as we have suggested, that Stalin's immediate lieutenants had as much or more to gain by the final elimination of the Old Bolshevik opposition as Stalin did. The Old Bolsheviks were more of a threat to them than to him. Of course, the position (and even life) of a Stalinist Politburo member was never secure, and Khrushchev recalls how he and his colleagues never knew whether a visit to Stalin would result in their arrest. But that precarious lieutenancy was not yet clear back in the 1930s. Until the spring of 1937 no Central Committee member had ever been arrested; until 1938 no Politburo member had fallen. Before then, the opposition was the former elite, and as long as its members survived, the positions of the current Politburo and Central Committee members seemed insecure. It would not have taken much for the Molotovs and Kaganoviches to take implacable and cruel positions toward the opposition, regardless of Stalin's plans or lack of them. In one of the very few glimpses we have of actual discussions in the Politburo, Stalin in 1930 had been outvoted by a Politburo majority that took a more aggressive stance than he did on punishment of oppositionists.[7] It may have been about this time, as Kaganovich later recalled, that younger members of the Central Committee asked Stalin why he was not tougher on the opposition.[8]

Indeed the politics of the 1930s—and there *was* a politics— cannot be understood in terms of Stalin alone. Below him were Politburo members, Central Committee members, powerful chiefs and secretaries of central and territorial organizations, district and city party secretaries, full-time party activists, and ordinary party members. Each of these groups had its own fears and its own

7. RTsKhIDNI, f. 17, op. 163, d. 1002, l. 218.
8. Lazar M. Kaganovich, *Pamiatnye zapiski,* Moscow, 1996, 557.

interests to defend vis-à-vis those above them and those below. Each grabbed as much autonomy as it could from above and used discursive, political, and/or repressive strategies to defend that autonomy and to ensure obedience from those below. If politics is defined as the deployment of power and influence, there was politics everywhere in the 1930s, as shifting issues and contingencies produced changing alignments among all these groups. This is the way bureaucratic politics works in other times and places, and indeed in all complex organizations. There is every reason to believe that these organizational practices also existed in the Soviet 1930s.

It is sometimes said that the political events and documents of 1932–37 were a prelude to terror, part of some building crescendo of repression. In some senses this is true. As we have seen, anxieties were growing among the elite, as was the perceived need for iron discipline in the party. But in another sense, the recourse to blind terror from the summer of 1937 was the opposite of the politics that had gone before. It was an abandonment not only of the varying hard-soft, moderate-radical, legalist-repressive discourse but of policy discourse itself. In the preceding period, even the repressive trend had always implied the primacy of Moscow and had been aimed at securing obedience and central control. The 1937–38 terror was different. Although it specified centrally planned quotas and procedures, it did not specify targets and left the selection of victims to local troikas and other bodies. Unlike the competing discourses about control and centralization in 1932–37, the 1937–38 terror was centrally authorized chaos. It was the negation of politics.

Legacies of the Terror

Because of the nature of the sources we have used, our focus has been on the apex of the pyramid, at the Politburo, and the nomenklatura elite that supported it. Within the sometimes severe constraints of social and political realities, this elite made policy and promulgated the hegemonic and normative discourse that both influenced and enforced those policies. The nomenklatura knew better than anyone just how unstable the social and political system of the USSR was in the 1930s, and it was afraid. As if they were in a besieged fortress, the party elite raised the drawbridge. This meant restricting membership, tightening their grip on all their weapons, increasing centralization on all fronts, and destroying those among the defenders whom they suspected of being (or having the potential to become) a fifth column.

Stalin wanted an orderly and predictably functioning state to fulfill economic and military plans and policies. This required a professionally competent bureaucracy with some kind of career security, functioning within a rule-based system. But the heritage of Bolshevik revolutionary voluntarism made him fear a bureaucratic class outside party control. Social opposition, dissidence, and alternative discourses of all kinds constantly encouraged the resort to terror and lawlessness to maintain Bolshevik control. In the long run, the problem of "two models in one," as one scholar described it, would be a basic contradiction of the Stalinist system.[9]

In the early years of the Soviet era, when the tension between the two models really began, the contradiction between legal-constitutional stability and voluntarist terror was relatively small. This was the time when the Stalinist system—and indeed the Soviet system as we knew it—was being born. In the first decade of the Stalin era, the regime was fighting for survival, or at least thought it was. There was an atmosphere of crisis on high, and the leaders thought that because of lingering "capitalist elements" in the country, they were in a "sharp struggle." They really believed that coups against the regime were possible.[10] The country was in chaos, populations were moving in unfathomable ways around the country, entire classes and strata were dissolving and new ones were forming. Party control on the ground thinned out the farther one moved from the cities; in rural outposts, the regime could enact policy changes only by violent and largely uncontrolled mobilizations. As Molotov said, "In our country, when you do things on such a scale, anything can happen." For Stalin and the nomenklatura elite, the problem was not deciding long-term grand strategies. There was no

9. See Moshe Lewin, *The Making of the Soviet System,* New York, 1985, 281–85.

10. Feliks Chuev, *Sto sorok besed s Molotovym,* Moscow, 1991, 391, 402, 407, 418, 428–29, 438; Kaganovich, *Pamiatnye zapiski,* 557–61.

time for that. The problem was week-to-week survival and finding ways simply to get control of the chaos they had unleashed.

In the long run, though, there was steady and growing tension between statism and voluntarism. Stalin and his circle used (or threatened to use) a number of tools to prevent the solidification of an independent bureaucratic class, including membership screenings, extralegal party interventions, and terror. The population of the GULAG camps continued to rise steadily until Stalin's death.[11] As long as Stalin lived—and, to a lesser extent, as long as his closest lieutenants remained in power—the state could not "normalize." As a result, the nomenklatura bureaucracy could not finally consolidate its hold on power. After Stalin's death in 1953, however, the bureaucracy was gradually freed. Terror was renounced, the rule of law was solidified, and a multipolar politics took shape in which a number of bureaucratic constituencies outside the Politburo became players in a system that did not constantly threaten their lives and interests. Rationalization and bureaucratic interests replaced high-level dictatorship and control. The fall of Khrushchev in 1964 was another significant landmark in the nomenklatura's freeing itself from Bolshevik political control and the power of a single leader.

In its wake, and for decades after, the terror left human disaster and titanic social change. Alexander Tivel's relatives were not alone in the 1950s as they tried to win legal and moral rehabilitation for their persecuted kin. Those who had survived the Stalinist camps would never be the same; even those who maintained their health were scarred forever. A generation of Soviet citizens never found out what happened to their friends and family; a generation of children wondered forever about their parents. Huge numbers of lives had been destroyed in one of the greatest human and personal tragedies of modern times.

People of the former Soviet Union still live with the social and political consequences of the 1930s terror. In the 1990s the victims, ghosts, and heirs of the terror still walk the earth. Stalin has been in

---

11. J. Arch Getty, Gábor T. Rittersporn, and V. N. Zemskov, "Victims of the Soviet Penal System in the Pre-war Years: A First Approach on the Basis of Archival Evidence," *American Historical Review*, 98(4), October 1993, 1049, based on NKVD archives found in GARF.

his grave for more than forty years, and even aside from the nostalgia some older people feel for him, his legacy in many ways has survived the formal collapse of the USSR. His victims are still being counted and remembered, and even today not many months go by without the discovery of new police documents, hidden mass graves, or nameless human bones washed up on some river bank. Stalin, his last henchmen Molotov and Kaganovich, and their countless victims have all now gone to their rewards. But in social and political terms, someone and something survives from that time.

The nomenklatura elite—though Stalin killed many members in the 1930s, though the Communist Party and Soviet Union were dismantled in the early 1990s—lives on. It survived Stalin and Stalinism. Although Stalin managed to destroy the elite of the 1930s, he did not and could not destroy the nomenklatura as a component of the regime. Back in the 1930s, Trotsky had predicted that the growing power of the nomenklatura could have one of two results. Either the workers would rise up and overthrow the elite, or that elite would ultimately be successful in converting itself into a true ruling class that not only wielded political power but owned the means of production outright.[12] As we know, there was no workers' revolution. Instead, the nomenklatura survived socialism and did in fact inherit the country. Its cohesion, connections, and experience were sufficient to allow its members to become not only the "new" governing elite of the 1990s but the legal owners of the country's assets and property.

---

12. Leon Trotsky, *The Revolution Betrayed*, New York, 1972, 248–49, 252–54, 284–85.

Numbers of Victims of the Terror

Scholars have long debated the precise numbers of victims of the terror of the 1930s. Their efforts have produced a wide gap, often of several millions, between high and low estimates. Using census and other data, they have proposed conflicting computations of birth, mortality, and arrests in order to calculate levels of famine deaths due to agricultural collectivization (1932–33), direct victims of the Great Terror (1936–39), and total "unnatural" population loss in the Stalin period.[1] Both high and low estimators have awaited solid archival evidence, which they have claimed would

1. For the most significant high estimates see S. Rosefielde, "An Assessment of the Sources and Uses of Gulag Forced Labour, 1929–56," *Soviet Studies,* 1981, no. 1, 51–87; S. Rosefielde, "Excess Mortality in the Soviet Union: A Reconstruction of Demographic Consequences of Forced Industrialization, 1929–1949," *Soviet Studies,* July 1983; Robert Conquest, "Forced Labour Statistics: Some Comments," *Soviet Studies,* July 1982; and Robert Conquest, *The Great Terror: A Reassessment,* Oxford, 1990, 484–89.

For low estimates see R. W. Davies and S. G. Wheatcroft, "Steven Rosefielde's 'Kliukva,'" *Slavic Review,* December 1980; S. G. Wheatcroft, "On Assessing the Size of Forced Concentration Camp Labour in the Soviet Union, 1929–56," *Soviet Studies,* 1981, no. 2; S. G. Wheatcroft, "Towards a Thorough Analysis of Soviet Forced Labour Statistics," *Soviet Studies,* 1983, no. 2; Jerry Hough and Merle Fainsod, *How the Soviet Union Is Governed,* Cambridge, Mass., 1979, 176–77; and Barbara Anderson and Brian Silver, "Demographic Analysis and Population Catastrophes in the USSR," *Slavic Review,* 1985, no. 3.

Table 5. Secret Police (GPU, OGPU, NKVD) Arrests and Sentences, 1921–39

	Arrests					Sentences			
Year	Total	For "counter-revolutionary" crimes	For "anti-Soviet agitation"	Other	Convictions	Shot	Camps and prison	Exiled	Other
1921	200,271	76,820		123,451	35,829	9,701	21,724	1,817	2,587
1922	119,329	45,405	0	73,924	6,003	1,962	2,656	166	1,219
1923	104,520	57,289	5,322	47,231	4,794	414	2,336	2,044	0
1924	92,849	74,055	0	18,794	12,425	2,550	4,151	5,724	0
1925	72,658	52,033	0	20,625	15,995	2,433	6,851	6,274	437
1926	62,817	30,676	0	32,141	17,804	990	7,547	8,571	696
1927	76,983	48,883	0	28,100	26,036	2,363	12,667	11,235	171
1928	112,803	72,186	0	40,617	33,757	869	16,211	15,640	1,037
1929	162,726	132,799	51,396	29,927	56,220	2,109	25,853	24,517	3,741
1930	331,544	266,679	0	64,865	208,069	20,201	114,443	58,816	14,609
1931	479,065	343,734	100,963	135,331	180,696	10,651	105,683	63,269	1,093
1932	410,433	195,540	23,484	214,893	141,919	2,728	73,946	36,017	29,228
1933	505,256	283,029	32,370	222,227	239,664	2,154	138,903	54,262	44,345
1934	205,173	90,417	16,788	114,756	78,999	2,056	59,451	5,994	11,498
1935	193,083	108,935	43,686	84,148	267,076	1,229	185,846	33,601	46,400
1936	131,168	91,127	32,110	40,041	274,670	1,118	219,418	23,719	30,415
1937	936,750	779,056	234,301	157,694	790,665	353,074	429,311	1,366	6,914
1938	638,509	593,326	57,366	45,183	554,258	328,618	205,509	16,842	3,289
1939						2,552	54,666	3,783	2,888

Source: Gosudarstvennyi arkhiv Rossisskoi Ferderatsii (GARF) f. 9401, op. 1, d. 4157, ll. 201–5.

confirm their respective projections. Both sides have accused the other of sloppy or incompetent scholarship, and the conversation has often been marked by an unseemly harsh tone.

Now, for the first time, Soviet secret police documents are available that permit us to narrow the range of estimates. These materials are from the archival records of the Secretariat of GULAG, the Main Camp Administration of the NKVD/MVD (the USSR Ministry of the Interior), housed in the formerly "special" (i.e., closed) sections of the State Archive of the Russian Federation (GARF). The data are summarized in Table 5.[2]

According to archival data, the total camp and exile population seems to have been less than 4 million before the war. Were we to extrapolate from the fragmentary prison data we do have, we might reasonably add a figure of 300,000–500,000 for each year, as well as an additional contingent of about 200,000 exiles other than "kulaks," to put the maximum detained population at around 3.5 million in the period of the Great Purges.[3]

Mainstream published estimates of the total number of arrests in the late 1930s have ranged from Dimitry Volkogonov's 3.5 million to Robert Conquest's 5–8 million to Olga Shatunovskaia's nearly 20 million.[4] The new archival materials suggest that Volkogonov was closest to the mark. A 1953 statistical report on NKVD cases shows that 1,575,259 people were arrested by the security police in the course of 1937–38, 87 percent of them on political grounds; 1,344,923, or 85 percent, were convicted. (The contrast is striking with the period 1930–36, when 61 percent were arrested for political reasons and 62 percent of all those arrested by the political police were eventually convicted, and especially with

2. The data discussed here and presented in the text of this book are analyzed in depth in J. Arch Getty, Gábor T. Rittersporn, and V. N. Zemskov, "Victims of the Soviet Penal System in the Prewar Years: A First Approach on the Basis of Archival Evidence," *American Historical Review*, 98(4), October 1993, 1017–49.

3. See GARF, f. 9414, op. 1, d. 1139, l. 88, for what is likely to be the record number of prison inmates at the beginning of 1938, and GARF, f. 9401, op. 1, d. 4157, ll., 202, 203–5, for figures on exile that may nevertheless contain a certain number of people banished in the wake of collectivization.

4. A. Antonov-Ovseenko, *The Time of Stalin: Portrait of a Tyranny*, New York, 1980, 212; Roy Medvedev, *Let History Judge: The Origins and Consequences of Stalinism*, rev. ed., New York, 1989, 455; *Moskovskie novosti*, 27 November 1988; O. Shatunovskaia, "Fal'sifikatsiia," *Argumenty i fakty*, 1990, no. 22; Conquest, *The Great Terror*, 485–86.

the years from 1920 through 1929, when 59 percent of security police arrests were for political reasons but only 21 percent of those arrested were convicted.)[5]

To be sure, the 1,575,259 people in the 1953 report do not include all 1937–38 arrests. Court statistics put the number of prosecutions unrelated to "counterrevolutionary" charges at 1,566,185,[6] but it is unlikely that all persons in this cohort count in the arrest figures. Especially if their sentences were noncustodial, such persons were often not formally arrested. Fifty-three percent of all court decisions in 1937 involved noncustodial sentences and 59 percent in 1938, so some 647,000 persons were executed or incarcerated in categories other than counterrevolution.[7]

Although we do not have exact figures for arrests in 1937–38, we do know that the population of the GULAG camps increased by 175,487 in 1937 and 320,828 in 1938 (it had declined in 1936).[8] The population of all labor camps, labor colonies, and prisons on 1 January 1939, near the end of the Great Purges, was 2,022,976. This gives us a total increase in the camp and prison population in 1937–38 of 1,006,030.[9] One must add to this figure the number of those who had been arrested but not sent to camps, either because they were released sometime later or because they were executed.

Popular estimates of executions in the Great Purges of 1937–38 vary from 500,000 to 7 million.[10] We do not have exact figures for the numbers of executions in these years, but we can now narrow the range considerably. According to a Gorbachev-era press release of the KGB, 786,098 persons were sentenced to death "for counter-

5. GARF, f. 9401, op. 1, d. 4157, ll. 203, 205. A handwritten note on this document tells us that 30 percent of those sentenced between 1921 and 1938 "upon cases of the security police" were "common criminals," and their number is given as 1,062,000. As the report speaks of 2,944,879 convicts, this figure constitutes 36 percent; 30 percent would amount to about 883,000 persons (l. 202).

6. GARF, f. 9492, op. 6, d. 14, l. 14.

7. This is calculated on the basis of GARF, f. 9492, op. 6, d. 14, l. 29, by subtracting the number of "counterrevolutionaries" indicated on l. 14. The actual figure is nevertheless somewhat smaller, for the data on death sentences include "political" cases. It therefore seems likely that the total number of arrests in 1937–38 is not too far from 2.5 million.

8. Getty, Rittersporn, and Zemskov, "Victims," 1048–49.

9. Getty, Rittersporn, and Zemskov, "Victims," 1048–49.

10. Medvedev, Let History Judge, 455; Moskovskie novosti, 27 November 1988; Shatunovskaia, "Fal'sifikatsiia."

revolutionary and state crimes" by various courts and extrajudicial bodies between 1930 and 1953.[11] According to the NKVD archival material currently available, 681,692 people were shot in 1937–38 (compared with 1,118 persons in 1936).[12] These archival figures, coming from a statistical report "on the quantity of people convicted upon cases of NKVD bodies," include victims who had not been arrested for political reasons,[13] whereas the KGB press release concerns only persons persecuted for "counterrevolutionary offenses." In any event, the data available at this point make it clear that the number shot in the two worst purge years was more likely in the hundreds of thousands than in the millions. The only period between 1930 and the outbreak of the war when the number of death sentences for nonpolitical crimes outstripped the ones meted out to "counterrevolutionaries" was from August 1932 to the last quarter of 1933.[14]

Aside from executions in the terror of 1937–38, many others died in the regime's custody during the 1930s. If we add the figure we have for executions up to 1940 to the number of persons who died in GULAG camps and the few figures we found on mortality in prisons and labor colonies,[15] then add to this the number of peasants known to have died in exile, we reach a figure of nearly 1.5 million deaths directly due to repression in the 1930s. If we put at hundreds of thousands the casualties of the most chaotic period of collectivization (deaths in exile, rather than from starvation in the 1932 famine), plus later victims of different categories for which we have no data, it is likely that "custodial mortality" figures of the

11. *Pravda*, 14 February 1990, 2.

12. *Pravda*, 22 June 1989, 3; *Kommunist*, 1990, no. 8, 103; GARF, f. 9401, op. 1, d. 4157, l. 202.

13. "Spravka o kolichestve osuzhdennykh po delam organov NKVD" (GARF, f. 9401, op. 1, d. 4157, l. 202). Judiciary statistics mention 4,387 death sentences pronounced by ordinary courts in 1937–38, but this figure includes also a certain number of "political" cases (GARF, f. 9492, op. 6, d. 14, l. 29).

14. Under a heavy-handed application of a particularly harsh decree against the theft of public property (the "Law of 7 August, 1932"), 5,338 people were condemned to death in 1932 and a further 11,463 in 1933 (GARF, f. 9474, op. 1, d. 76, l, 118; d. 83, l. 5). Not all these people were executed (d. 97, ll. 8, 61).

15. At least 69,566 deaths were recorded in prisons and colonies between January 1935 and the beginning of 1940 (GARF, f. 9414, op. 1, d. 2740, ll. 52, 60, 74). The other data are 288,307 for strict regime camps and 726,030 for people executed "upon cases of the political police."

1930s would reach 2 million: a huge number of "excess deaths." The figures we can document for deaths due to repression are inexact, but the available sources suggest that we are now within the right range, at least for the prewar period.

Accurate overall estimates of numbers of victims are difficult to make because of the fragmentary and dispersed nature of record keeping. Generally speaking, we have runs of quantitative data of several types: on arrests, formal charges and accusations, sentences, and camp populations. But these "events" could have taken place under the jurisdiction of a bewildering variety of institutions, each with its own statistical compilations and reports. These agencies included the several organizations of the secret police (NKVD troikas, special collegia, or special boards [osoboe soveshchanie]), the procuracy, the regular police, and various types of courts and tribunals. No single agency kept a master list reflecting the totality of repression, and great care is necessary to untangle the disparate events and actors in the penal process.

Further research is needed to locate the origins of inconsistencies and possible errors, especially where differences are significant. One must note, however, that the accuracy of Soviet records on much less mobile populations does not seem to give much hope that we can ever clarify each problem. For example, the Central Committee gave quite different figures for the total party membership and its composition as of 1 January 1937 in two documents that were compiled about the same time.[16] Yet another number was given in published party statistics.[17] The conditions of perpetual movement in the camp system created even greater difficulties than those posed by keeping track of supposedly disciplined party members immediately after two major attempts to improve the bookkeeping practices of the party.[18]

16. RTsKhIDNI, f. 17, op. 120, d. 278, ll. 8, 10, and TsKhSD (the Central Committee Archive), f. 77, op. 1, d. 1, l. 8.

17. Spravochnik partiinogo rabotnika, vyp. 18, Moscow, 1978, l. 366. This figure corresponds to that calculated by a Western scholar ten years earlier; one wonders whether the Soviet editors did not decide to rely more on the painstaking research of this scholar than on their own records. (See Thomas H. Rigby, Communist Party Membership in the USSR, 1917–1967, Princeton, 1968, 52.)

18. J. Arch Getty, Origins of the Great Purges: The Soviet Communist Party Reconsidered, 1933–1938, New York, 1985, 58–64, 86–90.

At times tens of thousands of inmates were listed in the category of "under way" in hard regime camp records,[19] though the likelihood that some of them would die before leaving jail or during the long and torturous transportation made their departure and especially their arrival uncertain. The situation is even more complicated for labor colonies, where, at any given moment, a considerable proportion of prisoners were being sent or taken to other places of detention, where a large number of convicts served rather short terms, and where many people had been held pending investigation, trial, or appeal of their sentences.[20]

Moreover, we do not yet know whether, in order to receive higher budgetary allocations, camp commandants inflated their reports on camp populations to include people slated for transfer to other places, prisoners who were only expected to arrive, and even the dead. Conversely, they may have been equally disposed to report as low a figure as possible in order to secure easily attainable production targets.

Because of these uncertainties, there is still controversy about the accuracy of these data, and no reason to believe them to be final or exact.[21] One cannot stress enough that with our current documentation, we can posit little more than general, though narrow, ranges. Still, these are the only data currently available from police archives. Moreover, there are good reasons for assuming that they are not wildly wrong because of the consistent way numbers from different sources compare with one another.[22]

Figures produced by researchers using other archival collections of different agencies show close similarities in scale. Documents of the People's Commissariat of Finance discuss a custodial popula-

19. See, for example, GARF, f. 9414, op. 1, d. 1138, l. 6.

20. See, for example, GARF, f. 9414, op. 1, d. 1139, ll. 88–89; d. 1140, l. 161.

21. See, for example, Robert Conquest, Letter to the Editor, *American Historical Review*, June 1994, 1038–40, and Robert Conquest, Letter to the Editor, *American Historical Review*, December 1994, 1821; Steven Rosefielde, "Stalinism in Post-Communist Perspective: New Evidence on Killings, Forced Labour, and Economic Growth in the 1930s," *Europe-Asia Studies*, 48(6), 1996, 959–87. Conquest believes that large numbers of victims remain hidden from the currently available archives. Rosefielde uses dubious statistical techniques in an attempt to find inconsistencies in the data.

22. See, for example, GARF, f. 8131sch, op. 27, d. 70, ll. 104, 141; f. 9414, op. 1, d. 20, ll. 135, 149.

tion whose size is not different from the one we have established.[23] Similarly, the labor force envisioned by the economic plans of the GULAG, found in the files of the Council of People's Commissars, does not imply figures in excess of these numbers.[24] The "NKVD contingent" of the 1937 and 1939 censuses is consistent with the data we have for detainees and exiles.[25]

Finally, in 1962–63 and 1988, secret, high-level government investigations produced results very similar to those presented above. On both occasions, the Politburo sought the most damning figures possible for use as political capital and commissioned blue-ribbon Politburo commissions to comb KGB files for data. In 1963 Khrushchev sought data condemning his current rivals Molotov and Kaganovich; in 1988 Gorbachev wanted to discredit Stalinism generally as part of his perestroika policy. In both cases, the results, recently published in the official *Bulletin of the Archive of the President of the Russian Federation,* are analogous to those presented here.[26]

23. V. V. Tsaplin, "Arkhivnye materialy o chisle zakliuchennykh v kontse 30-kh godov," *Voprosy istorii,* no. 4–5, 1991, 157–60.

24. See Oleg V. Khlevniuk, "Prinuditel'nyi trud v ekonomike SSSR, 1929–1941 gody," *Svobodnaia mysl',* no. 13, 1992, 73–84.

25. See E. M. Andreev, L. E. Darskii, T. L. Khar'kova, *Istoriia Naseleniia SSSR 1920–1959 gg.* (vypusk 3–5, chast' I of *Ekspress-informatsiia, seriia: Istoriia statistiki,* Moscow, 1990, 31, 37); V. N. Zemskov, "Ob uchete spetskontingenta NKVD vo vsesoiuznykh perepisiakh naseleniia 1937 i 1939 gg.," *Sotsiologicheskie issledovaniia,* 1991, no. 2, 74–75.

26. "Vestnik Arkhiva Prezidenta Rossiiskoi Federatsii: I.1995," *Istochnik,* no. 1, 1995, 117–30.

Biographical Sketches

The following biographical notes were compiled from archival materials at RTsKhIDNI and mainly encompass the period covered in this study. Many of the biographical sketches below include the notation "repressed." This has been standard terminology in Soviet sources since the 1950s and is still in use in archival files today. Punishments subsumed under the term could include noncustodial residence restrictions, expulsion from the party, exile to Siberia, confinement in various kinds of labor camps, imprisonment, or execution. Unfortunately, currently available archival sources in most cases do not specify the kind of level of repression the victim suffered.

Abashidze, M. (1873–1941). Publicist, public figure. Worked in cultural-educational and economic organizations.

Agranov, Ya. S. (1893–1938). From 1934 to 1937, first deputy people's commissar for internal affairs of the USSR. From May 1937, head of the NKVD for Saratov region. Repressed.

Aizenshtat, S. Sh. (1896–?). Professional journalist.

Akudzhava (Okudzhava), Sh. S. (1900–1937). From 1932, secretary of the Party Committee for Construction of the Ural Carriage-Building Works. From 1935, secretary of the Nizhni Tagil City Committee of the VKP(b) of Sverdlovsk region. Repressed.

Akulov, I. A. (1888–1937). From 1929 to 1930, secretary and member of the Presidium of the All-Union Central Council of Trade Unions (VTsSPS). From 1929, deputy people's commissar of the Workers' and Peasants' Inspectorate (RFI). From 1931 to 1933, deputy chairman of the OGPU. From 1933 to 1935, procurator of the USSR. From 1935 to 1937, secretary of the Central Executive Committee (TsIK) of the USSR. Repressed.

Alekseev, P. G. (1892–1947). From July 1935, worked in People's Commissariat for Heavy Industry.

Amatuni, A. S. (1900–1938). From October 1935, second secretary of the CC of the KP(b) of Armenia. From September 1936, first secretary of the CC of the KP(b) of Armenia. Repressed.

Andreev, A. A. (1895–1971). From 1930, chairman of the Central Control Commission (CCC) of the VKP(b), people's commissar of the Workers'-Peasants' Inspectorate (RKI), and deputy chairman of the Council of People's Commissars (SNK) of the USSR. From 1931 to 1935, USSR people's commissar for railway transport. From 1935 to 1946, secretary of the CC of the VKP(b).

Astrov, V. N. (1898–1995?). From 1924 to 1929, member of the editorial board of the journal *Bolshevik* and instructor at a number of universities and institutes of higher education in Moscow. From 1929 to 1931, professor of history of the USSR at the Ivanovo Regional Communist University (komvuz). From 1932, senior research officer at the Institute of History of the Communist Academy of Moscow. Arrested in February 1933 and exiled to Voronezh in 1934. In November 1936, arrested once again and gave evidence against Bukharin. In 1937 released and rehabilitated.

Bagirov, M. A. (1895–1956). From 1933 to 1953, first secretary of the CC of the Communist Party of Azerbaijan. In 1955 convicted and in 1956 shot for his association with L. P. Beria.

Bakaev, I. P. (1887–1936). In 1925 chairman of the Leningrad Regional Commission. From 1925 to 1927, member of the Central Control Commission (CCC) of the VKP(b). Expelled from the party at the Fifteenth Party Congress of the VKP(b) as a member of the Trotskyist opposition. Repressed.

Balashova (dates unknown). Weaver. Delegate to the Fifteenth All-Russian Congress of Soviets in 1931.

Bauman, K. Ya. (1892–1937). From 1931 to 1934, first secretary of the Mid-Asian Bureau of the CC of the VKP(b). From 1934 to 1937, director of the Department of Science, Scientific-Technical Discoveries, and Inventions of the CC of the VKP(b). Repressed.

Belenko, V. V. (dates unknown). During the 1930s, head of commodity circulation for the State Planning Commission (Gosplan) of the USSR.

Belenky, Z. M. (1888–1940). From 1938 to 1939, chairman of the Commission for Soviet Control attached to the Council of People's Commissars (SNK) of the USSR. Repressed.

Beloborodov, A. G. (1891–1938). From 1923 to 1927, RSFSR people's commissar for internal affairs. From 1927 to 1930, in internal exile. From 1930, worked for the Committee for State Procurement of the USSR and served as plenipotentiary of the People's Commissariat of the USSR for Internal Trade. Repeatedly expelled from the party (1927, 1936) for taking part in the Trotskyist opposition. Repressed.

Belsky, L. N. (1889–1941). From 1936 to 1938, USSR deputy people's commissar for internal affairs. From 1938 to 1939, USSR first deputy people's commissar for railway transport. Repressed.

Benek, K. F. (1895–1937). From 1927 to 1929, people's commissar of labor of the Belorussian SSR. From 1929 to 1930, people's commissar of trade of the Belorussian SSR. From 1933 to 1937, people's commissar of agriculture of the Belorussian SSR. From 1930 to 1934, deputy chairman of the Belorussian Council of People's Commissars (SNK). Repressed.

Berezin, A. V. (dates unknown). During the 1930s, elected secretary of the Nikolaev District Committee of the KP(b) of the Ukraine. In 1937 first secretary of the Azov–Black Sea Territorial Committee of the VKP(b). Repressed.

Beria, L. P. (1899–1953). From 1931, first secretary of the CC of the KP(b) of Georgia, from 1932, first secretary of the Trans-Caucasus Territorial Committee, and first secretary of the Tbilisi City Committee of the party. From 1938 to 1945, USSR people's commissar for internal affairs. In 1953 arrested and shot.

Berman, B. D. (1901–39). From 1937 to 1938, people's commissar of internal affairs of the Belorussian SSR. Repressed.

Berman, M. D. (1898–1939). From 1936 to 1937, USSR deputy people's commissar for internal affairs. From 1937 to 1938, USSR people's commissar for communications. Repressed.

Blagonravov, G. I. (1895–1938). From 1932 to 1934, USSR deputy people's commissar for railway transport. From 1935, head of the Main Administration for Highways. Repressed.

Bliukher, V. K. (1890–1938). From 1929 to 1938, commander of the Special Red Banner Far Eastern Army. Repressed.

Bubnov, A. S. (1884–1938). From 1929 to 1937, RSFSR people's commissar for education. Repressed.

Budenny, S. M. (1883–1973). From 1924 to 1937, inspector of the Cavalry of the Workers' and Peasants' Red Army (RKKA). From 1937 to 1938, commander of the troops of the Moscow Military District and member of the Chief Military Council of the USSR People's Commissariat for Defense.

Bukharin, N. I. (1888–1938). In the 1920s, Politburo member and leader of the rightist opposition. From 1929, head of a section of the Supreme Council for the National Economy of the USSR (VSNKh). From 1932, member of the Collegium of the People's Commissariat for Heavy Industry (NKTP). From 1934 to 1937, editor in chief of the newspaper *Izvestiia,* published by the Central Executive Committee (TsIK) of the USSR. In 1928–30 headed the rightist opposition in the VKP(b). Repressed.

Bulakh, V. S. (1903–36). In 1936 deputy chairman of the Proletarsky District Soviet of Moscow. Repressed.

Bulat, I. L. (1896–1939). From 1932, RSFSR deputy people's commissar of justice, chairman of the Supreme Court of the RSFSR, and then RSFSR people's commissar for justice. Repressed.

Bulatov, D. A. (1889–1941). From 1930, director of the Department for Organizational Instruction of the CC of the VKP(b). Subsequently, a member of the Collegium and head of the Department of Cadres of the OGPU. From 1934 to 1937, first secretary of the Omsk Regional Committee of the VKP(b). Repressed.

Bulganin, N. A. (1895–1975). From 1931, chairman of the Executive Committee of the Moscow Soviet. From 1937 to 1938, chairman of the Council of People's Commissars (SNK) of the RSFSR. From 1938 to 1941, deputy chairman of the Council of People's Commissars of the USSR.

Bulin, A. S. (1894–1938). After the civil war, head of the Political Directorate of the Moscow Military District. Subsequently, head of the Belorussian Military District. In

1937 appointed head of the Main Directorate of Cadres for the USSR People's Commissariat of Defense. Repressed.

Bykin, Ya. B. (1888–1937). From 1930 to 1937, first secretary of the Bashkir Regional Committee of the VKP(b). Repressed.

Chernov, M. A. (1891–1938). From 1930, worked for the USSR People's Commissariat for Trade and served as chairman of the Committee for State Procurement. From 1934 to 1937, USSR people's commissar of agriculture. Repressed.

Cherviakov, A. G. (1892–1937). From 1922, one of the chairmen of the Central Executive Committee (TsIK) of the USSR. From 1924, chairman of the TsIK of the Belorussian SSR. Repressed.

Chubar, V. Ya. (1891–1939). From 1923 to 1934, chairman of the Council of People's Commissars (SNK) of the Ukrainian SSR. From 1934 to 1938, deputy chairman of the Council of People's Commissars and of the Council for Labor and Defense (STO) of the USSR and USSR people's commissar for finance. Repressed.

Chudov, M. S. (1893–1937). From 1928 to 1936, second secretary of the Leningrad Regional Committee of the VKP(b). Repressed.

Dagin, I. Ya. (1895–1940). From 1937 to 1938, head of the First (Security) Department of the Main Administration for State Security (GUGB) of the USSR NKVD. Repressed.

Deich, Ya. A. (1898–1938). From 1936 to 1937, head of the Secretariat of the NKVD of the USSR. From 1937 to 1938, head of the Directorate of the NKVD for Rostov region. Died in prison.

Demchenko, N. N. (1896–1937). From 1932 to 1936, first secretary of the Kiev Regional Committee of the KP(b) of the Ukraine. From 1936, deputy USSR people's commissar for agriculture. Repressed.

Deniskevich, N. M. (1904–37). From 1934 to 1937, first secretary of the Liozno District Committee and secretary of the Vitebsk City Committee of the KP(b) of Belorussia. From June 1937, second secretary of the CC of the KP(b) of Belorussia. Repressed.

Deribas, T. D. (1883–1938). From February 1936, head of the directorate and commander of the Interior Border Guards of the NKVD for the Far Eastern region. Repressed.

Dmitriev, D. M. (1901–39). From 1936 to 1938, head of the directorate of the NKVD for the Sverdlovsk region. Repressed.

Drynshev (dates unknown). Official of the People's Commissariat for Justice.

Dvolaitsky, Sh. M. (1899–1937). From 1936 to 1937, director of the Department of Culture and Propaganda of the Azov–Black Sea Territorial Committee of the VKP(b). Repressed.

Dybenko, P. E. (1889–1938). From 1928 to 1938, commander of the troops of the Mid-Asian, Volga, Siberian, and Leningrad Military Districts. From February 1938, manager of the "Kamlesosplav" [Kama River Timber-Rafting] Trust in Perm. Repressed.

Eikhe, R. I. (1890–1940). From 1929 to 1937, first secretary of the Siberian and Western Siberian Territorial Committees and first secretary of the Novosibirsk City

Committee of the VKP(b). From 1937 to 1938, USSR people's commissar of agriculture. Repressed.

Eismont, N. B. (1891–1935). From 1926 to 1932, RSFSR people's commissar for trade, deputy USSR people's commissar for internal and foreign trade, and RSFSR people's commissar for supplies. Arrested in 1932, released in February 1935, and continued working as a free laborer in the Novy Tambov camp of the NKVD. Died in an automobile accident.

Friche, V. M. (1870–1929). Soviet literary critic and art historian. Professor at the Moscow State University and a member of the Academy of Sciences of the USSR.

Frinovsky, M. P. (1898–1940). From 1930 to 1933, chairman of the OGPU of the Azerbaijan SSR. In 1933 head of the Chief Directorate for Border Troops of the OGPU of the USSR. From 1936 to 1938, deputy, then first deputy USSR people's commissar for internal affairs. Repressed.

Furer, V. Ya. (?–1936). During the 1920s, secretary of a city committee of the VKP(b) in the Donetsk coalfields. During the 1930s, worked for the Communist International (Comintern). Committed suicide.

Gamarnik, Ya. B. (1894–1937). From 1929 to 1937, head of the Political Directorate of the Workers' and Peasants' Red Army (RKKA). During this time, also deputy USSR people's commissar for military and naval affairs and deputy chairman of the Revolutionary Military Council of the USSR. Committed suicide.

Gendin, S. G. (1902–39). In 1937 head of the Directorate of the NKVD for the Western region (Smolensk), then deputy head of the Fourth Department of the Main Administration for State Security (GUGB) of the NKVD of the USSR. From 1937 to 1938, deputy head of the Intelligence Directorate of the Workers' and Peasants' Red Army (RKKA). Repressed.

Gikalo, N. F. (1897–1938). From 1932 to 1937, secretary of the CC of the KP(b) of Belorussia. Repressed.

Ginzburg, I. V. (1887–1937). Veterinarian. From 1918 to 1925, served on the Veterinary Board of the Red Army. From 1927 to 1934, head of the Veterinary Board of the RSFSR People's Commissariat for Agriculture. From 1934 to 1937, head of the Veterinary Board of the USSR People's Commissariat for Agriculture. Repressed.

Glebov-Avilov, N. P. (1887–1937). From 1928, head of construction, then director of the Rostselmash [Rostov Agricultural Machinery] factory in Rostov-on-the-Don. Repressed.

Goglidze, S. A. (1901–53). From 1934 to 1938, people's commissar of Georgia for internal affairs. Repressed. In 1953 arrested and shot for his association with L. P. Beria.

Gogoberidze, L. D. (1896–1937). From May 1934, secretary of the Eisk District Committee of the VKP(b). From 1935, secretary of the Party Committee of the Rostselmash [Rostov Agricultural Machinery] factory. Repressed.

Goloded, N. M. (1894–1937). From 1927, chairman of the Council of People's Commissars (SNK) of the Belorussian SSR. Repressed.

Gorbachev, G. E. (1897–1942). Russian and Soviet critic and literary scholar. From 1923, associate professor *(dotsent)* at Leningrad University. A member of Litfront. Repressed.

Griadinsky, F. P. (1893–1938). From 1930 to 1937, chairman of the Western Siberian Territorial Executive Committee. Repressed.

Grinko, G. F. (1890–1938). From October 1930, USSR people's commissar for finance. Repressed.

Gubelman, M. I. (1885–1968). From 1937 to 1947, chairman of the CC of the Union of Workers of State Commerce.

Haeckel, Ernst (1834–1919). German scientist.

Ignatov, N. G. (1901–66). From 1937 to 1941, first secretary, subsequently second secretary, and once again first secretary of the Kuibyshev Regional Committee of the VKP(b).

Ikramov, A. I. (1898–1937). From 1929 to 1937, first secretary of the CC of the KP(b) of Uzbekistan and secretary of the Mid-Asian Bureau of the CC of the VKP(b). Repressed.

Isaev, U. D. (1899–1938). Until March 1934, plenipotentiary of the Committee of Commodity Funds attached to the Council for Labor and Defense (STO) for Kazakhstan. From 1934 to 1938, chairman of the Council of People's Commissars (SNK) of the Kazakh SSR. Repressed.

Ivanov, V. I. (1893–1938). In 1931 a member of the Presidium of the Supreme Council for the National Economy of the USSR (VSNKh). During this time, also a member of the Collegium of the People's Commissariat for Heavy Industry. From 1932 to 1936, first secretary of the Northern Regional Committee of the VKP(b). From 1936, USSR People's Commissar for Light Industry. Repressed.

Kaganovich, L. M. (1893–1991). From 1930 to 1935, first secretary of the Moscow Committee of the VKP(b). From 1934 to 1935, chairman of the Commission for Party Control (KPK) attached to the CC of the VKP(b). From 1935 to 1937 and from 1938 to 1942, USSR people's commissar for railway transport. From 1937 to 1939, USSR people's commissar for heavy industry. From 1928 to 1939, secretary of the CC of the VKP(b).

Kalinin, M. I. (1875–1946). From 1922 to 1938, chairman of the Central Executive Committee (TsIK) of the USSR. From 1938 to 1946, chairman of the Presidium of the Supreme Soviet of the USSR.

Kalmanovich, M. I. (1888–1937). From 1930 to 1934, both chairman of the board of the USSR State Bank (Gosbank) and USSR deputy people's commissar for finance. From 1934 to 1937, USSR people's commissar for grain and livestock sovkhozes. Repressed.

Kalygina, A. S. (1895–1937). From 1930 to 1935, secretary of the Kalinin City Committee of the VKP(b). From June 1935 to April 1936, second secretary of the Kalinin Regional Committee of the VKP(b). From 1936 to 1937, secretary of the Voronezh City Committee of the VKP(b). Repressed.

Kamenev, L. B. (1883–1936). From 1922, deputy chairman of the Council of People's Commissars (SNK) of the RSFSR. From 1924 to 1925, chairman of the Council for Labor and Defense (STO). From January 1926, USSR people's commissar for trade. From 1926 to 1927, plenipotentiary representative of the USSR in Italy. From 1929, chairman of the Main Concessionary Committee. Repressed.

Kamensky, G. N. (1895–1938). From 1930, secretary of the Moscow City Committee of the VKP(b). From 1932, chairman of the Executive Committee of the Moscow

Regional Council of Workers' Deputies. From 1934 to 1936, RSFSR people's commissar for health and chief health inspector of the USSR. From 1936 to 1937, USSR people's commissar for health. Repressed.

Karpov, G. G. (1898–1967). From 1922, worked for the GPU, NKVD, and MGB. From 1938 to 1939, head of the Directorate of the NKVD for the Pskov region.

Kartvelishvili, L. I. (Lavrentiev) (1890–1938). From 1931, secretary of the Trans-Caucasus Territorial Committee of the VKP(b). In 1932 second secretary of the Western Siberian Territorial Committee of the VKP(b). From 1933 to 1936, first secretary of the Far Eastern Territorial Committee of the VKP(b). From December 1936, first secretary of the Crimean Regional Committee of the VKP(b). Repressed.

Karutsky, V. A. (1900–1938). In 1937 deputy head of the Directorate of the NKVD for the Western region. From 1937 to 1938, deputy head of the Fourth Department of the Main Administration for State Security (GUGB) of the NKVD of the USSR. Committed suicide.

Kerensky, A. F. (1881–1970). After the February Revolution of 1917, minister of justice, then minister of war, then premier of the provisional government of Russia. Emigrated in 1918.

Khalatov, A. B. (1894–1938). From 1927 to 1929, rector of the Plekhanov Institute for the National Economy. From 1932 to 1935, member of the Collegium of the People's Commissariat for Railway Transport. From 1935, chairman of the All-Union Society of Inventors. Repressed.

Khandzhian, A. G. (1901–36). From 1928, second secretary of the CC of the KP(b) of Armenia. From 1930 to 1936, first secretary of the CC of the KP(b) of Armenia. Repressed.

Khataevich, M. M. (1893–1937). From 1930 to 1932, secretary for the Mid-Volga Territorial Committee of the VKP(b). From 1933, first secretary of the Dnepropetrovsk Regional Committee of the KP(b) of the Ukraine. From 1937, second secretary of the CC of the KP(b) of the Ukraine. Repressed.

Khrushchev, N. S. (1894–1971). From 1932 to 1934, second secretary of the Moscow City Committee of the VKP(b). From 1935 to 1938, first secretary of the Moscow Regional and City Committees of the VKP(b).

Kirov, S. M. (1886–1934). From 1926 to 1934, first secretary of the Leningrad Regional Committee of the VKP(b). In 1934 elected secretary of the CC of the VKP(b). Assassinated in Leningrad.

Knorin, V. G. (1890–1938). From 1928 to 1935, worked for the Executive Committee of the Communist International (ECCI). From 1935, deputy director of the Department for Agitation and Propaganda of the CC of the VKP(b). Repressed.

Kodatsky (Kadatsky), I. F. (1893–1937). From 1932, chairman of the Executive Committee of the Leningrad Soviet. In 1937 appointed head of the Main Directorate for the Construction of Light Machinery of the People's Commissariat for Heavy Industry. Repressed.

Kolotilin, N. T. (1902–37). From June 1935, secretary of the City Committee of the VKP(b) for Rostov-on-the-Don. Committed suicide.

Kosarev, A. V. (1903–39). From 1929 to 1939, secretary-general (first secretary) of the CC of the All-Union Leninist-Communist Youth League (VLKSM). Repressed.

Kosior, S. V. (1889–1939). From 1928 to 1937, secretary of the CC of the KP(b) of the Ukraine. In 1938 both deputy chairman of the Council of People's Commissars (SNK) of the USSR and chairman of the Commission for Soviet Control attached to the Council of People's Commissars of the USSR. Repressed.

Kotov, V. A. (1885–1937). From 1929, member of the Collegium of the USSR People's Commissariat for Labor. From 1935 to 1936, director of the Gosotdelstroi Construction Trust of the People's Commissariat for Utilities and Maintenance Enterprises. Repressed.

Krinitsky, A. I. (1894–1937). From 1933, head of the Political Board and deputy USSR people's commissar for agriculture. From 1934 to 1937, first secretary of the Saratov Regional Committee of the VKP(b). Repressed.

Krupskaia, N. K. (1869–1939). From 1929, RSFSR deputy people's commissar for education. Lenin's wife.

Krylenko, N. V. (1885–1938). From 1931, RSFSR people's commissar for justice. From 1936, USSR people's commissar for justice. Repressed.

Krylov, S. M. (1892–1938). During the 1930s, secretary of the Mid-Volga Territorial Committee of the VKP(b). Subsequently worked for the apparat of the CC of the VKP(b). Repressed.

Kudriavtsev, S. G. (1897–?). From September 1935, director of the Sector for Registering Leading Cadres of the CC of the VKP(b).

Kuibyshev, V. V. (1888–1935). From 1930 to 1934, chairman of the State Planning Commission (Gosplan) of the USSR and deputy chairman of the Council of People's Commissars (SNK) of the USSR and of the Council for Labor and Defense (STO) of the USSR. From 1934, chairman of the Commission for Soviet Control attached to the Council of People's Commissars of the USSR and first deputy chairman of the Council of People's Commissars of the USSR and of the Council for Labor and Defense of the USSR.

Kulikov, M. M. (1891–1939). From 1930 to 1935, first secretary of the Proletarsky District Committee of the VKP(b) of the city of Moscow. From March 1935, second secretary of the Moscow City Committee of the VKP(b). Subsequently representative of the Commission for Party Control (KPK) for Rostov region. Repressed.

Kuritsyn, V. I. (1892–1937). From 1935 to 1937, head of the Locomotive Board, then director of the Locomotive Repair Works Trust of the People's Commissariat for Railway Transport (NKPS). From April 1937, director of the Trust for Communal Equipment of the People's Commissariat for Local Industry. Repressed.

Kursky, V. M. (1897–1937). Until November 1936, head of the Directorate of the NKVD for the Western Siberian region. From November 1936, head of the Secret-Political Department of the Main Administration for State Security (GUGB) of the NKVD. In 1937 USSR acting deputy people's commissar for internal affairs. Repressed.

Lavrentiev. See Kartvelishvili, L. I.

Leoniuk, F. A. (1892–?). From 1935 to 1936, head of the Directorate of the NKVD for the Kuibyshev region. In 1937 head of the Directorate of the NKVD for the Krasnoiarsk region.

Lepa, A. K. (1896–1938). From 1933 to 1937, first secretary of the Tatar Regional Committee of the VKP(b). Repressed.

Leplevsky, I. M. (1896–1938). In 1931 deputy head, then head of the Special Section of the OGPU. In 1934 plenipotentiary of the OGPU for the Saratov region. In 1935 people's commissar of the Belorussian SSR for internal affairs. From November 1936, head of the Special Section of the Main Administration for State Security (GUGB) of the NKVD. In 1937 people's commissar of the Ukrainian SSR for internal affairs. From January 1938, head of the GUGB and deputy head of the NKVD USSR for transport and communications. Repressed.

Levin, A. M. (1889–1941). During the 1920s, plenipotentiary representative of the All-Russian Extraordinary Commission for Combating Counterrevolution and Sabotage (VChK) in the Far East.

Litvin, M. I. (1892–1938). From 1931 to 1932, director of a section, then deputy director of the Distribution Department of the CC of the VKP(b). From 1933, director of the Department of Cadres of the CC of the KP(b) of the Ukraine. From 1936, second secretary of the Kharkov Regional Committee of the KP(b) of the Ukraine. From 1937 to 1938, head of the Deparament of Cadres of the NKVD of the USSR. Committed suicide.

Litvinov, M. M. (1876–1951). From 1930 to 1939, USSR people's commissar for foreign affairs.

Liubchenko, P. P. (1897–1937). From 1933 to 1934, deputy chairman of the Council of People's Commissars (SNK) of the Ukrainian SSR. From 1934 to 1937, chairman of the Council of People's Commissars of the Ukrainian SSR. Committed suicide.

Liubimov, I. E. (1882–1937). From 1932 to 1937, USSR people's commissar for light industry. Repressed.

Liushkov, G. S. (1900–1945). From 1936 to June 1937, head of the Directorate of the NKVD for the Azov–Black Sea region. From 1937 to 1938, head of the Directorate of the NKVD for the Far Eastern region. Fled to Manchuria in 1938; executed by the Japanese.

Lobov, S. S. (1888–1937). From 1930, deputy people's commissar for supplies and provisions. From 1932, USSR people's commissar for forestry industries. From 1936 to 1937, RSFSR people's commissar for food industry. Repressed.

Lominadze, V. V. (1897–1935). In 1930 first secretary of the Trans-Caucasus Territorial Committee of the VKP(b). From August 1933, secretary of the Magnitogorsk City Committee of the VKP(b). Committed suicide.

Lozovsky, S. A. (Dridzo) (1878–1952). From 1921 to 1937, secretary-general of the Red International of Trade Unions (Profintern), director of the State Publishing House (Gosizdat) and USSR deputy people's commissar for foreign affairs. Repressed.

Lunacharsky, A. V. (1875–1933). From 1917 to 1929, RSFSR people's commissar for education. From August 1933, USSR ambassador to Spain.

Maiorsky, N. N. (dates unknown). Member of the scientific-research group of the Lenin Institute.

Makarov, I. G. (1888–1949). In 1931 head of the Donetsk Steel Board. From 1932 to 1937, director of the Donetsk Metallurgical Factory and head of the Chief Directorate for Special Steel (Glavspetsstal). From 1938 to 1939, USSR people's commissar for heavy industry.

Malenkov, G. M. (1902–88). From 1930, director of a department of the Moscow Committee of the VKP(b). From 1934 to 1939, director of the Department of Leading Party Organs of the CC of the VKP(b).

Malinov, M. M. (1893–?). From 1934, secretary of the Azov–Black Sea Territorial Committee of the VKP(b) in Rostov-on-Don.

Manuilsky, D. Z. (1883–1959). From 1928 to 1943, a secretary of the Executive Committee of the Communist International (ECCI).

Margolin, N. V. (1895–1938). From March 1935, secretary of the Moscow Committee of the VKP(b). Repressed.

Markitian, P. F. (1887–?). From 1932 to 1936, first secretary of the Chernigov Regional Committee of the KP(b) of the Ukraine. Repressed.

Mdivani, B. G. (1877–1937). From 1932 to 1934, people's commissar of Georgia for industry. Subsequently first deputy chairman of the Council of People's Commissars (SNK) of Georgia. Repressed.

Medvedev, A. V. (1884–?). From 1930 to 1934, a member of the Presidium of the Central Executive Committee (TsIK) of the USSR.

Mekhlis, M. Z. (1889–1953). From 1930 to 1937, director of the Department for the Press of the CC of the VKP(b) and editor of the newspaper *Pravda*. From 1937 to 1940, head of the Chief Political Directorate of the Workers' and Peasants' Red Army (RKKA).

Menzhinsky, V. R. (1874–1934). From 1926, chairman of the OGPU.

Mezhlauk, V. I. (1893–1938). From 1934, deputy chairman of the Council of People's Commissars (SNK) of the USSR, deputy chairman of the Council for Labor and Defense (STO) of the USSR, and then chairman of the State Planning Commission (Gosplan) of the USSR. From February to October 1937, USSR people's commissar for heavy industry. Repressed.

Mikhailov, M. E. (1902–38). In 1934 secretary of the Moscow Committee of the VKP(b). From 1935 to 1937, first secretary of the Kalinin Regional Committee of the VKP(b). From July to November 1937, first secretary of the Voronezh Regional Committee of the VKP(b). Repressed.

Miliutin, V. P. (1884–1937). People's commissar for agriculture in the first Soviet government. From 1928 to 1934, director of the Central Statistical Board (TsSU) of the USSR. Subsequently deputy chairman of the State Planning Commission (Gosplan) of the USSR. From 1934, chairman of the Council on Education attached to the Central Executive Committee (TsIK) of the USSR. Repressed.

Minaev (Tsikanovsky), A. M. (1888–1939). From 1937 to 1938, head of the Third Department of the Main Administration for State Security (GUGB) of the NKVD of the USSR. In 1938 USSR deputy people's commissar for heavy industry. Repressed.

Mironov, L. G. (1895–1938). From 1934 to 1938, head of the Economic Department (EKO) of the Main Administration for State Security (GUGB) of the NKVD of the USSR. From 1936 to 1937, head of the Third Department of the GUGB of the NKVD of the USSR. Repressed.

Mirzoian, L. I. (1897–1939). From 1933 first secretary of the Kazakhstan Territorial Committee of the Party. In 1937 first secretary of the CC of the KP(b) of Kazakhstan. Repressed.

Molchanov, G. A. (1897–1937). From 1930 to 1936, head of the Secret-Political Department of the Main Administration for State Security (GUGB) of the NKVD of the USSR. From 1936 to 1937, people's commissar of Belorussia for internal affairs. Repressed.

Molotov (Skriabin), V. M. (1890–1986). From 1921 to 1957, a member of the CC of the VKP(b). In 1921 candidate member, then from 1926 to 1957 member of the Politburo (Presidium) of the CC. From 1930 to 1941, chairman of the Council of People's Commissars (SNK) of the USSR.

Mrachkovsky, S. V. (1888–1936). From 1920 to 1925, commander of the Ural Military District and of the Western Siberian Military District. Expelled from the party in 1927 and in 1933. Up until his arrest, he was head of construction for the Baikal-Amur Railroad. Repressed.

Muralov, N. I. (1877–1937). From 1925, rector of the Timiriazev Agricultural Academy and member of the Presidium of the State Planning Commission (Gosplan) of the RSFSR. At the Fifteenth Party Congress of the VKP(b) expelled from the party as an active member of the Trotskyist opposition. Repressed.

Musabekov, G. M. (1888–1938). From 1931 to 1936, chairman of the Council of People's Commissars (SNK) of the Trans-Caucasus SFSR. From 1925 to 1937, one of the chairmen of the Central Executive Committee (TsIK) of the USSR. Repressed.

Nevsky, V. I. (1876–1937). From 1924, director of the Lenin State Library. Repressed.

Nikolaeva, K. I. (1893–1944). From 1936, secretary of the All-Union Central Council of Trade Unions (VTsSPS).

Nizovtsev, P. L. (dates unknown). In 1936 director of the Department of Leading Party Organs of the Leningrad Regional Committee of the VKP(b).

Nosov, I. P. (1888–1937). From 1932 to 1937, first secretary of the Ivanovo Regional Committee of the VKP(b). Repressed.

Okudzhava, Sh. S. See Akudzhava, Sh. S.

Ordzhonikidze, G. K. (1886–1937). From 1930, chairman of the Supreme Council for the National Economy of the USSR (VSNKh), then USSR people's commissar for heavy industry. Committed suicide.

Orlov, V. M. (1895–1938). From 1931 to 1937, head of Naval Forces of the Workers' and Peasants' Red Army (RKKA). From 1937, deputy USSR people's commissar for defense. Repressed.

Orzeszkowa, Eliza. (1841–1910). Polish writer. Her works were repeatedly translated into Russian and published (beginning in the 1880s) in Russian journals and in book form.

Osinsky, N. (V. V. Obolensky) (1887–1938). From 1929, deputy chairman of the Supreme Council for the National Economy of the USSR (VSNKh) and deputy chairman of the State Planning Commission (Gosplan) of the USSR. In 1933 chairman of the State Commission for Determining Crop Productivity attached to the Council of People's Commissars (SNK) of the USSR. Repressed.

Ovchinnikov, G. F. (1893–1937?). In 1933 first secretary of the Rostov City Committee of the VKP(b). From November 1933, head of the Northern Caucasus Regional Board for Communications. Repressed.

Pakhomov, N. I. (1890–1938). From 1928 to 1934, chairman of the Nizhni Novgorod Regional Executive Committee. From 1934 to 1936, USSR people's commissar for water transport. Repressed.

Pavlunovsky, I. P. (1888–1937). From 1932, USSR deputy people's commissar for heavy industry. In 1935 head of the Chief Directorate for Military Industry. From December 1936, head of the Main Administration for Machinery Construction in Transport (Glavtransmash) of the USSR People's Commissariat for Heavy Industry. In 1937 head of the Mobilization Department of the USSR People's Commissariat for Heavy Industry. Repressed.

Peterson, R. A. (1897–1940). From 1920 to 1935, commandant of the Kremlin. Subsequently, assistant commander of the troops of the Kiev Military District until 1937. Repressed.

Petrovsky, G. I. (1878–1958). From 1919 to 1938, chairman of the All-Ukrainian Central Executive Committee (TsIK) of the Ukrainian SSR and one of the chairmen of the Central Executive Committee of the USSR.

Piatakov, G. L. (1890–1937). From 1931 to 1936, deputy people's commissar of the USSR for heavy industry. Repressed.

Piatnitsky, I. A. (1882–1938). From 1922 to 1935, secretary of the Executive Committee of the Communist International (ECCI). From 1935, director of the Administrative-Political Department of the CC of the VKP(b). Repressed.

Polonsky, V. I. (1893–1937). From 1935 to 1937, secretary of the All-Union Central Council of Trade Unions (VTsSPS). From April to June 1937, deputy USSR people's commissar for communications. Repressed.

Popov, N. N. (1891–1938). From January 1933 to June 1937, secretary of the CC of the KP(b) of the Ukraine. Repressed.

Postyshev, P. P. (1887–1939). From 1930 to 1934, secretary of the CC of the VKP(b). From 1930 to 1933, director of departments of the CC of the VKP(b). From 1933 to 1937, second secretary of the CC of the KP(b) of the Ukraine, first secretary of the Kiev Regional Committee of the KP(b) of the Ukraine, then first secretary of the Kharkov Regional and City Committees. From 1937 to 1938, first secretary of the Kuibyshev Regional Committee of the VKP(b). Repressed.

Pramnek, Ye. K. (1899–1938). From 1930 to 1934, second secretary of the Gorky Territorial and Regional Committees of the VKP(b). From 1934 to 1937, first secretary of the Gorky Territorial and Regional Committees of the VKP(b). From 1937, secretary of the Donetsk Regional Committee of the KP(b) of the Ukraine. Repressed.

Preobrazhensky, Ye. A. (1886–1937). From 1921 to 1927, a member of the Collegium of the USSR People's Commissariat for Finances and member of the Presidium of the Communist Academy. Subsequently served as chairman of the Chief Directorate for Professional Education of the RSFSR People's Commissariat for Education. In 1927 expelled from the party. Repressed.

Prigozhin, V. G. (dates unknown). In 1936 director of the Azov–Black Sea Trust of the Main Board (GU) for Oil and Fat Industry. Member of the council attached to the USSR People's Commissariat for Food Industry.

Prokofiev, G. Ye. (1895–1937). From 1931 to 1932, deputy people's commissar of the Workers'-Peasants' Inspectorate (RKI). From 1932 to 1934, third deputy chairman of the OGPU. From 1934 to 1936, second deputy USSR people's commissar for internal affairs. From 1936 to 1937, first deputy USSR people's commissar for communications. Repressed.

Ptukha, V. V. (1894–1938). From 1934, first secretary of the Stalingrad Territorial Committee of the VKP(b). From 1935 to 1937, second secretary of the Far Eastern Territorial Committee of the VKP(b). Repressed.

Radek, K. B. (1885–1939). From 1925 to 1927, rector of the Chinese Workers' University of Moscow. Member of the editorial board of the newspaper *Izvestia*. In 1935, member of the Constitutional Commission of the Central Executive Committee (TsIK) of the USSR. Convicted in 1937 and murdered in prison.

Radin, Ye. P. (1872–1939). Physician. During the 1930s, worked at the State Scientific Institute for the Protection of the Health of Children and Adolescents.

Radzivilovsky, A. P. (1904–40). From 1935 to 1937, deputy head of the Directorate of the NKVD for Moscow region. From 1937 to 1938, head of the Directorate of the NKVD for Ivanovo region. Repressed.

Ramishvili, I. I. (1859–1937). Teacher. After 1918 a member of the Menshevik government of Georgia. Repressed.

Razumov, M. O. (1894–1937). From 1933 to 1937, first secretary of the Eastern Siberian Territorial Committee of the VKP(b). Repressed.

Redens, S. F. (1892–1940). From 1934 to 1938, head of the Directorate of the NKVD for Moscow region. In 1938 people's commissar of Kazakhstan for internal affairs. Repressed.

Reingold, I. I. (1897–1936). Member of the Trotskyist opposition. In 1927 expelled from the party. Restored to party membership in 1928. From 1932 to 1934, USSR deputy people's commissar for agriculture. Repressed.

Riazanov (Goldendakh), D. B. (1870–1938). A leading trade union official. From 1921 director of the Marx and Engels Institute. Expelled from the VKP(b) in 1931. Repressed.

Riutin, M. N. (1890–1937). In 1930 member of the Presidium of the Supreme Council for the National Economy (VSNKh) of the USSR. Subsequently, from March to October 1930, chairman of the board of the Photographic and Film Industry Association. Repressed.

Roshal, L. B. (1896–1940). From 1934 to 1938, head of the Political Department of the Chief Directorate of the Political-Military Section (GUPVO) of the NKVD of the USSR and deputy head of the GU PVO of the NKVD of the USSR. Repressed.

Rossiisky, D. M. (1887–1955). Well-known Soviet clinical physician-therapist and historian of medicine.

Rozenfeld, N. B. (1886–?). Book illustrator for the Akademia Publishing House. Convicted in July 1935. Brother of L. B. Kamenev.

Rozengolts, A. P. (1889–1941). From 1927 to 1937, deputy then USSR people's commissar for foreign trade. From 1937, head of the Board for State Reserves. Repressed.

Rud, P. G. (1896–1937). From January 1934 to August 1936, plenipotentiary representative of the OGPU for the Azov–Black Sea region, then head of the Directorate of the NKVD for the Azov–Black Sea region. From 1936 to 1937, people's commissar of the Tatar ASSR for internal affairs. Repressed.

Rudzutak, Ya. E. (1887–1938). From 1926 to 1937, deputy chairman of the Council of People's Commissars (SNK) and of the Council for Labor and Defense (STO) of the

USSR. Simultaneously, from 1931 to 1934, chairman of the Central Control Commission (CCC) and people's commissar of the Workers'-Peasants' Inspectorate (RKI) of the USSR. Repressed.

Rukhimovich, M. L. (1889–1938). From 1930 to 1931, USSR people's commissar of railway transport. Subsequently, director of the Kuzbassugol Trust. From 1934, deputy USSR people's commissar for heavy industry. From 1936 to 1937, USSR people's commissar for defense industries. Repressed.

Rumiantsev, I. P. (1886–1937). From 1929 to 1937, first secretary of the Western (Smolensk) Regional Committee of the VKP(b). Repressed.

Rykov, A. I. (1881–1938). From 1924 to 1930, chairman of the Council of People's Commissars (SNK) of the USSR, chairman of the RSFSR Council of People's Commissars, and chairman of the Council for Labor and Defense (STO) of the USSR. A leader of the rightist opposition. From 1931 to 1936, USSR people's commissar for communications (Postal and Telegraphic Services). Repressed.

Ryndin, R. V. (1893–1938). From 1934, first secretary of the Cheliabinsk Regional Committee of the VKP(b). Repressed.

Safarov, G. I. (1891–1942). From 1929, worked for the Executive Committee of the Communist International (ECCI). Affiliated with the Trotskyist opposition and repeatedly expelled from the VKP(b). Repressed.

Sapozhnikov, P. F. (1877–1937). During the 1930s, a member of the Presidium of the Voronezh Regional Planning Commission. Repressed.

Sarkisov, S. A. (1898–1937). From 1933, first secretary of the Donetsk Regional Committee of the KP(b) of the Ukraine. In 1937 head of the Donetsk coalfields. Repressed.

Saveliev, M. A. (1884–1939). From 1936 to 1939, deputy director of the Marx-Engels-Lenin Institute attached to the CC of the VKP(b).

Sedelnikov, A. I. (1894–1937). From 1930, a member of the Bureau of the Moscow Committee of the VKP(b). In 1937 director of a trust in the Kuibyshev region. Repressed.

Semenov, B. A. (dates unknown). From 1933 to 1935, first secretary of the Crimean Regional Committee of the VKP(b). Repressed.

Semiakin, P. A. (1869–1942). Statistician.

Serebriakov, L. P. (1888–1937). From 1929 to 1935, head of the Central Administration for Highways, Unpaved Roads, and Motor Transport in the RSFSR (Tsudortrans). From 1935 to 1936, deputy head of the Main Administration for Highways. Repeatedly expelled from the party. Repressed.

Serebrovsky, A. P. (1882–1938). From 1931 to 1937, deputy USSR people's commissar for heavy industry. Repressed.

Sevian (dates unknown). Second secretary of the Bazarny Syzgan District Committee of the VKP(b).

Shafransky, I. O. (1891–1954). During the 1930s, commander of a division of the Workers' and Peasants' Red Army (RKKA).

Shapiro, I. I. (1895–1940). Until 1936 worked for the apparat of the CC of the VKP(b). From 1936 to 1938, head of a department of the NKVD of the USSR, then head of the Secretariat of the NKVD of the USSR. Repressed.

Sharangovich, V. F. (1897–1938). During the 1930s, first secretary of the CC of the KP(b) of Belorussia. Repressed.

Shatunovsky, Ya. M. (1876–1932). From 1921, engaged in economic work. Member of the Transport Commission attached to the Council for Labor and Defense (STO) and of the Industrial Section of the State Planning Commission (Gosplan). In 1927 sided with the rightist deviationists but soon abandoned the opposition.

Sheboldaev, B. P. (1895–1937). From 1931 to 1934, secretary of the Northern Caucasus Territorial Committee of the VKP(b). From 1934 to 1937, secretary of the Azov–Black Sea Territorial Committee of the VKP(b). From 1937, secretary of the Kursk Regional Committee of the VKP(b). Repressed.

Shkiriatov, M. F. (1883–1954). From 1922 to 1934, member of the Central Control Commission (CCC) of the VKP(b). From 1927 to 1934, member of the Collegium of the People's Commissariat of the Workers'-Peasants' Inspectorate (RKI) of the USSR. From 1934 to 1939, secretary of the Party Collegium of the Commission for Party Control (KPK) attached to the CC of the VKP(b).

Shliapnikov, A. G. (1885–1937). People's commissar for labor in the first Soviet government. From 1920 to 1922, one of the leaders of the Workers' Opposition. From 1923 to 1932, member of the Collegium of the State Publishing House (Gosizdat) and a councillor to the Plenipotentiary Bureau of the USSR in France. From 1932 a member of the Presidium of the State Planning Commission (Gosplan). Expelled from the party in 1933. Repressed.

Shmidt, V. V. (1886–1938). From 1928 to 1930, deputy chairman of the Council of People's Commissars (SNK) and deputy chairman of the Council for Labor and Defense (STO) of the USSR. From 1930, USSR deputy people's commissar for agriculture. From 1931, principal state arbiter attached to the Council of People's Commissars of the USSR. From 1933, director of the Transugol Trust in the Far East. Repressed.

Shubrikov, V. P. (1895–1937). From 1932 to 1937, secretary of the Mid-Volga Territorial Committee and secretary of the Kuibyshev Regional Committee of the VKP(b). In 1937 second secretary of the Western Siberian Territorial Committee of the VKP(b). Repressed.

Shvernik, N. M. (1888–1970). From 1930 to 1944, chairman (first secretary) of the All-Union Central Council of Trade Unions (VTsSPS). At the same time, from 1938 to 1946, chairman of the Council of Nationalities of the Supreme Soviet of the USSR.

Skrypnik, N. A. (1872–1933). From 1927 to 1932, people's commissar of the Ukrainian SSR for education. In 1933 Ukrainian SSR deputy chairman of the Council of People's Commissars (SNK) and chairman of the State Planning Commission (Gosplan) of Ukraine. Committed suicide.

Slavinsky, A. S. (dates unknown). In 1929 chairman of a department of the Central Committee of the Trade Union of Artists. In 1935 head of the Political Department of the Moscow-Belorussian-Baltic Railroad.

Slepkov, A. N. (1899–1937). From 1928 to 1932, member and director of agitation and propaganda of the Mid-Volga Territorial Committee of the VKP(b). Repressed.

Smirnov, A. P. (1878–1938). From 1928 to 1930, deputy chairman of the Council of People's Commissars (SNK) of the RSFSR and secretary of the CC of the VKP(b). From 1931 to 1933, chairman of the All-Union Council for Utilities and Maintenance

Enterprises attached to the Central Executive Committee (TsIK) of the USSR. Expelled from the party in 1934. Repressed.

Smirnov, I. N. (1881–1936). From 1923 to 1927, people's commissar of the USSR for communications (Postal and Telegraphic Services). Member of the Trotskyist opposition. In 1933 convicted and sentenced to five years in prison. In 1936 sentenced to be shot as a member of the Trotskyist-Zinovievist center.

Smorodin, P. I. (1897–1939). From 1937 to 1938, first secretary of the Stalingrad Regional Committee of the VKP(b). Repressed.

Sokolnikov, G. Ya. (1888–1939). From 1929 to 1932, plenipotentiary representative of the USSR in Great Britain. Subsequently USSR deputy people's commissar for foreign affairs. From 1935 to 1936, first deputy USSR people's commissar for light industry. Arrested in July 1936. Murdered in prison by his cellmates.

Stalin (Dzhugashvili), I. V. (1878–1953). Secretary of the CC of the Communist Party of the Soviet Union (KPSS) from 1922 to 1953.

Stasova, Ye. D. (1873–1966). From 1927 to 1937, chairwoman of the CC of the International Organization for Assistance to Revolutionary Fighters (MOPR) of the USSR and deputy chairwoman of the Executive Committee of the MOPR. From 1935 to 1943, a member of the International Control Commission of the Communist International (Comintern).

Stetsky, A. I. (1896–1938). From 1930 to 1938, director of the Culture and Propaganda Department of the CC of the VKP(b). Also chief editor of the journal *Bolshevik*. Repressed.

Struppe, P. I. (1889–1937). From 1932 to 1936, chairman of the Leningrad Regional Executive Committee. Subsequently head of the Sverdlovsk Board of the People's Commissariat of the USSR for Grain and Livestock Sovkhozes. Repressed.

Sulebatov (Topuridze), Yu. D. (1889–?). From 1934 to 1938, people's commissar of Azerbaijan for internal affairs. From 1938 to 1947, head of the Administrative-Economic Directorate (AKhU-KhOZU) of the NKVD (MVD) of the USSR. In 1953 arrested in connection with the L. P. Beria case. From December 1955, under treatment at the Leningrad Prison Psychiatric Hospital.

Sulimov, D. Ye. (1890–1937). From 1930 to 1937, chairman of the RSFSR Council of People's Commissars (SNK). Repressed.

Ter-Vaganian, V. A. (1893–1936). During the 1920s, member of the editorial board of the newspaper *Pravda* and worked for the State Publishing House for Light Industry. Member of the editorial board of the journal *Krasnaia Nov'*. Expelled from the party in 1928, 1933, and 1935. Repressed.

Todorsky, A. I. (1894–1965). From 1930 to 1933, head of the Board of Military Training Institutes. From 1933 to 1936, head and military commissar of the Zhukovsky Air Force Academy. From 1936 to 1938, head of the Board of Supreme Military Training Institutes. Repressed. Released and rehabilitated in 1953.

Tolmachev, V. N. (1886–1937). From 1928 to 1930, RSFSR people's commissar for internal affairs. From 1931, head of the Main Administration for Highways, Unpaved Roads, and Motor Transport (Glavdortrans) attached to the Council of People's Commissars (SNK) of the RSFSR. Repressed.

Tomsky (Yefremov), M. P. (1880–1936). In the 1920s, chairman of Central Council of Trade Unions and a leader of the rightist opposition. From 1929, chairman of the All-

Union Association of the Chemical Industry and deputy chairman of the Supreme Council for the National Economy (VSNKh). From 1932 to 1936, director of the Association of State Publishing Houses (OGIZ). Committed suicide.

Tovstukha, I. P. (1889–1935). From 1931 to 1935, deputy director of the Marx-Engels-Lenin Institute attached to the CC of the VKP(b).

Trotsky (Bronshtein), L. D. (1879–1940). From 1918 to 1925, chairman of the Revolutionary Military Council (RVS) of the Soviet Republic. Member of the Politburo of the CC of the VKP(b) in 1917 and from 1919 to 1926. Deported from the USSR in 1929 and assassinated in 1940.

Tsekher, A. A. (dates unknown). In 1935 member of the Central Executive Committee (TsIK) of the USSR.

Tsesarsky, V. E. (1895–1940). From March 1935 to May 1936, a lecturer-consultant in the service of a secretary of the CC of the VKP(b). From 1936 to 1938, head of the Eighth Department of the Main Administration for State Security (GUGB) of the USSR NKVD. In 1938 head of the Directorate of the NKVD for the Moscow region. Repressed.

Tsetlin, E. V. (1898–?). In 1929 worked for the Scientific-Technical Board (NTU) of the Supreme Council for the National Economy of the USSR (VSNKh). From 1931 to 1933, deputy head of propaganda for technology (Tekhprop) of the USSR People's Commissariat for Heavy Industry. Repressed.

Tukhachevsky, M. N. (1893–1937). From 1931, deputy chairman of the Revolutionary Military Council (RVS) of the USSR and head of armaments and munitions of the Workers' and Peasants' Red Army (RKKA). From 1934, USSR deputy people's commissar for defense. From 1936, first deputy USSR people's commissar for defense and head of the Directorate for Military Preparedness of the Workers' and Peasants' Red Army. Repressed.

Ugarov, A. I. (1900–1939). From 1932 to 1936, secretary of the Leningrad City Committee of the VKP(b). In 1938 first secretary of the Moscow Regional and City Committees of the VKP(b). Repressed.

Uglanov, N. A. (1886–1937). From 1928 to 1930, USSR people's commissar for labor. From 1930 to 1932, engaged in economic work in Astrakhan. From 1932 to 1933, worked in the People's Commissariat for Heavy Machinery Construction. Imprisoned in 1933. Repeatedly expelled from the party. Repressed.

Ulianova, M. I. (1878–1937). From 1934 to 1937, a member of the Commission for Soviet Control and director of the Unified Bureau for Complaints of the People's Commissariat for the Workers'-Peasants' Inspectorate (RKI) of the USSR and of the RSFSR. (Lenin's sister.)

Unshlikht, I. S. (1879–1938). From 1930 to 1933, deputy chairman of the Supreme Council for the National Economy of the USSR (VSNKh). From 1933 to 1935, head of the Chief Directorate for Civil Aviation. From March 1935, secretary of the All-Union Council of the Central Executive Committee (TsIK) of the USSR. Repressed.

Vainov, A. R. [also Voinov] (1898–1937). During the 1930s, secretary of the Donetsk Regional Committee of the KP(b) of the Ukraine. From 1936, secretary of the Organizational Bureau (Orgburo) of the CC of the VKP(b) for Yaroslavl region. From February to September 1937, first secretary of the Yaroslavl Regional Committee of the VKP(b). Repressed.

Vardanian, S. Kh. (1900–1938). During the 1930s, second secretary of the CC of the KP(b) of Armenia. From 1932, first secretary of the Taganrog City Committee of the VKP(b). Repressed.

Vardin-Mgeladze, I. V. (1890–1941). From 1926, TASS correspondent in Teheran. Repressed.

Vareikis, I. M. (1894–1938). From 1935 to 1936, first secretary of the Stalingrad Territorial Committee of the VKP(b). Repressed.

Veger, E. I. (1899–1937). From 1933 to 1937, first secretary of the Odessa Regional Committee of the KP(b) of the Ukraine. Repressed.

Vinokurov, A. N. (1869–1944). From 1924 to 1938, chairman of the USSR Supreme Court. From 1938, worked for the USSR People's Commissariat for Health.

Volosevich, V. O. (1882–?). From 1924 to 1925, director of the Leningrad Section of the Central Board for Archives.

Voroshilov, K. Ye. (1881–1969). From 1925 to 1934, chairman of the Revolutionary Military Council (RVS) of the USSR. From 1934 to 1940, USSR people's commissar of defense.

Vyshinsky, A. Ya. (1883–1954). From 1931 to 1935, procurator of the RSFSR and deputy people's commissar of the RSFSR for justice. From 1935 to 1939, procurator of the USSR.

Yagoda, G. G. (1891–1938). From 1924, deputy chairman of the OGPU. From 1934 to 1936, USSR people's commissar for internal affairs. From 1936 to 1937, USSR people's commissar of communications. Repressed.

Yakir, I. E. (1896–1937). From 1925 to 1935, commander of the Ukrainian Military District. From 1935 to 1937, commander of the Kiev, Leningrad, and Trans-Caucasus Military Districts. Repressed.

Yakovlev (Epshtein), Ya. A. (1896–1938). From 1929 to 1934, USSR people's commissar of agriculture. From April 1934, director of the Department of Agriculture of the CC of the VKP(b). From 1931, first deputy chairman of the Commission for Party Control (KPK). Repressed.

Yaroslavsky, E. M. (1878–1943). From 1923 to 1939, member of the Central Control Commission (CCC) and of the Commission for Party Control (KPK) attached to the CC of the VKP(b). From 1931 to 1935, chairman of the All-Union Society of Old Bolsheviks.

Yavorsky, M. I. (dates unknown). Ukrainian historian. In 1928 chairman of the Kharkov Scientific Society attached to the All-Ukrainian Academy of Sciences. In 1930 expelled from the party.

Yegorov, A. I. (1883–1939). From July 1931, chief of headquarters of the Workers' and Peasants' Red Army (RKKA). From September 1935, chief of the general staff of the RKKA. From May 1937 to January 1938, first deputy USSR people's commissar of defense. From January to February 1938, commander of the troops of the Trans-Caucasus Military District. Repressed.

Yelvov, N. N. (dates unknown). During the 1930s a member of the Scientific-Research Group at the Lenin Institute.

Yenukidze, A. S. (1877–1937). From 1922 to 1935, secretary of the Central Executive Committee (TsIK) of the USSR. Repressed.

Yeremin, I. G. (1895–1937). From 1932 to 1937, second USSR deputy people's commissar for light industry. Repressed.

Yerofitsky, K. M. (1905–37). In 1930 chief instructor at the Saratov Territorial Committee of the VKP(b). From 1930 to 1932, a student at the Institute of Marxism-Leninism attached to the Central Executive Committee (TsIK) of the USSR. From 1932 to 1933, director of the Organizational Department of the Chechen Regional Committee of the VKP(b). From August 1933, first secretary of the Azov–Black Sea Territorial Committee of the All-Union Leninist-Communist Youth League (VLKSM). Repressed.

Yevdokimov, G. E. (1884–1936). From 1929 to 1934, chairman of the Samara Regional Union of Agricultural Cooperatives and head of the Main Directorate of the USSR People's Commissariat for Food Industry. Member of the Trotskyist opposition. Repeatedly expelled from the party. Repressed.

Yezhov, N. I. (1895–1940). From 1929, USSR deputy people's commissar of agriculture. From 1930, chief of the Distribution Section, then chief of the Department of Cadres and Chief of the Industrial Department of the CC of the VKP(b). From 1934 to 1935, deputy chairman of the Commission for Party Control (KPK). From 1935, chairman of the KPK. From 1936 to 1938, people's commissar of the USSR for internal affairs. From 1935 to 1939, secretary of the CC of the VKP(b). Executed on 4 February, 1940.

Zaidel, G. S. (1893–?). Historian. From 1926, worked for the Society of Marxist Historians of the Leningrad Section of the Communist Academy.

Zaitsev, F. I. (1894–1960). From 1930 to 1934, secretary of the CC of the KP(b) of the Ukraine.

Zakovsky (Shtubis) L. M. (1894–1938). From 1934 to 1938, head of the NKVD for Leningrad region. In 1938 simultaneously deputy USSR people's commissar for internal affairs and head of the Directorate of the NKVD for Moscow region. From April 1938, head of construction for the Kuibyshev hydroelectric complex of the NKVD. Repressed.

Zalin, L. B. (1897–1940). From 1935 to 1938, Kazakh SSR people's commissar for internal affairs. Repressed.

Zalpeter, A. K. (1899–1939). From 1937 to 1938, head of the Second (Operational) Department of the Main Administration for State Security (GUGB) of the USSR NKVD. Repressed.

Zalutsky, P. A. (1887–1937). From 1928 to 1934, chairman of the Lower-Volga Regional Council for the National Economy, head of construction for the Shatura hydroelectric power station, and manager of the Stroimashina Trust. For participation in the Trotskyist opposition, repeatedly expelled from the party (1928, 1934). Repressed.

Zaslavsky, P. S. (1890–1967). From 1927 to 1929, secretary of the Kostroma Regional Committee of the VKP(b). From 1931 to 1938, chairman of the CC of the Union of Financial and Banking Officials.

Zelensky, I. A. (1890–1938). From 1931, chairman of the board of the Central Union of Consumer Associations of the USSR (Tsentrsoyuz). Repressed.

Zhdanov, A. A. (1896–1948). From 1934 to 1944, secretary of the CC of the VKP(b) and first secretary of the Leningrad Regional and City Committees of the VKP(b).

Zhukov, I. P. (1889–1937). In 1932 USSR deputy people's commissar for heavy industry. From 1933 to 1936, USSR deputy people's commissar for communications. From 1936 to 1937, RSFSR people's commissar for local industry. Repressed.

Zhuravlev, V. P. (1902–46). From 1937 to 1938, head of the NKVD for Kuibyshev region. In 1938 head of the NKVD for Ivanovo region. From December 1938, head of the NKVD for Moscow region.

Zilberman, A. I. (dates unknown). Took part in the Trotskyist-Zinovievist opposition. In January 1935, sentenced to imprisonment in a concentration camp.

Zimin, N. N. (1895–?). During the 1930s, deputy director of the Department of Culture and Propaganda of the CC of the VKP(b). In 1933, deputy head of the Political Board of the USSR People's Commissariat for Railway Transport. From 1934, director of the Department of Transportation of the CC of the VKP(b). From 1935 to 1937, deputy USSR people's commissar for railway transport.

Zinoviev, G. Ye. (1883–1936). From 1919 to 1926, chairman of the Executive Committee of the Communist International (ECCI). From 1919 to 1926, one of the organizers of the united opposition and one of the leaders of the Trotskyist-Zinovievist bloc. Expelled in 1927 from the VKP(b). Repressed.

Index of Documents

Index